Václav Houžvička

Czechs and Germans 1848–2004

The Sudeten Question
and the Transformation
of Central Europe

Charles University in Prague
Karolinum Press 2016

Reviewed by: Prof. JUDr. Jan Kuklík
† PhDr. Václav Kural, CSc.
JUDr. Rudolf Jindrák
† Prof. Dr. Otto Pick

CATALOGUING-IN-PUBLICATION –
NATIONAL LIBRARY OF THE CZECH REPUBLIC

Houžvička, Václav
Czechs and Germans 1848–2004 : the Sudeten question and the transformation
of Central Europe / Václav Houžvička. – Vydání první. – Praha : Univerzita
Karlova v Praze, nakladatelství Karolinum, 2015
ISBN 978-80-246-2144-9

(=162.3):(=112.2) * 94(437.3+430) * (=112.2) * 314.151.1(=112.2) * 930:17.024.3 *
(437) * (437.3) * (430)
– 1848–2004
– Czechs and Germans – 19th–21st centuries
– Sudeten question
– Germans – Czechoslovakia
– displacement of Germans – Czechoslovakia – 1945–1948
– coming to terms with the past – Czechia – 1989–
– coming to terms with the past – Germany – 1989–
– monographs

943 – Central Europe, Germany [8]

The translation of this book was kindly supported by
Centrum pro studium demokracie a kultury (CDK).

ISBN 978-80-246-2144-9 (Karolinum)
ISBN 978-80-7325-284-7 (CDK)

Contents

Introduction – Historical Context and the Right to Memory

The Roman writer Terence said that books have fates of their own – habent sua fata libelli. He evidently meant that it is their reception among readers that determines whether books are read or sink into oblivion. To this classical insight I would add the observation that the need for a book, or in other words the fact that an author feels the need to write on a theme that is a live social issue, has much to do with the circumstances in which the idea for the book was born and developed. In the case of this particular book, the initial motivating circumstance for consideration of the theme was the stormy, mainly hostile response of Czech society to Václav Havel's statement in early November 1989 in which he condemned the postwar expulsion of the German-speaking population of Czechoslovakia. This public response was a patent signal that Czech-German relations were set to be a thorny subject even in the new context of the return of freedom. The widespread and emotionally impassioned debate was a telling sign of the sensitivity of Czech perceptions of Germany as a security partner and neighbor.

A dramatic dialogue involving almost all social groups, citizens, politicians and the academic sphere was set in motion. Passions that had been in hibernation during the frozen and apparently eternal Cold War erupted with unexpected force. The period of post-revolutionary euphoria was very brief and ended as early as 1991, when the Agreement on Good Neighbourly Relations and Friendly Cooperation between the Czech and Slovak Federative Republic and the Federal Republic of Germany was still in its preparatory phase. At this point I sensed that initial faith that the past could be rapidly left behind on the basis of the principle of *mene tekel* (numbered, weighed, divided), that magic verbal formulae could take the sting out of the heritage of historical conflict, and there could be instant solutions, was misplaced. The discovery confirmed me in the belief that we needed to explore the roots of the modern conflict between Czechs and Germans, and even if the results were incomplete and challengeable, to look into the contexts of the breakpoints in the dramatic story, and ask how far there had been genuine alternatives to the actual course of events. It was only over many years of research and preparatory work that I came to appreciate the immense scale and complexity of the task, and then to think about the need for a book that would offer a full retrospective treatment of the Czech-German relationship in the decisive period from the mid-19th century to the parting of the ways with the expulsion of the Germans after the end of the Second World War and beyond, i.e. also covering the difficult phase of attempts to pick up and in some way to repair the torn threads of continuity following the end of the Cold War. I should add that it is precisely in awareness of the scale of the problem that I make no claim to definitive judgments of the situation, when every year more specialized studies are appearing and more archival sources are opening up.

The culmination of the first phase of my involvement in Czech-German dialogue, and a powerful impulse for subsequent work, was the start of my collaboration with Pavel Tigrid, who in 1997, after the signing of the Czech-German Declaration, invited me to join him in founding the Czech-German Discussion Forum and its Coordination Board, of which I was a member from 1998 to 2004.

The idea of writing a book is usually just the start of a long journey. It took fifteen years of study, field research projects, and meetings with many academics and eye witnesses, before the Czech edition of the book now offered to readers in English translation by the Karolinum Press could appear in the bookshops. I am deeply grateful to Karolinum for long-term support going well beyond the usual relationship between an author and his publisher.

Since the end of the Cold War the postwar transfer/expulsion of ethnic Germans from Central Europe has become a prominent theme in the context of the whole subject of forced migrations of civilian populations in the 20th century, and has loomed large not only in debate within German society but also affected the bilateral relations of the Federal Republic of Germany with the Polish and Czech Republics. Following the retreat of Soviet hegemony, one key focus of discourse in the new situation has been the definition of the content and implications of the concept of "Central Europe", which all at once ceased to be a matter of mildly nostalgic retrospective views of the golden age of the Habsburg multi-ethnic state and the cosmopolitanism of the coffee-houses of Vienna, Prague and Budapest. Central Europe (has) reappeared unexpectedly rapidly in the sphere of real geopolitics, with signs of a "new" Central European order in which German influence has been making ever more headway, by no means just as a matter of power, but also as a model of a functional pluralist system with attractive elements of social market economy. Significantly this new Germany supports the eastwards expansion of the European Union, to which the new democracies looked with a whole range of expectations.

Before the fall of the Iron Curtain voices had been heard from the communist countries calling with apparent nostalgia for the resuscitation of Central Europe, although this is better understood not as a yearning for the "golden times" of the multi-ethnic Austrian monarchy, but more as a desperate appeal on the lines of, "Can't we belong somewhere else than the Soviet part of Europe?". Another ingredient in this wish has been the tendency to a romantic view of politics (affecting both social elites and society as a whole) that has been a long-term feature of Czech political thought and is one of the sources of the deep nationwide frustration that has followed the great but brief flowerings of Czech society (the typically breakpoint moments of 1938, 1968, and 1989).

The question of the expulsion of the Germans from Czechoslovakia has become part of thinking and debate on the transition of Central Europe from totalitarianism to democracy. Despite a whole range of elements of the new European order that might seem to undermine the preoccupation, including the shift of the aspirations of Germany into wider global space, one thing remains certain. Even though the coordinates of world politics have been shifting away from Europe, Central Europe remains politically important, because it evokes memories of the great catastrophes of the twentieth century: Nazism, two world wars, communism and the holocaust.

The divided Germany symbolized the bipolar world of the Cold War, when Central Europe represented the crucial stage and the most likely potential flashpoint of a fearfully expected devastating real war. With the disintegration of the Soviet bloc, history returned to Central Europe and in the course of the permanent process of "coming to terms" with its consequences, a number of conflictual factors have also come back into the relations between Germany and its Eastern neighbours, the Czech Republic and Poland. Decades of Soviet hegemony have left a legacy of Czech and Polish "heightened sensitivity" to any hint of hegemony. In this context the question inevitably arises: are efforts to "get over" history really having the expected positive and purgative effect for current cooperation between Germans and Czechs and Poles?

The modern history of the conflicts between Czechs and Germans, and also of periods of fruitful cooperation between them, needs to be studied in the interacting contexts of Central Europe in a way that enables historical memory to contribute to rapprochement and understanding between neighbouring nations. Failure to "remember" involves the risk of the re-emergence of past conflicts.

The President of the Czechoslovak Republic Tomáš Garrigue Masaryk
in the Library of the Prague Castle in 1930.

1 German Central Europe and Czech Emancipation

The rivalry between Czechs and Germans is not
a problem created by the Versailles Treaty, but has existed
in different forms for more than seven centuries.
Robert William Seton-Watson

The Sudeten German Question did not spring into existence suddenly and un-expectedly with the founding of the Czechoslovak Republic on the 28th of October 1918. It was the organic outcome of the earlier development of what has been called a "community of conflict"[1], in which there had been an escalation of the level of conflict in the latter half of the 19th century as the Czechs sought to achieve political emancipation within the Habsburg Monarchy. The Czech Question had always been the German Question as well, both because of the continuous co-existence and interaction of Czech and German society inside the Czech Lands and because of the constant overlap and broader implications of the issue in the wider Central European region. Czech constitutional and later national political and cultural aspirations indirectly presented a serious obstacle to a unified imperial Germany striving for hegemony in Central Europe. This close correlation between internal and broader issues was behind the development of the influence of Germany on Austrian government policy, and so indirectly on Czech efforts to obtain greater independence, especially in the 1860s and 70s.[2]

Every Czech political action, whether or not it had the slightest anti-German colouring, was essentially confronted and limited by the aspirations of German

---

[1] This term was coined for the relationship between the Czech- and German-speaking inhabitants of the historic lands up to the end of the First World War by Jan Křen. See Křen, J. 1990. *Konfliktní společenství Češi a Němci 1780–1918* [The Community of Conflict: Czechs and Germans 1780–1918]. Prague: Academia.

[2] *Dějiny Československa v datech* [The History of Czechoslovakia in Dates]. 1968. (Collective of authors). Prague: Svoboda. 245–246.

policy. The conflict between Czechs and Germans in the historic lands that has come to be known in a rather oversimplified and not entirely precise way as the Sudeten German Question, can only be understood in the context of its origins and development. These are directly bound up with the whole later nineteenth-century problem of how the Habsburg Monarchy was to be transformed, if at all, into a modern parliamentary democracy capable of tackling national (ethnic) questions in a consensual way.

The following chapter cannot and does not pretend to offer a comprehensive account of Czech-German contacts and conflicts in the 19th century, but will simply highlight a few key moments and issues in the period that set the "community of conflict" on its road to later divorce. A focus on the destructive aspects of development does not mean that the author denies that there were crossroads at which other more positive routes could have been taken, or that there were any lost opportunities for putting Czech-German co-existence on a better footing. It is simply dictated by his attempt to identify the process of the genesis of the destruction of the Czech-German relationship, a process with roots that go back well into the 19th century.

It was in fact in the second half of the 19th century that mutual trust between the two actors broke down in so profound and fundamental way that the gulf was only to deepen with every subsequent return of the Sudeten Question, until after many upheavals and reverses the story ended tragically with the postwar transfer of the Germans out of Czechoslovakia (Bohemia, Moravia, Silesia and Slovakia).

The growth of Czech national consciousness, so striking in the second half of the 19th century, was based on the expanding economic power of the Czech entrepreneurial class, the emerging intelligentsia and the established middle stratum of the bourgeoisie, which increasingly wanted a corresponding share in political power in Austria-Hungary. This was the background to the demands of Czech political leaders for greater political autonomy and less dependence on Vienna as political centre.[3]

During the 1830s and 40s, the Czech "revivalist" movement, as it was known, had started to transform political and cultural ideals into social reality. As soon as the idea of Czech identity had caught hold, the Czech revivalists started to mobilise their successors in social and cultural organisations and to expand and institutionalise Czech public life. It is essential to bear in mind, however, that while the rise of ethnically defined political consciousness and organisation on both the Czech and German sides gave a nationalist edge to their mu-

---

3   Perman, D. 1962. *The Shaping of the Czechoslovak State. Diplomatic History of the boundaries of Czechoslovakia, 1914–1920.* Leiden: Brill. 9.

tual relationship, Czech politics right up to the outbreak of the 1st World War was orientated to the Habsburg Monarchy rather than direct rivalry with Bohemian German neighbours, and in the long term to the goal of reviving Czech statehood within the Austrian multinational state.[4]

After defeat at the Battle of Solferino and the resulting Austrian loss of Lombardy (1859), the Habsburg state treasury finances were so exhausted by the ambitious war in Italy and by crooked machinations with war supplies that the imperial government had no option but to embark on a process of fundamental reforms. The Emperor Franz Josef I resolved that all more important decisions on financial matters would from now on be approved by the Imperial Council (an elected assembly). Calling the council was the first of a long series of measures that were supposed gradually to change the entire system.[5]

It soon became clear that the issue was not just a matter of finances, but of the basic need for critical reassessment of the whole government system of absolutism, which was bureaucratising every aspect of life and suppressing civic initiative. The trouble was that however radical the ensuing series of "state revolutions", from Bach's neo-absolutist reforms, the establishment of Austro-Hungarian dualism to Schmerling's pseudo-constitutionalism, they all took place without consultation with the broader public, as matters purely for "the government and key circles". The exclusion of public opinion in general (if one can even speak of such a thing at the time), applied doubly for Czechs in the monarchy. In contrast to the year 1848 and its aftermath, when civic initiative had played a key role, society now adopted a cautious "wait and see" attitude, reacting slowly and piecemeal to each of the constitutional "faits accomplis" with which it was presented.

The fall of the absolutist regime of Alexander Bach and Anton von Schmerling's appointment as prime minister opened up a little space for Czechs to pursue their own demands within the constitutional framework of the monarchy. Yet the new era was heralded by the constitution promulgated in February 1861, which with its moves toward dualism, bureaucratic centralism, retention of the decisive influence of the aristocracy and imperial court, and preference given to the German bourgoisie, in fact set the coordinates of the entire subsequent political fate of Austria.[6]

These coordinates did not allow for any serious participation by the Czechs as an equal partner. Any kind of Czech aspirations to national emancipation

---

[4]   Beneš, Z. Historické kořeny [Historical Roots], in *Rozumět dějinám* [Understanding History]. 2002. Kural, V. – Beneš, Z. (eds.). Prague: Gallery. 28.

[5]   Urban, O. 1982. *Česká společnost 1848–1918* [Czech Society 1848–1918]. Prague: Svoboda. 145.

[6]   Šolle, Z. 1998. *Století české politiky – od Palackého k Masarykovi* [Centuries of Czech Politics – from Palacký to Masaryk]. Prague: Mladá fronta. 52–53.

were considered to be in conflict with the model of a unified state, and all the more so when most of the leading Czech political figures had been compromised in government eyes by their activities in 1848. There was no serious reason to take account of any special wishes expressed by the "Ultra-Czechs" and no reason even to invite any of them to the debates of the duplicated imperial council or anywhere else where decisions were to be taken. Czech society simply did not exist for "decision-making circles" and the "subversive" Czech or Ultra-Czech party was under permanent and reliable police surveillance.[7]

In his historical study, O. Urban posed the question of how the existence of a nation five-million strong in the middle of the European continent could so easily be ignored? He found part of the answer in an article entitled "Our Homeland in the Eyes of Liberal Europe" by J. V. Frič in the newspaper *Čech* which he published as an emigrant in Switzerland.[8]

For centuries the Bohemian Lands had been inhabited by both Czechs and Germans. The Czech element had been very prominent in the medieval period, but in the new era after the defeat of the Bohemian Estates at the Battle of the White Mountain in 1620, the more that expressions of medieval culture and learning had been repressed or had faded, the more outwardly German the Bohemian Lands had become in character. This was not so much because of the attitude of the native German population. It was much more the result of governmental interference from the Enlightenment absolutist regime in Vienna and of the dominant influence of German high culture, which matured to classical greatness in the age of Goethe. For the wider 19th-century world a Czech was an Austrian and an Austrian was a German, and it was not just Frič who found it hard to explain to the external world that there were real differences. Urban nonetheless rejected as over-simplified the idea that external indifference or disparagement was just an expression of lack of understanding or ill-will; he argued that it was also to a significant extent a reflection of the internal strength (or weakness) and structure of Czech society.[9]

This situation had its deep historical roots, of course. The Bohemian Crown Lands (Bohemia, Moravia, Silesia) had for long centuries existed as a separate state formation within the Holy Roman Empire. After the dissolution of the lat-

---

[7]   Urban, O. *Česká společnost 1848–1918*. 155.

[8]   "They do not talk about us at all and know even less about us. And if they do know something about our existence, like the Polish and Hungarian emigrants, they speak with unconcealed criticism of Czechs as 'the most obedient Austrian officials', and 'the handiest policemen'", and if they are democrats, then they always add that Czechs are suspect Pan-Slavists." Ibidem.

[9]   In a leaflet of the period published in 1860, "Czech Sketches", and giving a detailed account of the Czech position, the author writes that, "it cannot be denied that the German bourgeois is more educated, much more formed by general and specialist education, by life itself, the press, numerous libraries, reading clubs and so on." The overall material and intellectual weakness of the Czech bourgeoisie was one of the main causes of the relative shakiness of Czech liberalism and democratism in this period. Ibidem. 158–159.

ter in the Napoleonic period, they became a part of the German Confederation, created in 1815 as an association of states (not a federal state) that included most of the former members of the Holy Roman Empire. The Bohemian and Alpine Lands were the only parts of the Habsburg Empire to be included in the German Confederation; the others, above all the whole Hungarian Kingdom and Galicia, remained outside it. This was one of the reasons why Polish and Hungarian liberals entirely diverged from Czech liberals in their attitude towards German aspirations and moves towards unification as represented in 1848 by the Frankfurt National Assembly.

The more that all but the most formal attributes of Bohemian statehood disappeared in the post-White Mountain period, the more real became the prospects for the integration of the Bohemian Lands into a larger Central European entity, regardless of whether the entity would reflect what was known as the Greater German (Grossdeutsche) solution (the frontiers to be those of the German Confederation), or the so-called Lesser German (Kleindeutsche) solution (i.e. with the exclusion of the relevant territories of the Habsburg Monarchy), or Schwarzenberg's concept of an empire of seventy million souls (i.e. the union of the lands of the Confederation with the other Lands of the Habsburg Monarchy).

Just how far things had gone in the direction of integration by the mid-19th century is evident enough from the fact that the then spokesmen of Czech society did not dare to raise the question of Czech statehood in emphatic and unambiguous terms. Instead they sought a "roof" for Czech aspirations to emancipation, and found one in the idea of a remoulded Austria. The outstretched wings of the Austrian eagle were supposed to protect the sleeping Bohemian lion. The shift of the centre of gravity to Austria – whatever the extent to which it corresponded to real conditions and possibilities – had eroded the distinctive identity of the Bohemian Lands.[10]

In the pursuit of their (still limited) aspirations the Czech liberals at first joined forces with the conservative nobility in a programme of "local patriotism" and appeal to continuity with the medieval Bohemian Kingdom as the basis for the right to limited statehood. In the spirit of this programme they called for the Emperor Franz Josef I to have himself crowned King of Bohemia. The German liberals, on the other hand, however much they desired constitutional reform, resolutely supported the government in its efforts to maintain the centralised form of the state.

After 1861 Czechs were already rejecting Germanisation as the price of social advancement, and were competing with the German elite for political power

---

[10] Ibidem. 156.

and social advantages as Czechs.[11] In the 1860s the trend in politics, in societies for entertainment and in various professional organisations was for separation on ethnic lines. Over the 1860s and 1870s a quite closely integrated network of German associations developed in the Bohemian Lands; there was a great deal of overlap in the top ranks of the associations involved and the Kasino Club of Prague Germans emerged as the leader of the whole group.[12]

The German liberal groups in Prague centred on the Kasino Club increasingly had to face not only their traditional enemies, such as clerical conservatives and Czech nationalists, but also the new and more problematic rise of anti-liberal, radical nationalism of *völkisch* type, which was gaining support among Germans in the Bohemian borderlands. These German nationalists blamed the problems of small German people on Czech interlopers, international socialists, Jewish crooks and their protectors in the corrupted Liberal Party. Criticism of the German liberals helped the *völkisch* movement to win over the lower social classes, who were attracted by the new, more prestigious consciousness of German identity based in a simple way on language and social identification.

Spokesmen of the *völkisch* movement blamed the liberals for rapid industrialisation and the emancipation of the Jews, which was allegedly the reason for the economic problems of the border areas (agrarian depression and the mechanisation of manufactures). Broad German national solidarity, the prospect of laws restricting the Jews, and the political separation of the Czech and German parts of Bohemia were causes with considerable appeal for the petit bourgeoisie and many workers in the German environment of the borderlands. G. Cohen argues that as extreme nationalism gained headway among the masses, the liberals were too obsessed with keeping a united German front against the conservative Slav coalition to take the fundamental step of distancing themselves from the programme principles of the *völkisch* movement.

All the same, the hostility of the borderland Germans to the moderate German liberals continued to grow. The groups of liberals around the Kasino tried to maintain their ties with moderate Germans in the border areas and sent campaigners to the German towns in Bohemia. They discovered to their cost, as the radical German nationalists were discovering to their benefit, that the revolt

---

[11]   Cohen, G. B. 2000. *Němci v Praze 1861–1914* [The Germans in Prague 1861–1914]. Prague: Karolinum. 28–46. Relevant here is the speech made by F. L. Rieger in the Imperial Council in the name of the Czech liberals on the 19th of June 1861, in which he developed the national theme to the full: "Nowhere in the world do people say 'science francaise' or 'English science', but I have heard and read the words 'Deutsche Wissenschaft' hundreds and thousands of times!! And how often have we had to hear that 'The German language is utterly unique, that it is our language of culture, science and that science can be cultivated only in the German language!" Urban, O. *Česká společnost 1848–1918*. 170.

[12]   For a detailed account see Vytváření německého společenského života v Praze [The Creation of German Social Life in Prague], in Cohen, G. B. *Němci v Praze 1861–1914*. 55–62.

against the old liberal elite was going beyond disputes over political power and influence and was increasingly bound up with fears for the very survival of the German minority in Bohemia.[13] In the Prague municipal government, Czech-German hostility entered a new phase in the 1880s when the council fell almost completely into the hands of Czech deputies, who thus became the beneficiaries of the considerable measure of autonomy that the German liberals had won for local government in Austria in the preceding period, when they had needed it to further their own interests.

The growing ethnic tension between Czechs and Germans involved revolt against the liberal Austrian state and turned against the Jews, the most conspicuous and vulnerable of the groups that had been benefitting from liberal constitutionalism.[14]

In the course of the 19th century both Czechs and Germans in the Austrian state were becoming increasingly aware of their different ethnic-linguistic identities and then consciously developing that sense of identity into increasingly clear-cut "national" positions that undermined their ability to co-exist. The head-start that the German-speaking inhabitants of the Bohemian Lands had enjoyed as a result of initially faster industrialisation was consistently diminishing in the second part of the 19th century, as was clear for example when Czech councillors came to dominate the Prague municipal council. This was partly because of the continuing advances of Czech society, with Czechs no longer disproportionately concentrated in lower social strata but developing a complete social structure through economic and cultural progress, and partly because of the marked slowdown of the economic development of German areas, which failed to exploit new trends (for example they showed a stubborn attachment to the textile industry that was falling behind). The loss of economic dynamism in the German areas had immediate results in the social sphere, where modernising processes were retarded with corresponding effects on the political choices of Bohemian Germans and their political leaders.

---

[13] Cohen, G. B. *Němci v Praze 1861–1914.* 116–118. The following opinion from the period press is characteristic: "The arrogance with which some Prague Germans look down on the artisan class is pushing it into the Czech circle and so today, as well informed individuals emphasise, there is not a single German tailor here… The Prague Germans lack the broad and firm base of an artisan middle class. They must therefore rely on the German towns and village districts or they will be lost." *Politik.* 30. 10. 1883.

[14] Cohen, G. B. *Němci v Praze 1861–1914.* 134–135. At the beginning of the 1880s the Prague Jews were facing antisemitism among some Czech radical nationalists, the German radicals in the Bohemian borderlands and the Prague German University, and also in sections of the lower class of Germans in Prague. G. Cohen considers the theory that the Jews were becoming progressively alienated from both Czech and German bourgeois society but this is uncertain. There are indications that as a result of the growing antisemitism of German society the Jews were gradually moving over to the Czech milieux. This trend was particularly evident after the establishment of the independent CSR.

Czechs and Germans had lived side by side for centuries. The two ethnic groups had led separate existences with language as the most powerful sign of their distinct identities. In the towns they attended their own churches, founded separate political parties, and lived their own cultural and economic lives. In Prague members of the two groups had even gone to their own different concert halls. Relative overall numbers was clearly a significant factor for the relations between, and political positions of, the two ethnic groups in Bohemian Lands, with demographic estimates of these provoking many disputes and challenges at the time.

In the mixed areas of Bohemia and Moravia it was hard to produce any reliable study of the ethnic composition of the population. The modern historian Z. Zeman draws attention to one detailed analysis (Rauchberg, H. *Der nationale Besitzstand in Böhmen* [National Assets in Bohemia]. 1905. Leipzig) of the first three censuses of the population carried out in Bohemia in 1880, 1890 and 1900, preceded in each case by heated debate in the Vienna Parliament on the criteria of nationality to be used.[15] The statistical censuses were supposed to identify a changing situation but in each case different statistical methods were employed. This opened the door to constant politically interested challenges to the results, for the census results were very politically sensitive, since they were used to justify direct political demands for schools teaching in one language or another or the use of the language in official contexts, and indeed were regarded as a measure of success or failure in the national struggle.[16]

In these circumstances the censuses themselves were difficult to carry out in the first place, as well as interpret. Professor Rauchberg had himself expressed fears that if a statistical census of the population was carried out there would be national/ethnic conflicts between Czechs and Germans that would go as far as the "division of individual families and individuals". In the preface to his study, however, he declared that he himself was striving for objectivity and was convinced that his work would contribute to the maintenance of internal peace in Austria. In fact Rauchberg was unable to resist the temptation to give his arguments a sharp political edge. He compared the strength of the Germans with the weakness of the Czechs, whose numbers in the Bohemian Lands (the core of the nation) did not even reach as much as six million, and stressed that the Slavs in Austria did not form a compact unit like the Germans and that only

---

15   Zeman, Z. 1998. *Vzestup a pád komunistické Evropy* [The Rise and Fall of Communist Europe]. Prague: Mladá fronta. 28. Rauchberg was aware of the provocative meanings of the term "national assets", which had already become a part of political vocabulary. In fact he saw the concept as covering "the whole current situation relating to all the national interests that are the subject of disputes between Czechs and Germans".

16   Ibidem. 31. After publication of Rauchberg's book there was yet another census, in 1910, the results of which were challenged even by the Austrian officials themselves. In the end the official publication of the census rated most of the results obtained using the criterion of *Umgangsprache*/language of social intercourse as "relatively reliable".

the Austrian state could secure peaceful ethnic relations. While he dismissed the possible Slav link between the Czechs and Russia as a piece of wishful thinking in politics, he insisted that the number of Germans in Bohemia was of international significance. He argued that the skill with which two and a half million Germans were defending their position in Bohemia was a positive influence on the attitudes of the further almost seven million Germans in Austria, and that the Austrian Germans were united by *Kulturgemeinschaft*/cultural community with the 60 million Germans of the Reich.[17]

The term "national assets" as used by Rauchberg thus becomes part of a geopolitical argument expressing the superior position of the German element in Central Europe – a position on which the Bohemian Germans could rely for the long-term prospects of their struggle with the Czechs. Yet even as he wrote, the situation sketched by Rauchberg was changing, and not only in Prague, where by the turn of the century the proportion of German inhabitants had fallen from 20.6 % to 8.5 %. The change in ethnic ratios in the mining and industrial areas of North Bohemia, for example, was even more radical.[18]

The political importance attributed to relative numbers of population is also evident from the fact that on the Czech side the *Národní jednota severočeská*/ North Bohemian National Union organised a "private census, because only these give a real picture of Czech minorities and will convince anyone of the incorrectness of the previous census based on the criterion to 'language of social intercourse'".[19] Using very detailed statistical data, the Union claimed that "in the official census of 1900 55,052 fewer Czechs were counted (than should have been), and similarly in the eastern part the figures were artificially low by a large margin, but precise numbers have not been established".

The long-term contiguity of Czechs and Germans in the Bohemian Lands was the reason why the notion of a "Mitteleuropa", characterised by German

---

[17] Ibidem. 33.

[18] E.g. in 1880 there were 31 thousand Germans and 2 thousand Czechs living in Most while 20 years later there were 54 thousand Germans and 20 thousand Czechs. Over the same period the overall numbers of German population of the North grew by 60% and of Czechs by 300%. After Prague, Vienna became the biggest Czech city, with 400–600 thousand inhabitants of Czech nationality living there in 1900. Ibidem. 34.

[19] Šubrt, J. 1908. *Vývoj a život českých menšin* [The Development and Life of Czech Minorities]. Vols. 1, 2. Most: Severočeské menšinové knihkupectví a nakladatelství (O. J. Bukač). 1. According to aggregate data at the end of the publication the official census gave the population numbers for the Bohemian Lands as a whole as 3 930 093 Czechs and 2 337 013 Germans, while the private census gave 4 069 000 Czechs and 2 198 106 Germans. The publication also challenges the school statistics and ends by stating that the private census had been undertaken, "in order to raise the awareness of the Czech public about its needs and to gain greater understanding for the North Czech Union and the Central School Foundation. This publication should serve to provide information during legislative debate on the next census in 1910, which ought to be taken using the criterion of mother tongue, for as has been demonstrated several times above, the previous conduct of official censuses has been illegal, because in districts with a German minority it violates Article XIX of the fundamental state laws. And therefore it should not serve as official information either for the legislature, executive or courts." Ibidem. 508.

political culture, survived here even after the 1st World War and establishment of new political frontiers.[20] At the heart of theories on the specific nature of this area was belief in the special, key role of Germany and Germanness in Central European space. The tragic consequences of the militant chauvinism and the political messianism that proved so resonant in the Sudeten German areas will be our subject in further chapters.

The national movement on both the Czech and German side was both established and strengthened by national political agitation. The fight for primacy between the two ethnic groups in one country continued and intensified throughout the 19th century, especially the latter half. It soon became clear that "Czech identity" (tchéquité) might well evaporate under the pressure of Austro-German authoritarian, anti-western and anti-liberal ideology, which was in any case deeply contrary to the traditional orientation of Czechs to western progressive thought. In this situation two possibilities remained to the Czech nation: either to strive for autonomy within a federal monarchy, i.e. for the same quasi-independence for which the Hungarian nobility were fighting with ever more energy, or to take the path of a radical political programme aiming for complete national independence.

In the course of the 19th century the Czechs as an ethnic group were increasingly meeting the "nation-building" requirement of possessing a "complete" social structure, above all with the emergence of their own social elites capable of formulating a national programme and pursuing it through the political and administrative structures of the Habsburg Monarchy. Paradoxically, this was in some ways a process of Germanisation, associated with the adoption of the German bourgeois life style, which for the Bohemian Lands represented an advanced model of society. Similar processes were taking place in parts of Western Europe, but to a lesser extent and only exceptionally in a form that linked cultural emulation to conflict (e.g. the Irish Question).[21]

---

[20]   Meyer, H. C. 1955. *Mitteleuropa in German Thought and Action 1815–1945*. The Hague: Martinus Nijhoff, 341. For more on this theme see also the series of articles by Bělohradský, V. "Sjednocené Německo a Západ: Tři lekce" [United Germany and the West; Three Lessons]. *Lidové noviny*. 12.–14. 6. 1995. With the exception of the repeated annexation and loss of the Cheb region (*Egerland*) in the 14th century, the Bohemian-German border (i.e. the border of the former hereditary lands of the Bohemian Crown, with Lusatia and Silesia) remained essentially unchanged despite many wars and violent changes. It was only with the annexation of the so-called Sudeten borderlands of the CSR after the Munich Agreement imposed on Czechoslovakia in September 1938 that this continuity was fundamentally disrupted. European history has been full of border conflicts, but this one was unusual in that both sides of the conflict, i.e. the Czech and German state, including the Sudeten Germans, had never until the Munich crisis challenged the border line itself despite the fact that it did not even roughly correspond to demarcation between language areas.

[21]   Křen, J. 1992. *Historické proměny češství* [The Historical Transformations of Czech Identity]. 60. On the 12th of December 1893 the Young Czech leader Eduard Grégr proclaimed in the Imperial Council in Vienna: "Yes, Gentlemen, Bohemia is the Ireland of Austria. Without a doubt. I could develop the comparison in detail, but still. After many centuries of persecution, bloody and cruel persecution, powerful England is having to

As has been noted, a major factor for the modern history of the relations between Czechs and Germans was the changing *population ratio* between them. From the 13th century, when the colonisation of the border areas by settlers from neighbouring Germany had begun, the proportion of Germans had risen smoothly from an original one quarter to a third of the overall population of the Bohemian Lands[22]. This ratio remained roughly stable overall up to 1945, when the fateful moment came in the form of the transfer of the German-speaking inhabitants of the Bohemian Lands.[23]

Western influences reached Central Europe partly but by no means exclusively from German milieux. Some Sudeten German publications have tendentiously claimed that German neighbours were the sole mediator of such influences on the cultural development of the Bohemian Lands, but this is not the case.[24] For example, W. K. Turnwald's work is informed by the frequent claims of Sudeten German authors about the "thousand-year cultural mission" of the Germans to the east (one aspect of the political messianism of pan-German concepts), and entirely overlooks the fact that Germany did not exist in its modern form until the second half of the 19th century. Before that it had been a mere tangle of medieval states and statelets, whose path to a unified national state was only to be opened up by the revolutionary situation of 1848.[25]

The physical and territorial proximity of Czechs and Germans laid the foundations for early manifestations of ethno-centric consciousness[26] which only

---

give back to poor Ireland its freedom and independence, it is only a matter of a short time. And in just the same way weak Austria too will be forced to give in to the just demands of the Czech nation." Urban, O. *Česká společnost 1848–1918*. 428.

[22] The year 1910 is generally considered to be the moment when the German population of the Bohemian Lands reached its highest point. According to some authors the percentage of German-speaking inhabitants of the Bohemians Lands dropped from 35% in 1910 to 29.2 % in 1930 and it was this trend that among other factors gave rise to fears about ultimate survival provoking the political demand for the division of the Bohemian Lands and later even the establishment of a closed Sudeten German territory within the CSR. See Bohmann, A. 1959. *Das Sudetendeutschtum in Zahlen*. München: Sudetendeutscher Rat. Handbuch über den Bestand und die Entwicklung der sudetendeutschen Volksgruppe in den Jahren von 1910 bis 1950. Die kulturellen, soziologischen und wirtschaftlichen Verhältnisse im Spiegel der Statistik. München: Sudetendeutscher Rat. 16. This was also why the situation of German settlement in 1910 was later taken as the basis for defining the territories to be annexed to Germany on the basis of the Munich Agreement.

[23] Hauner, M. 1993. "The Czechs and Germans: A One-Thousand Year Relationship", in *The Germans and Their Neighbours*. Boulder/San Francisco/Oxford: Westview Press. 258.

[24] "In their thousand years of history the inhabitants of Central Europe have belonged to Western culture and civilisation. This applies to Czechs as well as to Slovaks, Hungarians, Poles and other inhabitants of this region. It arises from the geographical and historical situation, the fact that the Germans brought them Christianity and many other elements of their culture and civilisation." Turnwald, W. K. 1954. *Renascence or Decline of Central Europe*. Munich: University Press Wolf & Sohn. 75.

[25] Šolle, Z. – Gajanová, A. 1969. *Po stopě dějin (Češi a Slováci v letech 1848–1938)* [On the Trail of History (Czechs and Slovaks in the Years 1848–1938)]. Prague: Orbis. 26.

[26] Modernising processes and social advance were accompanied in the Bohemian Lands by *assimilation and Germanisation*, but this was entirely utilitarian in nature, given by the need for a unifying language for official purposes in the multi-ethnic monarchy, and not by any campaign to forcibly strip ethnic groups of their iden-

later in the 19th century acquired the forms of modern nationalist rivalry. Continuity with earlier conflict, however, ensured that it was a concept of national/ethnic identity based on language that predominated among the Czech and German population over the land patriotism (Bohemian patriotism regardless of language) theoretically formulated by Bernard Bolzano.[27]

This latter noble but utopian idea was already at odds with the reality of Czech-German relations at the time of its formulation and was rejected by both sides, Czech and German. Bolzano with his fiction of a unified Bohemian nation (differentiated by language into Czech and German speaking parts) and a single homeland without regard to differences of language, custom and historical experience, sought to overcome differences that could no longer be smoothed over even in his time (he died in 1848).[28] Bolzano wanted to reconcile Czechs and Germans in a situation when they were no longer parts of one whole but represented two different wholes, consciously separate.

The increasingly potent ethnic-national factor ever more effectively marginalised the *böhmisch* idea (land patriotism) which reflected the attitudes and mode of thought of part of the land nobility, whose view was best expressed by Count Josef Matyáš Thun when he declared that "I am neither a Czech nor a German, but just an inhabitant of Bohemia (ein Böhme)".[29] The idea was, of course, linked to the specific political agenda of the land nobility in relation to the overall character of the Habsburg Monarchy, i.e. they were strongly against the centralising tendencies of the Austrian state.

---

tity in a way comparable to later nationalist Germanisation. "Fascinated by the centralist structure of French absolutism, Joseph II expressed his desire for linguistic uniformity. There is general agreement that Joseph was not motivated by nationalist considerations – the Habsburg embrace of German starts with Maria Theresa." Šamalík, F. 1996. *Úvahy o dějinách české politiky* [Reflections on the History of Czech Politics]. Prague: Victoria Publishing. 247.

[27] An elaborated vision of "Bohemism" as active land patriotism was formulated by B. Bolzano (1781–1848). His education at a Piarist gymnasium had given him a love of exact science and distaste for high-flown or speculative philosophy. His goal was usefulness for the common good as the criterion of justice – a concept showing traces of the influence of Rousseau's Social Contract. He understood patriotism in a similar light – as being useful to one's country. Bolzano was open in his criticism of the inequality suffered by the Czechs, such that social advancement in Bohemia inevitably meant the Germanisation of the individual. But his ideal of a depoliticised nationalism through simple sincere reform was a utopia that was accepted by neither side. For more detail see Loewenstein, B. "Vlastenectví jako otevřený projekt" [Patriotism as an Open Project], in *Češi a Němci 150 let po Bolzanovi (bilance a očekávání)* [Czechs and Germans 150 Years after Bolzano (Looking Back and Forward)]. 1998. Prague: Prago-Media-News. 60–61.

[28] According to Bolzano a true patriotism could only come into being when the people recognised the truth that Bohemia was the most fruitful and blessed land in Europe, and was capable of all sciences and virtues. He wanted to awaken in the nation and people an awareness of their own abilities and past values. This meant that the nation must be historically acquainted with its destiny, for only then will it believe in itself. For a detailed account see "Bolzanovo české vlastenectví" [Bolzano's Bohemian Patriotism], in Kutnar, F. 2003. *Obrozenské vlastenectví a nacionalismus* [Enlightenment Patriotism and Nationalism]. Prague: Karolinum. 237–244.

[29] Kořalka, J. 1996. *Češi v habsburské říši a v Evropě 1815–1914* [Czechs in the Habsburg Empire and in Europe 1815–1914]. Prague: Argo. 42.

Bohemian patriotism as the conservative, anti-centralising ideology of the nobility was encouraged both by the nature of noble property holdings (noble families often had estates in a number of different Austrian Lands) and cosmopolitan upbringing – their linguistic and intellectual horizons extended beyond the Bohemian Lands and often even Central Europe.[30] Inevitably, however, theirs was the standpoint of a small section of the social elite with only a limited influence on the course of nation-building processes and politics in the wider sense.

The opinions of Count Thun and others in fact show the efforts of the land nobility to remain "above" the growing tension between the two major ethnic groups in the Bohemian Lands, although lack of wider social support doomed most of these efforts to failure.

A smaller group among the old Bohemian nobility (according to F. M. Pelcl just ten noblemen[31]) saw the Czech language as an integral part of their political identity, understood in a wider sense as part of *land patriotism*.

M. Hroch has noted critically that "one of the stereotypes of historiography (not only German) is to talk about the *anti-German* character of the Czech national movement". He points out that in fact the first generation of Czech patriots (many of them scholars and clerics) used or indeed wavered between concepts of ethnic identity and land identity, and this suggests that their attitude to the Germans was far from as clear-cut and intolerant as is sometimes claimed. Their patriotism was based on the enlightenment ideal of the *moral code of the learned man*, who is responsible for the upbringing and education of "his" people, and for the prosperity and success of "his" homeland. On the other hand, this patriotism had in common with land patriotism little more than the fact that the object of its interest and engagement was in the Czech case a politically defined historical territory – the Bohemian Lands.[32]

The historical tradition of the existence of a Bohemian state was an important theme of the Czech national movement (and likewise of modern Czech politics), and for readers who do not speak Czech it should be noted that the Czech word for Bohemia (Čechy) and the Bohemian Lands (České země) has always been cognate with the word for ethnic Czech (Čech). History, together

---

[30] Ibidem.

[31] The same Professor Pelcl distinguished between "real Bohemians" otherwise called "Böhme" and "Non-Bohemians", whom he called "Deutschböhmen", see Hroch, M. 1999. *V národním zájmu* [In the National Interest]. Prague: Lidové noviny. 74. 63. This distinction is not connected in meaning with later similar terms at the time of the establishment of an independent CSR.

[32] J. Jungmann wrote in 1806 that responsibility for the fate of the nation rested entirely with the secular men of learning because the clergy was bound by its church duties, while teachers were very badly paid and not very well educated. The linguistic definition of the nation was not Jungmann's discovery but an organic development from an older Czech historiographical tradition reaching right back to the medieval chronicle of Dalimil. Ibidem. 62.

with cultural and linguistic roots provided the basic arguments for the demand for the revival of the Bohemian Lands (ie. Bohemia, Moravia, Silesia) in the form of a nation state. The importance of the historical dimension is clear from the fact that the very first years of the era of national revival saw a series of polemics between enlightenment historians on the interpretation of particular historical events and individual historical figures (e.g. F. M. Pelcl's monographs on Charles IV and Wenceslas IV, the controversy over the ethnic identity of Prince Samo etc.).

F. Seibt has claimed that it was purely and simply J. G. Herder and his romantic idea of the nation that woke Czech national consciousness, i.e. once again that Czech culture even in its self-affirmation was just a product of German influence. In fact there were many other major influences on Czech revivalist thought, a great many of them coming directly from France (the idea of equality of citizens, the influence of French enlightenment philosophers and the French Revolution – for example J. Jungmann's favourite philosopher was Voltaire). Nor was the revival simply a matter of anti-German reaction. The attitude of Czech patriots of the first generation, whose conception of their identity oscillated between the ethnic and the territorial, led at first more to reflection on themselves and their heritage than to uncompromising Czech-German confrontation.[33]

T. G. Masaryk in his declaration of political principles, *The New Europe – The Slav Standpoint*, wrote that "it makes no sense to speak of Germanism and Romanticism as the driving forces behind the struggle between western nations. All nations and states had been against each other up to then, and parts of the same nation against each other". He went on to argue that it was also mistaken to see external struggle between nations as the only basis for understanding the development and position of individual nations, including the Czech: "It is in no way sufficient for an interpretation of the history and development of individual nations to refer only to antagonism with neighbours: every nation has developed not only through hostility to its neighbours but from its own internal powers... I do not deny that the life of individuals and nations is to a significant extent a matter of competition and struggle, but both the individual and the nations develop through their own specific attributes and individuality."[34] Masaryk refused to accept that the origins and development of

---

[33] Hroch, M. *V národním zájmu*. 62, points out that the patriotism of the scholars and men of learning from the poorer classes differed from aristocratic land patriotism. All that it had in common with land patriotism, which was focused mainly on historic estates rights, was engagement in the cause of a politically defined historic entity, i.e. the Bohemian Lands. Otherwise the scholars embraced a different patriotism based on the Enlightenment moral codes of the educated man, responsible for the education and welfare of "his" people.

[34] Masaryk, T. G. 1920. *Nová Evropa – stanovisko slovanské* [The New Europe – The Slav View]. Prague: G. Dubský. 187.

a national community could be reduced purely to struggle, but with his characteristic positive approach he insisted on the no less important part played by
the emergence of national consciousness that he saw in the inner dynamism of
a national community, in its creative abilities, intellectual riches and its industrious development of its potential.

Other authors have also challenged the stress on the romantic "eastern" variant of nationalism as a type born exclusively out of struggle. In any case, Herder's philosophy was not distinctively "eastern" but can also be found among
Flemings, Catalans and even in the Irish and Norwegian national movements.[35]
There are good grounds for scepticism about the constant insistence (especially
in German literature) on the decisive influence of romanticism in the genesis
of national movements. The whole interpretation is founded on the unprovable
idea of a "spirit of nationalism" haunting Europe. The contribution of romanticism and romantics to national movements is indisputable, but their influence
was not confined to national movements with political programmes, nor is this
influence enough to explain and characterise them.

At this point we should also mention the requirement for a *complete social
structure* as a precondition for national aspirations, for this had an influence on
the content of the national programme and its realisation. The significant correlation between the social structure of a non-ruling ethnic group (in our case
Czechs within the Austrian monarchy) and the phases of the birth of a national
movement has been noted by M. Hroch and other authors such as J. Křen or
D. Perman[36]. The growth of Czech national consciousness in the later 19th century was based on the growing economic power of the Czech business class,
emergent intelligentsia and established bourgeoisie, who then wanted a corresponding share of political power in Austria-Hungary. This was the background to the increasingly urgent demands of the Czech political leadership
for political autonomy and greater independence from Vienna.[37]

An important role in the preservation and revival of historical consciousness
of Czech statehood was played in Czech society by historiography, especially

---

[35] Hroch, M. *V národním zájmu*. 74.
[36] Hroch identifies three phases in the development of every national movement. Phase A is the period of
scholarly interest, when the language of an ethnic group, its past, culture and way of life becomes the object of
enlightenment interest and study. At this point national identity is just being born. Phase B is the period of
national agitation, when a group of patriots (mainly scholars) convinces the members of an ethnic group that
they are members of a nation that has the same value and attributes as already existing nations. The national
movement is still in a reversible stage from the point of view of the secure formation of a nation. Phase C is
what Hroch calls *mass movements*, which develop out of national agitation and involve the mobilisation of
tens of thousands of people. The national movement has achieved a complete social structure and formed the
nation. Its role ends with the achievement of political independence or extensive autonomy.
[37] Perman, D. *The Shaping of the Czechoslovak State*. 9.

given the high levels of literacy[38] in the population of the Czech Lands. The cultivation of historical consciousness was an integral aspect of the formation of a modern nation whose primary demands were *political participation and the right to autonomous existence*, with leaders of the Czech *risorgimento* drawing on that history and the revived Czech language as supporting arguments.[39] In this respect F. Palacký and his book *The History of the Czech Nation*, which was the theoretical basis for his philosophy of Czech history and programme for a modern Czech politics for the later 19th century, were of crucial significance.

Whole books have been written on the multiple possible definitions of the "nation". Definition of the concept of the nation is difficult, often imprecise, and the content of the concept was constantly changing, as many authors have observed including the great expert on Central Europe and its national problems Seton-Watson, who confessed that, "I am therefore forced to conclude that no "scientific definition" of the nation can be constructed, even though this phenomenon has existed and continues to exist. All that can be said is that a nation exists when a significant number of people in a community share the view that it forms a nation or behave as if they formed a unity. It is not necessary for the whole population to feel or act in this way, nor is it possible to state dogmatically some minimum percentage of the population that needs to be affected. If the conviction is shared by a significant group of inhabitants, it is then the bearer of "national consciousness"."[40]

Anthony D. Smith has offered a more precise and material definition of the basic features (preconditions of the genesis) of national identity: a historical territory or homeland, common myths and historical memories, a shared mass public culture, shared legally secured rights and duties for all members, a shared economy with mobility across the territory for all members.[41]

---

[38] J. Křen draws attention to the precondition of modernising processes in the Habsburg Monarchy, education – and the fact that the Bohemian Lands soon took the lead in terms of literacy (through the introduction of compulsory elementary education). The new organisation of middle and higher schools allowed the emergence of a secular intelligentsia, administrative and technical. For ethnic Czechs, the arrival of a generation that had received a full-scale education in the national language, which had previously been German, was a decisive influence on their own development of national consciousness. Křen, J. *Historické proměny češství*. 59–61.

[39] The use of Czech as the language of the kings and estates of the Pre-White-Mountain era was an obvious argument against Vienna centralism. In addition, language represented a necessary integrating element for an ethnic community on the road to the formation of a cultural nation. H. Seton-Watson expressed the point vividly: "The leaders of the Czech national revival were technicians of the language, and language became the criterion of national identity." Seton-Watson, H. 1977. *Nations And States*. Boulder: Westview. 152.

[40] Ibidem. 5.

[41] Smith, A. D. 1991. *National Identity*. London/New York: Penguin Books. See also the inspiring article by Smith, A. D. "Nationalism and the Historians". *International Journal of Comparative Sociology* XXXIII/1–2 (1992). Smith sees the emergence of national identity as a process involving at least two phases. For the first, in developmental terms the lowest phase of the formation of ethnic identity, he proposes the term "ethnic category" which is an overall label for specific cultural features (linguistically close dialects, elements of life

One might identify Seton-Watson's definition and Smith's definition with Eastern and Western nationalism respectively, but in fact Smith's definition can usefully be applied to the development of Czech national consciousness in the 19th century. In general, as P. Barša and M. Strmiska have pointed out, the supposedly Western model of the nation, which includes the notion of a specific cultural community, unified collective memory and shared social values, among them myths about the origins of the nation and its mission, in many ways overlaps with the Eastern concept. A closer view reveals that the distinction between the genesis of the nations of Western and Eastern Europe is somewhat artificial.

The western and eastern models of the nation are ideal types that exist in pure form only as theoretical models. In reality they are always modified on the basis of concrete political, territorial and historical context. Not even in the case of "nations with established states", can civic-political membership of the nation ever be entirely divorced from ethnic-cultural membership.[42]

Despite certain reservations about the definition of different forms of nationalism, A. D. Smith regards the distinction between civic-territorial and ethnic-cultural national consciousness to be useful, but far from hard and fast. Ethnic and cultural identity always to a certain extent overlaps with or permeates territorial and political identity. All nations are at one and the same time cultural and political.[43] In the light of these facts the now traditional argument of Sudeten German historiography on the inferior position of the nations of Central and Eastern Europe (including the Czechs), whose emergence was allegedly accompanied by an intolerant ethnic nationalism foreign to the state-nations of the more advanced western Europe, fails to stand up.

The traditional state gave the major western nations a head-start in terms of civilisation, or in some cases the dynamics of revolution gave them greater integrational power. Smaller, more backward or less well-defined ethnic groups were usually entirely or partly swallowed up, neutralised or marginalised (Provencals, Scots, Welsh etc.). Given this background of disadvantage we can

---

style, customs, religion), whose bearers only have a very weak sense of their own group identity. The higher developmental step is "ethnic community", when a larger or smaller proportion of the ethnic group become clearly conscious of attributes of commonality such as a commonly accepted name, myth of common origin, consciousness of shared homeland, certain elements of historical consciousness and a certain shared solidarity with other members of the ethnic community.

[42] Barša, P. – Strmiska, M. 1999. *Národní stát a etnický konflikt* [The Nation State and Ethnic Conflict]. Brno: CDK. 33. In support of this argument the authors offer the example of the fragmentation of national consciousness among the French at the turn of the 19th/20th century, into an organic wing represented by the monarchist right and an associative wing representing the republican left. Even in moments of the most bitter ideological dispute, however, both republicans and monarchists agreed that France had a "natural" historical territory (including Alsace-Lorraine), and that there was a need to systematically instill a common national culture in all citizens. Both sides insisted on the exclusiveness of the French nation and their loyalty to the French language.

[43] Smith, A. D. *National Identity*. 99.

say that in the course of the 19th century the Czech performance in the field of cultural, economic and political emancipation was outstanding, especially in view of the predominantly German-speaking conditions; by creating a political nation the Czechs managed to create the conditions for the birth of an independent state.

Nonetheless, the specific character of Central Europe, where political subdivision did not correspond to linguistic territory and where large German-speaking countries were immediate neighbours, turned the territorial identity of Germans in the Bohemian Lands into a long-term problem. The situation is vividly summed up in a question posed by historian E. Hahn(ová): "Were the German-speaking inhabitants of the Bohemian Lands *Böhmen* in the original sense used by Palacký, Bohemian Germans, "Our Germans", Sudeten Germans, generally Germans, or Austrians?" There is probably no clear answer. What is more, not only did the Bohemian Germans define themselves in different ways at different times, but so did the Czechs. The way in which Sudeten Germans were perceived by Czech society is a classic case of *mental images*, an imprint in social consciousness founded not just on facts and historical events but on deep emotional experience forming the collective memory negatively over the long term.[44]

The problem of perception of Sudeten Germans and their territorial identity was not just an issue for Czechs. In Germany uncertainty about how and in what contexts the Sudeten identity should be defined persists to this day.[45] For example the frequently reprinted *Sudetendeutsche Geschichte*, well-known in Sudeten circles, states in the introduction that: "Sudeten German history has been in wide-ranging ways a function of European, German and Austrian history". It is a statement that testifies to an instability of identity caused by shifting frames of reference; here the frame of reference of Sudeten German history is constructed as that of Europe and Germany, while the author entirely ignores the manifest connection between Sudeten German history and the history of the Bohemian Lands, which in other contexts the Sudeten German political

---

[44]   On contemporary sociological studies see the last chapter of this book. In historical perspective see especially Křen, J. – Broklová, E. 1998. *Obraz Němců, Rakouska a Německa v české společnosti 19. a 20. století* [The Image of Germans, Austria and Germany in 19th- and 20th-Century Czech Society]. Prague: Karolinum.

[45]   Hahn, E. 1999. *Sudetoněmecký problém: obtížné loučení s minulostí* [The Sudeten German Problem: A Difficult Leave-Taking from the Past]. Ústí n. Labem: Albis International. 65. Hahn argues that among the German-speaking population of the Bohemian Lands there were ever fewer people who considered themselves Bohemian Land patriots and ever more who felt themselves to be German-speaking Austrians. The establishment of Czech cultural and scientific societies, political parties and economic associations was a striking feature of the last decades of the 19th century but so too was a similar development on the Bohemian German side. Common Czech-German structures were disintegrating and being replaced by separate Czech or German groups. The division of Charles University into a Czech university and a German university in 1882 can be regarded as a symbolic expression of this trend. Ibidem. 72.

leadership deliberately emphasised and still emphasises. This kind of approach is internally inconsistent and politically tendentious.[46]

In fact, right up to the collapse of the Austro-Hungarian Monarchy the Germans in the Bohemian Lands did not consider themselves to be an independent German "tribe" with a specific cultural and political identity. They saw themselves as Austrian Germans, although (as we shall see later) this Austrian identity had a number of secondary but by no means unimportant peculiarities that clearly arose partly from the changing state of relations between the German Reich and the Austrian Monarchy, and partly from the long-term national rivalry in the Bohemian Lands (ethnic mobilisation). This "borderland" or "frontiersman" identity (in the sense of the linguistic border/*Sprachgrenze* of the German- and Czech-speaking territories) was to be intensively developed by Bohemian Germans only after 1918, as a direct reaction to the founding of an independent Czechoslovak state and as a consequence of the ideology of *Sudeten Volkstumpolitik*.[47]

From the point of view of the development of the relations between Czechs and Germans in the Bohemian Lands, the key factor was the qualitative transformation of the Czech national identity that occurred through the emergence of Czechs as a political nation. Czech society was becoming politicised (this process accelerated in the later 19th century with the series of attempts to give Czechs equal status with Germans), and state-forming ideals taking root in Czech society.

Every serious attempt to find a political solution (i.e. solutions involving the political reform of the Habsburg Monarchy, specifically the emancipation of Czechs as a political nation), came up against the intensifying Czech-German rivalry in the Bohemian Lands. It was clear that the strength of the Bohemian German opposition increased in direct proportion to the pressure that Czechs exerted on the centralist power of Vienna, and that Germans saw themselves as having a vital interest in the maintenance of the constitutional arrangement that ensured their relative privilege.

A vivid example of the (Greater German) argument, and one that also demonstrates how far the radicalised views of the Germans in the Bohemian Lands were diverging from the Bolzano ideal (Bohemian land patriotism) as early as

---

[46]   Franzel, E. 1997. *Sudetendeutsche Geschichte*. (Eine Volkstümliche Darstellung). Augsburg: Bechtermünz Verlag. 8.

[47]   The movement of national struggle known as the *Volkstumkampf* proclaimed the need for systematic efforts to develop the distinctive identity of German ethnic groups/*Volksgruppen*, especially in what were known as the third zones *Reibungszonen* of contact between Germans and Slavs. Ideologically this was a mixture of militant nationalism, plebeian-radical social goals, Pan-Germanism and anti-democratism. For more details see Smelser, R. M. 1975. *The Sudeten Problem 1933–1938*. Middletown: Wesleyan University Press. 42–47. Also Kural, V. 1993. *Konflikt místo společenství* [Conflict instead of Community]. Prague: Ústav mezinárodních vztahů. 108–111.

the 1840s, is to be found in the publication *Ist Österreich deutsch?*. The author F. Schuselka makes no bones about speaking in the name of the German people, who in his opinion have a thousand-year right to the Bohemian Lands. To support his claim he presents the following arguments:

Bohemia is German, because it is an integral, inseparable part of the German Confederation. Bohemia is organically connected with Germany. Bohemia is inhabited by at least 1.5 million Germans forming a continuous part of the population of the land, and every Slav who wants to achieve a certain level of education has to have a German education. [48]

In the years 1843–1848 Schuselka repeated the same Greater German idea with variations in a series of published writings. In another book, *Deutsche Worte eines Österreichers*, he asked, "why Slavs and Hungarians in the Austrian lands have not been Germanised long ago, like the Slavs in the Baltic and Oder regions?".[49] In another work he claimed that the Slavs in Bohemia and Moravia were surrounded on all sides by Germans and that this situation together with their character meant that they could never create their own state. Schuselka's systematic publishing campaign unreservedly supporting Greater German unification won many supporters among Bohemian Germans and was a typical expression of the increasingly nationalist mood among Bohemian Germans.

In addition to his fame as a writer, Schuselka was an important political figure in the German Revolution in 1848 – a deputy in both the German National Assembly in Frankfurt and the Imperial Diet in Vienna. In his memoirs H. Kudlich gives us detailed information on the influence of Schuselka's articles in the journal *Die Grenzboten* and other works on the atmosphere in pre-revolutionary Austria. He writes that no copy of *Grenzboten*, no brochure by Schuselka, and no pamphlet concerned with the future, past or present of Austria, could escape the passionate interest of readers (he means specifically the Germans in the Bohemian Lands).[50]

In the revolutionary year 1848 the Society of Germans from Bohemia, Moravia and Silesia for the Defence of their Nationalities, of which Hans Kudlich was a member, met on a continuous basis. Through "open letters" the club urged Germans in the Bohemian Lands to refuse to vote for a responsible ministry in Prague, for separation from Germany, for the introduction of the Czech language into schools and courts in German districts, for the introduction of

---

[48]   Klíma, A. *Češi a Němci v revoluci 1848–1849*. 7. F. Schuselka was born in České Budějovice. His book *Ist Österreich deutsch?* came out in 1843 in Leipzig and his views on the relationship of Czechs to Germans and the Bohemian Lands to Germany were strongly influenced by the German revolutionary events of 1848. He consciously identified with the Greater German movement and defended the theory that the Bohemian Lands were German in a series of later publications.

[49]   Ibidem.

[50]   Kudlich, H. 1926. *Rückblicke und Erinnerungen*. Band I. Budweis. 93.

Czech as a teaching language at the university in Prague, or for the union of Bohemia, Moravia and Silesia.[51] One of Kudlich's letters gives a sense of the mood in the club, "Prussia was wise and Germanised its conquered territory, it unified while Austria divided. On account of its wisdom Prussia will now probably take first place in Germany."[52]

The campaign found an immediate response in the border areas of Bohemia. On the 15th of April 1848 the town committee and owners of the estate in Cheb approved a petition demanding that the Cheb area be detached from Bohemia and joined to the German Confederation, and should be allowed its own assembly.[53] In the same spirit the town of Žatec/Saatz sent the National Land Committee in Prague a text taken from the Vienna Society of Germans from Bohemia, Moravia and Silesia for the Defence of their Nationalities demanding immediate elections to the Frankfurt Assembly. The German national movement (above all in North Bohemia), received abundant support from its German neighbours across the border.

The 17th of April saw the establishment of the *Verein zur Wahrung der deutschen Interessen in den östlichen Grenzmarken/*The Association for the Protection of the German Interest in the Eastern Borderlands in Leipzig, headed by dr. H. Wuttke, dr. J. Fürst and dr G. Kühne. The association sent proclamations to the German regions of Bohemia appealing to the population to join the new Reich. This was followed by frequent meetings of Germans from Bohemia, Saxony, Silesia and Bavaria at what were known as border rallies, or *Grenzverbünderungsfeste.*[54]

In the political long-term, Greater German ideas helped to undermine the loyalty of Bohemian and Austrian Germans to the multi-national concept of the Habsburg Monarchy, and when Czech politicians were later to seek to achieve federalisation, this was the source of their rigid opposition to any kind of proposed reform directed at linguistic and ethnic equality for Czechs. The nationally radicalised section of the Austrian and Bohemian German population fatally blocked the way to internal reforms of the monarchy and contributed decisively to the dissolution of the Danubian common state; it was a role confirmed in the controversy over the Badeni language reforms in 1897.

There was marked divergence in the opinions of German politicians on the attitude that Germany in the process of revolt and unification should take to the small nations of Central Europe, including Czechs. Some believed that

51 *Letáky z roku 1848.* 1948. Novotný, Miloslav (ed.). Prague: Sfinx.
52 Kudlich, H. *Rückblicke und Erinnerungen.* 181.
53 Maršan, R. 1898. *Čechové a Němci roku 1848 a boj o Frankfurt* [Czechs and Germans of the Year 1848 and the Struggle for Frankfurt]. Prague. 100.
54 Klíma, A. *Češi a Němci v revoluci 1848–1849.* 27.

a united Germany should guarantee equality to Czechs, but the majority was convinced that the non-German peoples must submit to historical reality and could not prevent the emergence of a great Germany. For example the newspaper of the Viennese left, *Die Constitution*, published a series of articles in 1848 on the Slav-German question, the question of the Bohemian Lands and the Slavs in Austria. The leading idea was the defence of the German destiny and element, and insistence that Austrian Germans should join the new Germany sincerely as part of a great German homeland. If they failed to do so (it was claimed) they would be exposing themselves to the risk that the Slavs would gain numerical superiority in Austria and so win political control.[55]

In the revolutionary year 1848 the idea of the unification of Germany and of securing the hegemony of the German element over the smaller nations and states of Central and Eastern Europe was already dominant in all the key revolutionary currents of German politics, from the constitutionally monarchist liberals to the democrats (republicans – mostly supporters of unitarism) and even the most radical leftwing revolutionaries such as Marx and Engels.[56] All were united in the cause of a great national Germany, and shared a conviction that Germany had a legitimate historical vocation to fill the Central European vacuum between France and Russia. The Germans in the Bohemian Lands strove from the very beginning for an active part in this process.

Radicalisation was also underway on the Czech side, however, and nationalist sentiments gaining in intensity (although as A. Klíma rightly points out, Czech radicalism was incomparably less radical in its implications than the Greater German plans for the incorporation of the Bohemian Lands into Germany). One of the leading Czech politicans seeking a way out of the Czech-German dispute was the outstanding historian František Palacký.[57]

With carefully thought out, informed and rationally objective arguments, F. Palacký sought a solution acceptable to both sides and a way of blunting

---

55   *Die Constitution* 33. 29. 4. 1848. 503–504.

56   Influenced by the slogan "Do not grant liberty to the counter-revolution", extreme radicals like Marx and Engels openly supported the demand for the assimilation of the non-German nations (Czechs, Slovenes, Lusatian Serbs, Poznan Poles) inside the Habsburg Monarchy. The crucial problem of the German national revolution was, however, a lack of historical continuity to support the programme. There existed no important traditional centre of the German Lands aspiring to the integrating role of symbol of a renewed unified Germany.

57   F. Fejtö (who tended to be an apologist for the Habsburg Monarchy) had this to say of Palacký: "Thus the leading role in the Czech Revival was played by historians, and especially Palacký, the greatest of them all. Palacký restored dignity and pride to the Czechs by reminding them not only of the glorious kingdom of St. Wenceslas, which theoretically had never ceased to exist, but also of their Hussite forebears, the pioneers of the Reformation, admired by the whole of civilised Europe even after they succumbed to the greater strength of the Holy Roman Empire, bearer of Roman Catholicism, which then however turned ever more into a German empire." Fejtö, F. 1998. *Rekviem za mrtvou říši (o zkáze Rakouska-Uherska)* [Requiem for a Dead Empire (on the destruction of Austria-Hungary)]. Prague: Academia. 9.

the dangerous edge of nationalist radicalism through exploitation of the constitutional framework of the Danubian monarchy. In the heat of the struggle for Czech constitutional rights Palacký defended the principle that the Czech political nation also included the German-speaking inhabitants of Bohemia. He was very much aware of the split in the ranks of Bohemian Germans in the growing national conflict. Those of "our German-speaking compatriots" who recognised the ancient right of the Czech nation in Bohemia he called "the just and humanely minded Germans among us", whereas he condemned the political leadership of the Germans in Bohemia for rejecting Czech demands.

In this and the following era, the key supporting elements of Czech national identity were language and history, and here František Palacký's role was of unique importance. The linguistic conception of the nation had been successful in advancing Czech society to the stage at which there was a generally perceived need for arguments justifying and defining a process leading to the emancipation of Czechs within the Habsburg Monarchy. This process included the demand for equality for Czechs with members of the governing German elites.

The Czechs had progressed to the point of forming a political nation at the same time as the Germans, and this naturally generated potential ethnic rivalry both within the Bohemian Lands and internationally, in the relationship of the future nation states of Czechs and Germans. Despite the parallel course of the nation-creating processes, it was obvious that the central problem for Czech policy was the relationship with Germany and the need to confront various forms of pan-Germanism in Central Europe. Also important on the Czech side was the democratic dimension of the process, i.e. the desire to combine the emergence of the nation with the development of individual liberty for its citizens.

František Palacký refused to accept the automatic assumption that the Bohemian Lands were part of German space, as he made clear in the letter in which he declined to participate in the deliberations of what was known as the *Vorparlament* (which met on the 31ˢᵗ of March 1848 in Frankfurt), which was drawing up organisational plans for the future great and united Germany. Palacký gave three reasons for his attitude, which in fact represented the *consistent political programme* by which Czech policy defined itself against German policy.

First he declared that the Frankfurt Assembly was drawing up plans for a united Germany that would "multiply the power and strength of the German reich" and that he could not participate in this endeavour because he was not a German. His second reason was that the creation of a united Germany would result in the destruction of the Austrian Monarchy, in which he saw the guarantee of the continuing national existence of Czechs (on the condition of equality for Czechs). His third reason was his rejection of the proclamation of the two republics – Austrian and German – and their subsequent projected merger.[58]

Palacký's views on a solution for Central Europe found comprehensive expression in his thoughts on a new Austrian constitition, for which he drew up two alternative plans. He declared himself a resolute federalist and presented his position in a speech to the constitutional committee of the Kroměříž Assembly on the 23rd of January 1849. He said, "A principle has emerged in the historical development of our time that became manifest in its effects last year in the history of Austria, and this is the equal right of nations, which up to 1848 was rejected both in theory and in practice. With this, the emancipation of the Slavs and Rumanians in Austria has been declared in principle, but it has yet to be carried into practice. We need to structure Austria in such a way that the nations are happy to be in Austria; let that be our leading idea." He went on to say that, "I am in no way against the division of the German and Czech parts of Bohemia (Deutsch-Böhmens und Czechiens), and if it were only practically possible I would propose it. Bohemia is a a basin, however, and if a vessel is not to be destroyed it cannot be divided." [59]

Here Palacký was taking up the ideas of the *Manifesto Addressed to the European Nations*, the statement of principle approved by the Slav Congress[60] (opened on the 2nd of June 1848 in Prague) and expressing the political conception of *Austroslavism*, which Palacký himself had formulated. The manifesto elaborated and gave concrete form to the idea of the historical vocation of Austria expressed by Palacký earlier in his letter to Frankfurt ("certainly, if the Austrian state had not already existed from ages past, in the interests of Europe and even humanity we would have to make sure to create it as soon as possible"), which may be considered not just the founding document of Palacký's political programme, but also the foundation of all Czech politics right up to the First World War.[61]

The idea of recasting Austria as a federal state, which "should rest on the association of free and quite equally legitimate states", as a constitutional monarchy respecting equal rights for all citizens, represented an acceptable negotiating position both for the Czechs themselves and for the monarchy. Palacký's

---

[58] Klíma, A. *Češi a Němci v revoluci 1848–1849*. 20–21.

[59] Šolle, Z. *Století české politiky*. 28.

[60] The Slav Congress showed clearly – in terms of its main results – that the representatives of the Slav nations who attended were interested primarily in achieving equality with the other nations in the French revolutionary sense of Liberty, Equality, Fraternity. There was no talk of any unification of the Slav nations into some overall state. One of those who baselessly acused the congress of Pan-Slavism was Engels, who wrote that, "This ridiculous anti-historical movement, which intends nothing less than to subject the civilised West to the barbarian East, was born in the studies of a few Slav dilettantes of historical science." Klíma, A. *Češi a Němci v revoluci 1848–1849*. 69.

[61] Šolle, Z. – Gajanová, A. *Po stopě dějin*. 34–40.

greatness lay in the fact that with his arguments he put forward a *Czech national programme* but at the same time *offered the monarchy a way out of a crisis* that was undermining the very foundations of its existence. In the last years of his life this was only to deepen his disappointment that his hopes for peaceful reform of Austria in the spirit of the equality of all nations were never fulfilled. The meaning and legacy of Palacký's political and scholarly work remains the message that the Czech nation and its natural emancipatory movement was not the accidental by-product of the great modern current of history springing from the French Revolution, but a deeper and inevitable phenomenon, expressing the inalienable historical right of Czechs to their own independent existence.

Palacký and Havlíček's programme was the only Czech national programme that gave the impression of a real social force in the Revolution of 1848.[62] The influence of their views on Czech politics was to extend far beyond the horizon of this one revolutionary situation. Even though in his straightforward nationalism Havlíček seems simpler and more immediate than Palacký,[63] the American historian H. Kohn has argued that in Palacký and Havlíček the Czechs in the 1840s had two politicians with a keener sense of reality than any other people on the European continent.[64]

K. Havlíček Borovský pregnantly formulated his own idea of the principles of Czech politics in his article "Slav Policy", published in July 1850 in the journal *Slovan* [*Slav*].[65] Havlíček was only developing the principle that he had already formulated in the revolutionary year of 1848: "Let us remember the principal rule that we are taught by the experience of all ages: political freedom without national freedom is valueless, and in any nation where a foreign language rules in government, there is no true freedom, no democracy, because what exists there is an aristocracy, and indeed the most shameful aristocracy, the aristocracy of language."[66]

We cannot ignore Havlíček's contribution to the formulation of Austroslavism in his article "Slav and Czech" (1846), which expressed an approach

---

[62] There were certain differences of nuance between the approaches of the two men. Havlíček gave more prominence to the idea that more numerous Slav nations of the monarchy could shore up and secure Austria's political position and stability.

[63] Ibidem. 61.

[64] Klíma, A. *Češi a Němci v revoluci 1848–1849*. 73.

[65] "Our task is to bring to real life both the constitution and the nation, not allowing ourselves to be in any way confused by our national and political opponents, the first of whom (absolutists and aristocrats) promise us nationality if we abandon liberty, and the second (the Germans), liberty if we abandon nationality. Being Slavs and democrats, however, we cannot abandon either one or the other, for we do not want nationality without liberty, or liberty without nationality." Šolle, Z. – Gajanová, A. *Po stopě dějin*. 53.

[66] Havlíček Borovský, Karel. "Slovo v čas. O nepoctivosti našich nepřátel, Němců i Maďarů, aneb o tom, kdo jest reakcionář a kdo jest svobodomyslný" [A Timely Word. On the Dishonesty of Our Enemies, the Germans and Hungarians, or Who is Reactionary and who is Free-thinking]. *Národní noviny*. 29. 9. 1848.

that he subsequently sought to promote with Palacký in the revolutionary period 1848–49. The concept of Austroslavism was born in reaction to ideas of Greater-Germany (Pan-Germanism) and envisaged the participation of all the nations of Austria in the transformation of the monarchy into a federative state of autonomous countries. It thus inevitably met with opposition from the Pan-Germans and the Germans in Bohemia and Austria.

Havlíček's sober view that egoism was the main motive of human action (especially politics) differed sharply from the romanticising ideas and notions prevailing in Czech society. "Let us take the world as it is, and so expect friendship and harmony between people and nations only when both sides get some benefit out of it."[67]

In this spirit Havlíček realised that given the contradictory interests of the Slav nations, Pan-Slavism could not be a reliable foundation for Czechs feeling menaced by Germany. In the conclusion to his article he puts the point bluntly, "In short, I can say with national pride – I am a Czech, but never – I am a Slav". This earned him a storm of outrage and criticism among conservative patriots and Czech Slavophiles, including anger at his claim that, "The Austrian Monarchy is the best guarantee of the preservation of our and Illyrian (South Slav) nationality and the more the might of imperial Austria grows, the more secure will our nationalities be."[68]

Havlíček also fundamentally questioned some romantic ideas held by Czech leaders on the saviour role of Russia. He was one of the first in Bohemia to challenge (in his set of travel sketches *Pictures from Russia*, 1843) support for greater Russia and the Tsarist absolutist system. Just like Havlíček, Palacký rejected Germany for national reasons and for political reasons invested no hopes in Russia either (even though both saw the sheer existence of Russia as a kind of reinforcement for Slav aspirations). The absolutist and feudal Tsarist system they considered to be the most reactionary regime of the Europe of their day. All that remained was Austria, in which particularly after March 1848 both saw a bulwark against the engulfment of the Bohemian Lands by a Germany in the process of unification and ever more powerful.

Havlíček always saw the main problem of Czech politics as the relationship to Germany, and believed it to be essential for Czech policy to resist all forms of Pan-Germanism. At the same time, however, in line with his democratic principles he proposed a just settlement between Czechs and Germans in the Bohemian Lands, with each nationality having the right to administer the ter-

---

[67] Havlíček Borovský, K. 1906. *Epištoly kutnohorské a vybrané články politické* [Kutná Hora Epistles and Selected Political Articles). Prague: B. Kočí. 36–46.

[68] Klíma, A. *Češi a Němci v revoluci 1848–1849*. 71.

ritories (schools, offices, societies etc.) in which it represented a majority of the population.[69]

The revolutionary events of 1848–49 ultimately resulted in the defeat of the democrats, culminating in Bachian absolutism. The crushing defeat of attempts at emancipation also meant that Austrian-Hungarian relations were settled in 1867 without any participation by the Czechs, and the Czech struggle for what were known as the "fundamental points" ended in failure. From 1848 various different concepts and approaches succeeded each other in Czech political strategy – Austroslavism, constitutional right,[70] Slav and Russophile orientations, sharp uncompromising opposition, and "minor" rewards for supporting the Vienna government – without any leading to the desired goal. The successful and dynamic cultural and social advance of the Czech nation in the later half of the 19th century was in sharp contrast to the failure of Czech politics,[71] which for decades vainly tried to secure from the Austrian centre reform that would provide Czechs with a constitutional position within the monarchy and share in political decision-making corresponding to their new confidence and importance in the state.

The Czech nation was experiencing its own economic and social miracle. From a backward mass of peasants bound by labour dues in their villages, from poor merchants and artisans in the towns and from a handful of enthusiastic intellectuals, the Czechs had emerged by 1848 as a self-confident modern nation, equal in worth to all the other nations of Western and Central Europe. In 1899 the German consul in Prague already rated the Bohemian Lands as "the jewel in the crown of Austria". He also mentioned the Czech-German conflict, saying, "These disputes have been going on in the Bohemian Kingdom for a long time, but have only become acute under the Taaffe government, which started to extend special favour to Slavs, specifically Czechoslavs."[72]

---

[69] "In line with this principle we are leaving those regions in Bohemia where Germans live in continuous concentrations under German administration… we want decency and mutual neighbourly love and forbearance, standing by the first rule: What you do not want others to do to you, do not do to them!" Havlíček Borovský, K. *Epištoly kutnohorské*. 89.

[70] All the Czech political parties adhered to the doctrine of Bohemian historical state right. In the pre-war period Bohemian historical right was almost always presented in modified form as a loyalist doctrine that presupposed the continuing framework of the dynasty and empire. The great advantage of historical right was that it ruled out any division or fragmentation of the historic lands. The continuing existence of these historical individual entities within the Habsburg Monarchy in the form of administrative units had kept alive the hope that a Bohemian state could be born on that basis. In the mid-19th century Czech politics oscillated in their justifications between historical constitutional right and the ethnic principle, but as soon as the idea of the Bohemian state became dominant, even if as a part of the Austrian state, historical right was the victor. Galandauer, J. 1988. *Vznik Československé republiky 1918* [The Establishment of the Czechoslovak Republic 1918]. Prague: Svoboda. 153.

[71] J. Galandauer's postscript to the new edition of Masaryk, T. G. 1990. *Česká otázka* [The Czech Question]. Prague: Svoboda. 348.

[72] All quotations from Šolle, Z. *Století české politiky*. 74–78.

Z. Šolle however points out that the leading politician of the Hungarian liberal party, L. Láng, was a good deal more accurate in his assessment of the causes of the situation in the historic lands, writing that, "here we are confronted not with the work of the favour or antipathy of individual governments, but with the result of the slow but unstoppable effects of ethnographic and economic, moral and social factors. The lordship of the Germans in Austria rested mainly on the will of the monarch and the absolutist tradition. To the extent to which these traditions have become weaker, the hegemony of the Germans would inevitably have been shaken even had they not committed so many errors against their own interests". In this context the most important failure was arguably the disintegration of the German-Austrian liberals, which opened the way to rapprochement between the two German monarchies (Habsburg and Hohenzollern), whose Dual Alliance became the basis for the division of Europe into two hostile blocks and in the final phase resulted in the First World War.

The Czech political leadership represented by the two main political parties (Old Czechs and Young Czechs) found itself in crisis in the 1880s because Czech politics was unable to offer society enough in the way of alternatives to the approaches that seemed to have run into the ground. It was a problem of the possibility of choice, the possibility of an alternative, the possibility of choosing from a wider range of leading circles in cultural, social and political elites.[73]

At the same time it should be added that Czech politics was not lacking in documents setting out political programmes or people capable of the effective pursuit of political goals. The reason for the Czech failures was the rigid resistance of the bureaucratic, centralised political system of the Habsburg Monarchy, which rejected any kind of moves toward reform in the direction of a "settlement" with Czechs that would give the latter a share of state power corresponding to their social and economic importance. To make matters worse, the government in Vienna was under pressure from a number of political organisations and associations of Austrian and Bohemian Germans whose aim was to block, at any cost, the erosion of the position of ethnic Germans in the Danubian Monarchy.

The militant attitudes of the Pan-German agitators were characterised by an ideologically grounded and increasingly intransigent refusal to compromise. The tone of their arguments is clear from an extract from a letter written by the deputy Baernreither to Baron von Schönerer: "I consider the attempt to reach an understanding with the Czechs to be futile. The issue is simply whether we or the Slavs will have the upper hand in Austria", while Schönerer replied,

---

[73] Šolle, Z. Století české politiky. 77.

"there continues to be talk of equality between Germans and Slavs: this is like comparing a lion to a louse on the grounds that both are animals. In matters of nationality I cannot insist on the standpoint of equality."[74] Schönerer's colleague Iro put it entirely bluntly and openly: "We don't want any language decrees, any one-sided "settlement", and division of Bohemia – we want the complete acknowledgement of the supremacy of Germans in Austria."

The adherents of Pan-Germanism were convinced that the Danubian multinational monarchy was threatened in the long-term by the expansion of the Slav nations, which in their view the ruling Habsburgs were either simply unable to stop or were even effectively exacerbating with various reform proposals offering concessions of one sort or another that immediately menaced the privileged position of the nine million German-speaking inhabitants of the monarchy to the benefit of the fifteen million Slavs. J. W. Brügel cites publications of the Berlin Pan-German League/*Berliner Alldeutschen Verband* from the turn of the year 1900/1901 to show that the idea of the removal and resettlement of the non-German peoples of Central Europe had already appeared even at this early period.[75] Brügel adds that the Pan-Germans were only a fraction of German bourgeois society and that their dream of a new start from the *anno dazumal* (sic!) cannot be taken as typical of German opinion, whether in Germany itself or in Austria. The fact remains, however, that the ideas that the Nazi political theory of the need to "solve the Czech problem" sought to put into practice had already emerged in German milieux at this point.

Here it is appropriate to ask what exactly "Slav" identity meant in German milieux. It was not just nationality in the neutral sense of "Czech" or "Polish" but was seen as expressing an element of political challenge, and thus comparable to the charged concept "German" with all its associated notions of expansion and hegemony, i.e. it was the political identification of the enemy. From the outset, Pan-Germanism was not just a theory and a political ideal, but also a reflection and expression of the political advance of the German nation.[76]

---

[74] Chéradame, A. 1901. *Evropa a otázka rakouská na prahu XX. století* [Europe and the Austrian Question on the Threshold of the 20th Century]. Prague: Samostatnost. 111.

[75] "Inzwischen hört man... gegenüber der Idee, ein Alldeutschland zu schaffen, häufig die Entgegnung: Ja, wohin mit den Tschechen, Slowenen usw... Dann wird es aber auch, wenn Deutschlands siegerreichte Heere von der Moldau bis zur Adria stehen, möglich sein, *die nichtdeutsche Bevölkerung Zislethaniens* (Österreichs*) einfach auszuweisen*... und auf *deutsch zu kolonisieren*... So denken wir uns die Ausdehnung unserer Grenzen in Europa." *Deutschland bei Beginn des 20. Jahrhunderts*. 1900. Von einem Deutschen. Berlin: Militär-Verlag R. Felix. 212–213. "Meanwhile against the idea of the establishment of a Greater Germany one hears the frequent objection... Yes, but whither with Czechs, the Slovenians and others... Yet once the power of Germany is victorious from the Vltava to the Adriatic, it will be possible simply to expel the non-German population... and colonise the land with Germans... Thus we are thinking of expanding our land in Europe." Brügel, J. W. 1974. *Tschechen und Deutsche 1939–1946*. München: Nymphenburger Verlagshandlung. 98.

[76] Masaryk, T. G. *Nová Evropa*. Brno: Doplněk. 64.

After 1848, the Austrian Germans repeatedly and deliberately wrecked all attempts to reform the monarchy in a way that would offer a more equal status and share in political power to the non-German (Slav) peoples, especially the Czechs. In this sense the Austrian/Bohemian-German nationalists had a direct share of responsibility for the collapse of the Danubian Monarchy and the subsequent problems and tragedy of Central Europe that ensued.

The Austrian German nationalists took the view that the House of Habsburg had failed in its duty to Germanise its empire and link it to the German Union: "This the Hohenzollerns, in association with the other ruling lines, must and can bring to a successful conclusion."[77] This Prussian action was all the more needful, because" the Austrian German tribes (sic) have not proved equal to their cultural mission". K. Pröll believed that "if care is not taken, Austria will gradually be transformed into a group of individual states that will dissolve when the time is ripe".[78] The only possible way of preventing this fate was to demand that Austria be annexed to the German Reich.[79]

A consciousness of Pan-German ethnic identity was developing both in Austria and in Germany as an influential factor in domestic and foreign policy, albeit at different stages, to a different extent and modified depending on the character of leading politicians and programmes of their parties. Both in Austria and in Germany it was often said that national aspirations could not be limited just to the "ethnographic concept of Germany" but must be enlarged right up to the point, "where it will border strictly with France and Russia. There can only be one policy in Central Europe, because here the Germans are the only powerful nation... this must be German policy".[80]

At the latest from 1871, from the European point of view the German Question more or less boiled down to the crucial problem of how to preserve the peace and security of Europe while at the same time satisfying the political ambitions of Germany. In the real situation this meant that the Germany's neighbours had to choose whether to support a strong unitary German state in Central Europe or a power vacuum with the attendant risks of unforeseeable interventions from outside. Both alternatives, whether a strong power centre

[77]   *Österreichs Zusammenbruch und Wiederaufbau*. 1899. München: Lehmann. 20.
[78]   Pröll, K. 1890. *Die Kämpfe der Deutschen in Oesterreich*. Berlin: Lüstenöder. 7.
[79]   Chéradame, A. *Evropa a otázka rakouská*. 71.
[80]   Redlich, J. 1920. *Das österreichische Staats- und Reichs- problem I*. Leipzig. 30. Masaryk drew attention to the Pan-German geographical argument arising from the German sense of being endangered: "The geographical position of the Germans, surrounded on three sides by unfriendly nations, requires a rectification of the borders, and therefore also the occupation of non-German territory. Ratzel drew the attention of Pan-Germans to the political and strategic importance of a central position, to efforts generated from the centre (in contrast to efforts from the periphery etc.). Not just geography but geology too determines right: territory geologically similar to the German belongs – to Germans. And German geographers are already systematising the peculiar science – geopolitics." Masaryk, T. G. *Nová Evropa*. 70.

in Central Europe or a power vacuum, threatened to destabilise the balance of power between European states and presented a security risk for the whole continent. This view of Central Europe became a basic constant of European diplomacy (in different forms and with different levels of intensity) right up to the present.

European (and American) studies have generally preferred the concept of the German Problem to that of the German Question, thus emphasing the fact that from the beginning of the 19th century Germany was regarded as a difficult, uncontrollable and even dangerous neighbour. The German Problem (in the period up to 1945) is seen in historical perspective as a source of political instability in Central Europe, typified by the aggressive behaviour of the German state, militarism, expansionism and dubious "national character".[81] P. Alter, inspired by the formulations of the German historian T. Schieder,[82] defines the German questions as follows: the territorial and political organisation of Central Europe from the beginning of the 19th century; the constitutional order in which Germans live or for which they strive; the European *balance of power* – whether strengthened or threatened by the German-speaking part of Central Europe, and how other Europeans perceived the German state/states.[83]

From the mid-18th century to the constitution of the German Reich in 1871, Central Europe had been something close to a political vacuum, primarily because of the antagonism between the political interests of Berlin and Vienna – the two great German powers, Germany and the Habsburg Monarchy. The foundation of the German Reich in 1871 ushered in a period (relatively short, but extremely tragic in European history) when a strong German state became dominant in Central Europe with well-known results for European peace and balance.

In a classic study, the British historian A. J. P. Taylor characterised this phase as the *Prussian Conquest of Germany*.[84] Prussia won the competition for hegemony over Germany. Three successful "wars of unification" against Denmark (1864), Austria (1866) and France (1870) enabled Prussia to consolidate its leading position among the German states. In the words of Masaryk: "Suc-

---

[81]   Alter, P. 2000. *The German Question and Europe – A History*. London/New York: Arnold-Oxford University Press. 11.

[82]   Schieder, T. 1972. "Die deutsche Frage", in *Meyers Enzyklopädisches Lexikon*. (Collective of authors). Mannheim: Meyers.

[83]   Alter, P. *The German Question and Europe*. 11.

[84]   Taylor, A. J. P. 1945. *The Course of German History*. London/New York: Routledge. 111 f. (reprint 2001). P. Alter, however, considers Taylor's work to be very much a product of the atmosphere of the Second World War, and so typically presents the Anglo-Saxon wartime vision of Germany that reduces the issue to two well-known questions, i.e. (1) How are Europeans to be secured against further recidivist expressions of German aggression? and (2) How can Germans find a permanent peaceful form of political existence? Alter, P. *The German Question and Europe*. 12.

cessful industrialisation and world earnings evoked (the prospect of) world domination and so strengthened the traditional German imperialist ideal of the Holy Roman Empire: by the defeat of Napoleon III, Prussia revived the medieval imperium dissolved by Austria in 1806, and the *Zollverein* and *Bund* were a transition to industrialisation and to imperialism."[85]

The personality and policies of Otto von Bismarck played a major part in this development. His skilful and cynical approach enabled him first to win over and then entirely to eliminate the power of the German liberals, who were an obstacle to his ideas about German unification.[86] He did so by first presenting the Prussian government as a progressive and dynamic force backing the liberal concept of Greater German unification in contrast to the dilapidated particularism of the Habsburg court in Vienna. This strategy was made possible by the fact that in the minds of Prussian and the other German liberals, nationalism and liberalism were intrinsically linked – an attitude that was of course shared by their conservative enemies. Bismarck came to believe that in order to achieve an unchallengeable leading role in German Central Europe he had to exploit Pan-German national sentiment, which Prussia was incomparably better qualified to use than Austria.[87]

Bismarck's methods and ideas influenced, fascinated, and one might even say engulfed the rising generation of German politicians across the spectrum, including Catholics, social democrats and radical liberals. Many admired the exceptionally successful way in which Bismarck controlled German internal and foreign policy for three decades. The sharp dichotomy of "friends" and "enemies", both "domestic" and "external" made a deep impact on German politics. Reflection on this phenomenon led Max Weber to develop the concept of "negative integration", in which the scapegoat – the enemy – plays a key role in unifying opinion and achieving consensus in internal politics. A generation later Carl Schmitt offered a new formulation of this idea, arguing that division into friends and enemies was the primordial principle of politics.[88]

---

[85] Masaryk, T. G. *Nová Evropa*. 65. Masaryk likewise draws attention to the role of international trade by which Germany was building up and strengthening its own position: "The energetic industrialisation of Germany after 1870 was bonding not just colonies to Germany, but the other countries as well: The United States, Russia, England and India, Austria-Hungary, Italy, Holland, Switzerland, Brazil, Argentina, became intimately linked with Germany; the German *penetration pacifique*, as it is called now, was successful everywhere." Ibidem.

[86] After January 1871 the enthusiasm of the liberals for the New Germany was almost unbounded. In the Reichstag they were calling on Bismarck to continue with the process of nation building, the expansion of the area of free trade, the unification of currency and legislation and the setting up of a central bank. Soon, however, rifts in the liberal ranks began to emerge. For more detail see Stürmer, M. 2002. *The German Empire*. New York: Random House. 27–28.

[87] Hall, R. B. 1999. *National Collective Identity*. New York: Columbia University Press. 190–192.

[88] New insights and reflections on German politics in the period up to the outbreak of the First World War and on the development of the positions of the individual German parties, especially the Social Democrats

In 1871 the Second German Reich was proclaimed, established by military means rather than as the result of revolution, and with the exclusion of Austria. The states of North and South Germany merged in a new empire influenced more by Prussian authoritarianism than by bourgeois liberalism.[89] Bismarck intuitively grasped the correspondence between the institutionalised form of collective action suited to demonstrations of Pan-German nationalism and the actual constitution of individual and Pan-German national collective identity.[90] The dramatic period in German history that opened with Bismarck was only to end with the unconditional capitulation of Germany and its division into two states.[91]

The British historian P. Alter and others make it clear in their accounts that they regard the Austrian and the German politics of the 19th and 20th centuries as ultimately connecting vessels, with the Czech question (together with the Polish) being integral parts of the German problem because both implictly or explicitly set limits to the German power position in Central Europe.[92] Taylor takes a similar view when he argues that the conflict between Czechs and Germans in the Bohemian Lands determined German history almost as much as the conflict between Poles and Germans an Eastern Prussia.[93]

Although Alter is aware of the key role of Germany for the security of the Central European region (and by extension the continent as a whole), he has no qualms about dismissing the views of non-German authors as stereotypical and entirely uniform (on the grounds of their repeated emphasis on the manifest security implications of successive definitions of the German Question). He seems quietly to overlook the fact that for Germany's immediate neighbours (most of their political elites and populations) the security aspect has naturally loomed larger in historiography than the urge for originality of interpretative perspective. Neither for the first nor the last time, what we see here is the difference between views of the German Question from the East and the West. Another British historian and specialist on modern German history, R. J. Evans, has drawn attention to the phenomenon.[94]

---

as the main protagonists of anti-militarism can be found in Stargardt, N. 1994. *The German Idea of Militarism (Radical And Socialist Critics 1866–1914)*. Cambridge: Cambridge University Press. 150.

[89] Verheyen, D. 1999. *The German Question*. Boulder/Oxford: Westview Press. 8.

[90] Hall, R. B. *National Collective Identity*. 210.

[91] Alter, P. *The German Question and Europe*. 7. Alter argues that non-German authors past and present see the German Question primarily as a security problem, and more concretely as the question of the stabilisation of Central Europe to guarantee "tranquility in Europe", expressed by the period diplomatic term, "le repos de l'Europe".

[92] Taylor, A. J. P. *The Course of German History*. 47.

[93] Ibidem. xxi.

[94] Evans, R. J. 1997. *Rereading German History 1800–1996*. London: Routledge. Evans draws attention to some tendentious claims by the French historian and expert of German issues J. Rovan, who for example describes

The difference in angle of vision is evident for example in answers to the question: *What, or perhaps more relevantly, who is Europe?* In other words, whom have historians (and politicians) actually included in that rather abstract and fuzzy concept known as Europe. The distinguished American historian Gordon A. Craig offered a pragmatic answer: in the 19th century and later, Europe simply meant the five European states that as a result of their military, economic and other resources, and their size and position, were considered great powers, i.e. Britain, Russia, France, Austria-Hungary and Prussia/Germany.[95] Up to the outbreak of the First World War these five states represented the constitutive basis of legal theory and political reality: the so-called "pentarchy" of the European international system. This was reflected in all the more important negotiating forums, such as the Congress of Vienna, the Paris Peace Congress 1856, the Congress of Berlin 1878, and even the negotiations of the Paris Peace Conference of 1918, although the latter was dominated by the United States.

This context is crucial for exploration of our basic theme – the German Question and its Central European dimension – for if we talk about European attitudes to Germany, then we need to be aware that in any period up to 1914 these were the attitudes of the great powers mentioned. The smaller and less important states and peoples (including the Czechs) found themselves peripheral to political decision-making. This power constellation of the time has had a knock-on effect in historiography, i.e. it had been the basis for the relative weight accorded to the opinions of historians of different nationalities both in the past and the present, and this fact is relevant to contemporary Czech-(Sudeten) German discourse, which is the outcome of a dispute lasting decades, with generations of experts and politicians having successively joined and molded it.

In this context Alter has drawn attention to a number of less well-known German authors whose views he considers inspiring. One is Wilhelm Röpke and his book *The German Question*[96] (finished towards the end of the Second World War in Switzerland, where he emigrated to escape the Nazis), which Alter rates among the most penetrating analyses of the role of Germany in Central Europe. Röpke argued that modern German history represents no less than the negation of the idea of the German nation state.

Bismarck as a moderate modern conservative, a kind of 19th-century de Gaulle. In doing so Rovan gives no hint of how Bismarck deformed German political culture by creating "enemies of the Reich", cruelly persecuting Catholics, Social Democrats and ethnic minorities and using police informers and agents provocateurs on a considerable scale. Rovan is entirely silent on these and other facts. For detail see Evans' chapter The view from France. Ibidem. 54 ff.

[95] Craig, G. A. 1962. *Europe since 1815.* New York: Knopf. 10–11.

[96] Röpke, W. 1946. *The German Question.* London: Knopf.

The key situation for the future Nazi catastrophe was in his view the five years in the career of Chancellor Bismarck – 1866–1871, when in the name of unifying Germany, "by blood and iron", the problem of finding a new identity was addressed by the violent form used to make individual parts of Germany integral parts of "Greater Prussia". Röpke also saw the question of the organisation of Central Europe as a synonym for the German Question, which since its emergence has always alternated between two positions: either it is in the centre of interest and dominates European politics, or else it is "quietly resting" on the margins waiting to be re-evaluated and a re-included among the burning themes of international relations. Developing this theory, Alter argues that the events of 1989–1990 brought another variant of an answer to the German Question, this time after the fall of the Berlin Wall, collapse of communism and unification of the two German states. He immediately poses the question: Do these events really mean the end of the two-centuries long political disturbance and ferment radiating from Central Europe?

After all, from the beginning of the 19th century, whenever the German Question appeared on the political scene, the other Europeans asked how Germany would fit into the present and future geographical, political and mental maps of Europe. By the middle years of the same century it was already clear that the problem was not whether a German nation-state would emerge, but how it would be constituted and which territories it would include.

A retrospective overview of the whole course of discussions on the German question highlights the fact that the Germans themselves had a different view of the basis of the problem than non-Germans. Essentially, the axis of German perception and experience of the German question has been the problem of identity, with problems of national unity or the German role and influence in world affairs being judged in terms of their relationship to contexts derived from that identity. In contrast, the same question considered from the non-German perspective and especially Germany's neighbours, definitely appears more straightforwardly as the question of German power and the need to "control" it.[97]

From all this it will be evident that the two different interpretations (in fact of course there is a much wider and more differentiated range of approaches), of the same German Question as seen from the German and non-German angle of vision can be and have in fact repeatedly been the cause of problems for German diplomacy in relation to other states. In this respect the Czech Republic is no exception, as we shall see in the final chapters.

---

[97] Craig, G. A. 1982. *The Germans*. New York: Putnam's Sons. 15. See also Verheyen, D. *The German Question*. 9.

Identity and role on the one side, and unity and power on the other, may be regarded as connecting pairs of analytical concepts. Over the last two centuries the German search for national and political identity (including questions of choice of ideological orientation and political system) regularly came into competition (or conflict) with the interests of neighbouring peoples and states as a result of the way in which the effects of this search for identity were projected into the role of Germany in the system of international relations.

The German Question overlaps with the much more general question of why in modern history such striking differences in political thought and life developed between Germany and its Western European neighbours – differences that brought Germany into conflict with them. One answer has revolved round the well-known concept of the *Sonderweg*, the idea of the special German path to modernity that has been the subject of decades of controversy especially among historians. The results of the debate have not been persuasive in the sense of fully explaining the historical deviation of Germany in the course of the first half of the 20th century, but they remain a source of warning for politicians and scholars tempted by notions of the role of a united Germany as a bridge between East and West.[98] For example, while the work of the historian G. Ritter (a member of the German resistance movement during the Second World War) was first published in 1948, its message is to some extent still topical today for a Europe in process of integration.

When the birth of the German Reich was ceremonially declared in the Mirror Hall at Versailles in 1871, many were convinced that everything that the Germans had been demanding since 1843 had now been gloriously achieved.[99] Today we know that in 1871 the German Question had not been satisfactorily answered (just as the answer given in 1918–1919 was to be unsatisfactory too).[100] Germany was to remain a theme on the European political agenda for

---

[98] Ritter, G. 1965. *The German Problem: Basic Questions of German Political Life, Past And Present*. Columbus: Ohio State University. See introductory chapter. 10.

[99] For example the Prussian historian Heinrich von Sybel described his feelings in ecstatic style: "What have we done to keep God's mercy that it was granted to us to live through such superb and overwhelming things? What had been a mere wish and longing for us for twenty years was now fulfilled in so brilliant a way! What more remains for me to achieve in my life?" Heyderhoff, J. – Wentzcke, P. 1970. *Deutscher Liberalismus im Zeitalter Bismarcks. Eine politische Briefsammlung*. Vol. 1 (1925). Reprint. 494.

[100] Today we are also encountering the view that the Potsdam solution to the German Question likewise shows basic errors ("the limitations of the imperial horizon of the victors"), and that the famous *Historikerstreit* (the dispute between German historians) was a mere prefiguration of what awaits intellectual Europe after the enlargement of the European Union. Ch. S. Maier argues that the discourse of German historians (Nolte, Stürmer) in the 1980s was full of the same themes as were discussed in the period of the Weimar Republic: incompleteness, fragmentation, destructive subdivision that must be overcome, the echoes of an earlier yearning. In the preface to his work he says that it would be a mistake to exaggerate the importance of the provocations of the new conservatism (he regards E. Nolte as its main representative), which in itself is nothing new, and just an echo of rightwing radicalism in the Weimar Republic. Maier, Ch. S. 1997. *The Un-*

decades. It became apparent at the latest from the end of the 19th century that the issue was not just that of the fulfilment of German nation-building aspirations. Great-power visions of a "Greater" Germany were starting to threaten Europe, but above all Germany's smaller neighbours, among them the Czechs, who were at the same time striving for full political emancipation including ambitions for constitutional autonomy within the Habsburg Monarchy. Germany's unification by Bismarck was characterised not only by the victory of Prussia over Austria but also (and from the point of view of later development much more dangerously) by the triumph of authoritarianism and militarism over liberalism and a parliamentary form of government.[101]

The transformation of Germans and Germany from a mere cultural and ethnic collectivity into a distinctive political entity, the integration of the nation and its institutionalisation, gave birth to a project of a national Germany that in size and political influence would be a partner comparable to the two European great powers, France and Great Britain. The demand of the German revolutionary forces was for a great national Germany, in the light of which Slav "small statehood" looked most frequently like mere intrigue or an opportunity for interference by the hated Russia. This view persisted on the German left for decades, and Pan-German opinions even appeared in the revolutionary Spartacus movement at the end of the First World War.[102]

In fact it was not specifically the Slavs but Austria – to which according to the visions of the time the embrace of German unification was to be extended, that posed the biggest problem for the German Revolution. The Habsburgs' attitude to the German national movement was frigid to say the least. Vienna represented the main support for German fragmentation and even worse, the empire was the embodiment of reaction, which had burdened Germany with "the ballast of backward non-German nations". Here precisely lay the root of the problem of the position of Germany and Austria (in a wider sense the German problem), for only part of the German-speaking population of the empire was concentrated in a nationally homogenous territory, while the rest lived in territories with an ethnically mixed population where German-speakers were often in the position of ethnic minorities. Yet the identification of the Habsburg monarchy with Germanness was entrenched, since this strengthened its power and secured special weight and influence for the Austrian Germans in

---

masterable Past. History, Holocaust, and German National Identity. Cambridge/Massachusetts/London: Harvard University Press. 149–151.

[101] Gildea, R. 2003. *Barricades And Borders. Europe 1800–1914.* Oxford/New York: Oxford University Press.

[102] Taylor, A. J. P. *The Course of German History.* 197. Rosa Luxemburg expressed it by the term, "the great united German Republic", including – in line with Marx's demand of 1848 – Czechs and other Slav nations of the Austrian Monarchy.

the German *Gesamtvolk*.[103] Despite a number of attempts to modify the political system of the monarchy, Germanness played the role of important integrating factor in the multi-national state.

As has been noted, the problem of German status and identity increased in urgency in the latter half of the 19th century (after the Frankfurt Assembly of 1848), and generated a major discussion on the new form and new conception of German political life. Austria was to remain the recurrent problem of Pan-German unification. Eventually, from the tangle of contradictory standpoints and conflicts of interest and tradition there emerged three main currents of thought on how to solve the German problem, with a basic difference existing between the Greater German and Little German concept of the correct approach.

According to German historian F. W. Foerster, one was a *Prussian-Nordic-Little-German* approach committed to renouncing Austria because of its non-German elements, as the Slav nations of the multi-national Habsburg Empire were regarded. Another current, the Greater Germans in the narrower sense of the word, wanted to offer their fellow Germans in Austria the opportunity to break away from these elements and so create an exclusively German state entity. Finally the third current of opinion was that of the Greater Germans in the broader sense of the word, who strove for the preservation of the supra-national character of Germany with the aim of building a German Union encompassing all Central Europe, i.e. with the inclusion of all the nations of the Austro-Hungarian Empire.[104]

Some historians of German Central Europe (E. Wiskemann, H. C. Meyer, F. W. Foerster and others) agree that the Greater-German solution found supporters primarily in Austria "whose German elements were on the one hand reluctant to give up the traditional imperial community with non-German elements and were very well aware of the real benefits of German identity as a connecting link with faraway Danubian regions, but who on the other hand

---

[103] Křen, J. *Konfliktní společenství.* 88–95.

[104] Foerster, F. W. 1948. *Evropa a německá otázka* [Europe and the German Question]. Prague: Universum. 89. Friedrich Wilhelm Foerster was born on the 2nd of June 1869 to the family of W. Foerster, director of the Berlin state observatory. In 1895 he became editor of *Ethische Kultur* and after publishing an article sharply critical of Kaiser Wilhelm II he was imprisoned for half a year. He then moved to Switzerland, where he took his habilitation (second doctorate) in 1898 and spent the rest of his life. He made a name for himself with educational writings based on the ideal of the Christian harmonisation of man. His work *Europe and the German Question* first came out in 1937 and was translated into many different languages. The author was afraid not only of Nazism (and Prussian traditions), but of the spiritual devastation of human beings, desire for power, desire for self-promotion, desire for advance of the self at any cost. His book ends with the sentence, "If only one day a new generation will be born that wants to revive the old value of the German people and understands that the real task of a future spiritual world policy lies in the conciliation of the antagonised world and not in the escalation of tension." Ibidem. 506.

foresaw that they might get into a difficult situation if they stood in the way of the non-German population as only a fragment separated off from the wider German community".[105]

Chancellor Bismarck took a quite different view and as already noted refused to waste energy on solving the problems of the Austrian Germans, whom he saw as a disruptive element for the great-power ambitions of a unified Germany in the West, where he intended above all to compete with Great Britain. In a speech of 1865 he expressed his ideas on the future form of the greater Prussian state, asserting that the whole (possibly federative) Danubian region "with its population that stretches away into the Orient" was at odds with everything he wanted to achieve: "There is no German nation. Our policy is the dissolution of Germany in Prussia and thus the remoulding of Prussia into Germany".[106]

It is not without interest that Bismarck's desire to strengthen the German role on the European continent by concentrating and focusing it is the reason why from a geopolitical viewpoint he looks like a moderate statesman striving for balance. Thus for example Henry Kissinger can comment that "Bismarck tried to prevent the emergence of threats by creating close relations with the greatest possible number of partners, by building overlapping alliances and using the influence he gained by doing so to moderate the demands of contentious relations".[107]

Bismarck repeatedly stressed that the Germans in the Habsburg Monarchy, or in the Baltic regions of the Russian Empire, should not be included in the German Reich. He believed that the concept of "greater" Germany fashionable in his time was not relevant to the realities of the day and not in the interests of the community of competing European states.[108] Sebastian Haffner (like for example Alter) points out that the priority of Bismarck's foreign policy was the consolidation of the Reich, and in this context the German Question appeared to Bismarck as a matter of finding the form that would secure the German nation state and integrate it smoothly into the Concert of Europe.

This meant that Bismarck's policy involved the abandonment of several fundamental demands of the Austrian and German nationalists:

- Renunciation of any territorial expansion in Europe.
- Hence the suppression of all expansionist tendencies in Germany, especially all Greater German tendencies.

---

[105]   Ibidem. 90.
[106]   Ibidem. 90.
[107]   Kissinger, H. 1996. *Umění diplomacie* [The Art of Diplomacy]. Prague: Prostor. 172.
[108]   Alter, P. *The German Question and Europe*. 70.

- Consistent rejection of all wishes for the annexation of the "unemancipated" Germans who remained cut off from the foundation of the Reich, especially the Austrian and Baltic Germans.
- Strict refusal to get involved in the overseas colonial politics of the other European powers, which was to be regarded as a good thing in that it distracted the attention of the powers "to the periphery", minimising the risk of coalition against Mittel Europa.
- In case of need to seek to prevent internal European wars, even where the German Reich was not immediately involved or threatened. This principle was based on the premise that European wars had had and would have a tendency to spread.[109]

S. Haffner argues that this was a generally respectable policy that had no parallel in the German Reich after Bismarck. It should be noted, however, that while in practice Bismarck held to the first three points, he nonetheless embarked (with reservations) on closer relations with Austria, and this inconsistency on the chancellor's part inevitably encouraged Austrian and Bohemian Germans in their efforts to advance political linkage between the German-speaking states and regions in Central Europe. The striving for collaboration between Austrian and German supporters of a German Central Europe thus continued and deepened even under Bismarck, developing to the full after his resignation. One key aspect of any possible annexation of Austria to Germany has been the effect on the ratio of Catholics to Protestants, with one commentator of the time remarking that, "Prince Bismarck could in no way desire the exacerbation of the religious difficulties of the German Reich that would ensue if he brought into it a Catholic element as powerful as German Austria and the lands between the latter and Germany. The time is already past when Germany did not dare even to think about the possibility of enlargement to include Austria simply out of the sheer fear that by doing so it would multiply the number of its Catholic subjects."[110]

Bismarck himself and his insistence on a certain restraint (motivated more by a pragmatic assessment of the German Reich's resources than political moderation) eventually attracted attacks not only from Pan-Germans, but also from people like Paul de Lagarde, who wrote, "the obstacles that indeed exist are not insuperable. The more radiant the glory of the nation, the more difficult it is for its mission to be fulfilled."[111] Another example of the national radicalism of

---

[109] Haffner, S. 1995. *Od Bismarcka k Hitlerovi* [From Bismarck to Hitler]. Olomouc: Votobia. 41.

[110] Dilke, Sir Charles. 1887. *l'Europeen*. Paris: Quantin. 183.

[111] Lagarde, P. de. 1892. *Deutsche Schriften*. Göttingen: Dietrich Verlag. 110. See also Lagarde, P. de. *An die Deutschen*. Berlin: Deutsche Buch-Gemeinschaft.

Prussian military circles was the widespread opinion that the other European countries were threatening the very foundations of Germany: "If Bismarck constantly proclaims peace in his *Memoirs*, and if he advises Germany to take care not to be provocative, he is thereby encouraging our neighbours and good friends to impudence. In this sense Bismarck definitely did no service to his country."[112] After the First World War, the fear of foreign states, artificially nurtured by nationalists, fuelled the fires of criticism of the Versailles Treaty and became a key argument for the rising Nazi movement.[113]

The supporters of a Greater Germany (strongly numerically represented especially in the German-speaking border areas of the Bohemian Lands) claimed that of all the German-speaking Lands it was Austria (with Germany) that had the most to gain from Greater Germanism. Their argument was that it was Austria, especially in the Cisleithian part of the monarchy, that was menaced by the principle of nationality adopted as the only possible solution by Napoleon III. Paul de Lagarde enumerated the advantages of this approach[114]: "Pan-Germanism will rid Cisleithania of the danger that the non-German nations will assert their interests." He argued that Prussia had an insufficiently large body for its soul, and Austria an insufficient soul for its body, that Germany had too many princes and Austria too many nations, that Austria needed colonists and Germany needed Austria for its colonists. The policy of the state (the future Pan-German state) should then be to attract German emigrants and divide them into compact colonies on the furthest fronters, since the single vocation of Austria was to become the colonising state of Germany. Thus Austria would ensure its real interests: it needed a ruling race, and only Germans could rule in Austria.[115]

Lagarde's ideas were a step in the direction of claims of the racial superiority of the Germans. In his view there was no need to reckon with the rest of the population, because Hungarians and Czechs were no more than a historical burden of no political significance (*politisch werthlos*)[116], forming merely useful connecting filler for the new German state formations. A Pan-Germanism con-

---

[112] *Deutschland bei Beginn des 20. Jahrhunderts.* 41.

[113] Nationalist propaganda publications for example claimed in the 1920s that more than 10,000 pieces of heavy artillery were aimed at helpless Germany, including artillery in the CSR. Uhle-Wettler, F. *Das Versailler Diktat.* 1999. Kiel: Arndt-Verlag. 337.

[114] Paul Anton de Lagarde (1827–1891): professor of semitic languages at the University of Göttingen, an outstanding orientalist and theologian (works on the earliest period of church history and old canon law), but also admired in his time as the author of studies on the future of Germany. His proposed solution for the so-called Jewish Problem was the resettlement of Polish and German Jews in Palestine or their complete assimilation. See Lagarde, P. de. *Deutsche Schriften.* 34–36.

[115] Ibidem. 32–35, 111–113.

[116] Ibidem. 27.

ceived in this way would in his view prevent nationality conflicts in Austria by guaranteeing strong German rule.

H. C. Meyer has characterised the content of Lagarde's writings as "a strange mixture of Prussian dynastic conservatism, anti-semitism and radical nationalism".[117] The basis of his ardently expressed *Grossdeutsche* views was the conviction that complete German unity had to be achieved at any price. This meant that he vehemently attacked anything and anyone that might present an obstacle on the road to German unification and the fulfilment of this national (historical) mission.

Lagarde's views presented one of the possible versions of *Mitteleuropa* that sprang from radical nationalist thought. He proposed a conservative, monarchically governed German empire to include all the Germans in Central Europe and demanded expansion toward the "natural German borders, *MittelEuropa* (sic) as defined in a way that would allow the inhabitants of that territory sustenance and defence."[118] Lagarde may be regarded as the direct precursor of the later Pan-German movement and creator of a new vision of a German-dominated form of Central Europe. A collection of his essays published under the title *Deutsche Schriften* was among the most widely read works of the years 1895–97 and later representatives of the various ideological currents in Pan-German programmes often referred precisely to this source.

In the course of the second half of the 19th century the Pan-German movement increased markedly in intensity and virulence. At the German National Assembly in Frankfurt the view that *anyone who lived on German soil was a German* was voiced several times. This might be considered just an ideological slogan, but it acquired ever more serious content. In the autumn of 1848 the parliamentarians in Frankfurt had opened the question of how the German-speaking Austrians might be brought back into the Reich.[119] Subsequently this question returned with more urgency as a result of the the rapidly diminishing relative number of German-speaking inhabitants in the Austrian monarchy. After 1866 the strong current of immigration from the other German states had abated and a mere five years later the Austrian Germans were having difficulty maintaining control of a monarchy in which other nations were making fast headway, the Czechs being among the most dynamic in this respect.

It was as an answer to a feeling of supposed menace from the expanding Slav nations that the *concept of a Greater Germany* was elaborated, with increasingly organised support especially after 1870, when it became clear that the Austrian Monarchy had lost its struggle with Prussia for hegemony in Germany and

---

[117]   Meyer, H. C. *Mitteleuropa in German Thought and Action 1815–1945.* 31.

[118]   Ibidem. 31.

[119]   Alter, P. *The German Question and Europe.* 75.

Central Europe. Victorious Prussia transformed a united Germany into Prussia-Germany, which in line with Bismarck's ideas was supposed to implement the Bruck plan for a customs union that was in fact the prototype of the project of Mitteleuropa.[120]

The modern nationalism of the Austrian Germans was thus born in conditions of shock, out of an exaggerated sense of disillusion and psychological insecurity.[121] One of the first reactions to the feeling of national threat was the establishment of the *Deutscher Volksverein*/German People's Union (Vienna 1867) and *Verein der Deutschnationalen*/Association of German Nationalists (Graz, 1869) associations. Four groups of Austrian Germans pursuing nationalist demands in different variants were ultimately to emerge.

The first group, and the most active in the field of national agitation, were the *Bohemian Germans* (for whom the term Sudeten Germans, coined by the deputy and journalist Dr. Franz Jesser, was adopted into common usage in the period before the First World War). An extremely large group of people from the ranks of the intelligentsia and successful businessmen of the monarchy was recruited precisely from the Bohemian German milieu. One group with a special position in this context came from West Bohemia (Cheb region), and inclined to Germany rather than Austria. Henry C. Meyer has pointed out that it was in this region that local national sentiment started to form even before 1866. The second group were the *Alpine Germans* in East and South-East Austria – forming an ethnic group with a great deal of resistant solidarity in terms of psychological attitude and views.

A third group formed on the territory of Styria and Corinthia (*Südmark*) and showed radical nationalist features similar to those of the Bohemian Germans. Finally we can see Vienna as a separate group or more precisely a milieu where we can discern the emergence of a conglomerate of representatives of different classes, groups and provinces, subject intellectually to cosmopolitan and imperial influences and reacting only in a lukewarm way to expressions of ethnic tension (with the exception of academic circles).[122]

The year 1894 saw the founding of the Pan-German League (*Alldeutscher Verband*) headed by Dr. Hasse. It had close connections with The Navy League

---

[120] The clash took place on the diplomatic and economic field where the two great-power concepts faced each other: the Greater-Austrian Schwarzenberg-Bruck plan for an "empire for 70 million inhabitants" (the project for customs union between Austria and the German Confederation), and the Prussian Little German union (planning reforms on the principles of free trade). Jindra, Z. "Založení Německé říše v novém světle" [The Foundation of the German Reich in a New Light]. *Československý časopis historický* XVII. 719.

[121] This key moment in the awakening of aggressive nationalism is discussed by several authors, e.g. P. Molisch, E. Wiskemann, H. G. Skilling and others. Here cited from Meyer, H. C. *Mitteleuropa in German Thought and Action 1815–1945*. 39.

[122] This classification of groupings is based on the fundamental work Meyer, H. C., *Mitteleuropa in German Thought and Action 1815–1945*. Ibidem. 40.

(*Deutscher Flottenverein*), and its members included deputies from all political groupings except for the socialists.[123] Its views and influence were disseminated primarily through periodicals like *Heimdall* and *Alldeutsche Blätter.*

Austrian Pan-Germanism found a cult personality in the form of Ritter Georg von Schönerer. On public holidays the paper *Alldeutsche Tagblatt* would publish congratulatory messages to him of the type *"Heil dem Führer"* with grandiose tributes like "We love, honour and admire you, and glorify you as the best man to have arisen in our nation after Bismarck." Schönerer replied with the Bismarckian statement, "What is German will sooner or later return to Germany."[124]

As the national/ethnic composition of the monarchy changed, liberalism increasingly came into conflict with nationalism, with liberalism ever more often sacrificed in the cause of the defence of nationalist demands. These demands spread from the milieu of the Austrian *Südmark* through academic circles in Graz and Vienna into other areas of the monarchy, and especially Northern Bohemia. The programme defended by Georg von Schönerer represented the spirit of national radicalism, and while even at its most influential it was embraced by only an unconvincing minority of Austrian Germans, in the peripheral parts of the monarchy, in linguistically mixed areas (border territories of ethnic overlap and conflict (*Volkstumkampf*) it attracted strong support.

Many people who were later to become well-known in political life were among Schönerer's close colleagues and associates.[125] The fanatical antisemite von Schönerer was elected to the Imperial Council by votes from the Cheb and Opava regions and was made an honorary citizen there. The programme of his Anti-Semitic *Pan-German Party* was very similar to the programme of the DNSAP (Sudeten National Socialist Party) decades later. It is not without significance that Schönerer found support among members of the intelligentsia, the radical antisemitic student body, and among the doctors and lawyers who were later most often behind the moves to impose what were known as "Jewish quotas".[126]

---

[123] Wiskemann, E. 1967. *Czechs And Germans.* London/Melbourne/Toronto: Macmillan, St. Martin's Press. 47.

[124] Hamann, B. 1999. *Hitlerova Vídeň* [Hitler's Vienna]. 267. This work is comprehensive and penetrating account of the theme of Pan-German nationalists in Austrian milieux in the period before the First World War.

[125] Among them were then young German nationalist intellectuals such as Dr. Victor Adler, Dr. Heinrich Friedjung, Dr. Karl Lueger, and others, who at that time still formed a compact group in terms of views. Later their paths were to diverge, for various reasons including the fact that Schönerer became the best known and most persuasive voice of racial antisemitism, drawing on the work of the German philosopher Dühring, E. 1881. *Die Judenfrage als Racen, Sitten und Kulturfrage.* Karlsruhe/Leipzig.

[126] The territorial distribution of his supporters is indicated by a survey that Schönerer conducted in his own journal *Unverfälschte deutsche Worte.* He requested written declarations from voters that they were willing to support his programme. He received a total of 3260 answers: 16% were from the Bohemian borderlands, 20% from Austrian Silesia, and the remainder mainly from students in Vienna and Lower Austria. Later the Nazis were to speak in very approving terms of the "similarity between the temporarily successful Sudeten German wing of the Schönererians and the National Socialist antisemitic and anti-social-democratic programme".

Under Schönerer's leadership this circle developed the programme presented under the slogan "non-liberal, non-clerical, but national", the so-called *Linz Programme*. This fundamental document of German nationalism presented not only political demands but also quite an elaborate section concerned with social welfare. It demanded social reforms including old-age and injury insurance, restriction of the labour of women and children, but also the extension of civic rights and liberties – democratisation, freedom of the press and of asembly. To secure the leading role of Germans, the *Linz Programme* proposed basic changes in the structure of the multi-national monarchy. Galicia and Bukovina as the lands with the greatest proportion of non-German population were to be excluded (it was in these provinces that the greatest number of Jews lived, perhaps one million, and here that the largest amount of funds were sent as part of state redistribution of resources). The programme proposed the annexation of Dalmatia, Bosnia and Herzegovina together with Croatia to Hungary. The remainder of the Austrian hereditary holdings including the Bohemian Lands were to be more closely integrated and progressively create a customs union with the German Reich. The state language was to be German and the introduction of universal equal male franchise was to be hedged with measures to secure a permanent German majority.

The *Linz Programme* was not without attractions for the other Austrian civic political parties (ultimately it was playing on a common national string), and was also welcomed by the Hungarians and especially the Poles, to whom it opened the way to the establishment of the independent state that they had so long been denied. There were, however, two basic obstacles to the whole programme. First, the Emperor Franz Josef I would never agree to any kind of further division of the empire, and second, the Czechs would never accept German as state language.[127] For a full illustration of the Emperor's attitude we should add that the *Schönererian Programme* annoyed him so much that he refused the alliance with the Hohenzollern Empire for which Schönerer's supporters had been calling for years.[128]

With the radicalisation of nationalism in the 1880s and 1890s the position of the Jews was becoming ever more difficult. The collapse of German liberalism under the government of Count Taaffe and the rise of radical nationalism among Austrian and Bohemian Germans, often closely bound up with antisem-

---

For more detail see Míšková, A. "Od Schönerera ke genocidě" [From Schönerer to Genocide], in Otte, A. (et al.). *Židé v Sudetech* [Jews in the Sudetenland]. 2000. Prague: Ackermann-Gemeinde/Česká křesťanská akademie. 48–49.

[127] For more detail see Hamann, B. *Hitlerova Vídeň.* 270–272.

[128] Wiskemann, E. *Czechs and Germans.* 47. The author cites a despatch sent by Count A. Eulenburg to Prince Hohenlohe on the 5th of March 1898.

itism, led Jews to reconsider what had originally been pro-German sympathies and even their tendency to consider themselves German. The rise of clerical antisemitism among the Germans of Lower Austria, heralded by the Christian Social Party of Karl Lueger (himself an extreme antisemite), meant that Jews inevitably began to fear the German conservatives. Despite this, however, the majority of Jews, including those who considered Czech to be their "language of social intercourse" (*Umgangsprache*), attended German schools (including the German University and German Technical University in Prague) and remained attached to German culture and German way of life. In the case of the Jews in the Bohemian Lands, German antisemitism was generally driving them towards a degree of alignment with Czech society, which was growing and flourishing in terms of both economic power and cultural achievements. This put some brakes on the increasing level of antisemitism expressed by some Czech politicians.[129]

H. G. Skilling regards it as an irony that the antisemitism permeating into Czech political and public life was fed by German sources in Vienna, for example precisely the Pan-German G. von Schönerer, the Christian socialist K. Lueger, and sometimes the German nationalist parties and their press. Jewish hopes were pinned on the Young Czech Party, who identified with liberalism and democracy, but even here an extreme nationalism associated with antisemitism was gaining ground.

Hostility to Jews was an all-European phenomenon in the last quarter of the 19th century and found expression in France, Germany, Russia and other countries.[130] The basic shift away from it in Czech public opinion (and also the views of Czech cultural and political elites) owed a great deal to T. G. Masaryk, who at the time of the Hilsner Affair (an alleged case of ritual murder at the turn of the century) took an uncompromising stand against Czech antisemitism and achieved an "ethical catharsis of Czech thought". Masaryk had to struggle with his own nation on behalf of that nation and get through to the conscience of the Czech intelligentsia. His fight against prejudice and intolerance changed the way Czechs were seen abroad, and helped him during the First World War

---

[129]   For example some articles by Julius Grégr, and one wing of the radical constitutional party led by A. Hajn and K. Baxa. In an interview in 1901 the leader of the Old Czechs F. L. Rieger even described Jews as a:"destructive alien element" and attacked T. G. Masaryk on this score, calling him a "declared enemy of the Lord God". Skilling, H. G. 1995. *T. G. Masaryk proti proudu 1882–1914* [T. G. Masaryk against the Current]. Prague: Práh. 129–130.

[130]   The liberals in Southern Germany had been pushing through equal rights for Jews. Baden emancipated the Jews in 1862, Frankfurt and Württemberg in 1864. The Northern confederation followed in 1869 and imposed the same measure on Catholic Bavaria in 1870. In Austria and Hungary the Jews were given equal rights by a settlement of 1867. Great Britain followed suit in 1871. In France and Germany there was great pressure on Jews to assimilate to the dominant nation, whereas in the ethnically diverse Habsburg Monarchy it was easier for Jews to be politically Austrian, "culturally German" while also continuing to preserve aspects of Jewish identity. Gildea, R. *Barricades And Borders. Europe 1800–1914.* 258.

when he won the support of many Jews throughout the world for the "Czech cause".[131]

Mitteleuropa as a fully-fledged concept is generally considered to have been first formulated and published by F. Naumann in 1915, but in fact Pan-German circles had already come up with many similar visions characterised by political messianism and belief in the exclusive role of Germany in Central European territory. This was pointed out by A. Chéradame, who argued that all these programmes had one and the same basis and differed merely in form and details.[132]

By way of example Chéradame gave a leaflet published in 1895 by an anonymous author (who identifies himself simply as a member of the Pan-German League), *Greater Germany and Central Europe in 1950*.[133] Later developments confirmed that the League was indeed seeking to realise the principles set out in the leaflet. In the introduction the author states that the German Reich is incomplete because twenty-one million Germans live outside its borders: two million in Switzerland, ten million in Austria-Hungary, one million in Russia and eight million in Belgium and the Netherlands. On the basis of this claim he goes on to demand that linguistic territory must correspond to political territory, for only thus can Germany reach its natural frontiers. There follows a very detailed geographical definition of the territories that the author demands for Germany. Its western border should run through the Flemish part of Belgium, the Ardennes, the Alps right to Mont Blanc, while in the direction of Italy it should be defined by the Dolomite range. The author states that to the east and otherwise to the south there was no line established by nature. Where the limit of expansion should be remained an open question. For the moment, in the author's view, all endeavours should be concentrated on Austria, which needed to be annexed to the German Reich. "The collapse of the Habsburg Empire is near, and will happen as soon as the current ruler closes his eyes. Power will bring the Slav population to heel and the rapid fragmentation of the Habsburg Empire will make German supremacy easy."[134]

The author pursues his geopolitical arguments for extensive re-assignment of territories by recommending the partition of Galicia and Bukovina with Tsarist Russia. Rumania should be enlarged to include part of Hungary, while Croa-

---

[131] Skilling, H. G. *T. G. Masaryk proti proudu 1882–1914*. 137. Masaryk grasped that our greatest task was to prepare for that "fortunate constellation of 1917 and 1918". In fact, his whole life's work had prepared him for the task of highlighting and promoting the importanceof the Czech Question in Europe. He alone managed to find the right tone in dealing with the democratic west, and this was ultimately decisive. He alone had a major international reputation allowing him to hope that people would listen to him. Peroutka, F. 1927. *Kdo nás osvobodil* [Who Freed Us]. Prague: Svaz národního osvobození. 93.

[132] Chéradame, A. *Evropa a otázka rakouská*. 90–91.

[133] *Gross-Deutschland und Mitteleuropa um das Jahr 1950. Von einem Alldeutschen*. 1895. Berlin: Thormann.

[134] Ibidem. 10.

tia, Slavonia, Dalmatia, Montenegro, Bosnia and Herzegovina should together constitute a Serbian Kingdom connected with Austria by personal union, while Austria itself should be inseparably merged with the German Reich. "In order that the way should be clear as far as Trieste, control of which is essential for the German Reich, it remains only to humble the Czechs and Slovenes."

The author also anticipates the disintegration of Turkey, with Germany taking its share of the pickings. "The inevitable war between Germany and Russia will finish this work. If the result is fortunate, Germany will seize the Baltic provinces, Estonia, Livonia, Kurland, and create a Polish State and Rusine Kingdom destined to accept the Jews and Slavs, who will be moved out of the greater German Reich."[135]

From a map reproduced in the Debes atlas *Europa, Sprachen und Völkerkarte* published in 1899, it is evident that the plan reckoned with the establishment of two territorial entities in Central Europe conceived broadly as extending "from Hamburg to Trieste". The first was supposed to be the German Union (including the German empire, Luxemburg, the Netherlands, Belgium, German Switzerland and Austria-Hungary), and the second a customs union/*Zollverein* to include in addition the principalities in the Baltic, the Polish state, the Rusine Kingdom, Rumania and an enlarged Serbia.

This massive Pan-Germany was to encompass a population of 86 million, while the territories included in the customs union would with their population of 131 million offer a huge market for the expanding German economy. The author was in no doubt over who would have the decisive voice in the planned mega-state:

"Of course the Germans will not be the only inhabitants of a German Reich created in this way, but only they will exercise political rights, serve in the army and navy, and only they will have the power to acquire land. Thus they will regain the consciousness, with which they were suffused in the Middle Ages, that they are the governing nation, and will be happy to allow foreigners living among them to perform lower manual work."[136]

In 1901 Chéradame could still consider these demands ridiculously wild and unrealistic and could conclude in his analysis that there could be no serious debate about Pan-Germanism on the basis of such ideas. He suggests that these fantasy elements serving only to "awaken the imagination of the masses" should be brought down to politically realistic contents. Today we naturally view them rather differently in the light of the later variants of *Mitteleuropa* in the period of the First World War and the Nazi territorial expansion, intellectu-

---

[135] Ibidem. 40.
[136] Ibidem. 48.

ally grounded in ideas that derive directly from the visions of the Pan-German enthusiasts.

A great many books and leaflets of various kinds promoting different versions of the vision of a Central Europe dominated by the German "element" came out at the end of the 19th century. Another such booklet, entitled, *The Collapse and Rebuilding of Austria*[137] developed similar notions of territorial change arguing that the Bohemian Lands should become part of Saxony.

Chéradame's work offered a detailed analysis of a number of other plans, visions and ideas inspired by the belief that German-speaking territory in Central Europe had to expand as a consequence of its special mission, especially in regard to the Slavs. It is clear from his approach that Chéradame was strongly on the side of the "Slav element", which he believed was resisting a Pan-German conspiracy that threatened Europe, but while partisan he still made painstaking efforts to prove and document his claims with reference to published literature, the speeches of politicians, publicists and so on. Given his perspective, he describes only that part of the German and Austrian political spectrum associated with the extreme (but by no means marginal) ideas that he saw as a threat to the future development of Central Europe.

Chéradame points out that the Pan-Germans were an immediate menace to the existence of the multi-national Habsburg Empire, which he regarded as in some sense a guarantee of the peaceful future of this part of Europe. He believed that while moderate views existed in German circles, those who held them were being shouted down by the aggressive Pan-German campaigners: "Unfortunately we are forced to say that these expressions [of moderation] are very rare, and that organs like the *Süddeutsche Reichskorrespondenz* which never cease to accuse the Pan-German League of whipping up an irredentist movement among Austrian Germans remain entirely helpless to stem the tide."[138]

As we have noted elsewhere, the influence of the Schönerer programme started to fade at the turn of the century, but the traces that it left in the political thinking of the Austrian and above all Bohemian Germans in North and West Bohemia would turn out to be tragically deep for the future.

---

[137] *Österreichs Zusammenbruch und Wiederaufbau.* The pamphlet, seized by the Austrian police, was the work of the Pan-German League and was found harmful by six tribunals in Cisleithania.

[138] Chéradame, A. *Evropa a otázka rakouská.* 194. H. C. Meyer calls A. Chéradame's views anti-German (see bibliographical essay, ibidem. 352), but accordingly adds facts supporting Chéradame's opinion. The culminating point of the ever closer cooperation between Germany and Austria-Hungary was a confidential memorandum of November 1915, in which the Wilhelmine Ministry of Foreign Affairs proposed to Vienna an economic union of the two monarchies with the aim of strengthening political alliance, Meyer, H. C. *Mitteleuropa in German Thought and Action 1815–1945.* 172. H. W. Steed on the contrary asserts that with his studies on Pan-Germanism A. Chéradame made a strong contribution to the knowledge of the danger it posed. See Steed H. W. *Třicet let novinářem* [Thirty Years a Journalist]. 1927. Prague: Orbis. 339.

Another voice warning Austrian Germans (in the Bohemian Lands) against a lack of critical reflection that might have tragic results was that of H. Kudlich, a man considered the "liberator of the Austrian peasants".[139] In correspondence from the USA (where he had emigrated in the face of persecution by the Austrian authorities), he wrote bluntly to H. Krommer in Opava, that, "There are not many rich Austrian Germans here. The richest among them are Jews, for example the Fleischmanns… here they are multimillionaires, and generous with it, but they won't have a haller for the Germans in Opava. They know your situation better than I do. Personally I don't want to have anything to do with antisemites. Because it is from the [rise of such views] that the sad and criminal erosion of the foundations of German liberalism in Austria dates."[140] We should add that Kudlich disagreed with the national radicals more on tactical grounds than because he wanted any kind of Czech emancipation.

Those who attempted to overcome the national/ethnic conflict in the Habsburg Monarchy included the Social Democratic Workers' Party of Austria, which on the 4th of September 1897 organised a joint land conference in Prague devoted to national relations in the workers' movement, especially relations between Czechs and Germans. A large demonstration supporting the idea of peace and brotherhood took place, but in Vienna and the North Bohemian border areas there were no demonstrations against nationalism.[141]

Another effort to find a solution acceptable to both sides in a tolerant spirit of national reconciliation was the Brno National Programme presented by the Austrian Social Democratic Party in 1899. Although criticised for the deliberate vagueness of its formulation, allowing various possible interpretations, it was a genuine attempt to identify a positive way out of a difficult situation. The programme proclaimed the principle of the cultivation and development of the national identity of all the peoples of Austria on the basis of equal rights and without national oppression.

It was valuable that the Czech and Austrian Social Democrats managed to agree on a programme of national understanding and tolerance at a time when national conflict was intensifying, especially in the wake of the withdrawal of the Badeni language reforms. Indeed this was the time at which the Social

---

[139] Following his involvement in the 1848 revolution he had to emigrate to Switzerland and later he settled in the USA. He returned to his native Úvalno in the Opava region after an amnesty in 1872 and there he wrote his memoirs, in which he first expressed fears for the future of Germans in the Bohemian Lands. Hoffmann, R. J. – Harasko, A. 2000. *Odsun – Die Vertreibung der Sudetendeutschen*. München: Sudetendeutsches Archiv. 324.

[140] Ibidem. 360. At the end of his letter he does not, however, neglect to write, "You know my German sentiments! But sentiments alone are not enough for leading the nation. That requires a portion of tact and cleverness…" In another letter (17th September 1898) Kudlich prophecies: "If in 50 years time Opava and Silesia are Czech, then it will be you alone who are to blame for the change."

[141] Kořalka, J. *Češi v habsburské říši a v Evropě 1815–1914*. 287–288.

Democrats defined themselves as the leading supporters of a transformation of the Cisleithanian part of the Habsburg Monarchy into a federation of emancipated democratic states. Yet although in subsequent years the Social Democrats were among the most conciliatory on nationalist questions, the compromise represented by the Brno programme proved impossible to put into political practice and in 1910 a dispute in which the key factor was the national question erupted between the Czechoslovak Social Democrats and the All-Austria SD Party. Moreover, after the outbreak of the First World War, part of the Austrian (but also the German) Social Democratic party became much more strongly nationalist in approach.

It was clear to Austrian politicians that the continued existence of the monarchy depended on some degree of concession to Czech constitutional ambitions, since it was becoming ever harder to maintain the privileged position of the Germans in the Bohemian Lands including German over-representation in the electoral system. Austrian political elites faced a tough task that could not be solved by the mere political tacking with which they tried to defuse the explosive situation at the end of the 19th century – a stage when they were compelled to take on board the fact that the Slav nations now had the demographic upper hand in the monarchy. The central government in Vienna manoeuvred with greater or lesser success between the non-German nations, the government majority and the German liberal oppositions with just one aim: to strengthen the patriarchal semi-absolutism in which the crown, government and bureaucratic executive would always be able to tip the balance of power in the monarchy in its favour.[142]

Czech political life became more radicalised after the failure of Hohenwart's attempt at a settlement of the Czech question in 1871 – which showed up the unreality of hopes for implementation of a Czech constitutional programme. Czech politicians were increasingly forced to abandon the tactic of passive opposition. Their first and much celebrated success (however partial) was the promulgation of the Stremayr Language Decree, which imposed an obligation on state offices in the Bohemian Lands to accept submissions in Czech as well as German and to reply to them in Czech.

At the beginning of 1890 (4th–19th January), representatives of Czech and German political groupings met in Vienna, and their negotiations resulted in the signing of what is known as the *Vienna Punctations*, which proposed common principles for resolving relations between the two nations in Bohemia.[143] If

---

[142] Křen. J. *Konfliktní společenství*. 218.

[143] The principles agreed on were supposed to be realised in the form of land laws or government regulations. Apart from measures relating to education (the division of the Land School Council into two parts/a Czech and a German, the setting up of minority schools, the division of the Agricultural Council for the Bohemian

this provisional agreement had been implemented, it would have meant the division of Bohemia into a German part and a bilingual part. The Young Czechs rejected it on the grounds that it did not respect Czech national identity. The Bohemian Germans also rejected a number of points and as E. Wiskemann remarks, the whole material discussion between Czechs and Sudeten Germans was shipwrecked on the reluctance of both sides to agree to a *definition of linguistically mixed areas.*[144]

The Punctations were likewise rejected in a debate of the Bohemian Diet at the beginning of April 1892 by the then deputy T. G. Masaryk.[145] On both the Czech and German side it was obvious that even the remnants of loyalty to the supra-national principle of the Habsburg Empire were rapidly disappearing. Nonetheless, particularly in Czech politics there continued to be voices calling for moderation.

The year 1882 saw the opening of the Czech university in Prague. Profesor Tomáš G. Masaryk started to teach there and was soon a central figure in the community of Czech university intelligentsia publishing the *Atheneum* revue. Three men with pronounced political views and ambitions – Josef Kaizl, Karel Kramář and Tomáš G. Masaryk – rapidly parted company with the "Realist" Group. Before long Kaizl and Kramář were heading the Young Czech Party, while Masaryk took up a stance of opposition to a "confused, conservative and extreme nationalist interpretation of constitutional right".[146] He concentrated on the revival and development of the political programme of F. Palacký, believing that Palacký had grasped the basis of modern development and so placed greater emphasis on the modern idea of nationality than on historical rights.

In 1884 the Young Czech politician Julius Grégr made a major study tour of Germany, and then published a report in *Národní listy* which included his assessment of the goals of a united Germany. He wrote that this is "a state not only in

Kingdom, the revision of the electoral regulations for chambers of commerce and trade), the Punctations fulfilled the greatest wish of German politicians in Bohemia, since Points Six to Ten opened up the way to the establishment of a separate province of German Bohemians (*Deutschböhmen*). The borders of district and regional courts, regional authorities and electoral districts were to be revised with a view to the wishes of the local population so that as far as possible the higher-level whole should include communities of only one nationality. Other points related to the appointment of judges on the basis of linguistic knowledge and use of the land languages. Kořalka, J. *Češi v habsburské říši a v Evropě 1815–1914.* 164.

[144] For example, in the elections to the Bohemian Assembly in 1901 the slogans of Pan-Germans were, "Our motto is nothing but German, Pan-German and indivisible! Germans in Bohemia have to decide if they intend to become Slavs or if in accordance with their mission they will be Germans! There is no third way." Wiskemann, E. *Czechs and Germans.* 66.

[145] Masaryk declared that, "in the Punctations the Germans were being given deeds, but the Czechs only promises... [and] that the extreme demands of the Germans in recent years are met in the Punctations... the German programme is centralising, Germanising, unmodern, and that autonomy is the only possible political standpoint." Šolle, Z. *Století české politiky.* 114.

[146] Šolle, Z. – Gajanová, E. *Po stopě dějin.* 123.

full political and national but also economic development. For its neighbours this rise is a threat, but it is not yet an acute threat for the nations of the Habsburg Monarchy, because the *Prussification* of Germany is not yet certain and because Germany needs the friendship of the monarchy".[147]

The activist (in the sense of prepared to engage in the existing Austrian system) wing of Czech politics preferred to exploit the framework of the Austrian state and its potential transformation to ensure continuing dynamic Czech growth – essentially in the spirit of Palacký's programme. Typical in this context were the views of the experienced Czech politician J. Kaizl, who put forward the idea of Czech *pénetration pacifique* of the political centre in Vienna.[148] Behind this approach was Kaizl's desire to avoid the need for a settlement with the Germans in the Bohemian Lands by the strategy of having Czechs "negotiate" linguistic national autonomy directly with Vienna. Kaizl planned to push through Czech demands by exploiting the Austrian bureaucracy (the penetration of Czech officials into the ministries and other government organs of the monarchy) and favoured agreement with liberal Germans who hoped for the democratisation of the empire.

Yet it was as a challenge to these same German liberals that on the 18th of November 1892 Masaryk made a major speech in the Imperial Council in Vienna, claiming that the aim of the German liberals and the parties allied with them was the Germanisation of the non-German peoples in the monarchy, above all the Czechs. "When you speak of German reformation, you are extremely enthusiastic with all your liberalism... but the moment that you are supposed to grasp and acknowledge something in Czech history, you are absolutely incapable of it. And so Gentlemen, we are hearing time and time again about German culture as contrasted to the inferior culture that is ours."

In another speech he touched on all the points of the Czech-Austrian/German relationship as expressed in political programmes; he mentioned its international context, the alliance between Austria and German, and relationship of the Czech nation to the Triple Alliance: "We need peace for the Czech nation... the Triple Alliance will not guarantee peace, as is constantly claimed. In any case I wish just to say that the Triple Alliance is exploited by our opponents in a spirit that is anti-national and especially anti-Czech, and for that reason alone the Czech nation cannot regard this alliance without a great deal of distrust."

Masaryk cited the formulations of a series of promoters of Germanisation, initiated in his view by Bismarck and his policy towards the Poles in the Poznan area. "A statesman who has been so deified in Germany has been responsible –

---

[147] Křen, J. – Broklová, E. *Obraz Němců, Rakouska a Německa.* 23.
[148] Křen, J. *Konfliktní společenství.* 254.

and in Germany it seems there is no longer any doubt about this – for causing public opinion to run wild. He introduced into European politics a de-
moralisation of a kind that had not existed before, and if you are going to
point the finger gloatingly at Russia, which is reaching for Poland to strip it
of its nationality with an iron and brutal hand, it has to be said that the Russians learned this from Prussia, from Bismarck. The great ferment that is now
manifest in the Czech nation is just an answer to this systematic threat to the
nation... Face to face with these menacing tendencies we are struggling for our
independence."[149]

Masaryk was later to return to these themes, and for the purposes of our
study we should note his attitude to the connections between internal and foreign policy. In his view the Triple Alliance was an instrument of war by which
Austria was bound to Germany and its interests in the search for allies against
France and Russia. He asserted that Austria as a state union of smaller nations
was a great power "and we wish it to remain a great power, but we want it to be
powerful and great internally as well". In this he was opposing the spread of
the idea that Austria was some kind of hinterland for the German Reich, and
was to serve only for German colonisation. The Triple Alliance reinforced views
demanding the Germanisation of Bohemia, which provoked Czech resistance
to German demands for districts in the North of Bohemia to be separated off
on national criteria. "Yes, who will guarantee to us that a world situation of
the kind in which we shall live in eternal peace with Germany will endure? We
cannot allow independent German provinces to be set up in the north of our
empire, especially in our homeland."

The openly formulated demands for linguistic equality of Czechs with Germans in the Bohemian Lands put forward on the 13th of December 1895 by
J. Kaizl at a sitting of the Imperial Council represented an important stage in
the long-term campaign of Czech politicians for emancipation. In the same year
a new government had been appointed, headed as prime minister by K. Badeni, who from the start tried to find a way out that would be acceptable for
Czech aspirations. In April 1897 the government issued a language decree for
Bohemia and Moravia that extended the terms of the Stremayr government
decreee; Czech was now to be granted equal status with German not only in
the dealings of government offices with the public but also in internal official
business.[150]

---

[149] Šolle, Z. *Století české politiky*. 120.
[150] The reform consisted in the fact that documents submitted to the authorities would now be considered
and processed in the language of submitted document, so that Czech submissions would not need to be
translated into German. This did not of course mean full equality for Czech, which could only be secured by
a new language law. Masaryk pointed this out in the journal *Nová doba* but added that the "decree also has

This attempt by the Vienna government to move forward in finding a way to solve the Czech-German dispute provoked a tempest of opposition on the German side. Although it was a moderate reform of existing conditions (if one that was in the direction of giving equal status to both languages), obstruction by the German deputies paralysed the debates of the Imperial Council, which the government eventually had to close on the 2nd of June.

The influential Pan-German League[151] called a protest meeting in Dresden to support the Austrian and Bohemian Germans as early as the 9th of May 1897. It was held in the spirit of the declaration by the Austrian journalist Welker: "The Czech language question is a common matter for all nations of the German language, for the German people is not limited in its borders by black-white-red columns."[152] The meeting supported these words and unanimously approved a resolution "proclaiming the language decrees for Czechs a humiliation for the whole German nation, urging all Germans to struggle against the Slav lusts, using all means [...] and obliging Austrian compatriots to fight no matter what".

Throughout Cisleithania, German deputies immediately launched a campaign of clearly targeted agitation actions to whip up opposition to the government and the Czechs. The town of Cheb was a bastion of resistance to the Badeni language decrees, becoming on the 11th of June the scene of an anti-government and anti-Czech demonstration (known as the German People's Day) which culminated in what was known as the "Cheb Oath" – an act of solidarity by representatives of the German liberals and radical nationalist German politicians of the Sudeten and Alpine Lands, but also Reich Germans. The Czech *Národní listy* reporter wrote, "From today *Germania iredenta* is no mere empty

---

significant political and national value in the sense that it imposes the necessity of a knowledge of Czech on all German officials." Ibidem. 153.

[151] Of all the radical rightwing groups of the time, the Pan-German League has the worst historical reputation. It was founded in 1891 in furious reaction to Chancellor Caprivi's cession of the colonial holding Zanzibar, but soon its programme expanded to include a whole range of ultranationalist and expansionist demands. It defined itself as a force standing above politics in the cause of the national interest, but at the same time it appeared as an alternative opposition force in relation to – as it termed it – the moderate political line of the governments of Bülow (1894–1906) and von Bethmann Hollweg (1908–1916). When Heinrich Claß became leader of the Pan-German League in 1908 the antisemitic tone intensified and Claß and his colleages took the view that if Germany was to occupy a leading position in the world, war with Britain was unavoidable and even desirable. L. McGowan argues that the *völkisch* nationalists embodied a new current in politics. They started to promote ideas that are today generally regarded as the principles of contemporary radical extremism, i.e. aggressive nationalism with an openly antisemitic and racist programme, a fanatical faith in militarism and imperialism, antagonism to socialism and Marxism and the rejection of pluralist and democratic political arrangements. The origins of the ideas of the radical right in 20th-century Germany go back to the period of the Second Reich. McGowan, L. 2004. *Radikální pravice v Německu* [The Radical Right in Germany]. Prague: Prostor. 47–52.

[152] Chéradame, A. *Evropa a otázka rakouská*. 171.

phrase, and today our Germans with their deputies have openly confessed that they desire annexation to Greater Germany."[153]

In the Western and Northern borderlands of Bohemia the anti-Czech agitation led to disturbances and violence reported in Štětí, Chabařovice, Teplice, Most, Liberec, Ústí, Jablonec and other places. Demonstrations against the Badeni language decrees took place in all German areas and created long-term pressure on the Vienna government and Imperial Council, which was called again only at the end of October 1897.

In the summer of 1897 the atmosphere in the Cheb region was characterised by whipped up nationalist emotion and a deliberately cultivated fear of the allegedly aggressive Czechs and Slavs in general. "It is sad when political struggle has to go so far. But we are acting in necessary self-defence. They are attacking us from all sides and anyone who holds life dear simply has to defend himself to the last breath. War has been frivolously declared on the German nation, Count Badeni has frivolously thrown a burning torch into a powder keg and the Czechs are exploiting the folly of the government in the most flagrant way to justify unprecedented attacks on the life and property of Germans... we have to take off the kid gloves and strike with the feared German force".[154]

It is in this episode over the language reforms that we can already observe the genesis of one simple but important theory expressing the feelings of the German inhabitants of the Bohemian Lands. This was the highlighting of the "frontier" mentality of the society, "the fighting spirit of a frontier territory". According to this theory or rather shared myth, the Sudeten Germans had for centuries stood loyally and firmly on the German-Slav border as an advance guard.

The function as guards and borderer spirit was now believed to have maintained their sense of national identity in centuries past, to have made them peculiarly vigilant, toughened them and imposed on them the sacred duty of defending the soil on which they lived.[155] From the point of view of the development of relations between Czechs and Germans in the historic lands, this

---

[153] Šolle, Z. *Století české politiky*. 156. Evidence of the degree of national mobilisation and radicalisation can be found for example in the formulation of an article in the *Rumburger Zeitung* of the 24th of July 1897: "A friend of our paper has written us the following about the national movement in the Ohře Valley, "Now we'll really teach the Czechs a lesson in the Egerland (Chebsko). Czech workers, junior workers and servants will be dismissed, and Czech tenants will be given notice to move out." *Dux Zeitung* chose a similar tone: "Today we can inform you that as a consequence of the rape of Germans in Bohemia, the German Reich has begun to dismiss Czech workers and send them home. Every day a group of 10–20 workers passes through Duchcov on their way home from the German Reich. May it only continue – in an emergency we can start to do the same thing here." Hoffmann, R. J. – Harasko, A. *Odsun*. 288–289.

[154] "Deutsches Volk, erwache!" *Eggerer Nachrichten*. 21. 8. 1897. Hoffmann, R. J. – Harasko, A. *Odsun*. 300–301.

[155] Jaworski, R. "Mezi politikou a trivialitou – Sudetoněmecké grenzlandromány, 1918–1938" [Between Politics and Triviality – the Sudeten-German Frontiersmen]. *Dějiny a současnost* 1/2004. 28.

militant "frontiersmen" rhetoric and ethnic mobilisation of the German-speaking inhabitants of the border regions prefigured in outline the tragic course of events in the first half of the 20th century.

The calling of assemblies of the German electorate continued in Bohemia and outside it, and involved expressions of confidence in obstructive deputies and the approval of obstruction as the politically resolute and right way forward. The professors of the German University and Technical University in Prague protested against the language decree.[156] German local government bodies in Bohemia, in Silesia, Lower Austria, Styria and elsewhere threatened to strike.[157] When a new session of the lower house of the Imperial Council was called at the end of October 1897, German obstruction intensified as it was joined by K. Lueger's Christian Socialists, the clerical conservatives from the Alpine Lands, and even the Social Democrats. The conflict came to a climax in November, not only in parliament but with demonstrations in all areas settled by Germans. Austria-Hungary was shaken to its foundations.

One of those to become involved in the widespread anti-Czech campaign was the leading German historian Professor Theodor Mommsen, whose open letter, "An die Deutschen in Österreich" was printed on the 31st of October 1897 in the newspaper *Neue Freie Presse*. In his nationalist ecstasy the distinguished scholar used the vocabulary of gutter journalism, "Be hard! The skulls of Czechs won't accept reason, but even they will understand blows. Too many sins have been committed and much ruined by untimely acquiescence."[158]

No small role in further souring relations was played by the German-language media, both the liberally orientated and the radical nationalist organs. Czechs were presented in articles in an ever more negative way that was ever less justifiable in terms of reality, and according to J. Křen "racist aspects" even started to appear. Naturally the Czechs responded.[159]

---

[156] It was in the Badeni crisis that solidarity between Austrian and German nationalists manifested itself to the full. In the summer of 1897 on the initiative of the University of Heidelberg regular professors at the Reich universities (816 out of a total of 1100) sent an address to the professors at the German University in Prague appealing to the latter to join manly battle against the Czechs. University professors had considerable influence in Germany and a large number of them supported Pan-German ideals. For example there were more than 30 professors on the Committee of the Pan-German League. The front page of the Pan-German *Alldeutsche Blätter* declared, "Let us – they advise parents – send our German students from the Reich to study for a few semesters at the German University in Graz to be imbued with the fresh idealism of a German bourgeoisie fighting for its national existence." Chéradame, A. *Evropa a otázka rakouská*. 191.

[157] Tobolka, Z. V. 1936. *Politické dějiny československého národa od r. 1848 až do dnešní doby* [The Political History of the Czechoslovak Nation from 1848 to the Present Day]. Vol. 31. Prague: Kompas. 156–157.

[158] Hoffmann, R. J. – Harasko, A. *Odsun*. 307.

[159] On this aspect there is a relevant passage from a work by the Sudeten German historian E. Franzel: "Another attempt at a settlement was made in 1887 by Jiří Lobkowicz but once again it failed as a result of hesitation on the German side. In the meantime, however, new challenges were being planned in the Czech camp. The Young Czechs won the Land elections. The more conspicuously radical, democratic and free-thinking the programme of a party originally aimed against the state constitutional right concept became, the more

As is usual in such polarised situations, moderate voices urging caution tended to be drowned out. One such was the *Kölnische Zeitung*, which declared that, "Every nation undoubtedly has the right and duty to defend its national identity energetically, but it must accord the same right to the others and not obstruct them in the enjoyment of that right. This is particularly necessary in Austria, where such diverse nations are joined in one and the same state. The Germans must say to themselves: No one has the right to suppress our nationality, but nor do we have any right to suppress Slav identity artificially and with the use of force!"[160]

Militant support for Pan-German ideas coming from the German Reich was quite obviously threatening the statehood of the Austrian Monarchy. The Austrian authorities confiscated particular issues of the *Alldeutsche Blätter*, and the Pan-German League, as one of the main organisers of resistance, reacted with a series of protest demonstrations. Its responses were inspired by reports from an extensive network of contacts throughout the territory of the Austrian Monarchy.

In their reactions to the Badeni language reforms proposal German commentators accused the Emperor Franz Josef I and the house of Habsburg of failing to do their duty and of trying to repress the German cause.[161] "It is a fatal mistake, and one still made in many cases by Austrian Germans, to think that the Emperor Franz Josef is a friend to the German cause, the Austrian German cause."[162] The attitude of the Pan-Germans to Austria was vividly expressed by the Austrian deputy Wolf: "We care nothing for Austria if she acts against the interests of the Germans."[163]

---

they adopted the romantic dream of the "state right constitutionalists". But mixed in with the militant canonade of the Young Czech speakers there were already also tones that were to bear fruit some decades later. J. Grégr at that point said that the Czechs should sacrifice the historic borders and cede certain German districts – from Chebsko to roughly Kadaň, North Bohemia (with the exception of Liberec, Česká Lípa and Podmokly), a whole territory inhabited by about three quarters of a million Germans. And that it would then be easier in their own national kingdom to deal with the remaining one and a quarter Germans. These Germans would simply be Czechised." Franzel, E. *Sudetendeutsche Geschichte*. 281. Julius Grégr published his ideas in a series of articles in the newspaper *Národní listy* in September 1888. On the 27th of September he concluded his seventh letter with the words, "I believe that the fewer Germans we have in our stomach the more easily we can digest them." The proposal provoked a public debate and later T. G. Masaryk was to speak about the "Grégr Plan" at the end of the First World War. Evidently it also inspired E. Beneš to the proposals of the so-called Nečas Mission in September 1938. For more details see Hoffmann, R. J. – Harasko, A. *Odsun*. 251–255.

[160] Chéradame, A. *Evropa a otázka rakouská*. 193.

[161] Bley, F. 1897. *Die Weltstellung des Deutschtums*. München: Lehmann. 20.

[162] *Hannoverscher Kurier*. 8. 2. 1899.

[163] Chéradame, A. *Evropa a otázka rakouská*. 175. A programme document put out by the Pan-German League in 1900 was similarly unambiguous in its nationalist standpoint: "The Pan-German League sees the preservation of Austrian Germanhood as a matter of life or death for the German nation, and hopes that by their manly perseverance in the fight the German Austrians will succeed in achieving the position in the state that is theirs by right. On this assumption it wishes for the closer connection of Austria to the German Reich

The tense political situation in the Danubian monarchy was naturally of constant diplomatic concern to the German Reich, which at the turn of the 19th/20th century repeatedly confirmed its interest in the dualist constitutional settlement and the preservation of the ascendancy of Austrian Germans and Hungarians. With its interest in preserving the alliance of the two empires Germany was resolutely opposed to any kind of reform in the direction of federalisation of the Habsburg Monarchy. The German position was expressed by the diplomatic councillor K. M. von Lichnowsky in a report: "By far the most dangerous element of the federal programme for Germany is what is known as the "Bohemian Constitutional Right", the creation of a community consisting of the Sudeten Lands of Bohemia, Moravia and Silesia under Slav rule, which would rapidly acquire a leading position in Austria. The Germans of Bohemia and the secondary lands, who number more than three million, would then be exposed to the danger of extinction, i.e. Slavicisation from the side of the majority perhaps five and a half million Czechs, whose (ethnic) frontline positions would then be progressively moved up as far as Cheb and Podmokly."[164]

At the end of November the wave of demonstrations reached the streets of Vienna and on the 28th of November 1897 the emperor, fearing further escalation, dismissed the Badeni government and postponed the sitting of the Imperial Council. Thus ended what was clearly the last serious attempt by Vienna to find a way out of the Czech-German conflict, on the resolution of which the future of the monarchy depended. Under Count Thun's government the crisis only deepened. On the 21st of May 1899 the German parties formulated what was known as the All Souls Programme, which was an expression of the will of the Germans to maintain supremacy in Cisleithania. Its basic demands were as follows: 1) "Austria" as the official name of the Cisleithanian half of the empire, 2) German as the official language of communication of this Austria, 3) a closer and indissoluble alliance with Germany, 4) a privileged position for Germans in all the crown lands of Austria with the exception of Galicia and Dalmatia.[165]

These demands could only be met if all the other nations of the Habsburg Monarchy were prepared to accept the position of second-class citizenship, and thus the road to compromise between the German minority and the Slav majority of the population was blocked. The achievement of internal stability in the empire was made conditional on German supremacy, which the Czech political leadership in particular, but also Poles and others, was bound to reject.

---

through the German acceptance of German-Austrian confederation into Reich government, and by customs union." Ibidem.
[164] Kořalka, J. *Češi v habsburské říši a v Evropě 1815–1914.* 299.
[165] Šolle, Z. *Století české politiky.* 166.

The Thun government was likewise under pressure from the German Reich, which made it clear that, "for foreign policy reasons it is not possible for Austria to govern against Germans". Germany's disapproval of the Thun government, which had left the language decrees in force, was also expressed in a policy of barring Austrian citizens from travelling into German territory. When the Prussian government went as far as refusal to allow professors from the Polish universities of Krakow and Lvov (Lviv) to attend a medical congress in Poznan, the Thun government threatened to respond with counter-measures, but the emperor and the foreign minister intervened, preventing Thun from pursuing an independent policy. Thus Austria had became effectively subordinate to the German Reich and the room for manoeuvre in resolving the Czech question inside the monarchy became vanishingly small.[166]

Czech political leaders were forced to look for new approaches, this time already ultimately to be directed to the new goal of an entirely independent state. The later 19th century had, however, confirmed the virulence of the Czech-German conflict and its capacity to escalate into a form that threatened the stability of Central Europe as a whole. The crisis unleashed by the Badeni Language Decrees, like the foreign policy of Germany supporting the Pan-Germanist irredentism, showed clearly that the political emancipation of the Czech nation was coming into direct conflict with the aspirations of the German cause in Central Europe. As Prince von Lichnowsky expressed it in one of his reports to Berlin, "It is wholly clear that the whole German people inside and outside Austria is obliged to take a stand not only against a federalist state revolution, but also against the most remote promises of some federalist policy, or also any measures that might form a basis for the later revival of the empire of St. Wenceslas."[167]

Ethnic Tensions in the Monarchy and Masaryk's Programme

Masaryk's opinions, like those of Palacký, showed a development traditional in Czech politics. He started out on his political career convinced of the possibility of the internal reform of Austria into a democratic federation of equal Central European nations, only to be cured of his illusions "by the resistance of a rigid bureaucracy, influential aristocratic circles and above all the omnipotent influence of the German element relying on the power of the German Reich and permeated by the ideals of militant Pan-Germanism."[168]

---

[166] Ibidem. 168–169.
[167] Ibidem. 160.
[168] On this point we may cite Masaryk's direct words: "The Austria-Hungary of today is not a federation of small nations. This federation exists only on the paper of imbecile and court-apologist historians and politicians:

Masaryk rejected not only Prussian expansionism, but above all the Prussian political world view. In this context he wrote, "I reject Prussian etatism, the cult of the Prussian state and especially Prussian monarchism, I reject the ideal of Prussian kingship, the proclamation of the dynasty as divine revelation, I reject the Prussian negation of parliamentarianism, the deification of war, the cult of militarism and militarised bureaucratism".[169]

He saw the basis of international conflict in the clash of two world views, "between the powers of medieval theocratic monarchism (un-democratic and non-national absolutism) and constitutional, democratic, republican states recognising the right of all nations, the small as well as the large, to constitutional independence." It should be noted that Masaryk was never a national chauvinist. He always differentiated between the different currents of opinion in German politics. He spoke out against Germany and Austria-Hungary because he was profoundly convinced that they were the perpetrators of war catastrophes and obstacles to the realisation of the ideals of humanity that he saw as the new organising principle of the small states of Central and Eastern Europe.

As has been noted above, in Masaryk's view the Triple Alliance of Central Powers was an instrument of war by which Austria was bound to Germany and its interests. He wanted a great and strong Austria as a bulwark for non-German peoples refusing to succumb to German pressure. "We want it to remain a great power, but we also want Austria to be powerful and great within". In a speech made on the 18th of November 1892 Masaryk rejected views that conceived of Austria as just the hinterland of the German Reich and space for German colonisation. Such views implied the need to Germanise the Bohemian Lands and the formation of Central Powers was giving them greater weight. Masaryk justified Czech resistance to the German demands for the separation of districts in the North of Bohemia.

As is evident, the idea of amputating the border areas from the body of the Bohemian Lands was not born in the autumn of 1918 after the establishment of Czechoslovakia, or in the autumn of 1938. It was a political concept that had been shared for many years before in the circles of the political leadership of the Bohemian (Sudeten) Germans. It is here too that we should seek the ideological roots of opposition to Czech political aspirations to national emancipation. While Czech politicians considered the Czech question to be the problem of Austria, German politicians from the Bohemian Lands sought sup-

---

Austria-Hungary is the organised violence of the minority over the majority. In its entire essence, history, geography and ethnography Austria is the negation of the modern state and modern nationhood… it is merely an appendage to Germany." Tobolka, Z. V. 1925. "Česká politika za světové války" [Czech Politics in the First World War], in *Politika I*. Prague: Československý kompas. 124.

[169] Ibidem. 125.

port in the German Reich and its aspirations to hegemony in Central Europe. As soon as the Austrian Monarchy failed in its role of protector of the smaller nations in the face of the German nationalists, Czech politicians were forced sooner or later to look for an alternative solution outside the framework of the empire.[170]

As it happened, in the last years before the First World War, positive developments in Czech politics resulted in a diminution of the ethnic tension between Czechs and Germans. The whole resolution of their relationship came to seem less crucial and urgent. The space for political negotiation expanded with the concessions to some Czech aspirations made by the Vienna government. With the prospect of more of a voice in government, Czechs found local linguistic autonomy in the form that the Germans were seeking in the Bohemian Lands more acceptable. In retrospect we can say that here at last there was a window of opportunity for the establishment of a modus vivendi acceptable to both sides. Yet this depended on the maintenance and reform of the monarchy and on continuing peace in Europe. Neither condition was fulfilled. Austria failed to avoid being dragged into a world conflict by Wilhelmine Germany.

The gravity of the problem of the "Czech Question" and need for a solution if the Monarchy was to survive was obvious to the last pre-war government, headed by Count Stürgkh, who tried once again in February 1913 to achieve Czech-German agreement on the language issue in government offices in the Bohemian Lands. In July 1913, however, the Austrian government attempted to break through German obstruction of a solution to the financial situation in the Bohemian Lands (which was on the point of collapse) by suspending the constitution, replacing the Bohemian and Land Committee with new administrative commissions and issuing what were known as the Agnes Patents. All the Czech parties took a stand against these moves and the result was to strengthen the radical anti-government bloc.[171]

[170] Masaryk was far from the only one. For example, on the 18th of June 1891 the important Young Czech politician J. Kaizl said of the Austrian empire, that he "will not and cannot forget that the foundations on which the present internal order of this state rest are iniquitous and unnatural. The reason why agreement with the Czechs cannot be reached is the national arrogance and imperiousness of the Germans in Austria. This exaggerated nationalism harms not only the Czechs, but the Germans themselves, who are diminished by their small-minded prejudice and petty intolerance. But they also damage the state itself, for were it not for this small-minded prejudice and petty intolerance Austria would be able to do human progress one of the greatest of services in being an example of how to overcome national intolerance and how to substitute positive cooperation for the mutual antagonism of nations." Ibidem. 123.

[171] "The tide of events from the autumn (1913) showed the dependence of the decisions of Austria-Hungary in external policy, in the long-drawn out and finally acute conflict with Serbia, on cooperation with the German Reich and of course the German Reich's own interests. Given the need for support from the Reich the Monarchy had also to take account of the voice of Germany in its internal policy as far as the Czech-German question was concerned. It could not allow a situation in which the *Schmerzenschreie* (painful cries for help) of the Germans in Bohemia would reach the German Reich as in 1871. And in Germany people were fol-

Subsequent development showed that "mere national autonomy, without a clear form and moreover rationed out on a provincial basis, could only increase the frustration of the increasingly strong nation, because it did not satisfy its prestige and real needs, including a territory belonging to the nation and its language as an exclusive domain." Looking back after the war Masaryk defined this problem precisely when he pointed out that rights of national autonomy were used as a means to solve national disputes by defenders of mixed states (also including socialists like K. Renner or O. Bauer), such as Austria-Hungary. "Honestly implemented national autonomy, the recognition of a language in schools, government offices and parliament, would suffice in some cases, but does not suffice for national majorities, or whole nations like the Czechoslovak, Polish etc., who were unjustly deprived of their independence and who are claiming complete independence.[172]

It was obvious that the Czechs lacked the support within the Austrian Monarchy that the Sudeten Germans enjoyed by virtue of belonging to the Austrian German community, with its undoubted links to the huge potential of German economics, culture and politics. All the same, at the beginning of the 20th century Czech society was experiencing within the framework of the Austrian state a period of prosperity that *strengthened the state-forming potential of the Czech leadership*. On the Sudeten political scene, by contrast, a nationalist atmosphere dominated and nationalism was much more strongly on the rise than in Austria. The Bohemian German Social Democrats paid the price in terms of loss of votes, as became obvious in the elections of 1911 when the national radicals won almost a third of German mandates in the Bohemian Lands, which had become their main support. Furthermore, as Pan-Germanism gained ground among Austro-Germans at the time, the national struggles and goals of the Sudeten Germans no longer looked so problematic from the point of view of the future internal political development of the Habsburg Monarchy, and so the Austrian parties felt freer to express solidarity with them.[173]

---

lowing the progress of Czech-German negotiation carefully from the point of view of benefit to the German population. The bond between Austria-Hungary and Germany as allies, then hardened by the war, became the decisive, key factor for the way in which the question of national "settlement" in Bohemia would be tackled even after the war." In a conversation with the Austro-Hungarian Chief of Staff Conrad, the German ambassador in Vienna, von Tschirschky, expressed criticisms and worry over the conditions and status of Germans in Bohemia: he called the Germans in Bohemia the chain that held the Habsburg Monarchy together. In his view it is essential especially in Bohemia to sustain the Germans, that means to support them, for otherwise there is a danger that Austria will become the Western Slav Empire." For details see Kazbunda, K. 1995. *Otázka česko-německá v předvečer velké války* [The Czech-German Question]. Prague: Karolinum. 437–438. See also Tobolka, Z. V. 1936. *Politické dějiny československého národa od r. 1848 až do dnešní doby.* Vol. 3. Prague: Československý kompas. 580–586.

172 Masaryk, T. G. *Nová Evropa*. 95.

173 Křen, J. *Konfliktní společenství*. 341–342. The author points out how even culture was politicised in Czech-German relations. "For young Prague (German) writers open engagement to the benefit of Czechs was

The outbreak of the First World War reignited the smouldering ethnic rivalry between Czechs and Germans by bringing to the fore Pan-German concepts of a Central European order that naturally did not reckon with the Czechs as equal partners. The chance for peaceful settlement had either slipped by or was never allowed to materialise. The World War was a turning point that brought Pan-German nationalism into Austrian policy. Positions on the Czech side were radicalised in a similar way, as is clear in the changing views of T. G. Masaryk, who soon after the outbreak of war reached the conclusion that here was a unique historical opportunity to fulfil the long-term goal of Czech politics: an independent state.

K. Pichlík argues that Masaryk saw the victory of the Alliance and the defeat of the Central Powers, above all Germany, as the basic condition for the fulfilment of his aims. In conversations with Robert W. Seton-Watson in October 1914 in Rotterdam Masaryk argued that a Czechoslovak state was "completely unthinkable if and to the extent that Germany is not crushed... Without a decisive German defeat there can be no independent Bohemia".[174] This basic theory and assumption can be found repeated in many of the confidential memoranda that he drew up and sent in the course of the war to leading politicians of the Allies (e.g. *Independent Bohemia*/Samostatné Čechy, *At the Eleventh Hour*, *L'Europe centrale pangermanique ou Boheme indépendante?* and others).[175]

A passage from his *World Revolution* also testifies to the depth and breadth of his change of position: "I was resolved, and for good: opposition to Austria

literary suicide." In the Sudeten areas public opinion continued to be strongly influenced by a stereotypical form of popular nationalist literature, the so-called *grenzland novels* expressing the sense of danger that the Sudeten Germans felt in a situation where the German language border forming the "barrier against the Slav threat" was ceasing to be fully functional and becoming unstable as a result of internal migrations long before the First World War. These novels were intended to invoke the militant "spirit of the borderlands". They characteristically had titles like *Heimat in Ketten* (Homeland in Chains), *Noch steht ein Mann* (One Man Still Stands), *Das Dorf an der Grenze* (The Village on the Frontier) and so on. This low-grade literature became an instrument of agitation among the German nationalists and was later considered as such by the authorities of the Czechoslovak state. For example diffusion of the novel *Oh, Böhmen* by H. Watzlik was prohibited in the ČSR. For more detail see Jaworski, R. "Mezi politikou a trivialitou". 27–31.

174 Memorandum of Conversation between T. G. Masaryk and R. W. Seton-Watson at Rotterdam, on October 25–26. For the authentic text in the Foreign Office archives (FO 371/1900) see *R. W. Seton-Watson and his Relations with the Czechs and Slovaks*. (Documents 1906–1951). Vol. 1. 1995. Rychlík, J. – Marzik, T. D. – Bielik, M. (eds.). Prague/Martin. 209–215.

175 In his memorandum *Independent Bohemia* he argues that, "its central position tempts Germany into claiming supremacy over Europe". Masaryk then writes that the father of modern Pan-Germanism was Lagarde, who formulated the German programme as "The colonisation of Austria by Germany". Beneš, E. 1935. *Světová válka a naše revoluce* [World Revolution and Our Revolution]. Werstadt, J. – Opočenský, J. – Papoušek, J. (eds.). Prague: Orbis/Čin. 241. A list and overview of Masaryk's memoranda is given in the article by Pichlík, K. "Poválečná Evropa v představách T. G. Masaryka v exilu" [Postwar Europe in the Ideas of T. G. Masaryk in Exile], in Mommsen, H. – Kováč, D. – Malíř, J. – Marková, M. 2000. *První světová válka a vztahy mezi Čechy, Slováky a Němci* [The First World War and Relations between Czechs, Slovaks and Germans]. Brno: Matice moravská. 53–62.

had to become real, in earnest, a matter of life and death – the world situation made this imperative."[176] One can agree that "Masaryk did not abandon the political orientation of a lifetime, but he radicalised it."[177]

The hard line now voiced by Masaryk[178] is arresting given his concentrated (but futile) pre-war efforts to effect a reconciliation between Czechs and Germans. J. Galandauer shares the view (supported for example by the major work *Dějiny Maffie* [History of the Maffia] by M. Paulová, who was a great admirer of TGM), that Masaryk's striking change of view of the Austrian Monarchy has never been convincingly explained. After all, in the 1890s Masaryk had been an opponent of national radicalism, had expressed his support for Austria, and rejected the idea of a national revolution leading to the establishment of an independent state, especially if this would involve "foreign complications", yet in the course of the war when pushing for the Czechoslovak cause abroad he reversed all these positions. Paulová concludes that "despite Masaryk's own testimony we still lack a sufficiently detailed knowledge of how Masaryk reached the decision that the nation must unfurl the banner of armed resistance and that he must place himself at its head."[179]

Nonetheless, Masaryk's decision was obviously a response to the extreme conditions of war, and what he saw as the slide of world politics (including the position of the Austrian Monarchy) into the deep crisis of "world revolution". In this critical situation Masaryk necessarily saw the Czech cause, its possibilities and the external framework needed to realise them, in more simplified and radical terms consistent with the simplification and radicalisation of the circumstances. In the changed conditions of struggle between aristocratism and democratism, it was necessary to adopt an appropriately altered "realistic attitude and to respect the fact that matters are being resolved, will be resolved and should be resolved in a radical way corresponding to the internal tension of the 'world situation'".[180]

---

[176]   Masaryk, T. G. 1925. *Světová revoluce* [The World Revolution]. Prague: Orbis/Čin. 15.

[177]   Šabata, J. 1994. "Masarykova Nová Evropa" [Masaryk's New Europe] (preface), in Masaryk, T. G. *Nová Evropa*. 19.

[178]   The furthest point in terms of Masaryk's break with Austroslavism is to be found in his book *Nová Evropa* [The New Europe] 144–117.

[179]   Galandauer, J. *Vznik československé republiky 1918*. 30–31. In this context J. Křen writes that, "Even Czechophiles from the Allied camp were surprised at how resolutely Masaryk adopted historical right from the very beginning and how stubbornly he insisted on the thousand-year borders for the new state – and so the German borderlands as well... For Masaryk it was a break with his own past: an evolutionist and reformist set out on the path of the conspirator and revolutionary." Křen, J. *Konfliktní společenství*. 396–398.

[180]   Urban, O. "Masarykovo pojetí české otázky" [Masaryk's Conception of the Czech Question]. *Československý časopis historický* XVII. 545. Urban draws attention to an interesting aspect of Masaryk's interpretation of world conflict as the clash of progressive ideas (democracy) and outdated (absolutism), i.e. that he relatively underestimated the possibility of the institutional exploitation and ideologisation of nationalism which

His fundamental work *Nová Evropa* [The New Europe] includes some passages that in fact give us more detailed insight into Masaryk's thinking. It is clear that he had been systematically studying German politics long before the outbreak of the war, and in a spirit of critical detachment. On Pan-Germanism he writes, "I watched this movement carefully: this brought me into contact, personal and via correspondence, with a number of outstanding Pan-Germanists, with C. Frantz and Lagarde themselves, and my knowledge of Pan-Germanism, the movement and literature, led me to anticipate this war. I found it strange how little attention the English and French paid to Pan-Germanism, and I drew the attention of my compatriots to the threatening danger through articles and lectures. I made a start on writing an overview of Pan-Germanism and analogical movements and currents in other nations..."[181]

During the war the radicalisation of Masaryk's views on the national question involved him in a major political shift of view of the Germans. As soon as he was convinced of the necessity for an independent Czech state, he abandoned his pre-war concepts of settlement with the Germans in the Bohemian Lands. In terms of his new perspective, the Sudeten Germans would no longer be part of the Austro-German ethnic group and would become a national minority. In Masaryk's view they could, as such, be reconciled with the new state so long as the latter maintained correct relations with Germany and Austria and in domestic policy acted with restraint and moderation, leaving German schools and institutions their freedom. This was an idea of cultural autonomy that arose from Czech experience under the Austrian monarchy.[182]

---

could lead to the transformation of traditional forms of aristocratic institutions into "modern" totalitarian systems.

[181] Masaryk, T. G. *Nová Evropa*. 63–64. "My prediction, or to put it more modestly and better, my expectation of war was also based on a careful observation of Austria-Hungary and Germany and on the tracking of the Pan-Germanist movement and its historical and political literature... On this broad scientific and philosophical foundation Pan-Germanism has in recent times organised itself as the philosophy and policy of the German nation: Lagarde is its leading philosophical and theological representative, Treitschke its historian, Kaiser Wilhelm its politician. A whole system of theoretical and practical Pan-Germanism has been emerging in organised form – associations and societies spreading published writings, maps, journals and reviews, leaflets and so on." Masaryk's intuition here evidently did not fail him even in later years, in the times of the CSR. J. Šabata quotes contemporaries who recall that long before the rise of Nazism to power Masaryk asked chancellor Šámal the question, "And is anyone concerned with Pan-Germanism?" Šabata, J. "Masarykova Nová Evropa". (Preface to the new Czech edition of Masaryk's work.)

[182] Masaryk's ideas are presented in comprehensive form in his major work *Nová Evropa* [The New Europe], which he wrote in the later years of the war and which was not published in Czech until 1920 (G. Dubský). From TGM's preface it appears that the text first appeared in English and French in the spring of 1918 as an "internal" print. The book is important not just because it formulated the intellectual foundations of the future Czechoslovakia (the Slav viewpoint), but also because it offered allied statesmen a political interpretation of the European situation in terms of a positive programme. It was an interpretation that to a significant extent formed the starting point for the future, postwar Central European order. See Masaryk, T. G. *Nová Evropa*.

Clearly, not even Masaryk with his formidable powers of political analysis fully appreciated the extent of the trauma caused to the Sudeten Germans by the radical redefinition of their situation (the loss of privileged social status in the Bohemian Lands), their fall from the status of part of the governing nation to that of national minority in a state belonging to their old national-ethnic rivals – the Czechs.[183]

Masaryk's fundamental reassessment of the need for the existence of Austria from the point of view of the goals of Czech policy was based partly on his bitter experience of unsuccessful attempts to reform the monarchy, but also seems to have reflected the influence of important friends abroad. Among the most influential of these were the French historian E. Denis, the Scottish expert on Central European nationality problems R. W. Seton-Watson, the foreign policy commentator of *The Times* H. Wickham Steed and the French journalist A. Chéradame.[184] It is also important that Masaryk was deeply convinced that the Bohemian state had never actually legally ceased to exist as a separate entity. He considered the establishment of an independent Czechoslovak state to be an expression of political justice, which demanded that the Czech and Slovak peoples be provided with satisfaction for their centuries of struggle against German pressure on the East. "If the Czechoslovak nation were to remain in subjection to the Germans and Asiatics (Hungarians, Turks) allied with the Germans, or even to fall, Pan-German Central Europe would come into being with its further political consequences. The Czechoslovak Question is a world question and it is precisely the question of this war."[185]

In the mid-19th century the ethnic rivalry between Slavs and Germans in Central Europe had given rise to two movements – the Slavophile and the Pan-German. The ideas of the Slavophiles based on pan-Slav mutuality (solidarity) and Russia as the main "bastion of Slavdom" are sufficiently well known. According to Masaryk's interpretation, Pan-Slavism was actually Pan-Russianism, i.e. a set of sympathies and the expectation of help for smaller Slav nations, and in its political consequences was not comparable with the programme of Pan-Germanism, which had been conceived and practiced with the goal of subordinating non-German nations to German needs.[186] Masaryk was later to be sceptical about the possibility of Russia exercising a positive influence on developments

---

[183] Křen, J. *Konfliktní společenství*. 397.

[184] "For example Chéradame, with whom we have been in contact, had also written in favour of the preservation of Austria against Germany before the war, but during the war realised that Austria could no longer resist Germany." Masaryk, T. G. *Světová revoluce*. 317. Elsewhere, in his memoirs, TGM nevertheless states that while he was considered –an incurable pacifist and idealist, "in reality, inwardly, I expected war... that now I would be able to show my opposition to Austria and Austrian doctrine by deeds." Ibidem. 10.

[185] Tobolka, Z. V. *Politické dějiny čs. národa od r. 1848 až do dnešní doby*. Díl III. 580–586.

[186] Masaryk, T. G. *Nová Evropa*. 166.

in Central Europe ("Given my knowledge of the matter I could not expect salvation from Tsarist Russia"), just like other Czech politicians, including Edvard Beneš. Nonetheless, Masaryk appreciated the potential role of Russia as a political counterweight to Germany. Despite his postwar reservations about Tsarist Russia (see *Světová revoluce*), in the course of the war Masaryk assumed that Russia would play a key role in post-war Central Europe. The overthrow of Tsarist absolutism and constitution of the Provisional Government in March 1917 greatly raised his hopes and expections: "For Russia is now no longer an obstacle to democracy".[187]

Beneš was another who took a critical analytical view of Pan-Slavist sentiments, dating the origins and influence of this movement in the Bohemian Lands to the period 1856–1905."[188] Beneš noted the similarities between the doctrine of Pan-Slav mutuality and Pan-Germanism but argued that the fundamental difference was that Slavophilia had emerged as a defensive reaction to the pressure of Pan-Germanism. Its defensive character was implicit in the fact that the demands of the Slavophiles were mainly for the liberation of oppressed and unfree nations, whereas the Pan-German movement aimed for the unification of Germans who were already free, to whom the other non-German nations were supposed to be fully subordinated – i.e. a programme of German domination.[189]

Beneš likewise pointed out that the Pan-Slav programme had been politically unrealisable, for politically it had not addressed let alone resolved problems in the relationships between the Slav peoples (the Russian Slavophiles remained opponents of the Poles, for example) and in the end it had become a synonym for Russian nationalism in the sense of the reactionary Russian trinity: orthodoxy, samodzherzhavi (absolutism), nationality. Pan-Slav ideals had found their most convinced supporters in Russia, where the whole concept soon became an ideological instrument of Russian imperialism in the Bal-

---

[187] Masaryk, T. G. "Russia: From Theocracy to Democracy". *New Europe* 23/2. 23. 22. 3. 1917. For more detail on the development of Masaryk's views on the postwar organisation of Central Europe see Pichlík, K. "Poválečná Evropa v představách T. G. Masaryka v exilu". 53–62.

[188] He defines this political current (rather than a programme) as follows: "Political Pan-Slavism was a movement that formulated as its programme national liberation and political unification of some kind in a common state or governmental and legal entity composed of all Slav nations under the leadership of Russia. The best known propagandist of "Slavophilia with a Russian face" was the biologist Nikolai Y. Danilevsky, whose book *Russia and Europe* (1869) is often cited as the "bible of Pan-Slavism". Beneš, E. 1947. *Úvahy o slovanství* [Reflections on Slavhood]. Prague: Čin. 128.

[189] In *Nová Evropa* Masaryk writes that, "The Pan-Germans often proposed resettlement even for significant national minorities, the Zionist example and emigration in general suggesting this instrument. It is doubtful whether the thing can be carried out without compulsion and justly, and de facto the Pan-Germanists have in mind the weakening of non-German minorities, and not their national satisfaction." Masaryk, T. G. *Nová Evropa*. 108.

kans.[190] Among Czech leaders K. Kramář was an exception in his Pan-Slavism; at the beginning of the First World War he refused Masaryk's invitation to join him in emigration because he expected the Russians to solve the Czechoslovak Question themselves.[191] Before the war he had headed the Young Czech Party and had been considered the leader of the nation. He considered himself a royalist, "but was for a monarchy with a Russian dynasty" and maintained close contacts with Russian monarchists.

Kramář like Masaryk came to the conclusion that the future of the Czechs lay outside the framework of the Austrian Empire. In May 1914 he drew up a plan for the creation of a Slav empire headed by Russia. He produced a Constitution of the Slav Empire, which was supposed to include the Russian Empire, the Kingdom of Poland, the Kingdom of Bohemia, the Bulgarian Tsardom, the Kingdom of Serbia and the Kingdom of Montenegro. Kramář did not envisage the establishment of an independent Czech or Czechoslovak state but believed that it would be just a federal state in a huge empire led by the Russian tsar, which would be given extensive central powers.[192]

This political programme was a development of his pre-war "Slav Policy" of trying to bring the two great powers Russia and Austria-Hungary closer together. Kramář intended his grandiose project to be implemented the moment that the victorious Russian forces entered the Bohemian Lands. This did not happen, since in May 1915 the German and Austro-Hungarian army broke through the Russian position at Gorlica and pushed the front line back 200–300 kilometres to the east. Russia suffered a heavy defeat and the prospect of its troops entering Bohemia became remote. The revolution of 1917 swept away the Tsarist system and T. G. Masaryk's pro-Western orientation prevailed in Czech politics. Although Kramář was to return from Austrian prison as a national martyr (in 1916 he was sentenced to death for treason, but was amnestied in 1917), his influence on Czech politics had been greatly weakened.

In terms of foreign policy, after the Bolshevik Revolution Kramář remained in favour of the revival of Tsarist Russia and its great power role, but in the autumn of 1918 he was isolated in his view. Although he became the first Prime

---

[190]   Alter, P. 1994. *Nationalism*. London/N. York/Sydney: Arnold. 64.
[191]   Masaryk, T. G. *Světová revoluce*. 25. "On top of that he [talked about] Slavs and brothers, and that was swallowed by our public, uneducated in objective foreign politics and world politics."
[192]   The government of the empire was to be called the imperial council, and the parliament the imperial duma. Russia would have a decisive majority of 175 members in a duma of 300. The whole empire was supposed to be a unified customs territory and to have a single currency. The railways, commercial fleet, and in part the postal, telegraph and telephone system were supposed to be under central authority, and the court system was to be unified. Galandauer, J. *Vznik československé republiky 1918*. 22–27.

Minister in the new Czechoslovakia, it was Masaryk's influence that predominated with its orientation to the West while Kramář's vision of a Russian solution remained just an episode.

After the end of the First World War Slavophilia ebbed away as the smaller Slav nations of Central Europe freed themselves from Austrian rule, and having founded independent states and started to grapple with modernising processes looked for concepts of identity other than that of alliance with Russia. A certain renaissance of the idea of Russia as support, if in modified form, was observable in Czech society rather later, as a direct result of Nazi expansion in the 1930s and the Second World War.

The outbreak of the First World War provoked a wave of political activity among Germans in the Bohemian Lands. The new *Deutscher Nationalverband/* German National Union was the first important political organisation in which a major part was played by Sudeten nationalists "to whom the war seemed an opportunity for revolution in the Bohemian Lands and the pushing through of an unambiguous German line throughout Austria". The increasing passivity and opposition of Czechs to the war and the ever more militant attitudes of the Sudeten national radicals who accused "Czech saboteurs" of wrecking the war effort, deepened the gulf between Czechs and Germans and led to escalation of the conflict between them. As early as June 1917 the *German National Council for Bohemia* passed a *Resolution on the Self-Determination of Bohemian Germans*", "in the framework of a united Austrian state and with legal backing for the German state language", and demanded the prompt creation of a province of German Bohemia (*Deutschböhmen*) with its own land diet, land committee and regional constitution. The demand for an independent state (resting on the right to national self-determination), which was gaining ground among Czechs, thus also became part of the programme for the Sudeten Germans. The world conflict was intensifying even within the Bohemian Lands.

Supranational loyalty to the empire (already felt only by a minority of the population of the Bohemian Lands) collapsed together with the Habsburg Monarchy itself, and the cultural and political identity of Bohemian Germans came into conflict with the new geopolitical reality of the system of successor states that included a newly independent Czechoslovakia. Alongside cultural irredentism Bohemian Germans now discovered political irredentism as well (already familiar, for example, among Austrian Italians).

Just as from the point of view of the Austrian Germans a "Czech Question" had existed inside the Austrian Monarchy, so now a "German Question" emerged in the new Czechoslovak Republic. Although Czech leaders tried to win over Bohemian Germans to co-operate in the new state immediately after its establishment in 1918, both German leaders Dr Lodgman and J. Seliger insisted that there was now a German government in Bohemia as well as a Czechoslovak one.

Faced with the German politicians' unwillingness to compromise and their over-confident refusal to accept the reality of the changed situation, the Czech leaders proclaimed that they did not recognise the *Deutschböhmen* government and would not negotiate with it. They insisted that there had never been any question of independence for German-language territory in Bohemia, let alone Moravia and Silesia. It had always been conceived as an autonomous part of a greater whole, Bohemia or later German Austria or Germany. Self-determination for Germans was possible without the Sudetens, but independence for Czechs without the Sudetens would be no more than a fiction. This was in fact also the premise of Reich German diplomacy when it was considering what steps to take against the CSR at the end of the war.[193]

Relations between the Czechs and Sudeten Germans had become highly polarised during the war. The prevailing trend was for both groups to go for their own solutions – the Sudeten Germans for a place in a unified Germany or German Mitteleuropa, and the Czechs for an independent Czechoslovakia. It was clear that there was less and less room for agreement, not only because the notions of self-determination involved were obviously completely incompatible, but because of the escalation of mutual fear and distrust on both sides. The Sudeten Germans felt threatened by Czech economic, political and demographic expansion, while the experience of danger to the very existence of the nation, which had been present even in times of the best relations with Germany and Austria, remained encoded in the mentality of Czech society.

Given that the greater part of the Czech political leadership (at home and abroad) came to support the demand for an independent state sooner or later in the course of the First World War, it was only a question of time before there would be fundamental conflict between the two political nations and their political representatives in the Bohemian Lands.

While the preceding section has tried to give a brief outline of the growing antagonism in Czech-German relations in the Bohemian Lands at the time of the establishment of the independent Czechoslovakia, it is based on the understanding that the conflict between Czechs and Germans in the historic lands was not a matter of mere regional history in Central Europe, but the result of developments with wider international political causes and implications arising from German and Austrian neighbourhood, and also the territorially more distant influence of the decisions of the great powers, specifically Great Britain and France and at some points the United States of America.

---

[193] Křen, J. *Konfliktní společenství*. 396.

The relationship between Czechs and Germans cannot then be fully understood only through the Sudeten lens and the historical picture of this relationship needs to have three levels: the Sudeten, the Austrian and the German as a whole. In this triad of relations the Sudeten German politicians inclined to the nationalistic, Pan-German approach, but this was the approach that found it most difficult to come to terms with defeat. In the end the victorious Allied Powers accepted the French position (vigorously supported by Masaryk and his activities abroad) that the defeated Germany and Austria should not be granted the advantage of combination in a new state which by its size and influence in Central Europe would turn defeat into quiet victory.

Political forces in both the former monarchies underwent a rapid process of differentiation as they reacted to the new situation with different degrees of pragmatism. In this context we can see the position of the Sudeten German as one in which their own frame of history became the place where the Austrian and Pan-German frames of history overlapped and interlocked, and where action and attitudes in each of these frames was automatically influenced by, and affected, action and attitudes in the others.

This section offers merely a brief sketch of some of the more important events and processes involved in the antagonistic side of the Czech-German relationship, but it is based on the premise that the Sudeten German theme "requires the broadening of the field of analysis far into the past so that the perspective is widened and things acquire their proper dimensions"[194] In this wider perspective it becomes evident that the fateful conflict between Czechs and "their" Germans had its roots in the 19th century, where closer examination reveals the signs (antecedents) of the later parting of the ways.

---

[194] Ibidem. 20.

Mitteleuropa

von

Friedrich Naumann

Berlin 1915 · druck u. Verlag von Georg Reimer

Title page of the first edition of F. Naumann's *Mitteleuropa* of 1915.

2 Mitteleuropa – The vision of a dominant Germany

Prime Minister K. F. Badeni's *language reforms* of 1897, aimed at giving Czech equal status with German, were an important and as it turned out the last serious attempt at Austrian-Czech settlement in the framework of the Austrian Monarchy. These provoked outrage, however, not only in the circles of Austrian supporters of Pan-German ideas but also in neighbouring Germany, as has been described above. Other episodes in the rivalry between Austrian Germans and Slavs inside the Habsburg Empire also offered opportunities for Reich Germans to enthusiastically express their ethnic sympathy and support the patriotic activities of some of the Bohemian Germans, especially in the period 1880–1900.

For example, the Protestant *Gustav-Adolf-Verein* and the Evangelical *Evangelischer Verein* as well as the large organisation of "school" societies spontaneously responded to requests for money from the Austrian Germans. Activities of this kind were frequent, especially in Saxony. The reactions of the *Pan-German League* to the supposed plight of the Bohemian Germans were particularly melodramatic.[1] In the Reich Assembly the Republican deputy Hans Kudlich (Krnov electoral district, complained that "Wilhelm (the Kaiser) is more concerned about Kia-Chow than about the Bohemians and wants no more Catholics in the empire".

---

[1] The basic work on the theme is Wertheimer, M. 1924. *The Pan-German League*, 1890–1914. New York. See among others "Austrian-German Plans to recognize the Monarchy." In Meyer, H. C. 1955. *Mitteleuropa in German Thought and Action*. The Hague: Martinus Nijhoff. 175–182.

The state secretary of the foreign office prince B. von Bülow (and other members of the political elites of the Reich) did indeed cautiously distance himself from the particularist interests of the Austrian Germans and made it clear that the interests of the German Reich had a different dimension, to be understood in terms of a broader concept of *Mitteleuropa*). The nature of these ideas is clear from a letter that Bülow wrote in 1898 to Prince von Lichnowsky: "Our political interest, to which any kind of other sympathies must be subordinated, requires the recognition and preservation of Austria-Hungary as a great independent power. This interest requires that we should refrain from supporting any divisive influences in Austria, whether Polish, Czech or German. There is no doubt that the Austrian Germans have our full sympathy in their attempts to strengthen the German element where this serves the end of maintaining the present ties and future security of the Austrian state in its present form. But as soon as their efforts are directed towards the separation of the German areas of Austria in an attempt to revive the *status quo ante* 1866, then the Austro-German nationalists cannot count on our support for their plans."[2]

The rest of the letter also stresses the fact that Reich German support is based on such generally formulated principles of the long-term goals and interests of the Hohenzollerns and the new Reich, and not on the momentary situation of Austrian Germans competing for influence in the Habsburg Monarchy with other nations, especially the aspirations of the Czechs. Forty years later a Nazi author was still to be berating the Reich Germans for their lack of sympathy and understanding for the Austrian Germans in a situation of crisis and claimed that only a small group of Pan-Germans really understood the question of the day.[3] Despite the increasing skepticism of the Reich German public (for various reasons) about the Austrian Germans, attachment remained to the basic notion that the Austrian Germans were an essential bulwark against the "onslaught of the Slavs" and were the only guarantee against their being "inundated and washed away by the Czech flood".

Lichnowsky's correspondence expresses in condensed form the prevailing standpoint of the Reich Germans, who were satisfied by alliance with a monarchy that in their view could and should provide the Austrian Germans with

---

[2] Meyer, H. C. *Mitteleuropa in German Thought and Action.* 49.

[3] Ibidem. 48–50. In the course of the First World War the Reich German attitude to the German-Czech problem increasingly boiled down to just two alternatives: the first was based on the hope that the Czech population could be persuaded to remain on the German side as Czechs and so take part in German world politics, and the second on the old idea that the Habsburg Monarchy was for nationality and security reasons consolidating itself as a German power, as a kind of "German Eastern Mark", and so it would be essential for Bohemia to retain its "German character". Morgenbrodová, B. "Česká otázka v říšskoněmecké publicistice 1914–1918" [The Czech Question in Reich German Political Writings], in Mommsen, H. – Kováč, D. – Malíř, J. – Marková, M. *První světová válka a vztahy mezi Čechy, Slováky a Němci.* 179–194.

enough political and psychological support. As the opening up of world markets enlarged the potential influence of Wilhelmine Germany, the Reich Germans were finding new interests and avenues for their ambitions and the "small world" of the Austrian Germans was becoming less and less interesting to them.[4] This was to change only much later, in the redefined situation of the 1930s.

T. G. Masaryk developed a strongly negative position on Germany and its role in Central Europe in the course of the First World War, and this led him to his decision to break with the monarchy. It was a difficult decision and one based on the empirical experience of his political probes in Vienna at the beginning of the war in Vienna, which had confirmed him in the belief that victory for the Central Powers would inevitably lead to the harsh hegemony of the Germans in Austria and in *Mitteleuropa*.[5] His tough view of Germans and Germany, which according to J. Křen also had philosophical roots in his "animus against Kant", only hardened as the war years went by. Masaryk had a tendency to reduce Germany to Prussia and Prussia to no more than a bearer of aggression and militarism, but one cannot deny that he had reason to see a real threat to Central Europe and its peoples in the German position. He demanded not only the fall of Austria, but also the "crushing of Berlin".

In November 1915 he wrote the memorandum *At the Eleventh Hour* in which he warned the Allies not to underestimate Germany, which had been excellently prepared for war and had a programme for a Pan-German Central Europe. Masaryk appealed to the Allies to counter this with a programme for a Central Europe that would be "not German, but European", bringing freedom to the nations between the Baltic and the Black Sea, and especially the creation of an independent Poland, Bohemia and Serbia.[6]

In confidential memoranda the Czech leaders abroad offered the ruling circles of the Allied States a programme that would for the first time give the war with Germany a wider rationale, and tried to persuade the powers that it would be consistent with their war aims and advantageous to combine the war with democratic changes and with the liberation of nations lacking self-determination.[7]

Masaryk's anti-German attitude continued to harden as a result of war events, but he did not demand the destruction of Germany and was even willing to accept the annexation of German Austria to Germany – although in fact

---

[4]   Meyer, H. C. *Mitteleuropa in German Thought and Action*. 50.

[5]   Křen, J. *Konfliktní společenství*. 391.

[6]   Pichlík, K. 1968. *Zahraniční odboj 1914/1918 bez legend* [The Armed Resistance Abroad 1914/1918 without Legends]. Prague: Svoboda. 170–171.

[7]   Ibidem. 176.

it was precisely in this step that he saw a chance for the other nations of Central Europe to set up their own independent states.[8] It was not, however, easy for him to overcome the Allies' fears of the disturbance of the traditional European balance of power that might ensue from a major shift of borders in ethnically explosive Central Europe.

Like other politicians and statesmen of the time, Masaryk argued against the concept of *Mitteleuropa*, which had certain features of economic liberalism in the sense of enlarging a unified (customs-free) economic zone but completely marginalised the small nations and consigned them historically to the role of extras in a drama directed by Germany.

A passage from F. Naumann's famous formulation of the model of *Mitteleuropa* – Central Europe united around Germany, published in 1915, indicates in condensed form the projected role of small states: "Our conception of large states has entirely changed. Only truly large states can hope to have any kind of importance, all the other smaller states can exploit disputes between the big states or must gain permission if they wish to do anything unusual. Sovereignty is the freedom to take a decision of far-reaching historical importance, and now it is being concentrated in just a very few places on the globe."[9]

From the Pan-German point of view, this concept was the theoretical framework for the formulation of German geopolitical interests given by the needs of the expanding German economy.[10] In parallel with military conflict Germany sought various other possibilities for the political pursuit of its interests. The prevailing opinion was that a more active *Weltpolitik* would help open up world markets and gain for Germany new markets and sources of raw materials in the colonies. Furthermore, Germany leadership of Europe would be advanced by the creation of a continental bloc that would prevent any discrimination against German goods on the markets of neighbouring countries. It is not therefore surprising that as soon as the war broke out, plans for a European trading bloc in *Mitteleuropa* and German colonies in *Mittelafrica* started to take shape on the list of popular war aims.[11]

---

[8] Křen, J. *Konfliktní společenství*. 391.

[9] Cobban, A. 1969. *The Nation State and National Self-Determination*. London/Glasgow: Collins. 285. For the original edition see Naumann, F. 1915. *Mitteleuropa*. Berlin: Druck und Verlag von Georg Reimer.

[10] The principles of geopolitics were elaborated in detail in the work of the founder of German political geography Ratzel, F. *Politische Geographie*. 1897. München/Berlin: R. Oldenbourg. For an analysis of the individual theories of geopolitics see Hunter, James, M. 1983. *Perspective Ratzel's Political Geography*. Lanham/New York/London: University Press of America.

[11] Calleo, D. 1978. *The German Problem Reconsidered*. Cambridge/London/New York/Melbourne: Cambridge University Press. 40.

Naumann's Project

The author of the book *Mitteleuropa*, published in 1915, was the theologian, journalist, social thinker and deputy to the Reich Assembly Friedrich Naumann, who had been fascinated by the dynamic development of the capitalist economy in Germany at the turn of the 19th/20th century. In the years before the First World War he travelled widely through the countries of Central Europe and met many politicians in the Habsburg Empire with the clear aim of getting a better understanding of this socially, ethnically and complex region. His social reformist attitudes led him to seek contacts with Social Democratic leaders such as K. Renner, on whose recommendation he had a meeting with B. Šmeral, but also with representatives of the Bohemian Germans, including A. Spiethoff.

His many study journeys gave Naumann an insight into Central European problems and he was deeply influenced by the ideas of the Austrian statesman K. von Bruck, who criticised the historians of the Bismarck era for their short-sighted assessment of the more recent history of the Central European region. Naumann reached the conclusion that "economic union from Hamburg to Trieste could have been attained if the question of political domination could have been solved without the war of 1866."[12]

J. Kořalka sees the following passage of Naumann's vision of a Central Europe dominated by Germany as crucial: "It is necessary to achieve the establishment of a Central European economic union through joint customs agreements including France, Belgium, Holland, Denmark, Austria-Hungary, Poland and as the case arises, Italy, Sweden and Norway. This union, possibly without a common constitutional authority and with retention of the external equality of its members, must stabilise the economic supremacy of Germany over Central Europe."[13]

Naumann returned from his tours with an awareness that the *Grossdeutsch* conceptions were much more important and politically much more fruitful than the crude Schönererian nationalism that he encountered in Austria in 1899. In the journal *Die Hilfe* he regularly published commentaries and reflections, which are in fact the first fragments of the later book *Mitteleuropa* in which the basic argument was that a purely economic solution to the situation in Central Europe was insufficient. Revising his own earlier conclusions he argued that the situation was one that required political rebirth rather than

---

[12]   Meyer, H. C. *Mitteleuropa in German Thought and Action*. 196.
[13]   Kořalka, J. "Mitteleuropa Friedricha Naumanna jako plán německé hegemonie v Evropě za první světové války" [The Mitteleuropa of Friedrich Naumann as a Plan for German Hegemony in Europe during the First World War]. *Dějiny a současnost* 1/2003. 14.

simply economic agreement.[14] The Bohemian-German writer H. Ullmann took Naumann's idea still further, arguing that "Central Europe should be positively and energetically dominated and colonised by Germans" and promoting this notion as an "addendum" to Naumann's work without consulting the latter.[15] In Germany itself the response to Naumann's work was substantially more sober than in important Austrian German circles.

Naumann emphatically rejected the idea of Reich German intervention in Habsburg affairs, considering it a dangerous experiment. In March 1915 A. Spiethoff sent Naumann a "strictly secret memorandum" defending a dictatorial form for the reorganisation of Austria. It was not the first or the last time that a similar radicalism was voiced from the ranks of Bohemian German political representatives. Henry C. Meyer argues that *Grossdeutsch* sentiment was rampant in pre-war Austria.

Although Naumann had great sympathy for the Austrian Germans, he was aware of the extreme narrowness of their political aspirations, which threatened to create obstacles to a broader multinational Central European synthesis. It was in this spirit that he was also critical of Heinrich Friedjung's memorandum, on the grounds of its fundamentally anti-Slav tone and undemocratic suggestion that decision-making be left to both monarchs, i.e. Wilhelm II and Franz Josef I. The German historian R. Jaworski has drawn attention to the fact that Naumann rarely expressed interest in Bohemia and the Czech Question except in connection with larger problems.[16]

Naumann's views underwent some development, however. He initially formulated his opinion on the role of Bohemia in 1900 in his work *Deutschland und Österreich* (Germany and Austria), where he wrote that "the most dangerous point is the Bohemian Lands, geographically, materially and historically an important country. Here sits our most capable opponent, here the Czech has 62.9%."[17]

In the same work he also commented on the language dispute and its escalation in the Bohemian Lands at the end of the 19th century. "Language is only the clothing of power. Where Germans are victorious, German is spoken, and where they are losing, the old German streets are acquiring Czech names... The German nation, which could rule from Prague all the way to Belgrade, does not exist in the Danubian Empire of today. Let the Germans then glimpse their [possible] future as only one part of the nations among the others (*Teilvolk*).

---

[14]   Meyer, H. C. *Mitteleuropa in German Thought and Action*. 197.
[15]   Ullmann, H. *Die Tat* VII (1915–1916). 882–886.
[16]   Jaworski, R. 1996. *Friedrich Naumann a Češi* [F. Naumann and the Czechs]. Prague: Centrum liberálních studií. 23.
[17]   Ibidem. 25.

They should therefore try to secure their future above all by looking for support in the German Reich, and so together with the dynasty, the army and the Social Democratic Party guarantee the progress of the common state."[18]

Resignation, but also respect is evident in this passage. Here we see a nationally and politically motivated detachment that reckons with real political possibilities. The preservation of the Austro-Hungarian state was one of Naumann's core ideas. It was one to which he subordinated all other questions, including solidarity with the German cause in mixed language areas such as the Bohemian Lands.

H. C. Meyer argues that Naumann rediscovered the *Holy Roman Empire of the German Nation* as a Central European phenomenon and emancipated it from the meanings and emotions of the time. He also believes that it would be a mistake to judge Naumann as a mere unconditional adherent of Grossdeutsch concepts of history. He argues this with reference to the bibliographical apparatus of *Mitteleuropa*, which contains only a few *Grossdeutsch*-orientated works. Although Naumann refused to defend Grossdeutsch sentiment, he called on Germans to "be more deeply aware of their common destiny, to heal dissensions between groups and to open up their human spirit to audacious speculations."[19] He advised Reich Germans to try to understand the opinions of historians of the Austrian Germans such as E. Wertheimer, H. Friedjung and R. Charmatz.

Naumann's claim that if the interests of Austria-Hungary and Germany could be harmonised, the other countries would join this Central European core, might be considered evidence of a certain political messianism. He appealed to actors on the political scene – industrialists, union leaders, farmers, land owners, historians, lawyers, doctors and other important people of all nationalities – to talk about their mutual interests and problems and to develop mutual trust by getting to know one another. His core interest was the preservation of the state, in this case clearly represented by the Habsburg Monarchy. In a letter to the historian W. Goetz he wrote: "For my special task is to make visible the idea of *Mitteleuropa* not just for Austrian Germans, but also for other groups of inhabitants of the Austro-Hungarian Monarchy, and in particular I would like to see the development of more moderate and friendly understanding among Reich Germans for the Hungarians and Western Slavs."[20]

Let us note in this context that apart from his conviction of the irreplaceable role of Germany, its culture and above all the German language as the universal speech of Central Europeans, Naumann showed quite a strong grasp of the

---

[18]   Ibidem.
[19]   Meyer, H. C. *Mitteleuropa in German Thought and Action.* 200.
[20]   Ibidem. 199.

inherent right of non-German nationalities to retain their national individuality and pursue democratic political activities. Understood in terms of contemporary theory, this was a concept of *co-operative hegemony* which is, by the way, a contemporary paradigm of German foreign policy in the frame of European integration today.

On the basis of a detailed analysis of Naumann's work, H. C. Meyer has come to the conclusion that he had a better understanding of Hungarians than Slavs. Naumann believed that after the Hungarians, the Czechs were the second most important non-German people of the monarchy and repeatedly acknowledged the "ancient royal tradition" of the Czechs. Unlike in the cases of Poland and Hungary, however, he was not willing to concede constitutional rights to the Czechs for that reason.[21] He considered Bohemia and Moravia to be a "disputable German-Czech area" and believed that Czech demands could only complicate the anyway fragile balance of the Danubian Monarchy. Indeed, Naumann saw the demands of the Czech political nation in pursuit of emancipation exlusively through the prism of Austrian state interest, and from this point of view the Czechs often appeared as a subversive element damaging Austrian state interests through its contacts abroad. The creation of an independent Czech nation-state was in his view out of the question. Naumann did not believe that small states, let alone small stateless peoples, had any chance of survival. In his view there was only one option for the "*Zwischenvölker*", the nations occupying the space between Russia and the two empires led by Germans: "Anyone who does not want to be a Russian must become a Central European", with "Central European" meaning the zone of German influence. Wholly pragmatically, however, he assumed that "it cannot be expected of the non-German nations that they will have understanding or interest in German leadership, in having us, the Germans, sitting at the steering wheel of world history. We cannot expect them to share our understanding of history, for the heart of another lineage and another sensibility beats within them."[22]

The idea of the historical mission of the Germans is recurrent in Naumann's work: "Let us once again consider the supranational conception of *Mitteleuropa*. It will have a German core, it will manifestly use the German language, recognised as a universal language... through the combination of all cultural elements and forces the new generations will become the bearers of rich and diverse civilisations integrated into the German core."

Naumann contemplated pushing the idea of Czech-German settlement (*Ausgleich*) as far as possible. In this context he chose Prague for the role of "Centre

---

[21] Jaworski, R. *Friedrich Naumann a Češi*. 26.
[22] Ibidem. 29.

of Central Europe", as a way of showing that he also respected Czech interests in the choice of metropolis. But his ideas here operated only on the level of as it were demonstrating an ability for sympathy, which was scarcely the same as respect for an equal partner. In the framework of "universal humanity" he was prepared to reject some nationalist excesses, but again only in the interests of the *Oberstaat*, which in terms of structure he envisaged as a union of non-constitutional authorities and committees supposed to form the organisational basis for the existence of *Mitteleuropa*.

The principle of constitutional democracy and individual civil rights had no particular appeal for Naumann. He clearly looked back with admiration to the process of German unification in the Bismarck era. He considered the iron chancellor a creative genius, paid tribute to him, and shared his preference for the use of force in time of need. This historical sympathy revealed much more clearly to foreign observers than to Naumann himself that despite claims about guarantees of individual independence and about measures to secure equality, Germany was supposed to dominate *Mitteleuropa* in the same way as Prussia dominated Germany.[23]

Naumann was deeply disappointed when he discovered that his carefully chosen and in his view wholly neutral and in no way loaded term *Mitteleuropa* had made him famous in the non-German world as an *arch-Germaniser* and that his project became in the eyes of West Europeans and Germany's neighbours a kind of basic sketch for the later concept of *Drang nach Osten*.

Ideas of Greater Germany

From the point of view of our theme – the relationship between Czechs and Germans in the historic lands – it is important to note that Naumann's concept was enthusiastically received among Austrian Germans, and especially the political leaders of the conservative nationalist Bohemian Germans. In the years 1915–1916 Naumann gave a number of lectures in Prague, Brno and Vienna, each time attracting great attention from politicians, journalists and the public. Austrians and Germans in the Bohemian Lands were delighted by his words on their mediating role. He was particularly well received by historians who had been developing the ideology of the "frontiersman" struggle, where the Slav and German elements supposedly clashed and contended in three zones. For example, Friedjung sent a congratulatory telegram to Naumann which illustrates the importance that he and his supporters attached to the project:

23   Meyer, H. C. *Mitteleuropa in German Thought and Action*. 209.

"Two careful readings of your work have filled me with the certainty that you have provided the (German) nation with the finest fruits of the world war, an indispensable guide to the long-desired goal."[24] Meyer shares Masaryk's belief that the notions of *Mitteleuropa* and the *Drang nach Osten* were not incidental phenomena of the wartime atmosphere, but were key to understanding the principles of 20th-century German politics.

For a while it seemed to Naumann that a consensus might be developing in favour of his great synthesis, but sharp disagreement on the part of nationalists from the ranks of the Bohemian Germans soon cured him of this illusion. Ullmann was all for *Mitteleuropa* as the greatest idea of the war years, but at the same time lamented Naumann's "shallow" understanding of the German nationalist movement in the Habsburg Monarchy. In his view Prague was incapable of responding to tact, trust and compromise, but would have to be dragged into supporting the project with Bismarckian resolution. The Germans must positively and energetically dominate and colonise Central Europe so as to achieve a broader homeland (*Heimat*) from the Vosges to the Carpathians.[25]

The sharpest attacks on Naumann came, however, from the Pan-Germans who claimed that the idea of the economic unification of Central Europe was originally theirs, and one that they had been promoting since at least 1890. The East Prussian-born historian and deputy in the Reich Diet, G. von Bülow, rejected *Mitteleuropa* as an "incredible construction". On Pan-Germanism he said that, "with the same intensity as we from our point of view desire the establishment of a powerful economic zone from Berlin to Baghdad and further, we likewise know for certain that the future belongs to a racially determined German Central Europe."[26]

From the point of view of the relationship between Czechs and Germans (and not only on the Bohemian Lands), it is important to realise that the Pan-German plan for Central Europe aspired to solve three basic problems of integration in the region: a) the Grossdeutsche union of Germany and Austria, 2) the incorporation of the non-German peoples of Austria-Hungary, and 3) the annexation of other non-German nations, or in some cases states, whether or not they had a German language basis.[27]

German aspirations to hegemony in Central Europe found their most comprehensive form precisely in the *Mitteleuropa* project. Naumann's book became an effective propaganda tool for the Allies, who presented it as proof of the

---

[24] Ibidem. 210.

[25] Ibidem. 214.

[26] Ibidem.

[27] Krejčí, O. 2000. *Geopolitika středoevropského prostoru* [The Geopolitics of Central Europe]. Prague: Eko-press. 101.

intentions and aims of Wilhelmine Germany.[28] By the beginning of 1916 the highest Allied political circles were convinced that the German desire to establish *Mitteleruopa* had been one of the basic reasons for unleashing the war and was the Berlin government's primary war aim.[29] It is a mark of just how seriously the Allies took this project that in the course of 1916 they had two meetings in Paris to assess the extent of the threat of *Mitteleuropa* and decided that economic war should continue against the Central Powers even if a ceasefire were agreed.

The polemic counter-offensive on the Allied side was spearheaded by Tomáš G. Masaryk and R. W. Seton-Watson, who were its main sponsors,[30] but also by the authors of the *The New Europe* review, who saw the main mission of the journal as that of presenting alternative proposals and ideas for the reorganisation of Central Europe. Henry C. Meyer takes a rather sceptical and nor entirely accurate view of the results of this activity, seeing it as mainly an intellectual exercise intended primarily to upstage the well-publicised views of the French journalist, commentator and specialist on Central European problems A. Chéradame[31] about the Pan-German conspiracy. In fact Masaryk, together with R. W. Seton-Watson, H. W. Steed, E. Beneš and others, wanted to influence West European public opinion and political elites with their publications. In this respect Masaryk was remarkably successful, managing to win over previously indifferent influential circles to the idea of an independent Czechoslovakia.

It must be admitted, however, that the political leadership of the Allies failed to formulate any comprehensive vision of the postwar organisation of Central Europe until the declaration of President Woodrow Wilson's famous Fourteen Points.

The course of the military conflict inspired the Pan-Germans to feverish activity and war psychosis increasingly affected even the originally moderate Catholic organisations and social democrats. Reform liberals like Redlich or Baernreither also succumbed to war fever.[32] Similar positions were taken by most of

---

[28]   Up to 1916 Allied propaganda had been concentrating on the description of battle scenes and the greater losses of the enemy, or sometimes stories of submarine warfare. Now the Mitteleuropa project for the first time became the target of concentrated ideological attacks.

[29]   Ford, G. S. *American Historical Review.* LVII (1951).

[30]   The list of contributors and patrons is impressive, including such names as E. Denis, L. Eisenmann, N. Jorga, H. W. Steed, P. Struve and others. "I tried as soon as possible to put out journals that while political were guided by scientific method. This applied to Denis's *La Nation Tchéque*, and later *Le Monde Slave... The New Europe* was assiduously read not only in England, but also in France, America and Italy." Masaryk, T. G. *Světová revoluce.* 101.

[31]   T. G. Masaryk mentions his contacts with this influential expert, "Chéradame, with whom we were in contact: before the war he also wrote in favour of preserving Austria against Germany, but in the war he realised that Austria could no longer resist Germany." Ibidem. 317.

[32]   Křen, J. *Konfliktní společenství.* 402.

the Austrian intelligentsia and moderate writers like R. M. Rilke or F. Werfel were exceptions, their views a source of embarassment and so ignored. The polarisation of ideas in the wartime atmosphere was evident on both the Czech and the German side in Bohemia.

Characteristic of this process was the shift in the views of T. G. Masaryk, who eventually entirely abandoned the concept of Austroslavism according to which complete independence was unthinkable for a small nation in the Europe of great powers.[33] The war led Masaryk to the decision to take a radical step out of the traditional frame of Czech politics (already set out in its basics by Palacký), which had previously moved between Austria, Germany and Russia. Masaryk combined historical legal and natural legal doctrine in his vision of a new state that would bring together the Lands of the Bohemian Crown with Slovakia. Against a German *Mitteleuropa*, Masaryk set a programme for reorganisation of a belt of small Central European nations on the basis of national statehood. These were to replace the monarchy and form a sort of buffer zone against the German *Drang nach Osten*, or a potential Russian *Drang nach West*.[34]

In the course of the war Masaryk's opinions became more radical not only in terms of nationalism, but also in relation to internal politics. He modified the traditional concepts of liberalism and radicalism and developed a vision of an independent Czechoslovakia resting on the system of Western democracy. J. Křen argues that Masaryk's concept of republican independence, a clear western orientation and above all a democratic domestic order in the new state differed from standard Czech radical nationalism, which was as it were the mirror image of German nationalism.[35]

From the very outset, however, Masaryk insisted on the historical rights of Bohemia to its thousand-year borders,[36] i.e. territory that included the border areas settled by a German-speaking population. He premised this on the argument that while self-determination for the Germans as a whole was possible without the Sudetenland, independence for Czechs and their state would be a pure fiction without the Sudetenland. He thus revised his pre-war ideas about

---

[33] Ibidem. 398.

[34] Ibidem. For detail see the chapter Masarykova akce. 391–401.

[35] Ibidem.

[36] It was the historical right that was of fundamental importance for determining the borders of the Bohemian/ Czech state in a relatively unambiguous way: its borders were those of the three Austrian crown lands – Bohemia, Moravia and Silesia. Czech historical constitutional right had two characteristic features that distinguished the doctrine from irrational historicism: a) the borders according to historical right were the same as the actual borders of the existing state (now effectively provincial) entities – lands, b) the borders according to historical right defined natural geographically and economically coherent territories. If someone in Central Europe were to construct viable states without taking account of the national/ethnic principle and bearing in mind only geographical, economic, strategic and communications criteria, the result would not differ much from the work of history. Galandauer, J. *Vznik Československé republiky 1918.* 153.

Czech-German settlement and no longer saw the Sudeten Germans as a partner, as part of the Austro-German ethnic element. Instead they were now to
become a "mere" national minority, but Masaryk believed it would be possible
for the Sudeten Germans to reconcile themselves to the new state. Indeed, he
underestimated the trauma that the loss of their earlier status would cause the
Germans, but he was aware that the Sudeten Germans were numerically much
larger than the usual national minority and he considered reducing their numbers by ceding some marginal territories to Germany.[37]

The Sudeten nationalists found a voice particularly in the the *German National Union*, believing that the war could be an opportunity for revolution in
the Bohemian Lands and the imposition of a clear German line throughout
the monarchy. In June 1917 the German National Council for Bohemia passed
a resolution on self-determination for the Bohemian Germans "in the framework of a unified Austrian state and with the enshrinement of German as state
language". The resolution demanded the speedy creation of German Bohemia
as a province (*Deutschböhmen*) with its own land diet, land committee and district authorities. [38] It was with a demand formulated in these terms that the
leader of the association of German deputies in Bohemia, Lodgman von Auen,
responded to the Czech Epiphany Declaration (6th January 1918). At this moment it was already clear that the ethnic mobilisation of Czechs in the expectation of the end of the Austrian Monarchy was heading for its first climax in
modern history.

The desire for an independent state was intensifying among both Czechs and
Germans and despite certain complications became integral to the political programmes of both sides. Yet on both sides it was obvious that it would be very
difficult to form a functional state meeting the requirement for continuous territory that was one of the basic criteria for the establishment of a new state. The
Sudeten party DNSAP came up with demands for special rights for small German enclaves in towns and for the connection of the belts of German settlement
in the south and north of the Bohemian Lands to Austria and Silesia[39] while
totally ignoring the presence of a Czech population on the German territories.

For Czech politics the principle of self-determination was a double-edged
sword. It was useful as a revolutionary principle directed against the multinational Hasburg Empire because it gave a dynamic to Czech national demands;

---

[37]   In this he was developing the idea put forward in the 1890s by Grégr, i.e. the cession of a number of border
       "promontories" that were not essential to the viability of the new state (Cheb region, Southern Bohemia, and
       Moravia, Silesia). He estimates that this would reduce the number of Germans in the new state by around
       a million. The Czechoslovak delegation returned to the idea in 1919 and at the time of Munich so did Beneš,
       in the form of the so-called Nečas Mission.
[38]   Křen, J. *Konfliktní společenství*. 444.
[39]   Ibidem.

the principle of self-determination could be used as a basis for demanding Czech independence and denying the sovereign rights of the Austrian states. But the same principle could also be turned against the Czech programme. If the right of nations to self-determination were to be understood as the right of every individual to belong to his own nation state, this would mean that a Czech state could be founded only within the borders given by majority Czech settlement. As J. Galandauer concludes, a Czech state within ethnic borders would not be capable of economic prosperity and independence. This was something grasped by Czech politicians far back in the 19th century and was the main reason (rather than memories of the medieval Czech state) behind the persistent Czech opposition to the "splitting up of the state". The principle of self-determination therefore had to be interpreted in such a way as not to violate the historic borders. Czech political theory and propagandist praxis was therefore faced with the task of justifying Czech state borders of a kind that would secure the viability of the Czech state.[40]

The Austrian Social Democratic party, which was strongly represented in German areas of the Bohemian Lands, likewise committed itself to support the demands for rights of self-determination for the Bohemian Germans. Josef Seliger (the leader of the German Social Democrats in the Bohemian Lands), expressed this position with the term, "the principle of mutuality of rights of self-determination".[41] Two German Social Democratic conferences held in the Bohemian Lands in June (Prague) and September (Brno) 1917 agreed and proclaimed that the Czech right to statehood was a reactionary Utopia and that the Sudeten Germans would not submit to it even at the price of civil war. The only possible conclusion was: either national autonomy to be provided in the regions or a fight. The German-Austrian Social Democrats from the Sudeten areas and the whole German-Austrian side were turning the Sudeten Question into the acid test for the consistency of political claims based on nationality.

It was evident that K. Renner and B. Šmeral as the two leading representatives of "black and yellow internationalism" were incapable of agreement. The interpretations of the Austro-Marxist concept adopted by the Czechoslovak Social Democratic Party on the one hand and the German-Austrian Social Democratic Party on the others proved to be so divergent that no compromise between them could be found in the situation as it was. As a result the leadership of the Czechoslovak party experienced a loss of nerve and did not come out publicly with its standpoint based on natural law.[42]

[40] Galandauer, J. *Vznik Československé republiky 1918*. 154–155.
[41] Křen, J. *Konfliktní společenství*. 445.
[42] Kárník, Z. 1968. *Socialisté na rozcestí. Habsburk, Masaryk či Šmeral?* [Socialists at the Crossroads. Habsburg, Masaryk of Šmeral?]. Prague: Svoboda. 144–145.

In the spring of 1918 the outlines of collaboration between the German Social Democrats and the other German civic parties on the basis of a national programme were already emerging.[43] The growing tension between Czechs and Germans was exacerbated by the organic nature of interethnic relations in the Bohemian Lands and the deteriorating position of the Austrian Monarchy in the war. The first climax of the clash between the two nations of the historic lands was on the horizon. The result of decades of Czech efforts to gain their own state was in the balance. The Bohemian Germans did not intend to give up the privileges of a ruling majority without a fight. At that moment, however, the victorious powers, who had their own interests in Central Europe, entered the dispute.

It was this external, foreign-policy dimension that proved crucial for the outcome of the ethnic conflict for the moment and were also to play a decisive role in the further development of the conflict in the crisis situations yet to come (The Munich Agreement, the role of the Czechoslovak government in exile in London and its recognition, and the transfer of the Sudeten Germans after the Second World War).

---

[43] The social democrats sent representatives to a joint committee for national/ethnic organisation.

The Treaty of Versailles. Georges Clemenceau, Thomas Woodrow Wilson and David Lloyd George leaving the Trianon Palace after signing the treaty on the 28th of June 1919.

3 The Central Europe
of the Successor States

The key factor for the future fate of the Habsburg Monarchy was the change
in the attitudes of the Allied powers – France, Great Britain, the United States
and later also Italy – in the second half of the war. For all the campaigning led
by T. G. Masaryk abroad and Czech politicians at home, the views of the Allies
were the critical determinant for the cause of renewed Czech statehood. After
all, Central Europe has always provided plenty of confirmation of the truism
that the fortunes of small states unfold on the basis of the interest and decisions
of great(er) powers.[1]

The president of the USA, Woodrow Wilson, became the spokesman for the
Alliance, since it was to him that the Central Powers had turned with the offer
of an end to the state of war. Austria-Hungary's offer to accept the Fourteen
Points of the peace programme presented by Wilson to the US Congress of the
8th of January 1918 as a basis for negotiations was favourable for T. G. Masaryk
and E. Beneš. Wilson's programme clearly formulated the theory of the right of
nations to self-determination (as an overall political concept but not as a principle of international law), which could be fulfilled only by the creation of their
own nation states.[2] The Czech-German relationship provided a vivid example
of how difficult it would be to apply the principle in practice. There were political, technical and legal obstacles to its realisation in ideal form in Wilson's day,
as there still are today.

---

[1]   On T. G. Masaryk's post-war ideas see also Pichlík, K. "Poválečná Evropa v představách T. G. Masaryka
      v exilu".
[2]   Krejčí, O. 1997. *Mezinárodní politika* [International Politics]. Prague: Victoria Publishing. 164.

In the particular situation of the Czechs and Germans living side by side (rather than together) in the Bohemian Lands, the claims of both ethnic communities rested on the 9th point of Wilson's declaration, i.e. "the nations of Austria-Hungary, whose position among the nations we wish to see safeguarded and assured, should be guaranteed the greatest possible freedom of autonomous development".[3]

This formulation did not entirely meet the ideas and goals of Masaryk's campaign abroad. The right to self-determination had been explicitly acknowledged by the victorious powers as a universally applicable principle for the new world order, but what could be done about the hopes of the Bohemian Germans that it would also apply to them?[4]

The central powers explicitly accepted Wilson's Fourteen Points as the basis for negotiations on cessation of hostilities, and this necessarily implied that as a result there would be interference in the internal organisation of Germany and Austria-Hungary. On the other hand, democratisation of the political system and provision of autonomy to minorities did not yet automatically mean major change in the political structure of Germany and the disintegration of the Habsburg Empire. Austria could accept the American demands in the form stated (the British prime minister Lloyd George indicated that the Allies did not intend to insist on the territorial dismemberment of the central powers).

In this situation the *Czechoslovak National Council* based in Prague opted for the tactic of achieving the maximum number of *faits accomplis* with the evident aim of getting the still hesitating politicians of the Allied states, above all Wilson himself, to change their minds. The crown of their efforts and decisive turning-point was Wilson's note of the 18th of October 1918 in which he recognised the existence of the Czechoslovak government (and also the South Slav) and declared that an autonomist response to the demands of the Austrian nations was not enough unless those nations themselves decided that autonomy was sufficient.[5] In this way, of course, the Allied states placed the fate of the Habsburg Monarchy in the hands of the Czechoslovaks and South Slavs.

This was also the moment that fatefully changed the hitherto favourable political position of the Sudeten Germans in the Bohemian Lands. They lost the status of state nation and in the new republic became a large but "mere" national (ethnic) minority. Taking a lesson in reality from Wilson's note, they too now tried the tactic of *fait accompli*. Their idea was to unify all Austrian Germans in one state and settle the matter before any revolutionary chaos could arise. They were prepared to sacrifice the interests of the dynasty and "hurriedly

---

[3] Peroutka, F. 1991. *Budování státu I* [Building of the State I]. Prague: Lidové noviny. 49.
[4] Ibidem. 128.
[5] Ibidem. 51.

adjusted their tactics to make them credible", adopting the rhetoric of sincere pupils of Woodrow Wilson. From the idea of German hegemony in Austria they switched directly to the idea of self-determination and started to behave as if the real aim of the war had been to win the right of self-determination for the German people.

At the same time the Austrian Germans in fact "had to hand a number of incisive and tough programmes to reform the status of non-German peoples after the victorious end of the war". The core of these programmes was unprecedented and brutal Germanisation.[6] These political programmes had not prepared the political parties and groupings of the German peoples of the Monarchy for the dramatic situation of defeat. Most of these programmes worked on the assumption of the victory of the central powers, to be followed by the uncompromising Germanisation of the non-German territories of the Habsburg Monarchy in close collaboration with the German Reich. The ideological source of most of these nationalistically orientated programmes was the concept of a *Mitteleuropa* dominated by Germany, as drawn up by Naumann in 1915.

Nonetheless, it was from these sources, combined with the Pan-German ideas of G. von Schönerer (particularly the theory that national right abrogates state right),[7] which especially at the turn of the 19th/20th century had strongly influenced political life in Vienna, that the Sudeten Germans politicians now drew ideological inspiration. They thus interpreted Wilson's demand for the right to self-determination in the spirit of Pan-German ideals.

Three immediate factors helped to invigorate this traditional orientation of Austrian German politics. First there was the attempt to compensate for military defeat by German solidarity – a closing of German ranks. Second, the situation gave the Austrian Germans courage to appeal to the same principle of self-determination that previously every one of their political groupings (with the exception of the socialists) had rejected. Third, there was the removal of the two ruling dynasties, the Hohenzollerns and Habsburgs, which had been an obstacle to the unification of the German-speaking lands.[8]

It was these considerations that led the deputies of the Austrian Germans to take the decisive step towards the constitutional dissolution of the monarchy

---

[6]   Ibidem. 54. By their sudden abandonment of the Habsburg Monarch the leaders of the Sudeten Germans seemed to be confirming the fears of the Emperor Charles I, who tried to save the empire and dynasty by making a separate peace and in so doing was also seeking to protect the sovereignty of the monarchy from its ally Germany as well. He had a distrust for the politics of the Bohemian Germans and regarded only the Alpine Germans as the support of the throne. This attitude had its logic, which at the same time brings up the question of the loyalty of the Bohemian Germans in the critical moment for the survival of the state that had for centuries guaranteed them their privileged position. Galandauer, J. *Vznik Československé republiky 1918*. 156.

[7]   For more detail see the earlier mentioned thesis of the Linz Programme.

[8]   Kural, V. *Konflikt místo společenství*. 13.

on the 21st of October 1918. It was they who did so, and not the Czechs as Sudeten German propaganda frequently claimed afterwards. For various reasons
the Czechs were temporising, waiting for a favourable moment and reluctant to
open the way to possible federalisation of the state. In contrast the monarchy's
Germans had an interest in haste, because they intended to use the principle
of self-determination to establish an Austrian-German state in the spirit of the
ideal of Pan-German unification.

Thus as interpreted by the Germans of the Austrian monarchy, the concept
of self-determination meant "self-determination all the way to Pan-German unification". Such was the alternative (as a replacement for the extinct monarchy)
to the idea of a Central Europe of small, democratic and independent states as
ultimately adopted by the victorious western powers and Masaryk's active campaign abroad. The disadvantage of a chain of new states was, of course, their
relatively weak economic potential and associated political instability (and also
potential ethnic conflicts). Nor did this variant of a Central European order
provide any guarantee *ex definitione* of capacity to resist further potential expansionism on the part of Germany. On the other hand, another factor in the
calculations of the victorious powers was the prospect of being able to exploit
the principle of self-determination to their advantage: a system of weak states
in Central Europe would allow them both to intervene when their own national
interests made that necessary and to create a sort of *no man's land* insulating
Western Europe from the political influence of Bolshevik Russia, as well as to
put brakes on the traditional German *Drang nach Osten*.

The tragic developments of the later 1930s, which culminated in the destruction of independent Czechoslovakia, unfortunately showed the security mechanism of the Versailles System, including the principle of the *cordon sanitaire*
chain of successor states, to be a complete failure, with fatal results for the CSR
as one of its most thorough-going supporters.

Yet for the later assessment of the wisdom of the Versailles approach to settlement of the relations between Czechs and Bohemian Germans, we should
not forget the two alternatives as they presented themselves at the end of the
First World War, i.e. a Pan-German order with a dominant position for Germany (inclining to authoritarian forms of political decision-making) in Central
Europe, or a set of independent successor states. Both sides of the dispute, in
our case the Sudeten Germans and the Czech political leadership at home and
in the resistance abroad, effectively dismissed the concept of federalisation as
pointless in the real situation.

H. Haas argues that whatever could be done for the Sudeten provinces from
Vienna was done, i.e. that Sudeten policy did not fail because of the political
passivity of central Austrian institutions but because of political conditions in

a larger frame. After mature reflection, the Allied and affiliated victorious powers accepted the historical unity of the Bohemian Lands as the territorial basis of a Czechoslovak state and from this a different model emerged, i.e. that of an ethnically multinational Czechoslovakia including Bohemian Germans, who now for the first time acquired the unifying (to some extent) political identity of Sudeten Germans.[9]

A whole week before the declaration of an independent Czechoslovakia, i.e. on the 21st of October 1918, the German deputies to the Vienna Imperial Council-Parliament voted for the creation of a German-Austria. While formally they voted for the federalisation offered by the emperor on the basis of the Wilson principles, in fact they saw this as the first step to the creation of a Greater Germany to be constituted by the incorporation of Austria and the border areas of the Bohemian Lands into Germany. Thus political practice very quickly offered proof of how the humanism of the programme declared by the American president could be abused.

At the end of the First World War, the international community, and as a result international law, had only very limited experience of the application of the right to self-determination. Wilson's doctrines of self-determination and collective security took European diplomats into unknown territory.[10] Up to this point the assumption behind most European international agreements and treaties had been that the balance of power could be strengthened by the movement of borders and redistribution of territory. The British shared with the Austrians (both states at the head of multinational empires) the view that smaller states must subordinate their national ambitions to the broader interest, i.e. the maintenance of peace, and (let us add) the existing international order. They feared that newly emergent states would undermine international order.

Wilson entirely rejected this old-fashioned approach, arguing that it was not self-determination but the lack of it that had caused the war. In his view instability had not been produced by the absence of political equilibrium, but by the striving for it.[11] The striking novelty of Wilson's proposals and ideas was the notion that the international order would no longer be based on power and

---

[9]   All the reports of the period indicate the Germans' deep crisis of national identity in the hour of defeat and also civil fears of the destabilisation of social and political order. Omnipresent hunger and lack of energy ultimately reduced their capacity for political action. The author shares the view that this triple crisis of identity kept the immediate potential of the national idea within narrow limits. Haas also argues that the Deutschböhmen lacked a strong organisational base for politics. The social democratic workers movement was the only mass organisation supporting Sudeten politics, but it did not effectively manage to channel the social movement of the time into national opposition. Haas, H. "Konflikt při uplatňování nároků na právo na sebeurčení" [The Conflict in Claims to the Right of Self-Determination], in Mommsen, H. – Kováč, D. – Malíř, J. – Marková, M. *První světová válka a vztahy mezi Čechy, Slováky a Němci*. 176–177.

[10] Kissinger, H. *The Art of Diplomacy*. 233.

[11] Ibidem.

interests, but on principle embodied in law. For Wilson, self-determination was just another name for sovereignty. In this sense he was following the American and French rather than the British political tradition. He idealised the possibilities of democracy, and this was the foundation of his ideology.[12] He was genuinely convinced that *vox populi* was *vox legi* and so he had a tendency to address the people over the heads of their politicians. This was an effective approach that played a positive role in the course of the war, but his fellow statesmen colleagues were a great deal less enthusiastic about it in the course of the Versailles Peace Conference.[13]

To this day the principle of self-determination has remained a very sensitive issue in international law, and one that is hard to define. Indeed, bitter experience with its application in the inter-war period, especially demands for its application by groups of ethnic Germans (*Volksdeutsche*), led in post-war Western Europe to a universal demand for the borders and integrity of states to be considered inviolable as the premise for any kind of step towards integration. The supreme bodies of the European Union therefore currently prefer to use and refer to the concept of the cultural autonomy of national minorities and ethnic groups, i.e. right not to statehood but to identity (cultural difference).

The Paris Peace Conference

The acknowledged expert on the problem of self-determination in international law, Alfred Cobban, considers the basic weakness of Wilson's ideas to have been failure to see how indeterminate a criterion nationality could be in any decision on the real demarcation of the borders of newly formed states. It was with this key problem that the victorious powers struggled throughout the proceedings of the Versailles Peace Conference, as we shall describe elsewhere.

When the principle was tested in the conditions of real politics it very rapidly became clear that Wilson's idealism with its very good intentions could pave the road to catastrophe. The spread of democracy did not automatically – as Wilson believed – prevent states from becoming expansionist, and the right

---

[12]   Cobban, A. *The Nation State and National Self-Determination*. 63.

[13]   As a theory, Wilson's ideas form a logically integrated whole but in practical application they lead to a series of inconsistencies and contradictions. In the course of a hearing before the US Senate Committee for Foreign Affairs, Wilson himself was later to admit to doubts about his own approach, saying," When I gave utterance to those words (that all nations had a right to self-determination) I spoke without the knowledge that nationalities existed, which are coming to us... You do not know and cannot appreciate the anxieties that I have experienced as a result of many millions of people having their hopes raised by what I have said." Ibidem. 65.

to self-determination very quickly created new epicentres of conflict because it was inevitably impossible to satisfy the demands of all claimants.

One fundamental reason for the conflict-generating effects of the right to self-determination is its completely inadequate definition at the level of international law. Wilson's theses were a political programme lacking international legal instruments. Henry Kissinger commented that never before had such revolutionary aims been presented with so little in the way of guidelines for their implementation. Elsewhere he added that Wilson's approach tended too often to exacerbate the very problems that he had identified and wished to remove or reduce.

The Paris Peace Conference, with President Wilson as its star, was supposed to be conducted in the spirit of these new rules set out in the Fourteen Point Programme and to secure a just solution for all states. In fact, aspiring to be a forum for all the states of the world, it ultimately turned into a free-for-all of each state for itself. In particular, conflict developed between Wilson's conception of the natural harmony that he believed that all states would somehow spontaneously start to pursue, and the selfish interests of the European powers, distrustful and exhausted by war.[14]

It was in this situation that the clash between Czechs and Germans over the achievement of their own state on the basis of the right of self-determination came to a head. The situation was not quite symmetrical. The Czech right to self-determination came into conflict with the Sudeten German right, but not with the German right as a whole. The setting up of a Greater Germany would, by contrast, entirely call into question the viability of the CSR as an integral state. This was understood by the representatives of the powers at the Paris peace conference, for whom awareness of the possible threat to the CSR (the security viewpoint) was the main argument for approving the historical (militarily defensible) borders, even at the price of the incorporation of a large number of Germans into the territory of the new state.

From the point of view of the negotiators, acceptance of the principle of the historical borders greatly simplified the problem of defining the borders

---

[14]   Valuable insights in this context were provided by a direct participant in the conference – the foreign correspondent of *The Times* H. W. Steed, who from mid-January to the 19th of May 1919 wrote daily reports to Lord Northcliffe on the progress of negotiations. He was in close contact with Colonel House and other key actors at the conference. Steed was critical of the approach taken by Wilson, seeing him as a man full of good will, but incapable of penetrating the network of European diplomacy full of intrigues and tricks. House grasped the situation but this resulted in conflict between him and the president (again thanks to intrigues). Steed regarded the final break beween the two close colleagues and key figures of the American delegation as a tragedy that affected the results of the peace conference. He considered Wilson's main mistake to be his failure to understand that "at the right moment an unshakeable refusal to yield can reduce the necessity for later compromise", Steed, H. W. 1927. *Třicet let novinářem II* ['Thirty Years a Journalist II']. Chapters on the Peace conference I+II. 289–330.

of Czechoslovakia as a successor state. President Wilson's main negotiator and foreign policy advisor Colonel Edward M. House recorded in his diary that, "I arrived at the War Ministry around five or six minutes before Lloyd George and Orlando and Clemenceau arrived before them and I agreed that we would accept the old line of the historical borders and would not delineate a new one. This was much simpler and provided much less scope for problems to arise. We hardly had any difficulty persuading George and Orlando to accept our conclusions, and it seemed that George knew only little about the theme…"[15]

Colonel House summarised the results of debate in a very chaotic fashion, and noted that his decision increased rather than decreased the size of the German minority in Czechoslovakia.[16] The briefing that he had been given by American experts before the negotiations had evidently entirely failed to have any effect. It is also clear that he was indifferent to the fate of the German minority in Bohemia, and unworried by the question of whether 330 000 Bohemian Germans would become citizens of Germany or members of an irredenta in the CSR. Despite the proclaimed great ideals of President Woodrow Wilson, this arrogance and great-power distaste for addressing controversial details intensified the Czech-German conflict that accompanied the birth of the independent state. Indeed, a similar great-power arrogance (although not American) was later, in the 1930s, to seal the fate of the CSR in the face of Nazi aggression.[17]

The Paris conference applied the principle of self-determination to nations, not their citizens and national/ethnic groups living in foreign countries. The Treaty of Saint Germain eventually offered a basic formulation of minority rights that T. G. Masaryk intended to apply quite generously in the case of the Bohemian Germans.

At the beginning of 1918, however, the Allied powers were still far from united on the question of the acknowledgement of the rights of the nations of the Habsburg Monarchy to self-determination. Indeed, the disintegration of the monarchy was far from accepted as the one and only option for a post-war order in Central Europe.

In view of the fact that Wilson spoke explicitly about the principle of autonomy rather than just self-determination, it was evident that the federalisation of Austria-Hungary had not yet been ruled out. In this ambiguity the leaders of Czech politics both at home and abroad saw a threat to their constitu-

---

[15]   Perman, D. "The Bohemian-German Frontier", in *The Shaping of the Czechoslovak State*. 172.
[16]   Superficial or insufficient consultation, or even no consultation at all with the *Inquiry* team on the part of leading American negotiators was a repeated problem and cause of failure in decision-making on many complicated situations.
[17]   Kural, V. *Konflikt místo společenství*. 28.

tional ambitions. The stated positions of the Sudeten German politicians seriously complicated key aspects of the negotiation on the birth of the CSR and it was obvious to both sides that a breaking-point was imminent, a culmination of the struggle over the future status of inhabitants of the historic lands in postwar Europe.

Some new states had not been recognised, which meant that they were excluded from participation in the peace conferences of 1919–1920 that drew up the new postwar European order. Italy (despite recognition from the USA) blocked the participation of the delegation of Yugoslavia, for example, which was then represented only by the delegation of Serbia, although the latter in fact no longer legally existed because it had been merged into the new Serbo-Croatian-Slovenian state.

After the end of the world war, the decisive factor for the result of the struggle between Czechs and Sudeten Germans over the prospect of setting up their own states was once again the international context. Specifically the Conference of Saint-Germain-en-Laye (10th of September 1919), the Paris conference at which the details of settlement with Austria were worked out, was the key meeting for the Czech claim to self-determination.

The Czechoslovak delegation was led by K. Kramář, but its real moving spirit was Eduard Beneš, who presented the Czechoslovak conception of statehood to the conference in the form of a *Mémoire* (memorandum)[18] and verbal elaborations. It was Beneš who was the source of all the important decisions on the Czechoslovak side, after their approval by Masaryk and usually their written consultation with the government. The other members of the Czechoslovak delegation mostly accepted Beneš's views because they respected his knowledge of complicated questions of international relations.

In pushing through the claims of Czechoslovakia at the Versailles Conference, Beneš relied on close alliance with France. This approach was based on the rational consideration that France shared with Czechoslovakia a priority interest in weakening the role of Germany in Central Europe. He understood that France was capable of securing much more for its smaller ally than Czechoslovakia could achieve by itself.

At the same time it was clear that Great Britain, fearing the Balkanisation of Central Europe, gave priority to the maintenance of the basic outline of the political order of Central Europe whereas Wilson, wholly in the spirit of his own theoretical conceptions, demanded first and foremost the establishment of a *Society of Nations* as the guarantee of future peaceful development and an in-

---

[18]   On the theme from the Sudeten German point of view see the monograph by Gordon, H. 1990. *Die Beneš-Denkschriften* (Die Tschechoslowakei und das Reich 1918/19 – Kommentar und Kritik). Starnberg: Verlagsgemeinschaft-Druffel Verlag.

stitution ensuring harmony in international relations. Beneš characterised this attitude: "They (the Americans) are inclined to a very schematic solution… with every problem they look above all to the principle of nationality or to a plebiscite". For example, on the 1st of April 1919 when the Czechoslovak Committee presented a report on the situation on the Czech-German borders, there was a clash between state secretary Lansing and the French representatives. The Americans took the view that Rumburk should become part of Germany and demanded that a plebiscite be held in the area. The French delegate J. Laroche contended that there was no justification for a plebiscite in this one restricted area unless a plebiscite were held in all areas with a German-speaking population.

W. Jaksch comments that, "the resolve of the French delegates not to yield even a square metre of ground to Germany dominated the scene". He also claims that *"deliberate falsifications"*, allegedly used by Beneš to pull the wool over the eyes of the representatives of France, Britain, the USA and Italy in the course of negotiation, were later exploited by Neville Chamberlain and Lord Halifax as arguments for their revisionist stance.[19]

In fact, the views and programme promoted by Masaryk and Beneš fitted well with the opinions of the victorious powers, especially French governing circles. The primary consideration behind French foreign policy and that of the emergent CSR was the search for safeguards against any further German expansionism. This consonance of interests soon led to the development of a Franco-Czech alliance. Although the Czech delegation indicated a willingness to make some minor territorial concessions to Germany, the French were steadfast in their efforts to prevent even the smallest conciliatory gestures towards the defeated Germany. The prospect of any cession of parts of the border territories of the Bohemian Lands wase evidently regarded by the French representatives as raising the spectre of the annexation of Austria to Germany. "The French were striving to avoid the Pan-German consolidation of Central Europe at any cost."[20]

A similarly vigorous debate took place on the question of the Aš "promontory", the Cheb region and other areas.[21] This discussion was prompted by the American delegation. In the end the consideration that prevailed was the need to ensure economic communication between the border areas and the interior,

[19]   Jaksch, W. *Cesta Evropy do Postupimi.* 165. For polemic with these views see below.
[20]   In a report on the proposal for the Czechoslovak border the *Comité d'Etudes* group of French experts stated, "There is no doubt that it is within our interest to create a Czechoslovak state strong enough not only to live, but also to form one of the strongest barriers against the German Eastern expansion." Perman, D. *The Shaping of the Czechoslovak State.* 132–134.
[21]   Wiskemann, E. *Czechs and Germans.* 90.

and also the need to retain a demonstrable connection between the course of the historical border and natural geographic aspects of the landscape. Nonetheless, in the course of the discussions it became clear that the delegation of the USA took a rather different view – influenced above all by Professor Charles Seymour, (a member of the expert *The Inquiry* group) who specialised in the problems of the settlement of territorial borders in Central and Eastern Europe. He proposed that the question of the border with Germany be settled by annexation of the north-western "horn" of the Bohemian Lands to neighbouring Germany – a solution that would supposedly ease the situation of the new state by reducing the number of German-speaking inhabitants.

Beneš had been self-confident, sure that he would have no problem pushing through the Czech demands in the form of the historic borders including the Germans inhabiting the borderlands.[22] In this respect his task was now easier because the peace agreements explicitly mentioned a Czechoslovak state, *which already existed at the time of signature of the agreements*[23]. The arguments used by Masaryk and Beneš to convince Colonel House and his team that the historic borders of the Bohemian Lands could be preserved without excessive damage to the rights of the Bohemian Germans to self-determination are of some interest. They claimed that self-determination for Bohemian Germans was better guaranteed by leaving three and a half million of them inside Czechoslovakia than by reducing their number to a million, since the latter solution would so weaken the German population that it would be much less able to resist erosion of ethnic identity.[24]

Views on the borders of the future Czechoslovakia (or revived Czech state) had changed considerably since the days when the increasingly ambitious Czech political leadership had first seriously started to consider the re-establishment of statehood. The so-called *Grégr Plan* of 1888 (Julius Grégr published it in the Czech daily *Národní listy*) had proposed the reduction of the number of Germans in Bohemia by the cession of parts of the border areas with a German population including the Cheb region, the Karlovy Vary region, the Krušné Mountains region, the Šluknov "promontory" and the Liberec region.

Masaryk had initially presented his views on the borders of the future state in the confidential memorandum *Samostatné Čechy*/Independent Bohemia, which he wrote in May 1915 in London for the British Foreign Minister Lord Grey. As the opening note to the text says, the memorandum offers a programme for

---

[22] Klimek, A. 1989. *Jak se dělal mír roku 1919. Československo na konferenci ve Versailles* [How Peace was Made in 1919. Czechoslovakia at the Versailles Conference]. Prague: Melantrich. 20.

[23] Krčmář, J. 1923. "Právní základ československé republiky" [The Legal Basis of the Czechoslovak Republic], in Tobolka, Z. V. *Politika I*. 208.

[24] Perman, D. *The Shaping of Czechoslovak State*. 126.

the re-establishment of Bohemia as an independent state. Here the prospective new state is accorded the territories of the historic lands of Bohemia, Moravia and Silesia, with the addition of the Slovak regions of the Northern Hungarian Lands. Dating from the same time is Masaryk's sketch of the borders of the future state, which in the Czech part of the country keep to the historic borders of the Bohemian Kingdom, i.e. they incorporate the border lands with their German population.[25]

The existence of the CSR was considered by the victorious powers to be a fait accompli and not a problem in itself. What was subject to dispute was the conception of the state, and the main bone of contention was the demarcation of the borders, involving as it did the question of the incorporation of minorities, especially the Sudeten Germans and their legal status.[26] Beneš's optimism was initially rather shaken when the real negotiations started. The Americans in particular showed little enthusiasm for the historical arguments referring to the continuity of the existence of the Bohemian state and its borders.[27] They were guided by Wilson's idealism in the pure form that was so hard to apply in the complex and acrimonious ethnic conditions of Central Europe. Hence they hesitated at the proposal to incorporate within Czechoslovakia three million Sudeten Germans who were currently demanding the right to decide on their own destiny, in most cases wanting to be part of a potential Austro-German state that they resolutely supported and still hoped would be established.

In a note of the 20th of December 1918 to the foreign ministry of the USA Beneš urgently demanded the satisfaction of Czech territorial claims, and so a meeting was held between him and two members of House's team – W. Lippmann, the secretary of the *Inquiry* group and Colonel S. Bonsal. Aware of the views of American experts who favoured incorporating part of the Sudeten population in Germany, the two negotiators stressed the need for a cautious approach that would allow the USA to avoid creating an undesirable and binding precedent (e.g. the USA would be unable to refuse the demands of Poland

---

[25] Beneš, E. *Světová válka a naše revoluce.* 246. In a letter to Beneš written from Washington on the 3rd of November 1918 TGM writes: "Our Germans in Bohemia will not be high and mighty. They too are to blame for the war, for their stupid anti-Slav policy. Exploit moods against them in Berlin. But leave them in peace, even if we will defend the historic borders to the limit. In the worst case fall back on the Grégr Plan (in part). *Odsun – dokumentace* [Transfer-Documentation]. 496–497. Klimko, J. 1986. *Politické a právne dejiny hraníc predmníchovskej republiky (1918–1938)* [The Political and Legal History of the Pre-Munich Republic (1918–1938)]. Bratislava: Veda. 146.

[26] Kural, V. *Konflikt místo společenství.* 17–22.

[27] For example during a meeting of the Supreme Allied Council at the Paris Peace Conference an American delegate said the following on the question of borders: "Mr. Cambon said that there was only little to be added on the question of the border to the west towards Aš. The Czechoslovak government has already yielded this place as well. The committee has taken cognisance of this, but the American delegation expressed the wish to cut away a more substantial part of the territory in addition..." Miller, D. H. *My Diary at the Paris Conference.* New York. Vol. XVI. 15.

for former territories including areas with non-Polish populations). Colonel House and his advisers were caught in a dilemma arising from an American policy that on the one hand was negotiating the liberal transition of power to the new governments of the nation states, while on the other was putting off any decision on the territorial definition of the power of these governments. The Bohemian Germans were exploiting this situation, and continuing to send notes and protests to the Western powers, but in fact the question was no longer to be the subject of further discussions.

The diaries of David Hunter Miller[28] show that idealism and naivety – the terms most often used to characterise the attitude of the American representatives at the peace talks, are far from accurate as regards the US level of information and planning.[29] As early as September 1917 a team of specialists known as *The Inquiry* (led by W. Lippmann) was created at the State Department, and this drew up the basic materials and reports for the key decisions of US foreign policy then formulated by President Wilson in consultation with his personal advisor Colonel House and to a lesser extent with the Secretary of State for Foreign Affairs Lansing.

The *Inquiry* team brought together experts on economics, geography, history and ethnography and was entrusted with the study and production of memoranda summarising recommendations and information that were used as the basis for the negotiations conducted by the delegates at the peace conference.[30] These studies played a decisive role in the drawing up of the post-war order of Central Europe and the territories along the Baghdad Railway (a transport axis which had also played a key role in the well-known plans for *Mitteleuropa*).[31] Since most of the new borders were to be created in this area, it was the most important from the point of view of the peace conference.

---

[28] The leading legal expert of the American delegations, whose diaries provide a unique view of the backstage diplomacy and activities of the American delegation in the course of the Paris Preace Conference. The set of documents was later successively published in 21 volumes by the State Department in a print run of only 40 copies. See Ibidem. This under-appreciated source of expert information has been referred by S. Raková and also e.g. W. Jaksch.

[29] One example of strikingly pragmatic political thinking on the basis of American interests might be this extract from a memorandum drawn up by the *Inquiry* group, which was submitted to the secretary of state Lansing on the 22nd of December 1917: "Our policy must therefore consist above all in instigating ethnic unrest, but later refusing to agree with the extreme result of this unrest, which would destroy Austria-Hungary. If then on the one hand we threaten the current German-Hungarian combination with ethnic/national rebellions, and if on the other we show them a way of safely holding on, we shall reduce their resistance to the minimum and hugely strengthen their strivings for foreign policy independence from Germany. Austria-Hungary is in the position of having to be obedient to survive." *Papers Relating to the Foreign Relations of the United States*. Vol. I. 1945. The Paris Peace Conference 1919. 44–45.

[30] Raková, S. 1983. *Politika Spojených států ve střední Evropě po první světové válce* [The Policy of the United States in Central Europe after the First World War]. Prague: Academia. 21.

[31] For a detailed account see House, E. M. – Seymour, Ch. 1921. *What really happend at Paris*. New York.

As of August 1918, the *Inquiry* team (from February 1919 renamed *The Territorial Section of the Peace Conference*) devoted itself exclusively to the question of drawing the borders and study of data connected with this task. The team's specialist on the subject of Austria-Hungary and Central Europe in general (including the future Czechoslovak state) was the Harvard professor and official American historian of the peace conference Charles Seymour. It should also be noted that the *Inquiry* team included David Hunter Miller and J. Brown Scott, experts on international law and the creators of plans for the Charter of the League of Nations, which according to the American vision was to be the main instrument for neutralising German expansionism and for stabilising international relations.

German Bohemians versus Czechoslovakia

The world war had shifted Sudeten German opinion further towards the idea of Naumann's *Mitteleuropa*, even though this ignored the key fact that the central powers had lost the war – among other things to the benefit of the Slav nations who were resolved to exploit the historic chance to push through their own claims to the right of national self-determination.

In this "open situation" the Germans and Czechs chose different model solutions: the Germans envisaged the division of the Bohemian Lands on ethnic lines and the annexation of territories with a German population to German-Austria, or (possibly) the annexation of this whole territory to the German Reich. The Czechs on the other hand wanted to keep the historic Bohemian lands as part of Czechoslovak territory and to tackle the issue of German-Czech relations as an internal state matter. The instruments that the two sides used as the first constitutional steps to making these models a reality were, respectively, the Declaration of the Founding of Czecho-Slovakia on the 28th of October 1918 and two days later, on the 30th of October, the creation of German Austria on the basis of the Provisional Constitution. Executive power in the territories claimed was now taken over by national authorities: the Czecho-Slovak authorities by revolutionary act, and the German-Austrian from the hands of the emperor on the 31st of October. The imperial cabinet became a government without a country. The final steps in the formal establishment of national states was the emperor's resignation from the proceedings of the government of German Austria, the declaration of the Republic of German Austria and the proclamation of union with Germany on the 12th of November 1918.[32]

---

[32] Haas, H. "Konflikt při uplatňování nároků na právo na sebeurčení od habsburského státu k Československu – Němci v českých zemích v letech 1918 až 1919" [The conflict over the application of the right to self-determination from the Habsburg state to Czechoslovakia-Germans in the Bohemian Lands 1918–1919], in

This was the situation in which Sudeten Germans decided to declare the establishment of a German Bohemia/*Deutschböhmen* (29th of October). The proposals of the Czech side (a special minister for Germans, three mainly self-governing German regions, German as a second language, a just educational and cultural policy etc.) were rejected, and the Czech side immediately reacted with the distrust that had been latently present in preceding disputes and was now only intensifying. The threat posed by a Sudeten German irredenta to the Czecho-Slovak state at its very birth was to fatally taint the whole course of co-existence between Czechs and Germans in the republic. This mutual distrust was deepened by the military occupation of the "insurgent" borderlands by military units of the new Czechoslovak army in November and December 1918.

On the 21st of October the German deputies from the Bohemian Lands had already rejected the independent CSR declared on the 28th of October 1918 and announced their intention of dividing the historic lands by attaching the German regions of Bohemia and Moravia to German-Austria.[33] Four Sudeten German provinces were successively declared: *Deutschböhmen* (Western and Northern Bohemia, *Sudetenland* (Northern Moravia), *Böhmerwaldgau* (The Šumava Mountains and South Bohemia) and *Deutschsüdmähren* (South Moravia). The language enclaves of Brno, Jihlava and Olomouc were also supposed to become part of German-Austria, while the Ostrava Basin was to be declared neutral. It was clear that the Sudeten Germans were resolved to fulfil to the letter the goals of their programme announced as early as January 1918, when for the first time (as a direct reaction to Wilson's message) they put forward a claim for the constitution of a province of *Deutschböhmen* in these terms:

"The Czechs want to exploit the revolutionary forces of the war to destroy the Austro-Hungarian monarchy and impose the yoke of the Czechoslovak state on two and a half million Germans. We, the representatives of the German nation in Bohemia, ask that an independent province of Deutschböhmen be created... without any kind of dependence on the Czech part of Bohemia. The German nation will not rest until it has brought about the definitive libera-

---

Mommsen, H. – Kováč, D. – Malíř, J. – Marková, M. *První světová válka a vztahy mezi Čechy, Slováky a Němci.* 113–114. Germans living in the Bohamian Lands, or specifically in the areas to which they laid claim, were thus contributing to the creation of a German-Austrian state with all its consequences internal and international. H. Haas argues that this annexation of territory by German Austria necessarily went hand in hand with often strenuous agitation campaign against ties with Bohemia, which were deep among Germans as well, and against the often nationally indifferent attitudes of Germans who doubted the point and practicality of the experiment.

[33] Entirely in the spirit of the programme expressed on the 21st of October 1918 by the national socialist deputy Knirsch in a speech to the Imperial Council: "We reject in advance the idea of the incorporation of German Austria into a union of states with the Slav states that are emerging out of old Austria. In our national, social and cultural interest we demand the incorporation of German-Austria as a federal state into the German Reich." Peroutka, F. *Budování státu I.* 56.

tion of its fellow-kinsmen from the rule of the Czechs and – if need be by violence – prevented the setting up of a Czechoslovak state in which the German people would be enslaved... With this purpose we demand the demarcation of the borders and merger of German territory in Bohemia and all the central places, authorities and institutions appertaining to this territory that belong to the crown lands."[34]

From the point of view of Czech aspirations this directly threatened or even precluded the constitution of an independent Czechoslovak state. What is more, the threat appeared in an international context in which Czecho-Slovakia's international status was far from fully resolved, especially recognition by the other states. The strong terms in which T. G. Masaryk, in his first message from Prague castle (where he had arrived only the day before accompanied by legionaries) expressed his hostility to the idea of the cession of the borderlands underlined the drama of the situation: "I repeat. We have created our state, and this determines the status of our Germans, who originally came to this country as emigrants and colonists. We do not want and cannot sacrifice our considerable Czech minorities on so-called German territory. We are also convinced that it is to the economic advantage of our Germans to stay with us. It is up to them to take up the right position in regard to us. But I assure them that minorities in our state will enjoy complete national rights and civil equality. The American Republic preferred civil war to the prospect of permitting the secession of its south. We shall never permit the secession of our mixed north."[35]

Although the situation was unfavourable to German demands, the Bohemian Germans did have an opportunity – indirectly, via the Austrian delegation, – to express their views on the German and Austrian borders in the context of demarcation of the new frontiers of the Czecho-Slovak Republic at the Paris conference. The Austrian delegation at the Versailles negotiations included representatives of all the separatist Sudeten German provinces declared in the Bohemian Lands (R. Lodgman von Auen, J. Seliger, R. Freissler, A. Klement and Count H. Oldofredi).

Led by the Austrian chancellor K. Renner, the delegation submitted a memorandum demanding the application of the right to self-determination for the Sudeten Germans as well, proposing the incorporation of the border provinces into Austria and accusing the Czech government of the violent occupation of

---

[34] Ibidem. 57–58

[35] *Odsun – dokumentace.* 514–515. For a brief account of the Czechoslovak view on the circumstances of the foundation of the state see also the *Memorandum of the Czechoslovak Government* sent in November 1944 by the Czech government in exile in London to all the allied governments, especially Appendix I. "The Pan-Germanism of the Germans in Czechoslovakia." Král, V. *Die Deutschen in der Tschechoslowakei 1933–1947.* Prague: Nakladatelství Československé akademie věd (Acta occupationis Bohemicae and Moraviae). 544–546.

Sudeten German territories in breach of the principles of international law, thus allegedly destroying the possibility of peaceful settlement. The memorandum went on to argue that the new state would not have the necessary cohesion, because it would be ethnically complex (like the Habsburg Monarchy) and lacking in a unifying political ideal. Here, however, the memorandum was expressing only the view of ethnic Germans in the historic lands (around 3,700,000), i.e. 28% of the population of the new state.

On the course and results of the peace conference Wenzel Jaksch commented that: "The Prague government prevented the Sudeten Germans from taking part in the elections to the Austrian National Assembly. This was why they wanted to have their voices heard… The Czech army fired into peace-loving demonstrations in more than one town… No representative of the Sudeten Germans was allowed to speak a word at the peace conferences, while their supporters in their home country were being silenced. That was how… a model democratic state was born."[36]

Six months after the establishment of Czecho-Slovakia the Sudeten Germans were still refusing to accept the existence of the state. F. Peroutka showed some understanding for their attitude and argued that, "in their (the Sudeten Germans') minds, self-determination was uppermost, and before extending a hand they wanted to try everything that might save them from having to extend it… They saw that the act of independence of the 28th of October did not determine the borders, no authority challenged them to stop hoping, and they could still believe that the question of their self-determination was open and they would have a voice in the decision on the matter. Given all these causes one cannot call the actions of the Germans at the time treason. In this matter no law yet existed. There had as yet been no legal, international act incorporating them into the Czechoslovak state. Before the decision of the peace conference they were not legally the citizens of that state nor did the government later criminally prosecute them for any of their actions of the time since it knew that there could be no high treason where no state citizenship had yet been established."[37]

In the eyes of many Czech politicians (A. Rašín, who clearly never forgot the death sentence passed on him in 1916, was a particularly radical example), the situation confirmed the assessment of the Sudeten Germans contained in a report on Czecho-Slovakia discussed on the 16th of June 1919 by the committee of new states negotiating at the Paris Conference:

"The Germans in Bohemia have hitherto had a dominant influence on the state; they represent a highly developed and capable element and in the past

---

[36] Jaksch, W. *Cesta Evropy do Postupimi.* 61–63.
[37] Peroutka, F. *Budování státu I.* 128–129.

were a very aggressive population. It is clear that the prosperity and perhaps even the existence of this new state depends on the success with which it integrates Germans as citizens of good will. The huge extent of this task is entirely different in character from other minorities that the committee must consider and so deeply affects all institutions that it will evidently be best to leave the solution to the Czechs themselves."[38]

This text expresses in abbreviated and condensed form the feelings of resigned helplessness that seem to have afflicted most of those faced with tackling the complex web of national animosities and ethnic intolerance inherited by the successor states of the Habsburg Monarchy. The representatives of the victorious powers had a generally realistic view of their capacity to find solutions; they realised that their possibilities were very limited. Essentially it was clear that most of the successor states, including Czechoslovakia, were reproducing the ethnic problems that had brought about the fall of the Danubian Empire.

The Germans in Czechoslovakia were the largest and most advanced German minority in the states of Central and Eastern Europe.[39] They were a highly developed, industrious, professionally skilled and affluent group. Similarly they showed a high degree of discipline, and hard work, all of this encouraging a strong sense of duty to their ethnic group. The defeat of Germany deepened their fears of the increasing power of the Slav element and strengthened sentiments and romanticism that disdained the pragmatic values of civil society, which they believed liable to degenerate into egotism and opportunism. A sense of external threat had led them to develop a peculiar kind of escapism focused on the idealised national community/*Volksgemeinschaft*, supported by all the heroic virtues. R. Luža stresses that there was no one single form of Sudeten German thinking. Nonetheless, most of the German political leaders epitomized the latent nationalism that was always a part of any political movement among the Germans from the Czech lands. It was this emotional, aggressive nationalism of a somewhat provincial kind, stimulated by sublimated memories of past glories, that fanned Czech fears.[40]

The Sudeten Germans rejected the fully-fledged notion of the individual equality of citizens and insisted on the collective concept of the group rights of ethnic Germans in the sense of a community defined by a primordial common destiny – a *Volksgemeinschaft*. This basic conflict between two entirely different state-forming principles, the *civic* (promoted especially by T. G. Masaryk) and the *ethnic*, built into the very foundations of the independent CSR an explo-

[38] Wiskemann, E. *Czechs and Germans*. 93.
[39] In 1921 there were 513,000 Germans in Yugoslavia, 700,000 in Rumania in 1918 and 551,000 in Hungary in 1920. See Luža, R. 1964. *The Transfer of the Sudeten Germans*. New York University Press. 30.
[40] Ibidem.

sive charge that twenty years later was exploited by Nazi Germany to destroy a state that was not perfect, but provided on its territory a sufficiently democratic framework for the development of all its ethnic groups.

Democratic Reform of National-Ethnic Relations

In its search for a formulation of its relationship with the Bohemian Germans, the new Czecho-Slovakia was resolved to apply individual civic rights and other democratic principles, specifically universal, secret, equal and direct voting rights. Minorities were to be given favourable treatment by the principle of proportional representation instead of a purely majoritarian system.[41] Ideas on the position of Bohemian Germans were summarised in *Memorandum III* (*Mémoire III*), and later in similar terms in the note on the status of nationalities in the Czecho-Slovak Republic presented by Beneš on the 20th of May 1919 at the conference in Paris.

It was here that the first mention was made of a possible future arrangement along the lines of the Swiss Confederation. In view of the later frequent misinterpretation of this reference by Sudeten German authors, it is useful to cite the relevant passage of *Mémoire III*, where in Paragraph VI it speaks of the future position of the Germans of the Czechoslovak Republic: "The Republic of Czechoslovakia will be a perfectly democratic state, all elections there will be conducted by universal, direct and equal suffrage, all offices there will be open to all citizens, the language of national minorities will be permitted everywhere, no minority will be denied the right to their own schools, judges and courts. It is necessary to add that although they are aware that the Germans enjoyed huge privileges under the old regime, the Czechs have no intention of depriving the German population of e.g. its schools, universities, and its technical school, which in any case had few students before the war."

Beneš's promises in *Mémoire III* have often been attacked by German authors as deliberately deceitful, on the grounds that they were not fulfilled by the Czechoslovak state. Let us cite the key passage that has been subject to conflicting interpretations (original translation by K. Krofta):

"To sum up, the Germans in Bohemia should have the same rights as Czechoslovaks. German would be the second language of the country and the German population would never be subjected to any kind of oppression. The regime would be similar to the Swiss."[42]

---

[41] Kural, V. *Konflikt místo společenství.* 23.

[42] Krofta, K. 1939. *Z dob naší první republiky* [From the Times of Our First Republic]. Prague: Jan Laichter. 39–40.

In this context, Sudeten German publications (e.g. W. Jaksch or W. K. Turnwald) have often referred to the diaries of the American delegations expert D. H. Miller, which contain in several volumes all the documents, protocols and memoranda relating to the Paris peace negotiations.[43] On the theme of the future organisation of the Czechoslovak state Wilhelm Karl Turnwald cites the following passage from the diaries – supposedly a record of words spoken by Beneš in the course of the discussions of the Commission for National Minorities: "In the creation of the organs of the Czechoslovak state, the government to adopt as the basis the principles of the law on nationalities applied in the Swiss Republic. This will make the Czechoslovak Republic a kind of Switzerland, nevertheless with account taken of the special conditions of the Bohemian Lands."[44]

Beneš made this statement with the aim of convincing the representatives of the powers at the peace conference of the democratic character of the new state, but he did not neglect to stress the specific nature of the situation. With the expression "special conditions" he made it clear that in Czech conditions it was impossible to apply in full the model of the Swiss Confederation. The Swiss model was based on the different situation of every nationality having a support in a larger mother state in close proximity. Nor was Switzerland in the specific geopolitical situation of the Bohemian Lands, lying in the territory between Russia and Germany. Beneš's comparison was not a very happy one, as further events were to show.[45]

In political practice the ČSR fulfilled these promises only in part, but this was in no way the result of the bad faith of Beneš or Masaryk. V. Kural sees the failure to live up fully to these promises as a result of the role of Kramářian radicalism, but also of the way that the categorical rejection of the ČSR by Su-

---

[43]   Jaksch, W. *Cesta Evropy do Postupimi*. 67.

[44]   Miller, D. H. *My Diary at the Conference of Paris*. Vol. XIII. 96. Cited from Turnwald, W. K. *Renascence or Decline of Central Europe*. Jaksch refers to volumes XV-XVIII relating to the negotiations in Saint-Germain and Trianon, which only came out as late as 1935. On the theme of the "promises" Jaksch cites from a conversation of representatives of German activist parties at which he was supposedly present. Beneš allegedly said: "When we say that Switzerland will be a model for Czechoslovakia, or that the regime in Czechoslovakia will be similar to the Swiss: when we further say that we shall make Czechoslovakia into a certain kind of Switzerland, which, as is self-evident, will take into account the special conditions in Bohemia, and finally that it will be a regime significantly close to the Swiss regime, this does not mean the creation of a new Switzerland with identical institutions, but precisely, on the contrary, the creation of a state... which will adopt some main principles of the Swiss regime." Jaksch, W. *Cesta Evropy do Postupimi*. 160.

[45]   All the same in assessing the Versailles solution to international problems it is important not to succumb to a posteriori judgments. As a direct participant outstanding for his penetrating insights, David Hunter Miller writes in this context that, "The moral qualities of an act are to be judged as of its date, and not from subsequent events." Widenor, W. C. "The Construction of the American Interpretation", in *The Treaty of Versailles* (A Reassessment after 75 Years). 1998. Boemcke, M. et al. (ed.). German Historical Institute Washington/ Cambridge University Press. 547–548.

deten German politicians deepened mistrust on the Czech side.[46] Kural rejects the claim of deliberate deceit, instead considering the problem to be one of a formulation that was not fully thought out, but had a real basis.[47]

The failure to think the formulation through was basically a matter of neglecting the fact that the Swiss model would have meant federalisation, which no Czech political party had in its programme from the moment of decision for an independent state. On the other hand, the rational core of the Swiss analogy lay in the application of two principles: full democracy with just proportional representation and the principle of German self-government in 2–3 regions for which the word "cantons" was sometimes used. Combined with the assumption that German would be the second land language, the intended reforms could have been regarded as bearing a certain likeness to the Swiss constitution. The fact remains, however, that the content of *Mémoire III* remained unimplemented (largely due to the pressure of the Czech nationalist right) and that this later provided an excuse for attacks on E. Beneš, allegedly the guileful creator of a plan to deceive the Alliance politicians.[48]

The cantonal system as proposed by the Sudeten German leaders (each canton to have full governmental administrative autonomy, the different nationalities to be proportionately represented in the state according to their numbers, disputes to be decided by a constitutional court etc.) looks generally sensible even with the benefit of hindsight, and might theoretically have been an acceptable starting point for the incorporation of the Sudeten Germans into the CSR. But only on one condition, i.e. that these cantons would have wanted to remain in the union of the new republic. The Sudeten German politicians, however, ostentatiously rejected the CSR.[49] This was partly out of fear for their national/ethnic survival (fears that had been handed down from the preceding era of the monarchy), partly as a result of bitter disappointment at the German defeat and the collapse of a monarchy in which they had been part of the ruling

---

[46] Kural, V. *Konflikt místo společenství.* 24.

[47] Still it cannot be overlooked that the Map. no. 8 from the supplement to Memorandum no. 3 contained a sketched corridor of uninterrupted Czech settlement between from Ústí n. L. and Chomutov right up to the border, which did not correspond to reality. This map is often referred to in publications criticising the negotiators at the Paris Conference, e.g. Gordon, H. *Die Beneš-Denkschriften.* 216.

[48] Kural, V. *Konflikt místo společenství.* 24.

[49] For example the regional governor for the *Deutschböhmen* Rudolf Lodgman von Auen declared in this context in Innsbruck on the 8th of March 1919: "As far as the German-Czech problem is concerned, there are theoretically four possibilities: Deutschböhmen will 1) be annexed to the Czech state by declaration of the peace conference, 2) will entrust itself directly to the German Reich, 3) will become an independent state territory, or 4) will become part of the German-Austrian Republic. Incorporation into the Czech state is rejected by all Germans, and if the Czechs believe that it will be possible to hold down a whole nation of 3.5 million people and permanently force them into one state against their will, then they are definitely making a mistake. If the Entente assigns the *Deutschböhmen* and Sudetens to the Czechs, then in the enslaved lands it will experience a German irredenta of such power that the Czechs will be amazed." Hoffmann, R. J. – Harasko, A. *Odsun.* pp. 569.

Austro-German nation, but also the loss of the vision of the expected German hegemony in Central Europe.

The idea of a cantonal system was actually a kind of dream, part of the lingering illusion of democratic reform of the Habsburg Monarchy, but also a matter of the momentary need to offer the representatives of the powers a plausible way out of a complicated situation. The Swiss model was not in reality applicable in the conditions of the Bohemian Lands. Cantonal organisation could not have resolved the position of the Czech coal miners in the otherwise German region of North-West Bohemia, or the position of the German minorities in the Moravian towns.[50] Even more crucial, the internal stability of the Swiss state rested on the fact that each of its national groups had the support of a linguistically and culturally "kindred" state (France, Germany, Italy) in close territorial proximity. The balance of the cultural and political influence of these neighbouring states and the national/ethnic groups associated with them made long term stable political conditions possible for the Swiss Confederation. In the field of foreign policy the long-term Swiss policy of neutrality was an expression of this unique situation.

The exposed inter-war position of Czechoslovakia was such that comparison with Switzerland is more or less an irrelevance. Apart from that, Tomáš G. Masaryk famously asked for fifty years of peace and quiet to enable Czechoslovakia to work on the full development of its internal organisation and consolidation of its international position. The republic was to be granted a mere twenty years, the last ten already compromised by the tension and unrest caused in Central Europe by the rise of Nazism in Germany and authoritarian regimes in other direct neighbours of the CSR (Hungary, Poland).

The basic condition for a qualitatively new, less conflict-ridden and more permanent Central European order was the long-term development of democracy in neighbouring Germany – something for which Masaryk and his ruling circle longed with all their hearts, something on which they counted for the future, but something which ultimately did not happen. E. Kubů argues that what turned out to be crucial for the fate of the republic was unfortunately not territorially distant alliances, but relations with neighbouring states that cultivated the politics of territorial demands, with Germany playing the key role. He shares the view that from the outset Masaryk and Beneš grasped the problematic nature of the Versailles settlement, and in the same way understood the content and significance of the Locarno Treaty of 1925). Despite repeated attempts to maintain correct relations with Germany dating from the very first days of the existence of the CSR, these relations continued to be marked by

---

50   Wiskemann, E. *Czechs and Germans.* 93.

a tension that the German ambassador in Prague, W. Koch (1921–35) characterised as "an instinctive mutual rejection", and the Czechoslovak ambassador in Berlin, V. Mastný (1932–39) described as follows: "despite an externally consistently maintained official correctness and mutual assurance of wishes for improved relations, tension continues to prevail, with almost constant minor and serious differences, incidents and diplomatic protests."[51]

It proved possible to sustain a certain balance of power in Central Europe only during the 1920s. In 1928, the intermezzo of Beneš's strenuous efforts to reach rapprochement with Germany effectively ended.[52] The Hungarian government had adopted the method of "neither war nor peace" in regard to the CSR" and of pushing for the revision of the "unjust peace treaties" – a policy that constantly increased the tension in relations between the states of Central Europe and undermined the position of Czechoslovakia on the international scene.[53] Even in the period of relative stability there were already signs of potential threat to the fragile Central European equilibrium. For example in the spring of 1925 there was renewed talk of the possibility of a union between Austria and Germany.[54]

The sharpness with which the Czechoslovak foreign minister Beneš rejected this possibility[55] shows the urgency of his fears of a direct danger to Czechoslovak state interest. If to this international context we add the internal dimension of the hostile attitude of politicians and publicists from the ranks of the Bohemian Germans to the new state (which most of them regarded as imposed on them by force), it is obvious that comparisons with Switzerland are entirely beside the point. In the light of this development we can say that the analogy

---

[51] Kubů, E. "Zátěž dějinného dědictví, chybné kalkulace, osudová neschopnost, či neúprosná logika vývoje?" [The Burden of Historical Inheritance, Mistaken Calculations, Fateful Incapacity or the Inexorable Logic of Development?]. *Soudobé dějiny* 2–3/1995. 254–268. The author of this overview of the forms of foreign policy of interwar Czechoslovakia highlights the importance of the fact that the axiom of Czechoslovak foreign policy was a friendly relationship with the great Western democracies, which were, however, gradually politically and economically abandoning Central Europe.

[52] Klimek, A. – Kubů, E. 1995. *Československá zahraniční politika 1918–1938* [Czechoslovak Foreign Policy 1918–1938]. Prague: ISE. 57.

[53] Dejmek, J. 2002. *Československo – jeho sousedé a velmoci ve XX. století* [Czechoslovakia – its Neighbours and the Great Powers in the 20th Century]. Prague: SEP. 201–202.

[54] Břach, R. 1996. *Československo a Evropa v polovině dvacátých let* [Czechoslovakia and Europe in the Mid-1920s]. Litomyšl: Paseka. 181–182. "This was certainly the main reason why the Allies blocked Austria's road to Germany by the Treaty of St. Germain and Germany's road to Austria by the Versailles Treaty. Shifting the German frontier to the Danube would have substantially changed political conditions in Central Europe, and clearly to the disadvantage of the then CSR (a common Hungarian-German border, the intensification of German pressure on South-Eastern Europe, the centrifugal tendency of the Sudeten areas). There was no point in even talking about it." Ibidem.

[55] E. Beneš strictly refused the idea of Austrian anschluss as a threat at the least to the economic independence of the CSR and as its political encirclement by the German element. Dejmek, J. *Československo – jeho sousedé a velmoci*. 57.

used by Beneš in 1919 was unfortunate, but that he was speaking in good faith on the assumption that it would be possible to progressively fulfil this vision in a post-war democratic Europe. It was not his fault that events took a different turn.

The question of how far the views expressed by the Sudeten German politicians can be regarded as representative of the opinions of the German-speaking inhabitants of the Bohemian borderlands seems still, however, to be an open one (as a number of authors including V. Kural, J. W. Brügel and M. Alexander have suggested)[56] M. Alexander, for example, draws attention to a gap between words and deeds:

"The verbal rejection of the new state by politicians and political writers was generally at odds with the cooperation of Germans and Czechs at the communal or to a great extent the economic level." J. W. Brügel points out that the results of the first local government elections show that the militant attitude of Lodgman, distancing himself from the CSR, was supported by only a small minority of the German-speaking population of the borderlands, but it had the important effect of forcing the other German parties to take nationalist rhetoric into account when competing for votes in the Sudeten areas.[57]

The inhabitants of the Sudeten territories were exhausted by war, and worn down by food shortages, the wartime economy and human losses at the fronts of the First World War. It was therefore natural for the ordinary citizen or industrialist in the Sudeten areas to ask himself whether, despite all sympathies for great national aims, it was not more advantageous to join a new Czechoslovakia that enjoyed the advantages of alliance with the victorious powers rather than German states burdened by war reparations that were undermining their economies and by the stigma of starting the war. It was mainly these pragmatic considerations that led as early as 1919 to the appearance in embryonic form of future German activist (as opposed to separatist) parties willing to work with the new regime "on the basis of the [new] state".

Representatives of the larger German parties started to express some willingness to co-operate immediately following the signing of the peace agreements in May and June 1919 in the light of recognition of the historical borders of the

---

[56] Characteristic examples of resistance to the new republic include the text of a telegram sent by the so-called land government of German Czechs/*Deutschböhmen* to President Wilson via the Swedish government on the 21st of November 1918. It includes the passage, "In the name of the two and a half million Germans in Bohemia who with appeal to the right of self-determination consider themselves a constitutive part of the *German Republic,* we submit the most resolute protest against the oppression to which our territory has been exposed by the armed forces of the Czech states (sic)". Signed in the name of and as authorised by the National Representation of the German Czechs by leaders of all the important political parties in the Sudetenland – Dr Lodgman, Seliger, Maixner. *Odsun – dokumentace.* 502–504.

[57] Brügel, J. W. 1967. *Tschechen und Deutsche 1918–1938.* München: Nymphenburger Verlagshandlung. 111.

Bohemian Lands. Franz Křepek of the German Agrarian Party declared himself in Litoměřice in favour of collaboration between the Czech and German farmers, Prof. Mayr-Harting of the Christian Social People's Party responded positively to repeated Czech appeals for the co-option of German members to the provisional National Assembly, while Josef Seliger appealed in a major public speech for the creation of policy "on the basis of the [new] state". The embryo of later German "activism" [i.e. willingness to take a full part in Czechoslovak political life] thus appeared soon after it had become clear that the Czechoslovak state, and not the plan for a German common state, had won international recognition.[58]

The direct neighbourhood of the German-speaking lands of Austria and Germany was the defining characteristic of the Czechoslovak situation. Emotionally loaded ideas of a Pan-Slav solidarity (for example Kramář's modified version of Pan-Slavism) in which the new state might find support turned out to be unrealistic given the course of the Revolution in Russia. In any case, the pro-Western orientation of Masaryk and Beneš prevailed in setting the course for Czechoslovak foreign policy.

The peace conference in fact accepted the Czechoslovak proposals even without the "Swiss promise", since it required only that the CSR sign the international agreement on the protection of national minorities. Despite the repeated appeals of the politicians of the Sudeten Germans, who never ceased to send complaints on conditions in the Czechoslovak Republic from Vienna to Paris (and later to Geneva), the peace conference did not regard national minorities as independent legal subjects. It required on their behalf neither autonomy nor the federalisation of the state to which they belonged. The Sudeten Germans refused to be reconciled to this, however, for in the *right to self-determination* they saw a principle to which they appealed with the clear intention of avoiding incorporation into an unwanted state formation.[59] It was only when the peace conference had finally made its decision that they slowly, reluctantly, with con-

---

[58]   Ibidem. 109. Nonetheless, on the 28th of November 1918, Seliger in Vienna at a meeting of the provisional land assembly for Deutschböhmen had still been proclaiming that, "We, Social Democrats, recognise no solution of the German question in Bohemia other than through the right to self-determination of the German nation in Bohemia. We reject any other solution and any other decision, we shall accept no other... *Odsun – dokumentace*. 531.

[59]   See e.g. the standpoint of the so-called Sudeten Government issued on the 18th of December 1918 in Opava: The Sudeten Province and its government has been set up as part of the German-Austrian state because the German people in its closed (unmixed?) areas of settlement declares and demands as its inalienable right to establish its state allegiance and state form in free self-determination, this having been been repeatedly and solemnly confirmed by all warring states in the meaning of Wilson's proposals. For this reason the government of the Sudeten province considered the military occupation of towns and sites in closed German settlement areas to be unauthorised and protests against it. *Odsun – dokumentace*. 513.

stant complaints and above all under the pressure of economic interests, accepted the new republic.

In real political practice it soon became clear that the *principle of self-determination facilitates and reproduces the development of situations of conflict* in which two national groups claiming the right come into collision. A preceding conflict is not solved but only reproduced in the altered frame of the new state. Civic loyalty to the undesired state can be exacted only with difficulty, if at all. On the basis of the first unhappy post-war experiences of such situations, the *Minorities Section of the Secretariat for the Protection of Minorities at the League of Nations* adopted a resolution to insist that not only should the civil rights of members of minorities be respected, but that members of minorities had a reciprocal duty of loyalty to the given state.

"The commission, fully acknowledging the fundamental right of minorities to the protection of the *League of Nations* from any oppression, insists on the duty binding on minorities to co-operate with the nation state to which they now belong."[60]

Unusually, we find ourselves in agreement with the well-known proponent of Sudeten German separatism in the Bohemian Lands, Lodgman von Auen, when in 1938 he made the following pregnantly expressed comment:

"Yet let us not overlook that the right to self-determination has its limits and breaks down where one national group's right to self-determination contradicts another's – especially where the two groups are interknit without clear lines of division."

The main pitfall of the right to self-determination emerges in a centralised state where its application means the sacrifice of the smaller national entity. The post-war attempt to establish the borders of the states of Central and Eastern Europe on an ethnic basis inevitably meant exchange and evacuation of population groups. National minorities constituted a permanent source of internal disturbances and a permanent temptation to interference by external powers.[61]

What was in fact decisive for Czech success in winning the right to self-determination was the historical situation – the fact that Austria-Hungary with Germany had lost the war and that in their consequences for international law the constitutional demands of the Czechs were more or less in line with the ideas of the victors on the new organisation of the European balance of power. Specifically we could mention the French foreign policy goal of creating a belt of buffer states, a *cordon sanitaire*, across Europe, to hold back the growing influence of Bolshevik Russia.

---

[60]   Peroutka, F. 1991. *Budování státu II* [The Building of the State II]. Prague: Lidové noviny. 1607.
[61]   Cobban, A. *Nation State and National Self-determination*. 262.

Civic Nation versus Ethnic Community

A detailed examination of Wilson's concept of national self-determination and the way it was applied in Europe in the framework of the Versailles System, highlights its "impracticality" or very limited usefulness in the creation of states with frontiers not identical with ethnic and linguistic borders.[62] The victorious powers had no intention of applying the right to self-determination at the expense of their empires; in the demarcation of new borders it was impossible to avoid creating new minorities; and the most important obstacle was in any case the impossibility of defining the conditions that a national/ethnic group needed to fulfil in order to qualify for rights of self-determination.[63]

The successor states that arose on the ground plan of the Habsburg Monarchy were just as multi-ethnic and potentially charged with national conflicts (Czechoslovakia, Poland, Rumania and Yugoslavia). Thus Germans, Slovene and Croatian minorities in Italy were now in the position of Italian minorities in the former Habsburg Empire. E. J. Hobsbawm goes so far as to claim that the only difference was that the territory of the new states was smaller and "oppressed peoples" were now called "oppressed minorities".[64]

This is not an entirely accurate judgement, however, especially in the case of Czechoslovakia. There was definitely a clash over the priority of one group's right to self-determination over another's, but it is important to note that while the Czech right prejudiced the Sudeten German right, it did not threaten the German right as a whole, while in the opposite case of Greater Germany (what the Sudeten Germans were in effect demanding) the German right of self-determination fundamentally challenged the existence of Czechoslovakia.[65] Sudeten German writers have generally refused to take this fact on board. Jaksch for example claims that, "The decision was taken at Versailles to weaken Germany, but the very existence of Germany was not affected. By contrast the dividing up of Austria-Hungary was a decision on the overall structure of Europe. In the overall frame of European history it was of far-reaching importance that the principle of the linguistic nation was elevated as the decisive factor for the creation of states."[66]

---

[62] Hobsbawm, E. J. 1990. *Nations and Nationalism since 1780*. Cambridge: Cambridge University Press. Mainly Chapter V – The Apogee of Nationalism (1918–1950).

[63] Cobban, A. *Nation State and National Self-determination*. 68.

[64] Hobsbawm, E. J. *Nations and Nationalism since 1780*. 132–133.

[65] Kural, V. *Konflikt místo společenství*. 28.

[66] Jaksch, W. *Cesta Evropy do Postupimi*. In this context A. J. Toynbee wrote, "In Central and Eastern Europe the growing consciousness of nationality did not fix on traditional borders or new geographical conditions, but almost exclusively on mother tongue" in "The World after the Peace Conference". *Survey of International Affairs 1939–1946 Hitler's Europe*. 1954. Toynbee, A. J. – Toynbee, V. M. (eds.). London. 18.

What such a view ignores is that the Allied powers were seeking to apply the principle of the civic nation rather than simply the linguistic nation (and not the principle of the nation as an ethnic tribal entity defined in terms of blood and common destiny), nor were they interested in supporting the establishment of a large common state for German-speakers in Central Europe. France in particular had an extremely strong interest in creating an East European alliance system composed of strong nation states. The French position was the result of long-term strategic thinking on the distribution of forces on the post-war European continent. Indebted, with its earlier alliance system in ruins because of the Bolshevik Revolution, and weakened by its own considerable material and human losses, France was keen to minimise any prospect that it might once again have to confront a strong Germany with an undamaged industrial base and functioning transport communications, let alone do so single-handed. Furthermore, there was every reason to assume that Germany (like Hungary and partly Austria too) would be strongly motivated to strive for revision of the Versailles system. Both the British and French continued to fear the concept of *Mitteleuropa*, and of course T. G. Masaryk and E. Beneš had the same anxieties.

The incorporation of the Sudeten Germans and other border territories with German populations into the CSR was made definitive only with the Treaty on Austria signed on the 10th of September 1919 in Saint-Germain. Sudeten German separatism and unrealistic Sudeten demands on the new republic (demands which did not respect the international context in the application of the right to self-determination) fatefully tainted the relationship between Czechs and Germans in the new state. D. Salomon writes that, "In the circumstances, the Sudeten Germans considered this incorporation [into the new state] a violation of their right to self-determination and so could not recognise Czechoslovakia as their political homeland."[67]

D. H. Miller in his diaries likewise expressed scepticism about the union of Czechs and Germans in the new state, giving various reasons including the specific situation of the border regions of the Bohemian Lands. He wrote that its would be absurd to leave the Czech border with their mountains in German hands, but that the German population there was, "compact in its distribution, bitterly hostile to Slav neighbours, with German capitalists and a German nobility settled along borders with Saxons, Bavarians and Austrians with whom the population sympathises".[68]

---

[67] Salomon, D. "Od rozpadu podunajské monarchie do konce druhé světové války (1918–1945)" [From the Collapse of the Danubian Monarchy to the End of the Second World War (1918–1945)], in *Tisíc let česko-německých vztahů* [A Thousand Years of Czech-German Relations]. 1995. Bauer, F. (ed.). Prague: Panevropa. 191.

[68] Wiskemann, E. *Czechs and Germans*. 92.

On the Czech side the predominant feeling was of distrust for the German inhabitants who had threatened the integrity of the state at its birth. Representatives of the Germans were not invited (with reference to their earlier negative attitudes) to assist in drawing up the Constitution that decided on their status. The constitution was adopted on the 29th of February 1920 by the Revolutionary National Assembly, in which representatives of the Sudeten Germans refused to take part, just as they refused to fill the offered post of minister without portfolio.

This was the beginning of the end for any ideas of applying the Swiss model of ethnic coexistence in Central European conditions. The 1920s in fact brought some stabilisation in relations between Czechs and Sudeten Germans, largely as a result of the economic boom (which encouraged German activist parties willing to participate in national politics), but a latent tension remained, only to emerge again following the start of the great economic crisis at the turn of the decade.[69] Then, with the rise of Nazism in neighbouring Germany, the downward slide of Czech-German relations in the historic lands gathered ever more obvious momentum.

At this point, many Reich German organisations supporting cooperation with groups of ethnic Germans in Central and Eastern Europe emerged to exploit the period of negativism and their feverish activities soon brought results. Given that the development of external attitudes to the Sudeten German question in the course of the 1930s played a crucial role in the lead up to the tragic breaking-point in the autumn of 1938, we shall be considering its history in detail in the next chapter. After everything that had taken place between Czech and Germans at the birth of the independent Czechoslovakia, there is a prophetic edge to the sceptical words with which Emanuel Rádl, ended his book *Válka Čechů s Němci* [The War of the Czechs and Germans] in 1928:

"In this book I have shown the practical consequences of the error that has made race, tribe, and the state as it were the god of the modern age. The relationship between Czechs and Germans is so serious a phenomenon that its analysis might bring us an understanding of the great crisis in which humankind finds itself today. The way in which this problem is resolved will be decisive for the future not just of the Czechoslovak Republic but of Central and Eastern Europe altogether."[70]

---

[69] Rádl took a sceptical view of the situation of the CSR in the 1920s: "Today's joint government of Czechs and Germans is providing calmer conditions for communication and the solution of all kinds of important immediate national/ethnic issues; but it is only a ceasefire, in which both sides are holding to their principles in order to hurl themselves at each other at the next opportunity." Rádl, E. 1993. *Válka Čechů s Němci* [The War of the Czechs and Germans]. Prague: Melantrich. 9.

[70] Ibidem. 273.

I cannot quite agree, however, with Rádl's claim that the "great dilemma of war and peace between Czechs and Germans is not solved by the organisation of our state" I believe that the independent Czechoslovakia did in fact provide a sufficiently democratic framework in which the Czech-German relationship might eventually have sought and found an alternative to the previous period of ethnic intolerance. Unfortunately this historic "window of opportunity" turned out to be too fleeting for its potential to be realised.

Rádl's defence of the ČSR, written to persuade the Sudeten Germans of the need to defend a state that was also their homeland, is cited only rarely. It is as follows: "States based on ethnography are only Central European and manifestly transitional phenomena. Czechoslovakia is in no way a state of this kind. I am not thinking merely of the large minorities of our state. [I mean] that the history of Czechoslovakia also contradicts the conceptions of the racial theorists... Czechs demanded independence not in the name of the Czech race, but in the name of the freedom of the historic lands, i.e. in the name of a political ideal... To emphasise this fact is in no way to contradict the interest of the Sudeten Germans. The so-called "self-determination of nations" in the German sense, according to which nations understood as national tribes are set against "governments" as the true organic foundation of the state has remained a German fantasy, destined to extinction because it failed to understand the existence of the state."[71]

---

[71] Rádl, E. 2003. *O německé revoluci. K politické ideologii sudetských Němců* [On the German Revolution. The Political Ideology of the Sudeten Germans]. Prague: Masarykův ústav AV ČR. 118–119.

Poster advertising the Patriotic Day event organised by the DNSAP party
in Chomutov (then in the Sudetenland) in June 1925.

4 Germans in the New Republic

In Central and South-East Europe, the enshrinement of the rights of national minorities in the Versailles Treaty brought many improvements as compared to the situation before the First World War, especially in terms of recognition of the democratic civic principle of protection of the individual member of a national minority. Nonetheless, no one could claim that the problem had been fully solved. In a number of states, pressure continued for the assimilation of national groups and ethnic unification (or homogenisation) of the population. Furthermore, the legal anchorage of relatively wide-ranging rights for minorities in the cultural and political sphere did not preclude situations in which the demands of a minority (above all a minority with autonomist or irredentist aspirations), could threaten the functioning of a state organism or even the very existence of a state.[1]

Both Masaryk and Beneš were aware that the successful resolution of the problem of minority rights for all ethnic groups was a matter of life-or-death importance for the new republic, especially given the context of the autonomist ambitions of the Bohemian Germans. Another factor was pressure from the victorious powers, who required guarantees for ethnic minorities in return for recognition of the sovereignty of the new states. The representatives of some new states (Poland, Rumania) tried to resist the pressure and push for a definition of obligations universally binding on all the states of the international

---

[1] Šatava, L. 1994. *Národnostní menšiny v Evropě* [National Minorities in Europe]. Prague: Ivo Železný. 19.

community rather than unilateral undertakings.[2] Woodrow Wilson stood firm, however, declaring that the great powers could not afford to guarantee a division of territories that they did not believe to be just, nor could they agree to leave areas of potential unrest unaddressed, for these might disturb future world peace.[3]

Among the series of treaties and other sources of international law created at the Paris Peace Conference was the so-called Small (minority) Treaty binding on the CSR and signed as a "Treaty between the leading allied and affiliated powers and Czechoslovakia", on the 10th of September 1919 in Saint-Germain-en-Laye. Some of its provisions became part of, or otherwise embodied in, the Czechoslovak constitution. The demands of the treaty were not very extensive (they did not greatly restrict the republic's freedom of manoeuvre) and the efficacy of the system of protection in the framework of the League of Nations was very limited.

Czechoslovakia was part of a new map of Central Europe in which – as regards ethnic minorities – it anticipated support above all from France. France regarded special provisions on the protection of minorities as an interference in the internal affairs of states, and in fact it was the other great powers that finally got the treaty through, with the United States (the attitude of the delegation fundamentally influenced by Wilson's idealism), Britain and Italy being particularly active.

All the same, many politicians of the alliance continued to regard the new order and successor states with distinct distrust (this was particularly the case with the British representatives). In negotiations on the status of the League of Nations there were sharp disputes on the question of minorities. Originally it had been planned that the Charter of the League would include an article allowing for territorial changes based on the principle of national self-determination.[4] This idea was abandoned, however, once new frontiers that did not respect ethnic boundaries in full had actually been created. The problem was the subject of negotiations in the Supreme Council, in which Wilson demanded a provision protecting Jews and Germans in Poland. Indeed, provisions relating to Jews might be seen as a certain index of the faith of the great powers in individual states. Various Jewish organisations had a major influence on the creation of international law protection for minorities; they found support and

2   Broklová, E. 1992. *Československá demokracie 1918–1938* [Czechoslovak Democracy 1918–1938]. Prague: SLON. 69.

3   Peška, Z. 1932. *Národní menšiny a Československo* [National Minorities and Czechoslovakia]. Bratislava. 38. Peška, Z. 1929. "Otázka národnostních menšin na pařížské konferenci" [The Question of National Minorities at the Paris Conference]. *Zahraniční politika*. 1168–1182.

4   Petráš, R. "Mezinárodněprávní ochrana menšin po první světové válce" [The International-Legal Protection of Minorities after the First World War]. *Historický obzor* I.–II./2000. 33.

sympathy in President Wilson and Colonel House, who later did the most to push through protection for minorities, having been influenced *inter alia* by awareness of the bad position of Jews in Rumania (these had been leaving the country en masse before the outbreak of war and finding a refuge in the USA).

A committee for new states (known as the Minorities Commission) was set up with the task of negotiating obligations on the protection of minorities with the allies (Poland, the CSR, Rumania, the Kingdom of Slovenes, Croats and Serbs). The minority articles were to be included in the wording of the peace agreements, and the first negotiations of this kind were with Poland. Despite inevitable problems, the draft agreement was completed on the 14th of May 1919 and submitted to the Supreme Council and Polish delegation. All the other peace agreements including the agreement with the CSR were drawn up on this model.

The treaty of the 10th of September 1919 definitively incorporated the Sudeten Germans into the CSR. In Article 57 of this treaty Czechoslovakia undertook to "adopt in a special agreement provisions for the protection of the interests of those inhabitants of the republic who differ from the majority of the population by race, language or religion".

First and foremost, these provisions were a matter of Czechoslovak obligations arising from the Paris peace treaties themselves. The Revolutionary National Assembly adopted into its constitutional charter, and in some cases its constitutional laws, a number of regulations from the Treaty of St. Germain, thus fulfilling the obligation stipulated in Article 1 of this treaty that these articles be recognised as "fundamental law". The position of national minorities was then further governed by a number of other regulations.[5]

The position of Germans in the state was codified in the constitution passed on the 29th of February 1920 by the Revolutionary National Assembly, a legislative body that contained no German representatives because the latter had refused to take part in it. V. Kural argues that this act, the second unilateral measure after the actual founding of the CSR, seriously reduced the political credit of the new state, but it must be stressed that its unilateralism was a reaction to the secession of the German territories and German refusal to co-operate in creating the new state even after the signing of the peace treaty. In his farewell to the Austrian Parliament on the 24th of September 1919, Lodgman von Auen had declared that the Sudeten Germans would never give up their struggle for self-determination.[6]

---

[5]   Kocích, M. "K mezinárodněprávním aspektům ochrany národnostních menšin v předmnichovské republice" [On International Law Aspects of the Protection of National Minorities in the Pre-Munich Republic]. *Právněhistorické studie* 21/1978. Prague: Academia. 73–84.

[6]   Kural, V. *Konflikt místo společenství*. 30.

The Sudeten leaders had only recognised the new state *via facti* as late as the 20th of December 1919, and immediately started to demand a chance to co-operate in drawing up the new constitution, but their rhetoric left no one in any doubt that their internal aversion to the enforced state had not abated. Distrust on the Czech side, fuelled by Czech fears of German autonomist and federalist conceptions leading to close bonds with Germany and Austria, was likewise an important factor. In an atmosphere in which nationalism affected every issue, the space for cooperation between the two ethnic leaderships was very limited indeed.

The atmosphere of Czech-German relations in the initial days of the republic was summed up by the otherwise moderate prime minister V. Tusar: "There was almost no hope of agreement between Czechs and Germans on the constitution. There was no bridge between the prepared drafts of the constitution and the autonomist plans that every German politician and every German magazine was seething with at the time. The contradiction between Czech and German aspirations was insuperable: the Czechs wanted to unify the state, the Germans to separate themselves as much as possible from the Czechs."[7]

Ultimately the constitution of the new republic was forced on the German minority, and this was certainly not a good investment for the future. The Sudeten German movement of the 1930s was to exploit this fact with a range of arguments both in the domestic and international context.

The position of the Germans was regulated by the constitution in the framework of a state conceived in centralist, unitarist terms. Autonomy (with the special exception of Ruthenia, Sub-Carpathian Ukraine) was rejected as was federalisation. The introduction and application of universal and equal voting rights allowed the Germans to obtain 25.5% in the Assembly of Deputies and 26% in the Senate.

The way that the Czechoslovak Constitutional Charter (par. 106/2) formulated the matter was to state that all inhabitants were to enjoy full and uncondi-

---

[7] Ibidem. 32. The polarised atmosphere is also apparent for example from a passage in the draft answer of the government to the wording of a protocol submitted by the German deputies and senators to the League of Nations, in which they accused the Czechoslovak state of oppression: "If the German deputies and senators, elected on the basis of Czechoslovak electoral regulations and the Czechoslovak Constitution – German deputies and senators who accepted election in accordance with the constitution and Czechoslovak electoral laws and took their seats in the National Assembly of Czechoslovakia, claim that they do not accept either the constitutional or other laws of Czechoslovakia, this testifies only to the fact that they do not want to engage in real cooperation with the Czechoslovak nation… it is just another proof of the fact Germans have no sense of the equality and solidarity of nations and that their policies have until now been dominated in first place by a conviction of racial superiority and consequent attempts to achieve supremacy over other nations." Harna, J. – Šebek, J. 2002. *Státní politika vůči německé menšině v období konsolidace politické moci v Československu v letech 1918–1920* [State policy towards the German minority in the period of the consolidation of political power 1918–1920]. Prague: Historický ústav AV ČR. 344.

tional protection of their life and liberty regardless of their origin, state citizenship, language, race or religion. According to par. 128 all citizens of the CSR regardless of these criteria were equal and enjoyed full political rights. These provisions were further strengthened in par. 134 by the prohibition of forced assimilation (de-ethnicisation). These principles of the constitution were the basis for further provisions and legal norms that legally secured for Czechoslovak citizens equal rights to access to public services, offices, ranks/titles, the performance of any trade and occupation, the right to found their own schools with education in their ethnic language at their own expense, as well as "ethnic" humanitarian and religious institutions.[8]

Although this study is not specially focussed on the international law context of the Sudeten German question, it will be helpful for our later analysis of Sudeten German demands if we briefly list the obligations to protect national minorities that the CSR accepted and that it fulfilled.

Forced assimilation was prohibited. The constitution stipulated the equality of all state citizens of the Czechoslovak Republic in regard to civil and political rights, access to public service, offices and ranks, the performance of trades or occupation, and the use of any language in private relations, in matters of religion, in the press and any kind of publications or in public assemblies of the people. Citizens also had the right "consistent with practical possibilities" to use their language both aurally and in writing before the courts. Also guaranteed was the right to found schools with education in the national language, and humanitarian and religious institutions also using the national language.

Ethnicity was further safeguarded by Paragraph 1 on the protection of freedom in assemblies and a provision against the dismissal of employees on the basis of their national/ethnic identity. Legal protection against assimilation was applied in relation to school children and there were criminal penalties for incitement to hatred or violence against an ethnic group, religion or race.[9]

The theoretical constitutional framework of legal safeguards and the democratic rights of national minorities fulfilled the requirements of the Paris treaties and ranked Czechoslovak national minority law among the best. The practical fulfilment of the letter of the law had some weaknesses, however, to which V. Kural draws attention. He sees a very serious shortcoming in the fact that the

---

[8] Kural, V. *Konflikt místo společenství*. 33. Extensive documents relating to the subject are to be found in the edition of of sources Harna, J. – Šebek, J. *Státní politika*. 317–344. A full exposition of the standpoints and ideas of the creators of the new state on the extent and content of rights for national minorities can be found in the Supplement no. 2 – Draft response of the Czechoslovak government to a protocol of the German deputies and senators of the National Assembly of the Czechoslovak Republic to the League of Nations. Prepared for discussion by Ministerial Committee 31st October 1920.

[9] For more detail see Broklová, E. *Československá demokracie 1918–1938*. 69–72. Kural, V. *Konflikt místo společenství*. 32–34.

very term "národnost" (ethnicity/nationality), was not precisely defined. With appeal to the expert on nationality law Dr. Sobota,[10] he concludes that the legal regulation of relations between two or more nationalities/ethnic groups assumes that "the concept of nation be consistently described", but that in Czechoslovak law "this unfortunately is not the case". "Czechoslovak law did not develop a precise definition of nationality,"[11] and this theoretical problem had effects in practise, where mother tongue was generally considered the main external mark of an individual's nationality (with a secondary role for other criteria such as nationality of parents, etc.).

Another related shortcoming was the reduction of national/ethnic rights to individual civil rights, i.e. entirely inadequate respect for collective rights. Just as there existed no definition of nationality, so there existed no systematic lo-cal registers of nationality that might have formed a basis for defining national collectivities and been used for purposes of self-government. The data on na-tional/ethnic identity derived from censuses therefore remained just a list of individuals without further significance.[12]

The individual remained the alpha and omega of Czechoslovak nationality law and this purely individualistic conception excluded the possibility of re-form in the direction of autonomy or federalisation without change to the con-stitution. It was a conception that provided a constitutional guarantee of the administrative and territorial integrity of the state, but it restricted any future "manoeuvring space", that might have allowed for an alternative Czech policy in response to the demands of national minorities, especially the German mi-nority that constantly sought a larger share in national and local government. It remains an open question, however, whether a more positive response to these demands in the first years of the new republic would have been enough to prevent the later mass inclination of Bohemian Germans to the Henlein movement. Despite a certain calming of relations between Czechs and Ger-mans in the course of the 1920s, the potential for ethnically mobilising conflict remained. It continued to smoulder, and unfortunately, was to be reignited by changing circumstances.

Although it was clear that international law influenced internal state law at the very birth of the first law of the new republic, the Constitution of the new Czechoslovakia passed in 1920 did not set out any principles to govern the re-lationship between international and domestic law. J. Malenovský argues that this was because at the beginning of the 20th century the tendency to the inter-nationalisation of the life of states was not yet sufficiently marked for legisla-

[10] Sobota, E. 1931. *Das tschechoslowakische Nationalitätenrecht*. Prague. 43.
[11] Ibidem. 52–53.
[12] Kural, V. *Konflikt místo společenství*. 34.

tive bodies of the time to regard it as really essential to take a position on the relationship between the two spheres of law.

From the point of view of the later development of the Sudeten German question in the new CSR, however, it is obvious that internationalisation of the question was to play a key role, and that Czechoslovak law was not drawn up in a way adequate to the pitfalls of the situation. J. Malenovský comments: "Central Europe, in which the CSR was born, was a region with strong constitutionalist traditions. It is a territory where ethnically different groups have historically lived side by side, with one group or another having very often sought to identify with self-centred values that rationalised its right to self-determination, and to enshrine these in a constitution. This exclusivist angle of vision reduced the possibilities of international law, which with its universally binding rules tends on the contrary to erode the specificity of the ethnic/national group. In addition, international law had entered the life of Czechoslovakia as it were uninvited, as a sovereignty defining a group of obligations that had to be accepted if the new state was to come into existence and be internationally recognised."[13]

The Language Law

In line with the prevalent European legal approaches to the problem, Czechoslovak law considered language right to be the most fundamental and important mark of national identity. The main principles of Czechoslovak law included the declaration of the Czechoslovak language as the official language of the republic, a provision explicitly permitted by the wording of the St. Germain Treaty although the latter did not in fact speak of a "state" language. According to some authors (Z. Peška, E. Broklová), Czechoslovak law went further than the provisions of the minority treaty; for example while the treaty spoke only of the use of languages before courts of law, Czechoslovak law extended this use to other organs of state.[14]

The language law was adopted together with the Constitution of the Czechoslovak Republic on the 29th of February 1920, and legally enshrined the precedence of the Czechoslovak people (nation) in regard to language and hence the national character of the Czechoslovak Republic. The law guaranteed to every citizen the right to use any language in private relations, in matters of religion, in the press and in any kind of publications or at public assemblies of the peo-

---

[13]   Malenovský, J. 1993. *Mezinárodní právo veřejné* [International Public Law]. Brno: Doplněk 69.
[14]   Broklová, E. *Československá demokracie 1918–1938*. 71.

ple. The Czechoslovak language law was directly derived from the obligations incurred by signature of the Paris Treaty for the protection of minorities. The provisions of this treaty were then taken over into the treaty between Austria and the CSR of June 1920, from which they were consequently taken over into Czechoslovak law. This transmission mechanism also embodied in Czechoslovak law a number of other principles of Cisleithanian law on nationalities, which as the most fully worked out law of this kind had been used as a basis for the treaty on the protection of minorities as a whole.

The enactment of the law on state language was preceded by a bitter dispute on the Czech side about the very basis of language rights. The controversy was over the extent to which it was desirable to meet national minorities halfway, especially the German. Regardless of fundamental differences of opinion on this point, however, the resulting form of the legislation reflected a serious attempt by the state to reduce nationality problems to the smallest possible degree and to create conditions for rapprochement between the Germans (and other minorities) and the state.[15]

Naturally no challenges were made to the right of every citizen to use his mother tongue, but from the beginning, state institutions considered it essential to regulate the language of official communication by introducing Czech as the main official language. In official documents and later in the law itself, the term was "the Czechoslovak language", which was held to exist in two equal versions – Czech and Slovak. Before the new law was introduced, higher offices had tolerated the use of German in official documents without obstruction.[16]

The language law of the CSR, embodied in the constitution by the constitutional language law and pursuant laws of 1920–1922, represented a compromise reached after a sharp confrontation between Beneš, Tusar and other politicians and Kramář's militant nationalist wing of Czech politics, in the course of which the moderate Masarykian conception was sidelined.[17] More privileges were pushed through for Czech than had originally been intended and this was not desirable for the future peaceful development of a multi-ethnic state. The idea of German as the second language of the state, or a bilingual state, disappeared from the original Czech premises, and the language law became the second most contentious element of Czechoslovak nationality law.

---

[15] Harna, J. – Šebek, J. *Státní politika.* 9.

[16] Ibidem.

[17] "The state as an overall and unified organism and its army will have Czech (Slovak) as its language – this is given by the majority principle of democracy. It will therefore be a Czechoslovak state. But the national character is not secured by the state language, language does not exhaust the character of a nation, and the national character of our state must reside in the quality of a culturally inclusive programme... I regard the most practical solution under the new conditions as a two-language one... Chauvinist nationalism is not justified anywhere, least of all in our country." Masaryk, T. G. *Světová revoluce.* 528–529.

According to V. Kural, apart from the principle of the equality of individual citizens Czechoslovak nationality law also involved the principle of certain privileges for the "Czechoslovak" nation (ethnic group) that in some aspects recalled the privileges *de facto* enjoyed by the Germans in Cisleithania before the war. For example, public instruction was supposed to be in Czech or Slovak and public funds for educational and humanitarian purposes were supposed to be for the benefit of the "Czechoslovak" nation.

The resulting form of Czechoslovak nationality law and especially the legal status of Germans in the CSR has been characterised by V. Kural as the consequence of a "conflict of many wills", none of which achieved what it had originally been striving for. He considers one of the basic reasons for this situation to have been conflict with Sudeten German secessionism, which disturbed and weakened the moderates in Czech politics and radicalised Czech attitudes. Significantly, there was also conflict between the Czech and German socialists, whose shared approach on non-ethnic issues otherwise formed an important basis for potential rapprochement.

The struggle over language rights became hypertrophied and ceased to be confined to its cultural function. It was a proxy political theme in the Czech-German dispute, its content excessively politicised. As a result of the very emotional contexts it became a particularly neuralgic point in the projects of national self-realisation.[18]

The official language of the new republic was given a position of privilege similar to that of German in the times of the monarchy. German critics of this measure were, of course, able to appeal to the wording on the Note on the Position of Nationalities in the Czecho-Slovak Republic presented by Beneš on the 20th of May 1919 at the Paris Conference. In Article 8 this stated:

"Czech will be the official language and the state will be known abroad as Czecho-Slovak but in practice the German language will be the second language in the country, will be used in official communication in the courts and in the central parliament on an equal footing with Czech."[19]

This internationally made promise was not fulfilled (for more detail on the reasons see above) and Sudeten-German propaganda made all the capital it could from the fact, especially in gaining the sympathy of West European politicians and public in the latter half of the 1930s. It was further exploited as an argument demonstrating the need for an international solution to the Sudeten German question and as proof of alleged Czech hypocrisy. Yet practical politics is the art of the possible and in a situation when distrust for the Sudeten

---

[18]   Kural, V. *Konflikt místo společenství*. 36.
[19]   Wiskemann, E. *Czechs and Germans*. 93.

Germans was deepening in Czech political elites as a direct reaction to the irre-dentism of the border provinces of *Deutschböhmen*, the fulfilment of the original promise was simply not viable. We might say that the political will was lack-ing – but not without reason.

The Sudeten German leadership's view of the Czechoslovak Republic, as ex-pressed several decades later, shows the general distaste for the state imposed on the Germans. "In the initial years of the new republic the Sudeten Germans were excluded from participation in the creation of political life. From the start the state was led just by a cartel of Czech political parties. Masaryk ran this party cartel with a circle of professional politicians, lawyers, journalists, pro-fessors, unionists, bankers and industrialists – mostly atheists – that he had chosen and who had come to power with him". The castle, ironically entitled the "court camerillo" allegedly created a historical legend that glorified Hussit-ism, condemned the Habsburgs, Germans and Catholic Church and promoted ethnic intolerance. "The people who had previously been part of the political elite in the Danubian monarchy remained almost entirely excluded from politi-cal life: conservatives, catholics and aristocrats, even if they clearly offered their allegiance to the Czech national movement."[20]

The author of this account, D. Salomon, goes on to claim that the Sudeten German political parties could not be represented in the government of the CSR because in the first elected parliament they all agreed in proclaiming their intention to insist on the right to self-determination. This makes it clear that the political representatives of the Sudeten Germans were not excluded but excluded themselves from a share in the exercise of power by their own nega-tive attitude, even though they were repeatedly invited to co-operate both by moderate Czech politicians (V. Tusar) and by nationally more radical politi-cians such as A. Rašín or K. Kramář.[21] Masaryk's attempts to bring Germans into the government (he even considered setting up a minister for Bohemian Germans to safeguard their interests) were also evidently unrealistic, and the

---

[20] Salomon, D. "Od rozpadu podunajské monarchie do konce druhé světové války". 194. It is almost incredible that the editor of the book, E. Nittner, should consider this an objective assessment of the Czechoslovak state. In the preface to the enlarged edition of 1993 he writes: "Since our little volume – and its Czech trans-lation – has been received warmly and with interest, there is a need to republish it. And especially because the falsification and misrepresentation of the common history of Czechs and Germans, that has absolutely nothing in common with academic seriousness, has in the meantime reached unacceptable levels". The au-thor is not wrong: this has reached unacceptable levels, inter alia thanks to his publication.

[21] Regardless of Lodgman's provocative attitudes, which even the German ambassador in Prague, Saenger, considered impertinent, Masaryk considered the participation of Germans in the first parliamentary gov-ernment to be desirable. He offered ministerial posts to distinguished people – the ministry of trade to Prof. J. Redlich, the ministry of education to dr. R. Keller, publisher of the *Prager Tagblatt* newspaper. He supported the outlook of the social democratic politicians V. Tusar and R. Bechyně, who wanted to avoid a coalition of all the Czech parties, "which would destroy all bridges to the Germans". Kural, V. *Konflikt místo společenství*. 43.

significantly more hopeful attempts of Tusar to win over the German social democrats and agrarian party (*Bund der Landwirte*) likewise came to nothing.[22]

The language law provided for important exceptions allowing minorities to turn to the courts and other institutions in their own language provided that at least 20% of the state citizens in the relevant court district were members of that minority concerned (amendments to the law in 1926 even removed the 20% condition). This meant in practice that nine-tenths of the German-speaking citizens of the CSR could communicate with the authorities in their own language, but of course the privileged position of the state language in itself contributed to tension in areas with a mixed ethnic profile. E. Wiskemann, very well informed on the position of the Sudeten Germans, admitted that the language law of 1926 was a source of resentment, but considered it in no way oppressive or in violation of Czechoslovak obligations to minorities. As an example she gives the wording of Article 3, which imposes on officials a duty to give the greatest possible assistance to plaintiffs not able to speak the state language. Furthermore, Article 18 allows citizens to submit a request for the hearing of a case before a court or administrative organ in places other than their own district of residence, which meant for example that a resident of Prague could pursue a legal case in his mother tongue in Karlovy Vary.

In some respects Czechoslovak law provided national minorities with more than the rights required by the Treaty of Saint-Germain. Essentially, most Czech parties started from the premise that it was important not to give Bohemian Germans an excuse for dissatisfaction, and this policy was to a certain extent successfully developed in practice in the latter half of the 1920s when the emotional and embittered atmosphere of conflict provoked by the attempts of the border provinces at secession had subsided, and especially thanks to the activist policy of the German political parties and inclusion of German ministers in the Czechoslovak government.

Authors orientated to the defence of the Sudeten Germans (Salomon is a characteristic example) claim that from the start the policy of the state towards German fellow-citizens was one of retaliation.[23] They criticise the legal obligation to use the Czech language on state railways and in post-offices (but even these authors are relatively favourable in their assessment of the situation

---

[22] The real prospects of Masaryk's plans for linking the Czech and German political leadership are doubted by A. Klimek, the expert on conditions in the pre-war CSR: If in the presidential papers from the spring of 1920 we find some specific names from the ranks of our Germans that he was considering for ministerial functions (Czech, Lustig), we have to say that he did not know the Sudeten Germans well, because there was a danger that they would have reacted to the nominations with extreme outrage, and likewise the Czech chauvinists given the surviving antisemitic mood could well have been infuriated by the notion of the ties of the Castle with a Jewish coterie." Klimek, A. 1996. *Boj o Hrad* [The Struggle for the Castle]. Prague: Panevropa. 114.

[23] Salomon, D. "Od rozpadu podunajské monarchie do konce druhé světové války". 194.

of minorities in the education system, with 3,300 German general schools existing alongside 6,000 Czech general schools). They likewise regard as discriminatory the procedural regulation further to the language law of 1926, which meant that officials had to take a language test, a measure that allegedly led to more than 33,000 Germans being forced out of their posts by 1930.[24]

Supposedly as a defence against this constant pressure, the Sudeten Germans founded societies and auxiliary organisations independent of the state. The Czechoslovak authorities found that even after the German deputies from the Bohemian Lands had been compelled to leave the Austrian parliament, now the representative organ of a foreign state (the cut-off point was the Treaty of Saint Germain-en-Laye of the 10th of September 1919), their anti-CSR activities did not stop. Apart from irredentist organisations following on from the activities of the governments of the projected German provinces and most of the German political parties, an important role was played by societies like the *Hilfsverein für Deutschböhmen und Sudetenland*.[25]

The problem with these protection societies/*Schutzverbände* was not the mere fact that they were minority associations, but their nationalist rationale, their cultivation of the ideology of Germandom and *Volkstum*, a patriotic chauvinism encouraging nationalist intolerance especially among the younger generation.

The German Cultural Association/*Deutscher Kulturverband* with 500,000 members focused mainly on support for German schools and educational activity and was founded in the new CSR as a successor organisation to the Austrian *Schulverein*.[26] The German League in Bohemia/*Bund der Deutschen in Böhmen* was another very important and influential group. The fact that at the beginning of the 1930s it had more than a million members suggests the extent of its influence among the German-speaking inhabitants of the Bohemian Lands. Its close links to the *Kreditanstalt der Deutschen* bank enabled it to fund a wide range of activities[27]. In South and West Bohemia the German Šumava Association/*Deutscher Böhmerwaldbund* was particularly influential.

[24] Ibidem. 195.
[25] Harna, J. – Šebek, J. *Státní politika*. 11. Examples of irredentist activities recorded by the Czechoslovak authorities can be found in documents nos. 90, 96–98, 100–102.
[26] In 1929 it had 2,800 branches and 350,000 members, and was active throughout the republic including in Ruthenia. It published the *Mitteilungen des deutschen Kulturverbandes*. It helped to support German schools for example with a sum of 7 million Kc in 1929. In addition it did much to popularise the term Sudetendeutsche for Bohemian Germans in general. The term was first used in this sense by the journalist Franz Jesser in 1902, and then promoted especially by the so-called *Wanderlehrer* (travelling teachers), whose activities the *Kulturverband* funded. See Pleyer, W. 1949. *Heimat im Herzen – Wir Sudetendeutsche*. Salzburg: Akademischer Gemeinschaftsverlag. 202.
[27] It had different offshoots working in different fields of public life. For example it arranged (mediated) the purchase and sale of land parcels for Germans, obtained material and retail possibilities for craftsmen, and had an insurance society the *Brüderbund* etc. See Cesar, J. – Černý, B. 1962. *Politika německých buržoazních stran v Československu v letech 1918–1938* [The Politics of the German Bourgeois Parties in Czechoslova-

These associations were an expression of the Sudeten Germans' fear of the supposed expansionism of the "Czechoslovak" nation, but they also had a significant social side – mutual aid inside the community of German-speaking inhabitants. This aspect came to the fore particularly after the deterioration of the economic situation following the Great Economic Crisis. The organisations listed (and others) found jobs for members, organised domestic work, tried to keep land in German hands, and supported touring theatre companies and libraries, especially in the German language enclaves.[28] Indeed, the activities of the support societies characteristically combined ethnic/national (*Volkstum*) with social welfare programmes.

Other integral elements of the German cultural and social environment were the differentiated elements of the co-operative and trades union movement, and also the German Physical Education League/*Deutscher Turnverband*, which apart from promoting physical strength and health had other "important" national tasks, including the upbringing of youth in the spirit of German national solidarity (with elements of antisemitism and anti-Slavism).[29]

Other organisations included the *Böhmerlandbewegung*, which strove to maintain German culture and identity in the borderlands, or the semi-militarily organised *Wandervogel* (attracting mainly young war veterans and focused on building an "ethnic community"). The society of inhabitants of the Cheb region – the *Egerlander Gmoin*, which extended in membership and activity across the border into neighbouring Bavaria and Saxony (and used historicising arguments to encourage the Cheb Germans to feel a sense of belonging to the Reich), was another example.[30]

---

kia 1918–1938]. Prague: Nakladatelství ČSAV. 473. The *Bund der Deutschen in Böhmen* with its headquarters in Teplice-Šanov was founded in 1894 and by the end of the 1920s had 1,300 branches with a total of 140,000 members. It published the fortnightly *Bundesbote* and "by its great size and funds is a dangerous opponent of [Czech] national associations". Škába, J. "Národní organisace v Československé republice" [National Organisations in the Czechoslovak Republic]. *Československá vlastivěda* V. Stát. Prague: Sfinx – B. Janda. 244.

[28] Salomon, D. "Od rozpadu podunajské monarchie do konce druhé světové války". 196.

[29] Right back in the years of the Germans' struggle against Napoleon, F. L. Jahn imbued the Turnverein at its birth with the racial intolerance and antisemitism that continued to characterise the environment of the society throughout its existence. At the beginning of the 1930s it was in these circles that the *Sudetendeutsche Heimatfront* emerged, while Henlein and many other leaders of the Sudeten German movement came out of them as well. For more detail see Biman, S. – Malíř, J. 1983. *Kariéra učitele tělocviku* [The Career of a Physical Education Teacher]. Ústí n. L.: Severočeské nakladatelství. 36–40.

[30] The German nationalists sought to co-ordinate the political parties and a large number of societies with mass support, as a way of making campaigns for political demands more effective. They were never entirely successful in their efforts because of the diversity of sectional interests involved. In the period of the Austrian monarchy the *Deutscher Volksrat für Böhmen* had taken on this role, and at the beginning of the 1920s the *Deutschpolitisches Arbeitsamt* was formed with similar aspirations, and from the elections of 1925 it became an important element in the public life of Germans in the ČSR. For more detail see: Cesar, J. – Černý, B. *Politika německých buržoazních stran*. 76–478.

Behind these association activities was the desire to support and strengthen German identity in a situation in which the Sudeten German community felt itself encircled by an ever more expansive and confident Czech element. This vision, with its roots extending back into the times of the monarchy, was based on a feeling of the "threat to the closed community of an ethnic group on the boundaries of conflict with the Slav element", as mentioned above. The establishment of an independent ČSR intensified this feeling and it became one of the defining marks of the deep inner alienation from the republic felt by the majority of the German-speaking population of the Bohemian Lands.

German Parties and the Politics of Engagement

The year 1926 saw a significant turning-point in the attitude of some of the German parties to cooperation in the government of the state. While the *Deutsche Nationalpartei*/German National Party (DNP) rejected cooperation, calling it an opportunistic mistake or even a betrayal of national interests (the DNP programme called for the annexation of the Bohemian Lands as a whole to Germany), the second negativist fraction, the *Deutsche Nationalsozialistische Arbeiterpartei*/the German National Socialist Workers' Party (DNSAP), reacted rather more tactically.[31] The latter was coming to realise that German participation in the government had attractions and promised advantages for Sudeten Germans. Thus it did not reject involvement in government on principle, but only on the grounds that the two activist (pro-engagement) German parties – the *Bund der Landwirte*/The German Union of Agriculturists and the *Deutsche Christlich-Soziale Volkspartei*/The German Christian-Social People's Party – had entered the government without appropriate guarantees of an autonomist solution to the question of the Bohemian Germans.

There was a particularly bitter dispute over the plan put forward by the German agrarian representative F. Spina,[32] to overcome the entrenched form of Sudeten political thinking with its anti-Czech exaltation duly strengthened from Germany by the organised efforts of what was known as the *Volkstumar-*

---

31   Kural, V. *Konflikt místo společenství.* 67.
32   Dr. Franz Spina, professor of Slavonic studies at the German university in Prague and chairman of the club of agrarian party deputies in the National Assembly became minister of public works in the Czech government. He developed a conception of the social symbiosis of Czechs and Germans based on the premise that Czech-German coexistence was mutually beneficial and a challenge and opportunity for both sides. For a detailed treatment see Luža, R. *The Transfer of the Sudeten Germans.* 39.

beit, which was particularly active in the environment of the Sudeten German special interest associations.[33]

According to E. Broklová, the shift of some German parties to engagement – cooperation with the new republic was speeded up by professors of the German university in Prague, but also the politicians Bruno Kafka and Ludwig Spiegel from the German Free-Thinking Democratic Party, the Christian social party member Robert Mayr-Harting and Prof. Franz Spina from the German Union of Agriculturists. The steps taken by the political leaders of the Bohemian Germans also had an international dimension, of course, since the co-operative attitude of the activists was supported by the government of the Weimar Republic headed by G. Stresemann.[34]

R. Mayr-Harting entered the government as minister of justice with the political goal of maintaining both the existence of the state and the integrity of the German ethnic group, which was in his view under threat. In the period of activist cooperation the Christian Social Party also formulated a programme of ethnic local self-government.[35] According to this programme, the basis of local self-government was to be the settlement structure of the different ethnic groups-nationalities inhabiting the CSR as a nation state. National land registers were to be set up for this purpose, and national autonomy to be secured by a suitable organisation of representative corporations in the form of national curias or national land assemblies, the national division of government offices and definition of government districts. The armed forces should be transformed into a militia system as soon as possible and the school system should be placed under the control of the national group dominant in the area concerned. In the agrarian party's newspaper *Venkov*, readers were reminded that the Christian Social Party accepted as a basic document the "suggestion of the German National Socialists that national/ethnic self-government, according to the explicit declaration of their main organ, is nothing other than an intermediary step towards self-determination".[36]

From this and other evidence it is clear that there was a certain connecting bridge between the activist (engaged), to some extent pro-Czechoslovak policy

---

[33] Even in the period of the Weimar Republic, regarded by most authors as a democratic state, many organisations and societies with a racist or chauvinist orientation were active in Germany. For example the *Pan-German League*, *Verein für das Deutschtum im Ausland*, *Bund Deutscher Osten* or *Deutsches Ausland-Institut*, concerned with the study of German questions abroad. See Wiskemann, E. *Czechs and Germans*. 129.

[34] The attitude of the then German government is documented in detail in Dr. Koch's correspondence with Berlin. Koch was German ambassador in Prague in the years 1921–1935 and was considered a great expert on the relations between the two countries – his views were taken very seriously in Berlin. See Brügel, J. W. 1967. 'Ludwig Czech', in *Tschechen und Deutsche 1918–1938.*

[35] Broklová, E. 1999. *Politická kultura německých aktivistických stran v Československu 1918–1938.* [The Political Culture of German Activist Parties in Czechoslovakia 1918–1938] Prague: Karolinum. 89–90.

[36] Ibidem. 90.

of the German civic parties of the latter half of the 1920s and the later inclination to the nationalist programme of Henlein's *Sudeten German Party*, which was first strongly manifest in the elections of the autumn of 1935, when the SdP won 60% of the Sudeten German votes. This trend was undoubtedly speeded up by the economic problems experienced by the Sudeten areas as a consequence of the great depression at the turn of the 1920s/30s, but a certain linkage or basic continuity of ideas and programmes among the German political parties was important, as has been suggested.

The Economic Crisis and the Borderlands

The economic crisis of the first half of the 1930s had a truly cruel impact on Czechoslovakia's border areas, since they were economically dependent on Czechoslovakia's export capacities.[37] W. Jaksch states that in the Sudetenland the economic crisis led to a decline in production in the cotton industry by a half and in the glass and porcelain industry by a third. Jaksch quotes the opinion of an English observer of the situation in the Sudetenland: "the economic system and state finance in Czechoslovakia were not prepared to meet this terrible catastrophe. In a poverty almost bordering on starvation, the Sudeten Germans believed any explanation of their suffering and trusted every help offered to them."[38] A detailed study of the economic contexts of the development of relations between Czechs and Germans in the historic lands is not the subject of this work, but it will be relevant to give at least a short illustrative account of the social situation in the border areas of the Bohemian lands, which provided fertile ground for Henleinian agitation campaigns.

The economic crisis ended the first decade of the coexistence of Czechs and Sudeten Germans in the new state – a decade that had been one of diminishing conflict. The confrontational mood at the birth of the state had mellowed somewhat with the economic boom, and over the 1920s an atmosphere of greater tolerance had gradually developed, finding visible form in the rise of the German activist parties and their involvement in government at ministerial level. The crucial factor for the future was the fact that the crisis affected different areas and nationalities to different extents. In the case of the districts with a German-speaking population the level of unemployment rose in line with the percent-

---

[37] E. Wiskemann provides an overall table of the trends in Czechoslovak exports from 1926 and 1933, based on official Czechoslovak statistics. While in 1929 exports were still to a value of 20.5 milliard crowns, by 1933 this had fallen to 5.85 milliard crowns. Wiskemann, E. *Czechs And Germans*. 165.
[38] Grant Duff, S. 1939. *Europe And the Czechs*. London. 129.

age of German population.[39] At the height of the crisis a fifth of the German population capable of working was unemployed.

Wiskemann points out what she believes to have been a serious mistake on the part of the Prague government, i.e. that it sent unemployed Czechs to undertake public works in areas with a majority German-speaking population, and in a situation where it was obvious that public works were being organised to relieve the plight of the unemployed in the places where they lived. The import of Czech unemployed into German-speaking territories naturally seemed to the Sudeten Germans like a deliberate insult to their problems.[40]

The course of the economic crisis in both Germany and Czechoslovakia was a real social catastrophe that affected the whole structure of society – workers, the intelligentsia, the urban middle classes and the agricultural population. Given the importance of the consequences for Czech-German relations, it is useful to compare the impact on the two environments.

- In Germany the economic crisis led directly to a deep political crisis, but this did not happen in the CSR.
- In the CSR the impact of the economic crisis came somewhat later, and the beginnings of economic recovery were likewise delayed.
- In the CSR the different national groups were hit to different degrees, and this, combined with the faster recovery of production and employment rates in Germany, became dynamite of the most shattering kind for the CSR and Czech-German relations, helping to cause an accompanying ethnic/national crisis with direct consequences for the future of the Czechoslovak state and statehood.[41]

The Sudeten German economist J. Kislinger states that at the end of October 1935 there were on average 30.5 unemployed per thousand population on predominantly Czech territory and 80.9 per thousand on predominantly Bohemian German territory. The extent and duration of the unemployment was an important factor exacerbating German aversion to the state. While elsewhere in the world the economic crisis gradually abated, in 1936 there were still 525,000 unemployed among Bohemian Germans.[42] Unemployed glass-blowers and hosiery makers, machine weavers and textile workers in the borderlands of

---

[39] The view of the Czech demographer M. Weirich in Kural, V. *Konflikt místo společenství*. 104.

[40] Wiskemann, E. *Czechs and Germans*. 193.

[41] Kural, V. *Konflikt místo společenství*. 104.

[42] Seibt, F. 1993. *Německo a Češi* [Germany and the Czechs]. Prague: Academia. 306–307. In 1933 unemployment in the textile industry had risen to six times that of 1929, in the stone industry 27.9 times, in the glass industry 72.9 times and so on.

Western and Northern Bohemia could look over the border and see the well-known effects of the national socialist economic boom in Silesia, Bavaria and especially the adjacent areas of Saxony. For generations the feeling expressed by the phrase "Everything is better in the Reich" had been passed on among Bohemian Germans. Now this old idea was given fresh life by Hitler's economic "miracle", and had unsurprising political consequences. In these circumstances the faith of the Sudeten Germans in the CSR as a guarantee of their material existence was deeply shaken, and in the context of neighbouring Nazi Germany and its political ambitions this had serious domestic and international implications.

In this situation it could make no fundamental difference that unemployment benefits were allocated fairly by the state (the minister of social welfare, who was the German social democrat dr. L. Czech), and so that in this respect the CSR did not emerge as a nationalist state, but as J. W. Brügel put it, "as a state of absolute national/ethnic justice."[43]

The Sudeten Germans' latent hostility or at least lack of identification with the unwanted state was exploited by the demagogic propaganda of the Henleinian agitators, with their claim that the cause of the situation was the deliberate anti-German policy of the Czech side.[44] In fact the main cause of the economic problems of the German border regions was the structure of their manufacturing capacities, which had been failing to modernise even in the last period of the Austria-Hungarian monarchy. They had not been basically restructured even in the first decade of the new state, when their dependence on export markets became ever greater.

It is true that the state's economic policy played some part in exacerbating the problem, because the preference for customs protectionism of agriculture pushed through by the agrarian party and the deflationary measures championed by A. Rašín and the Živnobanka/Trades Bank, put light and export industry, i.e. the main Sudeten German form of industry, at a disadvantage.[45]

---

[43] Brügel, J. W. *Tschechen und Deutsche 1918–1939*. 191.

[44] For example the publication *Vom Kriegen zwischen den Kriege* asserts that unemployment destroyed the power of resistance of the German *Volksgruppe* in Czechoslovakia, as a result of the policy of redundancies/ *Entlassungspolitik*, allegedly systematically targetted against Sudeten Germans by the Czechs. The publicaton also claims that in 1918 as much as 80% of industrial enterprises in the Bohemian Lands had been in German hands, while in 1934 it was a mere 40%.

[45] Kural, V. *Konflikt místo společenství*. 105. The arguments of the Henleinians were frequently completely fraudulent. For example the ruins of the F. Preidl concern's weaving mill by České Kamenice, but also the demolition of old and entirely out-of-date factories closed before the crisis years, were used by the Henleinians for political agitation and the provocation of incidents. The liquidation of these old buildings was presented as the expression of a deliberate policy of deindustrialisation of territories with majority German population. Hoffman, J. 1996. *"Mnichov" a sudetoněmecký textilní průmysl* ["Munich" and the Sudeten-German Textile Industry]. Ústí n. L.: Univerzita J. E. Purkyně. 31.

The problems of the Czechoslovak textiles industry (which was fairly crucial for the economy of the Sudeten areas) have been pointed out by J. Hoffman, who shows that demand for its cotton goods had already been declining in the 1920s. The ability of our textile industry to compete with foreign suppliers was also diminished by its relatively limited experience and contacts in international trade.[46]

With the crisis, the share of the textile industry in the value of Czechoslovak exports dropped substantially, with the trading balance of 1,384 million crowns in 1929 falling to a mere 193 million in 1933. In the following period up to 1937 the Czechoslovak textile industry took only stumbling steps on the road to recovery, which was never complete. It was no accident that Northern Bohemia played so important a role in the Henlein movement; this was partly a direct result of the desperate problems of the local consumer industry, in which the textile industry had a key position. Similarly it was no accident that the closed gates of the textile factories or major cutbacks in their operations became a major and eagerly exploited argument for Henlein's agitators. The Bohemian German economic leaders and major businessmen also changed their tone; like the otherwise cautious major industrialist T. Liebieg, for example, they started to demand immediate aid from the Czechoslovak government and the establishment of extensive economic contacts with the neighbouring German Reich.

According to the Czech demographer M. Weirich, the state's failure to devote sufficient attention to the economic situation in the borderlands and general lack of systematic planning left the field open for unrestrained ethnic passions and power politics, and so "the ethnically most sensitive part of the state" was left to confront the most difficult situation in the crisis. [47]

It is true that aid from the state and its other interventions in the economic sphere was generally influenced by the power positions held by individual capital groups in state organs. The leading positions in these were occupied by the spokesmen of Czech capital, above all agricultural and heavy industrial capital, and so the capital group of Sudeten German light industry was exposed to a certain pressure and in the given situation its representatives had only minimal prospects of success in having their demands met, for example in getting state orders or the introduction of what were known as export bonuses.[48]

All the same, the Czech share of responsibility for the problems of the border areas may be considered secondary, since the main problem was the long-term

[46]   Before the First World War a major part of the textile production had been sold on the territory of the Monarchy, while export was usually an indirect matter, arranged mainly by Viennese and Reich German department stores, especially in Hamburg and Bremen. Ibidem. 27.

[47]   Weirich, M. 1938. *Staré a nové Československo* [Old and New Czechoslovakia]. Prague. 163.

[48]   Hoffman, J. *"Mnichov" a sudetoněmecký textilní průmysl.* 42.

unwillingness of Sudeten German capital to adapt, its refusal in the boom period to make risky investments in the modern branches of heavy industry, machine engineering and electrical engineering, which suffered significantly less from the effects of the crisis. This was the problem at the root of the striking differences in unemployment rates in the Czech and German territories of the CSR.

Yet without more detailed explanation of the course of modernising processes in the economy of the Czech Lands, to many it could easily seem to be the result of long-term Czech expansionism, with the Czechoslovak nation state employed as tool in pursuit of this overall goal. Demagogic arguments to this effect were a standard part of the conceptual apparatus of the Henleinian and Nazi propaganda, which claimed that businesses based in the CSR were being de-Germanised.

In this context, in a valuable and (on the Czech side) isolated study of the problem, J. Matějček has drawn attention to some hitherto neglected aspects of the economic development of the German-speaking border areas. In his view, treatment of the whole subject of the Sudeten German economy in the period of the First Republic has been a mass of obscurity and tendentious statements.

In the first place, he sees the very starting-point for assessing the whole situation, i.e. figures on the alleged share of Sudeten businessmen in the Czechoslovak economy, as debatable and unresolved. In his view it is not just a matter of statistical and other "hard data", but above all of the choice of criteria for judging the "Germanness" of businesses. It is extremely hard to establish these criteria (the economist and writer J. Hejda pointed out in the paper *Přítomnost* of 1927 and 1928), the data on the effects of the land reform on the German minority are questionable, and the data on unemployment, the real profitability of Sudeten German industry and other aspects are fragmentary.[49] Matějček considers Alfred Bohmann's lengthy study, *Das Sudetendeutschtum in Zahlen*, to be an example of the dubious use of figures and other data.

In the Czech context Matějček's work is a rare exploration of a problem very frequently instrumentalised in distorted form by the propaganda of the German nationalist parties. According to this propaganda the Prague government allowed the full weight of the economic crisis to fall on the borderlands with the clear aim of economically ruining the areas inhabited by the German-speaking population, and so breaking their political will to achieve an autonomist solution to their relationship to the CSR.

---

[49]   Matějček, J. – Machačová, J. 1999. *Sociální pozice národnostních menšin v českých zemích 1918–1938* [The Social Position of National Minorities in the Bohemian Lands 1918–1938]. Opava: Slezský ústav Slezského muzea. 211. Bohmann, A. *Das Sudetendeutschtum in Zahlen.*

One particular issue attracting Sudeten-German resentment and tendentious interpretation was the allocation of state orders, decisive for the survival of firms in the period of deepest depression. Czech firms were evidently preferred for some public orders for industrial production and public works, with state orders in German-majority areas allegedly allocated in a ratio of 81.9 and 18.1% in favour of Czech firms in the years 1933–1936, although in these German areas Czechs formed only about 16% of the population. Overall, from the total volume of public orders 23% went to German firms, 69.2% to Czech firms and 7.5% to mixed firms, which roughly corresponds to overall proportions of nationalities. Nonetheless, in the situation of the economic crisis, the Czechoslovak government was subject to constant pressure from "patriotic firms resolved to exploit their role in state building to gain economic advantages." "The fact that this only sharpened national antagonisms was not a matter of concern to these firms, just like the greater part of German elites before 1918 and in the later 1930s when the foundations of the post-1945 "final settlement of the German Question" were also created."[50]

Matějček points out some negative long-term trends in the economy of the border areas, where textile industry played a very important role. Most of the German textile manufacturers were aware of their lack of competitiveness (in relation to Reich German industry as well) and for this reason did not adopt a hostile stance to the new republic after 1918, unlike Sudeten German nationalist politicians.

The social and political climate in the borderlands was inevitably affected by the fact that the great economic crisis of the 1930s steeply reduced the production and export of fashion and luxury goods and thus had a particularly severe impact on the German industrial sector, laying bare the marked instability of the economy of the German areas. "The tendentious work of some Sudeten German authors, however, attributed this to Czechs and the Czech state, rather than the specific structure of "Sudeten" industry and its long term development."[51]

Long-term reliance on traditional light industries geared to the satisfaction of the increasingly out-dated consumer habits of lifestyle under the Habsburg

---

[50]   Matějček, J. – Machačová, J. *Sociální pozice národnostních menšin.* 214.

[51]   Similarly misleading and deceitful formulations have a tradition in the Nazi propaganda of the 1930s, which claimed that states with German minorities used economic instruments to undermine the viability of those minorities. Against this background, in the CSR the cyclical problems of the economic crisis were blamed by the SdP on a malicious plan aiming to weaken the Sudeten Germans. Thus for example, we find the claim, "In Czechoslovakia, Poland and Lithuania a particularly extensive attempt is being made to exploit this dangerously aggressive thesis: the German national groups/*Volksgruppen* of these states have lost the greater part of their ability to resist as a result of problems of unemployment." See Schumacher, R. – Hummel, H. 1938. *Vom Kriege zwischen den Kriegen.* Stuttgart: Union Deutsche Verlagsgesellschaft. 233.

Monarchy was ultimately fateful for the "Sudeten" economy. These industries missed the chance to modernise taken by "young" Czech capital, which at the turn of the 19th/20th century invested in the new, profitable branches of the second industrial revoltuion.

It was the "bad luck" of the Sudeten Germans that these long-term trends were to their disadvantage and that they were essentially dependent on the more or less unchangeable distribution of their settlements in the border mountains and hilly areas. Here we can see the effect of factors of a borderland structure of settlement formed roughly from the 13th to the 16th century! [52]

With this objective and de-ideologised assessment of the economic dimension of the rivalry between the Czechs and Sudeten Germans in the historic lands we can close this short account of the economic aspect of inter-war development, intended to show the destabilising influence of the economy on the political climate of Czech-German relations at the turn of the 1920s/30s.

---

[52] Matějček, J. – Machačová, J. *Sociální pozice národnostních menšin.* 228.

Edvard Beneš signing the Briand-Kellogg Pact on the 27th of August 1928 in Paris. The pact, prohibiting the use of force in international relations, was initiated by the French foreign minister Aristide Briand and the US secretary of state F. B. Kellogg. After WWII the pact was to be the legal basis for judgment on the Nazi aggression.

5 The Resurgence of Germany as a Great Power

The Sudeten Question was not just a local Czechoslovak problem,
but from the outset was objectively set in the wider context of attitudes
to the German Question in Europe generally.
Jan Křen: V emigraci [In Emigration]. 467

From the very foundation of the republic, which had a clearly international context when the CSR became part of the Versailles Treaty system, it was obvious that Sudeten leaders pinned their hopes of revision of the position of ethnic Germans in the Bohemian Lands precisely on this international framework. Given that after the First World War the League of Nations was set up as the instrument for protection of national minority rights, the Sudeten German politicians directed their complaints to this particular institution of international law.

The policy of the Bohemian German parties in the CSR was significantly related, however, to the question of the membership of Germany in the League of Nations, which became a live and urgent issue in the later part of 1924 when Ramsay MacDonald directly invited Germany to join.

Membership of the League of Nations held out the possibility of several benefits for Germany, some of them relating to the situation of German minorities in Central and Eastern Europe, including Czechoslovakia. While the treaty signed in October 1925 in Locarno (The Western Guarantee Pact known as the Rhineland Pact) confirmed for the victorious great powers their borders with Germany, it was forgotten in the general rejoicing that Germany had not been willing to guarantee its borders in the east. The result was a situation in which *two classes of border now existed in Europe* – those that Germany accepted and that the other powers guaranteed, and those that Germany had not accepted and the other powers refused to guarantee.[1] Stresemann soon took the oppor-

---

[1]   Kissinger, H. *The Art of Diplomacy.* 288. I mention this fact because it very directly impinged on the security of Czechoslovakia. Kissinger argues that confusion in the European international relations of the time was heightened by the absence of alliance obligations, which were replaced by French agreements with the

tunity to show Beneš what the new situation meant for Czech-German relations. In private negotiations Beneš rejected "Stresemann's attempt to discuss
the complaints of the Sudeten Germans, drawn up beforehand by the Berlin
Auswärtiges Amt", but at the same time Beneš's failed in his attempt to raise
the drafted Czechoslovak-German bilateral arbitrage agreement to the level
of a non-aggression pact. In his diary Stresemann recorded the brusque form of
his refusal of the clause on non-aggression proposed by Beneš: "Ohne Diskus-
sion a limine", quickly forgetting how he had recently eulogised Beneš when
asking him through his emissaries to take on the role of "mediator of good
services" in arranging negotiations with France.

Beneš nonetheless believed that the overall relaxation of tensions in Europe
after Locarno would ease the antagonism between Czechs and Sudeten-Germans. Fundamentally, however, what Locarno meant was that the CSR would
have to reconcile itself to the real possibility of future confrontation with Germany without the unambiguous protection of the West. At the same time it
was a clear signal that Germany was returning to its great power positions.[2]
The consequences for Czechoslovak-German relations appeared almost immediately in the form of intensified efforts by Germany to achieve economic and
political hegemony in Central and South-East Europe (economic penetration).

Through Equal Rights to Revision

Signing the treaty settlement in Locarno gave Germany political equality, thus
ending the post-war division of European states into victors and vanquished.
Membership of the League of Nations was next on the agenda and offered
Germany a chance to regain the privileges of great power status in European
context, giving it a direct influence in negotiations on the problems of disarmament, security, minority rights, mandate systems and other issues.[3] It brought
hope for the consolidation of a peaceful atmosphere in international relations,
and for Germany the eventual prospect of relief from the harsh conditions of

---

weaker new states in Eastern Europe. Great Britain refused to join this. Locarno gave the proof that the
League of Nations was incapable of providing guarantees of security even to its founding members.

[2] Dejmek, J. *Československo – jeho sousedé a velmoci*. 48–49. Klimek, A. – Kubů, E. *Československá zahraniční
politika*. 53. The authors mention the private diary of G. Stresemann, where on Czechoslovak policy at the
time of Locarno he notes, "Messrs Beneš and Skrzyński (the Polish foreign minister) had to sit in an adjacent
room until we let them in. This is the way it looks with states that have been spoilt in every possible way because they became servants of others, and that are dropped the moment it is believed that an understanding
with Germany can be achieved".

[3] Břach, R. *Československo a Evropa*. 48.

the Versailles Treaty, especially the reparations, which were undermining the German economy.

The League of Nations was part of the Versailles Treaty System and to accept membership involved a certain expression of recognition of the then international order. Article 1 of the Charter of the League of Nations explicitly bound member states to respect international agreements. As R. Břach points out, however, Article 19 did not exclude the revision of unworkable treaties. The international authority of the League of Nations in solving international disputes was limited by the fact that neither the USA or Russia were members. Entry into the League would bring Germany the chance of more rapprochement with France and Great Britain, but also some restriction of its freedom of action, i.e. through Article 16 which obliged member states to observe joint economic sanctions (in the case of unanimity in the Council of the League of Nations).

The German government agreed to the offer of membership, but on several conditions.[4] First and foremost it demanded an immediate seat on the Council of the League of Nations and all organs of the organisation. Second, it wanted the right to neutrality in the case of the application of Article 16 (with reference to the disarmament imposed on Germany on the basis of the Versailles Treaty), since it wished to preserving a manoeuvring space in relation to Russia, to which it had obligations undertaken in 1922 by the Treaty of Rapallo.[5] The third demand involved a dilution, by skilful formulation, of the acceptance of German's guilt in unleashing the First World War.[6] The fourth point related to a share in colonial administration: "Being since its defeat excluded

---

[4] Note the rapid qualitative turnaround in the international system made possible by the inconsistency of France and Britain, when a mere eight years from the end of a war provoked by Germany (the reparation agreements still in force), this state could dictate the conditions for the next step.

[5] Ibidem. 49. With the Rapallo Agreement Germany behaved as an independent actor in international politics for the first time since its defeat. It established full diplomatic relations with Russia, which explicitly waived its claim to reparations according to Article 116 of the Versailles Treaty and opened the way for close economic cooperation between the two countries. In Germany the agreement was supported by a variety of political forces including the communists and the conservative national block of generals and diplomats, who saw the agreement as the first, albeit limited, revolt against the spirit of Versailles. There was a convergence of the interests of Germany and Russia on change in the order of Eastern Europe, which became one of the constants of this period in European politics. The armies of the two states established important co-operative links, allowing Germany to keep up with the development and production of new weapons even in the years when it was under the strict supervision of the Alliance.

[6] It is worth quoting this in full to show the diplomatically ambiguous formulation: The German government "is willing to confirm to the League of Nations by formal declaration its firm intention to observe its international obligations. This declaration does not, however, affect declarations made by the German government on these obligations on earlier occasions, and specifically it should not be interpreted to mean that the German government recognises the correctness of the claims that served to justify these obligations and involve a moral burden on the German nation." Skilfulness of formulation creating a manoeuvring space in advance was characteristic of German foreign policy. Ibidem. 49–50.

from any kind of colonial activity, Germany expects that at a suitable time it will be called upon to participate effectively in the mandate administration of the League of Nations."[7] After a long and detailed debate all these points were conceded with one exception, which was the demand for the right to maintain German neutrality in disputed cases.

In the mid-1920s relations between Germany and Czechoslovakia were considered good and generally non-conflictual. While Polish-German relations (the main point of conflict was the Gdansk Corridor) were characterised by tension relating to German proposals for security agreements and to border disputes, there were no such remaining points of conflict between the CSR and Germany.[8] Or at least this was how German foreign policy ostentatiously presented the situation, and Stresemann "let Czechs believe", that it was so, since the border line between the two states had been taken over by the peace conference with small alterations from the period of the Austro-Hungarian monarchy (the exceptions were partial modifications in the Hlučín district). The Sudeten territories had never been part of the German Reich and at this time German policy was not even considering their annexation.[9]

Despite this, Sudeten German politicians relied on help from the Reich, although not necessarily help of a purely diplomatic kind. The German foreign ministry/*Auswärtiges Amt* (evidently in the spirit of the chancellor's policy of "model fulfilment of obligations") discretely but definitely encouraged Sudeten German activism (engagement) and in 1926 indirectly supported the decision of the agrarian party and Christian social party to join the government headed by premier A. Švehla.[10]

The Reich chancellor and foreign minister Stresemann strove in foreign policy for a faultless fulfilment of obligations arising from the Versailles Treaty, through which he hoped to secure the support of the Allied powers and increase trust in Germany as a basis for German return to the role of great power. This attitude earned Germany favourable reactions from the Western great powers and in the Central European region. For example, the Czechoslovak foreign minister Beneš offered his own place on the Council of the League of Nations to Stresemann as an ostentatious expression of honour for the latter's

---

[7] Memorandum of the German government sent on the 29th of September 1924 to the states-members of the Council of the League of Nations. *Zahraniční politika* 1–2/1925. 124.

[8] The entirely different positions of Poland and Czechoslovakia towards Germany were the subject of many debates of the time and some also raised the question of German sincerity in promoting a superficial view of the contrast. Břach cites the opinion of F. G. Campbell, that "Stresemann encouraged the Czechs to believe that the German refusal to guarantee the frontiers meant trouble for the Poles but not for the Czechs". Břach, R. *Československo a Evropa*. 119.

[9] Ibidem. 116.

[10] Kural, V. *Konflikt místo společenství*. 81.

restrained and moderate policies. When Stresemann first attended a sitting of the Council of the League of Nations as the permanent delegate of Germany on the council, he referred in his speech to his respect for Czechoslovakia. All the same, despite these showy gestures of good will, both politicians were aware that for Central Europe the full-scale return of Germany to the role of great power meant a fundamental change in the international power constellation.

Stresemann was the first post-war German leader to exploit the geopolitical advantages that the Versailles system gave to Germany.[11] He grasped the fact that the foundations of the Franco-British relationship were fragile, and managed to exploit its weak points to drive a wedge between the allies. His policy of "fulfilment" brought forward the day awaited by General von Seeckt: "We must regain strength and as soon as we achieve this, naturally we shall take back everything we have lost."[12] In the mid-1920s the international situation had changed to the extent that as a leader of defeated Germany Stresemann could influence the course of events far more than the leaders of the victorious states France and Great Britain, Briand and Chamberlain.

From as early as the spring of 1930, German foreign policy-makers (led by J. Curtius after the death of Stresemann) were working on the project of customs union with Austria, planned as a major step to de facto economic "anschluss" and opening the way to further economic expansion in Central Europe. In a Foreign Ministry circular depeche, Beneš accurately summed up the situation when he wrote that, "in essence this is the pre-war concept of *Mitteleuropa*, and the form that they give it is just a means of hiding it... The plan to include other members, Hungary, Yugoslavia and Rumania is just meant as a way of encircling Czechoslovakia and so forcing us into the same step. We are regarded as one of the main obstacles, principally for political reasons..."[13]

---

[11] After the opening up of Stresemann's personal archive, the earlier assessment of his personality changed considerably. As Kissinger (Kissinger, H. *Art of Diplomacy*. 297) put it, "the documents revealed the calculating practices of a real-politician, who pursued traditional German interests with ruthless obstinacy". For quite a long time before, Stresemann had been generally viewed as a democrat, a "good European" and a precursor of Konrad Adenauer. Commentators seemed to have forgotten that Stresemann was a friend of General E. Ludendorff (who was involved in Hitler's first putsch in 1923, and a deputy in the Reichstag for the Nazis 1924–28), a member of the Pan-German League and a man who during the 1st World War came forward with extensive demands for annexations. See *Encyklopedie osobností Evropy* [Personalities of Europe]. 1993. (Collective of authors). Prague: Nakladatelský dům OP. 616–617.

[12] Kissinger, H. 1994. *Diplomacy*. New York: Simon and Schuster. 285.

[13] Dejmek, J. *Československo – jeho sousedé a velmoci*. 50.

Complaints to the League of Nations

The League of Nations played an important role in the efforts of the Sudeten Germans to gain international support for their protests against the Czechoslovak state. In this context the Sudeten Germans exploited the provisions on the protection of national minorities, which the League was supposed to guarantee together with the existence and rights of the small states created in the framework of the Versailles System. The League was supposed to ensure the resolution of disputed issues in international relations through negotiation.

The basis of the repeated complaints was the expression of an alleged Sudeten German "collective will" to achieve a change in the conditions in which national minorities lived in Czechoslovakia. A publication of 1931 which came out in the USA[14] claimed that the "situation of minorities is unsatisfactory despite their numbers. Fifty-six complaints submitted by different national groups to the League of Nations is eloquent testimony to the state of the problem. The main complaints concern questions of administration and education, but also agrarian reform and language reforms prejudicial to minorities. Now as before, the efforts of the Czechs are directed to undermining continuous German-speaking districts, in the course of which the suppression of rights is the order of the day."

We could cite a whole series of similar formulations from a range of information and propagandist brochures and publications. Their German authors did not strive for an accurate and objective assessment of the situation of national minorities in Czechoslovakia (as described above), but for national agitation with the aim of influencing public opinion in Western countries and painting a picture of the CSR as the oppressor of its German inhabitants. Concretely, for example, for his pamphlets O. Junghahn took materials and "inspiration" from the Berlin institutions – the *Berlin-Steglitzer Institut für Grenz- und Auslandsstudien* and the *Deutsche Gesellschaft für Nationalitätenrecht* – whose activities had already been focussed on groups of ethnic Germans in the time of the Weimar state.[15]

The problem was that apart from the undoubted elements of fact in the Sudeten Germans' complaints at their treatment, the matter was always approached in an aggressively nationalist, anti-Czech tone.

---

[14] Junghahn, O. 1931. *National Minorities in Europe*. New York: Covici/Friede Publishers. 51.

[15] For an outstanding bibliographical overview of publications on the theme, see Low, Alfred D. 1984. *The Anschluss Movement, 1918–1938 Background and Aftermath (An Annotated Bibliography of German and Austrian Nationalism)*. New York & London: Garland Publishing Inc.

There were repeated extreme formulations of fears for the very existence of the Sudeten-German national group, which was allegedly exposed to a pressure from the Czech authorities designed to eliminate its ethnic identity entirely.

The claim that "the Sudeten German domain was weakened in all aspects and its very foundation threatened as years went by"[16] is characteristic.

Following the establishment of Czechoslovakia in 1918, the ownership of land, as an irreplaceable means of production, was viewed as a cardinal problem of the Czechoslovak economy and its development.[17] Not only emigration, but a gradual shift of population from the country to the urban industrial centres had been largely a consequence of the unjust distribution of land. The new CSR regarded land reform as the key to the dynamic development of the rural areas, but it was also a weapon that could be used to strengthen the Czech element in the territories with a German-speaking population, above all in the borderlands.

The political as opposed to purely economic rationale of land reform was admitted in 1922 by Dr. Viškovský, the President of the Land Office (entrusted with carrying the reform out), when he said that it was also a "work of political retaliation and redress for the wrongs of the Post-White Mountain period." F. Peroutka considered this a rather primitive view of the reform but one shared by the majority of the National Assembly. Indeed, he argued that the Land Reform was not based on economic considerations, citing the National Democrat Dr. Němec.[18] The National Assembly was not in fact entirely sure that the outcome of the Land Reform and land confiscations would be positive; the rapporteur of the committee for land reform, F. Modráček, who presented the draft law, said that only time would tell whether the land reform would turn out a blessing or a curse – a comment that evidently reflected the reservations of the experts.

The law itself (passed on the 30th of January 1920) gave no one the right to take up ownership of the land, nor in any way indicated the persons to whom

---

[16] V. Aschenbrenner: "Die Deutschen", in Kural, V. *Konflikt místo společenství*. 88.

[17] "The shortage of land in the hands of farmers as a consequence (almost half of agricultural producers farmed on leased land), was causing a great fragmentation of land ownership. Especially in areas dominated by a major noble land estate, the prevailing type of farming was on very small farms, which could not provide a family with a living. The small farmer could not obtain enough land to secure a minimum living standard, and this meant that each year tens of thousands of people left their homeland to seek a living abroad." Sommer, K. "Průběh a výsledky pozemkové reformy v pohraničí českých zemí" [The Course and Consequences of the Land Reform in the Borderlands of the Bohemian Lands], in *České národní aktivity v pohraničních oblastech první Československé republiky*. 2003. Šrajerová, O. (ed.). Ostrava: Tilia. 36.

[18] "It cannot be claimed that latifundia are malignant from the point of view of agricultural production. They are much more dangerous from the social viewpoint. With this land reform of ours we do not have great hopes that it will raise agricultural production, and for the first years we even fear that production may fall. We are motivated to carry out this reform by a desire to achieve social justice, and we also see the national question as involved in it." Peroutka, F. *Budování státu II*. 558.

land must be distributed. A great deal of power was left to the Land Office – a situation that particularly suited the agrarian party, which had influence there. Clearly a Czech or Slovak applicant found it much easier to acquire the land than a German, and this became a bone of contention. Resentment was all the more bitter because Germans had not been represented in parliament at the time of debate on the reform as a result of their policy of passive resistance and refusal to co-operate with the new state, and this meant that only Czechoslovak parties gained representation in the Land Fund.[19]

The rigid negativism of the German political leadership of all shades of party, which had launched a fierce, hate-filled campaign against the founding of the Czechoslovak Republic and refused any form of cooperation, thus rebounded on German interests. The Bohemian Germans naturally declared the land reform to be a Czech diktat because they had not been involved in its conception and discussion. Sections of the Austrian and Reich German press backed the invectives on the domestic scene with a massive campaign branding the Land reform "agrarian bolshevism" and an instrument of Czechification.[20] On the 13th of September 1921 at a meeting in Litoměřice the deputy W. Zierhut in his main speech for the German Union of Agriculturists/*Bund der Landwirte* appealed to Germans to defend purely German territory to prevent it being redistributed to the benefit of Czech national interests.

Peroutka saw the perceived rationale of the Land Reform as that of reversing preceding injustices in the distribution of land: "If it is considered in the context of the whole last century as a unilateral reaction to earlier unilateral acts, it gives more the impression of restorative justice... the Czechoslovak government decided to regard it as decent and right to exploit the favour of fortune on the other side and as far as possible redress the consequence of Germanisation, i.e. continuous tracts of German territory, by interspersing them with Czech colonists." The importance that Peroutka attributed to this step taken by the young state is clear from his claim that, "The Czechoslovak revolution stands on three pillars, – the takeover of the state, land reform, and adoption of the constitution."[21]

Yet although there can be no doubt that the reform had an ethnic/national dimension, this cannot be considered a completely dominant motive, since inter alia it involved an effort to adjust land holding to the actual economic and social situation of the state. E. Broklová writes: "Land reform was part of modernisation measures", but "the opening up of a democratic society with free movement of the population was in conflict with the traditions of the German

---

[19]   Ibidem. 563.
[20]   Sommer, K. 2003. "Průběh a výsledky pozemkové reformy v pohraničí českých zemí". 46.
[21]   Peroutka, F. *Budování státu II*. 564.

community, which believed in solidarity (*Gemeinschaft as against Gesellschaft*)."[22] She thus rightly points out that the political and economic dynamic of the new Czechoslovak state was based first and foremost on the idea of modernisation, and not exclusively on the notion of ensuring the ethnic dominance of Czechs.

Although as a result of the Land Reform the Germans in the Czech Lands lost the absolute ascendancy in property ownership that they had enjoyed in the times of the monarchy, their economic "holdings" continued to more than correspond to their numbers as percentage of the CSR population. The fact remains, however, that land reform took place in an atmosphere full of national sloganeering, on the Czech side too, for example with the Agrarian party leaders deploying the idea that the White Mountain had to be made up for: "After the White Mountain the Germans wanted to rule the Czechs and so took their land... if we want to give power back to the Czech people, first we must give the land back to them."[23]

In actual practice the situation was far less dramatic. F. Seibt soberly contends that the new Czech colonisation in German territory increased the share of Czech holdings overall by around 7,200 hectares (comparable in extent to about five larger villages). "Setting aside land losses in territories with scattered settlement or losses resulting from the great increase in state property especially in forestry, then this was not even a loss of three percent let alone the alarmist estimates of 30% of German settled territory."[24] All the same, Seibt regards it as a gross historical error that the Czechoslovak land reform took place under the ideological slogan of redress for the Battle of the White Mountain, and so these mistaken nationalist starting-points united the Bohemian Germans of all social classes and occupations in their opposition to the land reform.[25] Even though the real extent of land transfer into Czech hands was then very far from posing an economic threat to the material basis of the existence of the Sudeten-German ethnic group, as some of their leaders demagogically claimed.

Interesting facts challenging the arguments and data put forward by German nationalistically orientated historians on the subject of the Czechoslovak land reform have been presented in an extensive work by J. W. Brügel.[26] He shows that this data lacks serious value as evidence, among other things because the criteria of what are actually German lands (*Grund und Boden*) are not clearly defined. He adds that the entry of the German parties into the government

22 Broklová, E. "Dvě Hitlerovy lži o Československu" [Two of Hitler's Lies about Czechoslovakia], in *Spory o dějiny* I. 1999. Bednář, M. (ed.). Prague: Masarykův ústav AV ČR. 49.

23 Rašín, A., in *Národní listy*. 2. 12. 1920.

24 Seibt, F. 1993. *Německo a Češi*. Prague: Academia. 265.

25 Ibidem. 264.

26 Brügel, J. W. *Tschechen und Deutsche 1918–1939*. 145, 538–539, 631.

brought a change, enabling them prevent the nationalist abuse of land reform. Brügel even argues from the content of a memorandum drawn up on the 1st of December 1938 in Berlin by Dr. G. Klieber, "representative of the Reich commissioner and gauleiter K. Henlein", after the German annexation of the Sudetenland. Klieber, who had been a deputy in the National Assembly of the CSR in the years 1935–1938, drew up material as the basis for demands for compensation for damages caused to "Germandom" in the course of the Czechoslovak land reform, to be paid by the "residual" Czechoslovakia in the framework of settlement/*Wiedergutmachung*. Naturally he started from the thesis of the "loss of hundreds of thousands of hectares of land belonging to the German nation", but later by comparing data came to the unexpected conclusion that the Germans had not done so badly. For example, from the lands confiscated from major Bohemian landowners in German-speaking territory, Germans had obtained 5,527 hectares, and Czechs 2,937 hectares. Similarly, in closed solidly German territory Czech owners farmed 33,150 hectares, while in solidly Czech-language territory 250,000 hectares were in German hands.[27]

The real transfers of land were not therefore anything like as massive as claimed, but the bitter rhetoric reflected the atmosphere of ethnic tension between Czechs and Germans, which rightly disturbed foreign observers and experts on the ethnic conditions in Czechoslovakia. The extreme dramatising propagandist view regularly appeared in the texts of complaints addressed to the League of Nations. An expert on the subject par excellence, P. de Azcárate (the then director of the section for questions of national minorities at the League of Nations secretariat), asserted that, "exploiting the liberal regime of inter-war Czechoslovakia the German minority never stopped regularly sending petitions presenting demands that were both domestic and international in scope."[28]

Comparing the approaches of the German government to the problems of the German minorities in Poland and the CSR, Azcárate saw them as diametrically different in the sense that the Polish conditions were under constant public and private surveillance. The smallest details relating to the situation of the German minority in Poland were the subject of investigation by organs of the *League of Nations*[29]. The German government (publicly and privately) kept up demands that all questions affecting the German minority in Poland

---

[27]   Ibidem. 539.

[28]   Azcárate, de P. 1945. The *League of Nations and National Minorities – An Experiment*. Washington: Carnegie Endowment for International Peace. 38.

[29]   Azcárate contends, however, that even using the negotiating procedures of the League of Nations it was not possible to prevent the instrumentalisation of the problems of national minorities and their exploitation for certain political ends. For example, up to the signing of the German-Polish treaty one of the main aims of German foreign policy had been to prevent the consolidation of its Eastern borders with Poland. To achieve

be scrutinised. By contrast, the German Government's attitude even toward serious questions affecting the German minority of Czechoslovakia was one of complete indifference.

Azcárate sees two reasons for the difference in approach. The first was the fixed idea that the German minority in Czechoslovakia had traditionally always belonged to Austria by mentality and cultural orientation. The second was the view that the conditions of the German minority in Czechoslovakia were, generally speaking, satisfactory, and that they never had to endure a policy of persecution. Most of the [Sudeten German] complaints and claims were such as to be considered almost inevitable in the transition from the old régime of Central Europe, dominated by the Austro-Hungarian Empire, to the new régime of the Treaties of St. Germain and the Trianon, i.e. complaints concerning agrarian reform, additional schools for the minority, the use of the German language in the new law courts, etc."[30] All these complaints were judged groundless by the League, with the one exception of the Machník Decree (see further below).

For their complaints the Bohemian Germans primarily exploited the *institute of right of petition*. This right had first been formulated in a paragraph of the *Tittoni Report* adopted by the Council of the League of Nations in Brussels on the 22nd of October 1622. The same report also mentioned the procedure for accepting and judging petitions.[31] The petition had to be addressed to the League of Nations (or formally to its Secretary General). In the League secretariat there was a director of a special section whose job it was to organise further steps, above all to confirm receipt of the petition and its formal "admissibility" for further consideration, and then to pass the petition/complaint on to one of the members of the Council for study and production of a report.[32]

A petition could be submitted by any kind of subject,[33] but legally it had the status simply of source of information on the given problem and neither the Council nor any of its members had any duty to take any kind of step on its basis.[34] Thus submission of the petition/complaint was not in itself a legal act.

[ ] this aim, the German government instigated a feverish campaign of agitation motivated by the problems of the German minority in Poland. Ibidem.

[30] Ibidem. 38.

[31] Macartney, C. A. 1968. *National States And National Minorities*. New York: Russell. 311–312.

[32] Formally speaking, a petition had to fulfil the following criteria: "a) must have in view the protection of minorities in accordance with the treaties, b) in particular, must not be submitted in the form of a request for the severance of political relations between the minority in question and the state of which it forms a part, c) must abstain from violent language, d) must contain information or refer to facts which have not recently been the subject of a petition submitted to the ordinary procedure." Macartney, C. A. op. cit. 314.

[33] The one limitation was instituted on the 5th of September 1923 with the formulation that the petition could not come from "anonymous and unauthenticated sources". Ibidem.

[34] Ibidem. 313.

The usual procedure was for a petition, if judged admissible, to be discussed in what was known as a "Committee of Three", set up *ad hoc* for each case separately and consisting of the executive chairman of the Council and two other members.

The Sudeten Germans were not satisfied with the procedure and the nature of their objections can be more or less characterised in the view formulated by W. Jaksch, who writes, "This procedure very often placed assessment of disputed European questions in the hands of non-European powers, which as countries of settlers were committed to the idea of the assimilation of minorities (Brazil) or which were among the worst oppressors themselves, like Japan in Korea."[35]

Jaksch goes on to argue that in practice neither the Council of the League of Nations nor its individual members were keen to get into a dispute with the government of a member state on behalf of a helpless national minority. The mechanism for the protection of national minorities was in practice ineffectual above all because the implementation of any protective decision would come into conflict with the exercise of state sovereignty, one attribute of which was the clear priority of the legal norms of a given state, and this was why, in Jaksch's opinion, most of the complaints of the Sudeten Germans were ruled to be groundless.

In support of his argument Jaksch cites Macartney's view of the status of Sudeten Germans in Czechoslovakia: "The Germans have the feeling that their standing entitles them to full partnership in the state on the basis of full equality, practical and theoretical, of the kind enjoyed by the Swedes in Finland. The fact that they were not given such a position arouses in them a feeling of injustice of the kind that smaller minorities, whose liberties are not perhaps as extensive, would not feel."

Macartney ignored the significant fact that the Swedish minority in Finland had never demanded annexation to a neighbouring state or endangered the territorial integrity of the Finnish state. At the same time Jaksch fails to cite Macartney's praise for the liberal legislation of the CSR in the area of national minorities (not just towards the Germans, but also to Poles, Hungarians, Ukrainians and others), expressed as follows:

"In its attitude to its minorities Czechoslovakia in many respects represents a model for most of the other states of the Versailles system. In several points its laws go strikingly further than the demands set by the Treaty on Minorities".[36] This statement is followed by a list of concrete provisions in linguistic, political,

---

[35] Jaksch, W. *Cesta Evropy do Postupimi*. 113.
[36] Macartney, C. A. *National States a National Minorities*. 414–415.

governmental, cultural and other fields enabling minorities and their elected representatives effective exercise of their rights in the democratic state.[37]

The complaints of the Bohemian Germans were repeated on the agenda of discussions of relevant organs of the League of Nations. The number of complaints fell only during the second half of the 1920s as a result of the increasing activism (engagement) of sections of the German political leaders, and a general relaxation of ethnic tension between Czechs and Sudeten Germans based both on the economic boom of the time and favourable development on the international scene.

Over the whole inter-war period only in one case was a complaint accepted as worthy of consideration by the League of Nations. This was the complaint concerning the Machník Decree submitted on the 24th of April 1937 by K. Henlein for the *Sudeten German Party* (the SdP) together with deputies and senators of the Sudeten and Carpathian Germans. The complaint alleged that German firms were subject to discrimination by the wording of a decree on the allocation of state orders for the needs of the Czechoslovak army, because the decree required arms suppliers to ensure the loyalty of their employers to the state.[38]

In its reply to a query from the League of Nations, the Czechoslovak government stated that the disputed instruction had been issued by a subordinate organ and the matter had been settled in conciliatory spirit by the quashing of the instruction. After two months the SdP had submitted a related complaint to the League of Nations "that sought to give the impression that our government had drawn up a plan, implementation of which would result in mass dismissal of German employees". On the basis of the Czechoslovak government explanation, which included the information that not a single German employee had been dismissed, the three-member committee for the investigation of minority questions (consisting of A. Eden, V. Munters and R. Sandler) decided not to put the complaint forward for discussion by the Council of the League of Nations and to set it aside.[39]

---

[37] C. A. Macartney writes that in his opinion an important specific feature of the German national group in the Bohemian Lands is its size: "The Germans in Czechoslovakia are not in principle irredentists. It is true that at the end of the war they tried to form a federal state with Germany and Austria and they certainly would prefer a division of Europe along different lines than is the case at present (written in 1934 – author's note). Internally, however, they regard themselves as a natural integral part of the historic units of Bohemia, Moravia and Silesia. What they do not consider natural is that these units should form a Slav nation state, in which they are relegated to the position of national minorities." Ibidem. 413. This otherwise precise definition of the heart of the problem underestimates the centrifugal forces of Sudeten German separatism and shows just how far and how fast some western politicians and theorists (Macartney was an important British expert on ethnic problems in Central Europe) were ready to forget the lessons of the First World War.

[38] Krofta, K. *Z dob naší první republiky.* 186–187.

[39] Ibidem. 188.

In 1939 when the League of Nations definitively ceased to fulfil its role as the European order of international relations born at Versailles after the First World War collapsed, it was clear that the treaty system for the protection of the rights of national minorities had collapsed with it, and that if it was ever to be revived, it would be on the basis of a change of principles. The League of Nations system was unpopular with all the parties involved for a variety of reasons. The states that contained minorities were unsympathetic to the system because it limited their "sovereign rights". The minorities disliked the system because it was clumsy and failed to afford them the degree of protection that they were demanding. States ethnically related to the minorities were dissatisfied because it entirely excluded them from decision-making. The system functioned as a limited and by no means universally applicable set of rules for the treatment of national minorities, with states outside its range not being bound by its provisions even where they had minorities on their territories.

E. Chászár notes[40] that while Czechoslovakia made clear its will to co-operate in the protection of national minorities, Poland was irritable and in 1934 issued a declaration resolutely refusing obligations relating to the protection of minorities.[41]

Objectively speaking, Colonel Beck became an ally supporting Hitler in his decision to destroy the system of collective security in European international relations. He signed a pact with Germany in which Poland and Germany undertook to solve disputed questions on a bilateral basis. In the same year Germany announced its decision to leave the League of Nations, having earlier refused to answer the questions of several delegates on the treatment of German Jewish citizens. The German delegate insisted that this was a special case, sui generis, to which the provisions on the protection of minorities did not apply. The General Assembly nonetheless passed a resolution based on a resolution of the third General Assembly of the League of Nations of 1922 stating that "protection must extend without exceptions to all types of nation living in a state formation that differ from the majority by race, language or religion."[42]

In judging the role of the League of Nations in the protection of minorities we should note that in this context most authors use the word experiment, indicating the nature of a situation in which the international community was

---

[40] Chászár, E. "The Problem of National Minorities before and after the Paris Peace Treaties of 1947". *Nationality Papers* 2/1981 (IX). 198–199.

[41] On the 13th of September 1934 Colonel Beck declared to the general assembly of the League of Nations that, "in view of the introduction of a universal and unified system for the protection of minorities, my government feels compelled to reject from this day all cooperation with international organisations in the matter of oversight over the way Poland applies the system of protection of national minorities." Macartney, C. A. *National States And National Minorities*. 502.

[42] Ibidem.

forced following the First World War to try out untested procedures and instru-ments.

Application of the principle of self-determination proclaimed by President Wilson was very much at odds with the existing theory of international rela-tions, and so too was application of the instruments for protection of the rights of minorities, since any thorough-going use of such instruments interfered with the exercise of the sovereignty and freedom of action of individual states. Ap-plication of the principle was made even harder by the unstable international situation and non-participation of Russia (which joined as late as 1934) and Germany (member only in the period 1926–1933) in the work of the League of Nations. Assessment of the results of protection of minorities was likewise distorted by the abuse of the issue by German national groups in Central and Eastern Europe.[43]

In the course of the Second World War the Polish government-in-exile in London categorically proclaimed that Poland would never again accept agree-ments on national minorities. And as early as 1942 the exiled Czechoslovak President Beneš asserted with all the weight of his prestige that the League of Nations system "had failed and cannot be revived".[44] Let us add, in original form.

After the Second World War the creators of the legal framework of the Char-ter of the United Nations Organisation would accept the protection of the rights of national minorities in the form in which it had been formulated by President Beneš, i.e. as a principle of the individual "defence of human and civil rights, and not of the group rights of national minorities."[45]

German Minorities Abroad

As has been said, the defeated and disarmed Germany was aware that for some time to come it would not be capable of achieving by force a revision of the borders established at Versailles. The political leaders of the Weimar Republic therefore made it clear that they accepted the *status quo*, and showed no interest in the irredentist plans and goals of German minorities elsewhere.

---

[43] For example Prof. Oscar I. Janowsky argues that "the agitation of non-loyal elements such as the Sudeten Germans should not prevent us from seeing the unique successes of the League of Nations in the protection of national minorities". Janowsky, I. *Nationalities and National Minorities (with Special Reference to East-Central Europe)*. 1945. New York: Macmillan. 118.

[44] Beneš, E. 1942. In *Foreign Affairs*. 245. Viz též Chászár, E. "The Problem of National Minorities". 198.

[45] Macartney, C. A. *National States and National Minorities*. 507.

Latently, however, the theme of *Auslandsdeutschtum* remained a part of German policy, shelved only until the right moment would arrive. Germany never stopped hoping that a favourable set of circumstances would enable it to re-incorporate within its border the "kin" who had found themselves outside the territory of the Reich. Meanwhile, at Geneva Germany played the role not just of defender of German ethnic groups but of universal defender of the rights of oppressed national minorities.[46]

In fact the scope for Germany to champion its ethnic groups "lost" in foreign countries was limited for three reasons:

- because the protection of German ethnic minorities in Czechoslovakia, Hungary, Poland, Yugoslavia, Rumania, Lithuania, Latvia and Estonia was guaranteed by international treaties, as has been described above.
- because a procedure had been set up for dealing with petitions of complaint at the treatment of national minorities before the League of Nations.
- because internationally recognised principles of treatment of national minorities were being extended even to those states that had refused to make more precise undertakings in this respect – although Germany remained silent on the possibility of applying these principles to itself.

In the period before it joined the League of Nations Germany did, nonetheless, take a number of apparently ineffectual steps (in fact tactical in nature) in the forum of international organisations that expressed views on the subject of national minorities: these were the *Union Interparlementaire* (Commission des questions ethniques et coloniales), *Union Internationale des Associations pour la Société des Nations* (Commission spéciale sur les minorités de race, de langue et de religion), *International Law Association*, *Congrès des Groupes Nationaux Organisés des États Euopéens* and others. After 1926 Germany then took the same kind of initiatives at the League of Nations.

Failure to achieve concrete results did not put Germany's political leaders off the subject. The real purpose of their campaign for national minorities on the international scene (naturally ethnic Germans were those primarily mentioned) was simply to ensure that the "painful" problem of "lost Germans" was not forgotten, was constantly highlighted and so remained a focus of international attention.[47]

Open proposals for the revision of the Versailles System were not feasible in the course of the 1920s (there was no channel for them), at the very least up

---

[46] Schechtman, J. B. 1971. *European Population Transfers 1939–1945*. New York: Russell. 31.
[47] Ibidem. 30–31.

to Locarno. From the long-term German point of view (its desire to recover its great power status), however, Germany had an interest in maintaining contact with and influence on the groups of ethnic Germans that either by reason of the new European order or for much more long-standing historical reasons were outside the territory of the German state. The question of the reincorporation of certain areas of Germany into the state was due to be decided by plebiscite in the 1930s (Schleswig-Holstein, Upper Silesia, Eupen-Malmédy, the Saarland). Systematic efforts were therefore made to influence the future results by means of dozens of associations operating in ethnic German populations.

A German Foundation/*Deutsche Stiftung* was set up in the Weimar Republic as an instrument of general support for Germans outside the Reich shortly after the end of the First World War. It was devoted to funding, from Reich and Land institutions, research and promotion activities encouraging and cultivating German identity in the German territories recently ceded. Likewise, in relation to Czechoslovakia, several organisations were formed to focus on Sudeten German areas. These included, for example, the *Sudetendeutscher Heimatbund, Deutsche Pestalozzigesellschaft in der Tschechoslowakei* and the *Deutschpolitisches Arbeitsamt.*

Various societies orientated to conservative nationalist and Pan-German ideas came together in 1919 to form the German Defense Union/*Deutscher Schutzbund*, which played a decisive role in winning the support of the German-speaking populations in the territories where plebiscites were due to be held. In its arguments, the Union stressed the importance of the results of the eventual plebiscites for the future of the German people as a whole, reminded people of the extent of German's territorial losses following the war and urged them to prevent any further losses at any price. In commentaries on the plebiscite territories it warned against the alleged danger of a new outbreak of war, this time between Poland and Bolshevik Russia.[48]

The *Verband der deutschen Volksgruppen in Europa*/Association of German Ethnic Groups in Europe was formed, secretly and with the assistance of the German foreign ministry as early as 1922, and leaders of the German minorities helped to establish a *European Congress of Minorities*, which provided an international forum for continual complaints about the treatment of German minorities. After Hitler's rise to power this association changed in character and started to pursue a programme of cultural autonomy for the national minorities, involving anything from equality before the law for the majority and

---

[48] "Karte der Abstimmungsgebiete und Zusammenstellung einschlägigen Bestimmungen des Friedensvertrages." (1919, Berlin). Káňa, O. "Instituce a organizace protičeskoslovenské iredenty" [Institutions and Organisations of the Anti-Czechoslovak Irredenta], in *Severní Čechy a Mnichov* [North Bohemia and Munich]. 1969. Hájek, J. (ed.). Liberec/Ústí n. L. 11–12.

minority populations to complete autonomy for the German *Volksgruppen* as organic national entities inside other nation states. In this way one of the fundamental international legal principles championed by Wilson, the right to self-determination, became a perfect tool of Nazi geopolitics. Wilson could not, of course, have had any inkling of this possibility when he embraced and sought to apply the principle after the war, but in the real political world, policies and principles often have unintended consequences that their authors could never have imagined...[49]

Over the 1920s, institutions designed to support ethnic Germans outside the German state developed on the basis of the experience of many earlier German societies. Up to the point when the Nazis came to power, these institutions were mainly foundations and associations organised on a private basis without any deep or consistent linkage with each other. After 1933 they were to be systematically organised, their goals to be unified, their organisational remit to be expanded and an extensive system of support for them from German state funds to be built up.

The foreign or ethnic Germans/*Grenz- und Auslandsdeutsche* were then to be explicitly redefined as "outposts of the national whole"/*Aussenposten des nationalen Hauptkörper*, formed by "throngs of faithful compatriots, who remain united with the Germans in the Reich by origin, consciousness and language, even though at the present time they are under foreign rule".[50]

While in public Hitler ostentatiously ignored the problems of ethnic Germans in Poland, the South Tyrol and elsewhere (earning the reproaches of K. Henlein among others), R. Hess continued with the organisational planning of the covert activities of the Third Reich aimed at mobilising groups of ethnic Germans in Central and Eastern Europe. Among the key organisations in this policy were the *Verein für das Deutschtum im Ausland*/Association for Germandom Abroad and *Deutsches Ausland-Institut*/German Foreign Institute[51]

Two centres in Germany co-ordinated the work of a large number of societies and organisations. One was the Union of Germans Abroad/*Bund der Auslandsdeutschen* (BdA) and the other the Association for Germandom Abroad/*Verein* – later *Volksbund* – *für das Deutschtum im Ausland* (VDA), which was clearly directed to the support of irredentist tendencies with the aim of "supporting German-

---

[49]   Brown, MacAlister. "Fifth Column in Eastern Europe". *Journal of Central European Affairs*. July 1959 (XIX). 130.

[50]   *Severní Čechy a Mnichov*. 13.

[51]   Brown, MacAlister. "Fifth Column in Eastern Europe". The stress was placed on press propaganda, for example the Reich Office for the Support of German Literature/*Reichsstelle zur Förderung des deutschen Schrifttums* published the monthly *Zeitschrift für Geopolitik*. The publisher recommended it with the words: "This journal has by its achievements made a major contribution to the practice of education in a national spirit." Ibidem.

dom in foreign states in its political, economic and cultural endeavours".[52] Ronald M. Smelser is among those who argue that the VDA played a crucial role in the development of the Sudeten-German problem. This organisation was the strongest (largest) group with a traditionalist *Volkstum* orientation, and the only such group to retain a degree of independence and integrity even under the Nazi regime. It had been founded in 1881 as the *Deutscher Schulverein* and, as the name suggests, for many years concentrated on the development of German education in ethnic German communities abroad.

The VDA reacted to the shock of the defeat of Germany in 1918 by immediately stepping up its activities, and by 1932 it already boasted 27 Land Unions/ *Landesverbände* representing groups of ethnic Germans in the same number of states. It financed its work from annually organised collections in all the German towns and a certain contribution from the Foreign Ministry, which added to its political as well as financial strength. After the Nazis came to power in 1933, Dr. Hans Steinacher, a celebrated hero of nationalist struggles against the Slovenes in Carinthia, a veteran of the battles in the Ruhr in 1923 and an uncompromising supporter of German minorities in all countries, was elected to the function of association leader. In fact, as a conservative identified with the traditions of the Austrian defence associations/*Schutzverbände* (devoted to the "cultural, social and economic defence of the autonomously developing groups of ethnic Germans") Steinacher was primarily interested in promoting loyalty to the overall nation/*volk*, whereas Nazi policy was to insist on the priority of the Pan-German programme of the Nazi state and the primary Nazi demand was for unconditional loyalty to this state.[53]

In Germany and Austria, *die Völkischen* were the direct successors of the Greater German/*Alldeutsche* movements that had outwardly been more moderate in rhetoric, but in terms of content they nonetheless identified with the same goals as the emerging radicals – i.e. they demanded the annexation/unification of territories with a German-speaking population in such a way as to ultimately make possible the creation of a Greater Germany – a Greater Germany larger than had been the dream of the Frankfurt radical democrats in 1848 and with much greater ambitions to become a world power/*Weltmacht* than those

---

[52] Archives of the Ministry of Foreign Affairs, Prague (AMZV). Section 2, fasc. 307, in *Severní Čechy a Mnichov.* 14. MacAlister Brown regards the *Deutsches Ausland-Institut* as an organisation that played a central role. See The Third Reich's Mobilization of the German Fifth Column in Eastern Europe. Brown, MacAlister. "Fifth Column in Eastern Europe". 128. The *Deutsches Ausland-Institut* in Stuttgart was founded in 1917 and by 1932 had brought out fifty publications on the theme of German identity, ethnic conflicts, the role of German national groups etc.

[53] Smelser, R. M. "Germandom Organizations in the Reich", in *The Sudeten Problem 1933–1938.* 16–19.

of Wilhelmine Germany.[54] A certain megalomania of programme was not rare among such societies and organisations.

Groups of ethnic Germans abroad differed in the strength of their national sentiments, economic power and position, and specific cultural features. Together with other factors these affected the intensity with which different German populations responded to Nazi activities designed to exploit their presence in Central and East Europe for purposes of Nazi territorial ambitions in the east and the Nazi desire to achieve a "perfectly large space" (Hitler: *Mein Kampf*) for the needs of the development of the German nation.

Territorial expansionism relied on nationalist groups/*Volksgruppen* of ethnic Germans/*Volksdeutschen*, who played the role of Trojan horses (or *fifth columns*, to use the term employed for this phenomenon of irredentism of groups of ethnic Germans by experts on the theme such as Louis de Jong, MacAlister Brown, Henry C. Meyer, Ronald M. Smelser and others), undermining from within the integrity of the states within which they lived.

Using the excuse of defence of the rights of national minorities, demands were constantly raised on the gradualist principle with a view to ultimately destabilising the system of a given state and progressively crippling its capacity to function. The goal was to create situations in which the internal political problem posed by the German ethnic minority would become insoluble on a domestic basis and would require negotiation in the international forum, with appeals made for help from an influential power – Germany.[55]

The usual tactic was to set up a united national front, encouraged skilfully by the arguments of German propaganda. From the outside, such groupings looked "non-partisan", but in fact the national socialist forces were their prime movers. The formation of these fronts was usually secretly supported from Germany. Eventually the Anschluss with Austria and the annexation of the Sudetenland would extend this penetration even further, in a chain effect, as the Nazis gained the opportunity for direct contact with German minorities in Hungary and Yugoslavia. After a longer or shorter internal struggle, the united national fronts would force or manoeuvre into direct participation all bodies of *Volksdeutschen* opinion (groups) that had hitherto kept aloof, as happened in the Saarland, the Eupen-Malmédy district, Northern Schleswig, Poland, Estonia, Lithuania, Hungary and Yugoslavia, and outside Europe in South Africa.

---

54   Kural, V. *Konflikt místo společenství.* 108.

55   On the basis of the programme demands, Hedva Ben-Israel considers the Bohemian Germans to have been separatist but not an irredentist movement striving for annexation. He argues that they were pursuing the nationalism of German Bohemianism and the demand for self-determination was supposed to consolidate their national rights in the country. He defines this state as the pre-state phase of nationalism. See "Irredentism: Nationalism Reexamined", in *Irredentism and International Politics.* 1991. Chazan, N. (ed.). London: Adamantine Press Ltd. 28.

This tactic was to fail in Alsace and the USA, however, where it proved impossible to mobilise the German community for the cause.

Inside Czechoslovakia, protests against the "unfairness of the Versailles peace treaties" and demands for the revision of the Czechoslovak borders were often raised as a result of the efforts of the *Sudetendeutscher Heimatbund*. Claims about the cultural superiority and achievements of the German ethnic group were frequently deployed to whip up support. O. Spann became famous for his assertion that the Czechs had never been a nation but always just *Böhmen*.[56]

Until the coming of Nazism, these societies found their ideological inspiration in what was known as the *völkisch* movement, a blanket term for cultural, social and above all political movements among the German diaspora scattered on the territory of the new Central and Eastern European successor states. The *völkisch* ideology won enthusiastic supporters especially in border territories or "regions of friction" (*Reibungszone*), where there was a higher level of *interethnic tension* between the German-speaking and Slav populations.

The border territories of the Bohemian Lands with their ethnically overlapping areas of Czech-German settlement were one such zone as defined by this ideology. In the wake of the Great Economic Crisis, which had a particularly devastating impact on the border areas that made up the Sudetenland, a socially explosive situation developed that the nationalist agitators exploited to the full.

Jaksch argues that this was the last moment at which the leadership of the Czechoslovak state might have "undertaken a reform of the state so as to give the German population an objective choice between democracy and dictatorship. If the Germans had been accorded equality of language and proportional representation in government, and if generous measures had been taken to relieve the crisis in the border areas, no complicated structural problems would have arisen".[57]

Jaksch's claim sounds optimistic, yet given what we know today about the activities of the Nazi organisations and institutions geared towards Germans abroad (especially the Sudetenlanders), which gradually developed into a secretly directed movement under the veil of defence of the rights of national minorities, it is a disingenuous to exaggerate the room for manoeuvre available to the Czechoslovak government in both its domestic and foreign policy.

---

[56] Cesar, J. – Černý, B. *Politika německých buržoazních stran*. 55. Spann's doctrine was based on the "theory of the real state", in which government was the responsibility of a small group of leaders. The circle of Spann supporters remained in the background. In 1928 in Liberec the Working Group for Social Sciences transformed itself into the *Kameradschaftsbund für volks- und sozialpolitische Bildung*/The Friendly Society for Social-Political Education), from which nearly all the future leaders of the Sudeten German movement were to come, including K. Henlein. For more detail see Kural, V. *Konflikt místo společenství*. 120–121. Biman, S. – Malíř, J. *Kariéra učitele tělocviku*.

[57] Jaksch, W. *Cesta Evropy do Postupimi*. 134.

In the first half of the 1930s, the outlines of Nazi geopolitics, with their leit-motif of territorial expansion to the east, began to emerge. After a Polish-German treaty was signed in 1934, Czechoslovakia replaced neighbouring Poland in the role of main target of German expansion.

All contacts between the ethnic Germans' organisations and Berlin were kept a strict secret. The slogan *Heim ins Reich* scored its first major success in the Saarland, where there was an almost compact settlement of German-speaking population numbering approximately 820,000.[58] The demand for incorporation into Germany was alive here throughout the period of the French protectorate. In other countries, the activities of the national socialist fronts tried to exploit historical circumstances and popular aspirations that had existed long before anyone had ever heard the name Hitler. Such historical circumstances and aspirations were eminently exploitable in the Sudeten areas as a result of the Bohemian Germans' persisting hostility to the independent CSR and latent demand for self-determination.

In 1919 a youth organisation known as the *Böhmerlandbewegung* was founded in Ústí nad Labem, its representatives declaring that their programme was to strive for the "revival of Germandom", which they promoted by means that included the illegal periodical *Böhmerlandbewegung*. Its leading figures included H. Rutha, later an important colleague of Henlein, a member of the *Kameradschaftsbund* (KB) and of the Sudetendeutsche Heimatfront (SHF)/Sudeten German Homeland Front.[59]

Supporters of Spannism, based on the theory of a "real state" formulated by the Austrian sociologist and national economist Othmar Spann,[60] gained a majority in the leadership of the SHF. As the social basis of his utopian state, Spann took the concept of pre-industrial society, where the fundamental organisational unit is the domaine (feudal estate – holding), and conflicts be-

---

[58] According to the definition formulated at Versailles, the Saarland consisted of some 1,900 square kilometres. This densely populated region, at that time a centre of coal-mining, lay on the Franco-German frontier north of Lorraine. On the basis of the decision of the Congress of Vienna in 1815 the region had been assigned to Germany and German culture and language had become dominant there. After the victory in 1918 France had gained this territory with exclusive right to mine coal in the framework of reparation claims for 15 years. The attempts of the French government to establish the Saarland as an automonous state failed. In 1935 a plebiscite was held here, on the basis of which the territory was incorporated into Nazi Germany. See Anderson, M. "History And Territory", in *Frontiers*. 1996. Cambridge: Polity Press. 23.

[59] On the aims of the movement Rutha wrote, "In our work we recognise no parties, but only Germans. Age or class should not determine the leaders in public life. The self-sacrificing and industrious cooperation of the young will help to renew public life. We want to put all moral and spiritual forces in the service of Germandom. It does not matter to us which routes this work will take, or of what kind it will be." Fischer, J. – Patzak, V. – Perth, V. 1937. *Ihr Kampf: Die wahren Ziele der Sudetendeutschen Partei.* Karlsbad: Verlagsanstalt Graphia. 73.

[60] Prof. O. Spann taught until 1919 at the German Technical College in Brno and formulated his basic theory and ideas on the state and society particularly in his publications *Der Wahre Staat* (Jena 1932) and *Geschichtsphilosophie* (Jena 1931).

tween social classes could not theoretically occur. Like many other conservative revolutionary contemporaries, Spann was formulating a reactionary vision in reaction to both Marxism and liberalism.[61]

Essentially he argued that the democratic order should be replaced by an "estates" model organised on the leadership (führer) principle. The government of the state should be entrusted to a special state estate/*Staatstand*, represented by a special stratum of rulers/*Staatsführende Schicht*, created by purposive and systematic upbringing. The political elite would then run the so-called unified German community/*Volksgemeinschaft*. Germans would renounce any individual opinions and attitudes, which Spann uncompromisingly rejected in the interest of collective goals, above all the idea of the revival of the "Holy Roman Empire", because in his view only Germany had the potential to end the "Balkanisation of Central Europe" that he believed had occurred since the end of the First World War. He thought that the new state should extend from the Baltic to the Adriatic and from the Atlantic to the Black Sea.[62]

Spann's ideas had a fundamental influence on many members of the romantic German youth movement known as the *Wandervogel*, which was the seedbed of the *Kameradschaftsbund* circle, from which first the *Sudeten German Homeland Front* and eventually Henlein's *Sudeten German Party* developed. Spann's leadership principle, in which the "core of the nation", a privileged group, would lead the anonymous masses whose task would be to fulfil the will of the leaders unreservedly, remained a connecting ideological link.

The *Kameradschaftsbund* was a conspiratorial organisation with a structure inspired by masonic lodges.[63] It was also a strictly selective organisation of young German intellectuals and even at its height at the turn of the 1920s/30s possessed a mere two hundred members, the largest number on the territory of Czechoslovakia and the rest in Austria and Germany. Its influence, however, was very disproportionate to its small numbers. Members of the KB penetrated most of the German political parties, mass organisations and institutions, and influenced their activities without their special connections becoming particularly visible.[64,65]

---

[61] Smelser, R. M. *The Sudeten Problem 1933–1938*. 60.

[62] "For Spann, a society that avows liberalism and democratism is just a heap of individuals, a kind of human sand. In opposition to it he posits Gemeinschaft…, which is a kind of supra-personal collective unit in which the individual means about as much as a cell in an organism." *Přítomnost* XIII (1936). 241. For more detail see Cesar, J. – Černý, B. *Politika německých buržoazních stran*. 202–211.

[63] Especially the lodges of the so-called *Turngemeinden* in 1807–1813, created by the founder of the Turner movement Jahn for the preparation of a German rebellion against Napoleon. Ibidem. 206.

[64] Smelser, R. M. *The Sudeten Problem 1933–1938*. 60–65.

[65] KB members F. Künzel, Hodina and Preibsch were active in the Bund der Landwirte, W. Sebekowsky in the DNSAP, Liehm in the DNP. H. Neuwirth, H. Rutha and W. Brand were likewise active in the physical education organisation, the Turnverband, led by K. Henlein. E. Kundt had an important function in the

On the grounds that there was supposedly no political party in the Czecho-slovak government capable of consistently defending the German ethnic inter-est in the Bohemian Lands, the three largest German mass organisations, the *Bund der Deutschen in Böhmen, Kulturverband* and *Deutscher Turnverband,* made an agreement on mutual cooperation to make concentrated and co-ordinated work possible on all levels (local, district and regional) as a way of pushing through the political demands of ethnic Germans in the Sudetenland (e.g. "the rescue of German property", above all land, if there was a danger of it falling into Czech hands).

The preparations for creation of a new Sudeten German Party in 1933 in-volved not only the leaders of the DNSAP and DNP parties but also politicians from the other rightwing parties and leaders of mass non-political organisa-tions and interest associations. Members of the *Kameradschaftsbund* who had al-ready been working in the leadership of the Sudeten German Homeland Front played an important part in these preparations.

The founding of the Sudeten German Homeland Front/*Sudetendeutsche Hei-matfront* in 1933 (after the official banning of the DNSAP, i. e. the German Na-tional Socialist Workers' Party, and DNP, i. e. the German National Party) and then of Konrad Henlein's Sudeten German Party/*Sudetendeutsche Partei* in 1934 in Česká Lípa, followed the same pattern. The new party at first proceeded very cautiously, largely because the Czechoslovak police and judicial organs had been keeping a closer watch on the various Turner societies active mainly in the borderlands, the *hakenkreuzler,* but also the DNSAP. The Turner movement played a particularly important role in attracting a large number of supporters. It was an apparently entirely non-political movement of members of physical training societies, but offered its members not only training in physical fitness but also "national political education". In 1930 K. Henlein encapsulated its ethos with the words, "Our objective is the true heroic German way of life. It is the sign of any healthy movement."[66]

Initially it was SdP policy to seek to maintain the appearance of loyalty to the Czechoslovak state, but from 1935, (already demonstrably on the basis of instructions from Nazi Germany and with its financial, organisational and planning support), the goal of the *Sudetendeutsche Partei* became in practice the destruction of the republic. Before we look at the aspect of the close rela-

---

Deutschpolitisches Arbeitsamt, an institution set up to co-ordinate the policy of the German parties and organisations on the basis of national needs. The KB's propaganda instrument in the border areas was the publishing concern "Die Junge Front" which brought out a monthly of the same name. The society's organ was the *Rumburger Zeitung,* regarded as the most extreme (but also the most influential) nationalist paper. It also engaged in the internal disputes of the movement and was often the platform for attacks on "traditional-ists". Smelser, R. M. *The Sudeten Problem 1933–1938.* 56.

[66] Biman, S. – Malíř, J. *Kariéra učitele tělocviku.* 44.

tions of Henlein's party to Germany and the activities of the SdP in the field of international relations, it will be useful to characterise the activities of Sudeten German separatism in the wider context of the common factors affecting the dynamics of the behaviour of groups of Germans abroad (minority Germans) in the 1930s.

Ethnic Germans as an Instrument of Expansion

Although there were definitely some real violations of treaty obligations on the protection of minorities, it is clear that influential groups of ethnic Germans (the Sudeten Germans are regularly categorised among the most important groups – see below for the classification produced by Louis de Jong[67]) often provoked particularist conflicts, reviving old animosities and encouraging unwillingness to accept compromise solutions offered by governments in the states concerned. This strategy followed the general trend of increasing political resentment among German political associations in all states and confirmed them in feeling that any attempts to obtain satisfaction using the ordinary legal procedures of international relations were doomed to failure in advance. As a result, ethnic Germans looked to the "mother" country as the only possible source of salvation and hope.

A dissatisfied Sudeten German population would seem to have offered an ideal tool for the Nazis to "coordinate," mold, and use as they pursued an aggressive, expansionist foreign policy. In 1933, however, directly after Hitler's seizure of power, there could be no question of such a militant approach. The new régime had first to consolidate its power internally, a task which called for quiescence with Czechoslovakia and other Germany's neighbours, especially those to the east and southeast with considerable German minorities. If these countries had suspected that National Socialism was an export commodity, they might conceivably have been in a position to end the Thousand Year Reich before it even began.

The relationship of the Sudeten Germans to Germany in the 1930s can be defined using a set of factors that have been formulated at a general level (to analyse and compare the conditions of the German diaspora in different countries of the world) by the important Dutch historian, Louis de Jong. On the basis of detailed study he concluded that the position and character of the different

---

[67] "The Sudeten Germans were the largest German minority group in Europe, they were also the closest to the Reich. More important, their settlement areas included the strategically significant Bohemian mountain rim on Germany's border." Smelser, R. M. *The Sudeten Problem 1933–1938*. 10.

groups of *Volksdeutschen* showed a large measure of *diversity* arising from the different historical development of the different regions. He argued that these factors, formulated for the position before 1933, were the main determinants of the extent and depth to which the different *Volksgruppen* responded to the ideological impulses coming from national socialist Germany.

The following factors may be distinguished:

- *Relative size of the group in terms of population.* If the group is to form a mass movement that has a noticeable dislocating effect then it should be of considerable size as a proportion of the population of the state in which it finds itself.
- *Its situation with regard to Germany.* The nearer to Germany the more closely allied to Germany the group will feel, and the greater too will be the possibilities for intense contact between the two.
- *Geographical concentration.* The political activities developed by the group will be greater the more its settlements are continuous, even making it a regional majority.
- *Economic development.* In modern societies, political activities more often originate in towns than in the countryside. The less the group consists of farmers living scattered about, the faster their political activities will develop.
- *Socio-economic situation.* If the group is in social and economic difficulties then its discontent can express itself in political activity. People who are content do not start revolutions.
- *Historical ties to Germany.* If the group had once been part of Germany or has been separated from Germany against its will, or both, then it will be inclined to support any movement for re-integration or integration with Germany.
- *The feeling of being oppressed as a minority.* If a group feels oppressed, then the discontent thus engendered will be able to find an outlet in political activities.
- *Historical feeling of superiority.* The discontent will be the stronger in proportion as the group has the ingrained feeling that its members are the 'true rulers' in the country in question. If they are then oppressed, they will wish to 'take revenge'.
- *Existence of national socialist cadres.* If a national socialist nucleus of any permanency has already been formed, then the possibilities for a political movement in favour of the Third Reich will be greater.

Table 1: Factors influencing the formation of the role
of German ethnic groups in a given territory (state in 1933)

	GERMAN GROUP								
	Proportionately large population	Lives close to Germany	Lives in strong geographical concentration	Is economically highly advanced	Under economic pressure	Separated from Germany against its will	Feels oppressed as a minority	Conscious of former historical supremacy	Has nationalsocialist cadres
Saarland (99%)	■	■	■	▒		■			
Eupen-Malmédy (0.5%)		■	■			■	■		
Gdansk (98%)	■	■	■			■		▒	■
Memel (4%)	▒	■	■		▒	■		▒	▒
Alsace (2%)		■	■		▒				
Northern Schleswig (1%)		■	▒			■			
Gdansk Corridor, Poznan, East of Upper Silesia (3%)	▒	■	▒			■			
South-West Africa (35%)	■				▒				▒
Austria (98%)	■	■	■	▒		■			■
Sudetenland (22%)	■	■	■	▒		■	■		■
South Tyrol (0,5%)		▒	■	▒		■	▒		
Estonia (1.5%)	▒	▒		■		▒			
Lithuania (3%)	▒	■		■		▒			
Hungary (2%)		▒	▒				■	▒	
Rumania (2%)		▒	▒				■	▒	
Yugoslavia (3%)	▒		▒	▒				▒	▒
Soviet Union (0,5%)	▒			▒	■				▒
United States (1%)			▒	■					▒
Brazil (1.5%)			▒	▒				▒	
Argentina (1.5%)			▒	▒				▒	
Chile (0.66%)			▒	■				■	▒

Key:

Large share-proportion   ■

Small share   ▒

No or negligible share   □

(From the point of view of classification of the Sudeten German group, we should add for the sake of completeness that the Germans in Bohemia and Moravia had never been constitutionally a part of Germany, Upper or Lower Austria. The issue therefore could not be one of their re-incorporation in the Reich, but of the fulfilment of the demand for annexation to the German state after the Sudeten Germans lost their privileged position as a result of the collapse of the Habsburg Empire and establishment of an independent Czechoslovakia.).

De Jong made these factors the basis of a comparison that uses a three-degree scale (factor not operative at all – operative to a minor extent – acting to a major extent) to indicate the intensity of the effect of the different factors in different states. Having assigned a degree of effect to each factor in relation to each specific ethnic German group, he then evaluated their combined effect in each case. The characteristics of the different groups of ethnic Germans are presented with an indication of their percentage share in the overall population of the given state. As is evident, all significant groups of ethnic Germans living outside Germany are included: from Eupen-Malmédy, Austria, the Saarland, the Gdansk Corridor, Hungary and elsewhere, even including those overseas.

"Only in one case do we find all the factors present and operating at maximum intensity – in the Sudetenland – the border areas of the Bohemian Lands."[68]

Using a similar typology of circumstances influencing the relative intensity of the political activities of ethnic Germans in different areas of Czechoslovakia, R. M. Smelser arrived at a definition of three basic factors influencing the degree of development of the Henlein movement. These were as follows:

- *the geographical factor* expressing degree of proximity to Germany,
- *the ethnic factor* expressing the intensity of ethnic antagonism and the tension arising from it,
- *the economic factor* expressing the level of economic decline of the Sudeten territory.

Acording to Smelser all these factors worked in parallel and mutually reinforced each other. For example, the absence of only one of them in an area substantially reduced the number of active supporters of Nazism.[69]

---

[68] Jong, L. de. 1956. *The German Fifth Column in the Second World War*. London: Routledge & Kegan Paul, 290–292. The author was a leading expert on the Second World War, and specifically the role of German minorities in Nazi expansion. He spent the war in exile in Great Britain, where he worked as a commentator for the Dutch broadcasts of the BBC. In the 1950s he was executive director of the Dutch State Institute for War Documentation.

[69] On this issue Smelser gives the example of the districts of Jablonec n. N., Česká Lípa and Karlovy Vary, where the unemployment rate was the highest and membership of the SdP also at the highest level. In

Both these classifications are useful because they allow us to compare the course of ethnic mobilisation in the different conditions of different types of territory and states. Without exaggerating their explanatory power, we may consider them a contribution to deeper understanding of the "morphology" of the different variants of Nazi movements in the inter-war period.

Left only to themselves, groups of ethnic Germans could not, of course, have in any decisive way disrupted the stability of the political systems of the states in which they lived (this includes the Sudeten Germans in Czechoslovakia). This destabilisation required direct encouragement and support from Nazi Germany. Only in three territories – the Saarland, Gdansk and Austria, were German speaking inhabitants in a very substantial majority. In South Africa they had a substantial share, almost a third of the white population, and in Czechoslovakia just over a fifth. In all the other cases they were merely small and marginal minority groups.

The picture of the situation as defined using de Jong's nine "positive" factors would not be complete is we did not add three "negative" factors inhibiting influence from the Reich. These are:

- *Absolute isolation* – if an ethnic group was entirely cut off from Germany no further political activities connected to German plans were possible – this was the case of the Volga Germans inside the Soviet Union.
- *Ban imposed by Hitler* – if Hitler banned any sort of contact and support of the dissatisfaction of groups of ethnic Germans, as happened in the case of the South Tyrol.
- *Anti-nationalist social influences* – in cases where religious or political influences of a non-nationalist character predominated in a particular group, the effect of the "positive" factors was to a large extent eliminated.

Among these factors, the third "negative" factor was particularly important. It expresses the fact that in every group of ethnic Germans outside German territory the Nazis had first, in an initial phase, to gain a decisive influence, to overcome a greater or lesser degree of resistance to the ideology of violence. In all the ethnic German minorities there were other political forces and factors at work that were far from conducive to the spread of Nazi ideologies: primarily, these were groups of socialists, communists and liberals. In our case this

K. Vary there was 35–40% unemployed and 30.6% inhabitants were members of the SdP. By contrast, in the Znojmo district, where unemployment moved between 5 and 20%, 15% of the population was in the SdP. Smelser, R. M. 1975. "At the Limits of a Mass Movement: the Case of the Sudeten German Party, 1933–1938", in *Bohemia* (Jahrbuch des Collegium Carolinum). Band 17. 1976. München/Wien: Oldenbourg. 254–255.

applied to the politicial milieu of the democratic part of the Sudeten German population, which although a minority resisted the domination of the Nazi-orientated Henleinians until every last possibility had been exhausted. The most important group in this context were the German Social Democrats in the Sudetenland and their paramilitary units, the *Republikanische Wehr*, but the Communists, some of the German Christian Socialists and other groups of German democrats also played a role.[70]

To go back to the wider comparative perspective: in the Saarland, for example, a united anti-Nazi front was formed, and in the Gdansk corridor a third of the population remained loyal to the classic political parties. In Alsace, the great majority of ethnic Germans refused to have anything to do with the new forces of aggressive "Prussianism", even though they were not specially enthusiastic about French rule, and as a result the large movement in favour of autonomy in the 1920s dwindled into a Nazi sect whose influence remained limited. In 1937 Hitler had to intervene personally to force the cautious leaders of the ethnic Germans in Poland to resign in order to make way for the Nazi radicals. In Austria the number of supporters of Nazism was estimated at a third of the population. In Estonia, Lithuania, Latvia, Hungary and Yugoslavia the Nazis only succeeded in gaining control over the German minorities as late as 1938–39.[71]

In Sudeten conditions, too, Henlein's *Sudetendeutsche Partei* had to make concentrated efforts to win the majority of German-speaking inhabitants of Czechoslovakia over to his side. The economic crisis did much to encourage nationalist resentment, but so too did Henlein's gradualist policy, presenting what was in fact a programme of aggressive national chauvinism as a constitutional movement designed to improve the quality of Czech-German co-existence within the CSR. Where demagogy failed, terror was applied instead.

In the second half of the 1930s an atmosphere of intimidation prevailed in the German-speaking areas of the borderlands; it was designed to unify the ranks of Sudeten Germans and block any influence exercised by any Sudeten German supporters of Czechoslovak statehood. Fearing criticism from French and British appeasers, who were being encouraged by the propaganda of the Reich and SdP to see any strong Czechoslovak action as proof of oppression, the Prague government proceeded more defensively than confidently against

[70] Of the many studies dealing with the subject of democrats and antifascists among the Sudeten Germans, we shall mention the following: Mejdrová, H. 1997. *Trpký úděl. Výbor dokumentů k dějinám německé soc. dem. v ČSR 1937–1948* [Bitter Destiny. A Choice of Documents on the History of the German Social Democratic Party in the CSR 1937–1948]. Prague: Ústav mezinárodních vztahů. Brügel, J. W. *Deutsche und Tschechen I, II*. Grünwald, L. 1986. *Sudetendeutscher Widerstand gegen den Nationalsozialismus*. München: Sudetendeutsches Archiv.

[71] Jong, L. de. *The German Fifth Column in the Second World War*. 292–293.

reported cases of intimidation of democratically minded Germans. The German Social Democrats were thus to a considerable extent left to the mercy of the Henlein thugs.

In his later studies R. W. Seton-Watson recalled this atmosphere of terror, which he personally witnessed and which convinced him that Henlein's ostentatiously presented moderation in London was just a mask. For example, in the course of a visit to the Sudeten border areas in the summer of 1938 he went to a school in a small German town and saw a class teacher trying to persuade pupils in her class not to physically attack the small Jewish children. The fanaticised pupils pointed to the chandelier and said she would be hung from it when He (Hitler) came.

Meetings of the German Social Democratic part were regularly visited by photographers who declared that anyone whose face was caught in their photos would end up in a concentration camp or meet an even worse fate. Intimidation by members of the SdP and especially the party "ordners" was a daily occurrence.[72]

Despite this, Seton-Watson recalled a joint meeting of the Czech and German Social Democrats in Plzeň at which thousands of Czechs chanted, "Long live our German friends" and the Germans answered "Long live the Czechoslovak Republic". Another who often returned to the theme of the autumn of 1938 and the demonstrated solidarity of the Czech and German Democrats was Wenzel Jaksch.

As a result of energetic Henleinian propaganda the SdP won 88% of the German votes in the May community/local elections of 1938 (although this fell to 81% in the third round). The partial mobilisation of the Czechoslovak army in May, which decisively suppressed the Henleinian attempts at a coup in the border regions, helped somewhat to increase the self-confidence and chances of the democrats among the Sudeten Germans.[73]

In May 1938 an electoral meeting of the German Democratic bloc was held in the German House on Na Příkopě boulevard in Prague, where the German Social Democratic party leader Jaksch declared that, "The government of Czechoslovakia is offering a minority statute (which proposed to solve disputes over the Sudeten German demands by reviving land (provincial) self-government, with land assemblies to have legislative functions – author's note) which the SdP rejects. Being fully informed I can say that this rejection is wrong, because the conditions in the statute are acceptable, and we can certainly already come to an agreement"[74] On the last Sunday of August 1938 a series of

72 Seton-Watson, H. 1982. *Eastern Europe between the Wars 1918–1941*. London: Westview Press/Boulder. 282.
73 Cesar, J. – Černý, B. *Politika německých buržoazních stran*. 463. On the most recent doubts about the reasons for the May mobilisation see below.
74 Mejdrová, H. *Trpký úděl*. 49.

joint demonstrations by Czechs and Germans could still take place, appealing to the Czechoslovak government not to yield to the threats and blackmail of Henlein's SdP and Nazi Germany.[75]

The problem with Jaksch's view rests, however, in the weakness of the theory on which he repeatedly based his defence of the Sudeten Germans in Great Britain during the war and later in West Germany. He expressed this theory in concentrated form in the conclusion to his chapter entitled "The Burial of Saint-Germain and Preparation of Potsdam" where he says, "Munich showed that the will to maintain European democracy had been shaken. Inasmuch as the Sudeten Germans became scapegoats, this hides the all-European responsibility for this great failure. Furthermore, in the European crisis over the Sudeten German question, it was Prague that held the key to a good or bad solution."[76] Yet it is clear from the facts and context that it was not Prague that held the keys to the situation, but Berlin, Paris and London.

However much one may agree with Seton-Watson and other authors that it was Hitler who made German ethnic minorities abroad the instrument of his expansionist policies, one can hardly agree with the thesis that they did no more than play the part of unknowing executors of a "higher" will. After all, we are not talking of a one-off, short-term movement, but of the systematic destruction of a state – a destruction that was widely supported among the Sudeten German public. In this context H. Seton-Watson noted that, "after the fall of Nazism it will be impossible for the Germans to live side by side with those that they have betrayed and terrorised. Many will be massacred in revenge, others will be driven from their homes, and others will have to renounce their German identity. No one can predict the details, but it is probably certain that the historic mission of Germans in Eastern Europe has ended."[77] In retrospect Seton-Watson's prophecy in 1945 was not entirely inaccurate, and in any case it remains valid as a document of a period view of the German ethnic minorities in Central and Eastern Europe.

The Programme of International Isolation of the CSR

In the course of the 1930s German foreign policy was successfully geared to the progressive isolation of Czechoslovakia in Central Europe, particularly through the support of Hungarian revisionism and the systematic erosion of

[75]   Kural, V. – Hyršlová, K. 1999. *Češi a Němci společně proti Hitlerovi* [Czechs and Germans together against Hitler]. Katalog výstavy v pražském Karolinu [Catalogue of the exhibition of the Prague Karolinum]. 13.

[76]   Jaksch, W. *Cesta Evropy do Postupimi*. 199.

[77]   Seton-Watson, H. *Eastern Europe between the Wars 1918–1941*. 287.

economic cooperation between the states of the Little Entente. German propaganda from the summer of 1935 deliberately characterised the CSR as the tool of the Soviet Union (the republic was symbolically branded the "aircraft carrier of Bolshevism"), but above all as the oppressor of its German ethnic minority. These systematic propaganda efforts were to bear fruit in the crisis situation of autumn 1938.[78]

For the internationalisation of the Sudeten German question, a goal constantly pursued by Nazi Germany in co-ordination with the *Sudeten German Party*, the position of the great powers Great Britain and France, and to some extent also Italy, was crucial.

The SdP skilfully used propaganda activity in the League of Nations and other international forums to push forward its demands on the international level.

At a meeting of the *Congress of European National Minorities* in London in September 1936, Dr Neuwirth as head of the Sudeten German delegation made a speech about the right to life (*Lebensrecht*) of national minorities in European states. He argued that national minorities should be recognised as the foundation of development towards a new Europe. In his view this would not necessarily mean an immediate change in the current territorial arrangements, but the use of new forums in constitutional and new international law. He contended that the dynamics of change in the minorities were such that they needed to be regulated by law if they were not to have a destructive effect and lead to an undesirable situation.[79]

The line taken by the three-member Sudeten German delegation was typical; they were making strenuous efforts to influence foreign politicians, but above all journalists, and to convince them that the Germans in Czechoslovakia were threatened with complete extinction as a result of wide-ranging Czech efforts to de-ethnicise them, and because of the dire social and economic straits in which they found themselves. The constant dramatisation of the situation and effort to keep the Czechoslovak government under pressure of the time factor was characteristic. The views of the British journalist Vernon Bartlett in the *New Chronicle* testify to the success of this intense pressure.

"The leaders of the German minority assure me that if there is no improvement in the response to their next petition, which is to be presented to the League of Nations in September, this Mr. Henlein – who is a moderate man – will be replaced by other minority leaders who are far more radical and have far greater sympathy with national socialism in Germany."[80]

---

[78] Dejmek, J.*Československo – jeho sousedé a velmoci*. 52.
[79] Krofta, K. *Z časů naší první republiky*. 192.
[80] Ibidem. 93.

Great Britain, and the winning of its politicians and public opinion for the cause of the Sudeten German demands, played a crucial role from the moment that K. Henlein decided to concentrate on turning his cause into an issue on the international stage. He expressed this line on the 13th of October 1935 at a confidential meeting of SdP functionaries in Trutnov, saying, "With electoral victory we have shown the whole civilised world how three and a half million Germans are fighting for their rights. The Sudeten German question is a European concern, because our country is the balance wheel in the clock of Europe. Bohemia is and will remain its heartland. The world has an interest in ensuring that matters in this country take a good and right path. No one can turn back our development."[81]

It is interesting that Henlein's attempt to formulate his own foreign policy, setting the Sudeten German question in the context of European international relations and concentrating attention on it, failed to garner any very enthusiastic response from rank-and-file members or functionaries of the party. By this time, however, Henlein and his party were already directly run by the 2nd Department of the *Abwehr* (concerned with sabotage and diversionary activity).[82] It can therefore be supposed that his foreign political activities were part of wider Nazi plans which ignored the wishes of the "local" Germans, who played the role of mere tool. Indeed, other official organs and organisations in Nazi Germany were also interfering in the running of the political movements and parties of minority Germans; they included the Foreign Ministry, the Education Ministry, but also the Nazi party NSDAP, the SD, the SS, the German Foreign Institute, the *Deutsche Stiftung* and others, as well as most of the intelligence services.[83]

Henlein's first (official) journey abroad took him to Geneva, where he wanted "to sound out out the views of the politicians of Western, Central and Northern Europe on the Sudeten German question". On his return he stated self-confidently that, "With our struggle and our discipline we have become a European

---

[81] Biman, S. – Malíř, J. *Kariéra učitele tělocviku.* 124.

[82] The Czechoslovak intelligence service obtained its first more detailed information about the extensive network of Abwehr agents working with the support of the SdP in the Sudeten areas through P. Thümmel, known as Agent A-54. For example, on the 13th of November 1937 he reported that, "The New Department VII (of the *Abwehr*) is completely separate from the other elements and no unauthorised person has access to it. Its main task is to organise sabotage in Czechoslovakia. For this purpose it trains special agents from the ranks of the Sudeten Germans or completely reliable foreigners. It does not consider the use of Czechs. Currently the department is focusing on stepping up subversive activities among Slovaks." Kokoška, J. – Kokoška, S. 1994. *Spor o agenta A-54* [The Dispute over Agent A-54]. Prague: Naše vojsko. 66.

[83] In 1936, under the direction of Otto von Kursell, the *Party Office for the Ethnic German*, known as the *Büro Kursell* was set up, and from 1937 the direction and co-ordination of the whole field of activity was entrusted to Rudolf Hess through the *Volksdeutsche Mittelstelle (VoMi)* organisation. For details see Brown, MacAlister. "Fifth Column in Eastern Europe". 131–132. Also Smelser, R. M. *The Sudeten Problem 1933–1938*.

matter and will remain so as long as we are united."[84] On his next visit to the seat of the League of Nations Henlein established contact with Colonel Graham Christie, an expert on Central European affairs, former British air attaché in Berlin and an intermediary for the under-secretary of the British Foreign Office, Lord Vansittart.[85] It was Christie who as go-between paved the way for Henlein's lectures in London the following year, although the real rationale of Christie's mission remains unclear to this day.[86]

Likewise obscure are the circumstances of Henlein's first visit to Great Britain in August 1935, the first in a series of important SdP moves designed to win supporters among the British political elite. J. Dejmek notes that from the autumn of this year there was an increase in the number of reports from the British Embassy in Prague that in effect merely repeated the complaints being raised ever more militantly by the SdP leaders, without His Majesty's diplomats taking any critical view of them. Their attitude to Beneš was becoming correspondingly more disapproving. One British document of this period even commented that "the squeezing out of Beneš from the position of foreign minister in Prague might under certain circumstances be advantageous for London".[87]

In retrospect, the gamble on Great Britain proved to be the key decision of Sudeten German policy (and was undoubtedly made in close collaboration with Berlin). On the basis of a series of memoranda and reports from the British legation in Prague, and also from the Central Europe section of the Foreign Office headed by Sir Orme Sargent, from the beginning of 1936 onwards British leaders started to "advise" Czechoslovak politicians to respond to Sudeten German demands in a more generous and conciliatory way. One typical example of the unfortunate influence of one-sided information on the development of Czech-German relations was a memorandum drawn up by Sargent, at the time of Henlein's stay in London; this recommends explicitly that the Prague government should be pressured to make the boldest efforts to "remove the wrongs" of the Sudeten Germans, with an emphasis on the "European interest" in such reconciliation. This notion formed the basis of the later series of interferences in the purely internal affairs of the republic by British representatives. In this kind of atmosphere the intensified propaganda of Henlein's party was

---

[84] See Biman, S. – Malíř, J. *Kariéra učitele tělocviku*. 124.

[85] Colonel Christie was the former British air attaché in Berlin, and later an expert on Central European questions and probably also part of the British *Intelligence Service*. In 1934 Jan Masaryk said of him that, "although he is friendly to the national socialists, he has a very critical view of them." Ibidem. 126.

[86] R. M. Smelser claims that contrary to some views Christie was not in the IS. Smelser, R. M. *The Sudeten Problem 1933–1938*. 146.

[87] Dejmek, J. 2001. "Britská diplomacie, Československo a Sudetoněmecká strana" [British Diplomacy, Czechoslovakia and the Sudeten German Party], in *Moderní dějiny* 9. Prague: Historický ústav AV ČR. 166.

able to celebrate successes even in circles that were otherwise far from pro-German.[88]

Henlein made his first official appearance in Great Britain on the 9th of December 1935 (the first of several), with a lecture in the prestigious *Chatham House, The Royal Institute of International Affairs*, where he assured an influential audience that the SdP believed in the possibility of a peaceful settlement of the problem of the German minority in Czechoslovakia, that he believed it was the mission of Sudeten Germans to be mediators between the mother nation and Czechs, and that loyalty to one's own ethnic nation did not exclude loyalty to the Czechoslovak state. He expressed antipathy both for pan-Germanism and pan-Slavism and imperialist ideas, rejected antisemitism and did not hesitate to condemn the earlier excessive radicalism of the DNSAP in the CSR. The conclusion to his speech sounded truly positive about the state: "It is not our wish to work against this state, for we want to go with it entirely loyally."[89]

His speech, however, contained some other rather different claims. In the historical introduction he stated that in 1918 the Sudeten German territory had been annexed to the Czechoslovak Republic in violation of the rights of its German inhabitants to self-determination, and the Germans had been barred from the National Assembly which drew up a constitution proclaiming in the preamble that the republic was the national state of Czechs and Slovaks, thus allegedly condemning the Germans like other national minorities to the position of subjects. Henlein emphasised that he and his supporters wanted nothing more than the rights that had been promised them by the minority treaties and confirmed by the constitution of the republic. Kamil Krofta adds that Henlein, when repeatedly demanding equal rights for Germans with Czechs, evidently did not have just individual civic rights in mind, but the position of the whole national group in the state.

In his conversations in London, Henlein simply continued with his now established strategy of a politics that had two very different faces. In this context J. Dejmek cites the record of a conversation between Henlein and Sir Robert Vansittart that clearly shows the hints and nuances skilfully chosen in Sudeten German propaganda. Henlein characterised the state of Sudeten Germans as one of "great economic misery" and claimed that with its policy of "suspicion and persecution", the government was making the situation even worse. He repeatedly asserted that the Bohemian Germans did not wish for separation from Czechoslovakia, but that if the situation continued they would be driven in that direction. Vansittart, the experienced and influential permanent under-

---

[88]   Ibidem. 171.

[89]   Krofta, K. 1939. *Z časů naší první republiky* [From the Times of Our First Republic]. Prague: Jan Laichter. 191 and Biman, S. – Malíř, J. *Kariéra učitele tělocviku.* 129.

secretary at the Foreign Office, was persuaded to believe that by its policies Prague was providing Berlin with a useful excuse for possible action. Not even Jan Masaryk managed to counter the effects of the Sudeten German diplomacy and it was clear that British politicians and diplomats now believed they had a cogent reason to put pressure on "the Czechs".[90]

Another to devote similar vigorous efforts to promoting the Sudeten German cause abroad was Henlein's colleague, the architect H. Rutha (considered to be the SdP expert on foreign policy) with a group of North Bohemian industrialists. In May 1935 Rutha was appointed SdP commissioner to the League of Nations and and specialist consultant for nationality questions (a kind of shadow foreign minister).[91] He made several visits to Great Britain where he established a number of contacts in influential circles with the aim of winning support for Sudeten German demands. British public opinion was influenced systematically thanks to his work with leading papers such as *The Times, The Evening Standard* and others.

During another visit to Britain in 1936, which Rutha made together with Henlein, he had talks in London with the Czechoslovak envoy J. Masaryk and at one point explained to him the content of the Sudeten German demands, i.e. that in foreign policy it was necessary to create a block, "a united front against Bolshevism", to implement the "full autonomy" of Sudeten Germans in Czechoslovakia and for the republic to allow close cooperation between the Sudeten Germans and Nazi Germany.[92] At the same time he assured Masaryk that neither Hitler nor the *Sudeten German Party* wanted to deprive Czechoslovakia of even an inch of territory; all they wanted was for the spiritual and ideological cooperation of all Germans, whether in the Reich or outside it, to become the foundation stone of a new era for the German people. He insisted that for the German regions of Czechoslovakia to be able to administer their affairs in a German spirit, they had to have full autonomy, and the establishment of Czech settlers in German areas and all special preference for Czechs had to stop.[93]

On his visits to Great Britain Henlein met important politicians – W. Churchill, A. Sinclair, H. Nicolson and R. G. Vansittart. In most cases they found his conciliatory statements credible and he managed to convince them that, unlike and in defiance of Berlin and the radical wing of the SdP, he was a supporter of autonomist solutions.

---

[90] Dejmek, J. "Britská diplomacie, Československo a Sudetoněmecká strana". Vansittart's record of his conversation with Henlein on the 27th of July 1936. 172–173.

[91] Biman, S. – Malíř, J. *Kariéra učitele tělocviku.* 127.

[92] Archives of the Ministry of Foreign Affairs (AMZV). London Embassy. 22. 8. 1936.

[93] Krofta, K. *Z dob naší první republiky.* 191.

Henlein's success in deceiving Western politicians, reporters and the public remains puzzling to this day. The example of R. W. Seton-Watson suggests that even people with an excellent knowledge of the subject and sympathisers with the democratic CSR could be taken in. Krofta noted that, "After a lecture which clearly produced a generally good impression with its apparent moderation, Seton-Watson himself, who was present, reportedly did not hesitate to congratulate the speaker."[94] On other occasions too Seton-Watson expressed positive views of Henlein, for example remarking on one occasion that "I am sorry that some of my Czech friends are criticising Henlein, I regard that as unjust and politicising."[95]

It is obvious that initially even the leading British expert on nationality problems in Central Europe and long-term friend of T. G. Masaryk, R. W. Seton-Watson, was disposed to trust Henlein.[96] This gives even greater weight to his later insight and his verdict of 1943 that, "The Sudeten German agitation led by Henlein was the Trojan horse of the whole European tragedy. With unusual dexterity, sentimental Western European public opinion was deceived into thinking that it was defending the right to self-determination, when in reality it was singing to the tune of shameless pan-Germanism."[97]

Seton-Watson in fact changed his opinion quite soon. As early as 1938 he published an article on the Sudeten Germans in which he concluded that "Czecho-

---

[94] Ibidem. 183. R. W. Seton-Watson (1879–1951) was an outstanding expert on the national/ethnic problems of East-Central Europe. Before the First World War he travelled through Austria-Hungary and published many studies on the theme (including *Sarajevo*, in Czech – Prague: Melantrich 1930). On the basis of his knowledge and personal contacts he was an influential member of the *Intelligence Bureau of the War Cabinet* (1917) and *Enemy Propaganda Department* (1918), where he was responsible for war propaganda directed at the peoples of the Habsburg Monarchy. Together with T. G. Masaryk he edited the review *The New Europe* (1916–1920), which influenced the attitudes of the public in the monarchy and the political elites of the allies. He played a major part in the founding of the School of Slavonic Studies at King's College in London, founded and edited *The Slavonic Review* and after the outbreak of the Second World War he was once more in government service (1939–1940) *Foreign Research and Press Service*, (1940–1942) *Political Intelligence Bureau* of the British FO. http://www.aim25ac.uk/cats/58/7049.htm.

[95] Seton-Watson, R. W. "Henlein v Londýně". *Lidové noviny*. 26. 4. 1936.

[96] The director of the British *Royal Institute of International Affairs* Arnold Toynbee made a study trip through the CSR. He reported realistically and in depth on the Czech borderlands (including providing schematic maps of the industrial areas and language areas of the Bohemian Lands) and announced that in his view the chief cause of the constant unrest in the Sudetenland was a systematic campaign of Czechisation carried out from the very beginning of the republic. To quote, he stated that, "The Czechs pursue their policy of Czechisation and thereby antagonise the Germans on both sides of the border... that the Czechs are taking systematic steps to Czechise the Germans or else push them to the wall." Overall he concluded that in view of the ethnic tensions in Central Europe there evidently existed a radical flaw in the construction of the peace treaties, which would need to be changed – for example by affording Germany greater economic possibilities in the whole of Central Europe. Toynbee, A. J. "Czechoslovakia's German Problem". *The Economist*. London. 10. 7. 1937. 72–74. From the quotation, the extent to which the British elite had succumbed to the arguments of the Henleinians and the propaganda of the Reich is quite clear, Prof. Toynbee was an expert on ethnic conflicts in Central Europe and his influence on British foreign policy was considerable.

[97] Luža, R. *The Transfer of the Sudeten Germans.* 87.

slovakia has implemented rights of self-determination better than any other country... and its survival is vital to the interests of Western democracies"[98] In an article on the development of Central Europe and its ethnic conflicts in the inter-war period (first published in 1945), he argued that "Czechoslovakia was the only state east of Switzerland and South of the Baltic that managed to maintain political freedoms and progressive social institutions for a period of twenty years. Its fall meant not just a strategic but a moral loss for the whole of Europe."[99]

Concentrated efforts to represent the Sudeten German question as a major, urgent international issue, especially in the British press, continued and did not fail to find a response.[100] Signs of a deterioration in Czechoslovakia's international standing proliferated. The energetic activities of leaders of the *Sudeten German Party* in Berlin, London and Paris helped to fuel attacks in the foreign press on official Czechoslovak foreign policy and domestic conditions.[101] Nazi diplomacy resolutely insisted on a (more) speedy solution to the Sudeten German question and thus put the CSR under permanent pressure, supported by a disinformation campaign of Nazi propaganda declaring that Czechoslovakia planned to bomb cities in Germany, Austria and Hungary from 36 airports on its territory.[102]

The support from the Reich for the Sudeten German movement was complicated, however, by differences of view between individual Nazi leaders and institutions on strategy in regard to Czechoslovakia. Particularly significant in this context was the permanent and fundamental rivalry between the organisations of the Abwehr on the one side and the SS/SD on the other. These Nazi

---

[98] Seton-Watson, R. W. "The German Minority in Czechoslovakia". *Foreign Affairs*. 16. 7. 1938. 651–666.

[99] Seton-Watson. H. *Eastern Europe between the Wars 1918–1941*. 185. H. Seton-Watson argues, for example, that only in the case of the Bohemian Germans were there grounds for hoping that they would resist Nazi ideology, because they had a full social structure and political spectrum of parties. They were exposed to the whole range of political and religious influences – there were German socialists, communists, conservatives, fascists, liberals, agrarians and clericals. It might have been expected that most of them would reject Nazism. Yet this did not happen. Furthermore, most of the bourgeois (sic!) strata of Sudeten Germans always had radically nationalist views. Ibidem. 279–280.

[100] For example in mid-February 1937 the pro-revisionist press magnate Viscount Rothermere published an article "The Prisoners of Czechoslovakia" in *the Daily Mail,* in which he describes the CSR as a Czech prison for the majority of non-Czechs. The article was widely read, because it was reprinted by other papers in the USA and Australia. Dejmek, J. "Britská diplomacie, Československo a Sudetoněmecká strana". 178.

[101] The memorandum "The Problem of Czechoslovakia" drawn up by the Central Europe department of the Foreign Office as early as mid-January 1937 considered the eventuality of a German attack on the republic, although its author O. Sargent thought it was more likely that Berlin would try to get the state to disintegrate by supporting internal unrest and tensions. He predicted that the ultimate aim of Germany was not to absorb the CSR but complete German control of Central Europe. He saw the complete capitulation of Prague to Berlin in domestic and foreign policy as the only possible recipe for German-Czechoslovak agreement but believed this to be unlikely given Beneš's determination. Ibidem. 177.

[102] AMZV, Berlin embassy. 30. 9. 1938.

organisations directly influenced conditions in the Sudeten German movement by their activities.

The *Kameradschaftsbund*, close to Henlein in ideology, was a natural target for investigation and attack by the SD. The clerico-fascist model of the state defended by the KB was in almost all points in conflict with the racial, revolutionary elitism of Himmler and his SS. Like other Nazis of their generation, both Himmler and Heydrich were extremely anti-Catholic. This even went so far that the *Schwarze Korps* paper founded in 1935 and edited by Heydrich propagated anti-Catholicism even more vigorously than anti-semitism.

The distaste of the SS/SD for Spann and the KB soon led to them to ally with radical Sudeten emigrants in Germany and the *Aufbruch* circle active on Sudeten territory. The *Kameradschaftsbund – Aufbruch* conflict explains the ideological background of the SD/SS support provided to the radicals in the Sudetenland. There is evidence that R. Heydrich was personally involved in the active struggle for Germandom. W. Schellenberg later commented,

"Heydrich was kept informed on the position of the Sudeten German Party and Konrad Henlein by a special department. The National Socialist wing of the party, what was known as the *Aufbruch* led by K. H. Frank, pursued the policy of achieving the destruction of the whole Czechoslovakia as fast as possible. While Henlein was interested only in achieving autonomy for three and a half million Sudeten Germans. Heydrich therefore tried every available means to discredit the less radical Henlein in Hitler's eyes, for example with the repeated accusation that Henlein was in league with the British Secret Service."[103]

Leading critics of Spannian elitism also included the *Rumburger Zeitung* newspaper circle, which worked closely with Heydrich. An SD document entitled "Der Spannkreiss, Gefahren und Auswirkungen" [Spann's Circle – Dangers and Consequences] defined the influence of Spannism on the Sudeten Germans in the following words: "Since time immemorial Sudeten Germandom has been an intellectual battle field between Romance and German thinking. Before the world war it was entirely under the influence of Roman Catholicism of Viennese origin. After the war, the Sudeten Germans increasingly freed themselves from this influence as a result of the work of the DNSAP and found a connection to intellectual trends in Germany. This happy development, which was in the interest of all Germans, was undermined, however, by the successful activity of Spann's circle, which influenced Sudeten Germandom in the direction of Roman universalism, and alienated them from National Socialist Germany."

---

[103] Smelser, R. M. *The Sudeten Problem 1933–1938.* 174.

On the basis of this interpretation, an internal struggle developed inside the SdP against the architects of this ideological deviation, i.e. the leaders of the KB controlled the party and had been sidelining supporters of the DNSAP. A free-for-all broke out as the whole leadership including K. Henlein but particularly H. Rutha and W. Brand, Henlein's closest colleagues in the KB, became the target of radical attacks. Massive pressure caused a steep decline in the influence of Spannism on the Sudeten German movement and the Sudeten German Party eventually fully accepted the embrace of Nazi Germany with its "purely etatist solution".[104]

The Psychological War against Czechoslovakia

The press was the focus of the propaganda struggle in the "war of nerves" between Czechoslovakia and Germany. While the newspapers in the CSR in most cases belonged to political parties and were not directly controlled by the government, the German national socialist press fell directly under the Ministry of Propaganda headed by Goebbels. The basic difference in the conditions of press influence and influence on the press in the two countries was that in the Nazi state all the media were standardised and directly run by the ideological centres of the Reich, while in democratic Czechoslovakia the media had freedom of expression and were not dependent on the government, apart from the short period of September 1938 when censorship was introduced.

Most of the Czechoslovak press had taken a critical view of national socialism soon after Hitler seized power in January 1933. The ambassador in Berlin, Vojtěch Mastný, even had to ask that the overall tone of the press in the CSR be moderated so as not to risk upsetting German-Czechoslovak relations.[105] On the German side the Nazi press occupied itself more with attacks on the German immigrants who were finding a refuge from terror in the CSR. The aggression of the German press towards Czechoslovakia became more intense after Hitler announced his repudiation of the Locarno Treaty and on the 7th of March 1936 the wehrmacht occupied the contractually demilitarised Rhineland with-

---

[104] Kural, V. *Češi a Němci společně proti Hilterovi*. 143–145.

[105] Čelovský, B. 1999. *Mnichovská dohoda* [The Munich Agreement]. Ostrava: Tilia. 111. This outstanding Czechoslovak diplomat also drew attention to the influence of the German (specifically Nazi) environment on the attitudes and opinions of B. C. Newton, the new British ambassador in Prague (councillor at the embassy in Berlin 1929–1937). Like his predecessor Newton was irritated at the attitude of the Prague government to the SdP and its refusal to grant territorial autonomy to the German minority. He refused to accept the explanation of the Prime Minister M. Hodža, who said that the idea of territorial division of the CSR, with one part to be governed on totalitarian lines and the other on democratic principles, was completely unacceptable. Dejmek, J. "Britská diplomacie, Československo a Sudetoněmecká strana". 179–180.

out meeting any resistance. It was evidently at this point that the decision was taken to proceed uncompromisingly against the "aircraft carrier of Bolshevism" in Central Europe. The menace of Bolshevism was the main theme of German propaganda in this context; otherwise it avoided attacking Czechoslovakia as a democratic state and ally of France. Thus the strategy for discrediting the republic in the eyes of the West European public was the branding of the CSR a danger for "Western culture" and violator of the right to self-determination.[106]

The *exploitation of radio broadcasting*, and not only against Czechoslovakia, is a separate chapter in Nazi propaganda. Goebbels saw radio broadcasting as a much more effective instrument than the press for influencing public attitudes and thinking. As always, he had an ideological justification for his opinion. In his view the press was the exponent of the liberal spirit – the product and tool of the French Revolution, while radio broadcasting was in its essence authoritarian and so represented a suitable spiritual weapon for the totalitarian state.[107]

As soon as Goebbels took over the Ministry of Public Enlightenment and Propaganda (at his own wish not under the title Ministry of Information), he established direct government control over all radio stations in Germany. In the years 1933–1939 the number of radio receivers in Germany quadrupled and seventy percent of all households came to own a radio. In addition, radio loudspeakers were installed on wires in factories, offices and restaurants. Work would officially stop and listening would be obligatory when important speeches by Nazi chiefs were broadcast.[108]

Goebbels considered radio broadcasting the most valuable disseminator of the ideas of National Socialism abroad as well, and for the key reasons that broadcasting could be kept under central control, did not demand wasteful expenditure, and could get past the controls of foreign states on their territories.[109] Nazi radio broadcasting created a strong connection between listeners and the ideological goals of the Third Reich. In the case of the German minorities in foreign states this applied doubly. Here the primary aim was to create a fifth column of adherents of Nazism who could then be exploited as

---

[106] B. Čelovský describes the brilliant tactics employed by the journalist R. Kirchner in the *Frankfurter Zeitung* to undermine the international position of the CSR. Kirchner responded to Krofta's demand for the press campaign to be stopped by stressing that it had deep roots in the foundation of Czechoslovakia and its treatment of Sudeten Germans. In a mere three months he managed to create a major rift in opinion between Prague and Paris. Čelovský, B. *Mnichovská dohoda*. 113.

[107] Pohle, H. 1955. "Der Rundfunk als Instrument der Politik", in *Zur Geschichte des deutschen Rundfunks von 1923–38*. Hamburg: Hans Bredow Institut.

[108] Wasburn, P. C. 1992. *Broadcasting Propaganda*. Westport: Praeger. 14–15.

[109] Zeman, Z. A. B. 1964. *Nazi Propaganda*. London: Oxford University Press. 104–117. On this theme see also Klášterková, L. "Role německy vysílajících stanic ve vývoji Sudet v letech 1923–1938" [The Role of German Broadcasting Stations in the Development of the Sudetenland 1923–1938]. *Dějiny a současnost* 2/1999. 42–44.

a pressure group supporting the activities of the German diplomatic and other representative offices in their countries.[110]

This applied fully to the Sudeten German movement in Czechoslovakia. Goebbels's satisfaction in the crisis days of the for Czechoslovak democracy in September 1938 is apparent from his diaries: "In Bohemia the revolution is continuing according to plan. Attacks on banks and food shops. We are radio broadcasting all this in a great form. Panic is growing hour by hour. This state carcass is gradually decomposing into its parts. The only right thing that it can do."[111]

The *press and information offices* that the Sudeten German Party set up in 1937 in Paris and London likewise helped to influence the opinions of British and French political elites and public opinion. Systematic propagandist work with the press and public opinion both in Czechoslovakia and abroad were from the very beginning among the basic methods used by the Sudeten German Party. In fact one can say that in the second half of the thirties the Henlein movement, in close collaboration with the Third Reich, waged a psychological war of attrition against Czechoslovakia that culminated in the crisis month of September 1938.

From as early as 1933, the *Verein* (later the *Volksbund) für das Deutschtum im Ausland (VDA)*, which popularised the Henlein movement, was active as a source of irredentist propaganda from Germany. Links between the Reich and Sudeten German press were close. For example, when Henlein was elected chairman of the SdP at an assembly on the 19th–21st 1936 in Cheb, the organ of the Nazi Party NSDAP *Völkischer Beobachter* immediately praised his "cultured speech" and the address found a similar favourable reaction in the press of German minorities in other European countries. Henlein's speech was likewise praised by the *The Times* in Britain. The winning over of influential British papers for the cause of the SdP's demands may be considered a crucial success. Given the privileged standing of the British press on the international scene of the time, it was tragic for future events that it was precisely in British papers that Henlein's claims about the oppression of the Sudeten Germans in Czechoslovakia and the necessity of action by the Western powers to aid them should have been accepted.

---

[110] Hale, J. *Radio Power: Propaganda And International Broadcasting.* 1975. Philadelphia: Temple University, cited in Wasburn, P. C. *The Broadcasting Propaganda.* 16.

[111] Goebbels, J. 1992. *Deníky 1938* [Diaries 1938]. Liberec: Dialog. 223. In another place in the Diaries we find this passage, "Henlein has been giving me a description of the Czech people. Very interesting and lucid. This people has no national identity of its own. To give it a state is sheer nonsense. But Henlein thinks the Czechs will fight obstinately up to a certain point. Then, of course, they will necessarily completely collapse." Ibidem. 12. 9. 1938. 217.

This propaganda success owed a very great deal to Henlein's close colleague (from the *Kameradschaftsbund* circle) Heinrich Rutha, whose frequent visits to Great Britain were undertaken primarily with a few to systematically influencing British politicians and public opinion through the British press. He assumed the same role in relation to Anglo-Saxon journalists in the course of the 11th summer Olympic Games in Berlin in August 1936, when for example on the 17th of August he offered American and British journalists a lengthy account of the "oppression" of Sudeten Germans in the CSR. The only officially invited guest from Czechoslovakia at these Olympics was Konrad Henlein; here he took the opportunity to have talks with the Reich foreign minister Konstantin von Neurath, who gave him assurances of the financial and moral support of the Third Reich.[112]

In many foreign states, above all overseas states, the SdP gradually built a propaganda apparatus for the "Sudeten Question" in tandem with the promotion of the German light industry located in the border areas. The double purpose was to promote the export of Sudeten German manufactures but also to arouse interest abroad in the situation of the German minority and its demands.[113]

Soon after the elections of 1935 Henlein took a "health holiday" in Switzerland, the aim of which was to establish contacts at the League of Nations in Geneva. Not only with politicians, but also with journalists, whose ability to "create" public opinion he well understood, and for this reason he systematically supported the propaganda work of the SdP and its functionaries at all levels.

Press Propaganda

Programmatic arguments for the revision of Czechoslovak foreign policy, ideological solidarity with Nazi Germany and the demand for Sudeten German autonomy were the main themes of the Henleinian press. The party had its own print organs, which included the weekly *Rundschau*, the daily *Die Zeit*, the press bulletin SdP *Sudetendeutsche Pressebriefe*, the more academic monthly *Volk und Führung* and the satirical magazine *Igel*. Also important was the chain of regional and district magazines, 17 published in Bohemia and 18 in Moravia. From the 1st of October 1935, the SdP further brought out a regular selection from the press in the form of the (press monitor) *Presseschau der SdP.*

---

[112] Novák, O. 1987. *Henleinovci proti Československu* [Henleinians against Czechoslovakia]. Prague: Naše vojsko/ SPB. 93.
[113] Cesar, J. – Černý, B. *Politika německých buržoazních stran.* 313.

The daily *Die Zeit*, launched after the 1935 elections, can be used as an example of the massive but hidden funding from Berlin for the Sudeten German Party. Henlein requested financial aid to the level of 400,000 reichsmarks to enable the SdP to keep on publishing the daily, circulated with the *Presseschau* to 112 Czechoslovak and foreign editorial offices. Although the Reich Ministry of Finance initially refused to cover his request on the grounds of lack of funds, the money was provided after the personal intervention of Rudolf Hess supporting the request of the Berlin Propaganda Ministry for a special grant "to subsidise the new Prague daily, *Die Zeit*."[114] *The Foreign Ministry supported the regest because "the Sudeten German Party would suffer a severe blow" if the paper were forced to close.* The monthly losses of the daily *Die Zeit* amounted to 134,000 crowns, or 1,608,000 crowns a year, which was covered from Reich German sources.[115]

From 1934 Henlein was himself the publisher of the weekly *Rundschau*, with a print run reaching 70,000. The SdP built up an extensive press apparatus as the basis for an anti-Czechoslovak campaign with ever more damaging effects for Czechoslovak foreign policy in the later 1930s. Experienced journalists with strong ideologically pro-German views worked for the Sudeten German Party press. H. Hönig for example, who was entrusted with organising the SdP press, had worked from 1928 as the Czechoslovak correspondent of the Reich press concern *Scherl*, and in the 1930s was correspondent for Nazi papers coming out in Dresden and Munich. Contributors to *Die Zeit* included Prof. J. Pfitzner, historian at the Prague German University (during the occupation he became deputy mayor of Prague), and Dr. H. Neuwirth, who wrote on foreign policy problems.

The SdP Work Office set up by K. H. Frank was located in Prague at 4 Hybernská St. This building also housed the editorial offices of the daily *Die Zeit*, and the party propaganda department. Other *Die Zeit* offices were to be found in 7 Liliová St. on premises shared with the *Sudetendeutsche Presse-Briefe* office. Dr. W. Sebekowsky headed the SdP Press Office co-ordinating all these activities.[116]

---

[114] Luža, R. *Transfer of the Sudeten Germans*. 100. When Hitler consolidated his position in Germany he carried out a reorganisation and centralisation of the apparatus concerned with the problems of German minorities abroad. For this purpose he set up what was known as the *Büro Kursell,* which from 1935 functioned as the central office for contacts with Germans abroad. In January 1937 it was replaced by a new organisation, the *Volksdeutsche Mittelstelle* (VoMi). The Foreign Ministry's Cultural Policy Department recommended that the intra-Party autority of the VoMi be reinforced and that the VDA be restricted to purely cultural matters and barred from irredentist activities. The head VoMi, who was appointed by H. Himmler, was SS-Obergruppenführer W. Lorenz. He was directly subordinate to Rudolf Hess, but in public he continued to appear as head of an organ of the Foreign Ministry led by von Ribbentrop.

[115] For content of police report see Novák, O. *Henleinovci proti Československu*. 96.

[116] A leading functionary of the *Kameradschaftsbund*, he joined the DNSAP and later helped to found the SHF. He maintained contacts with the Reich through the *Volksbund für das Deutschtum im Ausland*. He also helped to soften up the atmosphere for the acceptance of Henleinian demands in Paris.

The characteristic "technology" of the Sudeten German propaganda machine and its "operating" techniques can be demonstrated using the example of what was known as the Teplice Case.

On the 17th of October 1937, district functionaries of the SdP had a meeting in the Teplice Municipal Theatre. Among those to address the meeting were K. H. Frank and K. Henlein, and the district leader of the SdP, F. Zippelius. Police present at the meeting merely monitored the Sudeten German leaders' attacks on the ČSR without intervening, but when the meeting was over there was an incident between Frank and the police inspector F. Fux, who was physically attacked by Frank. As a result, later in the afternoon the SdP deputies Kundt, Kellner and Richter were taken to the police station. That night the SdP leaders including Henlein met in Litoměřice, where they composed an open letter to President Beneš complaining that the behaviour of the state officials (police) had been in violation of the laws of the republic and was "intolerable for a courageous and honourable nation". Henlein saw only one remedy for this alleged outrage, i.e. "an immediate start on implementation of the autonomy that I and my party demand", which would hand over local government of Sudeten German areas to Germans alone, and thus avert "a deterioration in internal political conditions."[117]

An intensive information campaign against the ČSR followed. That very night the Reich radio broadcast news of the Teplice incident and the German press office the *Deutsche Nachrichtenbüro* immediately published the text of Henlein's open letter (banned from publication by the Czechoslovak censors) to President Beneš as well as details of the assault on Sudeten German deputies by Czechoslovak police. It is typical of the Nazi tactics that the text of the letter was broadcast before it was even delivered to its recipient.

In the Teplice case, co-ordination between the *Sudeten German Party*, its propaganda organs and the Nazi Reich was quite obvious. The culmination of the campaign was an attack on Czechoslovakia in the central party organ of the NSDAP, the *Völkischer Beobachter*, which alleged that "Sudeten German freedom... means – holding your tongue, cowering, and tolerating anything." The paper also claimed that this kind of incident was commonplace in the border areas. In line with the co-ordination policy, the SdP daily paper regularly published the views of the Reich press on the Sudeten German question.[118]

---

[117] Novák, O. *Henleinovci proti Československu.* 153.

[118] The Henleinians evidently dramatised the incident for yet another reason, i.e. to divert attention from the case of H. Rutha, the "foreign minister" of the SdP, who was arrested in mid-October 1937 by the Czechoslovak authorities and charged with "unnatural practices". His homosexual inclinations, like those of another of Henlein's close colleagues, W. Brand, were well known. Rutha hanged himself in a police cell and one piquant aspect of the whole affair was that he was arrested on the basis of information provided by another

In the case of the Teplice incident, precisely because of the lightning reaction of the Reich media Czechoslovak politicians feared that it might provide a pretext for war. In a secret report by Eisenlohr, the German ambassador in Prague, we find the comment, "In this context it caused an extraordinary fuss when the text of K. Henlein's "open letter" to the President of the Republic was read out on German Radio while the letter itself was still in the post from Litoměřice and Prague. Few believe that the speed with which the German information machinery was set in motion could be just the result of the perfect technical co-ordination between the Sudeten German press corps and the German Information Office, the DNB."[119]

In the final years of the 1930s journalists had agendas that had little to do with providing objective information. Czechoslovakia had for many years been out of favour with important British papers like the *Daily Mail*, whose owner Lord Rothermere could not bear to utter the republic's name even back in the 1920s. In 1938, the Prague correspondent of the *Daily Mail*, Ward-Price, wrote, for example, that President Beneš ought to go to Berlin and give up the borderlands of the republic to the Third Reich within ten weeks.[120] *The Times*, which recalled its Prague correspondent Douglas Reed at the end of May 1938 because his articles were insufficiently "conciliatory" in content, took a similar line. On the other hand, in its Prague correspondent S. Delmer, *The Daily Express* had a brilliant opponent of Sudeten German propaganda who knew how to see through the tissue of lies and half-truths with which it was supplying the world press. Henlein's information also failed to impress the correspondent of *The Daily Telegraph* and *The New York Times*, G. E. R. Gedye.

An authentic view of the work of the Sudeten German Party's press organs was given by the young British Journalist S. Morrell, working for the *Daily Express*. He had lived in Prague for some time and often moved between Aš and Liberec, in the heart of the Sudetenland, where the most important SdP activities were taking place. A passage in Morrell's book *I Saw the Crucifixion* on the organisation of the work of the SdP press department is eloquent testimony to the "effectiveness" of Sudeten German propaganda, which the Czechoslovak democracy failed to counter even at a time when it had all the relevant corresponding means to hand.

"Round the corner not far from the German House, in offices guarded by youths in black riding breeches and black high boots, youths who as visitors ar-

---

member of the Sudeten German Party. See *Documents on German Foreign Policy, 1918–1945*. 1949. U. S. Government Printing Office. Washington. 20.

[119] Ibidem. 21.

[120] Kvaček, R. "Předmluva k novému vydání" [Preface to a new edition], in Morrell, S. 1995. *Viděl jsem ukřižování* [I Saw the Crucifixion]. Brno: Jota. 6.

rived clicked their heels and raised their right hands with a throaty "Heil", the Sudeten German propaganda machine had been set in motion. The doors of these offices had concealed locks and opened only to carefully vetted visitors. Working nonstop in this building was Oskar Ullrich, the press chief of the Sudeten German Party. He knew all the correspondents. He could speak all their native languages. He had been in England for three years as the commercial representative of firms dealing in Jablonec goods and had even taught himself to speak in London Cockney... If Czechs and Sudeten Germans got into a fight in some remote little town or village, Ullrich would get on telephone in Prague and every correspondent would have the story in the German version before the Czechs even heard about the incident at all. When some important people – members of the English parliament, American senators – arrived in Prague, Ullrich would spring into action. He would promptly organise a trip to Sudeten German teritory and try to show that the industrial crisis was the fault of Czech persecution.

The Czechs were hopelessly outmaneouvred by this kind of propaganda. They would present historical reasons showing why Henlein's demands could not be implemented. They would defend the borders of their territories by pointing out that they had been there for a thousand years. And around nine at night, when my daily work was just starting and when the Sudeten German Party would be reporting clash after clash in Northern Bohemia, the officials of the Czech state press service would usually be in bed, or unavailable. I had Ullrich's day and night telephone numbers, and Ullrich was always at his post. I also had the telephone numbers of eight officials of the state press service of the Czechoslovak Foreign Ministry. But I was always having to drag these gentlemen out of bed or some restaurant. They were not used to it. They had finished their day's work and were off duty. They thought that an accurate account of an incident could wait until morning. They relied too much on the truth. The motto of their country was: Truth will Prevail!"[121]

Czechoslovak politicians, particularly E. Beneš, were familiar with the use of the media in political struggle. They had used such means themselves during the First World War when they were organising the anti-Austrian resistance. Masaryk and Beneš also understood the difficulties, in a democratic society, of pushing through the approach they considered desirable. After all, while newspapers and journalists were a potent instrument, what newspapers wrote depended on what their current owners wanted or tolerated, and owners saw

---

[121] Morrell, S. *Viděl jsem ukřižování.* 48–49.

nothing wrong in trading with a newspaper's profile.[122] Especially given the targeted Sudeten German propaganda, then, there had to be an active campaign to secure support for official Czechoslovak foreign policy, and the means adopted were similar, i.e. monetary gifts and favours to important French and British papers and journalists.

Although the head of the 3rd Section of the Foreign Ministry, Jan Hájek, and his staff provided an efficiently functioning information service, they proved unable to counter the influence of Sudeten German propaganda on high political circles in France, and especially in Great Britain, which were orientated to *appeasement*. Historians have continued to point out and criticise the inability of the Czechoslovak government to face up to the co-ordinated German propaganda, and effectively combat let alone reverse the effects of the Sudeten German Party media campaign on European public opinion, and above all France and Great Britain.

A Czechoslovak Ministry of Information headed by Dr. H. Vavrečka was set up on the 15th of September 1938, very belatedly and in fact too late to be able to make a successful impact in the war of information and ideas, in which the totalitarian centrally directed propaganda of Nazi Germany almost always enjoyed the initiative and advantage.

---

[122]   Urban, O. 1943. *Z tajných fondů III. sekce* (Z archivů Ministerstva zahraničí Republiky Česko-Slovenské) [From the Secret Funds of the 3rd Section (From the archives of the Foreign Ministry of the Czecho-Slovak Republic)]. Prague: Orbis. 12.

Hands clasped in friendship. Adolf Hitler and Neville Chamberlain in Munich on September 30, 1938. The day when premiers of France and Great Britain signed the Munich Agreement, sealing the fate of Czechoslovakia. Next to Chamberlain is Sir Nevile Henderson, British Ambassador to Germany. P. Schmidt, an interpreter, stands next to Hitler.

6 The Triumph of the Appeasers at Munich

The elevation of the Sudeten-German question to the status of real and major issue on the international stage was characterised by Henlein's proclamation of 1935: "Because the states of Central Europe are now unable to effectively tackle the minority problem as a result of the misunderstandings that have accumulated over 15 years, it is the duty of the League of Nations and powers to assist these governments in their tasks and to exert pressure on these governments if necessary. The goals of the minorities are not subversive. We ask only for justice. We have patiently waited for better times, but these have not come and will not come without help from outside."[1]

The SdP politicians constantly appealed to international law and the negotiation of remedy in the League of Nations, and especially to the pre-war interpretation of the protection of national minorities – which had been entrusted to the great powers. This is why K. Krofta had to explain repeatedly that this form of protection had been abandoned primarily and precisely out of fear that powers would abuse it to interfere in the affairs of other states. According to the more recent concept (which had been pushed through after the signing of the Paris peace treaties), the protection of minorities was entrusted to the Council of the League of Nations and the Permanent Court of International Justice. Especially authoritative in this respect was was the declaration of the Council of the League of Nations of the 22nd of October 1920 to the effect that the submissions of minorities to the League of Nations were to be considered

---

[1]   Krofta, K. *Z dob naší první republiky*. 186.

as petitions only, not legal acts that would authorise the Council to propose intervention on the territory of foreign states. It was also to the Council of the League of Nations and Permanent Court of International Justice that the powers had accorded the right to take steps for the protection of national minorities by the Minority Agreement of the 10th of September 1919.

From the point of view of the Czechoslovak situation in the later 1930s, the key statute meant that the initiative to take steps to protect a national minority could in theory come only from the member states of the Council, and not from Germany, which had resigned from the League of Nations in 1934.[2] At the time when the Czechoslovak crisis culminated, R. W. Seton-Watson saw Henlein's demands for self-determination as demands for racial (in the sense of *völkisch*[3]) autonomy, interpreted in terms of a poorly defined concept of Nazi ideology. The essential goal was to establish for every racial (ethnic) group (including Czechs and Slovaks) a far-reaching racial autonomy based on a system of "corporations", each one to have its own "racial distinctiveness".[4] Yet what was primarily meant by this was the collective right of the Sudeten German national minority to autonomy and eventually self-determination with the possibility of annexation to Germany on the basis of a plebiscite (as in the Saarland, which had been incorporated into Germany on the basis of referendum results).

The Czech–Sudeten German dispute took on an ever more dangerous dynamic and by the autumn of 1937 it was already not just a European problem but a problem of world politics. In the autumn of 1936 the Czechoslovak side had tried to get the existing anti-Hungarian Little Entente alliance transformed into a universal (i.e. primarily anti-German) alliance with the prospective aim of consolidating this grouping by a unified agreement with France.[5] In terms

---

2   Ibidem. 212.

3   The *völkisch* ideology involved an anti-liberal idea of the nation in which the nation was not defined by the territory of Germany, nor simply by shared history, language and culture, but in which there was an element of fundamental – indissoluble tribal identity – community of blood and race that could not be voluntarily adopted nor abandoned.

4   Seton-Watson, R. W. "The German Minority in Czechoslovakia". *Foreign Affairs*. 16. 7. 1938. 651–666.

5   Dejmek, J. "Britská diplomacie, Československo a Sudetoněmecká strana". 55. Here we need to draw attention to an exhaustive view of the diplomatic activities of Great Britain's Prague legation, which with its reports played a decisive role in forming the views of the British Foreign Office and thus influenced the decision-making of the British government. J. Dejmek's conclusions are based on study of the relevant archives of the Foreign Office – Czechoslovakia, kept in full at the Public Record Office in London, which contain the opinions of British diplomatic representatives in Prague on national-political events in the ČSR. Dejmek argues that, "The positive evaluation of Henlein's movement and of Henlein himself is one of the true debacles of British professional diplomacy in the 1930s, for which the greatest responsibility aside from the deceitful self-presentation of the SdP must be assigned to the entirely one-sided information provided by the British legation in Prague and the offices falling under it, especially the vice-consulate in Liberec." Dejmek considered the embassy secretary Robert Hadow and the consul in Liberec P. Pares to be flagrant representatives of the Germanophile perspective. Ibidem. 164.

of foreign policy the CSR was making intensive preparations for the defence of the republic, and also taking feverish steps to arm and modernise the Czechoslovak army. Despite this, in the same autumn diplomatic relations between Germany and Czechoslovakia still appeared "normal" and "correct".[6]

The government in Prague considered the Sudeten German question to be an internal problem, while Berlin was leaving it to Henlein to engineer a situation that would demand a solution by force.[7] The tension was projected into propagandist activities, as described above, rather than in the diplomatic field. The German ambassador Eisenlohr played an important role in "calming" diplomatic relations between the two states. Meanwhile the crucial development was the ongoing success of co-ordinated Reich and Sudeten German propaganda efforts in persuading public opinion and later the political leaders of France and Great Britain that the fate of the Sudeten Germans would eventually have to be solved in the international forum. Germany was able to achieve this breakthrough without increasing any diplomatic pressure. It was already clear that the tactic of exploiting the international lobbying potential of the German minority was highly effective. From now on this tried and tested instrument could be used to serve Nazi expansionist policy as Adolf Hitler had already formulated it in his *Mein Kampf*.

"If there is genuinely enough room in the world for the life of all, then we must get as much land as we need for life. To be sure, one does not enjoy doing it. But then the right of self-preservation comes into force: and what cannot be achieved amicably in this context, has then to be wrested by force."[8] Hitler's expansionist views and ideas drew on the work of the theorist of German geopolitics K. Haushofer, to whom he had been introduced by R. Hess in 1922. To support his arguments Haushofer had exploited the theoretical work of the "father" of geopolitics, H. Mackinder, who at the beginning of the 20th century had called the extensive territory of East Europe and Russia, "the heart of the world", or the *Heartland*. Taking up this idea, Haushofer was convinced that the vast extent of this territory would protect Germany against any attack and would be a source of invulnerability. He therefore called it the "citadel of rule over the world". Anyone who controlled this "heartland, controlled the world."[9]

---

[6] A series of bilateral agreements were signed, for example an agreement on air transport of 24th March 1937, an agreement on accounting (clearing?) on the 12th of November 1937 and even an agreement on the new marking and surveying of the border etc. Commercial contacts were also very intensive; Germany was the CSR's biggest trading partner in 1937 and in terms of import and export one might almost speak of economic dependence. See Čelovský, B. *Mnichovská dohoda*. 107.

[7] Ibidem. 106.

[8] Bauer, F. 1994. *Hitlerův Můj boj očima historiků I* [Hitler's Mein Kampf in the Eyes of Historians I]. Prague: Univers. 54.

[9] Hitler, A. *Mein Kampf*. 1993 (From the bible of German National Socialism with a commentary by J. Hájek). Liberec: Dialog. 205.

Secret Diplomatic Soundings in Prague

Although superficially Czech-German relations seemed to be functioning according to diplomatic norms, a German attack was obviously just a question of time. E. Beneš tried to put off this moment as long as possible. His methods included "secret" conversations with emissaries of Ribbentrop's unofficial foreign policy group, the *Dienststelle*, which he personally conducted as president at the end of 1936 outside normal diplomatic channels. These were evidently the most important Czech-German negotiations of the 1930s.[10]

What were known as the secret soundings took place on the 13th of November and then on the 18th of December, when President Beneš received Hitler's mediator Albrecht Haushofer (the son of the founder of German geopolitics Major General Karl Haushofer[11]) and Count Trauttmansdorff at Prague Castle. They had been instructed by Hitler to explore the possibilities of rapprochement between Nazi Germany and Czechoslovakia, and even the idea of a non-agression pact similar to that which the Reich had signed with Poland.[12]

V. Mastný, who took the minutes of negotiations with the German emissaries, records A. Haushofer as saying that, "Henlein had been with him in the summer and had indicated by some of his remarks, albeit not directly... a kind of iunctim in discussion with the question of Henlein's party... I commented in this context that for us the question of improving our relationship with Germans in Czechoslovakia could not be based on some kind of classification of Germans by their greater closeness to or distance from the ideology of the Third Reich... that for us what is key is solely the democratic concept of the equal-

---

[10]   Dejmek, J. "Britská diplomacie, Československo a Sudetoněmecká strana". 55.

[11]   For detail on the role of both Haushofers see Allen, M. 2003. *Podraz na Hitlera a Hesse* [Trick on Hitler and Hess]. Brno: Jota Military. The Haushofers father and son played what seems to be a much more important role in Hitler's foreign-policy designs than was supposed in the postwar period. Among other things they acted as middle men in 1940 for Rudolf Hess' secret negotiations with British representatives on a possible peace agreement between Great Britain and Nazi Germany, which would have freed Hitler's hands for military campaign in the east. This whole construction, however, seems to have been the work of the British intelligence service, which exploited the old contacts between A. Haushofer and some British circles and the confidence of the Nazis in the British appeasers, such as Lord Halifax or S. Hoare. The key records, however, are missing or non-existent. The materials in the British National Archives, London (Kew) therefore contain only part of the picture (most probably 30–50% of all information) of policy formation and the influence upon it. In detail see Brown, M. D. 2006. *Dealing with Democrats. The British Foreign Office and the Czechoslovak Émigrés in Great Britain, 1939 to 1945*. Frankfurt a. M.: Peter Lang Verlag (ed. Mitteleuropa/Osteuropa). 34–41ff. The theory of geopolitics as expounded by K. Haushofer was based on the premise that in the future the world would be divided into great territorial empires ruled from the "heartland", i.e. areas in Central Europe and Asia unassailable by sea power. According to Haushofer this situation would bring a revolution in the balance of world power and usher in a "new age" of stability, peace and prosperity for all. Ibidem. 33.

[12]   For a detailed account of the content of negotiations see Beneš, E. 1947. *Paměti* [Memoirs]. Prague: Orbis. 25–29, 30–31.

ity of the citizenry without distinction and the implementation of a nationality policy, of course by the parliamentary route and parliamentary parties."[13]

In the second half of March 1937, Hitler decided with the support of the Wilhelmstrasse to end the discussions because his instructions had not been fulfilled, i.e. *"1. Das Verhältnis der Tschechoslowakei zu Russland musste sich ändern. 2. Die Emigrantenfrage musste geregelt werden."* (see V. Mastný's minutes of the 21st of March 1937).[14]

The negotiations were terminated without results and their real goal remains unclear. It is not impossible that it was simply one of the Nazi camouflage manoeuvres designed to lull a future victim.

B. Čelovský, for example, believes that these were just tactical steps aimed at "softening up" the attitude of Prague, with nothing to be lost if they failed because it would always be possible to go on ratcheting up the tension in mutual relations.[15] It remains a puzzle, however, why Hitler should have first suddenly permitted the mission and then just as precipitately abandoned it without any kind of result. According to Haushofer's notes, Hitler had set out six points for negotiation, in an order that suggests their priority for him: 1. Ten-year non-aggression pact, 2. Neutralisation of Czechoslovakia in the event of Russian attack, 3. Habsburg Question, 4. Curtailing the activities of emigrants, 5. Trade agreement, 6. Substantial improvement of the situation of the Sudeten Germams. R. Smelser points out that significantly, the non-aggression pact point was crossed out in the notes.[16] He believes that Hitler decided that Germany was already sufficiently strong and any contractual restrictions would just hamper decision-making. The pact was simply no longer necessary...

From mid-1937 *rapprochement* between London and Berlin continued apace. In the process the CSR became an obstacle and as early as November of the same year Lord Halifax clearly indicated to the Nazi elite that Britain would not seek to obstruct changes in Central Europe if these took place by peaceful means.[17] The Czechoslovak foreign minister K. Krofta was convinced that Ber-

---

[13] Kvaček, R. – Vinš, V. "Materiály k německo-československým sondážím ve třicátých letech" [Materials on German-Czech Soundings in the 1930s]. *Československý časopis historický*. 1966. 889–890.

[14] Quoted ibidem. 895. There are grounds for believing that among the most important activities of German emigrants that Hitler wanted to see suppressed on Czechoslovak territory was the organisation *Schwarze Front* founded by O. Strasser, who had found refuge and support in the CSR. While Strasser "never managed entirely to free himself from some false and confused ideas of national socialism, as an unrelenting enemy of Hitler he was a potential – at least temporarily – ally of other antifascist forces". For more detail see Černý, B. "Schwarze Front v Československu (1933–1938)" [The Schwarze Front in Czechoslovakia (1933–1938)]. *Československý časopis historický*. 1966. 328.

[15] Čelovský, B. *Mnichovská dohoda*. 108.

[16] Smelser, R. M. *The Sudeten Problem 1933–1938*. 151.

[17] Lord Halifax visited in November 1937 Berlin and in the course of talks failed to respect A. Eden and R. Vansittart's wishes that he should not engage in debates on delicate problems with the Germans. In his first interview with Hitler he declared that Britain was not unconditionally interested in the status quo in Central

lin was seeking in the spirit of the former *Mitteleuropa* plan to create a Central European block with a population of 80 million, thus surpassing both Italy and France and controlling South-East Europe. In his view, this would entail the transformation of the CSR into a satellite state, whose bonds to the Berlin orbit would be strengthened by the SdP, entirely directed by Germany, joining the Czechoslovak governing coalition. In fact the aims of Nazi Germany went far beyond the contours of Mitteleuropa. Hitler's intention to destroy Czechoslovakia was suggested by the content of the so-called *Hossbach Document* drawn up before negotiations with Halifax.[18] In this document Hitler stated that he regarded the crushing of Czechoslovakia and the occupation of Austria as the first step to solving the "German Question".

The German side continued with the escalation of the psychological war against the CSR. On the 20th of February 1938 Hitler made a speech in which he openly spoke of a Sudeten-German crisis, attacking the League of Nations as an apparatus for the defence of the "Versailles iniquity" before going on to a threatening passage aimed directly at Czechoslovakia: "Only two states on our borders confine a mass of more than ten million Germans. Until 1866 they were united with the whole German people in a constitutional union. In the Great War they fought up to 1918 side by side with the German soldiers of the Reich. Union with the Reich was withheld from them against their will by the Peace Agreements. That in itself is painful enough. (But) Of one thing I can be in no doubt. Constitutional severing from the Reich cannot be allowed to lead to national political iniquity, and this means that the universal rights to national self-determination that were formally secured for us in Wilson's Fourteeen Points as the condition for peace, cannot simply be ignored because the people concerned are Germans."[19] The two states now on the agenda of Nazi expansion were Czechoslovakia and Austria. The *Anschluss* in March could leave Czechoslovak politicians in no doubt at all that their country was next in line.

At this point we should briefly mention the Austrian Chancellor Kurt Schuschnigg and his views on the Sudeten Germans and their role in the political development of the 1930s. He wrote his memoirs in exile in the USA

Europe as concerned Gdansk, Austria and Czechoslovakia, and that the only thing that London wanted to avoid was an approach that might cause problems, Dejmek, J. "Britská diplomacie, Československo a Sudetoněmecká strana". 199.

[18] Ibidem. Record of the discussion in the Reich Chancellery on the 5th of November 1937, when Hitler declared that the problem of German policy was the problem of living-space, in which Czechoslovakia with its geographical position and involvement in anti-German pacts played a key role. "The fuhrer personally believes that England and possibly France as well will in all likelihood tacitly renounce Czechoslovakia." For the full text see Šnejdárek, A. 1968. *Druhá světová válka* [The Second World War]. Prague: Svoboda. 60–67. See also Ečer, B. 1946. *Norimberský soud*. Prague: Orbis. 91–92.

[19] Čelovský, B. *Mnichovská dohoda*. 109.

where he took refuge after release from the Nazi prison in which he had been confined after the Anschluss.

"The Sudeten Germans, a tribe well schooled in battle as bordermen, – tough, hardworking, courageous and gifted in similar ways, played a peculiar role in the old as in the new Austria, and here again primarily in its capital city. A very substantial proportion of the high-ranking bureaucracy came from their ranks, and they were abundantly represented in the free academic professions. The leading strata in politics – on both extreme wings (the author means Austro-Marxism and Austro-Fascism) – were made up to great if not the most part of members of their strong tribal (folk) circle. This was true of the high and highest ranking Vienna Catholic clergy no less than of the various currents of strongly anti-church (anticlerical) movements. Sudeten Germans were no rarity among the leading Christian Socialists, and national socialist activism in Austria was almost completely inspired and led by Sudeten Germans."[20]

In the course of the Nuremberg Trials the American prosecutor Alderman read out a telegram that clearly proves the close connections betwen the SdP and the Reich and the fact that Henlein consulted all major steps with Berlin. The German ambassador E. Eisenlohr wrote from Prague to Berlin on the 16th of March that:

- The German foreign policy line, as it will be be communicated by the German embassy, is entirely decisive for the policy of the Sudeten German Party.
- Public speeches and the press will be co-ordinated on a unified basis with my agreement. The editorial work of the newspaper *Die Zeit* will be improved.
- Pushing through the Sudeten German demands.
- If a meeting with the Berlin authority is necessary before Henlein issues an important declaration about his programme, such a meeting will be requested and arranged by means of the embassy.
- All information from the Sudeten German Party destined for the German authorities will be given to the embassy.
- Henlein will be in contact with me every week and will come to Prague at any time I request it."

At the end of the telegram he states: "I hope that I now have the Sudeten German Party firmly in hand, which is especially necessary for the coming events in the interests of foreign policy."[21]

---

[20]   Schuschnigg, K. 1947. *Requiem v červeno-bílo-červené* [Requiem in Red-White-Blue]. Prague: Aventinum. 288.
[21]   Ečer, B. *Norimberský soud*. 162–163.

Henlein then had meetings with Hitler and Ribbentrop on the 28th and 29th of March 1938.[22] The meetings were also attended by K. H. Frank, the Reichs minister R. Hess and the VoMi chief W. Lorenz. The minutes of the meetings were marked secret twice over, and fell into the hands of the Americans as part of the archive of the Reich Minister of Foreign Affairs at the end of the war. At the meetings the SdP was given clear instructions for the imminent destruction of Czechoslovakia. At Nuremberg the American prosecutor also submitted documentary evidence that the Sudeten German Party had been supported by the German foreign ministry from 1935", both through the German embassy in Prague and through the Berlin contact office of the SdP – the *Büro Bürger.*

The prosecutor's comment on the document was that, "It convincingly proves that Henlein's movement was the tool and puppet of the Nazi conspirators. Henlein's party, as is clear from this document, was managed from Berlin and the German embassy in Prague. It did not have a politics of its own. Even the speeches of its leaders were checked and adjusted by the German authorities."[23] Henlein received unambiguous instructions to maintain the closest possible relations with the Reich minister Ribbentrop, the *Volksdeutsche Mittelstelle (VoMi)* and the German ambassador in Prague.

President E. Beneš, the Czech prime minister M. Hodža and the foreign minister K. Krofta realised, albeit under the pressure of events, the need to come up with offers for further negotiation that would demonstrate, especially to the Western powers, Czechoslovakia's willingness to solve the Sudeten German problem by peaceful means. From British Foreign Office internal documents it is evident that in late March and early April 1938, British foreign policy-makers were interested not in the possibilities for a thorough-going defence of the *status quo* in Central Europe, but in the options for a transformation of Czechoslovakia that might lead to a stable solution.

Following a radio speech from M. Hodža on the 28th of March 1938, in which he announced the project of a Nationality Statute, some British diplomats started to consider much more drastic steps to satisfy German and Sudeten German demands. For example, the ambassador B. C. Newton proposed the neutralisation of Czechoslovakia by liquidating its alliances with France and the USSR, while others suggested "the reconstitution of Czechoslovakia on a federal basis" through tough pressure on Beneš.[24]

---

[22] For the full wording of the text see "Záznam o poradě K. Henleina a K. H. Franka u Hitlera" [Record of the meeting between K. Henlein and K. H. Frank with Hitler], in Šnejdárek, A. 1968. *Druhá světová válka.* Prague: Svoboda. 75.

[23] Ečer, B. *Norimberský soud.* 162.

[24] Dejmek, J. "Britská diplomacie, Československo a Sudetoněmecká strana". 208.

On the 1st of April 1938, the prime minister M. Hodža opened negotiations with the Sudeten German Party on the Nationality Statute, in the drafting of which Beneš took an ever greater part since he was aware of the urgency of the situation and the need for more radical Czech concessions. On the 19th of May, the Czechoslovak government approved the framework draft of the Nationality Statute and on this basis M. Hodža resumed negotiations with the SdP representatives (Henlein and Kundt) on the 24th of May.

As Beneš saw it, the new statute would be a compromise between German national demands and the need to preserve the integrity of the state, which would be accomplished by reviving provincial self-government. The proposal involved a certain return to the arrangement of 1905, by which provincial assemblies had been divided into national curias and accorded legislative powers in the frame of nationwide laws. At the same time the powers of local government would be widened and deepened, again on the former Austrian model. The drafting of the statute was accompanied by disputes and delays that provided the SdP with an excuse to come up with a memorandum containing its own suggestions on the 8th of June. This was known as the *Skizze* ("Sketch for a new internal order in Czechoslovakia on the basis of the eight-points of the speech made by the chairman of the SdP K. Henlein, at Karlovy Vary on the 24th of April 1938").[25]

While the British saw it as a politically neutral matter of reform of local government, in the real context of the situation of the CSR it actually represented the old plan to divide the Bohemian Lands into Czech and German parts with the German parts to be governed on totalitarian lines (with the option of annexation to the Reich). On the 17th of June M. Hodža invited three German social democrats headed by the deputy W. Jaksch to a discussion of the reform. The move caused a storm of outrage in the ranks of the SdP, which had arrogated to itself the right to represent all Germans in the CSR.[26]

---

[25] 1. Recognition of nationalities as legal subjects, 2. the division of the territory into *Siedlungsgebiete* and a new demarcation of districts, 3. the extension of local self-government from the community right up to the Volkstag, 4. Volkstag and land national representative bodies, 5. cadastre (land register) of nationalities, 6. nationality sections in the ministries, 7. German officials for the German Siedlungsgebiet, 8. national proportionality in allocation of official appointments, 9. new language right (in government offices and parliament), 10. nationality key in the budget, 11. audit of the use of nationality key in the budget, 12. representation in central economic, financial, insurance, social, hygiene institutions etc. 13. damages for policy since 1918 (minority schools, bank rescue, land reform, university etc.). Beneš, E. 1968. *Mnichovské dny* [The Days of Munich]. Prague: Svoboda. 403. "No state and no government has ever yet been in a situation like ours. We are in close proximity to a unique elemental process in world history. This is the culmination of nationalism of a nation of 75 million people, who have entered a period in which they are moving from their rationalist roots into the nationalist field. This huge historical process cannot be administered away." From M. Hodža's address to representatives of the coalition press on the 15th of May 1938. Krofta, K. *Z dob naší první republiky*. 286.

[26] On the 26th of June, immediately after the attacks of the Henleinian paper *Die Zeit*, lists of "inconvenient" people from the ranks of German social democrats, which had been drawn up by the SdP secret service for the coming "day of retribution", were found in Liberec. Beneš, E. *Mnichovské dny*. 110.

Nonetheless, following British and French intervention, on the 15th of June Hodža announced that both documents, the draft Nationality Statute and the SdP memorandum, were being accepted as the basis for further negotiation. On the 27th of June, Lord Halifax repeatedly called on the Czechoslovak ambassador Jan Masaryk to communicate a new message to his government on the grounds that His Majesty's Government was disappointed at the slow progress of negotiation. It reiterated to the Czechoslovak government the need to act quickly and make wide-ranging concessions (allegedly Czechoslovak public opinion had not been sufficiently educated in the mentality of major concessions). Beneš commented that in his message Halifax was merely ventriloquising Henlein as well as the constant barrage of Reich propaganda being channelled to the Foreign Office by the British ambassador in Berlin Nevile Henderson. We should note here that according to the most recent findings, however, the major part of this relayed propaganda came from the British Prague legation (and its consulate in Liberec).[27]

In the good faith that an objective problem required a genuine solution, the leaders of the Czechoslovak state sought to find a positive way out of a situation in which it was ever more obvious that the goalposts were constantly being shifted to render such a solution impossible. The rationale of the permanent tension was not to solve the situation of the German minority but to show that the Czechoslovak government was no longer capable of resolving the problem with its own resources. The aim was to make intervention from outside and mediated negotiations unavoidable as the basis for ending the "intolerable oppression" of Sudeten Germans in the CSR. Precisely as Hitler later expressed the point in a speech in Nuremberg on the 11th of September:

"To the representatives of these (Western) democracies I can say only this… that if those tyrannically treated creatures (the Sudeten Germans) cannot find any justice and aid, then they will get both from us."[28]

The minutes of Henlein's talks in Berlin, read out by Alderman in the course of a hearing before the international court of justice in Nuremberg, make the planned strategy clear.

"The aim of the negotiations between the Sudeten German Party and the Czechoslovak government is ultimately this: to make entry into the government impossible by progressively broadening and increasing demands. In negotiations it must be clearly emphasised that the Sudeten German Party is the sole party for negotiations with the Czechoslovak government, and not the Reich government. The Reich government must reject any appearance of being the

---

[27]   Ibidem. 116. See also Dejmek, J. "Britská diplomacie, Československo a Sudetoněmecká strana".

[28]   Schmidt, P. 1997. *Paměti Hitlerova tlumočníka 1935–1945* [The Memoirs of Hitler's Interpreter 1935–1945]. Brno: Barrister & Principal. 116.

advocate or supporter of Sudeten German demands in the eyes of the Prague government or London and Paris. Obviously it is a condition that in discussions with the Czechoslovak government the Sudeten Germans will be firmly controlled by K. Henlein. They will observe calm and discipline and avoid any indiscretions."[29]

Efforts to draft legislative reform of the position of the Sudeten Germans in the state were underway from March 1938. On the 19th of March the government approved a decree to impose proportionality in appointments to government jobs. On the 16th of April Beneš signed an amnesty for 1,235 Sudeten Germans and on the 26th of April the Czechoslovak government submitted the draft new law on nationality to London.

Despite all these gestures of goodwill, it was clear to the Czechoslovak leadership that the moment of open clash with Nazi Germany was approaching. At the same time it was obvious that after the Anschluss with Austria, carried out without serious international opposition, Hitler was almost certain that the Western powers led by London would take no major steps to support Czechoslovakia in a situation where a large part of Western European public opinion had been won over to sympathy for the German minority in the CSR.

Henlein's Karlsbad Ultimatum

As tension mounted in the spring of 1938, the congress of Henlein's Sudeten German Party on the 24th of April in Karlsbad/Karlovy Vary brought further escalation. Here Henlein expounded the doctrine of his party in a form fully in line with his instructions from Berlin and left no one in doubt that at this point his position was totalitarian and pro-Nazi.

He declared that Bohemian Germans would continue to refuse to recognise Czechoslovakia in its present political and constitutional form and that he had finally turned his back on any "activist" politics, i.e. participatory engagement with the Czechoslovak state. Henlein demanded that Czechs change their political conception and also their whole mentality. In his view this meant that Czechs must abandon their national ideology and traditions and acknowledge them to be a historical error. Above all, they must revise their political conviction that their task was to form a barrier against German expansionism into South-Eastern Europe. He declared that without such change there could be no solution to the problem of coexistence between Czechs and Germans.

---

[29]   Ečer, B. *Norimberský soud.* 164.

His speech culminated in the presentation of the text known as the *Karlsbad Programme*.[30] In eight points he proposed the following reform of domestic and legal conditions in the CSR:

1. The negotiation of complete equality and equal status for the German national group with the Czech nation in the Czechoslovak Republic.
2. The recognition of the Sudeten German group as a legal subject, in order that its equality in the state should be safeguarded.
3. The demarcation and recognition of German national territory.
4. The establishment of self-government in German national territory in all areas of public life where the interests and concerns of the German national group were involved.
5. The creation of legislative protective measures for those citizens who lived outside the designated areas of national self-government.
6. The removal of the injustices inflicted on Sudeten Germans since 1918, and reparations for the material damages that they had unjustly suffered.
7. Recognition and implementation of the principle that only Germans should be public employees on German territory.
8. Complete freedom of identification with German national identity and the German world view (i.e. Nazism).[31]

The Reich press reacted by immediately proclaiming that Henlein's "demands are truly minimal" although it was clear that the autonomist demands were too extensive to be acceptable to any government that intended to maintain the independence and integrity of the state. The German historian J. W. Brügel considers the *Karlsbad Programme* to have been an "open declaration of war". In his report to the ministry in Berlin, ambassador Eisenlohr wrote that, "both in the Sudeten German camp and in the Czech camp, and also abroad, the opinion had gained ground that the Henlein Party was conducting only mock negotiations (with the Government), and intended to step up the demands in order to make an agreement impossible."[32]

It was typical of the information policy of the Sudeten German Party that the text of the *Karlsbad Programme* was made available to the British embassy

30   Quoted in Beneš, E. *Paměti*. 35–36. Henlein openly embraced national socialism when he said, "Sudeten Germandom, which despite the state frontiers feels itself to be part of *Deutschtum*, with which it has always lived in an indissoluble bond, cannot avoid the world view with which all Germans thoughout the world are joyfully identifying themselves. And precisely Sudeten Germandom, as a tribe that is endangered and fighting for its existence, may embrace none but this world view, whose highest law is *Volksgemeinschaft*."
31   Quoted ibidem. 36.
32   Brügel, J. W. 1961. "German Diplomacy and the Sudeten Question before 1938". *International Affairs*. 3/37. 331.

in Prague two days before its publication.[33] Henlein was still presenting himself to foreign politicians as the representative of the moderate wing. On the 28th of April he had talks on the *Karlsbad Programme* in Mariánské Lázně with a member of staff at the British embassy, N. Henderson, who came away convinced that "the demands are not exorbitant."

In mid-May 1938 Henlein made his fifth and final visit to London, where he once again undermined the situation of the Prague government in relation to the SdP by repeating the trick of pretending to be a moderate conservative attempting to control the radicals. Despite the intervention of J. Masaryk, he was received by a number of important figures including R. Vansittart, W. Churchill and prominent MPs from different parties. In discussion with Vansittart he slipped out of his "Karlsbad" role and posed as an "apostle of peace", reducing the demands of his party to cultural, local government and school autonomy. Vansittart, who had not ceased to regard him as a friend, advised him not to make impossible demands on Prague, such as a change in foreign policy or the adoption of a "Nazi Weltanschauung". To this Henlein several times repeated, hypocritically, that despite the radicalisation of his fellow Sudeten Germans the possibilities for agreement with the Prague government were not exhausted (at the same time, however, he ostentatiously expressed fears that the Czech side was unwilling to make any concessions).[34]

All the same, the direction that British policy was taking in these weeks and months was clear from an interview given to American journalists on the 10th of May by British prime minister N. Chamberlain, who expressed his support for the annexation of the Czechoslovak borderland to Germany. It was already evident in this phase of the crisis that Great Britain did not intend to risk open conflict with Germany on account of a small state in the centre of Europe. President Beneš found himself in an insoluble dilemma as a consequence of the attitudes of Britain and France. He was a supporter of a moderate policy, but saw its successs as dependent on the combination of Czechoslovakia's own defensive potential with the potential of its allies – yet those allies were indicating a lack of interest.

Beneš was well informed enough to form a realistic view of the situation and he tried (if under pressure and with time running out) to modify his policy in relation to the Western allies, but his room for manoeuvre had already become so restricted that is extremely hard to imagine any more effective, alter-

---

33 Biman, S. – Malíř, J. *Kariéra učitele tělocviku*. 190.
34 Yet again not only British politicians, but even J. Masaryk, and through Masaryk K. Krofta and others, believed this. In Prague the prevailing view was that Henlein would be "straightened out", from Berlin, and that the Germans now genuinely did not want to provoke a war. Dejmek, J. "Britská diplomacie, Československo a Sudetoněmecká strana". 217.

native approach to a virtually hopeless situation.[35] Evidently he could rely on no forces but his own. Especially when it was obvious that French policy was falling into line with decision-making in London, which had succumbed to the views of the *appeasers*.

Chamberlain in particular seemed possessed by a kind of fatefully mystical conviction on the necessity of justice for the Sudeten Germans.[36] This is something noted by Jaksch (Chamberlain's alleged "feeling of guilt for Versailles" of course suited Jaksch's position). R. Kvaček characterises the British view of Central Europe as a mixture of indifference, ignorance and power political calculations.[37] In one of his reports the Czechoslovak ambassador to London Jan Masaryk expressed himself quite openly, "the ignorance, disregard, reluctance and laziness in the assessment of urgent matters of political principle is amazing in this country (i.e. Britain)."[38]

The latest archival research has shown that a significant number of staff in the Central Europe department of the British Foreign Office were sympathetic to the cause of the Sudeten Germans (whose aspirations the Versailles Treaty had allegedly failed to fulfil) even after the fall of the political circle of appeasers. In any case, Central Europe had always been in the second-rank category in the hierarchy of British national interests as conceived by the Foreign Office, and its problems subordinated to wider strategic considerations, contexts and limits, too. What little information the British authorities had absorbed about

---

[35] H. Masařík draws attention to the "tragic dilemma that faced President Beneš just before Munich – either to agree to a general plebiscite or to the cession of part of the state territory." He takes the view that as a result of mistakes on the part of the CSR, Britain forced the Lord Runciman mission on Czechoslovakia in June 1938 as the mediator of negotiations with the SdP. Masařík, H. 2002. *V proměnách Evropy* [In the Transformations of Europe]. Prague: Paseka. 224.

[36] Highly eloquent in this connection is the record of a conversation between Chamberlain's confidante G. Steward and F. Hesse, an official at Ribbentrop's Ministry of Foreign Affairs and also a correspondent of the German Information Office (DNB). The conversation throws light on lesser known moments in the process of decision-making on the fate of the CSR. "The Prime Minister made his decisions in the last critical days genuinely completely by himself with just his two confidential advisors and in his last decisions he no longer even asked any members of the cabinet nor even the foreign minister Lord Halifax... Finally the Prime Minister did not even have any help and support from the *Foreign Office*, which in fact in the last three days tried to take a contrary stand and to engage Great Britain to military actions against Germany." Steward also declared that "the English decision-making in the Czech conflict and Chamberlain's attitude in particular was not dictated by consciousness of military weakness, but exclusively by a religious conviction that Germany must have justice and the wrong of Versailles must be redressed." *Documents on German foreign policy*. Series D (1937–1945)Volume 2. 1949. Germany and Czechoslovakia 1937–1938. Washington: US Government Printing Office. Doc. No. 579.

[37] Kvaček, R. "Tesařovo kritické tázání" [Tesař's Critical Questioning]. *Literární noviny* 53/2000. 18. On the 12th of August 1938, on the basis of information from Agent A-54, the 2nd Department of the Czechoslovak General Staff informed the British military attache that, "The Sudeten Germans are to get weapons from Germany... this will be a signal for members of the SA and SS to enter the territory (CSR) and protect the Sudeten Germans, and their expulsion will then be the signal for the German Army to attack". Kokoška, J. – Kokoška, S. *Spor o agenta A-54*. 94.

[38] Kvaček, R. 1966. *Nad Evropou zataženo* [Clouds over Europe]. Prague: Svoboda. 242.

Central European affairs by Munich crisis was shaped by the overriding consideration of Empire, an obsession with maintaining the 'balance of power', and by the constraining influences of geography.

Britain had long been a seafaring nation: her interests began and ended with control of the oceans and the British authorities were simply unable to project power into the landlocked heart of central Europe. These geographical limitations had a profound influence on all British policy made in reference to the Czechoslovak question between 1939 and 1945 and should not be discounted.[39]

In May 1938 there was a partial mobilisation of the Czechoslovak army (operation "Protection and Safeguarding of the Borders") in response to what were believed to be large-scale movements of German forces, and in a few days it suppressed a Henleinian attempt at a putsch in the borderlands.[40] The prelude to the crisis were talks on a Czech-German settlement for which the Czechoslovak government had drawn up a starting point in the form of a new "nationality statute" (responding to the British demand for a solution) while the Sudeten German side's starting point were the Karlsbad Demands (representing what was actually a programme for the federalisation of the CSR). Both approaches involved prospective wide-ranging changes to the constitution of the republic, and in terms of time and organisation would have needed a year even in calm, peaceful times, let alone in an atmosphere of unending pressure and threats from the Nazi Reich. In the circumstances, the mobilisation was problematic in terms of international reaction because it weakened the image of the CSR as a subject willing to negotiate on the future of the Sudeten Germans – as indeed some were keen that it should.

Nonetheless, the mobilisation did succeed in temporarily halting the rise of the Henlein movement and successfully tested the functioning of the Czechoslovak system of alliances. It is not entirely clear whether the May crisis was engineered by German intelligence, who may have pretended large-scale move-

---

[39] See e.g. the published dissertation by Brown, M. D. 2006. *Dealing with Democrats. The British Foreign Office and the Czechoslovak Émigrés in Great Britain, 1939 to 1945.* Frankfurt a. M.: Peter Lang Verlag. 31 ff.

[40] In recent years there has been speculation about the "strange" circumstances of the May mobilisation of 1938. The suggestion is that this was a matter of provocation inspired by the obscure plans of some of the European powers. Not excluding Germany. But the arguments for this theory are not very convincing and have remained on the level of pure hypothesis. See Lukeš, I. "Mimořádná vojenská opatření v květnu 1938: nová interpretace" [The Special Military Moves in May 1938: A new interpretation]. *Historie a vojenství* 5/1995 (XLIV). 79–97. The theory is that there might have been an attempt at creating an excuse for an attack on the CSR from the German side, as in the case of the Anschluss with Austria. The articles by the historians R. Kvaček, S. Kokoška and others do not lead to any consistent conclusion. Among scholars abroad the closest to the Czech interpretation is W. V. Wallace, when he argues that Hitler created the crisis himself. The German interpretations (Deutsche Militärgeschichte), however, prefer to see an underhand motive in the Czech reaction: the testing out of the Czechoslovak army and the political attitude of its allies, which these interpretations castigate as "the Czech leadership playing frivolously with the possibility of war."

ments of the *wehrmacht* close to the Czechoslovak border in order to provoke the Czechoslovak Leadership to retaliatory actions that could then be exploited on the international scene as proof of the "warlike" intentions of Czechoslovakia. Seen in this light, Czechoslovakia was to be presented to its allies (especially Britain) as a "troublemaker" to be got rid of at the first opportunity.

V. Kural has pointed out that Great Britain and its empire had always played an important role in Hitler's political thinking and that after 1925 Hitler definitely regarded it not as an enemy but as a valuable pillar of the world rule of the Arian race. The Nazi leader gambled on the growing isolationism of British political elites, from whom he hoped to gain a free hand in Central Eastern Europe. The Anglo-French meeting held on the 28th–29th May to discuss the Czechoslovak crisis, at which the two states decided to solve the problem by peaceful means, opened up Germany's path to the longed-for destruction of its unwanted neighbour. Czechoslovakia's allies asked Berlin to exercise restraint and asked the CSR to make the maximum possible concessions to the Sudeten Germans, i.e. the greatest possible concessions compatible with the maintenance of the territorial integrity of the state and, according to British ideas, the transformation of the CSR from a national state to a state of nationalities with Sudeten German autonomy.[41]

In the local elections on the 22nd, 29th of May, the Sudeten German Party won 90% of the votes. Together with the planned proclamation of a political amnesty by the Czechoslovak government, this situation might have been a starting point for talks on the Nationality Statute, which represented a peaceful way out of the crisis. In mid-May Henlein had presented the Karlsbad Demands in London as a programme of cultural, municipal and local autonomy. R. Vansittart's records show that the SdP was able to inspire more and more pressure on Prague from London. The gamble on winning round the British political elites had come off almost perfectly. This was why as early as June 1938 the British government was willing to give its agreement to the announcement of a plebiscite in the Sudetenland.[42]

Foreign Office internal documents suggest that in this phase of the conflict Czechoslovakia was written off in its existing form. For the first time the idea of calling an international conference of powers with an interest in the CSR appears. Czechoslovak military preparations, fully justified as they were in the shadow of aggressive German moves, continued to be a thorn in the side of the British and French; in the corridors of the Foreign Office the prevailing

---

[41]   Kural, V. "Případ čs. květnové mobilizace v roce 1938" [The case of the May mobilisation in 1938]. *Přísně tajné* 4/2002. 25–26.

[42]   Čelovský, B. *Mnichovská dohoda*. 221.

view, based on Nazi propaganda, was that President Beneš was hampering negotations by his hard line or at least his caution.[43]

It was in vain that Beneš tried to persuade the West that what was at stake in the Czechoslovak-German collision was not simply the fate of the German minority, or even of Czechoslovakia itself, and that the crisis was just a part of the overall struggle on the future of Europe, in which the CSR with its proportionately large and relatively well equipped army could – of course at the side of the democratic great powers in cooperation with the USSR – play an important role.[44] Unfortunately Beneš and his government's room for manoeuvre was continuing to disappear as a result of the adroit efforts of Nazi propaganda and diplomacy, which exploited the "Versailles guilt complex" of a section of French and British political elites to encourage constant appeasement of the categorical demands of Hitler.

The task of Henlein and German diplomacy was to work psychologically on Great Britain and France so that in any given case of aggression, as with the Austrian Anschluss, they would only stand back and watch as Nazi Germany "simply took back what belonged to it". To this end it was necessary to discredit Czechoslovakia and present it as the last barrier to a final peace in Europe.[45]

The blackmailing tactics of the Henleinians, who kept stepping up their demands, proved a success. As the Sudeten German Party increased its demands the Czechoslovak government was ready or rather forced to meet them to a significant degree in the interests of a peaceful solution (especially given the attitude of the French and British governments). One example from the summer of 1938 is a depeche from the Czechoslovak Foreign Ministry to CSR embassies, describing the next concession to the demands of the Henleinians (the Nationality Statute – so-called 2nd Plan):

"Land (provincial) assemblies with legislative powers will be set up in the framework of state laws... A provincial committee will be elected by the assembly from all nationalities, and will be the executive organ of the assembly... In the assembly national curias will be established that will be assigned part of the competence of the assembly, and in these curias the nationalities concerned will be complete masters of their national interests... A decentralisation of self-government to the districts will also be carried out... in this way minorities will be given real and wide-ranging local self-government."[46]

---

43   Dejmek, J. "Britská diplomacie, Československo a Sudetoněmecká strana". 227.

44   Ibidem. 56. The author draws attention to Beneš's comments to General E. Spears in mid-March 1938.

45   Čelovský, B. *Mnichovská dohoda*. 221.

46   The circular of the CSR Foreign Ministry on the state of negotiations on nationality questions of 20th July 1938. See Beneš, E. *Mnichovské dny*. 415–417.

The British government was not satisfied with this proposal either for, as the Czechoslovak ambassador in Paris Štefan Osuský reported after a meeting with the British delegation led by Lord Halifax, "London is of the opinion that governing circles in Prague are not proceeding sufficiently resolutely in the drafting of reforms that might produce a permanent *modus vivendi* between Czechoslovaks and Germans, and is afraid that this slow pace may provoke new complications."[47]

President Beneš commented on the escalating demands of the Sudeten German Party, as set out in a memorandum from M. Hodža of the 8th of June 1938, that they were now more or less openly intended to destroy the integrity of the state in violation of the Czechoslovak constitution, which would have to be massively changed if the Henleinian demands were to be met. This meant nothing less than the *creation of a closed independent territory, governed in totalitarian fashion, inside the democratic Czechoslovak Republic.* One part of the state would be governed on democratic principles, and the other by concentration camps, antisemitic regulations and the gestapo. In his comments on the Sudeten German memorandum Beneš pointed out that, "the whole system is based on the premise of weakening the power of the state (by no means just the central executive power) as much as possible. And unlike the tendency in authoritarian states, here the democratic state is to be weakened still further in its integrative power."[48]

The basic programme document *Grundplanung O.A.*, discovered in the archives of the Sudeten German Party, is tragic proof of the elaborate planning of the subversion of the state in the period before the Munich crisis. The methods and individual phases of the takeover of power are set out in detail in this document, together with the long term goals of the Henlein movement in regard to the Czech nation.

"Once the Czech nation has been broken apart we have an interest in maintaining it in that state and keeping the boundary between German and Czech in an unstable state to the benefit of Germandom. In this way we shall ensure that large sections of the Czech population identify with German nationality... It will be appropriate to meet all attempts at resistance with uncompromising harshness, whereas readiness to coexist with Germany will meet an open ear and open heart and effective action on our part. Anyone who has once found his path to us and out of Czechness during pervasive upheavals must feel that we value him as a citizen of Germany and also as a fellow-countryman."[49]

---

[47]   Ibidem. 420.

[48]   Ibidem. 404–405.

[49]   Fremund, K. 1961. *Chtěli nás vyhubit* [They Wanted to Exterminate Us] (Documents on the Nazi Extermination and Germanisation Policy in the Czech Lands in the Years of the Second World War). Prague: Naše

The *Grundplanung O.A.* was most probably produced in Henlein's staff office and represents the main political line of the Sudeten German Party, like another memorandum *On the Solution to the Czech Question* evidently drawn up on the 18th of September 1938, which argues that the Czechoslovak crisis "is not simply about the problem of the Sudeten Germans, but about the whole political order in the territory." It outlines four possible solutions to the relationship of the Czech state to the German Reich: 1. The creation of a rump Czech state without restrictions on its sovereign rights, 2. The creation of a neutralised rump Czech state, 3. The creation of a Czech state with special bonds to the German Reich, and 4. The incorporation of Bohemian territory into the German Reich. In the text of the document preference is unobtrusively given to the third variant, i.e. a rump Czech state with special ties to the German Reich.

In terms of content, the memorandum as it were returned to the conception developed by Spann, and characterised in his time by Henlein's first ideologue W. Brand from the *Kameradschaftsbund* circle: "The question is not that of the separation of the Sudeten German areas. It is much more about the holding of the entire territory, not through violent occupation but using political and economic influence – because what else can we do with the Czechs? They must be – more or less – pulled into the German sphere of influence."[50]

Typical of the maximalist demands of Spannism was the notion of the hegemony of the German element over the other Central European peoples, or the supremacy of the German totalitarian state as feudal lord over second-rank nations-vassals. Both documents, the *Grundplanung* and *On the Solution of the Czech Question*, are evidence that the planning of alternative scenarios of the destruction of the CSR was not conducted just in the limited context of a solution to the local Sudeten German problem, but that its geopolitical aim was a German Central Europe, this time conceived in a way that placed a question mark over the future existence of Czechs as a separate people.[51]

---

vojsko. 29–40. The document cited is not dated, but the compilers believe that it was drafted in the period between May and August 1938.

[50] Kural, V. "K problému tzv. Grundplanung O.A." [On the Problem of the so-called Grundplanung O.A.], in *Historie okupovaného pohraničí 1938–1945* [A History of the Occupied Borderlands 1938–1945]. 2000. Radvanovský, Z. (ed.). Ústí nad Labem: Univerzita J. E. Purkyně. 217.

[51] Ibidem. The Spannian conception (after 1989 its legacy has to some extent returned in terms of content) gave members of the *Kameradschaftsbund* (later the SHF and SdP) scope for adroit maneouvring: they could seem to be concerned only for Czechs to free themselves from the damaging influence of the West and go back to a "mutually creative cultural relationship with Germandom, to whose culture they owe so many stimuli for their own development. In this way Czechs can effect a very positive reversal of their state policy, the Sudeten Germans having already effected theirs, and do so by honourably embracing the policy in the framework of the given state, political-power conditions – it is then purely up to the Czechs whether the Germans have or do not have to revise their conception. The apparently moderate approach was supposed to create within the CSR a "true" state within a state in accordance with the Spannian idea, subordinate to the

President Beneš described the situation at the beginning of September when the SdP rejected the third plan with appeal to the demands of the *Karlsbad Programm*. Beneš immediately personally drew up an amended alternative solution, the so-called fourth plan, which made full concessions to the demands of the Sudeten German Party.[52] The whole paper now took the "form of a real agreement between two partners" and not a mere protocol on the conversation between the president of the republic and two members of the Sudeten German Party. This meant essentially *the complete acceptance of the eight points* that K. Henlein had put forward in Karlovy Vary. According to Beneš, Lord Runciman, in his capacity as international mediator in the dispute, said that no one in the world had a right to demand more from the Czechoslovak government, and that it had done everything for peace. [53]

On the German side, roles were skilfully allocated to ensure that as the crisis culminated in the summer of 1938 Germany could appear to remain aloof, since after all its interests were represented more by Henlein than by the ambassador Eisenlohr. At the start of August the only more serious bilateral dispute at international level concerned mutual complaints about the violation of air space by military aircraft of the two states.[54]

On the 31st of August, Germany repudiated the 1928 Austria-Czechoslovak agreement on borders. This was a move designed to unnerve the Czechoslovak government still further, placing it under huge international pressure. The Reich press, which had been intensifying its campaign of sensational articles on the repression of Sudeten Germans in the borderlands, ratchetted the campaign up even further.[55]

The propaganda pressure kept on mounting in the course of September, especially after Hitler's speech of the 12th of September at the NSDAP Congress in Nuremberg. "Mr. Beneš is playing tactics, talking and wanting to organise talks to solve the procedural question according to the Geneva model, and to give out small soothing little gifts. But this cannot go on for ever... What Germans are demanding is the right to self-determination, which every other nation has... But what I demand is that the oppression of three and a half million Germans in Czechoslovakia cease, and that it should be supplanted by the free right to self-determination... It is in any case a matter for the Czechoslovak government to make a settlement with the appointed representatives of the Su-

---

German universal state. A state where the hated democracy would be overcome and in which an elite "white" estate would govern. Kural, V. *Konflikt místo společenství.* 123–124.

[52] Beneš, E. *Mnichovské dny.* 205.

[53] Ibidem. 214.

[54] Čelovský, B. *Mnichovská dohoda.* 266.

[55] From 5th of September the Vienna Radio started to broadcast news in Czech under the title "Die Wahrheit siegt", allegedly "at the request of the Czech minority". Ibidem. 267.

deten Germans and reach an agreement, "so oder so."....For this is about German fellow-countrymen. Likewise, I have no intention of permitting, as a result of the actions of other state leaders, a second Palestine to be established in the very heart of Germany."[56]

Immediately, on the 13th of September, a series of incidents followed in the borderlands of the CSR which then grew into a Henleinian attempt at rebellion, but the Czechoslovak authorities restored law and order quite quickly. Yet Henlein had perfectly fulfilled his aim, which was to destroy negotiations whatever the cost. On the 15th of September the leadership of the SdP issued a proclamation stating that:

"Czechoslovak democracy has finally taken off its hypocritical mask. Helpless women and children, hundreds of dead and seriously wounded accuse it. Murder and robbery is committed under the pretence of humanitarian phrases. Through its national leaders, Sudeten Germandom declares before the whole world that it has sought for a peaceful solution until the very last minute. But the Czechoslovak government has refused all Konrad Henlein's demands."[57]

The Reich German dailies followed up with a wave of articles describing the ghastly atrocities perpetrated by Czech soldiers in the borderlands. The headlines alone are eloquent: "Czechs secretly bury corpses", "Sudeten German farms and factories burned to the ground", "Terrible crimes by Czech animals in Krumlov": this was just a selection of the titles of articles in the *Völkischer Beobachter* on the 18th of September. Who was the source of this "information"? We learn the answer from the testimony of Goebbels's personal press spokesman M. von Schirmeister to the Nuremberg Tribunal: "It was Alfred-Ingemar Berndt, the head of departments. He would sit for whole nights, with maps from the general staff, address books and lists of names in front of him, thinking up horrifying reports from the Sudetenland."[58]

German diplomats from the Prague mission, however, urged Berlin to moderate the stories in the Reich press, reporting that the situation was calm throughout the Sudetenland and that the Czechs were masters of the situation. They also drew attention to negative reactions among the Sudeten German population itself, with voices raised criticising the departure of the SdP leaders to Germany and interpreting it as flight after the unsuccessful attempt at a putsch in which the principal role had been played by units of the *Freikorps* – armed terrorist formations of the Sudeten German Party equipped and trained on the territory of the Third Reich.

---

[56] Ibidem. 272.
[57] Ibidem. 274.
[58] Ibidem. 275.

Czechoslovak propaganda sought to exploit the change in the mood of Bohemian Germans and on the 16th of September set up a Ministry of Information. Yet this very necessary step to co-ordinating the vital information activities of the CSR came too late to have any hope of reversing the march of events, especially if we remember the crucial importance of propaganda in the whole context of the conflict, as we have explored it above.

Munich 1938

The course of the Munich Conference is well-known, as are its consequences. On the basis of an agreement signed in Munich on the 29th of September 1938 by Germany, Great Britain, France and Italy, the borderlands of the CSR were to be ceded to Germany by the 1st of October.

It needs to be stressed that Hitler was fully resolved to militarily attack the CSR, and his pressure was no bluff. In fact he personally wanted to solve the conflict by armed force. In this sense the excessive readiness of the West to appease him, and the consequent lack of resistance from a cornered Prague, thwarted his plans. The British emphasised that if a war broke out on account of the CSR then even were Germany to be defeated Britain would not guarantee that there would be no change to the Czechoslovak borders. On the 27th of September the foreign secretary Lord Halifax sent the unfortunate document entitled the *Time-table* to Prague, setting out the deadlines for the cession of Czechoslovak territory to Germany. The hand-over was supposed to take place from the 1st to the 31st of October.

The Munich conference opened on the 29th of September with a speech by Hitler, in which the Führer declared himself the spokesman of the minority in the CSR, which in his view was "exposed to barbaric persecution", with allegedly two hundred and forty thousand people having already fled and the exodus continuing. He proclaimed that, "the existence of Czechoslovakia in its current form is a threat to peace in Europe".[59] The attitude of Britain, as Hitler's key opponent, is characterised by a sentence from Chamberlain's answer: "The Czechoslovak Question is a European question and its solution is not just a right but a duty for the great powers. They must also make sure that the Czechoslovak government does not refuse to evacuate the territory out of foolhardiness or obstinacy."[60]

---

[59] Klimek, A. – Kubů. E. *Československá zahraniční politika.* 92.
[60] Ibidem.

It is worth mentioning that as B. Čelovský has pointed out in his distinguished study of the Munich Agreements (*Münchner Abkommen*)[61], "the principle of the cession of the Sudetenland is of far greater significance historically and from the point of view of international law than the Munich Agreement itself." He draws attention to the way that the international law thesis propounded by H. Raschhofer (defending the validity of the Munich agreement in his work *Die Sudetenfrage* of 1953) rests primarily on the fact that on the 21st of September an agreement was made between France and Great Britain on the one hand and Czechoslovakia on the other on the principle of cession of the Sudetenland.[62]

The Munich Agreement, which Hitler was to violate in March 1939 and which the allied governments during the war declared invalid for that reason, was according to Raschhofer an agreement on the implementation of principles already accepted by Prague. In other words, the Munich Agreement merely represented the acceptance of principles earlier agreed to by Prague. For this reason Čelovský believes that what needs to be seen as the crucial period of the whole autumn crisis was the phase of negotiations between the 19th and 21st of September.[63]

An account of the September events as interpreted from the post-war Sudeten German perspective can also be found, in characteristic form, in the memoirs of W. Jaksch: "But on the 21st of September Beneš and his government capitulated. To his confidantes (advisors), who then deluged him with demands for explanation, Beneš said: "We were shamefully deceived." Thus was born the legend of a small country left in the lurch by its large allies. In actual fact, the state that was allegedly destroyed by the Munich Agreement had already

---

[61] For the full text of the Munich Agreement see *Documents of German Foreign Policy*. Vol. 2. Doc. No. 675. 1014–1017. For the Czech wording see *Mnichov v dokumentech* [Munich in Documents]. 1958. No. 131. Prague: SNPL. 271–272.

[62] The text of the Czech government's answer to the Franco-British aide-memoire of the 19th of September contains some ambiguous formulations, but it is not an expression of acceptance "The government of Czechoslovakia is aware of the efforts that the British and French governments have been investing... nonetheless for the reasons already stated it turns to them again with a last appeal and asks then to reassess their view." Ibidem. 151.

[63] Quoted in Čelovský, B. *Mnichovská dohoda*. 291. It is not without interest, and testifies to the roots of the argumentation of people like H. Raschhofer (legal advisor to K. H. Frank in the period of the occupation), who after the end of the war theoretically "elaborated" the Sudeten German question. The claim that the Prague government had accepted the Berchtesgaden Plan already on the 21st of September appeared first in the daily of the NSDAP *Völkischer Beobachter* and the Czechoslovak press pointed out that this was another psychological attack. See the leading article: "Negotiations continue in London – Roosevelt warns Hitler". *Polední Haló noviny*. 26. 9. 1938. According to H. Raschhofer, the Munich Agreement violated by Hitler in March 1939 was valid up to that point. See Raschhofer, H. *Die Sudetenfrage. Ihre völkerrechtliche Entwicklung vom ersten Weltkrieg bis zur Gegenwart*. 1953. München: Isar Verlag. See also the recent analysis of Raschhofer's theories in the study by Salzborn, S. "Zwischen Volksgruppentheorie, Völkerrechtslehre und Volkstumskampf. Hermann Raschhofer als Vordenker eines völkischen Minderheitenrechts". *Sozial Geschichte*. 21 3. 2006. 29–52.

capitulated on the 21st of September. From mid-September 1938, Beneš had no longer been fighting for the survival of Czechoslovakia, but only for his own personal alibi."[64]

According to the Sudeten German interpretation, Czechoslovak policy itself must bear the blame for the destruction of the state, having brought on itself the German pressure and indifference of the allied powers by its inability to co-operate constructively in the gradual demolition of the republic by all the politicians of the Henlein, Frank, and Krebs type and other "peacemakers" who managed to convince the democratic West that the CSR was a Versailles mistake that simply led to oppression of the German minority.

There is even some speculative suggestion that President Beneš "ordered" the pressure as a way to justify his own concessions, but such theories remain unproven and seem largely motivated more by the need to excuse the behaviour of the "appeasers". By contrast, there is incontrovertible evidence of the massive pressure brought to bear by the French but above all the British government on Beneš to accept all the German demands.[65]

The strange perverted logic of events in the autumn of 1938 has been identified as "the unique bestiality of Munich" by historian Zbyněk Zeman. As proof of the complete confusion of the concepts and values in the European conditions of the time, he quotes from the diary of H. Nicolson's response to the objection that Czechoslovakia was an artificial state which probably should never have come into existence was as follows: "That is perhaps true, but only God knows how we could have prevented the recognition of its existence in 1918. The reality today seems strange to me. Hitler has all the arguments on his side, but they are essentially false. And we, who have right on our side, are not permitted to say that in fact we are justified in resisting German hegemony. That would be "imperialistic". Never have opposite theories been so woven through with illusions."[66] Nicolson's words perfectly sum up the results of the systematic

[64] Jaksch, W. *Cesta Evropy do Postupimi.* 191.

[65] The question of the alleged "ultimatum produced to Czech order", in which the key role was played by M. Hodža was raised more than once among the Czechoslovak exiles in Great Britain in 1941. Beneš rejected the accusations against Hodža by the French ambassador V. de Lacroix and regarded the whole affair as an attempt by French politicians to put the blame for Munich on Czechoslovak politicians. Kuklík, J. – Němeček, J. 2004. *Proti Benešovi* [Against Beneš!]. Prague: Karolinum. 155. See also Lvová, M. 1968. *Edvard Beneš a Mnichov* [Edvard Beneš and Munich]. Prague: Svoboda. 34–36. Lvová, M. "K otázce tzv. objednaného ultimata" [On the Question of the so-called "ultimatum produced to order"]. *Československý časopis historický* 3/1965. 333–334. See also the entry for the 5th of February 1941 in the diary of J. Opočenský. *Válečné deníky Jana Opočenského* [The War Diaries of Jan Opočenský]. 2001. Čechurová, J. – Kuklík, J. – Čechura, J. – Němeček, J. (eds.). Prague: Karolinum. 91.

[66] Zeman, Z. 2002. *Edvard Beneš – politický životopis* [Edvard Beneš – A political biography]. Prague: Mladá fronta. 137.

efforts by which the genius of Nazi evil managed to invert values and paralyse the vacillating Western democracies.

Czechoslovak diplomatic documents of the time show that President Beneš pressed the Western allies to take a clear and uncompromising attitude to the German demands. On the 15ᵗʰ of September, the French ambassador V. de Lacroix was summoned to see the President, who asked him to convey to the French government a very urgent and emphatic communiqué in which he asked "France at this serious moment not to abandon the policy that we have pursued together for twenty years… in this historic moment a real appeal to France, because the issue concerns [!] the question of our very existence and because we are convinced that failure to hold the line at this moment would be extremely dangerous, even ruinous, not just for us but, in its consequences, for France itself."[67]

On the 17ᵗʰ of September the British cabinet heard reports from Lord Runciman and N. Chamberlain on the situation. These concurred in recommending the cession of the Sudetenland and neutral status for Czechoslovakia. On the 18ᵗʰ of September British-French discussions were held in London, but not on the question of whether or not to abandon Czechoslovakia. The only issue now was how to minimise the loss of prestige of the two European democracies and how to force Czechoslovakia to take the required steps. At the end of the conference, Daladier declared that there was a need to exert "the strongest pressure" on Beneš. "The fate of Czechoslovakia has been sealed since Versailles."[68] In any case, many of the British appeasers shared the same kind of "Czechophobia" as Lord Londonderry, who wrote that "Czechoslovakia is one of the unfortunate fruits of postwar developments, caused by the devilish cunning of (Edvard) Beneš and (Tomáš) Masaryk." Such views were not confined to extreme rightwing and pro-German circles, but were voiced regularly on the pages of such widely read and influential papers such as the *Daily Express*, *Daily Mail* and *The Times*. However, there was some divergence between the attitudes

---

67 Dejmek, J. *Československá zahraniční politika v roce 1938* [Czechoslovak Foreign Policy in 1938]. Vol. II. Prague: Ústav mezinárodních vztahů/Karolinum/Historický ústav AV ČR. 279. This two-volume publication also contains many other documents showing the determination of Beneš, but also the extent of the pressure, especially from the British side, for him to find a compromise that would avert war at any price. Nonetheless, J. Dejmek describes how Beneš repeatedly entertained the possibility of ceding some smaller sections of territory with solidly German population – a fact that could give rise to doubts about the firmness of his attitude over the key question of defence, e.g. in a conversation with B. Newton on the 17ᵗʰ of September or in instructions for the minister J. Nečas's negotiations in France of the 15ᵗʰ of September. See also the text of Š. Osuský's letter to Beneš of the 19ᵗʰ of September. Ibidem. 328.

68 Čelovský, B. *Mnichovská dohoda*. 284–285. The same author draws attention to Beneš's readiness to cede a certain part of the Sudetenland, a readiness expressed in conversations with Newton and Lacroix and possibly also in a message to L. Blum of the 17ᵗʰ of September, which encouraged French politicians in their view that the president would probably be prepared to make further concessions.

of ordinary people and political elites in Britain. The German Ambassador in London, Herbert von Dirksen, warned that while the British government was prepared to go a long way to accomodate the peaceful attainment of German aims, if Germany used force in the Czechoslovakia crisis 'England would without doubt march alongside France to war.'[69]

The pressure on the CSR culminated in a French-British *aide-mémoire*, in terms of tone more an ultimatum, delivered to the Czechoslovak side on the 19th of September 1938 after 2.00 p.m. This stated inter alia that "Both governments are convinced that after recent events a point has been reached where it is no longer possible for the areas predominantly inhabited by the Sudeten Germans to remain within the frontiers of the Czechoslovak state without this situation endangering the interests of Czechoslovakia itself and the interests of European peace. In view of these considerations, both governments have been forced to the conclusion that the preservation of peace and protection of the vital interests of Czechoslovakia can be effectively secured only if these districts are now ceded to the Reich."[70]

The text was delivered to Beneš with the warning that any delay in response could mean a German invasion of Czechoslovakia. Beneš's decision seems to have been crucially influenced by a message from Léon Blum, the leader of the governing Left block of parties in France, indicating that there was no hope of a change in the French government or a change in French policy of any kind that would mean help for the CSR. As a consequence there was altogether no hope of help from the West. Another factor in Beneš's decision was disunity in the Czechoslovak government, with some of its members expressing a willingness to accept the ultimatum. After a conversation between the French ambassador de Lacroix and the Czechoslovak prime minister Hodža on the 20th of September, London was informed that the Czechoslovak government was divided and would yield to pressure. While according to the ambassador de Lacroix, M. Hodža told him that Czechoslovakia would give in if pressure was applied, de Lacroix concluded that Hodža's words actually meant an order of a night demarche. However, Hodža denied he had said any such thing. At all events, at the crucial moment the lack of unity of Czechoslovak politicians and the tendency of part of the political spectrum (especially some members of the Agrarian Party) to favour appeasement of Germany played a role.[71]

---

[69] Kershaw, I. 2004. *Making friends with Hitler*. London: Allen Lane-Penguin. 240.

[70] *Mnichov v dokumentech*. 144–145.

[71] Zeman, Z. *Edvard Beneš*. 140. Zeman argues that Beneš was the main obstacle for the supporters of rapprochement with Germany who were scattered across the Czech political scene. The chairman of the Agrarian Party R. Beran believed that no agreement with Berlin was possible while Beneš remained head of state. As early as the time of the Anschluss with Austria J. Preiss in private conversations did not hide his view that Beneš ought to resign for the good of the state. Ibidem. 141.

In the late afternoon of the 21ˢᵗ of September the Czechoslovak foreign minister K. Krofta informed the ambassadors of France and Great Britain that his government was prepared to accept the ultimatum. Hodža resigned after the streets of Prague started to fill with demonstrators demanding that the government stand firm. Leadership of a new caretaker government was entrusted to General J. Syrový. Meanwhile, in the course of further negotiations with Hitler in Bad Godesberg on the 22ⁿᵈ of September, Chamberlain announced that the Czechoslovak government had assented to the preceding agreement. To his surprise Hitler then demanded a much larger part of the border territories (declaring at the same time his support for the territorial demands of Hungary and Poland against the CSR) and a devastated Chamberlain stated that there seemed no point in further mediation activities. [72]

On the 23ʳᵈ of September a meeting between Beneš and the prime minister Syrový, selected ministers and leaders of the coalition parties, decided on a mobilisation declared by the radio at 22.30 hours. The Czech population responded with a show of resolve to defend the republic. The international isolation of the CSR appeared to have breached but in fact the mobilisation measures taken by France were of a purely defensive character and Britain made almost no military preparations beyond putting the navy on alert.

Nonetheless the Western powers continued to hold intensive consultations, provoking Beneš to remark with prophetic anxiety, "These meetings terrify me".[73] His foreboding was fully justified. The lengths to which the British appeasers were prepared to go are illustrated by the emphatic statement of the former minister in Chamberlain's cabinet Lord Londonderry, who in discussion with Göring in mid-September 1938 commented on Chamberlain's negotiations with Hitler with the words "I have always been anxious, as you know, that this visit should take place, and I feel that nothing but good can come of it".[74]

Londonderry would no doubt have shown less enthusiasm if he had been present at the British Cabinet meeting when Chamberlain reported on his second discussion in Bad Godesberg. This time he faced opposition even from his otherwise reliably loyal "adjutant", the foreign secretary Lord Halifax, who said that this time Hitler had gone too far in his demands, that they sounded like the dictat of a victorious war leader and that it would be a mistake to require

---

[72] Ibidem. 142.
[73] Ibidem. 143.
[74] Kershaw, I. *Making friends with Hitler*. 244. Chamberlain was surprised by the reactions of his ministers. Duff Cooper resigned in protest at Munich, while O. Stanley and De La Warr demanded more efforts on armament. Halifax even repeatedly asked for the appointment of A. Eden and other Labour Party leaders to government posts with the aim of uniting national forces in the face of a threat. Even S. Hoare seconded him. Parker, R. A. C. 2000. *Churchill and Appeasement*. London: Macmillan. 181.

the Czechs to accept them. In his view this would look like complete capitulation to Germany, and war seemed a certainty.[75]

On the morning of the 27th of September the chief of the French general staff, M. Gamelin, arrived in London and surprisingly (from the point of view of the British and French appeasers), declared that France would take some offensive action if Germany attacked Czechoslovakia. In the afternoon of the same day Churchill met Halifax and Chamberlain in Downing Street. In the evening the Foreign Office released a press communiqué approved by Halifax to the effect that if Germany launched an assault on Czechoslovakia, "it will be the duty of the French to come to its aid, and Great Britain and Russia will assuredly stand with France." It is in this statement from the British government that we first hear the tones of Churchill's later Grand Alliance.[76] Yet while mention of Russia is important from the point of view of later development, at the time this was no more than a declaration. The Soviet Union was reportedly moving up military units to its Western frontier, but it had no common border with the CSR and Poland categorically refused to allow the Soviet armies to enter its territory, while negotiations with Rumania were dragging out with no results. Although on the 23rd of September Moscow sent an emphatic warning to a potential aggressor against Czechoslovakia, this was addressed to Warsaw and not to Berlin.[77]

It was not only the Soviets, however, who were playing a double game (in fact Beneš himself expressed doubts about the possibilities and effectiveness of any Soviet aid, and moreover feared the negative reactions of the West if Bolshevik Russia were to be drawn into the conflict). On the 26th of September Chamberlain made a speech on radio in which he famously declared, "How horrible, fantastic, incredible it is that we should be digging trenches and trying on gas-masks here because of a quarrel in a far-away country between people of whom we know nothing!... However much we may sympathize with a small nation confronted by a big and powerful neighbours, we cannot in all circumstances undertake to involve the whole British Empire in a war simply on her account."[78]

---

[75] Kershaw, I. *Making friends with Hitler.* 244–245.

[76] Parker, R. A. C. *Churchill and Appeasement.* 181.

[77] Zeman, Z. *Edvard Beneš.* 143. The text contained a warning that in the eventuality of an attack the USSR would consider itself dispensed from its obligations arising from the non-aggression pact signed with Poland.

[78] *Manchester Guardian.* 27. 9. 1938. The Czech press noticed the formulation of this speech indicating a dangerous turnaround in the British position, for example, "The historic day of the prime minister's first visit to Berchtesgarten was a historic milestone after which developments for us and for Europe greatly deteriorated... Chamberlain's comment on a small people in a faraway country, however, have distorted the existing line of the profferred English mediation even further." *Národní politika.* 30. 9. 1938.

A breakthrough (of a kind) came only with Mussolini's invitation issued on the 28th of September, proposing a conference of the four powers to resolve the tense situation. Hitler was aware that few, even in the circle of the Nazi leadership, shared his view that it was worth risking war with the Western powers when so many of the German demands over the Sudetenland could be satisfied by diplomatic means. Mussolini's initiative, supported by Göring, gave Hitler a way of entirely reversing his view without losing face by his readiness to invite Chamberlain, Daladier and Mussolini to a conference in Munich. Peace was to be preserved – at the expense of the Czechs. A distinguished British historian has argued that the the Munich agreement was not only morally repulsive but also politically disastrous for Britain.[79] Czechoslovakia, an ally, found itself cast in the role of a mischievous peace-breaker, not to be negotiated with but to be ordered about. The instructions sent by Chamberlain to the British ambassador in Prague, Newton, on the 30th of September are unambiguous in this respect:

"You should at once see President (Beneš) and on behalf of His Majesty's Government urge acceptance of plan that has been worked out today after prolonged discussion with a view to avoiding conflict. You will appreciate that there is no time for argument: it must be a plain acceptance."[80]

It would be hard to imagine a more categorical formulation in relations between two sovereign states (and what is more, allies).[81] It is possible that the peremptoriness of the wording was also partly the result of a Nazi tactic involving information gleaned by the espionage monitoring service of the *Research Institute at the Reich Ministry for Air Transport* during the Sudeten crisis of 22nd–23rd of September 1938. This service was of great value to Hitler, since we know, for example, that in the course of his negotiations with Chamberlain in Bad Godesberg the Reich Chancellor broke off his talks with the British for several hours to wait to be given the texts of radio-telegrams sent by Chamberlain to London. These were being picked up and deciphered by the *Research Institute*, and talks were resumed only after Hitler had read their contents. In this way the German chancellor could exploit what were known as the *Braune Blätter*, special intelligence reports supplied to the chancellor's office regularly from 1933 by the institute, directly during negotiations.

From the point of view of Chamberlain's attitude to the Czechs, it is significant that the text of intercepted telephone conversations between President

[79] Kershaw, I. *Making friends with Hitler*. 246.

[80] "You must immediately meet with President Beneš and in the name of His Majesty urge him to accept the plan drawn up today in a prolonged discussion with a view to the need to avoid conflict. Be aware that this is not a time for arguments, he simply must accept it." the same Chamberlain cynically remarked in private that while the Czechs might be in the right, today right does not exist". Zeman, Z. *Edvard Beneš*. 138.

[81] Čelovský, B. *Mnichovská dohoda*. 375.

Beneš and the ambassador J. Masaryk, Š. Osuský, Colonel Kalla and other diplomats in the period between the 14th and 26th of September 1938, was passed on at Göring's instructions and with Hitler's consent to the British ambassador in Berlin, N. Henderson, by the head of the ministerial office mentioned, General Bodenschatz. Evidently this information was made available to the English because on the telephone the Czechs had been less than flattering about English and French politicians. It is easy to suppose that this information did nothing to encourage Chamberlain to greater sympathy for Czechoslovakia.[82]

The German political leadership expected that in the ongoing negotiations the British and French politicians to whom the Czechs had referred to so disparagingly would react in an appropriately resentful way. Although only a hypothesis, it cannot be ruled out that this subjective factor played a role in the September crisis.

On the Czechoslovak side, the gloomy atmosphere of waiting for the verdict was described in his memoirs by H. Masařík,[83] who with V. Mastný was attached as advisor to the British delegation but was not allowed to take part in the actual negotiations at the Munich conference. Late in the evening on the 28th of September, the British diplomat F. T. Ashton-Gwatkin summoned both Czech representatives to inform them of the new plan for the cession of the border territories of the CSR and gave Mastný a map with the districts to be ceded marked. Ashton-Gwatkin told the two Czechs that the British delegation favoured the new German plan and added in a formal manner "If you do not accept this, it will mean you will have to settle the matter with Germany by yourselves. The French may tell you this with fine phrases, but believe me, they share our opinion and will not be interested in your fate."[84]

At half past one in the morning the two Czechoslovak diplomats were summoned to a conference room in the Regina Hotel (they were de facto interned in the hotel – the conference took place elsewhere) and here N. Chamberlain, É. Daladier, H. Wilson, A. Léger and F. Ashton-Gwatkin informed them of-

---

[82] Gellermann, G. W. 1995. ... *a naslouchali pro Hitlera* [... And They Listened in for Hitler] (Tappers of the Headquarters of the Third Reich). Brno: Bonus A. 120. Bonnet for example was called a pig, Chamberlain a crazy old man, and others: pigs, scoundrels, swine, shysters, rubbish. On the 27th of September 1938 the British ambassador in Berlin, Henderson, was still sending W. Strang (Foreign Office) the text of a conversation between J. Masaryk and Beneš that had been intercepted by the Germans and handed on to him by General Bodenschatz. Chamberlain had other sources of information, however, and specifically Sir J. Ball, the head of the research department of the Conservative Party (and former member of MI5, Chamberlain's agent for intelligence and secret propaganda) who "among other nefarious activities" inspired the bugging of the Czechoslovak ambassador J. Masaryk as well as W. Churchill and other important figures. Ball's intrigues prevented Churchill's intended visit to the CSR in April, 1938, for example. Parker, R. A. C. *Churchill and Appeasement*. 160.

[83] Masařík, H. *V proměnách Evropy*. 242.

[84] Ibidem.

ficially of the agreement just signed. Masařík had an especially bitter memory of Léger's brusque statement to the effect that "they were no longer waiting for any answer, that they regarded acceptance as something to be taken for granted. This was made brutally plain to us, and by a Frenchman, that this was a judgment without appeal and without the possibility of remedy." In his authentic account of the course of events on the 29th to 30th of September, Masařík convincingly describes the tragic final moments, in which "The Czechoslovak Republic ceased to exists in its 1918 borders".[85] Even years later, the approach of the Western politicians gives the impression that they were dealing with Czechoslovakia as an enemy – not an ally.

Shortly after six o'clock on the 30th of September, the German *chargé d'affaires* visited the Czechoslovak foreign minister K. Krofta to acquaint him with the results of the conference, and at 12.30 the ambassadors of France, Italy and Great Britain did the same. Krofta's answer was as follows:

"In the name of the President of the Republic and the government I declare that we are submitting to a decision made at Munich without us and against us. I would wish only to draw your attention to the fact that the press and radio war waged against us must now stop because otherwise the Munich programme cannot be implemented by peaceful means. I do not want to criticise, but for us this is a catastrophe that we have not deserved. We are submitting and we shall try to secure a peaceful life for our people. I do not know if your countries will benefit from the decision made in Munich. Certainly, however, we shall not be the last to suffer, and this will afflict others after us."[86]

President Beneš's ability to predict the subsequent tragic course of developments in Europe opened by Munich has often been cited. Study of the Czechoslovak press in the autumn of 1938 provides evidence that other Czechoslovak politicians and commentators also had a sober view of the political situation and were realistic in their assessment of the consequences of the policy of the Western great powers. One example may serve for all: the introduction to an analytical commentary written by F. Bauer of the 2nd of October 1938:

"This is a dreadful irony of history! What took place on the 29th of September in Munich was Germany's revenge for the Versailles dictat imposed on

---

[85]   Ibidem. 245. Also valuable are the author's memories of the personal attitudes and demanour or the individual protagonists immediately afterwards. He mentions Chamberlain's personal repugnance for Czechoslovakia and its leaders, Daladier's shame and disgust, and the fact that "none of the French spoke in a human way to us that day, none uttered a word of apology or regret. Only Ashton-Gwatkin, although a professional diplomat, spoke openly, in a human tone, and did not hide his depression at the negotiation with Hitler." For the full text of Masařík's report for E. Beneš and the Czechoslovak Foreign Ministry see: "Záznam čs. ministerstva zahraničních věcí o pobytu československé delegace v Mnichově" [Record of the Cz. Ministry of Foreign Affairs on the Stay of the Czechoslovak Delegation in Munich], in Šnejdárek, A. *Druhá světová válka v dokumentech a fotografiích.* 98–100. See the same text in *Mnichov v dokumentech.* 267–269.

[86]   Čelovský, B. *Mnichovská dohoda.* 375.

Germany twenty years ago. Let France and England make no mistake about it – the Reich chancellor Hitler is well aware of the fact that at Munich it was not just Czechoslovakia that fell, but France and England. By discerning this we do not mean even for a second to understate the depth of the national tragedy that is now afflicting us."[87]

In the immediate post-war period, R. Hilf (the personal secretary to Lodgman von Auen, with whom he parted company ideologically at the end of the 1950s), one of the important leaders of the organisations of deported Sudeten Germans and a protagonist of later reconciliatory activities, still shared the view that the reason for the destruction of the republic was not *the instrumentalised expansive application of the principle of self-determination* by Nazi geopolitics, but "the use of the two entirely incompatible principles of the historical continuity of the lands of the Bohemian crown and the principle of the self-determination of nations in the constitutional sense. At that moment, however, the politicians failed to have the foresight to conceive ethnic policy in a way that would have favoured a harmonious coexistence of peoples and averted internal tension and centrifugal tendencies."[88] The facts, however, lead me to believe that Hitler would still have been resolved to destroy Czechoslovakia even if it had provided the Sudeten Germans with the most extensive possible rights.

Jaksch makes the same kind of argument as Hilf when he discusses H. Ripka's book *Munich: Before and After*, which analyses the reasons for the defeat of democracy at Munich and seeks to define the contribution of Czech policy to the capitulation. Jaksch claims that Ripka "was just in his assessment of the struggle of the Sudeten democrats and also recognised the other German anti-Hitler opposition movements". Jaksch also claims that Ripka changed his position diametrically in the course of the war and so the book was never published in another edition.[89] In this book Ripka (307) argues that after the 21st of May 1938, following the partial mobilisation and in view of the "solid position of France and Great Britain", the Czechoslovak government should have pro-

---

[87] Bauer, F. "Od 21. května do 30. září" [From the 21st of May to the 30th of September]. *Národní politika*. 2. 10. 1938. 2.

[88] Hilf, R. 1996. *Němci a Češi* [Germans and Czechs]. Prague: Prago-Media. 188. If R. Hilf saw this view as a starting point for the "reconciliation" that he pursued after 1989, it is no surprise that he did not succeed with the Czechs. See e.g. the outraged reaction of L. Dobrovský to Hilf's analysis in the introduction to the Jihlava Conference Czechs-Germans in 1995, which the present author witnessed.

[89] Jaksch, W. *Cesta Evropy do Postupimi*. 382. Jaksch also draws attention to the often forgotten, "Proclamation of the German Social Democratic Party to the German People. The Sudeten Germans will be the first victims, and their future will be wiped out. Sudeten Germans! You are all now faced with a choice: equality through peace or destruction through war." Jaksch, W. in *Národní politika*. 14. 9. 1938. Often also mentioned in this context is the oath of the "Republikanische Wehr", the semi-military units of the Social Democratic Party in the Sudetenland, whose leadership sent a letter to E. Beneš in January 1936 with the words, "We swear that we shall fight among the German working class loyally and self-sacrificingly for your high ideas, peace, freedom and democracy." Mejdrová, H. *Trpký úděl*. 13.

posed a generous solution to the national problem. This solution would have had to be implemented fast, at the latest by the end of July, with or without the consent of the Sudeten German Party but in any case with the agreement of the democratic Germans.[90]

In my view the main reason why H. Ripka did not re-publish his book (written after Munich and published in Britain in 1939 soon after he had left Czechoslovakia) was that he came to realise that at the time of writing he had not had sufficient information (in particular he had not seen documents on British and German foreign policy), and in the light of this information he would have had to revise many of the arguments in his book.

The attitudes of the two great powers supposed by treaty to guarantee the security of the CSR were far from as solid as Ripka originally supposed (after the end of the war German foreign policy documents were published showing the willingness of the appeasers to concede).[91] Also published (likewise brought up before the Nuremberg Tribunal) were documents of the Sudeten German Party clearly showing that no proposals from the Czechoslovak government would have satisfied Henlein, who had clear instructions to manoeuvre Beneš into an impossible situation.[92]

The Historical Dilemma of Capitulation

Munich meant the definitive collapse of the French system of alliances in Central Europe, in which Czechoslovakia had been an important link. It also represented the failure of Beneš's one-sided orientation to France as the security anchor of the republic. The question that will evidently never be answered is

---

[90]   Jaksch, W. *Cesta Evropy do Postupimi*. 382. H. Masařík describes a dramatic meeting with W. Jaksch and O. Strasser in the period before Munich – they were reproaching the Czechs and Beneš for too yielding an attitude to Hitler, whom they claimed was only bluffing. Their reason seems to have been a secret report that Strasser had obtained from Germany from the generals and resistence movement suggesting that if war broke out they would plan to assassinate Hitler. Masařík, H. *V proměnách Evropy*. 231. There are also possible indications that Beneš was in confidential contact with Winston Churchill, who allegedly urged him to resist in the expectation of the fall of the British government. But this information is not confirmed by sufficiently reliable sources. Furthermore, in the summer of 1938 Churchill himself to a certain extent succumbed to the opinions pushed by Pro-Henleinian propaganda.

[91]   H. Masařík believes the main reason to have been that the CSR was not considered to lie in the sphere of the West's vital interests: "England had been saying it since 1922, and France adopted this viewpoint in the last two months before Munich." Ibidem. 250.

[92]   Often and rightly cited in this context is the speech made by Henlein in Vienna on the 4th of March 1941: "In any case it is certain that in the course of just a few years the Sudeten Germans succeeded in threatening the internal stability of Czechoslovakia so thoroughly and complicating its internal conditions to such an extent that it became ripe for liquidation in the sense of the new order of the continent that was cutting a path for itself. All this could happen only because all Sudeten Germandom became national socialist." Biman, S. – Malíř, J. *Kariéra učitele tělocviku*. 297.

whether President Beneš was tough enough in his attitudes face to face with the Nazi threat. The British press of the period mentioned that the most frequent question posed in London in September 1938 was whether the Czechs were really resolved to fight.[93]

R. Luža comments on the president's personality that "Beneš was a tenacious negotiator, but in negotiations with the West he was too often defensive. He failed to make it entirely clear to his Western allies that he did not intend to give up even an inch of territory under any conditions whatever." According to Luža, both Britain and France were afraid of such an unambiguous statement, because if Czechoslovakia had plainly declared that it would go to war even by itself, then that would have brought London closer to war and Paris would have been forced to come to the aid of its ally.

Such a declaration might have forced the British to put pressure on the Sudeten German Party. Luža further claims that despite having the moral, political and strategic advantage, Czechoslovakia failed to develop any kind of serious propaganda campaign of a kind that might have made an impression on public opinion in the Western countries. Generally he sees the fault on the Czechoslovak side in its political leader's neglect of the chance to demonstrate resolute intention to fight and will to resistance.[94] On this point one cannot but agree with his conclusions.

E. Táborský, Beneš's private secretary in his London exile and his advisor on questions of international law (as an insider in the Czechoslovak government in exile he was among the best informed individuals), wrote: "One criticism of Beneš's behaviour in 1938 is hard to refute, because its acceptance or rejection depends purely on highly subjective convictions, specifically on personal convictions about the moral duties of the nation and its leader in the kind of situation that confronted Beneš and Czechoslovakia in 1938. Is a leader obliged to send his people to war even when he is convinced, like Beneš in 1938, that there are no prospects of victory and that the nation is risking extermination? Does the heroic ethos of the nation demand from its leader not a practical but an ethical decision, as one of Beneš's critics declared, i.e. the demand that a dictat like that of Munich be rejected regardless of the consequences?"[95]

---

[93]   I cannot resist commenting that coming from British journalists this question may be regarded as the ultimate in pharisaism given the role that the British appeasers from the Cliveden clique played in the tragedy of Czechoslovakia. In his testimony before the International Tribunal in Nuremberg (24th–26th of April 1946) H. B. Gisevius stated that Chamberlain had been precisely informed by the German opposition from the spring of 1938 that Hitler intended to destroy Czechoslovakia. Ečer, B. *Norimberský soud*. 174.

[94]   Luža, R. *The Transfer of the Sudeten Germans*. 153–154.

[95]   Korbel, J. 1977. *Twentieth Century Czechoslovakia: The Meaning of Its History*. New York: Columbia University Press. Cited in Táborský, E. 1981. *President Beneš Between West and East, 1938–1948*. Stanford: Hoover Institu-

The historian J. Tesař rejects on principle any shifting of all the political responsibility of the social elites and people as a whole onto a single man, who is then made a scapegoat for the sins of all the other people involved, for the most part passively as bystanders.[96]

Tesař takes a critical view of Beneš, but does not in the least see this as reducing the guilt of Henlein and the Sudeten German Party for the destruction of the republic.[97] He criticises Beneš for accepting the so-called nationality settlement in the form pressed on him by Hitler and Runciman, since this involved acceptance of the principle that the Henleinians were the only authorised spokesmen of the Sudeten Germans. He believes that by doing so the president betrayed the ideal of the republic and its constitution (which categorically guaranteed the rights of every citizen/individual to free choice of nationality) by accepting the totalitarian idea of nationality as a collective entity in which the majority party can dictate binding rules of opinion and obligation to the minority.[98]

Tesař appreciates Beneš's ability always to "be sparing with the interests of the state", or – to paraphrase loosely, his ability to maintain loyalty to the *raison d'etre* of the republic under all circumstances. He argues that the president was right, at the time of culmination of the crisis, to consider the possibility of ceding part of Czechoslovak territory (Nečas's secret mission to Paris – the so-called fifth plan) if this would have meant that the republic got rid of one and a half or two million fanatic Henleinians and took the Sudeten German democrats and the Jewish population. The idea did not lack logic in relation to the defence of state interests and had significant moral cogency. Tesař claims that at Munich the West betrayed Beneš by forcing him to decide on capitulation without the chance to participate in negotiations rather than more overtly forcing him to compromise with Hitler before the eyes of the world and the domestic public.

In Tesař's view, the tragic situation of a critical threat to the state, the true gravity of which Beneš concealed right up to the 18th of September, was one

---

tion Press. Táborský's work is based not only on abundant secondary sources and unpublished documents from the American federal archives but also on the major part of Beneš's personal archives.

[96] Tesař, J. 2000. *Mnichovský komplex: jeho příčiny a důsledky* [The Munich Complex: Its causes and consequences]. Prague: Prostor. 81.

[97] "It was not within the power of any political republican leadership to prevent part or most of them from inclining to the side of Nazism", reproaches of this kind would be unjust. I feel not the slightest nostalgia for the Henleinian herd with its Hitler salutes. I am very familiar with the materials of the SD and so I know that it was this herd that was the support and driving force of Nazi fanaticism against our country throughout the war. Nor do I have anything in common with those of my countrymen who regret the fate of this herd. The object of my interest is the today general tendency to forget the anti-Nazi Sudeten Germans (citizens of the CSR) and the Germans (emigrants) – the first heroes of freedom." Ibidem. 81.

[98] Ibidem. 82.

that the president tackled in the same way as Masaryk before him in earlier critical situations. This meant that instead of engaging with criticism of Czech society and its alleged unwillingness to make sacrifices, Beneš substituted a legend of how the "nation wanted to fight" but was not allowed to. Well aware of the seriousness of the national predicament, the president understood that, "the question was whether the psychological strength of this people would be sufficient to the plan that he had resolved on and that from the very beinginng included a very ugly retreat followed by persevering fidelity to the principles of an independent and democratic state."[99]

Tesař grasps the dimension of President Beneš's distinctive attitude to the nation in a crisis situation and tries to explain (or reconstruct) it on the basis of known documents. In his view the key to Beneš's approach was the president's relief at avoiding the harsh moral crisis for the whole society that would have inevitably have arisen after a clash with reality, as a result of insufficient psychological readiness for war. The danger was that the lack of unity in attitudes to war would have come to light as soon as the political clans wishing for agreement with Germany, and representing almost half of Czech voters, and more than half Slovak voters spoke up – "the parties that from the moment of the anschluss had tactically kept silent and waited for the fruit to fall into their laps without their having to compromise themselves"[100] This judgment applied particularly to the Agrarian party, which had flirted with cooperation with the Sudeten German Party as early as the election campaign for a new president in 1935.[101] This view is perhaps supported by the way in which this disunity and disposition of forces expressed itself in full in the period of the so-called Second Republic.

Another important historian and expert on the Sudeten German movement, V. Kural, has also discussed the role of the people in the critical autumn of 1938.[102] Analysing the alternative strategies of defence of the CSR Kural ar-

---

[99] Ibidem. 94.

[100] Ibidem. 95.

[101] Interesting in the context of this study is the SdP view of Beneš's rival candidates. B. Němec, was proposed to the Henleinians by the anti-Castle wing of the Agrarians who stressed that he was not a man bound by association with a political party. W. Sebekowsky informed the Castle and Agrarians that the SdP had to pursue a radical national policy. And in the eyes of the Sudeten German politicians Prof. Němec was a "German-devourer", an ostentatious Czech nationalist. Therefore the Henleinians allegedly made it clear that they would, suprisingly, prefer K. Kramář, to whose "classic" nationalism they were used. See Klimek, A. 1998. *Boj o Hrad II* [The Struggle for the Castle II]. Prague: Panevropa. 444–445.

[102] Kural, V. *Konflikt místo společenství*. 206. On the military aspects of the September Crisis see also the study by Hauner, M. "Září 1938: Kapitulovat, či bojovat?" [September 1938: To capitulate or to fight?]. *Svědectví* 49/1975, and also Hauner, M. "Czechoslovakia as a Military Factor in British Considerations of 1938". *Journal of Strategic Studies*. 1978. A detailed analysis of the views and attitudes of the high command of the Czechoslovak Army in 1938 is to be found in the article by Šrámek, P. "Odhodlání versus loajalita" [Resolution versus Loyalty]. *Soudobé dějiny* 1–2/2004. 56–87.

gues that Czechoslovak politics and the Czechs as a people could in fact have been more active in decision-making on the further development of conditions in Central Europe, their own fate and the character of Czech-German relations than they ultimately were. Kural analyses the military aspects of the situation in the autumn of 1938 and shows that the September mobilisation of the Czechoslovak army, conducted at lightning speed,[103] crucially deprived the German army of the key factor of surprise and the CSR thus gained the necessary breathing space for further defensive activities.

Analysing the time factor in detail, Kural concludes that Germany was expecting a relatively long war and not just a short episode in which the isolated Czechoslovakia was supposed to fall. In his view, the border fortifications compensated for the qualitative superiority of German arms. He sees the existence of the "general's opposition" to Hitler in the wehrmacht command as a very significant consideration, and emphasises that after the talks in Godesberg on the 22nd–23rd of September Hitler used war as a tool of blackmail and an additional means of pressure. Kural concludes by considering capitulation to Hitler as "unjustified from a purely military point of view, and from this perspective it was not inevitable that Central Europe or the Czechs should have taken a path leading to German domination."[104]

Military resistance would have been a harsher alternative, full of sacrifice but not entirely impossible and morally superior.[105] Nonetheless, Kural argues that President Beneš's decision cannot be regarded as simple capitulation but as an acceptance merely of temporary defeat, after which Beneš immediately started to create the conditions for the future integration of Czechoslovaks (politicians and soldiers) into the ranks of the anti-Hitler coalition that he was convinced even in 1938 would inevitably be formed. It is particularly important to stress the attitude of the army, which alone unconditionally supported the president

---

[103] K. Bartošek quotes the words of the Chief of the Czechoslovak General Staff Krejčí: "our army will in about two days be entirely prepared to hold back an attack even by all German's forces so long as Poland does not move against us." Bartošek, K. "Mohli jsme se bránit?" [Could We have Defended Ourselves], in *Češi nemocní dějinami* [Czechs Sick with History]. Prague/Litomyšl: Paseka. 80–81.

[104] Kural, V. 1992. *Rok 1938. Mohli jsme se bránit?* [1938. Could We have Defended Ourselves?]. This was produced as a (non-sale) publication for the needs of the Czechoslovak Army. For an extract from this study see Kural, V. "Mohli jsme se bránit?" [Could We have Defended Ourselves?]. *Přísně tajné* 5/2003. 99–110.

[105] A central controversial point in assessment of the possibilities for defence of the CSR is Soviet military aid. Kural gives a concrete account of the military capacities that the USSR had put on military alert, but at the same time characterises the decisive political dimension of Beneš's choice: "The political aspect of the provision of Soviet military aid is well-known: An attempt to move the Red Army through Rumania and especially through Poland against the will of their governments might, given the known attitudes of Chamberlain's administration, have been exploited at Geneva to get the League of Nations to brand the USSR as the aggressor, with the consequent danger of the creation of just that continuous anti-Soviet and anti-Czechoslovak front that Beneš feared – a risk to which he ultimately preferred capitulation, although evidently Moscow too was afraid of it." Kural, V. "Mohli jsme se bránit?". 109.

of the republic and insisted in principle – if not now, then later – on the need for armed resistance to Nazi Germany. The Czechoslovak generals were a markedly compact group in terms of their political views – these were distinguished by loyalty to the political leadership of the state and a concentration exclusively on professional military problems.[106]

The dispute over "Munich" is essentially a dispute about Beneš, and raged not only in domestic conditions but also in the West, whether it was the Czechoslovak exiles or the Sudeten Germans who were trying to settle scores with Beneš using a positive or negative judgment of the man as weapon in the struggle to justify their own positions." H. Lemberg nonetheless argues that it is the Sudeten Germans themselves that represent the most contentious point of the problems surrounding Munich. He considers that the many aspects of the problem must include not only the question of how much or how little understanding for ethnicity the Czechoslovak Republic displayed, but how much real loyalty of disloyalty the Sudeten Germans actually exhibited.[107]

President Beneš's political actions and the many "ifs" of the crisis have been debated time and time again, but the military aspects of the Czechoslovak situation in the autumn of 1938 must also be considered crucial. Detailed discussion of the military aspect took place especially in the 1960s on the pages of the Czechoslovak academic journals.[108] The fundamental question of whether the republic should have militarily resisted in September 1938 found no clear answer. The later development of Czech-Sudeten German dialogue after 1989, however, has demonstrated the validity of the opinion expressed by H. Ripka in his letter to Beneš of 20th September 1938:

"Mr. President, it now depends on you alone whether we shall capitulate or resist, I know the risk of resistance: we may be defeated. But this defeat would not destroy the moral forces in the people – and these would pull themselves together at the first opportunity. Whereas capitulation means a rout for whole

[106] Šrámek, P. "Odhodlání versus loajalita". 57.

[107] Lemberg, H. "Mnichov 1938 a jeho dlouhodobé důsledky pro vztahy mezi Čechy a Němci" [Munich 1938 and its Long-term Consequences for Relations between Czechs and Germans]. *Soudobé dějiny.* 2–3/1995. 300–301. The author considers the particularly controversial points in the situation of the autumn of 1938 as follows: the theory that the Czechoslovak leadership "ordered" the Franco-British ultimatum of the 21st of September 1938, estimates of the military strength of both sides, the plans of the German resistance in German army circles, the possibility of military aid from the Soviet Union, the political role of appeasement as the intellectual background to Munich.

[108] In 1963 the journal *Odboj a revoluce* was launched together with further series of *Dokumenty a Studie*; in 1965 the publication *Odboj a revoluce 1938–1945* [Resistance and Revolution 1938–1945] came out, and in the latter half of the 1960s the broader public joined the discussion thanks to polemic articles in the military and historical academic journals. For more detail see for example Moulis, M. "Výbor pro dějiny národně osvobozeneckého boje" [Committee for the History of the Fight for National Liberation], in *Occurssus, Setkání, Begegnung* [Occurssus, Meeting, Begegnung]. (Collection in Honour of J. Křen). 1996. Pešek, J. – Pousta, Z. – Křen, J. (eds.). Prague: Karolinum. 20–25.

generations. We would not recover from this... I say openly, and it is the opinion of a great number of my friends: we prefer the most terrible risk of war to ignoble capitulation, which will destroy everything in us that is pure, strong and resolute."[109]

So it turned out, and Ripka became the first to define the phenomenon that was to bedevil the modern history of the Czech nation from this point onwards – the phenomenon known as the *Munich syndrome*. As symbol of helpless capitulation, Munich became deeply branded into the historical memory of the Czech people, afflicting the social consciousness not only of the generation of the autumn of 1938 but all subsequent generations. Its damaging effects would emerge again in the historically critical years of 1948 and 1968. In a sense, it can still be said to undermine Czech national self-confidence to this day. In this context let us cite yet another opinion – that of V. Černý, who says of Munich in his Memoirs that:

"There are fateful moments and historical situations that may be tragic, but in which even defeat, in a just fight, will be morally worth it for the future of a nation, and so that nation should and must face it, whatever the cost."[110]

H. Masařík was among the "insiders" of the September Munich crisis, and as someone with immediate experience and access to authentic information his view of the dilemma of capitulation has weight, and a certain objectivity particularly in the light of his later conflict with Beneš. Masařík writes: "If we look at the state of the European chessboard on the day of Munich with the eyes of a sober player we must concede that Beneš was right when in his speech on the 30th of September 1938 he recommended that the government accept the Munich agreement." As George Kennan says, this decision may have required more heroism than a romantic fight that would have equalled suicide."[111]

The historian K. Bartošek is among those who argue that Munich meant the definitive end of a centuries-long era in Central Europe characterised by the "meeting and jostling" of different cultures and civilisations: Western Slavs,

---

[109] Křen, J. 1963. *Do emigrace* [Into Emigration]. Prague: Naše vojsko. 55.

[110] Černý, V. 1992. *Paměti 1938–1945. Křik koruny české* [Memoirs 1938–1945. The Cry of the Czech Crown]. Brno: Atlantis. 58. Influential literary historian and critic V. Černý also recalls an episode described in Beneš's *Memoirs* – the night visit of generals Krejčí, Vojcechovský, Luža, Prchala and Syrový to try to persuade the president to order armed resistance even in a situation of abandonment by Western allies. Černý regards Beneš's response as shocking – the president let slip that *I will not lead the nation to the slaughterhouse for any empty heroism.* The last point in Beneš's own notes, however, reads, "I must act in such a way as to save the nation". I have no doubt that subjectively the president was deeply convinced of this. See the text of Beneš's notes in *Mnichovské dny*. 535.

[111] Masařík, H. *V proměnách Evropy*. 248. At the time of the Munich crisis H. M. was the deputy chief of the foreign minister K. Krofta's cabinet and undertook various confidential diplomatic missions, for example in November 1937 he conducted secret talks in Berlin with the state secretary von Mackensen. For detail see the postscript by Tomeš, J. "Solitér čs. diplomacie" [The Solitaire of Czechoslovak Diplomacy], in Masařík, H. *V proměnách Evropy*. 361–362.

Germans, and Jews. In this context Bartošek offers a "hierarchy of causes" for the change and for the level of responsibility. The prime responsibility is assigned to Nazi Germany (often overlooked in condemnations of the "Men of Munich") because the primary cause was its aggressive desire to control all Central Europe, implement the racist policy of liquidation of the Jewish minority, and also liquidate the Czechs as a nation. Second in terms of responsibility were the "Men of Munich" of the conservative circles of the West – and here Bartošek is surprised at their incomprehensible decision to clear the field for Hitler in Central Europe. The third in line are the "Men of Munich" of the small Central European states, where a "dreadfully limited nationalism and chauvinism was daily burying democracy." Yet Bartošek sees the key actor as Beneš, undoubtedly the tragic figure of the decade, and he argues that the "cool diplomat and calculator was evidently not the type of politician that the Czech interest in defending independence and democracy needed: this interest needed politicians of the Garibaldi type, or – in more contemporary terms – the de Gaulle or democratic Tito type."[112]

The historian Zbyněk Zeman is rather more critical of Beneš, arguing that the president became the victim of his own tactics, which were designed to show the world a maximum readiness for compromise on the part of his state. Zeman believes that through the September crisis Beneš made one mistake after another, and that under the growing pressure the flaws in his character came to the surface. He kept looking for compromise and could not find the necessary resolution when events turned against him. Zeman's view is that Beneš was incapable of making the basic decision – to lead a Czechoslovakia abandoned by its unreliable allies into an armed confrontation with Hitler. He was aware of the weakness of the state and the treacherousness of the international situation and was no warrior at any price.[113]

Of course, retrospectively we cannot see Munich as anything but a moment of dislocation in Czech history – the breakpoint that ushered in the period of systematic and repeated decimation of national elites (political, cultural, scientific), with consequences that emerged in full only after 1989, when once again the Sudeten German Question appeared in the centre of a society-wide

---

[112] Bartošek, K. "Mohli jsme se bránit?". 84–85. The hypothetical question of how TGM would have reacted to the September crisis is often brought up in connection with Munich. On this question Bartošek comments that when someone asked Masaryk's son Jan what his father would have done in the situation of Munich, Jan Masaryk replied that his father would not have calculated, but simply said: "Tož tedy budeme sedlat!" – "So we'll saddle up now!"

[113] Zeman, Z. *Edvard Beneš*. 145–146. However harsh, this assessment has some support in the facts. I cannot, however, accept the idea that one of the reasons for the hesitation of the western powers to support Czechoslovakia was their long-term experience of lack of far-sightedness and conciliatory spirit among the leaders of the successor states. The results of the foreign policy of the inter-war ČSR gives no grounds for such generalisations. See e.g. Dejmek, J. *Československo – jeho sousedé a velmoci*.

discourse that still continues. I shall consider this in more detail in the final chapter.

As I. Kershaw accurately summed it up: "The Munich Agreement had been morally repugnant and, in reality, politically humiliating for Britain (France, too). It had also left the rest of Czechoslovakia helpless and defenceless, had given Hitler another triumph without bloodshed, and had undermined the nascent internal opposition to the Nazi regime. Two years later, those in the British government who pursued the path of appeasement that led to Munich, Chamberlain in the vanguard, were polemically branded 'guilty men'."[114]

The Interval of the Second Republic

The extent of the last, so-called fifth annexation belt (without regard to the wording of preceding agreements) was in practice dictated by Germany entirely at will with a view to its own strategic plans. Germany took a territory of almost 30,000 km^2 and 3,860 thousand inhabitants, i.e. 38 % of the territory of the republic and 36 % of the population of the Czech Lands. Around 820–860 thousand inhabitants of the ceded territories were Czechs, of whom 120–160 thousand were expelled or fled to the interior, mainly just because they had identified their nationality as Czech. The alleged rationale of the Munich agreement as a means to just settlement of nationality conflicts was thus entirely vitiated immediately it was signed. [115] In any case, the shortness of the life of the so-called Second Republic was overwhelming proof of the real intentions of Germany.

The rump republic remained formally independent, although much reduced not only in territory but in sovereignty. Dependence on neighbouring Nazi Germany was reflected above all in the foreign political orientation of the state. In mid-October Hitler made it quite clear to the foreign minister F. Chvalkovský that he had no intention of tolerating any continuing Czech insolence. He emphasised that the only major power guarantee with any value came from Germany and in the event of "wobbling, catastrophe would follow for your state as fast as lightning".[116]

The new government headed by prime minister R. Beran adopted *the doctrine of survival* in which it proclaimed a government programme "of open cooperation with our biggest neighbour in our interests and the interest of future gen-

[114]   Kershaw, I. 2004. *Making friends with Hitler*. London: Allen Lane-Penguin Books. 246.
[115]   Bartoš, J. 1986. *Okupované pohraničí a české obyvatelstvo 1938–1945* [The Occupied Borderland and the Czech Population]. Prague: SPB. 18–21.
[116]   Dejmek, J. *Československo – jeho sousedé a velmoci*. 57.

erations." In the same document, however, the government also stated that "We shall be accommodating where this is essential, but we shall not renounce the defence of our state and national interests." A more detailed picture of R. Beran is offered by H. Masařík, who notes the way this agrarian leader and machine politician constantly shifted his views over a relatively short period.[117]

The process of demolition of the liberal, democratic political order went ahead fast, and the CSR found itself on the way to becoming an authoritarian state. J. Gebhart and J. Kuklík have suggestively characterised the new situation as a "discord of democracy and totalitarianism". A whole series of steps were taken that were in clear breach of the former and even more of the spirit of the Constitutional Charter of the 29th of February 1920. Constitutionally speaking, a peculiar state characterised by elements of continuity but also striking discontinuity was created in the Second Republic.[118]

The Second Republic, established in an atmosphere of deep frustration in Czech society (I consider the Munich Syndrome to be a useful abbreviation for this state) encouraged moral and political evasiveness (especially in part of the intelligentsia) and put a premium on tacking with the wind, thus opening the way for arrivistes, demagogues and marginal characters in Czech society. Practices previously unheard of rapidly found a way into official social and cultural life: their common denominator was desertion from formerly ostentatiously avowed national historical values.

Pliant adaptibility and the moral abdication expressed in the proverb "if we can't sing with the angels we shall howl with the wolves" (the equivalent of the English "if you can't beat them join them"), was presented as a model virtue of period pragmatism. The corruption was the most grievous, however, when spiritual and moral bankrupcy penetrated to the heart of Czech society not just as a direct result of external pressure from Germany and German policy, but also as a result of initiatives from inside the country.[119]

There was a feverish search for a rationale for the new Czech state to replace the values of the First Republic. The old dispute between T. G. Masaryk and the historian J. Pekař on the meaning of Czech history was brought up to date politically with assertions that Munich confirmed the truth of Pekař's position,

---

[117] R. Beran started to have doubts about the long-term prospects of German domination. Thus a peculiar situation arose. Beran supported the right, but only within certain limits, and definitely less than the Germans wanted; he allowed the worst elements of the right to rampage, but again only within certain limits, and intensified his contacts with people from the leftwing camp. He listened to the instructions and information provided by his press chief Z. Schmoranz, whose orientation was anti-German. Masařík, H. *V proměnách Evropy*. 268.

[118] Gebhart, J. – Kuklík, J. 2004. *Druhá republika 1938–1939* [The Second Republic 1938–1939]. Prague/Litomyšl: Paseka. 92–93.

[119] Ibidem. 180.

and especially his positive attitude to the Austria-Hungarian monarchy. The creators of the new state ideal put the emphasis on the tradition, dear to some conservatives, of the Bohemian lands as part of the Holy Roman Empire of the German Nation. Appeal to the historical tradition of St Wenceslas now led "to the revision of the Czech historical myth", in the search for a positive, realistic relationship to the German Reich.[120]

Shock and disillusion led Czech society to a crisis of confidence in the liberal and democratic norms and certainties that seemed to have failed entirely. Like insects, hidden under stones, the worst elements of the Czech people crawled out into the light, and with a sense of impunity started to organise witch hunts against victims, above all from the ranks of the Castle intellectuals, Jews, freemasons, communists, and leftist artists and cultural activitists. There were many who believed that the German hegemony in Central Europe was there to stay, and in a resigned spirit of "realism" started to collaborate with the Nazis.[121]

The Czech Fascists (members of the *Vlajka*/Czech Flag organisation) just waited for their chances and never ceased to terrorise the Beran government, whose position was a desperate result of the constant threat of armed intervention by the Reich. The Czech Flag supporters demanded "sincere" friendship with the Germans, and eagerly addressed denunciations to the Reich claiming that the Beran government was *secretly* just as anti-German and anti-Nazi as the former *openly* hostile Beneš government.[122]

J. Rataj argues that after Munich the image of Germany loomed much larger with the Czech public, who felt Germany to be "palpably closer" and to be taken more seriously than before. Generally the public was ready to believe in the possibility of cooperation with the "great neighbour", particularly as a result of propaganda about social benefits and particularly when it was systematically assured that German intentions were good and was deliberately kept in ignorance of the tension that Germany was deliberately injecting into relations with Czecho-Slovakia. The reverse side of the willingness to work with Germany was the appearance of self-appointed "saviours of the nation", who worked their way into influential positions by using the slogans of "a small state, but our own – united by Slavdom – a small but purely Czech nation", and unleashed a wave of "small Czech nationalism" (J. Rataj). An allegedly

---

[120] Ibidem. 183. Voices of this kind were heard particularly from the circles of integral Catholics associated with the weekly *Obnova (*National Revival) and the colleagues of the state president Dr. E. Hácha.

[121] Masařík, H. *V proměnách Evropy*. 269.

[122] Černý, V. *Paměti 1938–1945*. 66. The gutter press seethed with accusations like, "the government secretly supports Jews, Jew-lovers, communists, socialists, Masarykians, Benešites, Freemasons (all this meant the same in the the period jargon of the demagogic dregs) and is hampering the "purge" of Czecho-Slovakia.

new, and "integral nationalism" was presented as a sop to a humiliated nation suffering a crisis of self-confidence.

Among the symptoms of the collapsing moral integrity of the nation and its elites were such events as the press campaign for "purity of language", aimed at driving out and removing all foreign words from the Czech language, with all surnames to be fully Czechified by law and foreigners having to demonstrate a knowledge of Czech as the state language. A National Cultural Council was set up for the realisation of the ideal of "integral nationalism" and the preservation of "bare national existence", in practice a step towards the standardisation and totalitarianisation of social, political and national life. Its programme was based on the theory that "the blow that has been dealt to our nation and state was caused both by political reasons and by internal confusion in spiritual life".[123]

Journalists and politicians shared in reviving the conservative ideals associated with the tradition of St Wenceslas, which they adapted to the immediate needs of the time. The return of the Czech conservative state leaders to the idea of an integral national state involved the elevation of Czech historical statehood over Czechoslovak statehood. The latter was now presented but also perceived as artificial or "fabricated". The main ideologue of the Second Republic was the journalist E. Vajtauer, but he was joined by a series of other so-called activist journalists who succumbed to and later became tools of the Nazis (K. Lažnovský, F. Kahánek, V. Crha, J. Křemen, J. Trpák and others.)[124] Austroslavism was dusted off and taken out of historical context to become the basis of a wave of nostalgic apotheoses of the former Habsburg monarchy; this was summoned up by Czech conservative catholic rightwingers from the circle

---

[123] Gebhart, J. – Kuklík, J. *Druhá republika.* 185. The *National Cultural Council* (NCC) brought together conservative nationalist and militant Catholic-orientated representatives of culture and the arts, who during the First Republic mainly stayed in opposition to the liberal democratic and/or eventually leftist oriented stream of Czech culture and intellectual life. Leaders of the NCC consisted of J. Durych and R. Medek. One of the many targets of the rightwing press was the revue-style *Osvobozené divadlo* [Liberated Theatre] and its actor/writers J. Voskovec, J. Werich and composer J. Ježek. All three emigrated to the United States at the turn of 1938/39 and were followed into exile by other important cultural figures, such as the writers E. Hostovský, P. Fraenkl, V. Fischl, and A. Hoffmeister, actors like H. Haas, and the directors J. Weiss, W. Schorsch and many more, fleeing the rising tide of antisemitism. The idea of the "racial nation" took hold of most of the Czech non-democratic rightwing and conservative movements and groups. The integral Catholics (among others poet J. Deml) also identified with traditions of antisemitism inspired by Nazi Germany.

[124] As part of the effort to influence the press by various measures of the competent German organs (see in particular the activities of W. von Wolmar), in 1940 two special trips for Czech journalists were organised, one to the Western Front and the other across Germany. The second of these ended with a reception by Goebbels, who in his address appealed to the realism of the journalists and the Czech people. He proclaimed that when not even England could manage to do anything to prevent the incorporation of Bohemia into the German Reich, "the Czech nation will not manage it either". Brandes, D. 1999. *Češi pod německým protektorátem* [Czechs under the German Protectorate]. Prague: Prostor. 140.

of the traditional Czech pre-republican elite, and supported by a part of the young generation.[125]

The main target of the attacks of the right was Edvard Beneš and the parliamentary system of the First Republic.[126] Otherwise the most frequent targets were two organisations that had completely opposed views but were both actively resisting nazism – the Communists and the Freemasons. According to H. Masařík, members of the masonic lodges included Castle-orientated national democrats, former realists, national socialists, social democrats and here and there an agrarian intellectual. There were many protestants and Jews among the Freemasons. Various groups of Czech intelligentsia met in the masonic lodges and their ethos was strongly anti-Nazi and antifascist.

K. H. Frank was often to refer to freemasonry when criticising the Protectorate government of General A. Eliáš, in which he considered the situation to be the same as in the government of the Second Republic (there were five masons and two rotarians in the Beran government). The Henleinian leader H. Neuwirth was still proclaiming long after the war that the Castle camp of Beneš's circle was the "exclusive domaine of the Freemasons."

In assessing the Second Republic political leadership of "rump" Czechoslovakia, we ought to remember that at this stage Chamberlain's Britain and Daladier's France had become *de facto* allies of Hitler's Germany. That at least was the logic of the Munich Agreement and its solution to the "Czechoslovak Question".

Foreign policy and the domestic situation of the state were now basically under the influence of Germany. Even in normal times it had been very difficult for a medium-sized state to pursue an independent foreign policy, and for post-Munich Czechoslovakia it became progressively impossible.[127]

---

[125] For more detail on the course of political events in the period of the Second Republic see the monograph by Rataj, J. 1997. *O autoritativní národní stát* [On the Authoritarian National State]. Prague: Karolinum. 166–171. The strangely distorted world of the activist press can be illustrated by the story of the career of E. Vajtauer. Čelovský, B. 2002. *Strážce nové Evropy* [Guardian of the New Europe]. Ostrava: Tilia. Here we also find the passage, "Lažnovský and Crha evidently considered all printed materials written in Czech to be Czech papers, as if they did not know at first hand how Wolmar and Gregory issued orders on what and how these newspapers were to write. They considered the profession of journalists to be first and foremost a mere way of earning a living without any responsibility to society. This blindness has to some extent survived in this country to this day." Ibidem. 67.

[126] Even Ferdinand Peroutka changed his views radically. In the frame of K. Havlíček's theory that "politics is work according to circumstance", he reassessed his attitude to the West (he regarded alliance with them in future as impossible). Having originally supported Beneš, by the end of 1938 he did not want the president to return or any maintenance of continuity between the inhabitants of the CSR and Beneš's activity in London, on the grounds that this would complicate relations with Germany. Otáhal, M. 1992. "Ferdinand Peroutka – muž přítomnosti" [Ferdinand Peroutka – Man of the Present]. *Slovo k historii* 33. Prague: Melantrich. 20.

[127] Masařík, H. *V proměnách Evropy*. 271.

Germany insisted that the rump state repudiate its alliance agreements (especially with the Soviet Union) and join the Anticomintern Pact, and demanded that it resign from the League of Nations and stick closely to the German foreign policy line. The fulfilment of all the demands meant the loss of the remnants of state sovereignty.

The Germans also made demands relating to the domestic situation in the republic. Hitler insisted that the minister Chvalkovský radically suppress the influence of Beneš supporters and Jews, demilitarise completely, and hand over the Czechoslovak state gold reserve to Germany. He returned to the question of the Sudetenland, for which he required the complete opening of the Czechoslovak market to Sudeten products and a ban on any attempt to build in the republic factories to replace those in the ceded territories. In this context H. Masařík draws attention to the prevailing mistaken belief that the role of the Henleinians in the republic ended after Munich.

Henlein became *gauleiter* of the *Sudetenland Gau*/Sudeten areas annexed to the Reich, but the role of the Bohemian Germans in the rump state was far from over. Two of the Sudeten German Party leaders, Ernst Kundt and Hans Neuwirth, continued to operate in Prague. Kundt became the recognised "spokesman" of the remaining German minority in Czechoslovakia, which was far smaller than the number of Czechs who remained in the Sudetenland.[128] As Kundt saw it, on the whole territory of the Bohemian Lands the Bohemian Germans constituted a superior elite that would bring culture, economic structure and civilisation into Bohemia. In his view the dependence of the "small Czech nation on the great German nation" was a natural historical development that no one should be allowed to challenge with impunity. In a speech on the 17th of February 1939 he declared that, "We do not want to be and we will not be German-speaking Czechs, but shall feel and think in the spirit of the great men of our nation as Germans of a National Socialist world view!"[129]

In Henlein's staff headquarters in Liberec, but also in Prague, following Munich Sudeten German Party documents were drawn up proposing the liquidation of the state and national existence of post-Munich Czechoslovakia (in Nazi jargon *Rest-Tschechei*). One example is the the document "Interest Area of the German Reich" which outlined various alternative "solutions to the Czech Question" Here we find a sketch for the text of an "Agreement between the German Reich and the Czech Rump State" which includes the statement that

---

[128]   Ibidem. 276.
[129]   Rataj, J. *O autoritativní národní stát*. 164.

"All foreign policy measures for the Czech state would be undertaken by the German Reich in the name of the Czech state."[130]

In his proposal Kundt did not favour the extermination of the Czech people, but he wanted to change the mentality of the nation and replace the Hussite ideal with the ideal of King Přemysl Otakar II, who had supported everything German. Neuwirth recommended a radical solution to the Czech Question that almost amounted to extermination and in 1940 K. H. Frank came forward with a plan for the Germanisation, resettlement and liquidation of the Czech nation.[131]

The remaining German minority was once again to be an instrument to undermine and weaken the reduced CSR. Masařík notes that in the Second Republic the Germans had exterritorial rights, but not even this satisfied them. At the end of January 1939, on the instructions of Berlin, Kundt opened negotiations with the Beran government on the enhancement of the political positions of the German minority. His demands included the right of Germans to organise themselves in branches of the Reich NSDAP and live according to the guidelines of this party, the protection of their jobs from Czech refugees from the Sudetenland, complete self-government in education and culture, the sacking of Jews from places in state authorities where they would come into contact with the German minority and an improvement of the mutual relations of Germans and Czechs.[132]

Kundt negotiated successively with Beran, Chvalkovský and Masařík, all of whom found themselves faced with the insoluble problem of how to defend universally acknowledged legal norms from a representative of a "superior" and powerful nation and state that refused to acknowledge them. Masařík refused to grant further privileges to the German minority and insisted on the position that the Germans could not be accorded either priority rights (*Vorrecht*), nor superior rights (*Überrecht*). They had to be citizens with complete rights like the others, or to opt for German Reich citizenship according to the terms of the Munich agreement and leave the CSR. Hitler, however, refused to approve this option, because it would have meant the loss of an instrument of pressure, and the negotiations ended without a result for the German minority.

---

[130] Fremund, K. *Chtěli nás vyhubit.* 41–45. The document proposed four alternative solutions: 1. The creation of a Czech rump state without restriction of its sovereign rights, 2. The creation of a "neutralised" Czech rump state, 3. The creation of a Czech state with special ties to the German Reich, 4. The incorporation of Czech territory into the territory of the German Reich.

[131] Masařík, H. *V proměnách Evropy.* 277. For the full wording see Memorandum *Sonderbehandlung* presented on the 31st of September 1940 by K. H. Frank to Hitler with proposals also including "Memorandum on the Mode of Solution of the Czech Problem and the Future Organisation of Bohemian-Moravian territory." Fremund, K. *Chtěli nás vyhubit.* 62–75.

[132] Masařík, H. *V proměnách Evropy.* 277.

The Second Republic was not to last long, however, and the resistance of the Feierabend–Masařík–Čipera group was more or less purely symbolic in a situation where the ground was being prepared for the definitive liquidation of the independent republic.

V. Černý's summing up of this phase is telling: "We were still reeling from the hardest blows of Munich and now we were learning that although the Germans had crippled us in the name of their own national self-determination, they did not intend to accord us the right of national self-determination; as if in return for the million Czechs that they had torn from our body, they had left us a few tens of thousands of Germans, scattered through the remaining rump of the state, whose task was to chase us down."[133]

The Conflict-Ridden Principle of Self-determination

The right to self-determination formed the theoretical legal basis of the Sudeten German irredentist movement. It was the principle on which the movement demanded fulfilment of its claim to a compact ethnically defined territory contiguous with its ethnic "mother state", whose programme of territorial expansion produced a massive wave of political, ideological and social mobilisation. It is crucial to realise, however, that in the era founded by the Versailles system, the concept of self-determination was not a universally employable principle of international law but instead an ultimate political cultural ideal. In other words it was an ethnic group's ideal rather than actual legally fully defined right to its own state, or else to the opportunity to share that right in adapted form with its ethnic mother nation. As with other idealistic concepts that ignore political logic and the contradictions and pitfalls of context, it was thus wide open to abuse, and specifically to Nazi interpretation in the form in which the Sudeten German Party, inspired by the Third Reich, applied it.

In the 1950s the international lawyer H. Raschhofer made a detailed study of Sudeten German positions on the right to self-determination as related to the Munich Agreement.[134] Raschhofer's own interpretation was based on the theory

---

[133] Černý, V. *Paměti 1938–1945*. 67.

[134] Raschhofer, H. *Die Sudetenfrage*. See also the critical review of this work by Povolný, M. "Šedesát pět let od Mnichova" [Sixty Years after Munich]. *Slezský sborník* 3/2002. 264–270. The essay was first published as Povolný, M. "Mnichov po patnácti letech" [Munich after Fifteen Years]. *Tribuna* (The bulletin of the Czechoslovak Foreign Institute in Exile). Sept.-November 1953. 10–12. At the end of the essay Povolný offers his view on Czech-German relations in the context of the theme. "Friendly relations between Czechoslovakia and Germany will always be an essential component of peace and a just order in Central Europe. There has never been a reluctance on the Czechoslovak side in this regard, so long as friendship has not meant subjugation or the renunciation of our mission in Central Europe, which Czechoslovakia must defend against anyone."

that the Munich Agreement was in fact still valid, because it had effectively represented a remedy for the injustice of the agreements made in Versailles and St. Germain, by which the right of the Germans in the Bohemian Lands to self-determination had been violated in the system of peace treaties.

Raschhofer further argued that in terms of formal status in international law, the incorporation of the Sudeten German territory into the Czechoslovak Republic had been a collective award (adjudication) of part of Austro-Hungarian territory which found itself at the free disposition of the Allies. He then argued that formally the Sudeten German territory was also "adjudicated" to Germany by the collective decision of the great powers at Munich in the same way, but with the positive difference that the Munich Agreement had been the result of long negotiations in which the Czechoslovak government had also participated, and moreover that it had been in conformity with the right to self-determination. With some agile manipulation of the evidence for the individual standpoints of France and Great Britain during and shortly after the war, Raschhofer came up with the overall conclusion that from the point of view of international law, the Czechoslovak borderlands were still (he was writing in the 1953) a part of Germany under the "temporary occupation administration of Czechoslovakia".[135]

M. Povolný has drawn attention to the detailed refutation of Raschhofer's theories to be found in the works of Q. Wright and E. Táborský.[136] Prof. Wright pointed out that to be legally valid the Munich Agreement would have had to have been governed by the wording of Article 19 of the Pact on the League of Nations, which stipulated provisions for peaceful change of the *status quo.* A peaceful change according to this document was defined not just the absence of war, but also by the absence of injustice. Wright further noted that all the participants in the Munich "solution" were bound by the Briand-Kellogg Pact of 1923 forbidding war as an instrument of national policy, that most of the Munich signatories were also signatories to the Hague Conventions of 1899 and 1907, and that last but not least, the legal mechanism of the League of Nations for the peaceful solution of problems of national minorities had been entirely ignored at Munich. In addition, the Locarno Treaty of 1925 had imposed on Germany and Czechoslovakia the obligation to solve all legal disputes by arbitration or at the Permanent Court of International Justice, the Permanent Conciliation Commission and then the Council of the League of Nations.

---

[135]   Raschhofer, H. *Sudetenfrage.* 277. To try to prove the international legal validity of the Munich Agreement Raschhofer even appeals to Point 21 of Codicil C of the charges against the main Nazi war criminals, in which the violation of the Munich Agreement was included among "violations of international obligations, agreements and guarantees." He argues from this that the Munich Agreement could not have been an invalid international agreement from the beginning if it could later be "violated" in the sense of international law.

[136]   Wright, Q. "The Munich Settlement and International Law". *American Journal of International Law* 33 (1939)/1. 12–32. Táborský, E. 1946. *Naše věc* [Our Cause]. Prague: Melantrich.

To get round the problem posed to his thesis by this array of international legal collective and bilateral obligations, Raschhofer argued that the "concert" of European powers that came together at Munich did not in fact do so in order to agree the new borders of Czechoslovakia and the cession of the Sudeten territory to Germany, but that instead, "the main subject of the Munich Agreement in the narrower sense was to determine the procedure by which the evacuation of the Sudetenland would take place. The purpose of the agreement was the technical conduct of a transfer of territory that had already been agreed in principle and in rough outline."

The two decades of international relations between the world wars have been characterised by B. Čelovský as a diplomatic struggle between the revisionists, i.e. the opponents of the Versailles order, and its defenders. Up to the Anschluss with Austria, and in some eyes even up to the Munich Agreement, the aim of revision of the international order appeared to be correction of the imperfectly applied and later violated principle of the right of nations to self-determination.

The Versailles system was built on certain idealistic notions held by some politicians of the victorious side (mixed with lack of principle[137]) on how to tackle the complicated nationality situation in Central and South-East Europe by using the right to self-determination, but it also reflected the strategic power considerations and economic interests of its creators. The tension between the idealistic and the strategic was to be the reason for its fall. Hitler approached the Czechoslovak problem in terms of the pursuit of the strategic (the expansion of German territory) through the exploitation of the idealistic (the rights of ethnic German minorities in foreign states). He demanded the application of the right of self-determination for the Sudeten Germans, whose leaders had originally only campaigned for autonomy but later put themselves fully in the service of Nazi aggression.

The journalist Paul Ignotus showed a certain cynical insight when he commented that "the self-determination that triumphed in Danubian Europe in the autumn of 1918 and thereafter meant that a few gentlemen in Paris and its suburbs told the peoples affected what kind of future had been "determined" for them. And they were supposed to humbly do as they were told, for this system was degenerating into a form of terror and gang warfare."[138]

---

[137] H. W. Steed cites inter alia R. S. Baker's remark (vol. II, 47) about the British premier Lloyd George. "But no one could be entirely sure when hearing him express unalterable decisions one day that the next day he would not unalterably decide in some other way." Steed, H. W. *Tricet let novinářem II*. 312. In another passage Steed characterises the complicated relations between the allied politicians at the Versailles Conference – Clemenceau on Wilson: "Who can talk with a person who considers himself the only man in the last 2000 years who knows something about peace on earth? Wilson regards himself as a second Messiah." Ibidem. 304.

[138] Ignotus, P. "Czechs, Magyars, Slovaks". *Political Quarterly* 40/1969. 188.

Any attempt to apply the principle of self-determination necessarily involves definition of the territory affected, and above all definition of its size. Territorial claims thus automatically impact on the territorial integrity of one or more states, with direct consequences for the stability of international relations in a given region.[139]

The same applied to Central Europe in the later 1930s. By using the geopolitical principles of living space/*Lebensraum*, Germany could in fact be said to have completed the work begun at Versailles. In other words, Nazi Germany actually fully applied the principle of self-determination with which President W. Wilson had hoped to humanise the international relations of post-war Europe, but at the same time Nazi Germany subverted the political balance of international relations – a concept to which statesmen after Versailles had been ever less ready to refer to as a justification for the use of force.[140]

In his *Diplomacy* Henry Kissinger devotes considerable attention to the principle of the right to self-determination and the crisis in the autumn of 1938. He argues that the situation was complicated by the fact that the minorities of the CSR lived on territories adjacent to states in which their language was spoken, "which in the light of the Versailles orthodoxy requiring self-determination strengthened the arguments of those who demanded incorporation within their ethnic homeland."

Kissinger compares Czechoslovakia to Switzerland in terms of political maturity, but without regarding the "cantonisation", repeatedly mentioned and demanded by leaders of the Sudeten German movement as a viable path for the CSR. With regard to the CSR's ties of alliance, he identifies the dilemma of the Western powers: "from the point of view of traditional diplomacy it was easy to abandon (Czechoslovakia), and from the point of view of self-determination it was just as difficult to defend it... Munich was not then a capitulation but a state of mind, and at the same time an almost unavoidable consequence of the efforts of the democracies to preserve a geopolitically mistaken order by speeches about collective security and self-determination."[141]

---

[139] After 1945 the organisations of the expelled Germans repeatedly returned to the principle of self-determination with the evident intellectual background of Pan-German ideas. See e.g. the text of point 7 of the agreement made in Wiesbaden between the Czech National Council in exile represented by L. Prchala, and the representatives of the Sudeten Germans. "The right to self-determination is a complex idea, and in this special case admits of different territorial solutions. The Sudeten Germans will always consider themselves to be a part of the German nation. They are trying to be a bridge between Czechs and Germans." In the same publication of the Sudeten German Council we already find in the introduction the demand for use of a plebiscite as a means for the expression of the will of the people, to make possible a solution similar to that in the Saarland." See also Sudetendeutscher Rat e.V. *The Sudeten German Problem in International Politics*. (Documents on Central Europe Nr. 13). München: Dr. C. Wolf & Sohn. 27.

[140] Kissinger, H. *The Art of Diplomacy*. 327.

[141] Ibidem. 327–328.

Munich was the tragic culmination of the international legal consequences of the Versailles order in Europe, while the subsequent occupation of Czechoslovakia provided the Western powers with final proof that Hitler was aiming for control of Europe and not the application of the right of self-determination. Munich represented the organic outcome of the policy of concessions motivated in part by the reluctance of Britain and France to tackle a situation of conflict in Europe. This reluctance was conditioned by the fact that soon after the Paris treaties the USA had evacuated its political positions in Europe, and by a persistent sense of guilt for the problematic architecture of the peace agreements, its character (as Kissinger puts it) as a *punitive peace*.

Germany systematically broke free of the fetters imposed by the Versailles system with the direct assistance of the victorious powers, who were for example unwilling to compel it to recognise its eastern borders. *The victors themselves created the strongest reasons for revisionism and then collaborated in dismantling the order that they had brought into existence.*[142] And they did all this in the name of the noble ideal of a world order founded on a higher morality, while rejecting and ridiculing the principle of the balance of power. All we can say in fairness is that Wilson's moralistic conception of international relations was not ultimately completely useless, since at least it allowed Hitler to be condemned for an aggression unhampered by any moral principle.

The right to self-determination is a broad concept that can underpin a range of claims, – from the demand for ethnic self-government to territorial self-government, and from federal union to the right to incorporation into another state formation or to complete independence. The vagueness of the concept itself was skilfully exploited by Nazi Germany in international relations to support a demand based on the economic and demographic dimension of the right to self-determination: the notion of living space/lebensraum.[143] "The right to demand land country and soil can become a duty if a large nation is threatened with destruction and extinction without an increase in soil."[144] Nazi geopolitics as developed in theoretical form particularly by K. Haushofer was characterised by the linkage of territorial, economic and elitist claims against neighbouring states.[145]

---

[142] Ibidem. 331.

[143] Smutný, J. "Němci v Československu a jejich odsun z republiky" [Germans in Czechoslovakia and their Transfer from the Republic], in *Svědectví prezidentova kancléře* [Testimony of the President's Chancellor]. 1996. Prague: Mladá fronta. 315–316.

[144] Ensor, R. C. K. "Mein Kampf and Europe". *International Affairs* 18/1939. 486.

[145] Haushofer, K. 1939. *Grenzen in ihrer geographischen und politischen Bedeutung.* Heidelberg: K. Vowinckel. N. Hill summarises Haushofer's basic doctrine as follows: Every geographical region should belong to a people of certain precisely defined abilities and this superior race has the right to occupy a predetermined region even if this can be achieved only at the cost of liquidation of the other inferior ethnic groups. In this extremely radical form the theory already quite clearly served as a justification for Nazi aggressive territorial expansion.

A transport of Brno Jews arrives in the ghetto of Terezín. 270,000 Jewish citizens of pre-war Czechoslovakia were murdered in the years 1939–1945, 80,000 of them from Bohemia and Moravia (the territory of the Czech Republic today).

7 The Genesis of the Transfer of the Sudeten Germans

> *In the Balkans ethnic cleansing is a political goal,*
> *while the expulsion of the Germans from Poland and Czechoslovakia*
> *after the Second World War was a consequence*
> *of the war unleashed by the Germans.*
>
> Tadeusz Mazowiecki

Since 1989 we have witnessed a wide-ranging debate on the transfer of groups of ethnic Germans from areas of Central and South-Eastern Europe. It is a debate encouraged on the one hand by the work of historians and journalists interested in the history of Central Europe after the collapse of the Habsburg Monarchy[1], and on the other by the published or filmed recollections of people who were directly involved in the events concerned.[2]

In the wider context of the "postmodern" re-evaluation of history, an ahistorical application of the contemporary concept of human rights has been used as the basis for particularly crushing criticism of E. Beneš, who has been repeatedly branded the author of the idea of the expulsion of the Germans from

---

[1] Busek, E. "Střední Evropa v budoucí evropské konfederaci" [Central Europe in a Future European Confederation]. *Střední Evropa* 37/1994. Or e.g. the single-theme number of *Nová Přítomnost* 6/1996. The Central Europe Review deals systematically with the theme in content and title. See e.g. Hilf, R. "Plán pro střední Evropu: Jak předejít nacionální sebedestrukci" [A Plan for Central Europe. How to Prevent National Self-destruction]. *Střední Evropa* 35/1993. On the pages of *Střední Evropa* articles regularly appeared dealing with the idea of Pan-Europe in the form of a *United States of Europe* as formulated by H. Coudenhove-Kalergi and promoted from 1923 in inter-war Czechoslovakia through the local branch of *the Pan-European Union* (founded in Vienna in 1923). The rightwing *Národní Listy* on the 11th of December 1928 characterised the idea as "favouring Germany, supportive of the idea of Anschluss, sympathetic to Hungarian attempts to obtain revision of the Treaty of Trianon and to the plan of a Danubian federation". All the same, founders of the *Pan-European Union* included important politicians and intellectuals in the CSR like I. Dérer, K. Engliš, E. Rádl, J. S. Machar, A. Masaryková and others. For more detail see *Střední Evropa* 70, 71/1997.

[2] Turnwald, W. 1991. "Slyšme i druhou stranu" [Let us Hear the Other Side as Well], in Documents on the Expulsion of the Germans from the Czech Lands. Č. Budějovice: Infocentrum. *Svědkové zamlčené minulosti* [Witnesses to a Suppressed Past] I, II. 1995, 1996. Shromáždění Němců v Čechách, na Moravě a ve Slezsku (ed.). Pragomedia. *Vyhnání Čechů z pohraničí 1938* [The Expulsion of Czechs from the Borderlands 1938]. 1996. Zelený, K. (ed.). Prague: Ústav mezinárodních vztahů.

the Bohemian Lands.[3] Beneš has been demonised as a Czech chauvinist whose entire lifelong political career was directed to the liquidation of the Sudeten German presence in the republic.[4]

The question of who it was that first came up with the idea of the expulsion of the rival national community in the Bohemian Lands has been the subject of decades of fierce controversy in which some polemicists have shown an absurd disregard for context, above all the fact that *this extreme solution to an ethnic conflict* was not unique to the Sudeten German case. Such a solution had been applied earlier, and was also applied subsequently, in other ethnically mixed territories that had become seedbeds and excuses for international military conflicts.[5] It is also of more specific contextual relevance that the important Berlin political commentator Ernst Jäckh mentioned the possibility of the re-settlement of the non-German population of Central Europe as far back as 1913, in correspondence with F. Naumann.[6] J. W. Brügel has identified what he considers the first statement of a need to "expel the non-German population" from Central Europe in the publications of the Berlin Pan-German society *Alldeutscher Verband* at the turn of 1900/1901.[7]

---

[3] As one example among many see e.g. Jaksch, W. *Cesta Evropy do Postupimi*, or Churaň, M. 2001. *Postupim a Československo* [Potsdam and Czechoslovakia]. Prague: Libri. On the 11th–13th of September 1992 the Institut pro středoevropskou politiku a kulturu/Institute for Central European Politics and Culture in collaboration with the Sudeten German Academy of Sciences organised the international conference *The Policy of E. Beneš and Central Europe* (see the collection of the same title), in which such views were expressed as, "the Beneš Decrees and their implementation meet the material criteria of a crime against humanity in the meaning of the decision of the International Tribunal in Nuremberg", Blumenwitz, D. "Benešovy dekrety z roku 1945 z hlediska mezinárodního práva" [Beneš's Decrees of 1945 from the point of view of international law], in *Edvard Beneš a střední Evropa*. 1994. Drda, A. (ed.). Prague: ISE. 93. Similar views were expressed by Prof. O. Kimminich: "Much has been written on Beneš's guilt for the expulsion, but from the legal point of view this question falls into the area of criminal law, and in relation to Beneš is not material because Beneš is dead. The question is primarily one of the international legal responsibility of states... Beneš was head of state. Responsibility for the actions of a head of state that are in breach of international law is attributed to the state concerned. It is therefore impossible to dispute the responsibility of the Czechoslovak Republic." Kimminich, O. "Benešovy dekrety (posouzení z mezinárodněprávního hlediska)" [The Beneš Decrees (considered from the perspective of international law]. *Střední Evropa* 44–45/1994. 55.

[4] The tendentiousness of this claim, repeatedly made by Sudeten authors and Czech critics of Beneš (see especially E. Mandler) is pointed out by H. Lemberg: "Yet it was precisely the expelled Germans who attributed the "discovery" of the idea of expelling the Germans after the war mainly to two actors, Stalin and the Czechoslovak president Edvard Beneš." Lemberg, H. "Etnické čistky – řešení národnostních problémů?" [Ethnic Purges – A Solution to nationality problems?]. *Listy* 2/1993. 98.

[5] Pešek, J. "20. století – doba nucených migrací, vyhnání a transferů" [The 20th Century – A Time of Forced Migrations, Expulsions and Transfers]. *Dějiny a současnost* 1/2002. 42.

[6] Jäckh wrote the following to Naumann: "Have you already heard the term "to evacuate"? I heard it first today on board the battleship *Ostfriesland*. When we were debating German foreign policy and I kept insisting that Germany did not need a war, because it would obtain no benefit from it. We can genuinely pursue the aims of our *Weltpolitik* without provoking war... When I mentioned the impossibility of annexing non-German parts of neighbouring states, I received a simple answer: We shall have to evacuate them. I understood this to mean the dispossession and transfer of non-German elements." Meyer, H. C. *Mitteleuropa in German Thought and Action*. 108.

[7] On the content of these texts see the note on p. 33. Brügel, J. W. *Tschechen und Deutsche 1939–1946*. 98.

As far back as 1918, T. G. Masaryk drew attention to the repeated proposals made by pan-German ideologues during the First World War for the transfer of non-German ethnic groups and minority communities: "The Pan-Germans often suggested the *'transmigration'* of large national minorities... It is doubtful if this could be undertaken without compulsion and injustice. De facto, with these proposals the pan-Germanists were aiming to weaken the non-German minorities and not to satisfy the latter's national aspirations."[8]

A Century of Transfers of Populations

The idea that problems of national/ethnic minorities could be solved by disentangling the different groups of a population, i.e. by transfering one or more ethnic groups to their so-called "mother country". was first formulated by the Swiss anthropologist and ethnologist Georges Montandon during the First World War. In 1915 he drew up a Memorandum for the first *Conference on Nationalities*, which took place in June 1916 in Lausanne. Here he suggested that state borders should be defined in line with ethnic considerations, and the stability of the states concerned should be secured by the transfer of certain ethnic groups out of them. He noted that the populations with which he was concerned lived in agrarian areas and so had a deep attachment to the soil, which meant that compulsion and even drastic force would be needed to get them to leave the territory.

Borders and their adjustment in the frame of the post-war peace negotiations constituted one of the key problems of the new international order, since it soon became obvious that the powers were unable to come up with borders that would fully respect the territorial distribution of ethnic groups. During talks on the Statutes of the League of Nations there were bitter disputes on the question of national minorities. An article allowing for territorial changes on the grounds of rights of national self-determination was originally envisaged, and a provision on protection of minorities was subsequently mooted precisely because state borders were not fully based on ethnic borders (H. Lemberg commented that this approach showed "a remarkable tolerance for border changes on the part of the international system"[9]). While the USA was keen, in fact the other states including Great Britain displayed little enthusiasm for this new principle of international affairs. Finally it was agreed that minority articles would be part of the peace agreements with the individual states. The first of

---

8   Masaryk, T. G. 1918. *The New Europe: The Slav Standpoint*. London. 28. See also Janowsky, O. I. *Nationalities and National Minorities*. 140.

9   Lemberg, H. "Předmluva" [Preface], in Brandes, D. 2002. *Cesta k vyhnání 1938–1945*. Praha: Prostor. 12.

these was negotiated with Poland, and in this case Wilson emphasised the need to include provisions for the protection of Jews and Germans.[10]

During the First World War there had been a number of large-scale acts of transfer as punishment for the alleged treachery of certain national minorities. For example the Austro-Hungarian government branded dispersed Serbs as renegades and agents of Serbia and moved them to the Hungarian pusta (steppe). A similar fate was inflicted on the 130,000 Trentino Italians whom the Austrians deported to concentration camps in the pusta after Italy went over to the side of the Allies. A third of those interned are said to have died in the terrible conditions of the camps.

At the beginning of the 1920s the idea of resettlement as part of exchange of population was developed further by the French sociologist Bernard Lavergne. The very first inter-state agreements on the exchange of population in modern history were the *Adrianopolis Conventions* signed in November 1913 between Bulgaria and Turkey, which are considered the forerunners of the *Convention of Neuilly* of 1919 and the Convention of Lausanne.[11]

The 1920s saw several attempts to exploit the principle of exchange/resettlement of population with the aim of strengthening the human potential of a mother country, or of homogenising the ethnic profile of given state. In 1923 agreement was reached at an international conference in Lausanne under the aegis of the League of Nations on the organised resettlement of some populations of the Balkan peninsula in an exchange between Greece and Turkey which was intended to prevent further violence inflicted on civilians. Thus the principle of "*exchange of population*" emerged as a way of tackling problems of international relations. It was be an instrument of transfer and resettlement applied in the form of precedent right up to the end of the 1940s, with first the League of Nations and then United Nations as guarantor.[12]

During the Lausanne conference, diplomats received the first reports of the loss of human life and suffering associated with resettlement.[13] Of the half million transferred Greeks, allegedly only 190,000 survived "repatriation", while of the Turkish minority in Greece (Aegean Macedonia) approximately 366,000 evacuees reached the designated areas of Turkey.[14] J. Schechtman

---

[10] Petráš, R. "Mezinárodněprávní ochrana menšin po první světové válce". 32.

[11] Schechtman, J. B. *European Population Transfers*. 12.

[12] For a detailed study of the problem see Pallis, A. A. "Racial Migrations in the Balkans during the Years 1912–1924". *Geographical Journal* 66/1925. Likewise the study by J. Schechtman already mentioned.

[13] For a very detailed account see Ladas, S. P. 1932. *The Exchange of Minorities Bulgaria, Greece and Turkey*. New York: The Macmillan. Pallis, A. A. "Racial Migrations in the Balkans during the Years 1912–1924". 315–331.

[14] Pešek, J. "20. století – doba nucených migrací, vyhnání a transferů". *Dějiny a současnost* 1/2002. 42–43. J. Schechtman gives different figures for people transferred; in his view around 1.2 million Greeks were transferred from Turkey to Greece and 336 000 Turks from Greece to Turkey. The same author argues for the benefits of a high degree of ethnic homogenisation of the population of the state, which would not be attain-

claimed that the Turks left Greece in a more or less orderly fashion and that their transfer took place without major difficulties.[15] In 1944, in the context of later discussion on the possibilitity of solving the problem of German ethnic groups by the transfer of population in East Central Europe, the Mabbott Memorandum (see below) mentioned this Greek-Turkish precedent. Specifically Mabbott referred to it in a passage concluding that if relations between a majority and a minority are very hostile, members of the minority may give precedence to speed of transfer over elaborate preparations.[16] Although the British had discussed various options as to time scale, the ultimate preference was for a fast, radical "break", with the drastic phase of the operation to be kept as short as possible. The schedule of the transfer was so important from the "humanitarian and economic point of view" that it needed to be precisely agreed upon with the great powers and not left to the Polish and Czechoslovak governments. Mabbott feared the possible prolongation of the critical period in which there was a potential for massacres of the civilian population and uncontrollable outbreaks of mass revenge on ethnic Germans. In the plans of the allies, the phenomenon known to history as the "wild transfer" was intended to be kept to a mininum. As Mabbott noted, "...there are two main reasons for avoiding such a turn of events. First it would considerably increase the human suffering involved. Second, Germany has to absorb the migrants, and if it has to do so at a tempo of the kind determined by Czechs or Poles, the result would probably be economic collapse."[17]

It should be noted that the exchange of population that took place in the years 1919 to 1930 between Greece and Bulgaria was asymmetrical in the same way as the transfer of the Sudeten Germans. It resulted in the disappearance of the Greek minority in Bulgaria while the Bulgarian minority in Greece remained quite large.

Although the Greek-Turkish exchange of ethnic minority groups was not the first operation of its kind, it made a major impression on experts and politicians. In 1937 it was recommended as an instructive precedent by the British Royal Commission for the solution of the Arab-Jewish conflict in Palestine. It was similarly recommended as a functional model for the agreement between

---

able by methods other than transfer. The long-term German expert on the problem, the publicist Ernst Jäckh (a supporter of the project of *Mitteleuropa)* declared that "only be means of exchange of minorities could new Greek-Turkish relations be created. First it brought a relaxation of tension, which later changed into agreement and in the end grew in 1933 into alliance". Schechtman, J. *European Population Transfers.* 464. For more on this theme see Brandes, D. *Cesta k vyhnání 1938–1945.* 224 ff.

[15] Schechtman, J. *European Population Transfers.* 21.

[16] Brandes, D. *Cesta k vyhnání 1938–1945.* 224.

[17] Mabbott's memorandum also states that "fast and chaotic expulsion could be the cause of immense human suffering, as we already know from Hitler's violent transfers of population when migrants were hastily moved before preparations for their resettlement were ready". Ibidem. 136.

Mussolini and Hitler in 1939 on the South Tyrol, from which the German population was resettled. This latter agreement was in fact the first stage of the plans for population shifts envisaged by Nazi geopolitical schemes for the reorganisation of Central and Eastern Europe.[18]

In previous chapters we have suggested certain continuities in German foreign policy (in the sense of pursuit of the interests of Germany in Central Europe), regardless of the particular regime of the moment. As further evidence for a certain continuity we might mention the plan drawn up in 1923 by the Foreign Ministry of the Weimar Republic, which developed the concept of the *progressive withdrawal of groups of ethnic Germans from Eastern and Southern Europe to Reich territory*.[19] The German historian W. Mommsen argues that from today's point of view, and taking all contexts into account, the Weimar period 1918–1933 looks more like the last phase of the Kaiser's era than a real attempt at a fresh start.[20] Of course, there is a wide range of evidence for Stresemann's systematic efforts to recover Germany's position as a great power, but this plan is suggestive in the light of future developments.

Richard Evans has drawn attention to the role of the application of the theory of *selective social Darwinism*,[21] based on the idea of a struggle for domination of human society (the war of each against all), between races, individuals or families, in which only the strongest and the best prepared survive. In the period of the Weimar Republic this theory became widespread and influential, so preparing the ground for the mass acceptance of Nazi ideology. Transfers of population and the consolidation of Germandom were already widely accepted as potential tools of national policy in the interwar period. In the course of the Second World War, hundreds of thousands of Germans from the Baltic states, South Tyrol and other areas controlled by Nazi Germany were resettled as part of the plan to "*consolidate Germandom*". A total of 550,000 ethnic Germans (*Volksdeutsche*) were moved.

In the autumn of 1938 after the annexation of the border territories of the Czech Lands on the basis of the Munich Agreement, German democrats and opponents of Nazism, Jews and many Czechs domiciled in the border territories spontaneously fled or were driven out.[22]

---

[18]   Schechtman, J. *European Population Transfers*. 22.

[19]   Pešek, J. "20. století – doba nucených migrací, vyhnání a transferů". 43.

[20]   In this context Mommsen notes that the German Reich created under Bismarck even after reunification continues to represent a central point of orientation of national identity for Germans. See Evans, R. J. *Rereading German History 1800–1996*. 44.

[21]   See the chapter In search of German Social Darwinism, in Evans, R. J. *Rereading German History 1800–1996*. 119 ff.

[22]   *Konfliktní společenství, katastrofa, uvolnění* [Conflicting Communities, Catastrophe, Disengagement]. 1996. (Collective of authors). Prague: Ústav mezinárodních vztahů. 20.

The Munich Agreement contained a number of points formulated to allow for the possibility of further negotiations in response to increased demands on the German side and more forced concessions on the Czech side. In every case the wording played into the hands of the aggressor, making possible the annexation of far more territory than could be justified by the proclaimed principles of identifying such territory on the basis of "ethnographic designation by belt." England and France gave way to Germany's demand that areas with a more than 50% majority of German population (on the basis of the state of 1918) would be annexed. In practice this meant proceeding according to the census of 1910, in which the criterion had been not mother tongue but what was known as language of communication (*Umgangsprache*) – a criterion that favoured the Germans (in 1910 the German-speaking population of the Czech Lands had reached its peak numerically). In addition, since it was not stipulated whether the key territorial unit for calculation of percentage share was the administrative community, judicial or political district, the annexation came to include even political districts in which the minimum proportion of 50% Germans had never been reached even before 1918).[23]

The forced transfer of the Jewish population, first in Germany itself and then under occupation regimes in the individual European states, was carried out in several stages. In fictionalised conversations with Hitler H. Rauschning called this procedure, the "technique of depopulation".[24] Ruthless treatment of the population of the occupied territories characterised the creation of "living space for the German race", with the Jews, Poles and Gypsies in particular being first socially de-classed and then physically liquidated on the basis of the Nuremberg race laws of 1935.

After the attack on the Soviet Union, Hitler's original plan to resettle the Jewish population in Madagascar was abandoned and priority given to the deportation of the Jews to the East. Then, on the 31st of July 1941 Göring instructed the chief of the *Reich Main Security Office* to draw up a plan for the "final solution of the Jewish Problem". As Hitler said to his intimates on 16 July 1941: "it gives us the chance of exterminating anything that opposes us." Consequently Hitler passed instructions to the head of the Supreme Command of

---

[23] Bartoš, J. 1996. "Mnichov a československé pohraničí" [Munich and the Czechoslovak Borderlands], in *Vyhnání Čechů z pohraničí 1938*. 6–7. A summary report on immigrants designated refugees and fugitives was drawn up under the Protectorate of Bohemia and Moravia and gives a total number of 220,000, of which 162,000 were Czech and 23,000 foreign nationals. Munich evidently caused much more widespread movement in both directions than one might have expected. One special group were Jews: around 25,000 of them left the borderlands, and of these only a minority then managed to emigrate abroad and escape systematic liquidation. Ibidem. 18.

[24] See Lemberg, H. "Vývoj plánů na vysídlení Němců z Československa" [The Development of Plans for the Expulsion of the Germans from Czechoslovakia], in *Cesta do katastrofy* [The Road to Catastrophe]. 1992. Řezanková, I. – Kural, V. (eds.). Prague: Ústav mezinárodních vztahů. 61.

the Armed Forces/Oberkommando der Wehrmacht, Field Marshal W. Keitel: "No German participating in action against bands or their associates is to be held responsible for acts of violence either from a disciplinary or judicial point of view."[25]

On the 20th of January 1942 a meeting of the highest party functionaries and representatives of the Reich ministries was held at Wannsee, where Heydrich put forward his plan for all European countries within reach of the SS to be systematically "purged" of Jews and the Jews "settled in a suitable way in the East". This plan already anticipated that – Nazi jargon put it, "the majority will undoubtedly fall by the way through natural decrease."[26]

The German historian Golo Mann shares with others the view that Hitler's aim was not a pan-German national state. He was not striving for revision of the Versailles Treaty and the restoration of the Reich of 1914 – which had not been a purely ethnic state and had not included all ethnic Germans within its borders. He rejected these goals with contempt, or at best sometimes saw them just as stepping stones. His true aim was to subjugate or exterminate the non-German peoples, and to establish rule over territory limited neither by borders nor by the criterion of the historical presence of ethnic Germans.[27] To achieve his aim, Hitler needed to undertake mass shifts of population. Fortunately he only managed to carry out a small proportion of the transfers that he planned.

The Munich Agreement was conceived and justified as a rationalisation of borders, i.e. as a way of reducing the contradictions between the state borders and ethnic structure of settlement in the border areas. In fact it did not dramatically simplify the ethnic structure on either side, because 235,000 Germans remained in the unannexed interior and according to the informed estimate of J. Bartoš 578,000 Czechs remained in the annexed regions of the later Sudetenland Reichsgau. In the territories annexed to Bavaria and Austria 100,000 Czechs remained, and in the Těšín region (occupied by Poland) 95,000 Czechs and so on. Thus a total of at least 822,000 Czechs remained on all territories occupied in 1938. There was also flight from these territories by German antifascists and democrats (an estimated 10–30,000 seeking refuge from Nazism in Czechoslo-

---

[25] Burleigh, M. 1997. *Ethics and extermination (reflections on Nazi genocide)*. Cambridge: Cambridge University Press. 105–107.

[26] Müller, H. (et al.). "Konference ve Wannsee a 'konečné řešení židovské otázky'" [The Conference at Wannsee and the "Final Solution of the Jewish Problem"], in *Dějiny Německa* [History of Germany]. 1995. Prague: Lidové noviny. 299–230. For more detail on the subject of the genocide of Czech Jews, see e.g. Kárný, M. 1991. *Konečné řešení* [The Final Solution]. Prague: Academia. Kraus, O. – Kulka, E. 1966. *Noc a mlha* [Night and Mist]. Prague: Naše vojsko/SPB. Roseman, M. 2002. *The Wannsee Conference and the Final Solution*. New York: Metropolitan Books.

[27] Mann, G. 1993. *Dějiny Německa 1919–1945* [The History of Germany 1919–1945]. Prague: Československý spisovatel. 189.

vakia: their fates were particularly tragic), by almost the whole Jewish population of these territories (around 25,000) and others. Overall, the number of inhabitants who fled from or were expelled from the occupied borderlands is estimated at 152,000, including 115,000 Czechs.[28]

J. Šíma's unique study of *Czechoslovak Migrants*, gives a detailed view of the subject from the sociological point of view. The details of the motives that led the migrants to leave their homes are particularly valuable. Most respondents stated that they were afraid, and specifically deathly afraid of the "activists" among the German-speaking inhabitants of the CSR[29]. Almost 30% of respondents said that they had left their homes because of actual difficulties, and almost 40% because of fears of difficulties. A total of 19% stated that they had wanted to live either among citizens of Czech ethnicity or on the territory of the CSR. According to Šíma, by the 1st of July 1939 a total of 196,714 such migrants and 22,403 foreign nationals had moved from the borderlands to the interior.[30] *An Office for Care of Migrants* was set up to address their needs, and continued in operation right up to 1944.

H. Lemberg described the *Zamość Action* as probably the most grotesque example of Nazi settlement plans.[31] In a kind of laboratory experiment, the area around Zamość was to be transformed into part of an intended German "settlement bridge" ultimately supposed to stretch from the Baltic to Transylvania. Poles and Ukrainians were to be moved out to make way for German settlers. Another element of the scheme was supposed to be the *re-Germanisation* of families of former German migrants who had long been assimilated into Polish conditions. Only at this point in the plan was it realised that the resettlement of the Baltic Germans had been a mistake, because the selected groups of migrants rejected attempts to restore their original German identity.

---

[28] J. Bartoš, who is evidently the most informed Czech expert on movement of population in the border areas during the occupation, repeatedly points out the difficulty of reconstructing all the migration movements of the time, because the evidence is incomplete and existing sets of data hard to compare, partly as a result of conscious manipulation of data, and partly as a result of its collection by different criteria. One valuable contribution to the sociological understanding of movements of the Czech population after Munich is provided by Šíma, J. 1945. *Českoslovenští přestěhovalci v letech 1938–1945* [Czechoslovak Migration in the Years 1938–1945]. Prague: Societas. For more detail on the theme from the Czech side see especially the monographic study, Bartoš, J. *Okupované pohraničí a české obyvatelstvo 1938–1945*. The German view has been the subject of several studies of varying quality, among which we might mention Bohmann, A. *Das Sudetendeutschtum in Zahlen*.

[29] On the theme of the German anti-fascist exiles in Czechoslovakia, see e.g. Veselý, J. (et al.). 1983. *Azyl v Československu 1933–1938* [Exile in Czechoslovakia 1933–1938]. Prague: Naše vojsko. Kural, V. *Konflikt místo společenství*. 158–159. From March 15th to April 15th 1999, an exhibition was held in the Karolinum building in Prague on the theme "Czechs and Germans together against Hitler" (authors K. Hyršlová and V. Kural).

[30] Šíma, J. *Českoslovenští přestěhovalci 1938–1945*. 5–8, 103.

[31] Lemberg, H. "Etnické čistky – řešení národnostních problémů?". 97–98.

The relocation of populations which took place at the end of the Second World War and in the immediate postwar period was unprecented in scale. In Europe alone it affected more than 18 million people, more than 12 million of them ethnic Germans from the territory of Czechoslovakia, Poland, Hungary, Rumania and Yugoslavia.[32]

At the end of the Potsdam Conference (held from the 17th of July to the 2nd of August 1945) the Allied leaders issued a document called the "*Potsdam Communiqué*", which in Article XIII formulated special measures for implementation of "*orderly transfers of German populations*". The organisation and supervision of this unprecented operation – the scale, consequences and potential risks of which were well understood by the Allied powers, was entrusted to the *Allied Control Council in Germany*, which drew up a schedule of transfers in collaboration with the governments of affected countries to give the whole operation an overall international framework.[33] At the time when the decisions were being made on the fate of its German-speaking population, Czechoslovakia was part of Western political culture and the anti-Hitler alliance. I therefore consider it relevant to present the facts and contexts that allow us to judge the conduct of its politicians on the one hand by the acknowledged standards of international public law of the time, and on the other in the light of allied political planning of postwar measures in Germany.

This is not meant as a way of shifting responsibility for the decision to expel the Bohemian Germans onto the Allied powers, for this responsibility is something that the Czech Republic as the successor state to the former Czechoslovakia must accept. I am simply drawing attention to the fact that President Beneš's approach to postwar solution of the relations between Czechs and Germans was not something that went beyond generally shared ideas on the postwar order of Europe and the standards of international law of the time. Like those of other politicians of the allied coalition, his ideas moved within the limits of the contemporary concept of international law and the punitive paradigm of Allied thinking about Germany.[34]

---

[32] Schechtman, J. B. 1962. *Postwar Population Transfers in Europe 1945–1955*. VIII. University of Pennsylvania Press, Philadelphia. For a German view see e.g. *Die Flucht. Über die Vertreibung der Deutschen aus dem Osten*. 2002. Aust, S. – Burgdorff, S. (eds.). Stuttgart/München: Deutsche Verlags-Anstalt.

[33] Schechtman, J. B. *Postwar Population Transfers*. 38.

[34] Criticism of Beneš does not, however, come exclusively from Sudeten German circles. D. Brandes, for example, criticises and fundamentally challenges Beneš's role in the London government in exile, claiming that: "In negotiation on the composition of the provisional government he pushed through his own ideas and satisfied the British and opposition by accepting Hodža in the 'state council'. Behind the facade of this substitute parliament and government, he step-by-step built up his own absolute rule, which was to be challenged only by the communists. The British government left him freedom of action and was then surprised when the Czechoslovak exile institutions lost their internal political balance..." This respected German historian ignores the fact that Beneš enjoyed a natural authority both with most of the Czechoslovak exiled politicians

President Beneš was undoubtedly mistaken in some of his analyses and predictions (especially concerning the possible future role of the Soviet Union as guarantor of Czechoslovak security and sovereignty, but then other politicians hoped for positive changes in the Soviet system as a consequence of cooperation with the allies), but both in the eyes of the allies and the home resistance he was the key figure in Czech resistance to Nazism, and a democratic politician who managed to co-ordinate the very heterogeneous, ideologicially divergent currents of the resistance in the East, West and under the Protectorate in a way that meant Czechoslovaks were regarded as respected partners in the anti-Hitler coalition.[35]

The difficulty of finding appropriate norms of international law by which to judge the crimes of the Nazi era became fully apparent to the Allies after the war in the course of the proceedings of the International Tribunal in Nuremberg. It was almost impossible to find a precedent for events of a kind never before recorded in human history. Not surprisingly, in a situation in which the centuries-old ideals of European humanism had gone up in smoke in the ovens of Auschwitz, the view prevailed that the cruelty of the transfer was a lesser evil than the risk that the apocalypse would be repeated, once again, under the excuse of protection of the rights of German ethnic groups in the countries of Central and Eastern Europe.[36]

(including for example his long-term opponent Hodža), and many British authorities (Churchill, Eden, Lockhart, Sargent, Nichols and others), who regarded him as a democrat and a partner, and certainly not as a political adventurer who would "poison the postwar relations between national groups with his Greater-Czech ideas", as Brandes claims. (12). These relations were poisoned by Nazism, not by the governments in exile in London. Brandes, D. 2003. *Exil v Londýně 1939–1943* [Exile in London 1939–1943]. Prague: Karolinum. 423. Brandes' point here is also at odds with his view of the Sudeten Germans as expressed in another study: "The cooperation between the German nationalist groupings and parties in Poland under the Weimar Republic and from 1934, especially the concerted action between the Sudeten German Patriotic Front, later the Sudeten German Party and the national socialist leadership, suggested to Poles and Czechs, but also to the great powers and their advisors, that the long-term loyalty of German minorities to Czechoslovakia and the Polish Republic could not be counted upon." Brandes, D. *Cesta k vyhnání 1938–1945.* 367. An authentic and detailed insight into the atmosphere and internal relations in the Czechoslovak government in exile in London is provided by *Válečné deníky Jana Opočenského.*

[35] E. Táborský relates that Beneš often made official statements that were more optimistic than his private feelings, and that for example his repeated predictions of an early end to the war were not fulfilled. He also says, "No studies of Beneš's character and his actions through the decade 1938–1948 will of course be complete unless they mention his "Munich Complex". France and Britain sacrificed his country and his own vain attempt to satisfy the insatiable ambitions of Czechoslovakia's worst enemy. This feeling of betrayal inevitably distorted his attitude to the Western democracies during the war, and in the same way the opinions that he formed at the time of Munich influenced his later conduct and policy. The basic causes of Beneš's sudden political weakening lay beyond his reach. This was the huge Soviet support for the local communists unbalanced by corresponding countermeasures on the part of the West and a lack of civic courage among the demoralised masses. Táborský, E. *President Beneš between East and West.* 52–54.

[36] The first article of the programme of the Nazi Party NSDAP stated: "We are appealing for the unity of all Germans in order to form a greater Germany on the basis of the right to self-determination that nations enjoy." Feder, G. 1932. *The Program of the Party of Hitler.* München. 18.

The legend handed down in the spirit of the Henleinian propaganda of the later thirties, i.e. that Beneš was the author of the idea of the expulsion and it was a goal to which all his political activities were directed, must be firmly rejected.[37] Beneš arrived at the concept of expulsion of the Bohemian Germans by a very complex route in which the most important factors were the views of the British on the post-war organisation of Central Europe and the radical attitude of the Czech domestic resistance, which even threatened to withdraw recognition of his status as president in exile if he held back from demanding the complete expulsion of the Germans.[38] The attitude of resistance groups in the Protectorate, especially those formed by former officers of the Czechoslovak army, was in this respect uncompromising, and like that of the Polish government was justified with reference to the broadcasts made by Nazi Germany.

In London, of course, other governments-in-exile of the occupied countries of Europe were developing their own policies ("The National Committee of the Free French" and eight other governments in exile, of which four were Eastern European: Czechoslovak, Polish, Yugoslav and Greek).

The attitudes of the Polish government in exile headed by General W. E. Sikorski are particularly important for the development of ideas on the expulsion of the Sudeten Germans. The Polish government submitted to the Foreign Office its demands for the annexation of the territory of East Prussia and Upper Silesia, the shortening of the Polish-German frontier and the expulsion of the German population from the new Polish areas. These plans were premised on the idea that in combination with Czechoslovakia Poland would replace France as Great Britain's most important security partner on the continent, and ought therefore to be economically and strategically strengthened. Beneš's plans for tackling the Sudeten German problem seemed too moderate for the Polish government.[39] Poland was also an important factor in British

---

[37] Here we cannot of course overlook Wiskemann's mention of the fact that Ripka informed her in a letter about the first serious debate that he had on the practical possibilities of such a step (transfer) with Beneš in November 1938, in which they reportedly decided that after Munich war was inevitable. See Wiskemann, E. 1956. *Germany's Eastern Neighbours*. London: Oxford University Press. 62.

[38] When in September 1942 Beneš tried to win Jaksch over to the idea of partial transfer on the basis of the "principle of guilt", the Foreign Office told Beneš that this would be to set excessive limits on the desirable scale of the transfer. Brandes, D. *Exil v Londýně*. 434.

[39] Brandes, D. *Exil v Londýně*. 433. For an interpretation of the transfers from the perspective of Polish historiography see the overview by Borodziej, W. "Polská historiografie o "vyhnání" Němců" [Polish Historiography on the "Expulsion" of the Germans]. *Soudobé dějiny* 2/1997. 306–326. One of the views cited here is that of the historian K. Kersten: "If I claim, for example, that from the point of view of Polish national and state interest, the transfer of the Germans and the Ukrainians after the 2nd World War was in the situation of the time justified, however much it was in contradiction to human rights, I am not thereby relativising the truth, but placing it in a concrete normative order." Ibidem. 325. See also information on the major Polish-German research project led by W. Borodziej and H. Lemberg in the review by Pešek, J. "Poválečné osudy Němců

thinking on the postwar organisation of Central and Eastern Europe, which involved the reorganisation of the region into a confederation whose core would be formed by Poland and Czechoslovakia.[40]

M. Hodža in particular (supported by Gen. L. Prchala) favoured a great federation stretching all the way from Poland to Greece, and this fitted particularly well with British ideas of the formation of a post-war block of Central European states headed by Poland and Czechoslovakia. The British Foreign Office research centre (The Royal Institute of International Affairs and its Foreign Research and Press Service) recommended the creation of a Northern Federation made up of Poland, Czechoslovakia, Hungary and an autonomous Transylvania, which would reduce ethnic problems. Beneš agreed to the British and Polish plans and so took the wind out of the sails of the supporters of the more ambitious larger federation, such as Prchala, Hodža and Osuský.[41]

In the autumn of 1939 when Beneš was considering the idea of post-war creation of two ethnic territories inside the CSR, he envisaged a reduction in the German element to be achieved only through the expulsion of Nazis. In a BBC foreign broadcast, however, the home resistance learned through Jaksch of a possible imminent deal between him and Beneš on the entry of Sudeten-German representatives of the Jaksch group into the State Council.[42]

Beneš's efforts in 1939 to 1941 show a search for moderate solutions culminating in a proposal for a new status for Sudeten Germans in the framework of the post-war republic. In a policy programme document dated the 3rd of February 1941 he suggested the following solution for the minorities problem in

---

v Polsku pod drobnohledem" [The Postwar Fates of Germans in Poland under the Microscope]. *Soudobé dějiny* 3/2003. 351–356.

[40] At the beginning of the war Beneš envisaged the reduction of the Polish Republic to the ethnically Polish territory with a common border with Russia. On these premises he thought it would be possible to include Poland in a looser Danubian federation, which would however incorporate all the Danubian states. In the same spirit on the 28th of November 1939 M. Hodža presented the British government with a memorandim, "Collective Security in Europe", in which he argued above all for the economic cooperation of Poland, the Danubian states and Bulgaria. Hodža was willing to cede territory not only with German but also with Hungarian population. Brandes, D. *Exil v Londýně*. 61.

[41] Ibidem. 435. During a stay in the USA in the winter of 1943/44 Hodža sent the State Department a memorandum entitled *Europe at the Crossroads*, in which he warned against Stalin's neo-imperial policy based on the Soviet military factor and supported by the communist parties of individual countries. Hodža in his conclusions foresaw the events that actually happened. At the same time, however, he warned against the building of spheres of influence, which of course the great powers deliberately pursued at the end of the war. For more detail on the relations between the Czechoslovak and Polish governments in exile, including Beneš's negotiations with Sikorski on a possible postwar confederations, see Němeček, J. 2003. *Od spojenectví k roztržce* [From Alliance to Split]. Prague: Academia. 299.

[42] "After the provisional government had been recognised, Beneš offered Jaksch six seats in the State Council if he would agree with his conception of the creation of a "Czech living space" and partial transfer, but he then found himself in conflict with the Czech resistance movements and the government in exile." Brandes, D. *Exil v Londýně*. 433.

the revived republic: "For example in Czechoslovakia German, Czechoslovak, Hungarian and Ruthenian territories would be clearly created..."[43]

This latter memorandum was drawn up at the request of Bruce Lockhart, who asked Beneš to formulate the war aims of the Czechoslovak government in exile for presentation to the British government. In discussion of the document, some members of the government rejected the idea of a compact German territory. Fundamental objections to the concept were also expressed by H. Ripka. In his first note to Chapter X, he wrote, "I doubt that an "autonomous" mainly German territory located between the historic border and the borders of Czech living space would remain within the framework of Czechoslovakia for any longer or more lasting period. The Germans of this territory would have an interest in being incorporated within the framework of Czechoslovakia only in the first postwar years, so as to avoid suffering the political, economic and financial consequences of defeat with the rest of Germany. As soon as Germany regained some strength, there would be calls for annexation to it, or else the Germans would start theatening or trying to extort an anschluss of this kind."[44]

The home resistance reacted sharply to a series of critical radio programmes on Beneš's ideas about the postwar organisation of the restored republic, and eventually on the 19th of December 1941 the resistance organisation ÚVOD adopted a unified official viewpoint on the German problem. It recommended that the exile government in London should continue talks on the German question together with the other subjugated nations, but that it should ensure that the question be acknowledged to be its own internal affair. ÚVOD categorically rejected the idea of the establishment of three German (autonomous) regions, however, since this would risk the return of a closed German territory that could potentially be re-annexed from the CSR. It should be stressed, however, that although more radical than the president, above all because of the views of officers of the former Czechoslovak Army who from the beginning of the occupation took uncompromising attitudes of the "Germans out" type (and even demanded the annexation of Lusatia), ÚVOD did not cease to regard Beneš as the cornerstone of the resistance at home and abroad despite its reservations.[45]

---

[43] For detail see Chapter 10, Problém minorit ve střední Evropě. Memorandum "Mírové cíle československé" [The Problem of Minorities in Central Europe. Memorandum "Czechoslovak Peace Aims"], in Češi a sudetoněmecká otázka 1939–1945 [Czechs and the Sudeten German Problem 1939–1945]. 1994. Vondrová, J. (ed.). Prague: Ústav mezinárodních vztahů. 90–91. The editor draws attention to the fact that the opinions expressed by J. Nečas, J. Bečko and F. Němec have not yet been found in the archives. See also Luža, R. The Transfer of the Sudeten Germans. 229–230.

[44] Češi a sudetoněmecká otázka. 98.

[45] Kural, V. 1997. Vlastenci proti okupaci [Patriots agains the Occupation]. Prague: Karolinum/Ústav mezinárodních vztahů. 76.

Once again, however, a key role in forming Beneš's views was played by the British, specifically the Central Europe Section of the Foreign Office headed by Orme Sargent, which worked directly with the exiled governments of the occupied countries of Central Europe including the Czechoslovak. The British insisted that the Czechoslovak government negotiate with the Sudeten German emigrant group in Great Britain headed by W. Jaksch.[46]

The direction of Beneš's thinking on the post-war settlement of the Sudeten German question is expressed in a report to the domestic resistance of the 6th of September 1941. "If some Germans stay in our country in line with the minimal programme, however, it is in the interests of the matter that we win them for cooperation with us here, outside the country, and so undertake the expulsion of one million of the others with their agreement or at least silence… Refusing to co-operate with them is dangerous because this will easily be taken by the English and Americans to imply a renunciation on our side of the Sudeten territory and the acceptance of some improved Munich. Our people at home need to be aware that the international ramifications make the so-called Sudeten problem very complicated and that dealing with our Germans will not be as easy as many of us imagine."[47]

For Beneš, the key aspect was the need to maintain the theory of the continuity of the legal existence of the Czechoslovak state. He was very much aware of the connection between getting the Munich Agreement invalidated and the determination of final borders for the CSR[48], which he defined as the restoration of the *status quo ante*. Talks on the repudiation of Munich led on behalf of the government in exile by the state secretary in the Ministry of Foreign Affairs H. Ripka with British ambassador P. Nichols did not, however, prove at all easy. From the context of the discussions it is evident that the British insisted on the close connection between this issue and the future status of the German minority in the CSR. The British showed some willingness to refor-

---

[46] Here the English strenuously forced us to co-operate with Jaksch and our Germans generally. *Edvard Beneš – Vzkazy do vlasti* [Edvard Beneš – Messages to the Homeland]. 1996. Šolc, J. (ed.). Prague: Historický ústav AV ČR. 124. The views of the Foreign Office are analysed in detail in Brown, M. D. 2006 *Dealing with Democrats. The British Foreign Office's relations with the Czechoslovak emigrés in Great Britain, 1935–45*. Frankfurt a/M: Peter Lang. The same author says that it is very difficult to reconstruct some important activities on the basis of the FO archived documents, for example the bilateral negotiations between the Czechs and Poles on (con)federation, because some records are missing. Brown, M. D. "Never complain, never explain". The Foreign Office's influence on the formation of British policy with regard to Anglo-Polish-Czechoslovak relations in exile, 1939–1945', in P. Blažk, P. Jaworski, L. Kaminski (eds.), *Miedzy przymusowa przyjaznia a prawdziwa solidarnoscia: Czesi – Polacy – Slowacy, 1938/39 – 1945 – 1989*, vol. 1. Institute of National Memory, Warsaw, 2007, pp. 101–109.

[47] *Edvard Beneš – Vzkazy do vlasti*. 120.

[48] See also Beneš's Memorandum on the Question of the Borders of the CSR of January 1942, in Kuklík, J. 1998. *Londýnský exil a obnova československého státu 1938–1945* [The London Exile and the Restoration of the Czechoslovak State 1938–1945]. Prague: Karolinum. 171–175.

mulate their negative standpoint on the non-validity of the Munich Agreement and acknowledge the authority of the Czechoslovak government over the German immigrants with Czechoslovak citizenship, but only on condition that an agreement would be reached between Beneš and the leader of the exiled Sudeten German Social Democrats, Jaksch, on the representation of the Germans in the State Council.[49] The British and Czechoslovak legal interpretations of the situation diverged fundamentally.

The subsequent development of the situation was undoubtedly affected by other factors, particularly reports of the horrors of the occupation regime and the physical liquidation of entire groups of the population (Jews, gypsies, members of religious sects and so on) in the Protectorate of Bohemia and Moravia, and in the course of frontline war operations (the massacres of the civilian population and prisoners of war by the Sonderkommandos of the SS and Wehrmacht divisions), but also the demand for postwar autonomy for the Sudeten territories raised with Beneš in London by the leader of the Sudeten German Social Democrats Jaksch. Under the impression of Heydrich's terror and the destruction of Lidice, the British standpoint began to change, until finally in a note to Jan Masaryk. Anthony Eden declared that he regarded the Munich agreement as null and void.

The Sudeten Germans and the Protectorate

For assessment of the possible future co-existence of Czechs and Sudeten Germans a key consideration was undoubtedly the attitude of the Sudeten population both before the destruction of the CSR and subsequently, during the Occupation. The fanaticised Sudeten German supporters of Nazism were a perfect instrument of plans for the Germanisation of the Czech Lands, not just in the borderlands but also in the Protectorate. For example the head of the Reichsgau authority R. Staffen proposed, as the most viable route to Germanisation, the organisational merger of Czech and Sudeten German territory

---

[49] Ibidem. 126–127. I regard as one-sided the view of D. Brandes, that "As former and new president of the republic Beneš justified his claim to leadership with his theory of the legal continuity of the pre-Munich republic". Brandes, D. *Exil v Londýně*. 425. In my view, apart from the legal justification of his own position, another crucial factor in Beneš's attitude was the "Munich syndrome" caused by the internationally sanctioned injustice committed against the CSR. In his theory of the continuity of the Czechoslovak state Beneš built on the premise that if everything that had happened in Czechoslovakia and in connection with it since the 19th of September (Anglo-French proposal for the cession of the Sudetenland to Nazi Germany) had been based on "threats, terror and violence", then pre-Munich Czechoslovakia had never in fact ceased to exist legally, nor had he himself (who had left his office under the pressure of Hitler's threats), ever ceased to be legally president. Táborský, E. *President Beneš between East and West*. 65.

into a single whole that would facilitate the achievement of German dominance.[50]

Czech (but also serious German) historians see what is known as the *Grundplanung O.A.* (GPOA) as the fundamental programme document of the Sudeten German movement with regard to the solution of the "Czech Question". This strategic document was discovered in the so-called Führer Archive of the Sudeten German Party, lodged at the end of the war in the Chateau of Sukorady. The document focuses on the ethno-political angle/*volkspolitische Gesichtspunkte* of the conflict between Czechs and Germans and contains a set of proposals for elimination of the Czech language and culture (existing Czech educational institutions to be definitively liquidated), and the "dilution" of the Czech by the German element (on Czech language territory all important measures to divide and shatter Czech national integrity to be introduced in the period of military rule).

In the introduction to the document we find the statement that, "this is not just a Sudeten German problem, but involves the whole question of today's Czechoslovakia. As far as the Bohemian Lands are concerned, the German Reich on the basis of a thousand years of historical experience must once again implement Reich law and incorporate these lands in their entirety up to the old Reich (imperial) border valid until 1866 (the Little Carpathians)". In other sections of the document detailed instructions are formulated for the carrying out of subversive propaganda in the CSR in the period of mounting tension, and the destruction of symbols of Czech statehood such as memorials etc. The authors request that after the victorious annexation of the Czech state (not just the borderland) to Germany, "Prague should be granted in the order of cities the title "City of the Completion of the Reich". The leader of the Sudeten Germans, who according to internal rules was already as of 1937 the Gauleiter of the Sudeten Germans, should be appointed, "Reichs Governor for the Bohemian Lands".

Whether or not the Grundplanung O.A. was the official action plan of the SdP, it is evident from this and other documents originating from the "workshop" of Henlein's staff (where authorship has been proven) that the activities of the Sudeten German Party were directed to the internal subversion of a sovereign state with the goal of bringing about the intervention of the foreign

---

[50] "Penetration into Czech living space must have a clear goal of attack, which must also be very attractive: Prague. It would also be necessary to take account of the danger of German migration to the Czech Lands (position without fixed soil) and the danger of Czech infiltration into Sudeten German territory." Document no. 13: "The aim of advance: Prague", in Fremund, K. *Chtěli nás vyhubit.* 94–98. The author R. Staffen was a prominent functionary of the SdP, a close colleague of K. Henlein and in 1938 the special commissioner of the Gestapo for Prague. He also directed armed Nazi units in the borderland. After the war he was a functionary of the Sudeten German Homeland Association.

state to whose advantage the SdP was acting. In the verdict on K. H. Frank delivered by the Special People's Court in Prague on the 22nd of May 1946, this plan was described as a *plan for the destruction of the Czech people*.[51] The GPOA document was an important piece of evidence in the postwar trials not only of K. H. Frank but also of H. Krebs and a group of Sudeten German Party deputies. It figured in the justifications for the verdict and was considered a material source of inspiration for a series of other Sudeten German memoranda concerned with the "final solution" of the Czech Question.

V. Zimmermann argues that the hard core of fanatical Sudeten German supporters of violence towards Czechs was to be found primarily in the North-Bohemian industrial region. In the situation reports of the NSDAP Sudeten German organisations and SD security services there is conspicuously frequent emphasis on the fact that the Sudeten Germans know the Czech "mentality" and precisely for that reason support tough measures in the Protectorate, especially after the assassination of the Reichsprotektor R. Heydrich. They often demanded an even tougher approach from the German occupation organs on the territory of the Protectorate. The district NSDAP leaders in Teplice and Kraslice reported that the population approved of the destruction of Lidice and Ležáky. Similar attitudes were reported from the Cheb Government Region.[52]

These are just a few of the numerous examples of enthusiastic Nazi Sudeten Germans demanding even more severe measures against Czechs. As it turned out, however, the militant but excessively "local and traditional" view of the Sudeten German Nazis on the Czech Question had eventually to yield to the views and interests of the Reich authorities and especially the SS headed by H. Himmler.[53] The latter's views were more moderate, but only because of the practical need to maintain the smooth operation of war production for the needs of the Reich, not out of any sympathy for the lot of Czechs in the Protectorate.

The Reich German authorities did not wish to drive Czechs in the borderland (as in the Protectorate) into a corner and so provoke them to harm Ger-

---

[51] Zajíček, K. 1947. *Český národ soudí K. H. Franka* [The Czech Nation Judges K. H. Frank]. Prague: Ministerstvo informací. 176–177. See also Drábek, J. "Glosy k procesu s henleinovskými poslanci a senátory" [Glosses on the trial of the Henleinian deputies and senators]. *Dnešek* 46 (I.). 6. 2. 1947. 727–729.

[52] For example the (local) Government President in Ústí n. L. stated in June 1942: "If earlier it was not possible to suppress the hatred and antagonism of all Sudeten Germans towards the Czechs, (feelings) persisting from the time of the independent Czechoslovak state and also in reaction to their frequently provocative behaviour even after the incorporation of the Sudetenland into the Reich, then the assassination of Heydrich has brought existing detestation to boiling point once more. The Sudeten German population is of the opinion that Czechs are still provided with too many freedoms. We Sudeten Germans, we know this band of old; ultimately even the Germans of the Old Reich are beginning to understand what kind of people these Czechs really are." Zimmermann, V. 2001. *Sudetští Němci v nacistickém státě* [Sudeten Germans in the Nazi State]. Prague: Argo. 280–281.

[53] For more detail see Bartoš, J. *Okupované pohraničí a české obyvatelstvo 1938–1945*. 78–79.

many politically and economically. Nonetheless, all Czechs were excluded from state and local government on the territory of the Sudeten Reichsgau (an irony, given how in the years of the CSR the Sudeten Germans had constantly protested at the unfairness of their own small share in state service). The Czech population of the borderland was stripped of all fundamental political and national (ethnic) rights. Its task was to obey and work for the Reich.

Sudeten Germans replaced Czechs in local government and the management of concerns, companies and other legal entities in Czech areas of the borderlands, and were likewise installed in senior positions of government and in important arms factories in the Protectorate.[54]

Large towns such as Brno, Jihlava, Olomouc, Moravská Ostrava, Plzeň, and České Budějovice were now run by Sudeten German commissioners. In the eyes of Czechs, the Sudeten German K. H. Frank (the state secretary and Obergruppenführer of the SS and police) was the embodiment of German terror. The resistance groups on the territory of the Protectorate of Bohemia and Moravia, and the great majority of its inhabitants, regarded the terror involved in the occupation as final proof of the impossibility of the future co-existence of Czechs and Sudeten Germans in the same state. This opinion was conveyed in uncompromisingly formulated radio messages sent to Beneš in London. The demand for the removal of the German-speaking inhabitants of the historic lands became general and unshakeable after the wave of repression following the assassination of Heydrich.[55]

The Sudetenland Model Reichsgau

Terror against Czechs proceeded on the territory of the Sudetenland Reichsgau as well, although there is no surviving programme document of the organs of the NSDAP or SdP on the organised expulsion of Czechs from the Sudetenland and the character of the pressure was rather less visible. At first sight actions against the Czechs who stayed seem isolated and unconnected cases, but looked at altogether, a pattern emerges. On the one hand there was the expulsion of Czechs who had allegedly or in fact been involved in resistance to

---

[54] Luža, R. *The Transfer of the Sudeten Germans*. 195. See also Schieder, T. 1957. *Die Vertreibung der deutschen Bevölkerung aus Ost-Mitteleuropa IV/1*. Bonn. 17.

[55] This was far from being a demand confined to the communists, who in fact were the last to back the idea of the transfer. Ivo Ducháček, a deputy for the People's Party said on the matter: "Towards the end of 1943 all the members of the National Front agreed on this question: the expulsion of the Germans is thus the result of the common efforts of all members and parties of the National Front. It is a falsification of history if the communists claim that it is them we have to thank for the expulsion of the Germans." *Documents on the expulsion of the Germans from the Czech Lands*. 10.

the advance of the Wehrmacht into the territory, and on the other there were instances of "wild" expulsion carried out by radical Sudeten Germans, or of escape from the threat of violence.

Clear proof that the Munich "solution" to the nationality problems of the CSR failed to remove ethnic heterogenity and the complications arising from it is the fact that one of the distinctive features of the newly formed Reichsgau of the Sudetenland was its large Czech minority. The German authorities had actually ensured that a higher proportion of Czechs would remain in the annexed territory of the borderlands by successfully pushing through the demand that the border should be fixed "if possible" generously to the advantage of the Reich. On the 13th of October 1938, the international committee had unanimously withdrawn the requirement for the plebiscite that the Munich Agreement had stipulated in the case of areas without a clear German majority, and did so in response to the aggressive assurances of the German delegation that "the ethnographic border has already been identified on the demarcation line". In this context we find the leadership of the SdP exerting some influence on the decision-making of the German government by inflated territorial demands.[56]

Without protection, the future fortunes of this Czech minority were uncertain.[57] The reason why Czechs were not expelled en masse after the annexation of the Sudetenland was the Reich government's interest in maintaining a German minority in the "reduced" CSR as an instrument of foreign policy pressure. This was why the German government made an agreement with the Czechoslovak government to the effect that the deportation paragraph would be used only by mutual consent. The Reich authorities had no intention, however, of according any kinds of rights to Czechs in the Sudetenland (whether or not they opted for German national identity), and in this policy they found spontaneous support in the Sudetenland itself.

At a conference initiated by the Reich Ministry of Foreign Affairs at the Centre for Ethnic Germans (VoMi), where the Interior Ministry and the High Command of the Wehrmacht (OKW) were also represented, any legal protection for the rights of the Czech minority was resolutely rejected: "We have absolutely no intention of providing the Czech national group the kind of position that we expect for our own national group in Czechoslovakia."[58] It is a statement

---

56   Zimmermann, V. *Sudetští Němci v nacistickém státě.* 241.
57   Estimates of the number of Czechs in the border areas diverge. We can regard it as demonstrated that according to the Czechoslovak census, 726,416 Czechs lived in the areas ceded to the Reich in the autumn of 1938. With an eye to the unreliability of the various sources of data, V. Zimmermann regards as a working basis the number 291,000 Czechs in the Sudetenland Reichsgau, i.e. A total of 9.9% of the overall population of the ceded territories.
58   Ibidem. 243.

that casts the most curious and revealing light on the constant demands for ethnic tolerance and respect for minority rights that both the leaders of the Sudeten German Party and the leading Nazis of the Third Reich had voiced in relation to the ČSR before Munich.

From the start of negotiations between the German government and the "reduced" CSR on a joint declaration it was clear that the text was intended to be formulated in a way that effectively sidestepped any obligations towards the Czech minority in the Sudetenland. In any case, their fate was clearly of no great concern to the peacemakers of Munich either. An interstate committee for monitoring minority problems was formed, but never met. The Declaration of the Reich and the CSR of the 20th of November 1938 contained a formulation on the protection of minority rights that was nothing but empty phrases.

The later development of treatment of Czechs in the Sudetenland Reichsgau was more or less a matter of improvisation, with the only unifying thread being the general notion of a need to restore the "German character" of "Czechised" territory. The Reichsgau authorities, composed for the most part of members of the SdP, generally applied the principle that, "the Czech as a consequence of his Slav character observes order only when he feels a strong hand above him."[59] Up to 1942, the man responsible for the minority policy of the NSDAP (into which the SdP merged in November 1938) in the Sudetenland Reichsgau was Henlein's close colleague from the times of the *Kammeradschaftsbund*, F. Künzel, who in December 1938 was appointed chief of the Reichsgau Office of the NSDAP for the border areas. The office was staffed by Sudeten Germans who in the period of the CSR had worked in national protection societies such as for example the German League in Bohemia/*Bund der Deutschen in Böhmen*. Henlein gave the office greater weight by deciding to grant it the right of consultation with state authorities. Künzel used his position to press for a radical solution for Sudeten German territory: "In the Sudeten Reichsgau the Czechs will have to be displaced."[60]

As one example of such efforts, the German historian V. Zimmermann describes the expulsion of 40 Czechs from Nýřany in the Plzeň region, after they were accused of damaging a telephone cable. The Czechoslovak government protested against the expulsion on the 31st of October 1938 through its Berlin embassy; Heydrich denied everything but at the same time confirmed that on

[59] See e.g. Materials from the archive of the (district) government president in Ústí nad Labem. Ibidem. 247.

[60] Ibidem. 247. Despite the constant claims of Sudeten German authors that control of the government of the Sudetenland Reichsgau was to a decisive degree in the hands of "Reich" Germans, the author of this study produces a quantity of convincing evidence that the functionaries of the Sudeten German movement took a prominent share in management of the "model" Reichsgau and also significantly influenced the measures taken by the occupation authorities on the territory of the Protectorate.

this occasion all anti-German Czechoslovak railwaymen had been called on to leave Reich territory "as soon as possible".[61]

Generally, however, the Sudeten German leadership was unsuccessful in its attempts to get a policy of expulsion of Czechs off the ground. For example, in 1941 efforts to deport seven thousand Czech workers and their families from the Opava Government District came to nothing. The Sudeten German functionaries had to reconcile themselves to the presence of a Czech minority forced on them by the interests of a Reich policy enforced even more emphatically by Heydrich, who was appointed acting Reichs Protector in September 1941. He followed Reich policy in seeing the solution to the "Czech question" above all in systematic Germanisation with the aim of keeping production in the Czech Lands running smoothly in the service of the war machinery of the Third Reich.[62]

The agitation of the Sudeten German leadership for the transfer of Czechs to the territory of the Protectorate of Bohemia and Moravia ran into resistance from K. H. Frank and R. Heydrich. As early as the 22nd of September 1939, Frank in a letter to the Lower Danubian Reichsgau chief, Hugo Jury, rejected the idea of the resettlement of Czechs on the grounds of the need to maintain calm in the Czech Lands and not to provoke unrest among the population of the Protectorate. The Sudeten German leadership therefore had no choice but to get used to the continuing presence of the Czechs and address the situation simply by ethnic-political consolidation of territories with a high proportion of German-speaking inhabitants.

The Reich government was in fact conducting a similar active "border policy" on territories located by the state frontier. Surprisingly then, even after the annexation of the borderland to the Reich, a "struggle over the borderlands" was anticipated in areas with a large proportion of Czechs. As emerges from an SD report this expectation was fuelled primarily by the intervention of Sudeten German functionaries, as V. Zimmermann illustrates from a report of the 13th of December 1939: "Ethnic Germans in these territories are expecting that as part

---

[61]   Ibidem. 85–86.

[62]   "In view of the war and for tactical reasons we cannot allow a situation in which the Czech becomes furious and explodes in certain matters even though at the moment we must be for certain tactical reasons harsh… this territory must one day become German and *the Czech ultimately has no claims here*. In this territory I need calm, so that the worker, the Czech worker, should fully commit his work activity here to the German war effort and so we do not hold back progress and the further development of the arms industry in the huge war industry here… We must consider what to do with them. In the case of some of the people of good race but wrong sentiments there will be no option but to try and settle them in the Reich, in purely German conditions, Germanise them and re-educate their sentiments or, if this does not work, put them up against a wall, because I cannot transfer them since over there in the east they would form a leadership stratum that would set themselves against us." Text of the inauguration speech of R. Heydrich in the Černín Palace in Prague on the 2nd of October 1941. Fremund, K. *Chtěli nás vyhubit.* 125–137.

of the consolidation of the German national element in the Sudetenland, plans will be drawn up and implemented to ensure that the German national element pervades the named areas together with German cultural and economic measures."[63]

Initially generous financial aid from Reich sources for Sudeten German ethno-political activities soon diminished. The war efforts of the Reich were the priority, not *Volkstumkampf*. The three Sudeten German (local) goverment presidents (Ústí n. L., Karlovy Vary, Opava) nonetheless continued to voice demands for the "work for the borderland", which together with other Sudeten German national socialist functionaries they saw as their most distinctive and essential mission.

Propagandist literature glorifying the heroic period of the Sudeten German movement "in the time of struggles" in the CSR, and published in massive print-runs, became a major focus of their activities. The heroic vision of Sudeten Germandom standing on the far eastern tip of Germandom persisted. Henlein repeatedly declared that the territory entrusted to him had the "special role of a border gau". The authoritarian ideological viewpoint of the Sudeten Nazis was reflected in all spheres of social life. For example, the professional journal *Der sudetendeutsche Erzieher* appealed to all teachers from the Sudetenland to connect "the struggle over the borderlands with geopolitical national education." E. Lemberg described the situation in the Sudetenland Reichsgau at the beginning of March 1939: "It is necessary to encourage awareness of the special roles of the national frontier. Sudeten Germans now feel too secure, they are concentrating solely on tasks in the Reich and do not want to hear anything about the "hated" Czech and Slovak people. Work for the borderlands in the framework of the German Reich is an unambiguously formulated task."[64]

Demands of a similar type took up the themes of the decades-old inherited programme of Sudeten Germandom as the advance guard of German expansion into Central and Eastern Europe, now fighting "for our living space in Europe and the place allotted to us on Earth," The NSDAP found support among the former Sudeten-German protection societies such as the German Cultural Association/*Deutscher Kulturverband* (DKV) and the German League in Bohemia/*Bund der Deutschen in Böhmen* (BdD), which now together constituted the Sudeten department of the Reich German Organisation – the Union for the German East/*Bund Deutscher Osten* (BDO).

Yet the idea of continuing the ethnic struggle, on which the leadership of the Sudeten Reichsgau insisted, came into ever greater conflict with the ideas and

---

[63]   Zimmermann, V. *Sudetští Němci v nacistickém státě*. 248.
[64]   Ibidem. 249.

opinions of officials in SS circles, which were based on racial politics. According to K. H. Frank and K. von Neurath, the Czech nation, or more precisely the part of it whose "racial quality" was beyond doubt, should be the subject of "*Umvolkung*" or ethnic transposition (assimilation).

This plan was worked out in great detail in documents dealing with the "question of the future organisation of Czech-Moravian territory" (Supplement 1 formulated by Neurath, Supplement 2 by Frank) which the two rulers of the Protectorate drew up for Hitler on the 31st of August 1940. The steps described aimed to liquidate the Czech nation by the Germanisation of part of the Czech people, with expulsion and extermination of the rest, and the settlement of the Czech Lands by Germans.

Frank's "technological procedures" are charaterised by precise formulation: "*It is necessary through systematically conducted political neutralisation and depoliticisation to achieve first the political (spiritual) and then the national assimilation of the Czech nation, in order to bring about real changes of ethnicity/nationality...* My position is based on the intention to Germanise the territory and people in the Protectorate. It therefore does not engage with the question of the absolute "degradation" of the Czech people for racial reasons into a mere auxiliary nation (the Askari position), which would be under a social curse and with which marriages would have to be prohibited. I regard this degradation as probably impossible to implement in practice, and I envisage only individual degradation as a method of "special treatment"/*Sonderbehandlung* in accordance with D II/2. On the basis of the conclusions of this memorandum, total degradation appears neither necessary nor desirable, because the solution to the Czech question, and with it the final pacification of the centuries-old Czech-Moravian seedbed of conflict in Europe, is achievable by the path proposed."[65]

The Führer approved this approach and so preparations were put in train by the office of the Reichsprotektor for a racial census, on the basis of which the Czech nation was to be divided into different categories. The terminology used is in itself eloquent enough testimony to the nature of the Nazi "philosophy" of how to deal with Czechs: racially valuable (Slav racial characteristics do not predominate), racially unusable (nationally alien element), assigned for rejection or special procedure etc. The formulation of instructions related not just to the population of the Protectorate but also to the Czech minority in the Sudetenland Reichsgau.

The head of the Reichsgau office for the border area F. Künzel, on the other hand, regarded the concept of *Umvolkung* with deep suspicion. At a meeting with R. Hess (VoMi) on national problems in the German Eastern territories

---

[65]   Fremund, K. *Chtěli nás vyhubit.* 62–75. See also Zajíček, K. *Český národ soudí K. H. Franka.*

on the 12th of July 1940, he complained about a "creeping assimilation process", in his view extremely dangerous, because "unprincipled members of the Czech nation are insinuating themselves into the German people".[66] Künzel made his disagreement plain on other occasions, as SD reports show. What he saw as the problem was that Czechs "with a higher proportion of German blood" were the most resolute enemies of Germans, and so he considered *Umvolkung* on purely ethnic criteria as a risky policy. In his view there was a danger of "racial dilution", which could only be prevented by combining racial and political suitability as criteria in the selection of Czechs for assimilation.

The opinions of Künzel and other Sudeten German functionaries are the distilled essence of the aggressive intolerance of view that they had developed in their long years of resistance to the Czechoslovak state, and to a considerable extended represented the culmination of the long-term spirit of ethnic rivalry with which a substantial part of the Bohemian German community had repeatedly blocked all attempts at a peaceful and moderate approach to ethnic relations in the Czech Lands from as far back as the later 19th century. F. Künzel could not have put it more plainly: "These methods (infiltration to subvert another nation), failed to turn us into Czechs, and in the same way they will fail to turn a racially full-value Czech into a German."[67]

From the point of view of later, post-war developments and the possibility of further co-existence of Czechs and Sudeten Germans in one state, in my view the most crucial fact (confirmed by the work of V. Zimmermann and other historians) is that despite isolated expressions of partial disagreement, the "myth of the Führer" shared by large masses of the Sudeten-German population remained strong in the Sudetenland Reichsgau. This myth "enabled the population to put up with all kinds of difficulties in the faith that Hitler would solve every problem at the latest when the war was over." "Basic agreement" was already conditioned simply by the fact that the incorporation of the Sudeten Germans into the Reich had fulfilled a demand promoted for so many years, and the inhabitants of the Reichsgau expected it to bring an improvement of their social situation.

There were of course other reasons why the National Socialist regime functioned so smoothly in the Sudetenland. One factor was definitely effective propaganda. This might might give the impression that public opinion in the Sudetenland gau was manipulated by skilful policy, but why then do the situation reports of the SD continually contain reminders of the special loyalty of

---

[66] SD report on meeting of the Reichsgau chancellors for the border areas, Reichsgau party education chiefs and other representatives of the leadership of the Eastern reichsgaus. Sent to K. H. Frank on the 26th of July 1940 by the sector chief of the SD in Prague. Zimmermann, V. *Sudetští Němci v nacistickém státě.* 250.

[67] Lecture by F. Künzel on nationality questions in Liberec on the 17th of October 1940.

the Sudeten Germans? Dissatisfaction was only sporadic and resistance activities on the Sudeten side can be shown to have existed only among communists, social democrats, and a a certain number of clerics.[68] Not even this resistance, however, was on any impressive scale. Zimmermann concludes that cases of fundamental resistance to the regime and resolute rejection of its expressions were as few in the Sudetenland as in the rest of the Reich.[69]

The London Government in Exile and the Home Resistance

Eduard Beneš and Wenzel Jaksch who represented the Sudeten German Social Democrats (but in fact other groups of Sudeten German exiles as well) both emigrated to Great Britain before the Nazi occupation of Czechoslovakia, and in exile continued their dispute over the interpretation of the right to self-determination in the anticipated conditions of a restored republic. Jaksch's European concept of post-war organisation underwent various changes during the war, but was essentially based on the ethnic conception of the integration of all territories with a German-speaking population into a democratic pan-German empire.[70]

This concept inevitably not only led to conflict with the Czechoslovak exiles around Beneš, but was also completely unacceptable to the organisations of the home resistance in the Czech Lands, which insisted in their reports to President Beneš that they would never give up the principle of maintaining the legal continuity of the CSR – a principle that was the common denominator and bridge between groups otherwise extremely diverse and conflicting in views.

The most radical were the officers of the organisation *Obrana národa*/Defence of the Nation[71], which after the assassination of Heydrich in mid-1942 even threatened Beneš with withdrawal of recognition of his position as president in exile unless he immediately dropped negotiations with Jaksch. The home resist-

---

[68] V. Zimmermann draws attention to the different situation in the attitudes of the clergy to the National Socialist regime in the Reich and in the Sudetenland. He argues that according to the latest researches on the territory of the Reich, it was above all Catholics who distanced themselves from the church policy of the regime. When the Gestapo investigated the level of political reliability of priests/ministers on the territory of the Sudetenland in 1939, they found that 49.3% of Protestant and 92% of Catholic priests were former members of the SdP. One of those who personally remembered the situation characterised it in these terms: "A certain kind of protective national work was expected from a priest". Zimmermann, V. *Sudetští Němci v nacistickém státě*. 324–325.

[69] Ibidem. 368. For more detail on resistance acts and groups on Sudeten German territory see Grünwald, L. *Sudetendeutscher Widerstand gegen den Nationalsozialismus*.

[70] Hoensch, J. K. "Issues, going beyond an overall assessment", in *Coming to Terms With the Past, Opening up To The Future*. IGS Discussion Papers Series Number 98/19. 1998. Handl, V. (ed.). University of Birmingham. 35.

[71] Kural, V. *Místo společenství konflikt*. 108.

ance and the London exiles diverged in their ideas on the post-war organisation of the restored republic more than once, especially in the first years of the war.[72]

The basic formulation of the ideas of the Sudeten German exiles on the future approach to the national/ethnic question in the Czech Lands and the status of the Sudetenland was to be found in the *Holmhursts Declaration*, containing the programme of the *Treugemeinschaft* group which brought together the leaders of the Sudeten German exiles in Great Britain. The document demands a solution on the basis of the "urgent need for a federalist new order in Europe." The precise nature of this federalist order is not defined in detail, but from the context it is clear that Jaksch saw the idea as an instrument that would enable the right to self-determination to be applied. The term appears explicitly in the formulation: "We demand the right to self-determination (*Selbstbestimmungsrecht*) for three million Sudeten Germans. In line with the great tradition of our movement we are fighting for the application of the right to self-determination in the spirit of European solidarity. For this reason we are including in our declaration of commitment to the right to self-determination, our recognition of all the economic and geographical appurtenances of the Sudeten territories to the historic territory of Bohemia, Moravia and Silesia."[73]

These formulations were not entirely unambiguous, but Beneš evidently assessed them in the light of the secret document *Richtlinien für die Auslandspolitik der Sudetendeutschen Sozialdemokratie*, which he had managed to obtain shortly after it was drawn up by Jaksch as a draft of guidelines for the policy of the Sudeten German social democrats in exile in Britain. Here, already at the beginning of the war, the demand for the right to self-determination and an autonomous land government was quite clearly formulated. "Any lasting democratic solution to the relations between Czechs and Germans must be based on recognition of the closed German language areas in Bohemia and Moravia. The vital interests of the Sudeten Germans require an autonomist solution in the sense of

---

[72] Bartoš, J. *Okupované pohraničí a české obyvatelstvo 1938–1945.* 86. The views of one leading member of the military resistance, Karel Veselý-Štainer, are typical of relations between the government in exile and the home resistance. His retrospective account shows that the disagreements related not just to the question of the Sudeten Germans but also to the tactics and strategy of the resistance in the Protectorate.For example, he says "the high command in London advised us to undertake organisational work that we had already long ago completed. It assumed that actions would be launched progressively in Moravia, and before the launch of action in Bohemia. They wanted us to state the numbers of people in our organisations, which in practice varied greatly. They didn't understand our mobility, they did not know our situation, the new way of fighting, and imagined everything was as it had been here before they escaped abroad. They seemed to envisage some fixed resistance (organisation) skeleton working on preparation of its units, and didn't believe that we already had an organisation everywere and were only waiting for weapons, were deliberately not expanding it, that we had abandoned the old way of working and that we had everything in train." Veselý-Štainer, K. 1947. *Cestou národního odboje (Bojový vývoj domácího odbojového hnutí v letech 1938–1945)* [The Czech National Resistance (The Military Development of the Home Resistance Movement 1938–1945)]. Prague: Sfinx. 137.

[73] "Deklaration der Sudetendeutschen Sozialdemokratie", in *Češi a sudetoněmecká otázka.* 49–54.

a federalist solution."[74] There is no doubt that this was a variant of the demands that had been used to destroy Czechoslovakia.

In this context we might recall Elizabeth Wiskemann's aside on Jaksch's attitude to the Czech-German dispute – "Jaksch, who never lacked the feelings of strong racial identification of the typical Sudeten German."[75] The nature of Jaksch's ideas on a federalist solution is illuminated further by the record of interviews at the Royal Institute of International Affairs (*Chatham House*), where memoranda on the Czechoslovak question where prepared for the Foreign Office by the Czechoslovak department. F. M. Hník reported a new suggestion in a memorandum from Jaksch, "in which he proposes the creation of a special Sudeten German autonomous area, which together with Czechoslovakia, Austria and possibly other states would be parts of a broader Central European federation".[76]

The ideas of W. Jaksch on the post-war solution of the Sudeten German question had a great deal in common *with the vision of Mitteleuropa* as presented by F. Naumann in 1915. We can read about the proposed instruments by which the territory of the Sudeten Germans in the border areas of the Czech Lands would be defined in another document drawn up by Jaksch in mid-1943: "It is envisaged that none of the changes to European frontiers achieved by aggression and blackmail since the last peaceful modification will be recognised. As a result, nations in disputed areas should be allowed to decide by plebiscite in which state they want to vote on the choice of parliament to represent them at the peace conference, or whether they want to vote as an independent group under the administration of an international commission with the aim of sending their own representatives to the peace conference to defend their viewpoint there."[77]

The plebiscite was to be conducted under international supervision and on the basis of the elections governments would be formed that would then send their representative to a peace conference to negotiate on peace conditions and the future form of their national arrangements.

It is evident that in many respects Jaksch's ideas represented a return to 1918 as the point zero from which it would be possible to make another attempt at a Czech-German settlement in a liberated democratic Europe, this time with

---

[74]   *Češi a sudetoněmecká otázka.* 31.

[75]   Wiskemann, E. "Genesis of the Odsun", in *Germany's Eastern Neighbours.* See also the essay Křen, J. "Revanšisté s demokratickou minulostí" [Revanchists with a Democratic Past]. *Československý časopis historický.* 1961. 42.

[76]   Hník, F. M. "Záznam o rozhovorech v Chatham House" [Record of Discussions at Chatham House], in *Češi a sudetoněmecká otázka.* 239.

[77]   "Minority report of W. Jaksch" (July 1943), in *Češi a sudetoněmecká otázka.* 254.

a result more favourable for the Sudeten Germans. Beneš confronted a situation in which he had to decide whether – given his knowledge of the programme documents of the Sudeten German exiles (public and confidential) and on the basis of his bitter experience of the gradualism of Sudeten German demands – he should co-operate with the *Treugemeinschaft* and Jaksch in the interests of finding an acceptable compromise. He tried to do this yet again and proposed that the Jakschsites be represented in the State Council, a move that at the end of October 1940 was resolutely opposed by the leaders of the home armed resistance in the Protectorate, who from the beginning of the war had been proposing the expulsion of the Bohemian Germans to the Reich.[78]

O. Janowsky in his study (in 1945) pointed out the need to distinguish between population transfers on the criterion of motive, so as to underline the difference between democratic states compelled to adopt the policy and the Nazi transfers of population motivated above all *by racial reasons* (the settlement of eastern territories with German blood). He argued that the victorious democracies should see the forced transfer of minorities as a last resort, a "surgical cut" after all other remedies had failed. Furthermore, he saw the main motive behind so drastic a solution as the *preventive goal* of averting ethnic tension in future conflict situations. All the same, he took the view that to solve the national/ethnic problems of Central and Eastern Europe it would be necessary to move many millions of people. He openly argues that Hitler started this work on his own resettlement policies, which in the years 1939–1944 involved the resettlement of twelve groups (around 770,000) of ethnic Germans/*Volksdeutsche*, not into the territory of Germany, but to the conquered territory of Poznań, West Prussia, Łódź and Pomerania.[79]

Janowsky (who was generally one of the opponents of transfer as a method of solving ethnic conflicts) also considered other ways of solving such conflicts, such as assimilation. He wrote "If then minorities remain in Central and Eastern Europe and nation states of Western type are formed, it will be necessary to condone assimilation. But this approach too, as we have seen, offers only poor prospects for a real solution."[80] He saw a possible way forward (appealing in this inter alia to the ideas of H. Ripka and E. Beneš) in the creation of one or

---

[78]   Kural, V. *Místo společenství konflikt.* 125.
[79]   Janowsky, O. *Nationalities and National Minorities.* 138. He praises the level-headed approach of Beneš, whom he regards as a cautious and thoughtful politician aware of the risks of great transfers of population and said that "not even after the end of the Second World War will it be possible to create ethnically homogenous states in Europe." He quotes Beneš's report to the State Council in which he recommends that part of the German population be allowed to remain in the ČSR after the war and emphatically warns against unconsidered steps in the context of the national question. ("even after this war (the Second World War) it still will be impossible in Europe to create states which are nationally homogenous.") 138.
[80]   Ibidem. 142.

more federative states, but this of course assumed that the economic, political and social conditions would be sufficiently compatible in the different areas concerned to make a (con)federative order possible. As is well known, the federative idea was abandoned in the middle of the war; the disputes between the governments in exile in London made its lack of realism clear enough, not to mention the question of the real conditions in which states would have to be restored in a Central Europe devastated by occupation, war operations and an atmosphere of intolerance.

Debate on the merits and demerits of transfer continued throughout the war. Transfer was not ruled out even by the former director of the section for national minority questions of the League of Nations Prof. de Azcárate, who had extensive experience of this subject. One of the best informed experts on European territorial and ethnic problems, Bernard Newman declared in 1943: "whether or not we like the idea, the system of resettling of population has become a matter of European policy." Newman proposed transfer and exchange of population as a solution to the problems between Poland and Germany, and Poland and the Soviet Union, and a similar solution to the problems on the Soviet-Finnish border, and also saw transfer as the only solution to the Hungarian-Rumanian conflict over Transylvania, the Italian-Yugoslav conflict in the Istrian peninsula and elsewhere. L. C. Klausner, the former chairman of the *Pan-European Union* expressed the belief that population transfer had to be considered the best solution for minority problems in dangerous areas.

Nonetheless, there were also plenty of opponents of this method. To stand for many, let us mention the distinguished lawyer and expert on Balkan resettlement processes Stephen P. Ladas, who expressed doubts as to whether this was the only possible solution to the problem. In his view, a statesman of wisdom and foresight would prefer to avoid such surgical operations. J. L. Kunz pointed out that this step (transfer) would create a huge problem of international policy in the form of masses of refugees. In later years after the Second World War Eugene M. Kulischer was critical of transfers of population, but in the case of Czechoslovakia he made an exception. The views (mentioned above) of O. I. Janowsky, a recognised American authority on questions of ethnic groups, were thus in no way extreme but fairly mainstream.[81]

All these views highlight the very difficult situation not only of President Beneš, but also the Allied politicians planning the post-war order of Europe. It

---

[81] For a lucid assessment of the problem of population transfers see especially the last chapter Pro and Contra Population Transfer, in Schechtman, J. B. *Postwar Population Transfers in Europe: 1945–1955*. 389–398.

was clear to all of them that the solution of the minority problems was one of the key tasks in forging a new peace on the old continent.

The short period of Nazi rule over a large part of Europe altered perceptions of the idea of moving populations because of the sheer unprecedented cynicism of the various "scientific" transfer experiments conducted by the Nazis, and their brutal lawlessness. H. Lemberg argued that Hitler lowered the threshold of acceptability of what could be done with people and social groups. Even though defeated, Hitler set in motion shifts of borders that were in the spirit of the geopolitical and racial "theories" that he had himself formulated.[82]

The way that Beneš's idea of transfer developed is illuminated if we consider his thoughts in his work *Democracy Today and Tomorrow*, first published in London in 1939. This book was still far from claiming that the nationality problems of postwar Europe could only by solved by the transfer of the German-speaking inhabitants of Czechoslovakia (a fact that undermines the claims of critics today that this was his clear long-term goal). On the contrary, he expressed himself very cautiously on the matter – an attitude which many of the politicians and experts on the problem including O. I. Janowsky appreciated.[83]

It is true that in this book Beneš wrote of the necessity for postwar resettlement of minorities on a much greater scale than after the First World War, but he also concluded that linguistically mixed areas would still exist and that only exceptionally would it be possible to incorporate the linguistically compact territories of minorities into the territory of the neighbouring state.[84] Beneš premised his plans and thoughts on the need to restore the pre-Munich borders of the CSR, but in this of course he constantly came up against the national/ethnic problem.

Given the attitude of Great Britain, it was clear that any proposed solution would have no hope of acceptance unless it offered participation to the Sudeten Germans. In November 1940 Beneš stated, "We want Germans to be in the republic again and we must of course proceed on that basis. Otherwise it would be concluded everywhere that we are abandoning our historic borders, and even here there are still people who would like us to return to the (status quo) of Munich."[85] This reference clearly indicates the "personnel factor" in the continuity of British policy at the time of Munich and later in the course of the war.

---

[82] "We must direct our surplus population to the East and only to the East. This is the direction of German expansion given by nature." Hitler's politisches Testament (Bormann's records), in Jäckel, E. 1999. *Hitlerův světový názor* [Hitler's World View]. Litomyšl: Paseka. 46.

[83] "Hence President Beneš's approach to population transfer is highly qualified and precisely defined." Janowsky, O. *Nationalities and National Minorities*. 138.

[84] Beneš, E. 1948. *Demokracie dnes a zítra*. Prague: Čin. 209–210.

[85] Kural, V. *Vlastenci proti okupaci*. 75.

In the years 1939–1941 Beneš was looking for a moderate solution, and this earned him sharp criticism from the home resistance groups, especially ÚVOD. Bořek-Dohalský from the *Politické ústředí*/Political Centre group[86] (the group closest in views to Beneš) warned against cooperation with the London Germans because this would provoke "bitterness and incline the public to the Prague government, which explains its own policy in this way." Beneš evidently commissioned an expert opinion on the possible expulsion of the Sudeten Germans from Czechoslovakia as early as May 1939. A legal committee at the Political Centre led by Z. Peška started work on it. It was here that there first appeared an argument appealing to the Greek-Turkish exchange of population based on the Treaty of St. Lausanne with reference to the fundamental study of this subject by the author S. P. Ladas. The text of the Memorandum inter alia points out the difficulty of complete removal of the German-speaking inhabitants of the CSR but recommends the alternative of "removal of all people who are unable to prove that they actively helped to save the CSR."[87]

At the end of the report it is already clearly suggested that the eventual return of the government in exile to Prague could be jeopardised by the dispute.[88] The resistance group *Obrana národa*/Defence of the Nation had responded to a request from London (Gen. S. Ingr) at the beginning of August (1. 8.) 1941 for an opinion on the Sudeten question in the following terms: "According to the general conviction of the people, the CSR must be restored in its historic borders and the Germans expelled. We are nonetheless aware of the international context in the solution of the domestic problem and the determination of the border… The reduction of the number of Germans in this country is necessary, the exchange of population desirable but without losses of territory."[89]

---

[86] The initially moderate Political Centre led by the expert on national questions Z. Peška (professor of constitutional law at Charles University), saw the best solution as that of exchange of population, the ending of language islands in the interior, and the transfer of all Germans who could not prove a share in the defence of the republic. Prof. Z. Peška had been involved in the theoretical treatment of the minority question in the interwar period. See e.g. Peška, Z. "Historický vývoj mezinárodní menšinové ochrany před světovou válkou" [The Historical Development of Protection for Minorities before the World War]. *Zahraniční politika*. 1929. 1168–1182.

[87] "Pamětní spis o výměně obyvatelstva" [Memorandum on Exchange of Population]. August 1939. Prof. Z. Peška's Memorandum on Exchange of Population, in *Češi a sudetoněmecká otázka*. 21–23. The text of the memorandum is based on analysis of the study by Ladas, S. P. *The Exchange of Minorities Bulgaria, Greece and Turkey*.

[88] Kural, V. *Vlastenci proti okupaci*. 75.

[89] Brandes, D. *Cesta k vyhnání 1938–1945*. 111.

Edvard Beneš and British Plans

Independently of the development of opinions among the Czech Resistance at home and in exile, the idea that German minority groups had to be removed from Central and Eastern Europe because they were the main reason for international conflicts was gaining ground in British political thinking. In fact, there is evidence that the concept of "ethnic homogenisation" was alive in Great Britain from the very beginning of the war. Expert teams set up by the *British Foreign Office* in ever more intensive cooperation with the East European governments-in-exile were "spinning" plans for a new order in Central and Eastern Europe. The basic concencus here was that the states that would be reconstituted after the defeat of Hitler's Germany ought not to have national minorities, and certainly not German minorities, and that this homogenisation of states was to be achieved by massive transfer of population.[90]

At the instigation of the Foreign Office a special group was set up – *the Foreign Research and Press Service*, which put together expert teams to draw up and discuss proposals that included alternative suggestions for the national/ethnic organisation of postwar Central Europe.[91] One particular group of experts was supposed to answer a fundamental question posed by the *Foreign Office*: what points of view needed to be taken into account in determining the borders of the two federations planned for the postwar period in the Eastern part of Central Europe and in South-West Europe (Poland-Czechoslovakia and Yugoslavia-Rumania-Bulgaria). In the early years of the war the FO strongly supported and welcomed the creation of these new federations, evidently because of persistent fondness for the idea of a *cordon sanitaire*, as applied after the First World War. Yet although projects of this kind were discussed with various degrees of intensity at the FO in the first half of the war, the continuing hostility in Polish-Soviet relations rendered them ever less realistic, and increasingly unacceptable. It became clear that Britain no longer had the power to implement its political plans in Central Europe.

It was in the context of the earlier discussion of the character of a post-war European order that in May 1940 the expert group presented to the Foreign

---

[90] Lemberg, H. "Předmluva" [Preface], in Brandes, D. *Cesta k vyhnání 1938–1945*. 13.

[91] Rychlík, J. "Memorandum Britského královského institutu mezinárodních vztahů o transferu národnostních menšin z roku 1940" [The Memorandum of the British Royal Institute of International Relations on the Transfer of National Minorities]. *Český časopis historický* 4/1993. 612. The memorandum was fully drafted in its first version on the 14th of May 1940. The director of the FRPS was A. Toynbee and the head of the South-East Europe Section was R. W. Seton-Watson. Also on the team were C. A. Macartney, former secretary of the Commission for National Minorities of the *League of Nations*, the author of the outstanding study National States and National Minorities, D. Mitrany (Rumania) and R. G. D. Laffan (Yugoslavia). According to M. D. Brown the text of the memorandum almost immediately reached the hands of Beneš, to whom it was provided by Seton-Watson. M. D. Brown refers to a memorandum of B. Lockhart.

Office a memorandum proposing the transfer of German national minorities to the territory of Germany. It was drawn up by John David Mabbott and entitled *The Transfer of Minorities*. It not only recommended transfers as a feasible solution on the basis of previous experience with exchanges of population, but concluded that they were the best solution for Czechoslovakia's minority problems.[92] Indeed, in the thinking of the expert and energetic group of experts (one of its members was R. W. Seton-Watson), changes of envisaged borders in Eastern Europe almost always involved the idea of the exchange or transfer of population.[93]

The memorandum entirely ruled out application of the principle of voluntary transfer of population. In a passage considering the possibility of transfer it expressly stated that, "No transfer of Germans in the post-war period will be comparable with the German injustice and inhumanity in the treatment of Poles and Czechs. Furthermore the pre-war line of ethnic demarcation need not be regarded as an unchangeable border, since Hitler has destroyed it forever by his own transfers."

Part III of the memorandum deals with individual countries and areas from the point of view of specific proposed transfers. Paragraph 2 of the memorandum, which is devoted to the relationship between Germany and Czechoslovakia, starts by asserting the "ethnic correctness" of the borders defined by the Munich Agreement (Seton-Watson protested against this formulation). It goes on to argue that if these were to be modified in detail to the advantage of Czechoslovakia, a mutual exchange of population could then be undertaken to eliminate minorities from either side of the border.

According to the proposal, the transfer of Bohemian Germans should be judged only in terms of two criteria, i.e. its benefits for the Czechs and its ultimate effect for peace. At the same time it was noted that among the Sudeten

---

[92] Brown, M. D. "Forcible Population Transfers. A flawed legacy or an unavoidable necessity in protracted ethnic conflicts? The Case of the Sudeten Germans", *RUSI Journal* (The Royal United Services Institute) 148/4. August 2003. 83. First consideration of the transfer of ethnic Germans from Central Europe appeared in a study of the Chatham House prepared for Rockefeller Foundation (M.D. Brown).

[93] Lemberg, H. "Etnické čistky – řešení národnostních problémů?". 98. Like H. Lemberg, D. Brandes does not mention in his works the existence of the memorandum of the spring of 1940, despite the fact that detailed information on its existence was published by J. Rychlík in *Český časopis historický* 4/1993. According to Brandes, the British position on plans for the transfer based on the memorandum of the Foreign Research and Press Service of the Foreign Office was not ready until the 12th of February 1942. In the context of Beneš's attempts to get the British government to declare the Munich Agreement invalid, the mention of the British undertaking to the American government that they would make no promises relating to the borderland questions is important. From P. Nichols (the ambassador to the Czechoslovak government-in-exile), Beneš received only the compromise proposal that in the peace negotiations Great Britain would commit itself to ensuring for Czechoslovakia the kind of borders that will secure strength and stability for this country." Beneš officially gave the British ambassador to understand that if Poland was to be compensated for eventual losses of territory in the East, then it was "unthinkable" that "the question of Germans in his country should not likewise be solved". Brandes, D. *Cesta k vyhnání 1938–1945*. 129–132.

Germans there were many skilled workers whose loss might cause crises in industrial production for many years. These Germans were not new colonists, but "Bohemians" whose communities had lived on the territory for centuries. The proposed solution required the fulfilment of two conditions if the mistakes of the past were to be avoided. First, Czechoslovakia must provide Germans with the highest degree of local self-government. Second, Germany itself must be permanently weakened or permanently cured of racial Pan-Germanism (the Sudeten Germans are the most deeply and intensely pan-German of all the German minorities in Europe).

The memorandum states that the value of the expulsion of the Germans for the preservation of peace depends on factors that are outside its scope. It notes that the transfer will be a permanent injury to German "pride and honour". In this context it is recalled that even G. Stresemann had said that the creation of the Polish corridor must be regarded as an eternal injury to all German parties when in fact the creation of the corridor was *fair to Germany in every respect*.

Even with these optimum borders, the strongest economic position and the strongest military resources and armaments, J. D. Mabbott considers that Czechoslovakia will never be able to stand up to a continually unsatisfied Germany without help.[94] The prospects for peace will therefore be seriously threatened by the expulsion of two million Germans if Czechoslovakia does not join a political and military federation with the other states of Eastern Europe as the framework of some universal security system. Even in this situation its position will be unenviable unless Austria is separated from Germany and included in the federation. Transfer is not then to be recommended unless reliable forces of collective security are to hand.

At a meeting on the 6th of July 1942 the British war cabinet expressed approval of the principle of the transfer of German minorities from Central and

---

[94] In this context we need to draw attention to the essay by Colonel E. Moravec (pseudonym Yester), who in the second half of the 1930s systematically studied the military-political aspects of the defence capabilities of the CSR. He argued that the difference between the strategic position of states is also a matter of the *factor of neighbourhood*. Basing his thought on the geopolitical conceptions of the time, he claimed that the strategic position of a country is made more difficult by having more powerful neighbours. These neighbours exercise pressure. With appeal to the theorist Reinhard, he introduced for this situation the notion of the *co-efficient of pressure* which is given by share of aggregate number of citizens of the neighbouring state and own state. The dimensions of the pressure are further modified by the size of the state territory, its economic potential, communications infrastructure and so on. Moravec goes on to say that, "The problems of the *defense geography* of a state like ours, i.e. a Central European state, are given by the policy of the more powerful factor in Central Europe, and that is Germany. This policy pursues control of three great European industrial bases: the Rhine, the Silesian and the Don basis. This control would make Germany master of Europe." Moravec, E. 1935. *Obrana státu (Vojáci a doba)* [The Defence of the State (Soldiers and the Age). Prague: Svaz čs. důstojnictva. 37–39.

Eastern Europe.[95] In view of the fact that Great Britain evidently played a key role in Allied planning (especially in the first half of the war), this act by the British cabinent can be regarded as a turning point – the moment when it was decided that instead of the implementation of the right to self-determination, as demanded by W. Jaksch, the Allies would apply another model of the solution of nationality conflicts in Central Europe, i.e. resettlement of population. This moment meant the end of the Versailles Treaty system of protection of national minorities and made it impossible for the Sudeten Germans to appeal to the right to self-determination in post-war Europe.[96]

From the point of view of attacks on E. Beneš today, the sequence of the individual steps and shifts of opinion of the individual actors involved in decision-making on the transfer are of some relevance. The argument frequently repeated by Jaksch (see below), and many others afterwards, is that the author and driving force behind acceptance of the idea of transfer was in fact Stalin. This is a claim challenged by H. Lemberg, who argues that it is very doubtful to see the origin of the idea of expulsion purely in Soviet and so retrospectively in a Russian "political culture" allegedly going back to the Middle Ages, as some German authors insisted after the war.

In chronological sequence, the first plan to emerge envisaged (after the repudiation of Munich) the cession of the territorial "promontories" of the Cheb, Šluknov and certain other smaller areas beyond the border fortification line, which were almost exclusively inhabited by a German-speaking population (around 800–900,000). Following on from this suggestion, according to the so-called Beneš Plan,[97] Germany would accept another approximately 1 million Sudeten Germans. The remaining 1–1.5 million ("half of them democrats, socialists and Jews") would stay in the CSR as a controllable national minority.[98] In its conclusions of the 17th of May 1944, the Committee for Postwar Planning returned to the idea of cession of the "promontories", expressing the view that the cession of the Rumburk and Šluknov, Frýdlant and Aš and Cheb promontories would not endanger the strategic position of Czechoslovakia. Later, in

---

[95] Nonetheless, in the British civil service there existed a group of skeptics, whose main exponent was John Troutbeck, the *Chairman of the Interdepartmental Committee on the Transfer of German Populations*, which pointed out the difficulties and risks of large transfers of population. Troutbeck and his supporters claimed that the larger the territory conceded by Germany to Poland, the greater the potential threat of German revanchism. For more detail see Lemberg, H. "Etnické čistky – řešení národnostních problémů?". 99.

[96] Ripka, H. "Záznam rozhovoru s A. Edenem" [Record of a Conversation with A. Eden], in *Češi a sudetoněmecká otázka*. 172.

[97] In mid-September 1938, Beneš had sent Minister J. Nečas with a secret mission to Paris. He was supposed to present Léon Blum with a compromise, the so-*called fifth plan* for the solution of the Sudeten German crisis. The plan was to inspire (in the greatest possible secrecy) a Franco-British proposal that Hitler would be forced to accept.

[98] Pešek, J. "20. století – doba nucených migrací, vyhnání a transferů". 44.

November 1944, this Committee proposed the reduction of the number of Germans in Czechoslovakia to 800,000 and in February 1945 Beneš was still considering the possibility of exchanging the part of the territory densely populated by Germans for other sparsely settled territory, i.e. not the complete expulsion of the Sudeten Germans.

In this context J. Tesař, who generally takes a critical view of Czechoslovak foreign policy and military possibilities in the period of the Munich Crisis, actually praises Beneš's approach and rejects criticism of the president: "Crucially we ought first of all to ask what was actually at bottom antidemocratic about these ideas. I would rate them unusually positively for not writing off the Sudeten Jews and democrats, and indeed for showing a clear sense of obligation towards the latter! Getting rid of the fanaticised Henleinians would have been a huge victory for the state. This was not at bottom either a violation of democracy or a betrayal of the state."[99]

To repeat, it was only in the later years of the war that the national homogenisation of Czechoslovakia came to the fore as a solution, and it did so by a complicated route. The Czechoslovak government in exile in Britain had a partner in the exiled leadership of the Sudeten Social Democratic Party and its leader W. Jaksch. It was with Jaksch that Beneš negotiated in the first half of the war on the future relationship between Czechs and Germans in the restored state. The bone of contention between the two politicians was the conclusion that Jaksch drew from the successes of the Henlein Party in the 1930s, i.e. that if his own party wanted to lead the majority of the Sudeten Germans back into a democratic republic after the war, it would have to be transformed from a party based on a class principle into a (national) people's party, and so must defend the national demands of Sudeten Germans, which consisted in federalisation and territorial autonomy.[100] Beneš, however, after his experience with the demands of an SdP that had deployed the same principles, inevitably associated both with the development ending in the destruction of the territorial integrity of the CSR.[101]

---

[99] Tesař, J. *Mnichovský komplex*. 91.

[100] Brandes, D. *Cesta k vyhnání 1938–1945*. 368.

[101] J. W. Brügel reminds us that for Beneš Jaksch was a valuable witness for a number of reasons. One was that on his first visit to London in 1937 as an unknown deputy Jaksch had defended the cause of Czechoslovak democracy at a Foreign Office that was strongly prejudiced. He had declared at the time in front of a high-ranking official that Beneš respected rights and would bring the excessively zealous Czech officials to their senses – and that between a democratic state such as Czechoslovakia and the Hitler regime there could never be any justice and lasting agreement. He also did Beneš a service by being himself living proof that not all Germans were supporters of Henleinism. Finally he unwittingly did Beneš a service by showing that democrats too, as his own case exemplified, could have pan-German attitudes and nationalistic tendencies. Brügel, J. W. *Tschechen und Deutsche 1939–1946*. 260.

Despite this, after several interruptions, discussions between the two politicians continued, and in the autumn of 1940 Beneš suggested to Jaksch the possibility of his accepting Sudeten German social democrats onto the State Council,[102] and in the context of this initiative a group of ministers of the government in exile had talks with Jaksch on the creation of three cantons and various smaller-scale transfers within the territory of the Czechoslovak state. The talks were broken off because of the resolute protests of the home resistance – as happened in similar circumstances a year later. In the autumn of 1942 Beneš proposed the resumption of negotiations and a new solution including the expulsion of the "guilty", i.e. the variant of the reduction of the German minority to a maximum of 1 million. The Foreign Office opposed the application of the principle of guilt (because this threatened to limit the extent of the transfer planned by the British), and so Beneš once again broke off talks and Jaksch engaged in efforts to try to persuade the British public to reject transfer plans. In effect he returned to his federalist programme of the first months of the war and demanded that the Sudeten territories be occupied by "non-partisan Allied forces".[103]

In assessing this critical rupture in the development of Czech-Sudeten German relations (as with earlier turning points), it is natural to ask whether Beneš and Jaksch missed any real opportunity to establish a basis for postwar cooperation. Dostál Raška rejects as oversimplified J. W. Brügel's view that Jaksch's refusal to accept seats in the State Council was a great mistake which fundamentally influenced the final outcome.[104] He considers it unlikely that the presence of Sudeten Germans in the State Council would have prevented the transfer. The Liberal Democrats and the Zinner Group had for a long time taken an "unambiguously positive" pro-Czechoslovak standpoint, but they rejected

---

[102] F. Dostál Raška, however, cites in his work the view of the German historian F. Prinz that Beneš was not sincere in his offer, but intended it only as a sop to the British. According to Prinz, Beneš had lost hope of winning the Sudeten Germans over to the side of the CSR as early as 1935. Raška rejects these conclusions but admits that some of Beneš's later statements seem to give credence to them. Otherwise it is allegedly impossible to explain the fact that Beneš informed Jaksch of the need to expel a million Germans only a few days after he had proposed to the Treugemeinschaft that it nominate its own representatives for the State Council. But then did Jaksch behave any differently? – asks Raška. In 1940 Jaksch adopted a wait-and-see attitude, and the Foreign Office doubted that he had any real intention of coming to an agreement with Beneš. Raška, F. D. 2002. *The Czechoslovak exile government in London and the Sudeten German issue*. Prague: Karolinum. 199.

[103] Brandes, D. *Cesta k vyhnání 1938–1945*. 371. There was a split inside Jaksch's grouping – The Community of Loyal Social Democrats and what was known as the Zinner Group separated off. The latter tried by distancing itself from nationalist demands to win the favour of the Czechoslovak government-in-exile, which from March 1944 together with the communists it supported fully (in Brandes's phrase "it was under the Czech thumb").

[104] "Hier ergab sich die Gelegenheit, einen Geburtsfehler gutzumachen, wenn eine organisierte deutsche Gruppe sich schon an der Errichtung des neuen Staates aktiv beteiligt hätte." Brügel, J. W. *Tschechen und Deutsche 1939–1946*. 24.

the transfer and Beneš did not accept their offer to join the State Council. The clearly constructive position of this group had no impact on the final outcome and so there is no reason to think that Jaksch might have had such an impact if he had acted in the same way. Dostál Raška put the same question (of the possibility of an agreement between Beneš and Jaksch) to Eduard Goldstücker (from 1942 an official at the Czech Foreign Ministry in London) and the answer was an emphatic "no".[105] Apart from this, we should remember that Jaksch represented only part of the Social Democratic Party which itself was only part of a larger Sudeten German exile community in London.

Study of the archives of both the Czechoslovak government in exile and the Foreign Office is making it increasingly clear that Beneš basically respected the views of the British, which he regarded as direction-setting if not entirely binding on him. For example, in 1942 the Foreign Office and Sir Alexander Cadogan personally rejected his own original idea of expelling Sudeten Germans (see proposals on the reduction of the number of Sudeten Germans) on the principle of guilt alone, because in the British view it limited the prospective extent of transfer. The British also considered it impossible to establish a generally acceptable criterion of "guilt". When Beneš presented his list of "criteria" of guilt as a basis for the transfer of roughly one million Germans (active support (not just voting in elections) for the Henlein party and occupation government, contact with the youth movements, the SS and Gestapo and so on), P. Nichols expressed skepticism. In his view the Sudeten problem was one of the causes of the war, and so measures to solve it would be carefully followed in Great Britain and the whole world and it could be considered a certain test. This meant that clear and comprehensible criteria had to be established for the expulsion of this million and in the application of such criteria there could be no room for any "suspicion of horse-trading".

Nor did other FO officials F. K. Roberts and D. Allen see any other way of separating "the wheat from the chaff" (and to base the transfers merely on "war guilt" would hopelessly tie British hands).

Alexander Cadogan (1938–1946 permanent undersecretary at the FO) agreed, saying that the principle of guilt, "would probably lead to the curtailment of our right to carry out population transfers. Clearly we shall want (and possibly the Americans too will suggest this) to apply this instrument on quite a wide scale, without regard to "guilt", and so we should have a free hand in this respect." Cadogan's arguments were supported by A. Eden, and the For-

---

[105] Question: "Professor, do you think that with the different nuances in their talks there was ever any hope that Beneš and Jaksch might come to some form of agreement?" Answer: "No, their positions were clearly irreconcilable from the beginning and in fact had already entirely diverged in 1941..." Raška, F. D. *The Czechoslovak exile government*. 199–200.

eign Office told P. Nichols that "guilt" was a difficult criterion and that it would limit freedom of action in regard to expulsion of Germans.[106]

The British attitudes were based partly on the bitter realisation that groups of ethnic Germans had been exploited to facilitate Nazi expansionism, and partly on the interwar failure of processes of integration of ethnic minorities into majority societies and states. Transfer plans were agreed by the British government with the exiled governments of Eastern Europe, the United States, the *European Advisory Commission* and other organisations.[107] In fact, far more drastic proposals than transfer appeared in British reports and materials on the post-war organisation of Central Europe in the wake of the shock of news of Nazi terror in the occupired territories. For example one of the plans suggested letting Germans transferred from East Prussia and Upper Silesia, "disappear in Siberia".[108]

In the case of Czechoslovakia a major shift in British attitudes was caused by the barbaric extermination of the villagers of Lidice and Ležáky as part of the massive Nazi revenge for the assassination of the acting Reichsprotektor Heydrich on the 4th of June 1942.[109]

Evidence of the important role of the British in Allied planning (and particularly in relation to the exiled governments) includes the record of confidential

---

[106] Brown, M. D. "Forcible Population Transfers". 83. Cadogan's actual words were: "I'm rather doubtful about this principle of ejecting the "guilty" ...because I fear that it might lead to the restriction of our right to make major population transfers." D. Allen's, F. Roberts's, O. Sargent's, A. Cadogan's and A. Eden's records of 27. 9.–1. 10. 1942 F. Roberts to P. Nichols on 6. 10. 1942. FO 371/30835, C9161/326/12. In Brandes, D. *Cesta k vyhnání 1938–1945*. 159–160.

[107] In November 1944 when the Czechoslovak government presented its demands for the transfer in the form of a memorandum to the *European Advisory Commission,* it added a supplement entitled *(The Pan-Germanism of the Germans in Czechoslovakia* containing an analysis of the destructive historical role of the German minority in the Czech Lands. Brandes, D. *Cesta k vyhnání 1938–1945*. 152.

[108] Lemberg, H. "Etnické čistky – řešení národnostních problémů?". 99.

[109] Heydrich took up his Prague function in September 1941, and immediately had General Eliáš arrested, executed many members of the resistance and stepped up the occupation terror on the territory of the Protectorate. On the 2nd of October 1941, he made his notorious speech "on the problem of Czech territory". Here he said, "It must be clear to us that in German history Bohemia and Moravia were the heart of the Reich, a heart that in favourable times was always a fortress of Germandom... and as Bismarck put it, the "citadel of Europe". The final solution of the Czech Question included a combination of physical liquidation, transfer and "the Germanisation of the Czech rabble using old methods". Fremund, K. *Chtěli nás vyhubit*. 125–137. Major R. Littledale of the British Army, who was under cover in Prague at this period, wrote that "The SS men were real lunatics. They shot everyone they believed suspicious. They shot Eliáš and several dozen people arrested on suspicion of being in the resistance... They found Kubiš a Gabčík [part of the team that had assasinated Heydrich] who were hiding in the crypt of a church... After a long fight Kubiš and Gabčík preferred to shoot themselves than to fall into the hands of the SS... Lidice and Ležáky, both were razed to the ground, and the soil ploughed up, as if this was defeated Carthage. All the adult inhabitants of these villages were shot... most of the children suffered gunshot injuries. The cruelty perpetrated by the Germans provided the excuse after the re-establishment of the borders for the transfer of three million Germans from their homes in the Czech borderlands, which Bohemia and Moravia had lost because of Munich." As many as 5000 people were executed in connection with the assassination. Foot, M. R. D. 1997. *S.O.E. Sbor pro speciální operace* [S.O.E. Special Operations Executive]. Brno: Nakladatelství Bonus. 260–261.

talks held on the 3ʳᵈ of April 1943 at Chequers between Beneš and Churchill in the presence of Jan Masaryk (who kept the minutes of the meeting). Here Churchill said: "We need to think about the structure of post-war Europe. The main enemy is Prussia. It must be destroyed – that means destroying the general staff once and for all – they are guilty. It is absolutely necessary to divide Germany and separate it from Prussia and then begin with some federation or confederation... a Europe in little pieces is a danger... After the destruction of Prussia and the first post-war crisis it will be possible to deal more moderately with the other parts of Germany... Once Germany grasps that Prussianism is finished once and for all, cooperation will be possible, but this presupposes complete disarmament... Population transfer will be necessary. Those who want to get out of the Baltic states, let them go – the same from East Prussia, or Poland and also from the *Sudetenland*. – Give them a short deadline and let them take what is most necessary and go – I hope we shall get this through with the Russians."[110]

From this and many other documents it is obvious that Beneš's ideas on the postwar expulsion of the Sudeten Germans were fully within the frame of reference of politicians of the Western Allies and their political culture, which considered the relocation and exchange of population to be a legitimate way of solving ethnic conflicts. Indeed, the British had abundant experience of this kind in the modern history of their empire and projected this into their foreign policy in the course of the war.[111]

During 1944 a debate on the modalities of the transfer of ethnic Germans continued between different departments of the FO. The British government had approved the principle but not the method. According to a memorandum

---

[110] Sum, A. 1996. *Osudové kroky Jana Masaryka* [The Fateful Steps of Jan Masaryk]. Prague: Státní ústřední archiv. 76–77. Churchill repeated his views in similar terms in the House of Commons, when he informed the house that the British government had agreed to the shifting of the Polish border to the West at the Yalta Conference: "I believe that the expulsion of the population will be a satisfactory and lasting solution. There will be no mixing of populations causing endless complications... A clean sweep will be made." Chászár, E. "The problem of National Minorities". 199.

[111] A great deal of information has been provided by the historian Martin D. Brown, who has been engaged in research on the document of the Foreign Office (particularly its Central Europe section) in the British National Archives (earlier the Public Record Office) in Kew Garden in London. He reports that currently only 30–50% of the materials from the years 1939–1945 is available. Nonetheless, the elaborate system of registration of documents introduced in 1906 provides a good overall picture of the functioning of the Foreign Office. He points out that the FO was only one source of decision-making on foreign policy since the government took its own initiatives that circumvented the competence of the FO. I would add that the existence of multiple centres of decision-making on foreign policy is hardly specific to one nation or era and that we can still find examples today. Brown, M. D. 2004. *"Never complain, never explain." The Foreign Office's influence on the formation of British policy in regard to Anglo-Polish-Czechoslovak relations in exile, 1939–1945.* Unpublished paper. On the two fires that destroyed 90% of the SOE archives: "The work of the SOE was mostly so top secret that it was never recorded in writing... The second fire was started deliberately; the relentless spoliation of archives seems to be almost endemic in bureaucracies." Foot, M. R. D. *S.O.E. Sbor pro speciální operace.* 334.

of the *Foreign Office Research Department*, the transfer should be phased over a longer time period of five to ten years and subject to international supervision, and the German government, or German authorities, should co-operate in the resettlement. With a view to the difficulties of population transfer on such a scale and the need to co-ordinate the opinions of the relevant British ministries, in April 1944 a special *Interdepartmental Committee on the Transfer of German Populations* was set up at the instigation of the Foreign Office.[112] The committee discussed the economic, political and other consequences of the momentous step.

The memorandum "Alternative Policies towards Minorities", presented by J. D. Mabbott on the 20th of January 1944, provided the basis for a debate in the FO on the connections between the protection of minorities, assimilation and transfer. Once again it was asserted that the ideal solution to a minority problem would be to set the borders in a way that corresponded to the ethnic lines of division. Transfer could then only be used to solve the problem entirely if it was complete, i.e. if it was carried out by force. Mabbott also argued that the alternative, forced assimilation, had never been successful anywhere. Depending on the situation and character of the minority, "full protection", "voluntary assimilation" or transfer might be considered as solutions.

The key passage of the Mabbott memorandum on choice of solution runs as follows: "A minority that hates and is hated by its fellow citizens, that faces the danger of certain persecution, that has earlier been misused to divide the state in which it lived, and has oppressed its inhabitants, is a clear and serious candidate for transfer if the state borders have for some reason to be set in such a way as to include this minority."[113]

In the course of debate on the Sudeten German problem, P. Nichols commented that any solution to the problem of German minorities in Europe had to be assessed in terms of how far it contributed to prevention of a third world war. Since German minorities strengthened the position of Germany and tempted her to meddle in the internal affairs of the other states, they should be reduced to a minimum by transfer. O'Malley (the British representative with the Polish government in exile) stated in a report to Eden that while Beneš talked of "democratic human rights", in his own view it would be better to

---

[112] Brandes, D. *Cesta k vyhnání 1938–1945.* The committee gained the status of a sub-committee afiliated to the *Armistice and Post-War Committee* attached to the War Cabinet. The committee was chaired by R. Law and brought together representatives of the *Foreign Office, Treasury, War Cabinet Office, Dominions Office, Ministry of Economic Warfare* and *War Cabinet Office.*

[113] Brandes, D. *Cesta k vyhnání 1938–1945.* 220. It was commented on other variant solutions that "the policy of transfer and assimilarion would be a regression in comparison to the decisions of the peace agreements of 1878 and 1919, it would be an 'abandonment of principles of protection and their replacement by demands arising from irreconcilable nationalist sentiment.'

say openly "that minorities should be either eliminated or left *to sink or swim*), depending on how large they were or whether they were connected with other states ready to defend their cause."[114]

The Committee for Transfer (picking up on the text of the Mabbott Memorandum) drew attention to the fact that the transfer would be hampered by guarantees of minority rights, but would conversely be facilitated if the remaining people were threatened with loss of ethnic identity and assimilation. If large German minorities remained in place and were allowed to retain their national identity, a resurgent Germany would be tempted to exploit them. Whatever decision was made, it should not be a half-baked solution. The final report of the committee included Beneš's suggestion that Czechoslovak reparation claims should be amortised by the property of those expelled (the Sudeten Germans), and also that all persons who had German citizenship by German law should be considered German and that the Czechoslovak or Polish government should have the right to allow certain persons to retain original Polish or Czechoslovak citizenship or to be granted it.[115]

The committee likewise drew attention to the common features of the situation of German settlement in Poland and Czechoslovakia, but also to the striking differences. The text expresses fears that a very large number of refugees might complicate the situation in post-war Germany, "causing a major political and economic problem there and creating the basis for a widespread impoverished, embittered and restless element, urgently demanding revenge on the successor states, while at the same time leaving in the future Poland large compact blocks of German population that would create political problems, and for Germany would be a permanent temptation to further intervention. Rather different considerations are thought to apply to the Sudeten territories, and evidently the Czechoslovak government is the best judge of its own needs."[116]

One of the major charges against President Beneš underlies what is currently the basic postulate of views calling for the revision of the modern history of Czechoslovakia. It consists in the claim that the transfer of the Germans opened the way for communism in Czechoslovakia, which is alleged to have

---

[114] O'Malley to Eden 20th January 1944. FO 371/34355, C9894/12. See Brandes, D. *Cesta k vyhnání 1938–1945.* 222.

[115] Beneš's memorandum "Transfer of Population from Czechoslovakia" (with Nichols' note to Roberts of the 28th of January 1944), in Brandes, D. *Cesta k vyhnání 1938–1945.* 223, 240. See also "Transfer obyvatelstva v ČSR (Desetibodový plán E. Beneše k transferu sudetských Němců z Československa)" [The Transfer of Population in the CSR (E. Beneš's Ten-Point Plan for the Transfer of the Sudeten Germans from Czechoslovakia]. November 1943. London. And also "Návrh řešení menšinové otázky v ČSR. Prozatímní memorandum o řešení sudetoněmecké otázky" [Proposal for a Solution to the Minority Question in the CSR. A provisional memorandum on the solution of the Sudeten German Question'], drawn up by J. Císař. Study department of the Czech Foreign Ministry. London. *Češi a sudetoněmecká otázka.* 264–265, 272–278.

[116] Brandes, D. *Cesta k vyhnání 1938–1945.* 223.

been Beneš's aim. Jaksch for example expressed this idea in concentrated form when he wrote, "Potsdam inaugurated the last stage of Czech independence... The expulsion of the strongly anti-communist Sudeten Germans and the liquidation of most of the important private firms on the grounds that they had worked for Hitler were actions aimed at eliminating the forces standing in the way of the gradually spreading communist power, i.e. they were preparation of the ground for the decisive step in the strategy of the People's National Front – the transition to complete communist lordship."[117]

R. Hilf takes a rather different view, arguing that, "Beneš and with him a substantial part of the Czech nation certainly did not intend by the expulsion to decide for the East and against the West. The direction in which this decision led was given by objective circumstances rather than intentions. History is determined much more by unwanted consequences than by plans."[118] With this we can agree, because to attribute to Beneš a premeditated policy of driving the CSR into the arms of Stalin is misleading to the point of smear. Beneš was looking for support against a possible renewed German *Drang nach Osten* and found it, given the actual configuration of political forces (and with the blessing of the British and Americans), in the Soviet Union. President Roosevelt expressed his attitude to the treaty in a conversation with J. Masaryk: "I agree, and fully agree with your policy. Tell Beneš that he pulled off a remarkable success by his treaty with Russia. It should be a very sound precedent... Of course, the precipitate way in which Russia is announcing wide-ranging changes, is complicating the inter-ally situation and will be exploited in domestic politics here, in England and elsewhere. But I am not afraid of that. I believe that Russia wants to co-operate and will co-operate... Give Beneš my regards and tell him that I understand and approve."[119]

The tragedy of Beneš's decision-making lay in the rapid disintegration of the anti-Hitler coalition and start of the Cold War, which transformed the geopolitical situation of post-war Central Europe and ended the cooperation of the powers in which he had hoped after the end of the war. It soon turned out that President had been mistaken when in an interview for *Reynold's News* on the 20th of February 1944 he had commented on the Czechoslovak-Soviet Treaty with the words, "The pact that we have negotiated with the USSR will strengthen the security of the Czechoslovak Republic in a fundamental way.

[117] Jaksch, W. *Cesta Evropy do Postupimi*. 331.

[118] Hilf, R. *Němci a Češi*. 90.

[119] Record of J. Masaryk on conversation with F. D. Roosevelt 4th of February 1944. *Československo-sovětské vztahy. Vztahy v diplomatických jednáních 1939–1945* [Czechoslovak-Soviet Relations in Diplomatic Negotiations]. (Documents). 1996. Němeček, J. – Nováčková, H. – Šťovíček, I. – Tejchman, M. (eds.). Prague: Státní ústřední archiv. 229–230.

But in our judgement the pact with the USSR also confirms its [the CSR's] independence. The USSR has promised that it does not intend to interfere in the internal affairs of our state. Our friendship with the USSR is not supposed to mean our dependence on Soviet Russia, but on the contrary mutual cooperation and the strengthening of the independence of a state that wishes to live genuinely in sincere friendship with the USSR but also in full freedom and with full sovereignty." At this moment Beneš still believed that he had found a safe refuge for his state, but soon the case of Ruthenia (Sub-Carpathian Ukraine) would show what Stalin understood by partnership.

The main target of the attacks of critics (and not only from the ranks of Sudeten German authors) is Beneš's attitude to Stalin and the Soviet Union. Specifically the charge is that Beneš made a terrible mistake in trusting the word of the Soviet dictator and considering him a reasonable man who would be deterred from the violent communisation of as much of Europe as he could dominate by the desire to maintain good relations with Great Britain and the United States. Beneš is also alleged to have made the same mistake when, following the Soviet veto, he abandoned the plan to create a Czechoslovak-Polish confederation and in 1943 concluded a treaty on friendship, mutual aid and post-war cooperation with the Soviet Union.[120]

One important document in this context is the memorandum of the British government to the Czechoslovak government of 16th of October 1943, expressing its continuing reservations about the planned agreement between the Czechoslovak government in exile and the Soviet Union.[121] Despite these reservations, however, in the course of the October conference of foreign ministers of the allied states in Moscow, Eden ultimately approved the signing of this agreement by the Czechoslovaks.[122] The British position reflected an attitude of

---

[120] Authors who criticise Beneš's policy do in fact admit the real reasons for his negotiations with the Soviets. "Beneš's general attitude to the Soviets was free of any sentimental or vulgar "class" aspects and was purely utilitarian. For Beneš, who remained a Western-thinking man and an anti-communist, the Soviet Union represented a powerful factor in Europe and he regarded it... from his perspective of his conception of European politics." Brod, T. 1992. *Československo a Sovětský svaz 1939–1945* [Czechoslovakia and the Soviet Union 1939–1945]. Prague: Nakladatelství Listopad/Práce/SPB. 11–12.

[121] "The attitude of His Majesty's Government remains unchanged to-day. They understand the desires of the Czechoslovak Government to conclude a treaty of alliance with the Soviet Government as soon as possible... Pending the further discussion of the important issues involved, which they hope will take place during the forthcoming conversations at Moscow, His Majesty's Government feels bound to maintain towards the Czechoslovak Government's proposal the attitude of reserve which they have hitherto consistently adopted." *Československo-sovětské vztahy. Vztahy v diplomatických jednáních 1939–1945.* 84.

[122] Eden unexpectedly abandoned his negative attitude to the treaty in the course of the Moscow Conference at the end of October 1943 without consulting London. The Foreign Office was so surprised by this change of attitude that it felt compelled in agreement with the Prime Minister to remind Eden of the declared position of the government on the matter. The FO's intervention did not have the desired effect, however, and the treaty was signed in December. Brown, M. D. *Never complain, never explain.* Eden's volte face is partly explained by Z. Fierlinger's report to Beneš on his talks with Eden in Moscow, of the 25th of October 1943:

suspicion towards agreements between the great powers and the smaller states in the course of the war – a suspicion motivated above all by fear that post-war Europe might well be divided into two blocs, East and West.[123] If the British had been applying this idea as a fundamental doctrine, their objections would have been entirely legitimate. The question remained, however, the extent to which Beneš could in fact rely on the unambiguous support of the West, given his experiences from the sutumn of 1938 and in a situation in which there were once again indications that the Western allies were considering "parallel" scenarios and possibilities.[124]

E. Táborský considers the criticism of Beneš to be partially justified, but at the same time points out the retrospective analysis produced by a group of exiled Czechoslovak politicians and diplomats in 1949[125], which concluded that Beneš's pact with the USSR had been justifiable as holding out a certain chance, even if this later proved vain. These authors argue that in fact, regardless of the sequence and content of Beneš's steps, the fate of Czechoslovakia was already sealed. Táborský considers it absurd to criticise Beneš for his trips to Moscow in 1943 and 1945, and for making the pact with the USSR. He asks, "Would Czechoslovakia have avoided being swallowed up by the Soviet sphere if he had not gone to Moscow and not signed the agreement?" a question to

---

"Eden told me that Molotov has showed him the text of our treaty today and that he had been pleasantly surprised. The treaty is very good and there can be no objection to it. He said that he regretted not having known the text before and that we had made a great secret of it at the beginning. If that had not happened, the whole thing would have been settled long ago... I am not supposed to telegraph this to London, because he has exceeded his instructions. The original instructions were to ensure that the treaty was not signed." *Československo-sovětské vztahy. Vztahy v diplomatických jednáních 1939–1945.* Vol. 2. 97.

[123] H. Ripka's record on the treaty: "The bilateral treaty with Russia, says Lias (head of the Czechoslovak Political Warfare Executive) is a mistake. We should have done it on a broader base, with the Poles, Yugoslavs etc, and also within the framework of an Anglo-Soviet agreement. If Moscow had refused to join a geographically broader treaty, then the whole thing would have had to be dropped. To my reply, which was that we have emphasised that it is within the intentions and framework of the Anglo-Soviet agreement, Lias responded, 'Within the framework means exclusively that England is party to the agreement, a partner of such an agreement – i.e. a British-Russian-Czechoslovak agreement;' I said that we would welcome that even more, and Lias replied that, 'The one flaw in that would be the impossibility of making such an agreement with a relatively small state'." Ibidem. 86.

[124] V. Fischl (exile Czechoslovak Foreign Ministry) reported information of the following kind: From a conversation with a former FO official: "After the war Europe will inevitably be divided into spheres of interest, with Poland, Czechoslovakia, Bulgaria, Rumania and Hungary falling into the Russian sphere.' The same former FO official then said, 'You need to know that if the Soviet union decided tomorrow that Czechoslovakia should become a Soviet Republic, the Western powers would not lift a finger.' On the 26th of February Fischl reported, "I had a long talk with an English official (Smollett), who for reasons of his official position has a detailed interest in Russian affairs and so naturally also takes note of Polish and our affairs. He is one of several people who have alerted me to the fact that in English circles the opinion that Czechoslovakia has unambiguously gone over to the Russian camp is ever more widespread. Partly thanks to Polish propaganda, and partly because of the influential Catholic group at the Foreign Office, the belief is growing that we do not much care about relations with the West." Ibidem. 231.

[125] Táborský, E. *President Beneš between East and West.* 280. The author mentions an unpublished record of a meeting held in London on the 6th of December 1949, kept in his personal archives.

which the 1949 analysis replies: "The Czechoslovak government could not sit and wait in London because they could not expect anything better there than in Moscow, and then at home". Táborský rejects the claims that Beneš deliberately dragged the CSR into the Soviet embrace.[126] Beneš wanted to have the best possible relations with the Soviet leaders. Despite his bitter experiences from the years 1938–39 he tried to somehow bind the Western great powers to the Eastern countries of Central Europe in order that they should balance the Soviet influence there. It was not his fault that this policy came to nothing and that his vision of the Soviets and West having equal shares of influence in Czechoslovakia was not fulfilled. At the end of the war there were nonethelesss more and more voices claiming that Czechoslovakia was succumbing to Soviet aspirations to a dangerous degree.[127]

It would be outside the scope of this study to analyse the development of Beneš's political opinions on relations with the West and USSR in exhaustive detail, but given that his critics often relate this theme to the decision on the transfer I have regarded it necessary at least briefly to mention the context.[128]

Táborský takes the view that in the search for a satisfactory *modus vivendi* with the Third Reich and the Sudeten Germans, Beneš went as far as it was possible for him to go. He was willing to grant the Sudeten Germans everything they demanded except the annexation of the Sudetenland to the Reich. It could well be said that he exhausted all the possibilities as required of him by Western leaders, and only then turned to the drastic solution of population transfer.

[126] When studying Š. Osuský's literary estate at the Hoover Institution Táborský was surprised to discover evidence that Beneš's greatest opponent and relentless critic in the period 1939–1945 had shared Beneš's assumption and expectation that cooperation between the Soviet Union and the West was desirable and likely. Ibidem. 316.

[127] Z. Zeman relates that President Beneš was particularly put out by an article in *The Economist* of the 25th of March 1941 entitled "Will Czechoslovakia Turn to the East". According to the article, Beneš's appeal in a message of the 4th of February for the nation to prepare for armed struggle related to Soviet criticisms that in this respect Czechs and Slovaks were dragging their feet compared to other occupied nations. *The Economist* also took exception to Beneš's argument that the German nation, which had provoked two world wars, "deserves ignominy of the kind that will come after this war, and deserves a truly great national decline for centuries to come." The article further claims that Munich and the role of the Soviet Union in the war strengthened the pro-Russian and Pan-Slavist sentiments of Czechs and Slovaks. Beneš's policy is not based on historical reminiscences, but on reality. This is given by the fact that "Eastern Europe is becoming a Russian sphere of influence". No-one knows what role Czechoslovakia will play in this sphere and by what methods the Russians intend to exercise their influence. Zeman, Z. *Edvard Beneš.* 219.

[128] Controversy over the key moments and aspects of the Czech-Sudeten-German problem is at the same time a debate on the individual decisions of President Beneš and particularly in the context of the planning of the transfer of the Sudeten Germans it is evident that the dispute is also a dispute about his character. One useful source on this is the bibliographical essay by Dejmek, J. "Edvard Beneš – obtížná cesta k politické biografii" [Edvard Beneš – The difficult road to political biography]. *Český časopis historický* 3/2003. 624–662.

Transfer or Expulsion?[129]

The end of the war meant that the Czech-German conflict embodied in the "Sudeten German Question" had reached a historic crossroads. It was obvious that something fundamental had to happen to resolve a relationship in which so much antagonistic energy had been building up for decades. Given the tragic experience of the population in the occupied Czech Lands, and in the rest of Europe that had been the target of Nazi aggression and expansionism, it was evident that this time the solution would not be a matter of carefully untangling complex threads of guilt and responsibility, but would necessarily involve a radical break, and implementation of some version of the ideas examined in the preceding chapter.

The motives for the cutting of the Gordian knot of the Czecho-Sudeten relationship were not simply those of more or less just retribution, logical in the relation between victors and vanquished, but also involved the perceived need to prevent any possible further conflicts that might arise from a coexistence so deeply compromised. The whole of Europe was swept by a huge wave of repugnance and hatred for everything German and all the steps taken on the territory of liberated Czechoslovakia have to be seen in this widely shared European context. If there was a difference between the policy of transfer pursued by the Western allies and the policy of expulsion and depopulation pushed through by the Czechoslovak government and resistance movements, it was nonetheless predicated on the fact that the Allies saw no prospects for the success of any experiment in cohabitation between Germans and Czechs in the restored Czechoslovak state.[130]

For example, in the Prague Lucerna Palace on the 18th of May 1945 the leader of the Czechoslovak National Socialist Party [translator's note: not a fascist party despite the name] P. Drtina made an emotive speech which opened the floodgates to the spontaneous expulsion of the German population: "What is and must be our first task in laying the foundation for a new life is to cleanse the republic, all of it and wholly, of Germans. This is the order of the day for each one of us, this is the historical task of our generation... Our new repub-

---

[129] I am deliberately referring to the difference between the two alternative terms used in period documents and Allied decisions – terms that express different interpretations of the action – transfer/expulsion/*Vertreibung*.

[130] *Konfliktní společenství, katastrofa, uvolnění.* 28. The Potsdam summit considered the problem of the transfer from the ČSR in its fifth and ninth sessions. On the 25th of July it prompted the following exchange: "Eden: We have received a report from Dr. Beneš who wishes us to discuss the transfer of the Germans from Czechoslovakia. Might the foreign ministers consider this question? Stalin: My impression is that the transfer has already taken place. Churchill: We do not think a great many Germans have left, so we are still facing a problem that needs to be resolved. Stalin: Please. Churchill: Let the foreign ministers take up this question and identify the facts. Stalin: Good. Truman: I agree." Šnejdárek, A. *Druhá světová válka v dokumentech a fotografiích.* 429.

lic cannot be built otherwise than as a purely national state… But in order to achieve this goal, we must make a start on the expulsion of the Germans from our lands right away, this moment, using all means, and we must not stop or hesitate at anything."[131] He was expressing the predominant sentiments of most of the population, and isolated voices demanding a less radical approach mostly fell silent in the euphoric atmosphere of the restored republic.[132] Nonetheless, it was clear that President Beneš and other politicians were aware of the need to keep the emotional calls for revenge under control. In addition to humanitarian considerations, certain critical reactions apparent in Western public opinion played a role here. President Beneš responded to the situation with a speech on the 14th of October 1945 in Mělník, in which he declared that the only solution left was the "departure of the Germans from our country", but at the same time he insisted that "our whole procedure in the matter of their transfer to the Reich must be humane, decent, correct, morally justified, precisely planned and carried out on the basis of firm agreement with our allies. Our nation must not in any way taint its democratic and humane reputation even here. All subordinate organs that violate this principle will be very resolutely called to account."[133] There continued to be universal agreement on the basic questions, i.e. above all on attitude to the transfer and in its justifications, but behind the scenes there were signs of party political rivalry and some emerging differences of opinion.[134]

---

[131] Biman, S. – Cílek, R. 1989. *Poslední mrtví, první živí* [The Last Dead, the First Living]. Ústí n. L.: Severočeské nakladatelství. 101. The National Socialist Party was among the most zealous supporters of an uncompromising solution.

[132] For example, in October 1945 J. Macek wrote in the journal *Naše doba*: "The ethnically mixed character of the of the Czechoslovak Republic used to give our democracy a special quality… Regard for other ethnic stratas of the population moderated Czechoslovak nationalism, reduced political passion and was a spur to political good sense. The nation problem was a constant reminder in our internal policy. We shall be stripped of this reminder." Staněk, T. 1991. *Odsun Němců z Československa 1945–1947* [The Transfer of the Germans from Czechoslovakia 1945–1947]. Prague: Academia/Naše vojsko. 25.

[133] Ibidem. 123–124.

[134] The press of the period, however, provides some evidence of how quickly acute rage against the Sudeten Germans and their leaders subsided. The autumn of 1946 saw the start of the trial of H. Krebs and other parliamentary deputies of Henlein's Sudeten German Party (only 12 of the 70 deputies and senators indicted were present – five had left in the transfer and the others were evidently on the run). The state prosecutor Dr. J. Drábek wrote a long article about the trial, which took place in an empty court "with a complete lack of interest on the part of the public." Most of the daily papers devoted only a few lines in back pages to the course and outcome of the trial. The concluding words of the former extreme Nazi Krebs resounded through an empty room where a few journalists and guards dozed. "This is the last speech that a former German deputy will make before the Czechoslovak public and the high court. We stand today as defendants before you and you are our judges. With this period ends a whole millenium of a shared, difficult but also great historical epoch. The Czech nation will now finally live by itself in its own nation state, which has become a real nation state not just in name but in reality… Let us hope that the parting of the ways between Germans and Czechs will bring peace to both." The author concludes, "It is a pity, a tremendous pity, that the nation has learned almost nothing about all this." Drábek, J. "Glosy k procesu s henleinovskými poslanci a senátory". 729.

308 | CZECHS AND GERMANS 1848–2004

Given the wave of post-war anti-German feeling, there were justified fears for the fate of any German population living on the territory of a state that had been under German occupation during the war. This applied doubly to the community of Sudeten Germans, many of whom had taken an active part in the organs of the occupation authorities on the territory of the Protectorate of Bohemia and Moravia.[135] It was also from the ranks of Sudeten Germans that many fanatically devoted and efficient government officials and members of the security apparatus of the "model" Sudetenland Reichsgau had been recruited.[136] It could therefore be expected that with the defeat of Nazism there would be an explosion of spontaneous desire for revenge (see e.g. the statements of Churchill in 1943 cited in the preceding chapter). Towards the end of the war, experts generally agreed in anticipating a cruel revenge on the part of the victors. Most Germans regarded collective penance after the defeat as inevitable.[137]

It was clear that the solution of the German problem would be the cornerstone of the future of the European continent. From the 17th of July to the 2nd of August 1945, the leaders of the victorious anti-Hitler coalition (The USSR, Great Britain and the USA) met in Potsdam for a tripartite conference to agree on the principles of the future European order. Its closing document included the formulation, "The allied armies have completed the occupation of all Germany and the German people has started to atone for the terrible crimes that they committed under the leadership of men who in the times of their successes they (the people) openly approved and blindly obeyed... The conference has reached this agreement on the transfer of Germans from Poland, Czechoslovakia and Hungary: the three governments have studied this question in all its aspects and recognised that the German population or its components that remain in Poland, Czechoslovakia and Hungary, will have to be transferred

---

[135]   Luža, R. *The Transfer of the Sudeten Germans*. 195 ff. On their role in aryanisation and the running of local government, commerce and industry see Grant Duff, S. 1942. *A German Protectorate. The Czechs under Nazi Rule*. London. 196. *Survey of International Affairs 1939–1946. Hitler's Europe*. 1954. Toynbee, A. – Toynbee, V. M. (eds.). London. 589. See also the chapter by E. Wiskemann.

[136]   "October 1938, for Czechs tragic, was supremely a month of celebrations, and the intensity of these was not weakened by the anti-Jewish and anti-Czech actions that were underway, not to mention the pitiless "settling of scores" with the Germans' own social democrats or communists. The informing and spying activities of the local fanatics, on the basis of which there were extensive arrests of political opponents in the first days after annexation to the Reich, is a sad chapter in Sudeten German history." Míšková, A. "Nadšení i rozčarování ve jménu vůdce-osvoboditele" [Enthusiasm and Disillusion in the Name of the Fuhrer/Liberator], in Zimmermann, V. *Sudetští Němci v nacistickém státě*. 572–573.

[137]   Kershaw, I. 1987. *The Hitler Myth. Image and Reality in the Third Reich*. Oxford University Press. Chapter VIII. See also Hon, J. – Šitler, J. 1996. "Trestněprávní důsledky událostí v období německé nacistické okupace Československa a v době těsně po jejím skončení a jejich řešení" [Criminal-law consequences of events in the period of German Nazi occupation of Czechoslovakia and and immediately therafter and the way these were handled], in *Studie o sudetoněmecké otázce* [Studies on the Sudeten German Question]. 1996. Kural, V. (ed.). Prague: Ústav mezinárodních vztahů. 165–179.

to Germany. We are at one in agreeing that any kind of transfer must be conducted in an orderly and humane way."[138]

If after 1989 the Federation of Expellees and Sudeten German Homeland Association/Sudetendeutsche Landsmannschaft have repeatedly raised the question of the legitimacy of the expulsion processes by which 12 million ethnic Germans were transferred from Central and Eastern Europe to the territory of Germany, it is appropriate to draw attention to the sentiments of the time. These formed the views of the Allied powers on the solution to the situation, leading them to accept a *punitive principle* which related directly to the question of the collective guilt of the German people for the crimes of Nazism. This was well formulated by the outstanding expert on the problem, Joseph Schechtman, whose book *European Population Transfers 1939–1945* first came out in the United States in 1946. It reflects the views of the time on population transfers:

"Undoubtedly the most serious issue raised by the plan for exchange of population is its forced implementation. Yet given that this problem relates to individual rights, and not to the procedures themselves, it is a matter of political philosophy. What is certain is that considerations of this nature have very little relevance to the future location of German minorities, because theirs is the fate of a defeated people."[139]

Schechtman nevertheless himself provides an example of the shift in views that occurred in Western democracies as the events of the Second World War receded into the past, to be succeeded by the bipolarity of the Cold War era. In 1962 Schechtman was to write the following on the problem of the transfer:

"In the end, even if the majority of the members of an ethnic group are considered guilty of specific wrongdoings, the group as a whole cannot be morally or legally accused and punished for the actions of its members. The idea forming the basis of the decision on forced transfer of a whole popula-

---

[138] Extracts from the wording of heads III and XIII. "Zpráva o třístranné konferenci v Berlíně" [Reports on the tripartite conference in Berlin]. *Právní aspekty odsunu sudetských Němců* [Legal Aspects of the Transfer of the Sudeten Germans]. (Collection of documents.) 1995. Matějka, D. (ed.). Prague: Ústav mezinárodních vztahů. 73, 80. The English text of the key formulation of Head XIII: "The conference reached the following agreement on the removal of Germans from Poland, Czechoslovakia, and Hungary: The three Governments, having considered the question in all aspects, recognize that the transfer to Germany of German populations, or elements thereof, remaining in Poland, Czechoslovakia, and Hungary will have to be undertaken. They agree that any transfers that take place should be effected in an orderly and humane manner."

[139] Schechtman, J. B. *European Population Transfers.* 473. The concept of solving ethnic problems by transfer inevitably had opponents as well as supporters, and Luža offers a list of both. According to his classification supporters included Bernard Lavergne, William C. Bullitt, Leopold C. Klausner, Harold Butler, Warren S. Thompson, Nicolas Politis, Bernard Newman, Jacob Robinson, Herbert Hoover, Hugh Gibson, Nansen and Venizelos. Opponents included Stephen P. Ladas, Stélio Séfériadès, David Thompson and Erich Hula. Luža, R. *The Transfer of the Sudeten Germans.* 250.

tion thus has nothing to do with guilt and punishment or even with justice. The forced transfer of population is essentially a preventive not a retributive measure." This measure, according to Schechtman, "may be used if an ethnic group as a whole takes a radical attitude that threatens the long-term existence of the state of which it is a part. The repression of such group attitudes of disloyalty cannot solve the basis of the problem in a situation where by its mentality of disagreement and resistance such a group displays an incompatibility with the state formation, whose survival and security it systematically menaces. In that case there is no alternative to complete transfer of the disloyal population to a nationally kindred state to which they show loyalty in the long term."[140]

This assessment applied in full measure to the situation of the restored Czechoslovakia, where in fact both sides had felt after Munich that they would now never be able to be citizens of the same common state.[141]

If today we are seeing attempts retrospectively to challenge and reassess the Allied decisions as well as Beneš's approach to the transfers of German population, it is legitimate to illustrate the thinking of the time about guilt and punishment by citing the views of C. G. Jung. In an essay published immediately after the end of the Second World War he wrote that, "Just as Europe must render account to the the world, so must Germany render account to Europe. Just as a European cannot excuse himself to the Indians on the grounds that Germany is nothing to do with him and doesn't lie in Europe, or that he knows nothing about Germany, so a German cannot shake off his guilt before a European by pretending ignorance. In doing so he just compounds his collective guilt with the sin of ignorance. Psychological collective guilt is a tragic curse: it affects everyone, the just and the unjust, who were somehow present close to the place where the horror took place... If the German intends to get on with Europe, he should be aware that he stands before Europe as a culprit. As a German he betrayed European culture and its values; he brought such shame on his European family that a man must blush to be called a European; he robbed, attacked, persecuted and killed his European brothers. The German cannot

---

[140] Schechtman, J. B. *Postwar Population Transfers in Europe:1945–1955.* In his outstanding study J. Schechtman comments thus on potential alternative solutions to the Czech-Sudeten-German dispute: "The twenty years between the wars as well as five years of war have empirically established the utter impossibility of peaceful co-habitation of a German majority in the Sudetenland and a Czecho-Slovak majority in the rest of the state, within the common framework of one state. The only conceivable alternatives were thus Munich or transfer. The Munich solution had been applied by the Axis: the Axis and all its work were overthrown by the victorious Allies. Hence, only transfer remained... This is not a punitive measure, but a prophylactic one: a matter of highest state expedience, not of retribution." Ibidem. 364–367.

[141] Wiskemann, E. *Germany's Eastern Neighbours.* 65.

expect Europe to rise to the "refinements" of investigating in each case whether the criminal was named Müller or Meier."[142]

It was similar thinking on the guilt of Germany for unleashing the war that led to the decisions of the Potsdam Conference, and it was in the same spirit that the soldiers and politicians of the Czechoslovak resistance took the decision on the future destiny of the Sudeten Germans. But as a consequence of the Cold War, the collapse of the anti-Hitler coalition and the rapid integration of the Western occupied zones of Germany into the Euro-Atlantic alliance, this way of seeing the matter was sidelined. As early as April 1949 the Governor of the US Occupation zone in Germany, General Lucius Clay, issued a directive halting the denazification process. Not just this decision, but also the bipolar division of Europe into East and West, shifted the Czech-Sudeten dispute into the ideological co-ordinates of the Cold War, so modifying or entirely reversing judgments of some of the steps that had been taken before.[143] We shall look at this in more detail, however, in the next chapter.

There is no doubt that the consequences of the need to face up to a common enemy, the Soviet Union and its satellites, soon created a sense of the solidarity of the West (in Western European countries the intensity of wartime resentment against the Germany diminished), which Czech society, on the basis of its different historical experiences, did not get the chance to share. This is why the post-1989 debate on the transfer of the Sudeten Germans, its causes and consequences, is so complicated and still has the power to cause ethnic tension projected into Czech-German relations that otherwise show a positive dynamic.

We have already touched on the general problems of population transfers several times above. The "transfer" (in the German vocabulary the "expulsion") of the German-speaking inhabitants of Czechoslovakia represented a historical breaking point, a drastic outcome to the decades of disputes between the two nations of the Bohemian Lands. Certainly, the question of whether another solution less dramatic than complete divorce might have been possible is worth posing. Certainly, a more moderate solution can be imagined hypothetically, in a situation in which moderate approaches had prevailed on both sides. This situation did not arise, however, and given the universally known characteristics of Nazism, we may consider the idea irrelevant to an understanding of the

---

[142] Jung, C. G. "After the Catastrophe" (first published in *Neue Schweizer Rundschau*. Neue Folge 13/2, Zürich. 1945).

[143] As a brief postscript to the subject of the use of the instrument of population transfer we might mention that the hitherto largest and most dramatic exchange of population occurred at the beginning of the Cold War era in 1949 between India and Pakistan at the end of the bloody Kashmir conflict – and under the supervision of the UN.

real situation. The arguments (as described above) that finally issued in the solution by transfer mounted up in the course of the war. Since I regard the most important factor in the decision to expel the German minorities from Central and Eastern Europe to have been the attitude of the Western Allies, especially British policy, I have devoted greater attention to their decision-making in preceding chapters. The position of the home resistance was clear from the beginning of the war.

I am leaving aside the question of the extent to which the transfers opened the way to victory of communism in the whole territory of Central Europe, as a number of authors have claimed, including for example W. Jaksch. However evident it is that Stalin brilliantly politically exploited the removal of the Germans, I tend to the view that he would have pushed through his plans for expansion even without the transfers.[144]

Symptomatic of the impossibility of further coexistence between Czechs and Germans were the post-war fates of German antifascists and democrats living for the most part in the border areas of the former Sudetenland. According to some reports from the beginning of 1946, almost 80,000 applications for the retention or return of Czechoslovak state citizenship were submitted in Czechoslovakia.[145] The relevant persons were mostly pre-war members of the Communist Party of Czechoslovakia and then members of the DSAP/German Social Democratic Party. Some of them (at start 1946 it was about 30,000 antifascists with families) were prepared to leave for the Soviet Occupation Sector of Germany.

On the basis of a resolution of the government of the CSR in February 1946, the secretariats of the CPCz and Czech Social Democrats appointed commissioners for German antifascists in individual districts. In many cases the applications for the return of citizenship were dealt with in lukewarm and desultory fashion, one reason being the widespread opinion that the German anti-fascists, especially from the ranks of the pre-war communists, had a duty to con-

---

[144] International law recognises the institution of resettlement (transfer) of part of the population of one state to the territory of another state. In resettlement (transfer) there is a mass change of state citizenship associated with transfer and without the option of choice. The loss of existing state citizenship and obligation to leave state territory are independent of the will of individuals. For this reason the instrument is employed only in exceptional cases, if there are genuinely serious reasons – of a security, ethnic, religious or other nature. Potočný, M. "Mezinárodní právo a transfer Němců z Československa" [International Law and the Transfer of the Germans out of Czechoslovakia], in *Právní aspekty odsunu sudetských Němců*. 14.

[145] According to draft guidelines of the Ministry of Interior of the 17th of January 1946, transfer (departure from the republic) should be permitted to former members of the CPCz and German Social Democratic Party in in the CSR, who fulfilled all the conditions of the so-called antifascist paragraph of constitutional decree no. 33/1945. The lists of applicants for transfer should be drawn up by secretariats of the CPCz and Czechoslovak Social Democratic Party in cooperation with antifascist committees. Antifascists, whose non-moveable property was not subject to confiscation, would designate trustees to represent their interests until the final resolution of claims to compensation. Staněk, T. *Odsun Němců z Československa*. 274–275.

tribute to the democratic transformation of Germany. Another reason was the perception of the Czech public that there had been very few real German antifascists who fought for the republic and that the behaviour of the others had not been such as to suggest that the Czechoslovak state would have any need for them.

Quite frequently there were reports in the press that antifascist Germans were helping the other Germans, taking over their property to avoid its confiscation, abusing concessions etc. The screening proceedings accompanying the checking of already issued Model B certificates (a condition for obtaining the status and advantages of an antifascist) were tightened up, and sometimes these certificates were cancelled and concessions suspended. The pressure for the German antifascists to emigrate mounted and it was no surprise that the number of German antifascists who preferred to do so kept on rising. The depth of the quarrel between the two nations became fully evident and bitterness grew, especially among the real German democrats, one of whom wrote. "I admit we present a very difficult problem. To allow exceptions from the concept of collective guilt would be too objective... But a slap from a beloved person always hurts more than a punch from an enemy."[146] As the government commissioner for the transfer J. Kučera noted, antifascists felt that they would be better off leaving the republic. According to the final report of the Ministry of Interior on the implementation of the transfer, by the 1st of December 1946 a total of 94, 614 antifascists had left Czechoslovakia (although there are some slightly divergent data), of whom 53,187 went to the American and 42,989 to the Soviet zone of occupation.[147] The fates and decisions of those Bohemian Germans who had the option of staying in the restored republic thus to some extent answer the question of whether further co-existence was a realistic alternative.

The post-war transfers of German minorities affected Czechoslovakia, Poland, and partially Hungary and Yugoslavia. Several countries of West-Central and Western Europe got rid of their mainly small German minorities and also their much larger groups of German war colonists, civilian employees of the occupation authorities and refugees, without great formalities or special legislative changes immediately after liberation by the Allied armies. The phase of what was known as "wild" transfer was not just a Czech peculiarity. Some politicians, including Churchill, de Gaulle and Beneš, expected it and even reckoned with it. It had after all been evident even in the course of the war

---

[146] Staněk, T. *Odsun Němců z Československa*. 282. The journal *Dnešek* run by F. Peroutka offered regular information on the problem of the transfer, the border areas and the German question in general. It also provided a platform for discussion where minority opinions could be voiced as well.

[147] Ibidem. 283.

that the terror and atrocities of the occupation regimes had caused a build-up of such hatred and negative energy in societies that it would be difficult to prevent revenge and illegality at the start. There was a risk that the complicated investigation of the degree of guilt and collaboration in the case of specific individuals or whole groups would lead the search for justice into a blind alley. Furthermore, the formal and real transfer of power on the liberated territories took a certain amount of time, which was exploited by groups of self-appointed "judges", people who needed an alibi for the new situation fast, and antisocial elements using the "interregnum" for self enrichment at the expense of a German ethnic group with no remaining rights.

The several weeks of "wild" transfer in some areas of the Czech borderland are most certainly not among the episodes in modern Czech history in which Czechs can take any pride.[148] There is no doubt that sympathy with the defeated was much diminished by Nazi brutalities that had lowered the "threshhold of sensitivity" among those who had suffered under the occupation. This was not a phenomenon limited to Czech treatment of Germans. There are many well-known cases in which the commanders of Allied forces had great difficulty controlling the emotional reactions of their soldiers when they liberated concentration camps.[149] Can we categorically condemn the behaviour of the Czechs (if it is even possible to generalise about Czechs) when as late as the 2nd of May 1945 Czech prisoners were still being executed in the Small Fortress in Terezín, SS units were executing women and children in the Prague Pankrác district in efforts to suppress the Prague Uprising, and mass executions were being carried out in Western Bohemia (and elsewhere in the Czech Lands)[150], when the death transports from the concentration camps were fresh in memory, not to mention

---

[148] Reference is made in particular to the executions of German inhabitants in Postoloprty, the expulsion of Germans from Brno (they were marched and harried all the way to the Austrian frontier), the massacre of Carpathian Germans near Přerov and other incidents. Many of these cases were investigated shortly afterwards and accusations brought. In the hectic postwar atmosphere full of intrigues, justice also became the subject of the political infighting and struggle for power that culminated in the communist putsch of February 1948. Nonetheless, some perpetrators were charged and convicted, including for example the mass murderer K. Pazúr sentenced to twenty years. For detailed information on the theme of the inhumane treatment of German expellees in the first weeks of peace in areas of the Czech borderlands see Staněk, T. 1996. *Perzekuce 1945* [Persecution 1945]. Prague: ISE. Staněk, T. 1996. *Tábory v českých zemích 1945–1948* [Camps in the Czech Lands 1945–1948]. Ostrava: Tilia.

[149] One example was the reaction of American soldiers at the liberation of Dachau, or the British who opened the gates of Bergen-Belsen. In some cases they immediately shot anyone in German uniform: "In many instances German troops taken prisoner in or near the concentration camps were killed on the spot by Allied troops and former inmates unable to contain their rage." Hastings, M. – Stevens, G. 1985. *Victory in Europe*. London: Weidenfeld and Nicholson. 166.

[150] The documentation of the brutal mass killings at the end of the calvary of the death marches on Czech territory was entrusted to the National Land Committee in Prague's Exhumation Commission composed of medical and police experts. The results of the investigation were published: Anděl, J. – Bautz, R. – Filip, O. – Knobloch, E. 1947. *Hromadné hroby v Čechách* [Mass Graves in Bohemia]. Prague: Ministerstvo informací.

the six years of terror exercised by the occupation regime in the Protectorate of Bohemia and Moravia, in which tens of thousands of Czech patriots were murdered and the greater part of the Jewish population of the Czech lands was exterminated?[151]

All the liberated territories of Europe were settling accounts with the Nazi era. In Denmark, Norway and the Netherlands the death penalty was reintroduced. 80,000 people were tried by the Danish courts, and 90,000 by the Norwegian courts, a third of these losing their civic rights. In the Netherlands 200,000 people were tried and 60,000 were stripped of their civil rights and had their property confiscated; special courts brought in 14,562 verdicts and courts of honour 49,920 verdicts; 200 people were sentenced to death and 36 were executed. In Belgium the treatment of those suspected of collaboration was similarly harsh: 448,160 people were investigated, 87,000 tried and 64,000 found guilty.

At the end of the 1950s most of those imprisoned were released but had difficulty regaining their civic rights. The settling of accounts with traitors and collaborators was vigorously pursued, as statistics show. Out of every 100,000 inhabitants of France 94 collaborators were condemned, in Belgium 596 out of the same number and in Norway 633.[152] It is only in recent years that historians and journalists have been addressing the question of whether mass murders were committed in the course of the liberation or immediately thereafter, or whether these are only rumours. In Denmark, for example, there is on ongoing debate on whether thousands of Germans were shot after the liberation.[153]

The end of the war was complicated in France, where to this day there are no reliable and precise figures on the scale of repression. Immediately after the war, in the interregnum period when the new state power had not yet been established, spontaneous "people's courts" were held with the aim of dispensing justice even of an arbitrary kind. The number of victims in the first weeks after liberation is the subject of guesses but definitely in the order of thousands (10,000 to 100,000 and more).

---

[151] Czech solidarity with the persecuted Jews was also an expression of Czech resistance to the occupying power as such. The SS security service was well aware of this and often commented in their reports, "The Czech has so far refused to understand the Jewish problem. With the exception of members of certain rightwing opposition groups the Czech has a friendly attitude to Jews, even if often this is not a matter of goodwill so much as for political reasons. Our enemy is his friend and our measures against the Jews seem to the Czech to be a foreshadowing of our future treatment of Czechs." Groscurth, H. 1970. *Tagebücher eines Abwehroffiziers 1938–1940*. Stuttgart: H. Krausnick/H. C. Deutsch. 166–167. Cited from Kárný, M. *Konečné řešení*. 11. "The Protectorate was the only territory under Nazi influence which did not promulgate anti-Jewish laws." After the repeated refusal to do so by the Protectorate government the Reichsprotector von Neurath had to impose the Nuremberg Laws. Feierabend, L. K. 1994. *Politické vzpomínky I* [Political Memoirs 1]. Brno: Atlantis. 179.

[152] Jiřík, V. 2000. *Nedaleko od Norimberku* [Not Far from Nuremberg]. Cheb: Svět křídel. 9.

[153] Pešek, J. "20. století – doba nucených migrací, vyhnání a transferů". 47.

Overall 130,000 people were tried by courts of one kind or another. The numbers arrested are also unreliable. The official statistics of 80,000 are evidently a very low estimate. French post-war justice brought in 7037 sentences of death, of which 4397 were in absence and 791 were carried out.[154]

Under the recent impression of war events, demands for harsh retribution against Germany were voiced throughout Europe. For example, the Netherlands repeatedly demanded the annexation of part of what is today the Rhineland-Westphalia, as large as a third of the Netherlands itself, as territorial compensation for the polder land flooded by the wehrmacht with sea water in the course of military actions.[155] The Dutch demands envisaged the transfer of the population of this territory to deep within Germany. These ambitious demands were opposed by both the American occupation authorities and the Dutch bishops. All the same, the dispute ended only in 1948 with the onset of the Cold War, which also brought denazification to a halt in Germany itself. In the new situation of confrontation with the East, Germany rapidly changed into a valuable ally and this meant that the war experience of the countries of Western Europe was reconfigured (although by no means forgotten).

There is no doubt that any expulsion and forced transfer is at odds with current ideas of fundamental human rights, but an understanding of context is essential. The eventual adoption of the plan ending the conflictual coexistence with Germans in the CSR once and for all was motivated by experience with the policy of the Sudeten German Party and with the repressive German occupation policies. Over half a century ago, the transfer was one of the repercussions of a war provoked by the German political leadership, and the consequence of resettlement actions and the liquidation of whole groups of population carried out by that leadership.[156]

Following military victory the Allied powers set up occupation zones, dividing the defeated Germany into four parts that became the basis of the two states later created on German territory. The Federal Republic of Germany was created from the so-called *Tri-zone* (occupation zones of the USA, Great Britain and France), to which full sovereignty was restored in 1954, and the German Democratic Republic was established in September 1955 on the territory of the

---

[154] "It is easy to take a cynical view of the [French] Resistance: so many thousands of new defenders hurried to join it in July and August 1944 after having done nothing in the course of the dismal, dangerous years of the occupation, so many of them vied with each other over the chance to execute their fellow countryman who had collaborated, to torture German prisoners or shave the heads of women who had been seen too often in the close proximity of German soldiers." Hastings, M. – Stevens, G. *Victory in Europe*. 60. For detail on the French retribution actions see Rousso, H. L. "L'Épuration. Die politische Säuberung in Frankreich", in *Politische Säuberung in Europe. Die Abrechnung mit Faschismus und Kollaboration nach dem Zweiten Weltkrieg*. 1991. Henke, K.-D. – Woller, H. (eds.). München. 216–219.

[155] Pešek, J. "20. století – doba nucených migrací, vyhnání a transferů". 47.

[156] "Vyhnání a vysídlení Němců", in *Konfliktní společenství, katastrofa, uvolnění*. 29.

Soviet occupation zone. At the turn of 1947–48 it was becoming ever clearer that Europe was being divided by a descending Iron Curtain – the expression coined by Winston Churchill in a famous speech at Fulton University in the USA.

Communist governments were sooner or later installed in all the countries of Eastern and South-Eastern Europe that now found themselves in the Soviet sphere of influence. In Czechoslovakia this occurred in February 1948 when the CPCz seized power. The military balance of power now rested on the deterrent effect of the nuclear weapons held by both sides in the East-West conflict. This state of neither peace nor war acquired the name Cold War and in subsequent years the world was several times to find itself on the brink of armed conflict. A divided Germany and above all a divided Berlin (the new conflict in concentrated form) became the symbol of a newly divided world.

Cutting the Gordian Knot

The Czechoslovak government was informed of the Allied decision to transfer the Sudeten Germans out of Czechoslovakia, i.e. in this matter it did not have to decide on the principle, but only on the way in which the decision of the three great powers would be implemented.[157] This is incidentally why there exists no presidential decree ordering the transfer of the Germans out of Czechoslovak territory. This act was carried out on the basis of a multilateral agreement. Any kind of challenge to the legitimacy of this act therefore implies challenge to the legitimacy of the actions and policy of the victorious great powers in relation to the end of a war for which the responsibility (as these great powers explicitly formulated it) lay with the German people as well as their leaders.[158]

The status of the decrees of the president of the republic as normative acts promulgated by the president in collaboration with the Czechoslovak government in the years 1940–1945 is a matter that relates above all to both Czechoslovak constitutional and political development, and to international legal

---

[157] The Czechoslovak government accepted the decision of the great powers in a letter from the Foreign Ministry of the CSR (V. Clementis) to the British ambassador in Prague P. Nichols of 16ᵗʰ of August 1945. The last sentence of the letter reads, "If the three Allied great powers have agreed that the transfer should be conducted in an orderly and humane way, they have thereby only added emphasis to the policy that the Czechoslovak government has been putting into practice from the beginning." *Právní aspekty odsunu sudetských Němců*. 1996 (2ⁿᵈ enlarged edition). Matějka, D. (ed.). Prague: Ústav mezinárodních vztahů. 107.

[158] Šedivý, J. "Multilaterální aspekt problému německé menšiny na našem území v r. 1945" [The multilateral aspect of the problem of the German minority on our territory in 1945], in *Právní aspekty odsunu sudetských Němců*. 7.

development after Munich in 1938. The Munich Agreement, to which Czecho-slovakia was not a party, just like the later "agreement" on the incorporation of the "remnant of the Czecho-Slovak Republic" into the then Greater German Reich, and the creation of the Protectorate of Bohemia and Moravia, was never constitutionally approved on the Czechoslovak side. The legal continuity of the Czechoslovak Republic in its pre-Munich borders was recognised by many states in the course of the war, and it was on this basis that the republic was restored in practice in 1945.[159]

The crucial aspect of the whole legal construction of the theory of continuity was the continuity of Beneš's presidential function, which was the subject of debate in the London exile and is still the subject of academic and political disputes today. J. Kuklík takes the view that "today its original version can be accepted without reservation only with considerable difficulties." He considers the compromise conception that best corresponds to the real historical facts to be the formulation proposed by professor of constitutional law V. Pavlíček, which regards Beneš's abdication as valid, but judges that the president took up his position again in 1940 after British recognition.[160]

From the theory of the legal continuity of the CSR Beneš derived the legal basis for the provisional state organisation in Great Britain, consisting of the President of the Republic, the government and the State Council (an organ of consultation and supervision, "a sort of provisional parliament"). The government and State Council appointed the president of the republic. Later a Legal

---

[159] Mikule, V. "Dekrety prezidenta republiky a nynější právo" [The Decrees of the President of the Republic and Current Law], in *Právní aspekty odsunu sudetských Němců*. 57. There is a large body of academic literature on this theme dealing with all aspects and connections both in domestic and international context. J. Kuklík describes the very detailed debate on questions of the legal continuity of the CSR that took place in the government in exile and other exile groups. See e.g. K. B. Palkovský's polemic with H. Ripka (*Munich Before and After*). Palkovský (see *Londýnské epištoly* [London Epistles]. 1946. Prague: V. Petr) declared that in Czechoslovakia a constitutional-legal state *ex lex* occurred as of the 21st of September 1938 at 1:00 p.m. when the government submitted to the British-French ultimatum without a constitutional assembly being able to express a view of the matter. In exile, the Society of Czechoslovak Advocates Abroad published E. Schwelb's *Obnovení právního pořádku* [The Restoration of a Legal Order]. 1945. London. The problem of the position of the head of state was examined by E. Táborský, P. Körbel and others. Contemporary studies reacting to the current polemic challenging the legal aspects of the transfer of the Sudeten Germans include the following: Kuklík, J. 2002. *Mýty a realita takzvaných Benešových dekretů* [Myths and Reality of the Beneš Decrees]. Prague: Linde. Pavlíček, V. 2002. *O české státnosti, díl 1. Český stát a Němci* [On Czech Statehood. Vol. 1. The Czech State and the Germans]. Prague: Karolinum. Dejmek, J. – Kuklík, J. – Němeček, J. 1999. *Kauza tzv. Benešovy dekrety. Historické kořeny a souvislosti* [Controversy: The So-called Beneš Decrees. Historical roots and contexts]. Prague: Historický ústav AV ČR. *Právní aspekty odsunu sudetských Němců. Rozumět dějinám* (particularly chapter VII.). Jech, K. – Kaplan, K. 1995. *Dekrety prezidenta republiky 1+2* [The Decrees of the President of the Republic]. (Documents). Vols. 1 and 2. Brno: Doplněk. A number of works by leading Czech historians whose works are cited in the context of this work likewise deal with this legal side of the argument. One example of a negative German view of the decrees is to be found in Blumenwitz, D. "Benešovy dekrety z roku 1945 z hlediska mezinárodního práva".

[160] Kuklík, J. *Mýty a realita takzvaných Benešových dekretů*. 29. Jech, K. – Kaplan, K. *Dekrety prezidenta republiky 1940–1945*. Vol. 1.

Council[161] was set up, temporarily replacing the Administrative Court, and the powers of the Supreme Audit Office were revived. In July 1940 the provisional Czechoslovak government was recognised by Great Britain, where the government was based together with other governments in exile from occupied Europe.

In view of the state of legislative emergency (the phrase defined the state in which the government was temporarily unable to carry out the powers entrusted to it on state territory illegally occupied by Germany), in October 1940 the president issued a constitutional decree stipulating *inter alia* that, "Regulations by which laws are altered, abolished or newly promulgated will be promulgated for the period of validity of the provisional state constitution in essential cases by the president of the republic on the proposal of the government, in the form of decrees that will be co-signed by the chairman of the government/prime minister or members of the government entrusted with their implementation." This solution was a reaction to a situation in which the functioning of a democratic state had been made absolutely impossible by violence.[162]

Challenges today to the legitimacy of law-making by decree, which brand it a form of arbitrary rule by Beneš, do not correspond to the reality. As V. Mikule argues, it was clear that this was a modification forced on the exiled government in an extraordinary situation that the Constitution of the Republic could simply not have predicted. According to the Constitutional Decree of the 3rd of August 1944, all decrees were subject to a process of approval by the appropriate functionaries, ratification of which was confirmed in the form of the constitutional law passed by the Provisional National Assembly on the 28th of April 1946 (no. 57/1945 Coll.) and by the fact that the decrees were from the outset regarded as law, and constitutional decrees as constitutional law. The Decrees of the President of the Republic were tightly bound to the establishment and functioning of the Provisional State Constitution of the CSR in exile and so cannot be challenged without calling into question the restoration of Czecho-

---

[161] The Legal Council was used by the president and government to draw up expert evaluations of drafts of postwar legislation, and so also the draft presidential decrees. Members of the Legal Council also took part in drawing up a number of key decrees as experts on the inter-ministerial committes or as individuals for example in the framework of the activities of the Society of Czechoslovak Advocates in exile. The idea suggested in current attacks on Beneš that he was the only creator and originator of the decrees is therefore entirely false and misleading. Preparation of the decrees involved a plurality of opinions. For example E. Schwelb right at the beginning of 1945 produced a detailed commentary on the constitutional decree for the restoration of a legal order, and this became an important aid to interpretation even though Schwelb himself declared that his opinions, just like the final wording of the constitutional decree, differed from the original evaluation of the Legal Council. In addition to this, expert committees contributed to the drawing up of the decrees. Kuklík, J. *Mýty a realita takzvaných Benešových dekretů.* 79.

[162] Mikule, V. "Dekrety prezidenta republiky a nynější právo". 57.

slovakia in its pre-Munich borders. The range of subjects covered by the decrees is unusually wide and in fact includes all key aspects of the life of postwar Czechoslovakia, including the nationalisation of heavy industry, the mines and banks, but here we are concerned only with the decrees relating to the fate of the German minority in the CSR.

The assent to the demand for the transfer of the Sudeten Germans (which was supposed to start only after the Allied Control Council in Berlin had debated and stipulated concrete organisational measures) given by leaders of the victorious coalition, provided the Czechoslovak government with legal support for the expulsion of the Germans following the revocation of their citizenship on the basis of Presidential Decree no. 33/1945 on amendment of the Czechoslovak state citizenship of persons of German and Hungarian nationality, of the 2nd of October 1945.[163] The implementation of this decree was based on the theory that the Czechoslovak state citizenship of these persons had lasted throughout the war and that only by this decree did the CSR (retroactively) release them from this state bond.[164]

According to this decree, Czechoslovakia released from its state bond those people who "according to the regulations of the foreign occupation power had acquired German or Hungarian identity/citizenship. Germans who at the time of increased danger to the Republic had officially identified as Czech or those who had demonstrated "loyalty to the Czechoslovak Republic, had never transgressed against the Czech and Slovak peoples and had either actively participated in the fight for liberation or had suffered under Nazi or fascist terror" were permitted to retain Czechoslovak citizenship.[165]

Other decrees covered the confiscation of what was known as "enemy property". The initial measures in this respect were Decree no. 2/1945 of the 1st of February and then specifically Decree no. 5/1945 of the 3rd of June 1945, which

---

[163] Staněk, T. *Odsun Němců z Československa*. 99.

[164] Kuklík, J. "Odsun a jeho právní aspekty". 224. The decree on state citizenship related closely to the decision at Potsdam including in the fact that while it had been drawn up and approved by the government in June 1945, E. Beneš did not actually sign it until the 3rd of August 1945 with the date 2nd of August. Czechoslovak Law did not recognise either post-Munich legal development nor the legal state that came into existence after the 15th of March 1939 and on the basis of which most citizens of German nationality became Reich or Hungarian citizens, i.e. citizens of states with which Czechoslovakia was in a state of war from September 1938.

[165] Archive of documents – *Dekrety prezidenta republiky z let 1940–1945* [Decrees of the President of the Republic 1940–1945]. Prague: Ministerstvo zahraničních věcí CR. http://www.mzv.cz/archiv/dekrety.html. For more detail see in particular Jech, K. – Kaplan, K. *Dekrety prezidenta republiky 1+2*. For collected Czech legal interpretation see *Právní aspekty odsunu sudetských Němců*. The Sudeten German view is represented by the detailed expert opinion of Ermacora, F. 1991. *Rechtsgutachten über die Sudetendeutschen Fragen*. Wien/Innsbruck. Blumenwitz, D. "Benešovy dekrety z roku 1945 z hlediska mezinárodního práva". 86–96. O. Kimminich claims in his essay Kimminich, O. "Benešovy dekrety (Posouzení z mezinárodněprávního hlediska)" that "the comprehensiveness of the measures to destroy the basis of the life of Sudeten Germans as they are contained in the Beneš Decrees meet the material criteria of genocide".

stated that any kind of property transfers and any kind of dealing concerned with property rights, whether relating to property that was moveable or immoveable, public or private, was null and void if it had taken place after the 29th of September 1938 under the pressure of the occupation or national, racial and political persecution." This law therefore invalidated Nazi confiscation measures against the victims of Nazism. At the same time, national administration was imposed on the property of persons "unreliable in relation to the state." These and other measures were fully comparable with the legal denazification acts of other European states that had also been subjected to a regime of occupation by Nazi Germany.[166]

From the polemics produced from the side of Sudeten German organisations in the 1990s, the lay observer may well get the impression that the presidential decrees represent an approach unique and specific to the former CSR. In fact the Czechoslovak retributive laws differed little from those of other states that had been drawing up their norms in the conditions of exile, i.e. from the laws of the French, Belgian, Dutch, Luxemburg or Norwegian governments in exile. The Minister of Justice P. Drtina pointed out the international context and scope of the decrees in his report on retributive measures for the National Assembly submitted on the 29th of May 1947.[167]

For example, in France retributive measures were given legal form by the government ordinances (ordonances) signed by Charles de Gaulle as the prime minister of the provisional government and by ministers entrusted with their implementation – ordinances that originated in the period of the existence of the French Committee for National Liberation. As J. Kuklík writes, the Czechoslovak demand for the severe punishment of domestic collaborators and above all the protectorate government had a parallel particularly in the

---

[166] A complete catalogue of these norms was published in stages in three volumes in the years 1951–1955 by the Federal Ministry of Justice. See *Deutsches Vermögen im Ausland. 1951–1955*. 3 Bde. Bundesministerium für Justitz (Dokumentation). Bonn. For example, Ch. Tomuschat's relatively objective opinion on the presidential decrees which states, "Overall then it can be concluded that the relevant organs of the international community do not regard the confiscation measures of the Czechoslovak state to be a gross offence of the *international crime* type. The theory that compensation to the Sudeten Germans is the necessary condition for the admission of both countries into the European Union is therefore unsustainable." Tomuschat, Ch. "Die Benesch-Dekrete – ein Hinderniss für die Aufnahme der Tschechischen Republik in die Europäische Union?", in *Je již český právní řád v souladu s právem EU?* [Is the Czech legal order now in harmony with EU Law?]. 2002. (Collective of authors). Prague: Friedrich-Ebert Stiftung e.V. 70–98.

[167] For the purposes of their application, the presidential decrees governing Czechoslovak state citizenship, national administration, and the confiscation or nationalisation of property use terms relating to retributory actions which were already legally regulated by the London presidential decree on the punishment of Nazi criminals, traitors and their abettors and on special courts of the 3nd of February 1945 (Decree no. 16/1945 of 19th of June 1945) known also as the "Great Retributionary Decree". Issued together with this decree on the 19th of June 1945 was Decree no. 17/1945, which set up what was known as the National Court, and both were supplemented by the "Small Retributionary Decree" no. 138/1945 on the punishment of some offences against national honour. Kuklík, J. *Mýty a realita takzvaných Benešových dekretů*. 353.

French punishment of the leaders of the Vichy government.[168] France also had its equivalent of "wild transfer", characterised as "wild retribution", including the execution of people by "revolutionary tribunals".

For instance, in Montpelier the prefect, chief of police and eight other Vichy leaders were condemned to death. The question of French retributive actions was likewise linked to the process of the establishment of the new French regime and the "revolutionary" provisional committees taking power, among them the *Comité départemental de libération*. Nor was the state confiscation of property a phenomenon exclusive to Czechoslovakia. The umbrella French Trade Union the CGT exploited the connection between the punishment of collaborators and nationalisation, for example in the case of the factory of L. Renault, whose defence that he had collaborated only to protect his workers from being transported to Germany as forced labour was not accepted.[169]

The Norwegian government in exile in London drew up a decree on high treason of the 15th of December 1944 and new norms on special courts (decree of the 15th of February 1945). Interesting from the Czech point of view are the postwar Norwegian discussions on the constitutionality and legitimacy of the Norwegian government in exile in issuing criminal law regulations, a power normally reserved only to parliament. There were likewise criticisms of the retroactivity of retributive norms. As in the Czech case, this dispute was resolved by acceptance of the theory of the legal existence of one Norwegian government, the exile government, while the period from the 10th of June 1940 to the 8th of May 1945 was designated a period when Norway was at war with Germany.[170]

In the course of exile in London and the drafting of the presidential decrees, cooperation with the Polish government in exile played a major role for the Czechoslovak government, but the situation changed fundamentally in 1944 both from the international and domestic Polish point of view. The formation and recognition of a new provisional Polish government meant that the laws

---

[168] Ibidem. 354. Chapter XI.1 "A Comparison with the Planning and Implementation of Retribution in Selected European States" contains a concise comparative view of the legal instruments by which formerly occupied European states dealt with cases of collaboration. On the basis of an ordonance of the 29th of November 1944 (*Journal Officiel* 136) "on the amendment and codification of regulations relating to the punishment of acts of collaboration", the French provisional government set up a special tribunal which tried as "acts of collaboration" acts committed from the 16th of June 1940 to the liberation that had not been in breach of criminal law in force from that date. Several special crimes or newly severe definitions of crimes and punishments appeared – especially what was known as *degradation nationale* and *indignité nationale* punishable by loss of citizenship, or the forfeit of citizen rights. Ordonance no. 102 of the 19th of October 1944 confiscated all profits from the beginning of the war, i.e. from the 1st of September 1939 to the liberation. Less serious acts of collaboration were dealt with by the *Chambres civique*, which were in operation up to the end of 1949. Kuklík, J. *Mýty a realita takzvaných Benešových dekretů*. 355.

[169] Ibidem. 357.

[170] Ibidem. 358.

prepared by the Polish government in exile in London could not be implemented. The eventual basis for the radically implemented Polish retributive actions was to be the decrees of the Lublin Committee – the Polish Committee of National Liberation. The retributive Polish measures were distinctive for the enlargement of the material basis of war crimes to include "the violation of wartime right", to be judged according to customary international law and "according to the postulates of conscience". The decrees of the 31st of August 1944 and the 16th of February 1945 introduced a distinction between "war crimes", used above all for leaders of the German occupation administration, and "traitors to the nation" used for Polish collaborators.[171]

The Czechoslovak retributive legislation concerned with the judgment of the seriousness of offences committed against the republic by the Sudeten Germans (but also Czech and Slovak collaborators) needs to be seen in the context of the period. The retributive laws used by the previously occupied states included the use of special courts and changes to the procedural side of hearings for acts committed during the Second World War. Insofar as the presidential decrees promulgated half a century ago under historically and legally specific conditions, and already implemented with regard to the purposes for which they were framed, later came into conflict with the *Charter of Fundamental Rights and Liberties* they ceased to have legal force as of the 31st of December 1991 (without prejudice to legal relationships arising before this date), and cannot be applied in law (although of course given their purpose this would hardly be possible anyway). In these circumstances the obligations and rights to which they gave rise would not be affected even if the Constitutional Court were to give a specific ruling finding them null and void. Thus the *problem of the presidential decrees is today above all a political problem.*[172] This is how the German side also understands them.

In Point I of his *Expert Opinion on the Sudeten German Question*, Felix Ermacora states that he is submitting this opinion in connection with the unification of Germany. He thus essentially admits the political reasons and political approach behind his opinion and so its evident tendentiousness based on the new position and power of Germany. Ermacora approaches the matter as if the state of war with Germany and the conduct of the Germans in the war were

---

[171] Ibidem. 364. The special nature of Polish retributory judicial arrangements, but also their political basis, was expressed by the participation of two "people's judges" appointed by the presidium of the Land National Council on the basis of the recommentation of the presidium of the voivode people's committees mainly controlled by the communists. The institution of special courts became an important element of "sovietisation". On retribution see also Borák, M. 1998. *Spravedlnost podle dekretu, Retribuční soudnictví v ČSR a Mimořádný lidový soud v Ostravě (1945–1948)* [Justice by Decree, Retributive Justice in the CSR and the Special People's Court in Ostrava]. Ostrava: Tilia.

[172] Mikule, V. "Dekrety prezidenta republiky a nynější právo". 61.

wholly irrelevant to mutual property relations. He does not explain the post-war changes including the changes of property and confiscations in the context of the war or the international agreements of the time (i.e. Czechoslovakia was undoubtedly in a state of war with Germany and its demands for reparations were internationally recognised, specifically in 1945 when it was party to *the Paris Agreement on Reparations* from Germany and the founding of the *Interallied Reparations Office and return of Currency Gold*, which was based on this agreement and dealt with the responsibility of Germans and Germany) but considers them simply as facts that occurred after the war and independently of it. Not at all as consequences of the war.[173]

Important from the point of view of current attempts to pursue revision of post-war legal acts is Ermacora's claim that recognition of the domestic and international responsibility of the organs of Czechoslovakia is blocked by Law no. 115 of the 8th of May 1946 on the legitimacy of actions associated with the fight for the recovery of the freedom of Czechs and Slovaks (Article 240). He therefore sees a need for this law to be abrogated. I consider it significant in this context that another important legal opinion on the German side, that of Ch. Tomuschat, argues that "In the case of the Law of the 8th of May 1946, in contrast to the confiscation decrees, the legal effects last to this day." Although Tomuschat stresses that "Ermacora's theory that in the expulsion of the Sude-ten Germans the Czechoslovak state deliberately and purposively committed an act of genocide should in no case be repeated", in another text he argues that the official standpoint of the Czech side, "entails above all the denial of the rights of the German and Hungarian groups of the population to existence, and is evidence of an official view that the life and health of individual mem-bers of these ethnic groups are not legal goods worthy of protection. So radical a renunciation of the protective function of the state, which is incumbent on the state by virtue of its legal power, cannot be consistent with the standards of a community of *nations civilisées*."[174]

On the basis of the facts he adduces, and the wording of Paragraph 3 of the Czech-German Declaration of the 21st of January 1997, Tomuschat proposes that criminal proceedings be started against the persons most responsible for

---

[173] Pavlíček, V. – Suchánek, R. "O některých otázkách majetkových nároků v česko-německých vztazích" [Some Questions of Property Claims in Czech-German Relations], in *Krajanské organizace sudetských Němců v SRN* [Compatriot Organisations of the Sudeten Germans in the FRG]. Prague: Ústav mezinárodních vztahů. 82–83.

[174] Tomuschat, Ch. *Benešovy dekrety – překážka přijetí České republiky do Evropské unie?* 32 ff. The unpublished ex-pert opinion of the important German expert on international law who lectures at the Humboldt University in Berlin. The author considers it significant that "the final operative date of the law on impunity was not set as the end of the Second World War but as the 28th of October 1945. According to this law, then, for a period of six months from the termination of enmity every Czechoslovak citizen was authorised to commit violent acts for the purpose of "just retribution".

excesses that occurred in connection with the transfer. He concludes with the words, "Just as the Federal Republic of Germany has come to the conclusion that it is responsible in the field of criminal law, the Czech Republic must do so too."[175] As far as the possibility of the return of the Sudeten German ethnic group as a whole is concerned, however, Tomuschat argues that, "It would be practically absurd to argue that the Czech Republic should not be allowed to become a member of the European Union because it has so far refused the expelled Sudeten Germans the right of return, and so to close the gate to the desired free movement."[176]

Another decisive moment in the process of the accession of the CR to the EU was the expert opinion on the legal status of the decrees that formed the basis of the post-war transfer of the German-speaking inhabitants of the CR presented by Prof. J. Frowein (former director of the Max Planck Institute for comparative public law and international law in Heidelberg and the former vice president of the European Commission for Human Rights), Prof. U. Bernitz and the Rt. Hon. Lord Kingsland Q.C., who arrived at the following conclusions, which I quote here in full because of the importance of their argumentation:

1. The confiscations on the basis of the Beneš-decrees do not raise an issue under EU law which has no retroactive effect.
2. The Decrees on Citizenship are outside the competence of the EU.
3. The Czech system of restitution, although in some respects discriminatory as held by the UN-Human Rights Committee, does not raise an issue under EU-law.
4. It must be clarified during the accession procedure that criminal convictions on the basis of the Beneš Decrees cannot be enforced after accession.
5. A repeal of Law no. 115 of 1946, excempting "just reprisals" from criminal responsibility, does not seem to be mandatory in the context of accession. The reason is that individuals have relied on these provisions for more than 50 years, and as such have a legitimate expectation that they will not now be prosecuted for these actions. However, we are of the opinion that the Czech Republic should formally recognise that this law is repugnant to human rights and all fundamental legal principles.
6. We have based our opinions on the understanding that from accession all EU-citizens will have the same rights on the territory of the Czech Republic.

---

175 Ibidem. 44.
176 Ibidem. 32.

The Conference of the Heads of State of the European Parliament had ordered this study and it was completed at the end of September/beginning of October 2002.[177]

The actual transfer of the German population was not the subject of any decree/law or any other Czechoslovak legal norm. The act of transfer was based exclusively on the decision of the Potsdam Conference. This measure was part and parcel of the punitive approach taken by the Allies to Germany and Germans as expressed in extreme form for example by the US Secretary for the Treasure Henry Morgenthau's *Program to Prevent Germany from Starting a World War III*, which envisaged the complete destruction of German industrial potential and the transformation of Germany into an agrarian country. Ultimately, the fears of the allies that an excessively punitive approach might result in the same development as after the First World War (and also the anticipated East-West conflict) led to more moderate treatment of the defeated Germany.

The numbers of inhabitants that the transfer affected are very much disputed to this day and have remained a regular subject of polemics between experts on the Czech and German sides.

Table 2: Numbers of German population in the Borderlands as of 9th of December 1945

Germans	Of which Antifascists	Czechs and other Slavs	Total population in borderlands
1 918 181	51 776	1 730 956	3 649 137

Source: Srb, V. "Demografický profil německé menšiny" [Demographic Profile of the German Minority]. Tvorba. 12. 2. 1947. 31.

Most authors incline to the figure of 600,000 Germans who fled or were expelled from the Czech Lands in the period of April-May 1945 outside the framework of the "official" transfer.[178] Overall estimates of numbers of Germans transferred diverge massively, but we consider the most solid to be the estimates made by T. Staněk, who calculates that a total of 1,446,059 persons (including 53,187 people considered to be antifascist) were transferred to the American zone and 786,482 (including 42,989 antifascists) to the Soviet zone of occupation.[179]

---

[177] For the full wording of the expert opinions by leading experts see Frowein, J. A. – Bernitz, U. – Kingsland, Q. C. 2002. *Legal Opinion on the Beneš Decrees and the Accession of the Czech Republic to the EU*. Working document of the General Directorate for Research. European Parliament: Luxemburg.

[178] Staněk, T. *Odsun Němců z Československa*. 116.

[179] In total in the course of the transfer 1646 trains including 4 hospital trains, and 67,748 automobiles were deployed. At the height of the transfer in the first half of 1946 12 trains a day were used transporting 14,400 in-

The Czechoslovak authorities made all the necessary efforts to ensure that the transfer was conducted in accordance with the principles established by the Potsdam Conference. In the course of the transfer, foreign journalists, observers and diplomats had unrestricted access to all internment centres and assembly camps and the opportunity to talk to those being expelled and to inspect any facility associated with the transfer. When receiving a Czechoslovak delegation after the major part of the operation had been accomplished, the American delegate in the Allied Control Council, General Clay, declared that the transfer had been organised and conducted so efficiently and humanely that he wished to express his thanks to the Czechoslovak government.[180]

Throughout the operation a permanent attaché from the US army worked at the general staff of the Czechoslovak army entrusted with the organisation and conduct of the transfer, and dealt with problems arising in the course of transfer to the American occupation zone of Germany. The American authorities accepted and took charge of transports only after inspecting the trains and checking that all the rules stipulated[181] by agreement between the Czechoslovak and Allied leaders had been observed in an appropriate way.

The overall drop in the German-speaking population of the Czech Lands (not only by transfer but including the fallen, missing, prisoners, those who had fled etc.), is estimated at 2.9–3 million people. If to this is added an estimate of numbers of others who left the territory of the republic by various routes, we cannot exclude a possible drop of as many as 3.5 million people.[182]

In this work we cannot go into the course of the transfer in more detail, but we can certainly state that the transfer represented a very drastic solution to the ethnic conflict in the Czech Lands. It was a cruel tax on the decision of the clear majority of Sudeten Germans to embrace Nazism or at least passively accept a dictatorial regime. The understandable post-war wave of anti-German sentiment, which affected all Europe, resulted in the enforcement of the concept of collective responsibility[183] in relation to the whole German community. Today, when revisionist opinions constantly reiterate the theory of the immoral-

---

dividals, who were delivered to German border stations (Furth im Wald, Schirnding aj.). Luža, R. *The Transfer of the Sudeten Germans*. 288.

[180] Ibidem. 289. Inspection tours of the Czech borderlands were regularly undertaken by the ambassadors of the USA, Great Britain and France – L. Steinhardt, P. Nichols and Dejean. Steinhardt in particular often took the opportunity to visit various towns, transports and internment camps with the escort of a Czechoslovak army officer and to ask officials and expellees about conditions in situ.

[181] The American control report on redistribution centres drawn up at the end of July 1946 states that the expelled people, "were in a good state of health, appropriate clothing, and with the sum of 500 reich marks that had been provided to them by agreement". Ibidem. 285.

[182] Staněk, T. *Odsun Němců z Československa*. 237.

[183] In this, however, I see a fine but not insignificant nuance that distinguishes it from the concept of collective guilt that Sudeten authors and politicians claim was used against them.

ity of the principle of collective guilt, it is worth remembering the words of the outstanding philosopher and thinker Karl Jaspers, addressed to his German fellow citizens:

"That the spiritual conditions of German life provided an opportunity for such a regime is a fact for which all of us are co-responsible... It means that our national tradition contains something, mighty and threatening, which is our moral ruin.[184] We Germans differ from each other greatly in the manner and degree of our involvement in national socialism or resistance to it... In all this we cannot reduce ourselves to a single denominator. We have to be mutually open to each other and move forward from fundamentally different starting points. The common denominator is perhaps only our nationality. In this lies the collective guilt and responsibility of everyone who allowed 1933 to happen without dying."[185]

Immediately following the end of the war, the national/ethnic principle prevailed (although it should not be overlooked that the presidential decrees made distinctions in defining the guilty), and in the given conditions this was quite logical in view of the arguments on how to achieve internal security for the CSR and a lasting peace in Europe.[186] The main phase of the transfer ended in the autumn of 1946 after a summer in which most of the Sudeten Germans had been expelled. It is interesting to consider the evaluation of the transfer produced by the Commander of the US Armed Forces in the European theatre of war in his "Concluding Report on the transfer of the German population out of Czechoslovakia and into the American zone in Germany" by Colonel John H. Fye, an officer of the American liaison mission at the Czechoslovak General Staff who was entrusted with the task of co-ordinating the transfer of Sudeten Germans into the American occupatrion zone.[187] In the final passage of this document he writes:

"The Czechs are a strongly nationalistic and patriotic people. To say that they are by temperament extreme is not meant as an insult. They will give a friend everything they have, and stick a knife in the back of an enemy. There is no middle way for them. The Germans were their worst enemies. They tried

---

[184] Jaspers, K. *Otázka viny* [The Question of Guilt]. 1991. Prague: Mladá fronta. 51.

[185] Ibidem. 73.

[186] Staněk, T. *Odsun Němců z Československa*. 374.

[187] Colonel Fye was sometimes critical of the Czechs, however, as is evident from his answers to a questionnaire from the 2nd Army dated the 28th of August 1947, where he writes, "The Potsdam Agreement urged humane treatment of the Sudeten Germans during the transfer. The Czechs had been under German domination for seven years. The result was that I was engaged in a constant struggle with the Czech authorities to ensure that they treated the Germans as human beings... My relations with the Czechs were always very cordial, regardless of our problems over the harshness with which they treated the Sudeten Germans." Hrbek, J. "Americký dokument o odsunu Němců z Československa" [An American Document on the Transfer of the Germans from Czechslovakia]. *Historie a vojenství* 5/1995 (XLIV). 141.

to subjugate or destroy the Czechs, and so the Czechs see no reason why they should show any consideration for the Germans. Let them vanish from the face of the earth. The Czechs do not understand the Americans and their protective attitude to the Germans. The honest question is, what would the attitude of the Americans be if they were in the position of the Czechs? As far as the plan and goal are concerned, the expulsion of the German minority is complete. Some people, including a few Czechs, think that mass transfer was a mistake. But to find and expel only genuinely Nazi types would have been almost impossible from a practical point of view and would have taken years. Only time will tell."[188]

---

[188] *Final Report. Transfer of German Population From Czechoslovakia to U.S. Zone, Germany.* Translation of a document from the estate of Colonel J. H. Fye kept in the archives of the *U.S. Army Military History Institute* in Carlisle, Pennsylvania (John H. Fye Papers). Hrbek, J. "Americký dokument o odsunu Němců z Československa". 139–171. It is interesting to compare this with the authentic recollections of a direct actor in the transfer describing the act of handing over a transfer transport. "On the order of a US military guard the transport could proceed through the neutral zone to the receiving station. I would personally go through the details with the US liaison officer Samuel Wraytem and with the member of the reception committee Major Krištof. German functionaries would also be present – I think these were the mayors in the reception places, or sometimes the chief of the railway station in which the transport was handed over. The negotiation and handover took place in German and English. This reception committee, to which I gave the personal documents of the transferred German citizens, would go from coach to coach and the US liaison officer in his broken German would ask the commander of each coach, "Sind alle Familien zusammen? Wie wurde mit Ihnen während des Transports behandelt?" When the commander said that he had no comments or complaints on the course of the transfer the people in the coach were accepted and immediately handed over to the care of the German Red Cross." Smutný, F. "Byl jsem velitelem transportu odsunutých" [I was commander of a transfer transport]. *Národní osvobození* 25–26/2004. 13.

Prague, May 1945. The phase of the so-called "wild transfer" of Germans from the ČSR was a spontaneous reaction to the years of terror during the Occupation. Photograph of German civilians waiting for departure in Strossmayer Square.

8 The Transferred Sudeten Germans in Post-war Germany

You don't belong here but you can't go back.
Alena Wagnerová: Transferred Memories

The expelled Germans who arrived in Germany as a result of the transfer policy of the Allies after the Second World War confronted three crucial questions from the start: how to secure a basic livelihood, how to explain their expulsion from their homes and centuries-old settlements to themselves, and finally how and in what form to find a political voice in their new environment.

The situation of the expelled Germans was truly hard since in a Germany devastated by war the new environment had nothing to offer new arrivals, especially in a situation where they could expect little sympathy from the local population. Ordinary Germans tended to see them as a burden, and many even blamed them for their own troubles, considering them the cause of a lost war fought in the name of the liberation of the ethnic Germans/*Volksdeutsche* in the East.

In Bavaria and later in Würtemberg, elements of Sudeten German expellee selforganisation began to develop immediately after the war and soon laid the foundations for the main and most effective organised link of the whole postwar Sudeten German movement. The main focus at the beginning was social and humanitarian aid. As early as August 1945 an organisation of aid centres for Sudeten Germans (*Hilfstellen der Sudetendeutschen*) was set up in Bavaria, and while primarily concerned with charitable activities it was also already seeking a political profile.

Although the British in their own occupation zone set up advisory committees for expellees, the level of every community and district in November 1945, in the spring of the next year the occupying powers the USA and Britain forebade the formation of autonomous Sudeten German organisations on the basis of a resolution of the *Allied Control Council*. As General G. Marshall put it, the problem was "the need to minimise unavoidable irredentist pressure in Germany."[1] The measure reflected the fact that in the immediate post-war period the Sudeten German organisations were already returning to the right to self-determination as the fundamental principle of their political programme. Certain differences of opinion were becoming apparent in the attitudes of different groups of transferees, but one thing united them – a basic rejection of the transfer.[2]

Despite the dissolution of the transferees' organisational centre, printed bulletins, *Heimatbriefe* designed for Sudeten Germans from particular larger cities and areas in their former homeland, were increasingly produced and disseminated. R. Hilf claims that 19,000 titles of this kind of printed material were counted in 1949.[3] Sources of arguments for the gradually emerging Sudeten German "national exiled group" (E. Lemberg) or national community (*Volksgemeinschaft*) included E. Reichenberger's *Ostdeutsche Passion* and W. Jaksch's *Benesch war gewarnt* published in 1948–9. Jaksch's work in particular was later to be cited abundantly and used as a source of arguments by the Sudeten German associations.

Immediately after May 1945, i.e. still in the period of the "wild" transfers and expulsions, the Sudeten Germans sought aid and support for their self-help groups with the so-called Reich Union for Catholic Germandom Abroad/ *Reichsverband für das katholische Deutschtum im Ausland*. Thanks to pre-war contacts, they succeeded as early as October 1945 in setting up church aid agencies in Frankfurt am Main and Munich, and these became centres for various "circles" and planning for the future.[4]

Crucial for future development was the decision of the transferred Catholics not to renew the old Sudeten organisations but to found a new organisation. The *Kirchliche Hilfstelle* led by father Paulus Sladek and H. Schütz established an important position (partly thanks to support from the Vatican) among Christian-orientated expellees. August 1946 then saw the founding of the organisation *Ackermann-Gemeinde*, named after the famous medieval theological treatise The Ploughman from Bohemia (*Der Ackermann aus Böhmen*). The Ackermann community was a Catholic interest organisation with roots in the Christian-Socialist German party of interwar Czechoslovakia.

---

[1]   Wiskemann, E. *Germans and their eastern Neighbours*. 179.

[2]   Čelovský, B. "The Transferred Sudeten-Germans and their political activity". *Journal of Central European Affairs*. April 1957 (VI). 127–149.

[3]   Hilf, R. *Die Presse der Sudetendeutschen nach 1945 und ihre Stellungnahme zum Schicksal der vetriebenen Volksgruppe*. (Dissertation). 1951. München. See also Šnejdárek, A. "Počátky revanšistického Sudetoněmeckého krajanstva v západním Německu". 192–201.

[4]   Kural, V. "Organizace sudetoněmeckých vysídlenců v SRN 1945–1989" [The Organisation of the Sudeten German Expellees in the FRG 1945–1989], in *Studie o sudetoněmecké otázce*. 23 ff.

The Formation of the Sudeten German Expellee Organisations

1947 saw a gradual relaxation of restrictions on political life in the Western zones of occupation and the Ackermann Community formulated the basic thesis in which the hopes and directions of the time were reflected. "Expulsion from our old country, which was our homeland for centuries, was the worst injustice (*Unrecht*) inflicted on us... We shall never give up our right to our homeland. We definitely reject, however, all illusions promising a swift return to our homeland or ideas that even invest hope of this kind in a Third World War."[5]

From the first, the *Ackermann-Gemeinde* (A-G) profiled itself as an exile organisation working for the peaceful return of the Sudeten Germans to Bohemia, Moravia and Silesia. It officially embraced the view that the origin of all the evil and the war was the nationalist fragmentation of Central Europe. It blamed both sides involved, the Czech and German. The A-G standpoint is embodied in the following passage from the principles set out in the A-G Statutes published in 1948: "All the Central European nations need to realise that by their extreme nationalism of roughly the last 100 years they have not only destroyed the federative basis of their coexistence over a thousand years... but have finally made this region a helpless object in the disputes of the great powers and thereby brought themselves to the brink of destruction."[6]

This text exhibits the moderate tone, critical of German chauvinism, that has remained characteristic for other basic documents and standpoints of the A-G. Nonetheless, a sense of the sequence of causes and effects is lacking, and it must also be noted that in the Czech political environment the term *federalism of Central Europe* is not entirely neutral in meaning. Its resonance with the multiform project of *Mitteleuropa*, or one of the forms of the Danubian multinational state, is hard to overlook. All the same, the officially embraced tolerance of the A-G position has played a positive role in Czech-German debate over many years, reducing the potential for conflict. From the start the A-G has put the emphasis on systematic education (see for example its extensive publishing activity including the weekly *Volksbote*, and the series *Institutum Bohemicum – Beiträge*).

Like the A-G, the Sudeten German Social Democrat organisation, the *Seliger Gemeinde* (S-G) made efforts to set the specific experiences of the transferees in a wider political framework, which in its own case was one founded on cooper-

---

[5] Olbert, F. 1992. *Cesta ke smíření (prameny k dějinám sudetoněmecké otázky)* [The Road to Conciliation (sources on the history of the Sudeten German question)]. Prague: ISE. 24–25.

[6] "Statut sdružení Ackermann-Gemeinde vyhlášený roku 1948" [The Statutes of the Ackermann-Gemeinde issued in 1948], in Olbert, F. *Cesta ke smíření*. 23.

ation with European socialist parties. The Seliger-Gemeinde decided to address only the "Sudeten German Workers' Movement" and saw its main mission as that of placing "the intellectual tradition of all-Austrian and Sudeten socialism in the service of a new federalist order of all Europe."[7]

The S-G was formed in 1947 after Wenzel Jaksch, the former president of the Social Democratic Party in the CSR, returned from emigration in Great Britain and after he and another leader of the Sudeten German Social Democrats, Richard Reitzner, had managed to overcome their earlier differences. Since the Social Democrats were cautious in developing their political activities because they respected the prohibition imposed by the Allies, the S-G was not formally constituted until 1951.

The S-G's basic programme principles were very similar to those of the A-G and even the *Witikobund* in the sense of insisting on the Sudeten Germans' right to their homeland and return, and on the unification of Germany. The S-G also declared the establishment of Czechoslovakia in 1918 to have been "*eine Fehlkonstruktion*" (mistaken construction) of the Versailles Treaty. According to the S-G, the Munich Agreement represented a gross interference with the European order, but also redress of the wrongs of 1918–1919. On the question of German unification, the S-G was even more radical than the others, demanding the revision of the Potsdam Agreement and asserting that the border on the Oder and Nisa was an open matter.

Given that we are now hearing claims that the Social Democrats held views on the principle of self-determination that were diametrically opposed to those of other Sudeten Germans, it is worth remembering R. Reitzner's speech of 1955: "We are saying nothing about future borders, because we distinguish between statehood (*Statentum*) and ethnicity (*Volkstum*), between the state and the right to homeland."[8]

The right to self-determination, in any case a traditional part of Austro-Marxism (see especially K. Renner and others), was at the core of all S-G. thinking on the future, and the political orientations of the Sudeten German Social Democrats. As the Cold War set in, Jaksch was soon able to rehabilitate German ideas on Central Europe and the special mission of Germans in the struggle between good and evil: "After 1945 the pressure on the centre of Europe that started with the rise of Tsarist Russia hit the whole of Germany. The strong

[7]   Hahn, E. "Sudetskí Nemci v nemeckej spoločnosti: polstoročie politických dejín mezi 'vlasťou' a 'domovom'" [The Sudeten Germans in German Society (a half-century of political history between "homeland" and "home")], in *V rozdelenej Európe. Česi, Slováci, Nemci a ich štáty v rokoch 1948–1989* [In a Divided Europe. Czechs, Slovaks, Germans and their States in 1948–1989]. 1998. Kováč, D. – Křen, J. – Lemberg, H. (eds.). Bratislava: AEP. 78.

[8]   *Schicksalfrage Osteuropa*. Referate auf der Landeskonferenz der S-G zu Weissenburg/Bayern am 30. 6.–1. 7. 1956. Undated and with no place of publication given. 22.

German will for unification and the moral strength of West Germany became a factor of European self-confirmation."[9]

In terms of influence on the formation of theoretical, intellectual and organisational resources, however, the most important Sudeten German organisation was and still remains the *Witikobund*[10] Like the others, the Witikobund (WB) drew on the pre-war organisation of Sudeten Germans in Czechoslovakia. From the outset, however, its ambition was not to the role of mass organisation of the expellees, but to the role of a circle of adherents/*Kreis Gesinungsgenossen* in the spirit of the *Aufbruchkreiss* and *Bereitschaft* circles but above all the *Kameradschaftsbund*. This "philosophy" of a closed society meant that its membership was only of the order of hundreds.[11] The WB defined itself as "a union of people who in the tradition of the struggle for self-preservation in the former fatherland felt it to be a duty in the future too to work together in all spheres of life in creating the destiny of a national group expelled from its homeland."[12]

The opponents of the Witikobund warned that this was a secret organisation with an entryist strategy towards other Sudeten German organisational structures, where it tried to exercise influence using the method of the "second man" (in the foreground a man with a public, moderate image, and in second position a loyal, active and militant Nazi) in a way similar to that of the Kameradschaftsbund when it had drawn German organisations in inter-war Czechoslovakia over to its side, and so achieved the unexpectedly rapid formation of a *Sudetendeutsche Heimatfront*. Of course, the open declaration of these traditions and "technological" approaches from the period of prewar undermining of the political stability of the CSR was obviously undesirable.

All the same, in the spirit of its precursors the Witikobund concentrated on infiltration of the newly emerging Sudeten German Homeland Association/ *Sudetendeutsche Landsmannschaft* (SL), and made a major contribution to building it up and improving its organisational capabilities. The important member of the WB Walter Becher[13] became the president of the SL and another

---

[9]   Jaksch, W. *Cesta Evropy do Postupimi*. 350.

[10] Named after the medieval hero of the novel *Witiko*, by the famous Bohemian German Adalbert Stifter.

[11] It is said that in 1986 the number of members of the WB was around a thousand. From the start the WB has been highly selective in membership policy. The WB systematically strove to obtain important positions in the state apparatus, political parties, economy and the media. At the same time it made sure to continue to replenish its ranks with young supporters with the goal of ensuring *intergenerational continuity*. The policy of the CDU/CSU made it possible for former functionaries of Nazi organisations in the Sudetenland Reichsgau and the Protectorate of Bohemia and Moravia, and in the clerico-fascist Slovak state, to return to the scene. For details see Herde, G. – Stolze, A. 1987. *Die Sudetendeutsche Landsmannschaft*. Köln/Pahl-Rugenstein. 113 ff.

[12] Cited from Kural, V. "Hlavní organizace sudetoněmeckých vysídlenců v SRN 1945–1989" [The Main Organisation of Sudeten German Organisations in the FRG 1945–1989], in *Studie o sudetoněmecké otázce*. 27.

[13] Walter Becher (CSU), in the Henleinian era the editor of the Art, Science and Entertainment column in the Sudetenland NSDAP paper *Die Zeit*, was known for articles inflaming antisemitism. Like e.g. Walter Brand (CSU) he was among the leaders of the Sudeten German Party and he was the head of Henlein's office – on

Witikobund member, Theo Keil, became chairman of the working society of Sudeten German educators.

The WB intellectually continued the tradition of the Kameradschaftsbund and Othmar Spann's doctrine of the spiritual role of an elite entrusted with the mission of leading the masses and running the state. According to its exponent Walter Brand, the decisive factor is not the masses, but the activist core of the "enlightened", small groups of people equipped with spiritual discipline, who *are one world-second ahead*, and so have a better grasp of when the time for decision has come.[14] In terms of political theory, for the WB the relational pair of concepts *state – people* (*nation*) is central. The existing state is not an organic form, but a kind of apparatus for controlling society using authority, order, discipline and similar attributes of Prussianism. The type of states known hitherto, especially the liberal democratic and communist, needs to be reformed because it is demonstrably unable to meet the needs of contemporary society. The solution is a synthesis of democracy and authority, centralism and federalism.

The WB programme placed particularly heavy stress on the *exploitation of European integration processes*. In line with Brand's revised concept, it stressed the decline of the importance of nation states. Which side of a border a man lived on would now become less important than his affiliation to a particular ethnic entity/*Volkstum*, because if the significance of borders decline, nations in the ethnic sense would remain very real. Anyone who clearly identified with a *Volkstum*, would also at the same time be a full and valued member of a spiritual society unifying and embracing all the European nations.[15]

Brand's Witikobund guidelines of 1969 were no mere theoretical vision. In their treatment of the future relationship between a federalised Europe and Germany they prefigured real future developments following the fall of the communist regimes in Eastern Europe. Thus far his requirement for the fall of the totalitarian regimes has been fulfilled; from the WB point of view it remains to make a reality of the practical consequences of Brand's intellectual legacy.

As Brand saw it, the First World War had been an attempt by Wilhelmine Germany to save the West from the East. With the Treaties of Versailles, Saint-

---

the 1st of December 1938 he was appointed general officer for the four-year plan. Siegfried Zoglmann was territory head of the *Hitlerjugend* in the Protectorate of Bohemia and Moravia, Willy Sebekowsky was press director of the Henlein Party and later an SA Brigadeführer, Konstantin Höss was former regional chief of the NSDAP in Prague, Karl Kraus former head of the Gestapo in Belgrade and so on. We could find examples of similar biographical data in the case of many leading members of the WB, see Herde, G. – Stolze, A. *Die Sudetendeutsche Landsmannschaft.*

14   Brand, W. 1969. *Zwanzig Jahre Witikobund.* Beiträge, kleine Reihe des Institutum Bohemicum. München: A-G. 30. For more detail on the ideology and views of O. Spann see Hoensch, J. K. "Othmar Spann, Kameradschaftsbund a Sudetoněmecká vlastenecká fronta" [Othmar Spann, the Kameradschaftsbund and the Sudeten Patriotic Front]. *Dějiny a současnost* 5/1999. 31–35.

15   Kural, V. "Hlavní organizace sudetoněmeckých vysídlenců v SRN 1945–1989". 31.

Germain and Trianon, the powers of the victorious entente sowed the fatal seeds that finally led to the confusions of the Thirties and the storms of the Second World War." Hitler's national socialism abused the good intentions of Germans. The system as a whole was deviant, but also contained a measure of honourable idealism. The problem of collective guilt could therefore not be solved by a new injustice. *"In addition to this, there is the guilt of other nations (for crimes) against Germans."*[16]

This interpretation propounded by the Witikobund exonerates Germans of guilt or responsibility for the outbreak of both world wars[17] in the spirit of the principle of *Vergangenheitsbewältigung*. In this way Brand was building on the ongoing *re-evaluation of the Nazi era* and the associated phenomenon of the Holocaust that had become evident in some currents of German historiography from the earlier 1960s, which were responding not only to the needs of school education, but also to the purely pragmatic needs of practical policy. The historian Wulf Kansteiner considers this process of re-evaluation to be a self-centred (the culprit identifying himself with the victim) form of psychotherapy for descendants and perpetrators, but also fellow travellers of Nazism.[18]

A number of British historians[19] have explored the complications and difficulties of German national identity post-1945. The problem was even more intractable for the expelled ethnic Germans, who brought to their new home a *völkisch* identity further complicated by the challenge of integration into German society, especially in the economic and political conditions of post-war revival of a devastated country.

---

[16] For this approach today see media treatment of the subject of *Flucht/Vertreibung* (the flight and expulsion of ethnic Germans from East and Central Europe) and the *Luftterror* (the air offensive of the Allied forces in the Second World War) in German journalism and historiography. One example to stand for many is *Die Flucht (über die Vertreibung der Deutschen aus dem Osten)*.

[17] After the First World War, German historians tried to exonerate Wilhelm II of blame for the outbreak of the conflict. At the beginning of the 1960s the Hamburg historian F. Fischer reopened this debate by claiming that the German unleashing of the the First World War was an attempt to seize control of Europe if not the world. A number of West German historians furiously attacked Fischer for the theory. The controversy drew the attention of the mixed committee of historians of West Germany and France, which asserted, "Germany did not want general war in Europe. If Fischer takes a contrary view, we must point out that his arguments and proofs for the theory are inadequate." For a bibliography of the dispute see Šnejdárek, A. "Počátky revanšistického Sudetoněmeckého krajanstva v západním Německu". 43.

[18] Kansteiner, W. "Mandarins in the Public Sphere (Vergangenheitsbewältigung and the Paradigm of Social History in the Federal Republic of Germany)". *German Politics and Society* 3/1999 (XVII). 84. Kansteiner goes on to quip that, "It seems that the Germans, who were better fascists than the other Europeans, are also compelled to excel in the revision of the picture of the era of Nazism and the Second World War... Their successes in the kingdom of *Vergangenheitsbewältigung* have become a subject of pride, but in places it is unclear whether this pride represents remarkable self-critical elements of German historiography or the exceptional character of Nazi crimes."

[19] See e.g. Evans, R. J. *Rereading German History 1800–1996*. Especially the chapter Rebirth of the German Right. 225 ff.

The onset of the Cold War deformed the whole process by which German society was seeking to come to terms with the Nazi era. In the American Zone, the process of denazification was halted in 1949 by decision of the supreme representative of the Military Government General Lucius Clay in the context of the termination of the military phase of the occupation and the handover of government to German civil authorities. The decision to give *priority to a pragmatic approach* (in a situation in which denazification was far from complete), was clearly motivated by the Western powers need for a German ally in the new world conflict between East and West,[20] i.e. the Cold War.[21]

The business of restoring sovereignty to Germans and drawing up the Constitution of a revived German state required the concept of "settlement with the past"/*Vergangenheitsbewältigung*, which was employed by a number of conservative German politicians and historians not only with regard to domestic conditions but also with regard to neighbouring states including Czechoslovakia (especially given the presence and influence of Sudeten German organisations).

In the post-war period, conservatively orientated neo-nationalist historians boulstered the shaken self-belief of the Germans with relativising arguments on how many other regimes in history had committed crimes comparable with those of the Nazis. Also, crucially, they stressed the anti-communist identity of a West Germany which at the end of the day constituted the "front line" of the free world in the era of the Cold War.[22] The views of the expelled Germans on the causes and consequences of the Second World War to a considerable

---

[20] One officer in the American occupation authority expressed this as a matter of the need to give priority "to an effective administration without regard to the political consequences of the occupation government of Germany". For more detail see Boehling, R. L. "The Stunde Null. American Occupiers, German Appointees and Predemocratic Municipal Administration", in *A Question of Priorities – Democratic Reform and Economic Recovery in Postwar Germany*. 1998. Oxford: Berghahn Books. 116–155. See also Houžvička, V. "Poválečné Německo – tehdy v nulté hodině" [Postwar Germany – Zero Hour]. *Mezinárodní vztahy* 2/2000. 92–95.

[21] A concise but (in terms of content and argument) quite comprehensive overview of the role of the expellee organisations in post-war Germany, including consideration of the influence of their activities on the development of post-war German relarions with Central European neighbours, is provided in a study by the historian J. Dejmek, who specialises in the history of Czechoslovak foreign policy. See Dejmek, J. "Tzv. sudetoněmecká otázka a vztahy Československa a České republiky s německy mluvícími zeměmi po druhé světové válce" [The So-Called Sudeten German Question and the Relations of Czechoslovakia and the Czech Republic with the German-Speaking Countries after the Second World War], in *Kauza tzv. Benešovy dekrety. Historické kořeny a souvislosti*.

[22] The *Opinion Survey Section of the Information Control Division, Office of Military Government* started work immediately after the occupation of the territory of Germany. After the formal end to American military occupation of Germany in September 1949, regular sociological surveys of opinion and attitudes among the population of the American zone continued, now in the framework of *The Reaction Analysis Staff* which was part of the *U.S. High Commission for Germany*. In the early 1950s these surveys showed that only a third of respondents in the American zone rejected National Socialism as immoral. In eight surveys conducted between May 1951 and December 1952 more than 41% of the respondents saw more good than bad in Nazi ideals. Only a tiny group (4%) believed that all Germans, "bear a certain guilt for the actions of the period of the Third Reich". See Merritt, A. J. – Merritt, R. L. 1980. *Public Opinion in Semisovereign Germany*. Chicago: University of Illinois Press. 7.

extent appealed to and resonated with public opinion throughout Germany, as sociological surveys conducted by the American occupation administration at the time showed.

For German public opinion, the tragic fate of the expelled Germans provided the necessary proof of the "inhuman" approach of the victors. Important historians like H. Diwald in the 1970s and A. Hillgruber in the 1980s drew parallels between the post-war expulsion of the Germans from Central and East Europe and the genocide of the Jews (in West German society this culminated in the the so-called "clash of the historians" – *Historikerstreit*,[23] starting in the mid-1980s, which involved a major shift in judgement of the Nazi era involving reinterpretation of the concepts of guilt and punishment and a tangled and relativising view of Nazi crimes). According to Hillgruber, the twin catastrophes of the Holocaust and the transfer were part and parcel of the same historical processes of dehumanisation. He further claimed that the approach of the Allies to Germany and the Nazi genocide were based on the same policy of movements of population and extermination, and so essentially ethically equated the two phenomena.[24] Moral judgment that took into account the causal connection of causes and consequences was thus banished; it seems that this too can be a way of "coming to terms" with history.

As the main ideologue of the former Kameradschaftsbund and the contemporary Witikobund, Walter Brand promoted a systematic repudiation of German responsibility for both world wars to a much more radical degree than the other Sudeten German organisations.[25] For him, and other adherents of this concept of German excision from the sequence of historical events, the year 1945 was constructed as a "zero hour" or zero point from which a new history would unfold, enabling Sudeten Germans to distance themselves from the Nazi era. In this foreshortened perspective Sudeten Germans could be regarded sim-

---

[23]   The most important figure in the discussion of modern German history was E. Nolte, who opened up a new form of investigating the dictatorships of the 20th century. He entered the debate on the Nazi era with his study *Fascism in its Epoch* (1963) after the trial of Adolf Eichmann had set off trials of former Nazis in the FRG and a wave of doubt especially in the young German generation as to how comprehensively and thoroughly the FRG had really come to terms with the era of National Socialism. The previous approach characterised as *asymmetrical discretion* took into account the large-scale involvement of the German population in the Nazi regime. It allowed a certain *modus vivendi* between the compromised majority and the minority group of the uncompromised. J. Dobeš points out that the German way of coming to terms with the past is definitely not a simple and desirable model for Czechs, as is often mistakenly claimed. For more detail see Dobeš, J. "Nolte a studium dějin fašismu" [Nolte and the Study of Fascism], in Nolte, E. 1999. *Fašismus ve své epoše.* Prague: Argo. 671–672. For a comprehensive account of the debate see *Historikerstreit. Die Dokumentation der Kontroverse um die Einzigartigkeit der national sozialistischen Judenvernichtung.* 1991. Augstein, R. (et al.) München/Zürich: Piper.

[24]   For more details see Lipstadt, D. E. 2001. *Popírání holocaustu (Sílící útok na pravdu a paměť)* [Holocaust Denial (The intensifying attack on truth and memory)]. Litomyšl: Paseka. 263–264.

[25]   Kural, V. "Hlavní organizace sudetoněmeckých vysídlenců v SRN 1945–1989". 32.

ply as the object of the power struggles of a tragic era, and in no way as actors who actively contributed to the course of events. In other words they were not among the perpetrators of evil, but only among its victims. Thus "purified" of the unfortunate past, they could once again enter into events on the German and European political scene.

In Brand's vision as formulated in 1969, we can see the return of the messianic idea of *Mitteleuropa*, but this time built into a European democratic context. In fact he had already formulated the basic thesis (with the evident use of a geopolitical conceptual vocabulary) in 1949, as follows:

"The idea of the return of our national group home needs to be seen as a question affecting the whole of Europe. The re-establishment of a protective European line from the Baltic through Bohemian-Moravian-Silesian space and Panonian space right down to the Adriatic. This is not a matter of simple return, but of a new initiative/*Aufbruch*, a regaining of the homeland through its new settlement, which would be of the same genus as the medieval colonisation although it would be implemented by means of today's technology. Recolonisation – and this is crucial – would not this time take place under some imperialist banner, but would in a certain sense be a commission of Europe as a whole."[26]

Looking back over several decades, we have to accord Brand's vision a degree of genuine foresight. His *strategic priorities* as set out in the documents not only of the Witikobund, but also the Sudetendeutsche Landsmannschaft, were rapidly fulfilled following 1989.

The *Soviet empire collapsed* and communist influence in Central and Eastern Europe was reduced to a minimum. The process of the *unification of Germany took place* at incredible speed and Germany immediately regained the role of European great power. The process *of European integration reduced the role of borders* and national states and created conditions for the regional concept of a federation of European states with the expected wave of the expansion of the European Union to the East, i.e. the areas from which ethnic Germans had been expelled after the war.

Exploiting some of the principles of the functioning of the European Union (also binding on the Czech Republic since the 1st of May 2004), the Sudeten German organisations have now been striving in practice for the realisation of their political programme.[27] The theoretical basis of their approach is the

---

[26]   Ibidem. 33.
[27]   The Sudeten Germans have found particularly important support in the ranks of the CDU/CSU – parties that are strongly represented in the European Parliament (see e.g. B. Posselt as a Euro-MP) especially thanks to the strength of the European People's Party. The EPP was founded on the 8th of July 1976 in Luxemburg. "The German CDU was under its long-term chairman Helmut Kohl the driving force behind this process

promotion of a return (in a certain modified form via European integration principles) to a Christian universalist Europe rejecting the specific features of the nation state, which is branded an anachronistic expression of nationalism. Paradoxically, however, the Sudeten German organisations reject civic constitutions/institutions (likewise representing a universalist ethic even if based on a different principle) and identify with a "tribal" concept of national (ethnic) community. The evident inconsistency between these two approaches is apparently to be "bridged" by a new Europeanism.[28]

The 1990s witnessed the fulfilment of the conditions defined in the WB and SL documents as the basic prerequisites for fundamental revision of the facts created by the results of the Second World War. The question remains, however, whether and to what extent this political programme is still attractive for the mass of transferred Sudeten Germans or their descendants. Their integration into German society/*Eingliederung* was ultimately successful. The great majority eventually managed to settle down and prosper, and the idea of a mass return to Bohemia or Moravia evidently has little appeal to them.[29] All the same, a feeling of bitterness and injury undoubtedly persists among the Sudeten Germans.

Surveys of opinion among the transferees and their children, while these are partial and not entirely representative, indicate almost negligible interest in a life in the former fatherland.[30] There are grounds for concluding that many transferees who were not directly guilty of any crimes yet nonetheless suffered expulsion would be satisfied with expressions of regret and apology for their tragic human fate.

(European integration) and as a consequence of its status as the largest party in the EPP had a great deal of influence". This state has persisted following the enlargement of the EU to the East until the present, when the chairman of this largest European parliamentary grouping is H-G. Pöttering.

[28] For more detail on the development and programme principles of the EPP see Kubes, M. – Kučera, R. 2002. *Evropská lidová strana* [The European People's Party]. Prague: ISE.

[29] In 1998 a small opinion survey was carried out in the FRG among expellees from the Podbořany region. In reponse to a question asking which country they regarded as their homeland all the respondents (16) replied the Federal Republic of Germany. They considered the transfer of the Germans from the Bohemian Land to be unjust and called it an expulsion. As a solution to the Sudeten German question they stated: right to self-determination, right of return to original homeland, financial compensation, and wanted the Czech government to negotiate with representatives of the Sudeten Germans. Vinškovská, M. 1998. *Odsunutí Němci z Podbořanska* [Transferred Germans from Podbořany]. Unpublished degree thesis. Ústí n. L.: Pedagogická fakulta Univerzity J. E. Purkyně. 47.

[30] See e.g. the survey (cited in more detail below) conducted by the *EMNID* agency commissioned by the weekly magazine *Der Spiegel* in 1996. In the age group over 60, a total of 10,6 % of respondents would like to live in the old country. In the age group up to 24, however, this rises to 25% of respondents, which is surprising, because the motive evidently cannot be nostalgia for a remembered old country. In view of the fact that this group is marked by a lower level of education and social status, we can deduce that they expect social advance in a Czech environment. The survey was conducted in the period 6th of Feb. – 7th of April 1996 on a selected sample of 3,525 people.

The Unification of the Expellees

The first and primary impulse towards both solidarity and integration in their new country was undoubtedly the shared traumatic experience of having been forced to leave their homes when as a result of the crimes of the National Socialist regime everyone was stripped of civic rights and at the mercy of the victors. In Czechoslovakia, Presidential Decree no. 33/1945 of the 2nd of September 1945 "regulating the state citizenship of persons of German and Hungarian nationality" may be considered key for the future of the Sudeten Germans: in paragraph 1, point 1 it stated that, "Czechoslovak state citizens of German or Hungarian nationality who acquired German or Hungarian state citizenship according to the regulations of the foreign occupying power, forfeited Czechoslovak state citizenship on the date of acquisition of this citizenship."

Although this decree stripped persons of German nationality of Czechoslovak citizenship on a mass basis, it was not based exclusively on the application of the principle of collective guilt because it admitted certain exceptions, i.e. "Persons falling under the provisions of paragraph 1 who are able to prove that they remained loyal to the Czechoslovak Republic, never transgressed against the Czech and Slovak peoples and either took part in the fight for their liberation or suffered under Nazi and fascist terror, may retain Czechoslovak citizenship."[31] In addition, the decree did not apply (see para 3, article 3) to Germans and Hungarians who during the period of heightened danger to the republic had declared themselves in official documents to be Czechs or Slovaks.

As a result of the decree, which was in fact an executive instrument of the agreement on the orderly transfer of ethnic Germans out of Central and Eastern Europe reached at the Potsdam conference on the 2nd of August 1945 by representatives of the states of the victorious anti-Hitler coalition, most of the Sudeten Germans were expelled from the CSR.[32]

---

[31] Both quotations from Winkler, P. "Dekrety prezidenta republiky z období 1940–1945", in *Právní aspekty odsunu sudetských Němců*. 23–24. P. Winkler, like Beneš himself and others, stresses that the wording of the decrees also covered Czechs who had shown disloyalty to the state in the period of heightened threat to it. For instance, at a London meeting on the project at the turn of 1942/43 Beneš had said, "It is in principle out of the question that a distinction should be made between Germans and Czechs. The eventual decree or law on this question must in no circumstances appear as retribution against Germans. Such a legal provision would be unsustainable for international political reasons. It is necessary to take action just as resolutely and using the same measurement against Quislings and international traitors" minutes of Beneš's opinions on the punishment of war criminals. *Dekrety prezidenta republiky 1940–1945*. (Documents). Vol. 1. 179.

[32] Heading XIII. Protocol of *The Potsdam Conference of the Three Great Powers* on the transfer of the German population from Poland, Czechoslovakia and Hungary to Germany. (Orderly Transfers of German Population). The French government expressed its agreement with the conclusions of the conference in August 1945. The conference rejected the idea of unity for Germany, and agreed the principles of occupation, reparation,

The transferrees from Czechoslovakia went to the American and Soviet occupation zones, where they were relocated on the basis of the orders of the occupation authorities. In the Western zone they settled mainly in three federal lands: Bavaria, Lower Saxony and Schleswig-Holstein (but also in Hessen). The largest number, more than two million, went to Bavaria, where in 1970 they made up approximately one fifth of the population. They arrived in places where often there was no more than a decommissioned and desolate factory; at the beginning they lived just in emergency military barracks and they gradually built new centres. Through their efforts several entirely new towns grew up in Bavaria – Geretsried, Neu Gablonz, Waldkraiburg, Traunreut, Neutraubling, Neuwildflecken and others.[33]

To their new environment the Sudeten Germans brought expert skills, motivation and hard work, but also, in the political sphere, the baneful tradition of *Völkisch* ideology intensified by the suffering of the transfer, and a bitter feeling of historical injustice repeatedly expressed in the demand for the right to self-determination.

The first attempt to found an organisation defending the interests of the transferees was the Working Society for the Defence of Sudeten German Interests (*Arbeitsgemeinschaft zur Wahrung sudetendeutscher Interessen*), which developed out of the non-political *Block of the Expelled and Disenfranchised*. This Council represented one current of opinion working for the constitution of a Sudeten German umbrella organisation, and in its relations with the emerging *Sudetendeutsche Landsmannschaft* it alternated between cooperation and opposition. Federation of Expellees aimed mainly at tackling the social problems of their members represented a second organisational form, but these never developed a higher profile.[34]

June 1948 saw another move to find a common platform for the transferred Sudeten Germans when a Whitsun congress was called in the Bavarian spa town of Bad Aibling. Eight hundred people attended and the event founded the tradition of the annual Sudeten German Day/*Sudetendeutscher Tag* (known as Pfingsten), which regularly demonstrates the existence and strength of the Sudeten German national group.[35]

---

the drawing up of peace treaties, the border of Poland on the Oder and Nisa and the transfer of the German population from the countries of Central Europe.

[33] Ohlbaum, R. 1981. *Bayerns vierter Stamm – die Sudetendeutschen*. München: Sudetedeutschen Archiv/Aufstieg-Verlag. 46.

[34] Berounská, O. "Postavení a činnost přesídleneckých organizací a zejména sudetoněmeckého landsmanschaftu v SRN po 2. světové válce" [The Status and Activity of the Expellee Organisations and Especially the Sudetendeutsch Landsmannschaft in the FRG after the Second World War], in *Severní Čechy a Mnichov*. 241.

[35] For detail see Hahn, E. *Sudetoněmecký problém: obtížné loučení s minulostí*. 67.

In all sections of opinion there was a gradually increasing conviction of the practical necessity for the various Sudeten German associations to join forces in one umbrella organisation. What may be considered key in this respect, however, was the idea common to all three organisations of transferees, i.e. the *Seliger-Gemeinde, Ackermann-Gemeinde* and *Witikobund*, that the return of the Sudeten Germans should not suffer from the stigma of nationalism, but should take place in the frame of a new European order, federalist and embodying the right of transferees to self-determination.[36]

It is noteworthy that the process of creation of a centralised structure for the expellee organisations took place in circumstances in which the international legal status of the Sudeten Germans remained unclear, and so the basis on which they could formulate their demands arising from the position of victims of illegal actions and decisions was also unclear.[37]

This situation changed later following the establishment in 1949 of the Federal Republic of Germany, which considered itself the only legitimate successor state to Nazi Germany and thus took over responsibility for the ethnic Germans resettled from Eastern Europe. In 1949 Germans previously living in former German territories were granted citizenship of the FRG by constitutional law.[38]

In 1953 ethnic Germans still living in Central and Eastern Europe were defined as citizens of Germany by the Constitution of the FRG and as a consequence were enabled by a special law to request resettlement in West Germany. For ethnic Germans from Central and Eastern Europe this established a privileged access to the FRG which has been more or less maintained ever since. The measure implicitly confirmed and strengthened the traditional German perception of ethnic identity and citizenship by emphasising the political significance of ethnic origin.[39] However, it was precisely this exceptionally strong ethnic loyalty that had been a root of the tragedy of "Eastern" Germandom at the end of the war and in the immediate post-war period.

Ethnic Germans were defined as former citizens of Germany living on territories that had belonged to Germany[40] in 1937, and so were distinguished from

---

36 Kural, V. "Hlavní organizace sudetoněmeckých vysídlenců v SRN 1945–1989". 33.

37 Hahn, E. "Sudetskí Nemci v nemeckej spoločnosti: polstoročie politických dejín". 81. The divided and occupied German at first had no sovereignty at all, and later only a semi-sovereignty.

38 For more detail and abundant documentation see Marshall, B. 2000. *The New Germany and Migration in Europe*. The chapter, West Germany and Migration 1945–89. Manchester University Press. 10–19.

39 Münz, R. – Ohliger, R. "Long-Distance Citizens (Ethnic Germans and their Immigration to Germany)", in *Path to Inclusion: The Integration of Migrants in the United States and Germany*. 1998. Oxford University Press. 159.

40 To justify the acceptance of ethnic Germans the German Government used three lines of argument: legal, historical-political and socio-economic. The first appealed to the wording of Article 116 of the Constitution of the FRG, which defined ethnic Germans as Germans who had suffered specially in the course of the Sec-

people living in Austria, Bohemia and Moravia, the South Tyrol, France, Luxemburg and Slovenia, who had only become German citizens after their states (or parts of them) were annexed by Germany (Austria, the Sudeten areas, West Prussia, North Slovenia, Alsace-Lorraine, Luxemburg) or "governed by an occupation administration"[41] such as the so-called *General Gouvernement in Poland* or the Protectorate of Bohemia and Moravia.

Legislation influenced the incorporation of the standpoints of the expellees' organisations in the internal and foreign policy of the Federal Republic of Germany, the most important of the measures concerned being the Federal Expellee and Refugee Law passed in 1953 and confirmed again in 1957.[42] By the terms of this law, the definition of expellees was extended from persons actually expelled from a certain territory to Germany after the war to include all their family members and spouses of children of such families, and even their grandchildren. The Expellee Law thus envisages the inter-generational inheritance of property claims relating to the territories from which the transfer occurred.[43]

Eva Hahn has drawn attention to the often neglected fact that a large number of expellees never involved themselves in the search for collective identity and the creation of common political will (membership in the *Sudetendeutsche Landsmannschaft* or other organisations), and likewise never responded to the activities of the expellee organisations. T. Grosser, however, takes a rather different view on the basis of his detailed study of the processes by which the expellees were integrated into German society. He argues that immediately after the transfer, the expellees' desire to return home was extremely intense and there was little differentiation of view in this respect.[44] Deepening differences

---

ond World War and for their connection with Germany after the war. For this reason their demand for the provision of assistance and the possibility of settlement was legal, while Germany had a moral obligation to accept this demand. Paragraph 1 of the 1953 Federal Law on Refugees and Expellees of 1953 defined an ethnic German as a person belonging to the German people/*deutscher Volkszugehöriger* or of German state citizenship/*deutscher Staatsangehöriger*. The second reason in support of acceptance into the FRG was the long-term repressive treatment of persons from German milieux directed to their expulsion/*Vertreibungsdruckrichtlinie*. Finally, the third reason was the need for demographic renewal of the human resoures of the FRG. For more detail see Marshall, B. *The New Germany and Migration in Europe.* 9.

[41] This euphemistic term for the somewhat modified form of Nazi occupation government can be found in otherwise respectable current academic studies. The "game" of terminology seems to be a reflection of certain relativising approaches in some quarters in German historiography, as has been mentioned in relation to the *Historikerstreit*. It may also be a reflection of the differentiation of approach to individual countries of Central and Eastern Europe adopted by Germany in the inter-war period for functional goal-related purposes – and which finds an echo today as well.

[42] For a detailed overview of the legal norms and literature on the subject of refugees and expellees see Krallert-Sattler, G. *Recht und Verwaltung, Lastenausgleich.* For the full wording of the documents see "Anhang I. Charta der deutschen Heimatvertriebene, II. Grundsätzliches aus dem deutschen Vertriebenenrecht", in *Die Vertriebenen in Westdeutschland.* Lemberg, E. – Edding, F. (eds.). Kiel: Ferdinand Hirt. Band III. 597–684.

[43] Bundesgesetztblatt I. 22. 5. 1953. *Sudetendeutsche Zeitung* 14. 8. 4. 1961.

[44] Grosser, T. 1998. "Integrácia odsunutých v Spolkovej republike Nemecko" [The Integration of Expelled Germans in the Federal Republic of Germany], *V rozdelenej Európe.* 40.

of attitude developed among the expellees only as they came to achieve a certain degree of structural and social integration in the new environment. For example, in 1949 43 % of those expelled (from all Eastern territories) considered return to their homeland to be top of the list of desirable measures that would remedy their "refugee misery". The Sudeten Germans in fact exceeded this average, with 47.6% of them agreeing on this point. More than 70% of the respondents with a white collar occupation stated that they felt "just as respected as before the expulsion", while among manual workers only 57% of respondents felt the same way.[45]

The process of integration was in fact to be long and complicated, as is clear from sociological surveys conducted among expellees in the course of the 1950s and 1960s, the decades in which they were gradually having to accept that the prospect of a return based on the outbreak and successful outcome of a new armed conflict between East and West was receding.[46] All the same, the level of organised participation in the regional homeland associations of expellees showed a tendency to decline[47], and on the basis of sociological surveys Grosser notes that eagerness to return declined faster among Sudeten Germans than in the groups expelled from Silesia, Pomerania or Eastern Prussia. Clearly this trend was unfavourable to the aims of the leaders of the Landmannschafts and their long term efforts to keep the question of the expellees open as a highly political issue demanding care, attention and systematic pursuit of a solution on the part of the federal government.

In 1949 at the suggestion of the *Ackermann-Gemeinde*, representatives of the three currents of opinion of the Sudeten German organisations, i.e. the national

---

[45] Data taken from a large-scale sociological survey carried out by the Bavarian Land Statistical Office and published in *Die Vertriebenen in Westdeutschland*, 65. A series of surveys on the theme of the expellees was conducted by the *Office of Military Government for Germany of the United States (OMGUS)*, Information Control Division, Surveys Branch: *German Attitudes toward the Expulsion of German Nationals from Neighbouring Countries.* Report No. 14A. 8 July 1946 and others. The theme of the expellees was likewise investigated by the *Institut für Demoskopie*, Allensbach, *EMNID-Institute* aj.

[46] Among the many sociological surveys of individual groups of expellees we might mention the results of the survey conducted by Prof. Dr. Hans-Heinrich Herlemann in the winter of 1950/51 on a selected sample of 1,592 respondents defined as *former owners of agricultural land*. All the areas from which ethnic Germans had been expelled in the East were proportionately represented (East Prussia, Silesia, the Baltics, Yugoslavia, Rumania etc.). The survey was entitled *Das Schicksal der ehemaligen landwirtschaftlichen Betriebsinhaber unter den Vertriebenen* and showed in detail the attitudes and expectations of expellees of all age categories in the course of integration into German society. Half of the Sudeten German respondents expressed a wish to return to their former homeland. Herlemann, H.-H. "Vertriebene Bauern im Strukturwandel der Landwirtschaft", in *Die Vertriebenen in Westdeutschland*. 128.

[47] In 1963 the proportion of Sudeten Germans organised in the SL was in federal terms 16%. In northern Rhineland-Westphalia it was 8%, in Bavaria 15%, but in the age category over 60 it was 28%. In 1985, 90% of Sudeten Germans surveyed in the FRG felt "in every respect a full-value member of society", but surveys also indicate that in Bavaria the proportion of the fully satisfed is the lowest (66%). See Grosser, T. *Integrácia odsunutých*, on the basis of data provided by the EMNID agency.

(völkisch), Catholic and Social Democratic, met in Eichstätt to find a new common platform. This was formulated in the *Eichstätt Declaration*. Here once again we find the formulation that, "This is no longer a matter just of the right of self-determination for Sudeten Germans, but for all Europe... The nations behind the Iron Curtain must realise that the restoration of their own rights and liberties is inextricably linked to the acknowledgment and restoration of the rights of all the expelled to their country and home."[48] What we find for the first time in this document, however, is clear rejection of revenge for the transfer: "We Sudeten Germans do not ask for reprisal, but for justice."

From the very beginning the right to self-determination was part of the basic armoury of arguments of the expellee organisations and it also appeared in the preamble to the Constitution of the FRG of the 23rd of May 1949, where there is a mention of the unity of Germany as goal to be reached on the basis of the right to self-determination: "in freier Selbstbestimmung die Einheit und Freiheit Deutschlands zu vollenden."

Dr. Lodgman was immediately inspired to produce his own document in the form of the *Detmold Declaration*, which defined the Sudeten German ethnic group as part of the German nation, but in other sections came close to the *Eichstätt Declaration*, including the declared demand for self-determination. The same Lodgman von Auen, however, had presented his own idea of the role of the expellees earlier in a speech of June 1948 to the congress of Sudeten German organisations in Heppenheim.[49] This event was attended by 265 representatives of organisations already existing or in process of formation, who in the two days of discussion expressed support for the revision of the existing situation and the need to create a common organ for all these organisations. They rejected the suggestion that organisations aimed at integrating expellees into German society were different in character, as proposed for example by the association of new citizens, the *Neubürgerbund* which renounced ideas of revenge and the revision of the post-war order.

The title of Lodgman's speech in itself characterises its content: "The International Legal Basis of the Sudeten Problem and Political Development since 1945". His basic claim was that the appurtenance of the Sudeten areas to the Bohemian Lands and the Czechoslovak State must never be recognised. Closely related to this point was his insistence on the continuing validity of the Munich

---

[48] The full text of the *Eichstätts Declaration* of November 1949 can be found in *Cesta ke smíření*. 28–30.

[49] For more detail see Šnejdárek, A. "Počátky revanšistického Sudetoněmeckého krajanstva v západním Německu". *Příspěvky k dějinám KSČ* 2/1962. 199–201. The Heppenheim Conference took place under the slogans *Menschenrechte, Heimatrecht, Selbstbestimmungrecht gefördert*. A provisional *Sudetendeutscher Ausschuss* was established. For more detail see *Entschliessung der Heppenheimer Tagung*, in Habel, F. P. 1984. *Dokumente zur Sudetenfrage*. München: Langen Müller. 307.

Agreement[50] and his argument that post-war developments indicated that the Potsdam Coalition had finally fallen apart and the need now was to prepare for the redress of Potsdam and all its consequences, including the territorial settlement in Central Europe and the expulsion of the German minorities from Central European countries. According to Lodgman, the Sudeten Germans had to work to create political conditions of a kind that would enable them to exploit the coming opportunity for redress of Potsdam as soon as the state of affairs created in Central Europe after 1945 changed. What he meant was the territorial revision of the postwar settlement that would most likely occur following the third world war that he regarded as the almost inevitable outcome of competition between East and West. The end of the Soviet bloc, then, was to mean the end of sanctions against the defeated, and also a return to 1938.

Also discussed at Heppenheim was the form that an umbrella organisation for Sudeten Germans ought to take, i.e. whether it should be a government-in-exile on the model of the Czechoslovak State Council in London during the war, or merely an interest organisation without any claim to larger ambitions as far as the German and international public were concerned. The solution accepted was the establishment of a Sudeten German Homeland Association/ *Sudetendeutsche Landsmannschaft*, which would fulfil the role of an exile government without actually calling itself one and so having to face the complications that would ensue. The congress drew up a plan for a solid organisational structure including a form of elected representation that would enable it to transform itself into a government at any time. A proposal for the creation of a joint committee with groups of Czech political emigrant groups in the West was

---

[50] Prof. H. Raschhofer developed his conception of the continuing validity of the Munich Agreement and other legal arguments in detail in his work *Die Sudetenfrage*. Křen, J. "Poválečná německá historická literatura v českých zemích" [Postwar German historical literature in the Czech Lands], in *V rozdelenej Európe*. 149, points out the important role played by Raschhofer, who with his book *Die tschechoslowakischen Denkschfriten für die Friedenskonferenz von Paris 1919/1920*. 1937. Berlin, and other publications contributed substantially to the Hitlererian and anti-Czechoslovak campaign of the 1930s. In the role of advisor to K. H. Frank, he continued to develop these views with practical consequences for occupation policy in the Protectorate of Bohemia and Moravia. In 1988 his Denkschriften were supplemented and "rehabilitated" by Prof. O. Kimminich. B. Čelovský considers Raschhofer to be the key author and father of the legalistic theory that the Munich Agreemen is a valid act of international law (he initially presented this thesis in the article Raschhofer, H. "Das Münchener Abkommen". *Volk und Reich* 19/1946. 313–320).). In essence, he asserts that the Munich Agreement resolved only technical problems of the Czechoslovak evacuation of the Sudeten German territories, the evacuation being already determined by the Czechoslovak acceptance of the so-called French-British Plan on the 21st of September 1938. At first sight this seems a logical construction. Closer examination, however, reveals a central weakness: the deliberate omission of all circumstances leading up to the preparation of the French-British Plan. This interpretation entirely ignored all the circumstances (especially the inadmissible form of ultimatum and pressure, and the non-participation of the CSR), which led to Munich, and in particular Hitler's exploitation of the Sudeten Germans as an instrument for starting a war and extortion against President Beneš. See Čelovský, B. "The transferred Sudeten Germans and their political activity." *Journal of Central European Affairs* VI (April 1957). 141–142.

rejected on the grounds that the influential circle of Czech exiled politicians including P. Zenkl, H. Ripka, A. Procházka, J. Lettrich and others, most of them sitting on the Council of Free Czechoslovakia, inclined to the views of Beneš.

A year after the Heppenheim conference, the first *Sudeten German Day [Rally]* was held on the 16th and 17th of June 1949 in Memmingen, and was attended by 20,000 expellees.[51] For comparison – in 1961 the rally in Cologne was attended by 380,000 people. The mass rallies of expellees, which in the nineties were still attracting around 100,000 participants, give the Sudeten German Homeland Association legitimacy and increase its weight on the German political scene. To this day the Sudeten German organisations continue to confirm their reputation as the best organised and united community of all groups of ethnic Germans.

From 1950, the position of SL spokesman (according to the original ideas – president in exile), was held successively by R. Lodgman von Auen, H.-Ch. Seebohm, W. Becher and F. Neubauer. Today the positions of SL spokesman (B. Posselt) and SL president (J. Böhm) are separate.

The political board (association) on which political parties, and politically active institutions and individuals are represented is the Sudeten German Council/*Sudetendeutscher Rat*. The Catholic Church also plays an important role in Sudeten German circles. Apart from the influential Catholic Ackermann-Gemeinde, we should mention the association of Sudeten German priests – the *Sudetendeutsches Priestwerk*, the system of clerical administration for expellees and the bishops' conference with the institution of a bishop for refugees. The Society of Protestant Sudeten Germans/*Gemeinschaft evangelischer Sudetendeutscher* is said to bring together 150,000 Sudeten Germans.

A number of conservatively orientated periodicals were also founded and still appear, among them the *Sudetendeutsche Zeitung*, the *Sudetendeutsche Post* (Austria), the quarterly for art, literature, science and folk culture *Sudetenland*, and the lavish cultural yearbook *A. Stifter Jahrbuch*. There exist a range of educational institutions such as the *Collegium Carolinum* which publishes the theoretical review *Bohemia*, the Sudeten German Archive/*Sudetendeutsches Archiv*, the Sudeten German Academie of Sciences and Art/*Sudetendeutsche Akademie der Wissenschaften und Künste*, the *Sudetendeutsches Musikinstitut* and others.

In 1951 Prof. R. Laun, then an important lawyer and legal theorist on the right to self-determination, set out what he considered the task of the expellees'

---

[51] In 1949 the proportion of Sudeten German organised in the *Landsmannschaft* was quite high – 2.7%. In 1963 the *Demoscopic Institute* in Allensbach conducted a survey which identified membership of the expellee organisation at the federal level as 16% – and at the land level as 8% in the North Rhineland-Westphalia and in Bavaria 15% of those surveyed. For details see Grosser, T. "Integrácia odsunutých v Spolkovej republike Nemecko". 40.

organisations: "Homeland associations are a political novelty among German organisational forms. They are in the highest degree political without being tied to political parties. What is clearly reflected in the homeland associations is the fact that after the war the German nation lost a third of its territory and each homeland association represents part of that third in the rest of Germany. The idea of the homeland associations constitutes a particular area in the formation of German consciousness and is finding a positive response in the domestic population, because the concepts of the fatherland [among the expellees and the domestic Germans – translator's note] meet on the same platform."[52]

Views on this concept of the SL as a unifying force were not, however, unanimous. For example, a number of critical articles were published in *Der Neue Ackermann* journal in the 1950s challenging the ideological basis of the Sudetendeutsche Landsmannschaft and the traditions from which it drew its conception of itself and its political-strategic positions. E. Lemberg in particular opposed every attempt to subordinate political and cultural diversity to one single vision and explictly warned against attempts to incorporate the whole ethnic group and identify it with one single organisation. "This would impose a deadly rigidity and constraint on [the group] and – depending on the situation – would cost it the trust of the surrounding world."[53]

Disputes over the leading role of the SL continued, although the importance of the Sudetendeutsche Landsmannschaft was boulstered by the official patronage of the Bavarian government, which declared the Sudeten Germans "a tribe among the tribes of Bavaria" and recognised the Landsmannschaft and its individual parts as the representatives of this tribe. This was a step that guaranteed the privileged position of the Landsmannschaft among the other Sudeten German associations, and to this day no German politician has challenged the recognition of the SL as empowered to speak for Sudeten Germans.[54]

The leading role and weight of the SL has in fact been acknowledged by all Sudeten German organisations with the possible exception of the *Circle of Friends of German-Czech Understanding* based in the border town of Furth im Wald. Small but significant for its very existence, this club evidently represents the only attempt to resist the dominance of the SL. However, it is unable to offer expellees an alternative identity. Indeed, it is impossible to construct any form of collective Sudeten German identity to rival the form promoted by the

---

[52] Laun, R., *Sudetendeutsche Zeitung* 39. 29. 9. 1961. In detail see Laun, R. 1951. *Das Recht auf die Heimat*. Schroedel: Hannover/Darmstadt.

[53] Lemberg, E. "Aufbau und Führung einer Volksgruppe im Exil. Das sudetendeutsche Problem heute". *Der Neue Ackermann* 1/1953 (IV). Cited from Hahn, E. "Sudetskí Nemci v nemeckej spoločnosti: polstoročie politických dejín". 82.

[54] Ibidem. 83.

Landsmannschaft, however vehemently the criticism it has sometimes attracted from other associations.[55]

In 1950 all the parties represented in the *Bundestag* supported what was called the Declaration on Protection/*Obhutserklärung*, rejecting the Prague Agreement between the Czechoslovak and East German governments which declared the expulsion of the German-speaking inhabitants of the CSR borderlands to be final and confirmed the borders between the two states. The second paragraph of the *Bundestag* declaration reads, "The Prague Agreement is incompatible with the inalienable right of peoples to their homeland. The German Parliament therefore opposes the renunciation of right to homeland, takes the Germans from Czechoslovakia under the protection of the Federal Republic of Germany, and rejects the validity of the Prague Agreement."[56]

This declaration, strengthened and supported by the Free State of Bavaria's declared patronage of the Sudeten Germans in 1962 (the *Urkunde zur Schirmherrschaft*) forms the political basis within Germany for the demands of the leaders of the *Sudeten German Homeland Association*.

The Twenty-Point Programme

In 1961 the Sudeten German Council/*Sudetendeutscher Rat*, as the authoritative organ of the Sudeten German organisations for foreign policy, approved a new and updated programme in reponse to the changing international situation of the late 1950s and early 1960s, when following the initiatives of N. S. Khrushchev[57] there was a certain relaxation of tension between East and West. Despite some shifts, however, the Sudeten German leadership once again made the right to homeland and self-determination the cornerstone of their approach, and thus formulated the programe remained and remains unacceptable in its implications for the integrity of the Czechoslovak state.

The *Position on the Sudeten Question* (the so-called Twenty Points) was approved on the 15th of January 1951 by a plenary session of the Sudeten German Council and on the 7th of May 1961 it was confirmed by the Federal Assembly

---

[55]   Ibidem. 85.

[56]   "Erklärung des (1.) Deutschen Bundestages", in Habel, F. P. *Dokumente zur Sudetenfrage*. 315.

[57]   On the 10th of January 1959 the Chairman of the Council of Ministers of the USSR, Nikita S. Khrushchev put forward the draft of a peace treaty with Germany involving the demand that the government of the FRG should renounce the Munich Agreement entirely. In Article 10 the draft stated, "Germany recognises the Munich Agreement to be invalid with all the consequences that flowed from it, and declares that it will always acknowledge the territory of the former so-called Sudeten area to be an inalienable part of the state territory of the Czechoslovak Republic." Hajdů, V. – Líska, L. – Šnejdárek, A. 1964. *Německá otázka 1945–1963*. Prague: NPL. 506. At the Geneva Conference (11th May – 5th August 1959) with the participation of both German states the Soviet plan for the unification of Germany was rejected by the other three Great Powers.

of the Sudetendeutsche Landsmannschaft. The document is thus the official SL programme.[58]

In the very first article, the programme states that the Sudeten Question can be properly understood only against the background of the establishment of Czechoslovakia in 1918/19, when 3.5 million Sudeten Germans were "incorporated into a multi-national state against their declared will." This is followed up by the claim that up to 1806 the Bohemian Lands had belonged to the Holy Roman (German) Empire, up to 1866 to the German Federation and up to 1918 to Austria-Hungary. There is absolutely no mention of Czech statehood in history. Article 3 contains the statement, "With no respect for the right to self-determination, the founders of Czechoslovakia forced through the incorporation of 3.5 million Sudeten Germans and 1.3 million Hungarians, Ukrainians and Poles against their declared will into a multinational state that was, however, constituted as a "Czechoslovak" national state. In this way many decades of attempts to reach a German-Czech settlement came to naught." Article 6 refers to the fateful year 1938 and Munich and includes the statement that "England and France, however, would never have imposed on Czechoslovakia an obligation to cede the Sudeten German territory had the liberation of the Sudeten Germans from Czech hegemony not fundamentally conformed to the right to self-determination."

Although in the period following the German-Czech Declaration there have been signs of differences of views on the Sudeten German side (e.g. the Seliger-Gemeinde programme or the Ellwangen Declaration by the Ackermann-Gemeinde), no organisation in the *Sudeten German Homeland Association* has yet revised its support for the 20-Point Political Programme.

To stand for many instances, I shall mention just one more characteristic example of the truly remarkable reluctance of the SL to reflect soberly, and with some historical objectivity and grasp of causes and consequences on the tragic historical events concerned, and to distance itself clearly from Henleinian irredentism. The position of the Sudeten German Council on the autumn crisis of 1938, which was provoked by the Sudeten German movement, reads as follows: "The Sudeten Germans had been appealing for the aid of the League of Nations as the depository of the agreement made with Czechoslovakia for the protection of minorities, against the forced assimilation measures of the Czechs – but they had no great success. Great Britain particularly, however, started to follow the development of the national problem in Czechoslovakia with growing interest. The proposals of the Sudeten German Party were aimed at the transformation of the CSR into a state fully recognising more than one

---

[58]   For the full wording see Habel, F. P. *Dokumente zur Sudetenfrage.* 346–348.

nation and at the introduction of autonomy. These issues were expressed in abbreviated form in the concepts: school, native soil, and work. When the Reich Chancellor Hitler then began to take a public interest in the fate of the Sudeten Germans, after the annexation of Austria to the German Reich (13. 3. 1938), the so-called Sudeten Crisis arose in the summer of 1938."

The Sudeten Germans "in the framework of the institutions imposed on them strove vainly to achieve security for their economic, social and national existence". The programme goes on to claim that in 1938, "the Sudeten Germans were the mere object of the policies of the great powers". England and France would never have forced Czechoslovakia to cede the Sudeten territory unless this had not been in fundamental accord with the right to self-determination, and (we then read), "our political efforts are based on the right to homeland and the right of nations to self-determination in the framework of European integration, and independently of the disputed Munich Agreement of 1938."

There is no word here of the key role of Henlein's Sudeten German Party, which in "exemplary fashion" fulfilled the honourable Reich assignment of ratcheting up extortionate demands so as to force President Beneš and the CSR into an impossible situation requiring international intervention – without the participation of the state affected. The propagandist media campaign against the Czech Republic in the first half of 2002 (originating particularly in Bavarian, Austrian and Hungarian conservatively orientated political circles)[59] was in many respects reminiscent of the psychological war waged against Czechoslovakia in the period of the Munich crisis itself.

Point 11 of the programme states that not just the Sudeten Germans but the whole German nation will never be reconciled to the expulsion of the Sudeten Germans from the homeland in which they had lived for centuries. It declares that it will never be possible to consider conditions in Europe and the relations between the Federal Republic of Germany and Czechoslovakia (now the Czech Republic) normalised until the right of the Sudeten German national group to return to its homeland and live undisturbed in free self-determination is secured in practice. Article 12 states that, "We shall never give up our demands for the reinstatement of the right violated by expulsion and for compensation for the damages suffered."

---

[59]   For example, the Austrian Chancellor W. Schüssel made several statements on the Beneš Decrees, and did so even after the Commissioner for the Enlargement of the EU, G. Verheugen had assured the Prime Minister of the CR and other functionaries in Prague that the presidential decrees were in no way an obstacle for the admission of the CR into the European Union. Schüssel declared on the 12th of April 2002, for example, that "there is a suspicion, that has recently been confirmed, that by means of conversion laws the decrees remain in force. This force continues to have discriminatory effects in the CR and is definitely not compatible with EU law". *APA agency*. 13. 4. 2002.

The content of the last three points is especially revealing. Here we find the formulation, "In the special geographical conditions of the Bohemian-Moravian-Silesian territory the principle of the right of nations to self-determination permits *various constitutional and international legal solutions.* No solution respecting the right to self-determination, however, is compatible with any kind of attempt to incorporate Germans and Slovaks into a centralist Czech nation state in which they would be accorded a subordinate position (Czechoslovakism)." The division of the former Czechoslovakia into two states has made part of this latter point redundant, but nevertheless in view of the unclear formulation there is a need to clarify *which different solutions* are permissible and possible according to the *Sudeten German Homeland Association.*

"Constitutional community with the Czech and Slovak nation is not excluded in advance (sic!), provided that it rests on the principle of equal and free partnership, i.e. the free expression of the will of those involved, and provided that this is guaranteed by the community of the free nations of Europe." This paragraph might be interpreted as a demand for a plebiscite, and possible eventual autonomy for the borderland territories of the CR neighbouring with Germany, which would create the conditions for the establishment of a new territorial administrative whole (separated from the CR) in the frame of a new form of federalised Europe of regions as promoted by the FRG.

The final point predicted the future: "The relationship between the Sudeten Germans, Czechs and Slovaks can be satisfactorily solved only in the framework of European-wide integration. The precondition is reconciliation between the German nation and its Eastern neighbours conceived on a long-term basis."[60]

The Support of the Political Spectrum of the FRG for the Expellees

The Twenty-Point Programme triggered a process in which the Sudeten German Council and Sudeten German Homeland Association (SL), directed from the background, by the Witikobund worked to ensure that the ethnic and social integration of expellees into German society would be crowned by the identification of German political parties and the German state with the aims and aspiration of the expellee organisation. The first step in this direction had been the *Obhutserklärung* of 1950, mentioned above.

---

[60] "Stanovisko k sudetské otázce (20 bodů)" [Position on the Sudeten Question (20 Points)], in Olbert, F. *Cesta ke smíření.* 35–39.

The first major successes on the path to this goal were the agreements made between the Sudetendeutsche Landsmannschaft and the SPD and CSU in 1961. The Bergneustadt Declaration, issued by the German Social Democratic Party of the 22nd of January 1961 summarised in six points all the basic demands of the SL including the claim that "the Sudeten German Question has not been settled by the expulsion" and the possibility of a "different constitutional arrangement", in other words the possibility of a change in Czechoslovak state borders. On the 3rd of June 1961 the Social Democrats were followed by the Bavarian Christian Democrats, who not only accepted the SL programme but added statements on the recognition of the status of the Sudeten Germans in Bavaria.[61] After a certain interval, the final phase of garnering support for Sudeten German demands came in 1964. This phase was typified in terms of ideological content by H.-Ch. Seebohm[62] in a speech at the Sudeten German Day in Nuremberg, where he declared that, "The springs of the struggle of the Sudeten Germans are not material but exclusively ideal conditions: the rights to homeland and self-determination, which cannot be bought off by material compensation, because they are given by God. Nor can they be bought off by the fact that the Sudeten Germans have been able to integrate themselves economically and socially into the Federal Republic of Germany and Austria, nor is anything changed by the departure of the old generation and the rise of the young." Seebohm's arguments in building up the Sudeten German legal position also included the theory that, "we" bear no burden of guilt for historical events, since in this century "we" have been nothing but the object of the politics of the great powers.[63]

The mode of argument elaborated by Seebohm is relevant because it is still, to this day, employed by leaders of the SL, including typically misty phrases about an *integrated Europe rid of the old blight of nationalism*, where borders and national states will disappear to the benefit of a "regionalised Europe".

---

[61] For the texts of all documents in full see Habel, F. P. *Dokumente zur Sudetenfrage*. See also Kural, V. "Hlavní organizace sudetoněmeckých vysídlenců v SRN 1945–1989". 42–43.

[62] The second spokesman of the SL in 1959–1967 and federal minister of transport 1949–1966.

[63] Ibidem. 43. The weekly magazine *Der Spiegel* published an interview with H.-Ch. Seebohm, in which in answer to questions he answered mainly in a misty and vague way. Nonetheless the journalist reconstructed the content of his answers in the form of three programme points and asked if Seebohm's position could be interpreted as follows: Phase 1 – internal transformation of Czechoslovakia into a democratic state; Phase 2 – after negotiations between the FRG and a transformed ČSR the Sudeten Germans will return to the home territory; Phase 3 – in virtue of their right to self-determination the Sudeten Germans will decide on their future status. If we believe in the Europe without state frontiers, they will probably form a special ethnic region in a united Europe, or attach themselves to another administrative region. Seebohm responded that "cases outside the 1937 borders, like the German-Czech problem, demand *a new form of solution, probably as you have described it*".

In October 1964, the FDP followed the SPD and CSU with a declaration branding the expulsion an inhuman act and expressing support for the right to homeland and self-determination. At the same time the party undertook to seek to prevent German foreign policy from abandoning its commitments to pursue these rights. The last party to express its support was the CDU: on the 16th of November 1964 Chancellor Ludwig Erhard held a meeting with SL representatives which resulted in *clear commitments for the future*. The CDU recognised the major contribution of the Sudeten Germans to the social, economic and cultural reconstruction of the FRG, acknowledged the SL to be the legitimate representative of the Sudeten German ethnic group in the period of expulsion and expressed the conviction that this commitment would be respected by all future governments. The CDU also confirmed that it did not regard the Sudeten German Question as having been settled by the expulsion, and considered that the principle of the continuity of Germany in its 1937 borders did not exclude "a national and constitutional solution on the basis of the Sudeten Germans' right to homeland and self-determination".[64]

The clearly demonstrated support of all the major political parties and the land governments of the FRG culminated in a declaration by Chancellor Erhard which essentially repeated the points in the CDU statement with the addition of what was later to be the repeated standard formulation that "the FRG makes no territorial claims against the CSSR, but this assurance does not exclude the Sudeten German right to homeland and self-determination." Precisely this formulation expressed the shared standpoint of the Sudetendeutsche Landsmannschaft and the federal government, on behalf of which Chancellor Erhard promised that finding a solution to the unjust expulsion would be a matter "for the whole German nation and its constitutional organs". Immediately after his speech all the political parties (the CDU, CSU, SPD and FDP) issued a joint declaration on the question of the expellees in the Federal Parliament.

Following the 1966 elections, a Grand CDU/SPD Coalition was formed with Willy Brandt as deputy chancellor and foreign minister, and the outlines of a new direction in Bonn foreign policy, to be known as *Ostpolitik*, began to emerge. It was not a policy that included Sudeten German demands, and dissension started to develop between the Sudetendeutsche Landsmannschaft and the federal government.

One telling illustration of the new situation was the changed interpretation of the Munich Agreement evident in the text of the Grand Coalition government declaration of the 13th of December 1966, when a new tone appears in relation to Czechoslovakia: "The German nation would like to come to an un-

---

[64]   Ibidem. 44.

derstanding with Czechoslovakia as well. The federal government condemns the policy of Hitler, which was directed at the destruction of the integrity of the Czechoslovak state. It agrees with the view that the Munich Agreement, made under threat of violence, is no longer valid." This change of tone opened the way to the *Agreement on Mutual Relations between the CSSR and the FRG* signed on the 11th of December 1973 in the course of the visit of Chancellor Willy Brandt and Foreign Minister Walter Scheel to Prague.

The agreement was a fundamental breakthrough because the establishment of mutual diplomatic relations on the day of signing meant that the FRG had abandoned the *Hallstein doktrine* (rejecting diplomatic relations with states that had official contacts with the GDR). From the Czechoslovak point of view, what was crucial was the statement that, "In view of their mutual relations in accordance with this agreement, the CSSR and FRG consider the Munich Agreement of the 29th of September 1938 to be null and void."[65] The road to this agreement had been neither short nor easy, but the subject of the expellees had not been mentioned, except once when in the course of negotiations the view had been expressed that time and the change of generations would solve the problem of the residue of grudge on the part of the Sudetendeutsche Landsmannschaft.[66]

W. Brandt counselled "greater orientation to the future than to the past, for otherwise we might become prisoners of the past". I find his words still relevant today.

While successful, the negotiations had confirmed the difficulties and pitfalls in Czech-German relations, and after six rounds of exploratory talks the state secretary Frank had found it necessary to remind others of the only method by which the two sides could reach agreement – this was "to find the kind of wording that allows both sides to retain their own legal conception". This principle was to be employed in all subsequent Czech-German negotiations, even in the euphoric phase of international relations after the fall of the iron curtain and collapse of the Soviet Bloc. Both sides seek a formulation that allows them to maintain their own position intact in their own eyes. A "breakthrough" formula is evidently not on the cards.

Sudeten German identity involves a somewhat contradiction-ridden concept of duality between "homeland" and "home". The home of the expellees is de

---

[65] Břach, R. 1994. *Smlouva o vzájemných vztazích mezi ČSSR a SRN z roku 1973* [The Agreement on Mutual Relations between the CSSR and the FRG of 1973]. Prague: Ústav pro soudobé dějiny AV ČR. 73. This is the full wording of Article 1.

[66] Ibidem. 52. Brandt had at that point gone on to say, "Do not make it unnecessarily hard for yourselves and for us. Do not connect questions of future cooperation with questions of the past... Most people living in the FRG know what Nazism was, from reading. This does not mean that they are relieved of a certain historical responsibility, but it is very difficult for them to accept any kind of individual guilt, they do not have it." Does a similar situation not apply to the current inhabitants of the CR in relation to the excesses of the transfer?

facto the Federal Republic of Germany, but this home has provided the Sudeten Germans as a group with special rights, represented by the Sudetendeutsche Landsmannschaft and relating to a "homeland" exterior to the "home".
The problem with this "double" or "split" identity is that it demands collective
membership and loyalty to two different wholes. The SL presents itself not as
a union of former Czechoslovak nationals/state citizens (nor does it demand
restitution of this citizenship) but as a "tribe among the tribes of Bavaria" and
as an association of German state citizens that additionally demands state civil
rights in the Czech Republic. According to E. Hahn, it sees its goal in the ag-
gregation of homeland and home. Thus the special status of the Sudeten German group among Germans continues to imply the pursuit of a clearly expansionist aim under the guise of the restitution of its historical rights.[67]

The Sudetendeutsche Landsmannschaft is able to influence the Bonn government in *two ways: indirectly* – via the political parties, *and directly* – via its
own organisations. It has exploited both possibilities especially at times when
the governing formation is the CDU/CSU, which officially and over the long
term supports expellee organisations (reaping its reward at elections in the
form of a reliable number of votes estimated at anything from several hundred
thousand to a million).

In this situation it is, however, very difficult to ask the Czech political leadership or Czech public to adopt a new, different view of the goals of the Sudeten
German movement, which continue to be perceived on both the level of explicit
programmes and through the lens of history as a threat. The situation makes it
logical for the Czechs to wonder whether the Sudeten claims against the Czech
republic do not also represent Bavarian attempts to expand into Bohemia. After all, the demand that the Czechs engage in dialogue on the Sudeten German
Question is voiced not just by representatives of the Landsmannschaft but also
by politicians representing Bavaria. Is this not in fact the expression of *a demand for a share in decision-making in the affairs of a neighbouring state*?[68]

The year 1987 saw the organisation in Regensburg of the *First Sudeten German
National Congress*. It was attended by numerous Sudeten German associations
and approved a *Manifesto* declaring that 250 representatives of 105 Sudeten
German organisations representing 400,0000 Sudeten Germans, "consider the
Sudeten German Assembly to be the legitimate, democratically elected repre-

---

[67]   E. Hahn writes that, "the understandable and legitimate desire of many expelled Sudeten Germans for Czech
society to recognise the wrongs that they suffered, is therefore not comparable with the aims and claims
that the Sudeten German Landsmannschaft has set out for itself." Hahn, E. "Sudetskí Nemci v nemeckej
spoločnosti: polstoročie politických dejín". 86.

[68]   In 1990, for example, R. Hilf demanded as part of Czech-Sudeten German settlement that the Czechoslovaks
"provide the Sudeten Germans access to the media, policy, economy and cultural life of the CSFR". Hilf, R.
"Sudetoněmecká otázka dnes" [The Sudeten German Question Today]. *Přítomnost* 6/1990. 16–19.

sentative of the Sudeten Germans.". The manifesto was signed by most important figures from the various ideological sections of the movement including the Ackermann-Gemeinde, Seliger-Gemeinde and Adalbert Stifter Verein.

Eva Hahn has expressed doubts over whether the membership base gave its representatives a mandate to take a step of this kind, but given the tendency of Sudeten German organisations to behave to the outside world as a monolithic bloc (despite a great many internal disputes and differences), I do not find these doubts persuasive.[69] In the second edition of her book Hahn pursues this point and claims that some of the signatory organisations were just very small remnants of former associations (for example the former student *Burschenschaft* societies) or mere groups of family members.

Hahn puts forward the interesting but controversial theory that the Sudeten German group constituted itself in definitive form only after it had become a solid component of German society. However, this only highlights the question of how we are to understand the relationship of a "tribe" constituted (or constructed) in this way to its claimed homeland in the Bohemian Lands. Once again we confront the dual (parallel) identity of the expelled Sudeten Germans. All of this, of course, is predicated on the assumption that the political opinions voiced by the SL leaders express the views of the expelled population, and this once again raises the question of the legitimacy of the organisation and its organs, which has been discussed above.

Disputes over its political legitimacy and mandate to represent the entire group of expelled Sudeten Germans have continued for the whole period of the existence of the association. Nonetheless, it remains unchallengeable that the influence of the Sudetendeutsche Landsmannschaft has gradually become dominant, with all the consequences that this has had (including ideological and political influence exercised by the Witikobund).

---

[69] Hahn, E. "Sudetskí Nemci v nemeckej spolocnosti: polstoročie politických dejín". 84.

SVĚDECTVÍ

čtvrtletník pro politiku a kulturu

ročník XV ——————— číslo 57 ——————— 1978

Cover of the exile journal *Svědectví* (*Testimony*, a political and cultural quarterly), published by Pavel Tigrid. In No. 57 (1978), Danubius's "Theses on the Expulsion of the Czechoslovak Germans" were first printed, opening up debate on the transfer among dissidents at home and in exile.

9 The Sudeten German Question between Home and Exile

The Sudeten German question was a point of controversy among exiled Czechoslovaks in both the two major waves of emigration from the republic in the postwar period, i.e. the post-February 1948 wave (following the communist takeover) and the post-August 1968 wave (following the Soviet invasion). Judgments on and attitudes to the fateful divorce between Czechs and Sudeten Germans sometimes united and sometimes divided Czech emigrés and their organised bodies. The leaders of all political currents represented in these waves expressed their opinions both on the fact of the transfer and on possible future approaches to the question of cooperation with Sudeten German organisations.

Leaving aside the differences between the initial positions of the democrats who dominated the first wave and the former communists who dominated the second, one distinctive feature of post-August discourse was the subsequent greater degree of interaction between exiled and internal dissent, which had not been possible in the fifties when the iron curtain had been much less permeable. Yet in both cases the opinions of the exiles were to a certain extent projected into the domestic internal political situation, and of course, such opinions had immensely greater influence on developments post-1989, when many of the participants in the old debates in exile took a direct share in the creation of the internal and foreign policy of the restored democracy.

The limited scope of this study means that I shall focus only on two elements in the pre-1989 emigré engagement with the Sudeten German question. The first is the debate that was generated at the beginning of the 1950s in connection with the activities of the *Council of Free Czechoslovakia*, a body that brought together a number of politicians of the pre-February period, and the second is the discussion provoked by what were known as the Danubius Theses at the end of the 1970s and beginning of the 1980s, and later in the early 1990s.

R. Luža has pointed out that the double destruction of Czechoslovak democracy – in 1938 and then in February 1948, left deep traces on the views and attitudes of the political leaders who moved to the West in the post-February 1948 wave of emigration. He shares the opinion that in a way this situation created conditions for Czechoslovak-German reconciliation, since the Czechoslovak exile (organisation) was an ally of the Federal Republic of Germany from its foundation in 1949, yet at the same time he sees question of the Sudeten Germans as the main source of dissension in Czech-German relations (Czech in the sense of the democratic Czech exiles). The Czech democrats in exile were very sensitive about Sudeten German propaganda praising the "civilising" achievement of the Nazi occupation of the Czech Lands in 1939–1945.[1]

E. Táborský characterised the heart of the dispute,[2] showing that the basic reasons for quarrel between Czechs and Sudeten Germans were carried over in unresolved form from Czechoslovakia into the emigrant communities, and that they remained unresolvable even though the former rivals now found themselves on the same side in the struggle between the forces of totalitarianism and democracy.

"Members of the Council of Free Czechoslovakia regarded the expelled Germans as potentially the most serious threat to the Czechoslovak state after its prospective liberation from the communist yoke.[3] Many leading members of

---

[1] R. Luža states that in the Sudeten German press the Czech people was often wrongly accused of having murdered hundreds of thousands of Sudeten Germans, but was silent on the fate of the 200,000 Czech Jews, although 26,500 of them were of German nationality. The Sudeten German press boasted of how well-off Czechs had been in the Protectorate. The CSR (they claimed) was a disturber of the peace and as the artificial creation of the Versailles Treaty had died of its contradictions before the Second World War. The policy of the Henlein party had been "constructively European, universally national and genuinely social". "Perhaps no one has every yet treated their subordinated neightbours as decently and justly as the Sudeten Germans treated the Czechs after 1938". Luža, R. 2001. *Československá sociální demokracie (Kapitoly z let exilu 1948–1989)* [The Czechoslovak Social Democratic Party (Chapters from the years of exile 1948–1989]. Brno: Doplněk. 107.

[2] "For several years now the Sudeten Germans have been conducting a furious campaign against Czechoslovakia. I do not mean communist Czechoslovakia but democratic Czechoslovakia. They distort the facts, denounce the late Dr. Edvard Beneš, vilify his colleagues, negotiate agreements with the Prchala-ites and make threats. You would almost think that the blame for the Second World War and all its consequences lay with Beneš and not Hitler. And that in all this the Sudeten Germans were just an innocent sacrificial lamb whose neck was wrung by the Czech barbarians. The Sudeten Social Democrats under Jaksch's leadership are at their side in this campaign. Many Czechoslovak Social Democrats once genuinely respected Jaksch. I was among them. His courageous fight against the far more numerous Henleinians deserves the greatest honour." Táborský, E. in "Naše cesta" [Our Road]. č. 4 (duben), 1954. April 1954. See also Zpráva ústředního sekretariátu ČSSD z 30. 6. 1951, Londýn. (archiv R. Luži).

[3] Čelovský, B. 2000. *Politici bez moci* [Politicians without Power]. Ostrava: Tilia. 103.

the Council had been members of the resistance at home or abroad, and many had experienced concentration camps. With almost no exceptions (dr. J. Černý was an isolated case) they approved the expulsion of the German-speaking inhabitants of the CSR, and indeed this was the one and only point on which they agreed with communist Prague. Dr. Lettrich, who proposed that the Council condemn the cruelties accompanying the transfer, nevertheless foresaw that "with the growing importance of the Germans, the question of the transfer of the inhabitants of the Sudetenland with German nationality will become more acute." The Council continued in its resolve to monitor the activities of the Sudeten German organisations.[4]

Another who warned the CFC of the Sudeten German problem and its likely importance in the event of another war that would re-open the situation in Central Europe was Vojta Beneš, the elder brother of President Beneš. In a letter of the 16th of May 1950, he called it "one of the most dangerous (questions) that the CFC will have to confront in the future when a new European order is created. We all know that the Sudeten Germans are working hard to prepare for this moment with the help of the rest of Germany... Even though, or perhaps precisely because we do not know the day or the hour, it would be a mistake to put off this question to the future."[5]

The situation was fundamentally complicated, however, by the circumstances of the Cold War. The three democratic great powers (the USA, Great Britain and France), connected the problem of the defence of Europe against possible attack by the Soviet Union with the arming of West Germany (or rather the need to develop defence capacity on German soil with the consent of West Germany). This, and the commitments to West Germany as an ally arising from it, substantially restricted their freedom of diplomatic action in Europe.[6] The Czechoslovak chancellor in exile, J. Smutný, noted that, "twice in a period of thirty years Germany has been responsible for a world war, brutalities and destruction going beyond anything known in the history of wars. This has left an indelible mark, even though in political actions in which Germany is concerned, today (the 1950s), the past is not mentioned more than is absolutely necessary. Yet the great historical lesson that has emerged from the militant policy of the German nation remains an unwritten and unspoken warning."

---

[4] Pavel Tigrid agreed to the *Council's* request and for a whole year 1949/50 sent regular reports to Washington. For example in July 1951 he concluded his analysis with the following words. "The situation suggests that the political influence of the expelled and so also the Sudeten Germans is growing fast throughout West Germany, and that the ruling parties will be fighting for the favour of these groups using political and social concessions and reliefs on the one hand and by strengthening the political power of the leaders of the expelled Germans on the other." Ibidem. 106.

[5] Ibidem. 108.

[6] Smutný, J. "Němci v Československu a jejich odsun z republiky". 251.

Smutný drew attention to the activities of the expellees in the FRG demanding "the right of return and self-determination." He pointed out that among the former Czechoslovak Germans the question of the Czechoslovak-German border and the transfer had for years remained a live one, with the prospects of return still hotly debated. He argued, indeed, that the century-old Czech-German problem had been revived (he was writing in 1956) through skilful and systematic German propaganda, but above all as a result of the situation into which Europe. and the whole world, had been thrown by communism after the war. This meant that there was growing interest in the German problem among the Czech emigrants.

Unease at the new Cold War role of the Sudeten Germans as allies of the West, especially the United States, was soon expressed by Ferdinand Peroutka, who from 1950 directed the Czech broadcasts of *Radio Free Europe* (RFE). At a meeting of the Council of Free Czechoslovakia on the 23rd of June 1950, he declared that "in connection with RFE activities a major attack has been launched on the Czechoslovak state cause by a coalition of Sudeten Germans, separatist and Prchala supporters. These elements are challenging the right of the Czechoslovak exiles to defend the Czechoslovak state."[7]

At a meeting on the 23rd of June 1951, the Board of the Council of Free Czechoslovakia decided to draw up a memorandum on the transfer, and the activities of General Prchala.[8] Many passages of this document remain relevant even today, especially in view of the current pressure from Bavaria, Austria and Hungary for the nullification of the presidential decrees.

The memorandum agrees that Germany has a vital interest in Western resistance to the communist threat, but condemns as lacking in foresight any political concessions of a kind "that would enable Germany to reassert German imperialism following the exorcism of the communist-Soviet menace. One of the most effective contributions to [the possible resurgence of German imperialism]... would be for the Western powers to permit the Sudeten Germans to incorporate themselves into Germany with so-called Sudeten German territory,

---

[7]　Čelovský, B. *Politici bez moci*. 109. Peroutka was forced to react to the intervention of the American official W. E. Griffith, who wrote to him that, "As you know, we are coming under attack from the German press. The article in the *Münchener Allgemeine* need not be taken too seriously, but the article in the *Frankfurter Allgemeine Zeitung*, although not so extreme, is something quite different... I think the Sudeten Germans are following all our broadcasts, and so it would be unwise to broadcast ten programmes about Beneš in succession." Ibidem.

[8]　The commander of the 4th army deployed in the South of Bohemia and Moravia during the crisis year of 1938, General Prchala already had political ambitions at the start of the Second World War when in 1940 he founded *the Czechoslovak National Committee* which opposed Beneš. He had very good relations with the Slovak separatists F. Ďurčanský and M. Polák. In exile after 1948, on the 4th of August 1950, Prchala and Vladimír Pekelský for the London *Czechoslovak National Committee* made an agreement with the *Arbeitsgemeinschaft zur Wahrung sudetendeutscher Interessen*, which was represented by Rudolf Lodgman von Auen, R. Reitzner and H. Schütz. This agreement declared the return of the Sudeten Germans to be "just and so self-evident".

or to become a federative component of Czechoslovakia and so empowered to join a Central European federation. The inclusion of the German element would transform a Central European federation into a certain variant of *Mitteleuropa*, because in this eventuality, apart from this German component many other federative components would succumb to the attraction of Reich German power." Evidently, like Masaryk and Beneš, the leaders of the post-war democratic exile considered Sudeten Germandom to be an element endangering the sovereignty and integrity of the Czechoslovak state.[9]

In a letter from John F. Leich[10] the Americans appealed to the CFC to take a more positive attitude in the Sudeten German question, because "the West German Republic will be in some way a participant in the liberation of the countries of Eastern and Central Europe... The further we move away from Potsdam, the less the reasons for the expulsion have validity".

The next sentence of Leich's letter I regard as key. It characterises the situation of the Czechoslovaks at the time and perhaps to some extent Czech Republic even today I regard: "Do you consider it possible that a public declaration on the part of the *Council* recognising that at Potsdam and after Potsdam there may have been mistakes, might be a useful step? We believe that it might lead to better mutual understanding between Czechoslovakia and West Germany."

The letter provoked a stormy discussion in the CFC, in which Peroutka tried to calm his outraged colleagues by saying that while the Germans were trying to force discussions on the German question in the sense intended by General Prchala, the Americans only wanted "to accommodate the West German government psychologically" rather than to accommodate the Sudeten Germans materially by invalidating the transfer.

The debate in the CFC continued and in another memorandum of the 6th of December 1951 it was argued that "the transfer was not retribution for Hitler's crimes but a contribution to preventing the repeat of the German *Drang nach Osten*. The transfer was not even complete when the Sudeten Germans started to claim that the Potsdam Agreement had ceased to apply because the Czechoslovak government had not acted in accordance with its provisions... As far as the return of property is concerned, this is a question settled in 1946 in the Paris Agreement on Reparations."[11]

---

[9]   Ibidem. 110.

[10] John F. Leich – the deputy director of the nationalities department of the *National Committee for a Free Europe*. R. Luža reports that Leich's letter was met with deep disagreement in both camps of the divided exiled community, The Council of Free Czechoslovakia and National Committee. Luža, R. *The Transfer of the Sudeten Germans*. 109.

[11] Minutes of the meeting of the presidium of the CFC on the 6th of December 1957. See Čelovský, B. *Politici bez moci*. 113.

In the context of the current development of Czech-German relations since 1989, it is clear that the arguments on both sides of the dispute had already formed at the very beginning – at the start of the 1950s. In my view this is proof of the depth of the gulf between the two positions, for after all, this was a point at which the international framework of the Cold War offered almost ideal conditions for possible conciliation between the Czechoslovak democratic exile and the Sudeten German organisations. Yet even in these almost ideal conditions, no reconciliation occurred.

Disputes over the Sudeten German question, post-war transfer and possible return of the Sudeten Germans (which would have had to be resolved for any serious negotiation with representatives of the expellees to begin), continued to divide the Czechoslovak exile community in the West. Further CFC negotiation with US bodies showed that the Americans considered an attitude of complete opposition to the revision of the conclusions of the post-war decisions of the Allies to be extremely tactless and even dangerous, specifically with regard to "the grave consequences for the question of the consolidation of conditions in West Germany."

At another meeting, confidentially recorded by P. Zenkl, J. Papánek told representatives of the National Committee, that "all three representatives of the Council would be destroyed at home if they departed from the accepted standpoint on the question of the Sudeten Germans, or even just wavered on it."[12] Everything testified to the ever more important role of the political interests of a restored Germany. In April 1953, deputies in the Bundestag interpellated a question to the government that was targeted at the relationship between the Council of Free Czechoslovakia and the station Radio Free Europe based in Munich. The deputies challenged the government of the FRG to condemn the transfer of the Sudeten Germans.[13] In the context of this issue the CFC commissioner in Germany, General F. Dastich, was later to warn colleagues of the seriousness of the situation: "It is very uncertain how long Radio Free Europe can resist the pressure of the Germans for power to determine the policy of broadcasting to Czechoslovakia."[14]

Another storm among the exiles and their organisations was provoked by the views of F. Peroutka, who was coming to embrace the idea of dialogue with the Sudeten Germans. On the 20th of April 1953, he talked in New York with a representative of Lodgman von Auen, who was seeking a new Czech partner since it was now clear to him that General Prchala had almost negligible influence among the Czechoslovak exiles. According to his own record of the talk,

---

[12]   Unsigned "Confidential record" made by Dr. Zenkl on the 1st of July 1952. Ibidem. 116.

[13]   *Sudetendeutsche Zeitung*, 4th of April 1953 (press report from Bonn). Ibidem. 119.

[14]   Čelovský cites a letter from F. Dastich to the CFC of the 9th of November 1952.

Peroutka said the following about the Sudeten German problem: "I shall tell you my position but I do not want to be quoted. My position on the return of the Germans is that without it I cannot imagine a lasting settlement of conditions... But this does not mean that I can openly express this position at RFE... What is absolutely necessary for us today, if we are to fulfil our task, is that under no circumstances should RFE give the impression that it is controlled by Germans."[15]

Peroutka continued to have discussions with Sudeten Germans, and two years later talked with Lodgman von Auen's representative in America, Paul Fiala, who conveyed to him Lodgman's desire to open negotiations between Czechs and Germans. According to Peroutka's record, Fiala predicted that as soon as Germany gained its independence it would take control of RFE and demand that Sudeten Germans be allowed to speak on the RFE airwaves to their people in the CSR. In response to a question from Peroutka, he said that the Sudeten German programme was to create a "federative state of Czechs and Germans" in which Czech and German presidents would alternate. Lodgman expressed the wish to make a formal agreement with the Council of Free Czechoslovakia.[16] Peroutka, however, was aware that it was beyond his power to push through anything of the kind.

The shift in Peroutka's views over the transfer of the Sudeten Germans later caused what was known as the Peroutka Affair, which erupted after a German newspaper published in New York printed an interview with him by the journalist Hermann W. Gaertner: "Die Geschichte von Bärenfell: Zum tschechisch-sudetendeutschen Verhältniss."[17] Here Peroutka said, "It is my personal opinion that the almost complete expulsion of the Sudeten Germans was a mistake. What is more, what happened during the implementation of this action was shameful." He also expressed willingness to negotiate with representatives of the Sudetendeutsche Landsmannschaft. Faced by an avalanche of outraged reactions, he claimed the newspaper had not presented his views accurately, but in fact he later repeatedly confirmed them.

Certain attempts at rapprochement with the Sudeten Germans were also made by the exiled Czech Social Democrats. On the 16th of May 1959, the Seliger-Gemeinde's weekly *Die Brücke* published a report on talks with Sudeten Germans held by two CSSD representatives, V. Bernard and A. Mokrý in Wiesbaden. R. Luža states that they were not empowered to engage in such

---

[15] Peroutka's record in his own hand in the *Hoover Institution on War, Revolution and Peace*. Stanford, Ca., Fond Ferdinand Peroutka. Ibidem. 121.

[16] Ibidem. 122.

[17] Gaertner, H. W. Die Geschichte von Bärentell: Zum tschechisch-sudetendeutschen Verhältniss. *Staats-Zeitung und Herold*. New York. 11th of March 1956.

negotiations by anyone and neither of them had asked for the permission of the party's central executive committee.[18] At this meeting the president of the S-G, W. Jaksch and the Bundestag deputies R. Reitzner and E. Paul asked for recognition of the Munich Agreement and Slovak independence. They accepted the pre-Munich borders of the republic and presented requests for the recognition of the "right to homeland" and for material compensation for the transfer. In Luža's view they therefore merely confirmed once again "the universally known greater German and anti-Czechoslovak" standpoint of the S-G. It was clear that not even the shared social and political principles of the two social democratic parties could provide a basis for overcoming diametrically opposed approaches to the Sudeten German question. In the autumn of 1959 the central executive committee of the exiled CSSD decided not to proceed with further negotiations with the S-G.

Talks between the exiled Social Democrats were held once again two decades later on the basis of an invitation sent by the President of the Seliger-Gemeinde on the 7th of November 1978. The meeting took place on the 24th of May 1979 and essentially both sides simply repeated their established positions. The S-G president, A. Hasenöhrl, said that it had to be recognised that the transfer had not been a suitable solution. R. Luža replied that, "the transfer was certainly a brutal act. I understand the Sudeten German position in not agreeing with it, but the Czech nation did not start a world war and did not conduct a policy of genocide. It was the victim of this."[19]

The Danubius Theses on the Expulsion of the Czechoslovak Germans

As already indicated, the Sudeten German question entered a new phase after the Soviet invasion of Czechoslovakia in August 1968, which violently terminated the reforms of the Prague Spring and sent another wave of emigrants, this time mainly left-wing in orientation, heading for the West. In a difficult life situation, some of them found support in Sudeten German circles where there was some feeling of solidarity with the fate of the new emigrants. It was only a matter of time before the Sudeten German debate erupted among the exiles with a new intensity.

On the initiative of the *Opus Bonum* society (and above all the charismatic Benedictine abbot A. Opasek), a symposium was held in Franken in Bavaria at

---

[18] Luža, R. *Československá sociální demokracie*. 110.
[19] Ibidem. 155.

the end of February 1978 on events in Czechoslovakia 1945–1948 and involved discussion of the planning and course of the transfer of the Czechoslovak Germans after the war. The debate was summed up in the text of the *Franken Declaration*, which included the statement that, "after 1945 millions of citizens of German ethnicity were the first to be placed outside the law and the principle of retaliation triumphed over the principle of justice and right."[20] The text condemned the principle of exclusion of inconvenient groups of citizens from political liberties and rights, and expresses the view of supporters living in exile that the indivisibility of human rights and political liberties is "the fundamental social acknowledged value, regardless of differences of faith, philosophical and political conviction."

What was to some degree a turning point in views of the post-war expulsion came in the late 1970s, when the exiles' quarterly for politics and culture *Svědectví* [Testimony] 57/1978 published the highly controversial *Theses on the Expulsion of the Czechoslovak Germans*.[21] The theses, signed under the pseudonym Danubius, provoked heated discussion that by this time involved considerable interaction between exiled circles and dissent inside Czechoslovakia.

The discussion was launched by J. Příbram (P. Příhoda) in his article "A Story with a Bad End" (*Svědectví* 55/1978, 384–389), which was a response to Danubius (J. Mlynárik)'s Theses. Příhoda starts by asserting that "the transfer of three million Germans is an act that has no parallel in Western and Central Europe... To be honest, we have to look away from "political prudence", and in doing so have to admit that the expulsion of the Bohemian Germans was unjustified." He also claims that "the victory of nationalism helped to unify Germany or Italy, but it threatened the Czech Lands because for centuries their historic borders had not been linguistic borders. Here, nationalist conflict inevitably resulted in internal political conflict, in one or another form of civil war. A problem of this kind can be only removed either by getting over nationalism or by disenfranchising one of the nationalities."[22]

He goes on to argue that in the newborn CSR the Germans were treated essentially as persons without full legal rights, and that this provoked a feeling of injustice among Bohemian Germans. This in his view was the reason why after the disintegration of the old Europe (which allegedly the founders of the

---

[20]   The Franken Declaration was signed by R. Belcredi. A. Heidler, K. Kaplan, A. Kratochvil, Z. Mlynář, A. Opasek, L. Pachman, J. Pecháček, V. Prečan, R. Selucký, K. Skalický, J. Sláma, R. Ströbinger, and P. Tigrid. The full text can be found in Olbert, F. *Cesta ke smíření*. 44–45.

[21]   The text of the *Theses* was first published under the pseudonym Danubius (Ján Mlynárik) in *Svědectví* in shortened form. It was published in full form on the collection of: "Danubius" debate, *Češi, Němci, odsun* [Czechs, Germans, the Transfer]. 1990. Černý, B. (ed.). Prague: Academia. 55–90. All further citations here come from this edition.

[22]   Příbram, J. "Příběh s nedobrým koncem", in *Češi, Němci, odsun*. 46.

CSR also failed to notice), and especially after the economic crisis of 1929–1932 and the rise of Nazism in neighbouring Germany, the population of the Sudeten territories turned away from Czechoslovakia. According to P. Příhoda, one result of the transfer was the depopulation of the borderlands, which were resettled by people unable to sustain the necessary cultural continuity, which was lost. The interior then went the same way as the borderlands: "In the interior as well, towns capitulated to factories and housing estates, old books vanished, people became grey and coarse, and their lives became superficial. There too the wayside shrines have been torn down and much is overgrown by weeds."[23]

Although there is some truth in these claims, their basic tone is one of emotive simplification of the whole relationship between Czechs and Germans in the Czech Lands. The approach as it were excises the "conflictual society" from its period correlations and factors out an "unexamined Czech guilt complex". The assessment of the role of nationalism (especially its "nation-building" phase) in the Czech Lands and the comparison with other European countries are both in my view particularly ahistorical and downright inaccurate. The attempt to delegitimise Czech national consciousness root and branch is facile. National consciousness everywhere in Europe has had both positive (integrative) aspects and destructive (conflictual) aspects. In any case there is a continuum, rather than a clearcut semantic break, between what we positively view as patriotism and negatively view as nationalism. A certain degree of patriotism/nationalism may be considered a legitimate part of the emergence of modern political nations at a particular period, both in the case of Germans and Czechs.[24] Beyond general questions of the legitimacy of national consciousness, the issue must be one of the specific level of national mobilisation and degree of extremism of attitudes in concrete social and political context.

Emanuel Rádl (distinguished Czech philospoher and scientist), for example, who otherwise showed considerable sympathy for the Bohemian Germans and their aspirations for self-determination, makes this point:"The Czech na-

---

[23]   Ibidem. 50–51. In the mid-1980s P. Příhoda (under the pseudonym F. Jedermann) expressed his view of the transfer and its consequences in the spirit of Danubius's theses (I walk through the borderlands today and see and know that the Germans should not have been transferred, 8) and in highly dramatic expressive form (with many unacceptable and factually inaccurate generalisations of the type – the reconciliation of the double nation on the soil of the Czech Lands was somehow unimaginable to the Czechs as a fact of a social psychological order, 25), printed in Jedermann, F. *Ztracené dějiny* (postscript by F. Neubauer). 1991. Prague: ISE.

[24]   The tragic dimension of the Czech-German Relationship is the clash of two identities, in which the "search for own identity is as a rule linked with trauma at the loss of life in the given real world. Especially after great social upheavals or in times of great crisis, historical consciousness and historical "unconsciousness" appear with the same intensity and intervene in the whole business of our life. In this context J. Pešková poses the question: Are we capable together with the other heirs of "Auschwitz" of getting beyond the events of the Second World War as a way of realising the European principle in the real business of our lives? Pešková, J. 1997. *Role vědomí v dějinách* [The Role of Consciousness in History]. Prague: Lidové noviny. 38 ff.

tion had never been the main issue of the Czech national programme, it concerned... the rule of reason, the Czech brother-hood, reasonable policy, humanity." According to Rádl, Czech Germans, by contrast, were not very conscious of the fact that the "struggle for the preservation of German nationality is an insufficient political programme."[25]

Danubius sees the population transfers of the 20th century as the expression of over-exposed violence, as the fruit of totalitarian dictatorships (specifically he gives the example of the deportation of national and ethnic groups in the Soviet Union in the Stalin era). He even claims that the Central European transfers after the Second world war were umbilically linked precisely with these Soviet deportations, and that "they are congruent with the orientally Asiatic transfers of the Russian imperium in terms of mass scale (they affected more than 11 million people), in scope (they involved more than one state – Poland, Czechoslovakia, Hungary and some Balkan states) and in the principle of collective guilt (all Germans are to blame for the Second World War and its massacres).

Danubius asserts that the cultural elite of the nation has the moral burden of coming to terms with the problems of this most momentous act of violation of human rights. He reproaches regime (i.e. Communist) historiography for defending and trying to justify the transfer, and criticises *non-regime* historiography and literature for not having sufficient moral courage or material grounding to openly confront the problem.

According to Danubius "the general foot-dragging over this open problem is prolonging the reign of a morally unsustainable situation". He repeats the false claims of the Sudeten German historians and politicians that Beneš was the key originator and architect of the justifications for the transfer of the Bohemian Germans. In complete contradiction to the findings of historians, he insists that the opinions of the Czechoslovak resistance groups, sections of the population and individuals were not a significant factor from the beginning of the occupation.

The passage in the *Theses* describing the international political consequences of the transfer is rarely cited but is in fact remarkable for its congruence with an assessment that Danubius could not have known at the time he was writing, since it was only discovered in British archives at the beginning of the 1990s. This was *Memorandum of the British Expert Group* set up to consider the question of the ethnic Germans in Central Europe that I have cited at length in the chapter on the genesis of plans for the transfer. The passage on possible conse-

---

[25] Rádl, E. 2003. *O německé revoluci/K politické ideologii sudetských Němců.* [On the German Revolution/Towards Political Ideology of Sudeten Germans] Praha: Masarykův ústav AV ČR. 131.

quences of the option of transfer is strikingly similar to the following thoughts of Danubius:

"In its consequences for state borders, transfer therefore means the end, or the extreme complication of the Western, German alternative by the threat of revanche (to which Germans have always been prone), so leaving the Czechs and Slovaks with only the Eastern Russian alternative, co-existence or slow and gradual assimilation in the last greatest colonial power. There is nothing encouraging for the Czechoslovak future in either the first or the second eventuality."[26]

In 1940 this British *Memorandum* had pointed out the power and depth of the "wounded legal consciousness" of the Sudeten Germans as a source of future threat to a restored Czechoslovakia and several decades later we find Danubius arguing after the event in similar terms. All the same, I see a problem in Danubius's text in the implicit idea that the only path to the West for a Czechoslovakia rid of Soviet domination would be the path through Germany. Certainly Germany always has been and remains the powerful and influential neighbour of the Czech Lands, but Czech ties with the West are far more diverse and multilateral, especially in the current situation when the CR is part of the North Atlantic Alliance and has joined the European Union.

Another weakness of Danubius's *Theses* is the one-sided, inflated caricature of the consequences of the transfer for Czechoslovak society. For example, he claims that the appropriation of property into socialist ownership on an unprecedented scale had roots not only in socialist doctrine, but in the unprecedented stealing and looting of the property of three million (German) people. "This is only one, but a particularly important syndrome of Czechoslovak reality – the result of what happens to a nation when the opportunity for so colossal a robbery is politically provided."[27]

By seeking to present Czechoslovakia as uniquely corrupted, Danubius entirely ignores the fact that confiscation of German property took place in many other European countries that had experienced occupation regimes (including Western Europe)[28] on the basis of the *punitive* approach of the Allies to Germany. Furthermore, although in the disturbed post-war years there were cases of loss, theft and destruction of former Sudeten German property (partly as a result of the moral failure of individuals and groups, partly as a consequence

[26]   Danubius (J. Mlynárik). "Teze k vysídlení" [Theses on the Expulsion], in *Češi, Němci, odsun*. 82.

[27]   Ibidem. 87.

[28]   See e.g. "Soupis německého majetku konfiskovaného v evropských státech" [List of German Property Confiscated in European States], in *Češi, Němci, odsun*. Very recently on the problems of confiscation of German property see the British government material, "British policy towards enemy property during the Second World War (April 1998) and the expert opinion of the Rt. Hon Lord Archer of Sandwell, Q. C. *Enemy Property Independent Third Party Consultation*. July 1998. http://www.enemyproperty.gov.uk/index.html.

of the difficulty of restoring the values and practices of a legal state and establishing its legal structures), it is illegitimate to equate acts of denazification law based on the principles of the *punitive approach* with colossal robbery.[29] Essentially Danubius is seeking to introduce into the Czech – (Sudeten) German relationship the permanent stigma of the guilt of the Czech nation – a stigma based precisely on the principle of collective guilt that he rejects with indignation in the case of the Germans.

Most of those who contributed to the discussion engendered by Danubius's Theses rejected the one-sidedness of his conclusions. The historian J. Křen, who himself launched a debate on the transfer of the Sudeten Germans in 1967[30] refused to engage on this level and branded the *Theses* a text of dubious standard and motivation. The critics basically agreed that Danubius's jeremiad was moralisation rather than history – an attempt to undo deeds that could not be undone and could not even by usefully judged through the lens of a later period.

Commenting on the national introspection and self-criticism demanded by Danubius and later by the group writing under the pseudonym of Bohemus (P. Pithart, T. Brod, M. Otáhal, J. Doležal, M. Pojar, P. Příhoda), Křen rightly noted that this could not be turned into the methodological starting point of historical analysis. "The idea that the Czech side should re-examine itself (and logically, that the German side should do the same too), may perhaps fulfil the function of intellectual provocation designed to break through the damn of taboo and national prejudices, but it is inadequate as a basis for objective analysis. A picture with the attributes of scholarly objectivity cannot emerge from two one-sided approaches."[31]

In this context Křen remarks that just as German history was neither the constant repetition of one and the same thing, nor some clearcut and fatal linear process leading to Hitler (as B. Loewenstein put it in 1965), so neither Czech history nor the history of Czech-German relations was ever just a road that "inevitably led to the dramatic end of mutual coexistence" (P. Pithart).

---

[29] In December 1945 in Paris the CSR was party to the signing of *the Agreement on Reparations from Germany*, in which in Paragraph D it was stated that every signatory government would retain enemy German property within its jurisdiction by a form that it would choose for itself. On the basis of this provision the CSR had a right to German reparations and this claim was to be satisfied from German property left and confiscated on the territory of the republic, including the property of the Sudeten Germans. Czechoslovakia calculated war damages to be 19 milliard and 471.6 million dollars (1945), of which only a tiny amount – 0.4% had been genuinely covered. "Dekrety prezidenta z hlediska současnosti a práva" [The Presidential Decrees from the Perspective of the Present and Law] (text of expert opinion of the CR government). *Právo*. 15. 5. 2002. 10.

[30] Křen, J. 1967. "Odsun Němců ve světle nových pramenů" [The Transfer of the Germans in the Light of New Sources]. *Dialog* 4–6.

[31] See Bohemus. "Stanovisko k odsunu Němců z Československa" [Position on the Transfer of the Germans from Czechoslovakia], in *Češi, Němci, odsun*. Křen, J. "Češi a Němci: kritické poznámky" [Czechs and Germans: Critical notes], in *Češi, Němci, odsun*. 203.

Bohemus agreed with Danubius's insistence that the Sudeten Germans had suffered great injustice, but added that the Czechs had suffered a similar injustice earlier. He recalled the "bilingual" Bohemian, Bernard Bolzano (1781–1848) whose ideas were based on land patriotism (the idea of Bohemism) and who felt responsibility for both peoples, Czechs and Germans, in their common homeland, the Kingdom of Bohemia. Bolzano's ideal was the creation of a Bohemian political nation out of the two "language tribes" settled in Bohemia. What Bohemus neglected to add, however, was that this was a Utopian vision, rejected by both ethnic groups, Czech and German, since even back in this early period of the formation of political nations, ethnic loyalty was clearly coming to the fore as the basic condition for the achievement of a national entity of one's own.

We cannot but agree with the claim that "it is foolish to squabble over whether Czech nationalism provoked German nationalism or vice versa. The linguistic basis of these nationalisms in both cases provided the potential for intolerant exclusivivity."[32] We must add, however, that this was not a situation specific to the Czech-German relationship; it also characterised the course of the national *risorgimento* of other European nations. Bohemus poses questions that are intellectually provocative and lofty (Munich should be a moral challenge compelling Czechs to ask whether they did everything possible to solve the problem of coexistence with the Germans in one state democratically? Was the path that Czechs embarked on with the National Revival in the 19th century truly the right path?). On the other hand, set against the tragic end of Czechoslovakia (including the direct threat to the physical existence of the Czech people), which the Sudeten German movement did so much to bring about, these questions sound somewhat irrelevant.

I consider it absurd to claim that, "the Allies (especially the USA) had no idea how to deal with the problem of Germany, and allowed themselves to be carried away by vengefulness with the aim of destroying Germany". Of course, the Allies did indeed hesitate on how to treat the defeated Nazi Germany, but this was above all because they were faced with the task of judging crimes more monstrous than any previously known to history (the physical liquidation of entire racial and ethnic groups), and because the first priority seemed therefore the difficult task of ensuring, at any price, that there could be no possible repetition of the catastrophe.[33] Calls for merciless retribution were heard even

---

[32] Bohemus. "Stanovisko k odsunu Němců z Československa". 186–187.

[33] At the beginning of June 1945 the *Gallup Institute* conducted a survey of US public opinion which showed that 67% of Americans wanted Göring to be executed without trial and 45% of Americans wanted agents of the Gestapo and members of the Nazi party to be liquidated in the same way. Typical reactions were, "Kill them… Hang them… Erase them from then surface of the planet." The War Department informed

in the USA, whose civilians had experienced the war "only at second hand"; in European countries these feelings were naturally much more intense.

Bohemus categorises the consequences of the transfer for the later development of the Czech society and CSR as follows: *historical* (the removal of one of the two historical peoples gave rise to an ethnically homogeous state), *legal* (the sanction given to expressions of arbitrary power), *ethical* (the undermining of values, the de-moralisation of Czech society), *political* (the weakening of civic and democratic parties, *foreign political* (orientation to the Soviet Union), *economic* (destruction of material goods in the borderland), *sociological-demographic* (the depopulation of the border territory and its destabilisation) and *cultural* (the loss of German cultural and intellectual background and resources). Bohemus sees the greatest mistake in the fact that Czech politicians and society failed to seek a solution other than the expulsion of a whole ethnic group.

Implicit in the whole series of claims centred on the need for "complete" re-evaluation of the meaning of Czech history is the belief that Czech policy was simply incapable of rising to the challenge of the time, events and the imperative for a generous approach in relation both to Germany and to its own Bohemian Germans. The interpretation here is psychological, i.e. the deeper layer of the Czech attitude was full of fear of those who were seen as ancient enemies intrinsically bent on *Drang nach Osten*, but the Czech mind was unable to admit this fear because in doing so it would have admitted the insufficiency of any power of its own, not merely derived from others."[34]

In another passage Bohemus complains, "The Czechs, having decided to become a state nation, practically never managed to create good neighbourly relations with the countries around then: instead a deep antipathy predominated here... The source of the mistakes of Czech foreign policy can evidently be found in the Janus-faced "strongman-weakling" character of Czech defensively integral or integrally defensive nationalism. Failing to reflect on what they actually were, the Czechs pretended to be something they were not... Thus

Eisenhower that, "Dr. Gallup has discovered that Americans want no delay in the punishment of war criminals. They demand immediate punishment, without further delay." Irving, D. 1997. *Norimberk – poslední bitva* [Nuremberg – The last battle]. Prague: Grafoprint-Neubert. 58. The standpoint of the CFC (R. Luža, J. Horák, M. Povolný and others) referred to the fact that in the debate on retribution Churchill had considered the alternative of just hanging the main culprits without trial. At the same time it notes that the victor should show generosity and that "we should have pardoned and expelled the Sudeten German politicians who were condemned to death." *Svědectví* 58/1979. 383. On the atmosphere at the end of the war in relation to Germany Churchill commented, "In the ranks of the Allies universally shared passionate desires for retribution against the common enemy were manifest. These entirely dominated our minds." Churchill, W. 1995. *Druhá světová válka V. (Kruh se uzavírá)* [The Second World War V (Closing the Ring)]. Prague: Lidové noviny. 398.

34   Podiven (the pseudonym of a collective of authors: P. Příhoda, P. Pithart, M. Otáhal). 1991. *Češi v dějinách nové doby* [Czechs in the History of the Modern Age]. Prague: Rozmluvy. 400.

a remarkable "darling of the Entente" complex formed among Czechs, i.e. an automatic reliance on the allegedly automatic goodwill of the powerful, which contrasted unpleasingly with a lack of will to fend for themselves through their own unaided efforts. This complex was at work even in the period preceding the Munich crisis. Munich itself was a shattering awakening from the dream of "sweet France" and "proud Albion", but unfortunately this was never later subjected to scrutiny. Ordinary political reality was branded "betrayal", and after the end of the Second World War the complex awakened again. It was at work in 1945, 1948 and in 1968 and there is no certainty that it has finally been extinguished."[35]

This quintessentially *flagellant concept of history*, put forward as a kind of brilliant intellectual self-criticism without which the Czech nation would have no right to any further existence in civilised Europe, was formulated in a way that prefigured the development of certain views post-1989 on the key events in Czech history. In the preface to the second, now official rather than samizdat edition of their book, the authors referred to the reactions of critics who condemned the "Czech national self-flagellatory tendency" that they found in the work. In the view of the authors, however, such reactions merely confirmed Czechs in a self-confidence based on self-delusion.

The whole intellectual amalgam that re-evaluates modern Czech history from the point of view of the "critical socialist, the critical conservative liberal and the critical Catholic" is indeed extremely critical of the performance of the Czech nation and its political and intellectual elites. In my view, however, its whole interpretative framework context is vitiated by its uninhibited tendency to substitute moralising judgments for the objective analysis of facts and events. It is also very noteworthy that the theory that "greater Czech" ambitions were at the core of the Czech policy that founded an independent state in the centre of Europe before the nation hard "matured" to the responsibility necessary for state building, is a commonplace of argumentation regularly employed by authors of Sudeten German provenience.[36]

At the end of the last chapter, Podiven claims that, "The failure of 1938–9 was undoubtedly additionally the result of the dissposition of forces at the time, which was unfavourable to us. It was *also*, however, an unconscious settling of accounts with the whole two inter-war decades of the Czech state. It was the basis not only of Beneš's personal "Munich Complex" but also caused

---

[35] Ibidem. 407–410.

[36] See e.g. Grünwald, L. "Die Ursache der Katastrofe von 1938–1939 in der "grosstschechischen" bzw. Tschechoslowakischen Einstellung der Gründer der Republik", in *Wir haben uns selbst aus Europa vertrieben. Tschechische Selbstkritik an der Vertreibung der Sudetendeutschen*. 1985. München: Sudetendeutsche Stiftung. 13.

something worse: unacknowledged national self-doubt. The future chapters of Czech history would be proof of this."

In his polemic with this approach, Václav Kural argues that "Bohemus (like Podiven-author's note) prefers moral judgment on history to historical research and analysis". Kural considers Bohemus's "constitutional objections" to the demand for the priority of concrete understanding to be intellectual "Nadelstich" [embroidery] and several times recommends a little of that pedestrian, grey work "of the positivist type" which might "support the lofty arches of moral judgment on history on more solid pillars".

In place of objective analysis of the events that led to the tragic, dislocated and catastrophic outcome of the relationship between Czechs and Bohemian Germans, and the causal relations of these events, Bohemus merely reconstructs more or less exclusively Czech (and Allied) mistakes and adduces reasons for guilt. Even the best intentions cannot make such non-methods instruments of sober scholarly understanding.[37] A. Haman takes the view that the "approach based on a Christian universalist perspective (from which the whole 19th century appears as the climax of the disintegration of medieval Europe and the period of nationalist particularism), takes authors beyond the bounds of objective thinking and generates unanchored value judgments on the Czech literature of the time."[38]

The Czech Fate in Central Europe

Lack of space, and the specific focus of this work, means that I shall not attempt to reconstruct in full the course of the discussions on the problem of the transfer among exiles and in dissident circles inside Czechoslovakia. Represented in these discussions we find almost the complete spectrum of views that would be heard after 1989. Of course, following the fall of communism, the various different positions were all developed much more comprehensively and systematically, but the ideologisation of the theme that had already been evident in some dissident circles evident soon became very marked and even temporarily dominant in post-revolution conditions. This development was associated with the conspicious withdrawal of most leftwing intellectuals from public forums

---

[37]   Kural, V. "Ještě několik glos" [Some Further Glosses], in *Češi, Němci, odsun*. 316.

[38]   Haman, A. "Masochistický pohled na české dějiny" [The Masochistic View of Czech History]. *Dějiny a současnost* 3/1992. 59. See other critical reactions to the book *Češi v dějinách nové doby* in the same journal issue, in the Discussion-Debate section. J. Havránek takes the view that "one thing remains common to the whole book. That is its dependence on the time in which it was written. The attitude of the authors is predetermined by the fact that they are seeking answers to the question: how could it have happened that we are today a country of the socialist bloc". Ibidem. 56.

and above all the media in the first half of the 1990s. The diversity of their views on the transfer, and in the case of historians their understanding of sources and contexts, was all but buried under an avalanche of mainly journalistic polemic from writers demanding a fundamental revision of the official Czech position on the transfer.

Aggressive and trivialising deployment of ideological labels (for example, the present author and V. Pavlíček were sneeringly branded "patriots" by E. Mandler – but there are many other instances) led to a reduction of the number of participants in the exchange of views, and in any case the media preferred to offer a platform to those calling for an "innovative" approach. Many authors fell silent and withdrew. The result was a latent frustration and discontent in sections of the public (expressed for example in the position of the Union of Fighters for Freedom in the journal *Národní osvobození*, printed repeatedly but ignored) which found some partial vent in the course of preparations for the FRG-CSFR Treaty and the Czech-German Declaration, and most recently in the spring of 2002 in the debate on national interests provoked by external pressure from Bavaria, Austria and Hungary for the nullification of the presidential decrees as a condition for Czech accession to the European Union.

Debate on the specific character of Central Europe and its intellectual milieu had been going on among Czechs since the 1960s. One of the leading protagonists in the debate was Milan Kundera, who gave a lengthy speech on the theme at the 4th Congress of Czechoslovak Writers, then took up the subject again at the end of 1970s ("From the Cultural Testament of Central Europe"[39]) and developed it in the 1980s with the seminal essay, "The Tragedy of Central Europe".[40] In polemic with Václav Havel on the fate of the Czech nation in

---

[39] One of Kundera's themes was the distance between the experience and Central- and West- Europeans: "Large nations are deeply convinced that they make history. A Russian, even if extremely anti-Soviet, is proud in the depths of his heart to belong to a large nation that has changed the course of the world. This is not the case of the small nations of Central Europe. We have not made history, but have undergone it. We do not like it, because it does not like us. We do not identify with its meaning, assumed or real. We accord it no greatness or respect. The first Austrian emigrants to arrive in France and England at the end of the 1930s were amazed at the carefree indifference of their hosts. They had the impression that they were a generation ahead of the West in experience. We who have escaped from the laboratory of History that is Central Europe have the same feeling today." Kundera, M. "Z kulturního testamentu střední Evropy" [From the Cultural Testament of Central Europe]. *Listy 3/*2000 (XXX). 89–90. (Reprint of article first published in *Listy* 6/1978.)

[40] Milan Kundera's essay, "The Tragedy of Central Europe". *The New York Review of Books*. 26th April 1984, inspired a wide-ranging discussion. The journal *Svědectví* reviewed it and then carried the first part of a discussion which after November 1989 continued in the country that it most concerned, Czechoslovakia. Kundera is wrongly marginalised in Czech culural life today, since his texts on the theme of Czechs and Europe have always been key sources and stimuli. One example was Kundera's speech at the 4th Congress of Czechoslovak writers in June 1967, which included the passage: "for the great European nations with a so-called classic history, the European context is somehow self-evident. But Czechs have experienced alternating periods of wakefulness and periods of deep sleep, and so have missed some of the basic phases of development of the European spirit and have always had to relay, adopt and create a European context anew for themselves.

1968, Kundera expressed a thought that has lost nothing of its urgency: "The Czech nation is integrally connected to its culture in a way that means it could not survive the decline of that culture, and so freedom of speech is a question of life or death for it – to be or not to be."

The relevance of this idea today arises from the the fundamental redefinition of the international political framework in which the Czech state finds itself, having in the meantime also become smaller. Freedom of speech and opinion here is no longer threatened by Soviet and domestic totalitarianism, but instead by its trivialisation by the tabloid-style media, by the Berlusconisation of public political space (to use a shorthand symbol of the manipulation of information and social consciousness), and also by the monopolisation of the national and regional press in the hands of German owners.[41]

These ominous trends have been developing in a situation in which most of the print media supports the views of the Sudeten German organisations on the need for nullification of the post-war presidential decrees (which were in fact Czechoslovak denazification legislation), views which in the spring of 2002 received the backing of the German federal government when at the 53rd Sudeten German Days in Nuremberg, the interior minister O. Schily declared that, "in the spirit of the Czech-German Declaration the Czech side should take the decision to abolish the Beneš Decrees."[42]

Similar views have been expressed repeatedly by the Austrian federal chancellor Wolfgang Schüssel and the Hungarian prime minister Viktor Orbán. Not only Sudeten German campaigning materials but serious academic studies are now using the term "ethnic cleansing" to describe events at the end of the Second World War and just after it.[43] Every re-interpretation of historical realities and definitions inevitably finds its reflection in the field of real politics sooner or later. The same applies to the reassessment of the post-war population transfers in Central and Eastern Europe.

An old spirit returned to haunt Central Europe in the wake of the euphoria at the fall of communism – the spirit of "Central Europe", but less as Kundera understood it than as it had been identified and explored in 1992 by the Austrian-born British historian Eric Hobsbawm. Hobsbawm argued that the term

---

Nothing for the Czechs has every been automatic and to be taken for granted, not even their language. Not even their European identity." Kundera, M. "IV. sjezd SČSS" překlad. *Svědectví* 29–32/1966–67 (VIII) (reprint). 493. Kundera, M. "Český úděl" [The Czech Fate]. *Svědectví* 89/90 (XXIII). 357–362.

[41] For more detail see the concise but pithy analysis in Čelovský, B. 2001. *Konec českého tisku?* [The End of the Czech Press?]. Ostrava: Tilia.

[42] "Sudetští Němci přitvrzují, budou volby" [Sudeten German attitudes harden, elections ahead]. *MF Dnes.* 20. 5. 2002. A/3.

[43] E.g. *Redrawing Nations (Ethnic Cleansing in East-Central Europe, 1944–1948.* 2001. Ther, P. – Siljak, A. (eds.). Lanham/Boulder/New York/Oxford: Rowman & Littlefield Publishers, Inc.

Central Europe was politically normative rather than just geographical, that it was more a goal and a vision of what ought to be than a description of what is. Of course, every historian and diplomat is familiar with the phenomenon of *words and 'facts' that conceal an agenda*. In this context Hobsbawm repeatedly drew attention to the concept of *Mitteleuropa* formulated by Friedrich Naumann, i.e. "a unified territory from the Visla to the Vogéza and from Galicia to the Bodensee, economic and political supremacy over South Europe on the road from Berlin to Baghdad."

This is a very different and arguably a far more substantial concept of Central Europe than any intellectual nostalgia for "Kakania" [translator's note: the expression for the old Austro-Hungarian monarchy as a state of mind, associated with the Austrian author Robert Musil] cultivated among dissidents who were aware that as a result of the Second World War and its aftermath, "political freedom and human rights on a large part of the former territory of the Habsburg Monarchy... [are in a worse state] today than in 1913."[44] Hobsbawm by contrast tells us not to delude ourselves, for in his view the concept of Central Europe tends dangerously towards racism and possibly imperialism as well. Indeed, "was it not always the Austrians who from the founding of the German Reich offered themselves and their country to their powerful neighbours as experts on questions of the South-East, and experts in the art of how to deal with Slivovitz drinkers?" He argues that we must reject Central Europe as a political term.

Not that Hobsbawm denies that a valuable Central European culture once existed. He identifies this as the culture of emancipated Jews, educated and integrated into bourgeois society in the period when German learning was dominant. It was these German-speaking Jews who liked to consider themselves Central Europeans because in this way they could distance themselves from Eastern Jews who spoke only Yiddish and were in many cases moving Westwards especially after the First World War – until both groups ended in the same crematoria.[45]

The original bearers of this Central European culture were crushed and massacred. In any case, from the times of the Weimar Republic, German culture no longer set the tone and the German language was no longer the *lingua franca* of educated people from the Baltic to Albania. The Central Europe of a broad educated middle class (orientated to German culture) no longer exists.

---

[44] Somewhat aphoristically, but accurately, Hobsbawm points out that the collapse of Austria-Hungary was the only case of a state whose fall was the impetus for the writing of great literature (K. Kraus, R. Musil, J. Hašek, M. Krleža and others). Hobsbawm, E. "Rakousko a střední Evropa". *Lettre Internationale* 5/1992. 52–53.

[45] Ibidem.

Hobsbawm, just like Milan Šimečka in his criticism of Kundera's demonisation of the destructive influence of the Russian communist imperium on Central European culture, argues that "there should be no evasion of the the the fact that it was not Russia that was the first cause of the end of the Central European tradition… First and foremost it was the insane actions of the Nazis that turned the nations of Central Europe into victims and outsiders of history. The tragedy of Central Europe started without the influence of the Eastern element, and without any substantial Russian contribution; the cancer that destroyed what had existed here, grew out of West European history and was nourished on the waste materials of West European intellectual discoveries. That was the real sequence of events; it was only the remnants of old Central Europe that breathed their last breath in the embrace of Russia."[46]

In 1988 (*Historische Zeitschrift*), the German historian R. Jaworski offered a similar view. He noted that "It seems to be particularly the independent voices from Eastern Europe that are locked into a Yalta complex. We need to be understanding about this, since after all, the people who are expressing their opinions here are precisely those who were harmed by the division of Europe," but he questioned whether the decisions made in February 1945 in the Crimea were really the primary reasons for the break up of Central Europe. What – he asks – actually remained of Central Europe after its decimation as a result of national socialist rule?[47]

In much the same vein, Milan Hauner in polemic with Kundera argues that Kundera's concept of the Central European tragedy is incomplete and distorted because it lacks any deeper understanding of Hitler and Nazism. After all, Hitler himself, who never makes any appearance in Kundera's lengthy article, was a product of Central European culture *par excellence*; Stalin not at all. Hauner also argues that the Red Army advance into Central Europe was primarily a matter of revenge after a desperate struggle with German aggressors who had planned and to some extent succeeded in bringing about a far worse enslavement of the peoples of Central Europe. He considers that the striking rise of pan-Slavism among Czechs after the war should be understood in this context and not branded an ideological deviation with no intelligible historical causes.[48]

---

[46] Šimečka, M. "Jiná civilizace?" [A Different Civilisation?]. *Svědectví* 89–90/1984–1985 (XXIII). 377.

[47] What he objects to in the polemics against Yalta is the attempt to explain all the misfortunes of the nations of Central Europe purely in terms of external origins, i.e. the effects of the actions of the great powers. Jaworski, R. "Aktuální diskuse o střední Evropě v historické perspektivě" [Current Discussion on Central Europe in Historical Perspective]. *Listy* 4/1990 (XX). 29.

[48] Hauner, M. "Dopis redakci" [Letter to the Editor of The New York Review of Books]. *Svědectví* 89–90/1984–1985. 381.

Hauner brings up the views of the 19th-century Czech historian and patriot František Palacký, who wanted Central Europe to remain under the Habsburg, not just as a bulwark against Russian imperialism, but also as a defence against the equally dangerous ambitions of Prussian Pan-Germanism. He also points out that Kundera systematically views Central Europe as "culture or fate" ("a bold but of course an ahistorical metaphor") and not as an historical and geopolitical entity. Here Hauner puts his finger on the problematic status of a concept that has so strikingly moulded the understanding of Central Europe among those Czech intellectuals who tend to an emotionally romanticising view of history, and one that they also believe must be "come to terms with" in the spirit of *Vergangenheitsbewältigung*.

Hobsbawm interpreted the voices calling for the revival of Central Europe in communist countries in the 1980s as less a genuine expression of longing for the "golden age" of the multi-ethnic monarchy and more as the plea, "Can't we belong somewhere else than in the Soviet part of Europe?" My view, however, is that another reason for this wish was a tendency to a romantic conception of politics that has always been present in Czech political milieux and is one source of the deep, society-wide frustration that has followed the great, but short-term phases of upswing in Czech society (typically the turning-point moments of 1938 and 1968).

The difficulty with "Central Europe" is its utter vagueness, whether with regard to territory or other objective criteria. It is of course precisely this vagueness that makes the concept so perfect for the deployment of a "peculiar sense of irreplaceable cultural feeling", and the sheer number of interpretations that it can be made to bear may be precisely what has so fascinated the imagination of intellectuals. M. Schulze Wessel argues that the immense influence that Kundera's essay has exercised derives mainly just from the term "Central Europe" itself.[49] Kundera's concept of Europe offers resonances and and invites correlations with the concepts propounded by Arnold Toynbee and Oswald Spengler, who spoke not of "European" but "Western" culture and regarded only the Western part of Europe as truly European. We can find associated ideas today in the comments of T. G. Ash: "We have to understand that what used to be genuinely Central European (for Poles and Czechs) was always Western, ra-

---

[49]   He points out that Kundera had published the same theses five years before in *Le Monde, Le Nouvelle Observateur* and elsewhere without the same success – he had been speaking then of "Eastern Europe" and got no reaction. Perhaps the right key word had to be found, or perhaps the situation changed the perceived nature and urgency of the theme. See also other views of the problem: Schulze Wessel, M. "Střed je na Západě – střední Evropa v české diskusi osmdesátých let" [The Centre is in the West – Eastern Europe in Czech Discussion of the 1980], in *Evropa očima Čechů* [Europe through the Eyes of Czechs]. 1997. Hahn, E. (ed.). Prague: Nakladatelství Franze Kafky. 73–77.

tional, humanist, democratic, sceptical and tolerant. Everything else was East European, Russian, or perhaps German."[50]

We have already mentioned the concept of *Mitteleuropa* as published in 1915 by F. Naumann, and now need to ask whether all this continues to play some kind of role in the context of Czech-German relations as of 1989. P. Katzenstein argues that the return of the construct of Central Europe is a sign of profound political change after 1989. Despite the various modifying elements of the new European order, including the transposition of German aspirations into wider global context, and despite the fact that the co-ordinates of world politics are shifting away from Europe, "Central Europe" remains important. This is because it evokes memories of the great catastrophes of the 20th century: fascism, two world wars, and the Holocaust. It is also because Central Europe was a theatre of the Cold War: the flashpoint where war was most likely to have become a reality, but also an area of diplomatic tacking and weaving.[51] Czech-German and in some cases Polish-German relations provide a good illustration of this claim.

We can identify certain conditions making for a continuity of meanings lasting into the present day, above all if we remember that the alternative and rival vision to that of F. Naumann's Mitteleuropa was T. G. Masaryk's concept of Central Europe as a belt of small states reaching from Estonia, Latvia and Lithuania right down to Albania and Greece.[52] Germany and Austria do not belong to Central Europe according to this schema. Of course, at first sight it might seem outdated and irrelevant to the current framework of the international political situation of the CR, which is about to join the European Union.[53] Yet have all Masaryk's ideas on Germany and its role in Central Europe ceased to

---

[50] Ash, T. G. "Does Central Europe Exist?" *New York Review of Books*. 9. 10. 1986. The essay begins with the words: Central Europe has returned. J. Dienstbier quotes another comment from Garton Ash, "On my repeated journeys it has occurred to me more than once that the real dividing line is between those (in the West), who have Europe, and those (in the East) who believe in it. The sentence with which people in all these countries try to express what they care about is "return to Europe". Ash, T. G. *Rok zázraků* [Year of Miracles]. 123.

[51] Katzenstein, P. J. 1997. *Mitteleuropa – between Europe and Germany*. Oxford, Providence: Berghahn Books. 4. On this theme see also Markovits, A. S. – Reich, S. 1997. *The German Predicament: Memory and Power in the New Europe*. Ithaca: Cornell University Press. Markovits, A. S. – Reich. S. 1998. *Das deutsche Dilemma (Die Berliner Republik zwischen Macht und Machtverzicht)*. Berlin: Alexander Fest Verlag.

[52] Masaryk, T. G. *Světová revoluce*. 299.

[53] K. Kosík is another who takes the side of Masaryk and his concept in the context of debate on Central Europe: "Palacký made the same arguments for the necessity of a Central European federation as Masaryk made for the necessity of a common state for Czechs and Slovaks – the defence against the expansionism of old and modernised Prussianism and Tsarism. Central Europe is a historical territory of a peculiar, unique and irreplaceable kind. This territory lies between two great powers who from time to time (i.e. whenever an opportunity presents itself) make a claim to "protect" or annex it (these are two different words for the same thing)." Kosík, K. "Třetí Mnichov?" [A Third Munich?]. *Listy* 6/1992 (XXII). 35.

be relevant? The key question here is whether and to what extent Germany is ready, willing and able to return to the plan of *Mitteleuropa*.

M. Schulze Wessel points out that Masaryk's and Naumann's concepts of Central Europe were mutually exclusive and "in their way correspond ideologically to the basic dualism between Eastern Central Europe and Western Central Europe (Germany, German Austria)." More specifically he writes:

"If we review the journalistic discussion of the time on Central Europe [he is referring to the 1980s], we cannot avoid the impression that this is a continuation of the conceptual dispute between Naumann and Masaryk. Kundera located his Central Europe between Germany and Russia and so aligned himself with the Masarykian tradition. Václav Havel likewise excluded Germany from his thoughts on Central Europe."[54]

The Redefinition of the German Role in Central Europe

With regard to Czech-German relations at the beginning of the Third Millenium, however, the question is one of trying to identify their present forms and prospects in the redefined situation following the collapse of the Russian imperium, the membership of both the CR and FRG in NATO and the accession of the CR to the European Union. One leading British expert on German foreign policy considers that, "Germany's *Europapolitik* has two strategic lines: the deepening of integration processes and the expansion of the European Union to the East."[55] According to this interpretation, Germany has a special interest in the entry of Poland, the Czech Republic and Germany into the EU, and this interest is conditioned by four basic factors:

a) The need to stabilise the security environment along the Eastern borders, since this will help Germany and its neighbours find a co-operative solution for many security-agenda problems following the end of the Cold War, specifically economic transformation and the process of building states and nations.

b) Enlargement promises Germany major economic benefits in the form of trade and investment together with the creation of a single Central Euro-

---

54 Schulze Wessel, M. "Střed je na Západě". 81–82. The author ends his overview study of the debate on Central Europe by pointing out that there is no one Czech discussion on Central Europe. The three basic approaches to the theme, however – Kundera's clearly anti-Russia essay, the Catholic conception of Central Europe and the devaluation of the Slavophile tradition – all share one direction, i.e. the trend towards rejection of historical conceptions focused only on the past of the nation itself.

55 Hyde-Price, A. 2000. *Germany and European Order (enlarging NATO and the EU)*. Manchester/New York: Manchester University Press. 181.

pean market that possesses a skilled and cheap workforce. According to G. Verheugen, the alternative is a "border of poverty" running through the centre of Europe, which would be in no-one's interests, least of all Germany's.

c) Enlargement will create a multilateral basis for Germany's relations with smaller neighbours in East and Central Europe, and this will help to reduce the unease about German dominance in *Mitteleuropa*[56] that remains widespread in the region. It will likewise help spread some of the costs associated with the stabilisation of Central and Eastern Europe to other EU member states.

d) The broad support for enlargement in the German political and economic elites reflects the deep-rootedness of ideas of multilateralism, which have become parts of the "genetic code" of these elites. Germany is convinced that the result will be the further "Europeanisation" of its own state identity and believes that the new democracies will benefit from multilateral relations of cooperation and integration.[57]

Yet despite these generally formulated goals of German foreign policy (which are hard to fault), there are still areas where the specific form of the fulfilment of these goals remains unclarified (i.e. where the practice may potentially be less altruistic than Hyde-Price believes), and there is also a continuing situation of *very marked and many-sided asymmetry* between the Western European states (represented above all by Germany) and their neighbours in Central Europe. For Germany, expansion to the East opens up prospects of the institutional exploitation of geopolitical and cultural asymmetry.[58] V. Handl draws attention to the arguments of Markovits and Reich, who believe that following unification Germany is now in a position that will allow it to dominate East Central Europe economically and culturally.[59]

One of the theories that seek to explain Germany's support for enlargement towards the East is that this is the result of Germany's decision to cease to play the role of "buffer zone" in regard to Eastern Europe and to shift this role onto the shoulders of the Visegrad States. From this perspective the region itself is

---

[56] British academic literature regularly uses the term Mitteleuropa, often simply as an alternative to "East-Central Europe", without seeing in it any important specific connotations of the kind immediately evident to Czechs.

[57] For more detail see ibidem. 182–183.

[58] Pedersen, T. 1998. *Germany, France and the Integration of Europe*. London/New York: Pinter. 192.

[59] Handl, V. "Německý multilateralismus a vztahy k státům visegrádské skupiny" [German Multilateralism and Relations with the States of the Visegrad Group]. *Mezinárodní vztahy* 1/2003. 13.

defined as an "economic, institutional and migrational buffer zone", and in less controversial form as a kind of "inter-zone".[60]

The post-communist states seeking the opportunity to "rejoin Europe" have found themselves in the role of petitioner vis-a-vis the Euro-Atlantic community, and subject to demands and conditions that they have to accept or reject. This position, reinforced by the asymmetry of the Czech-German relationship, has been provoking a trend to negative attitudes towards the Brussels Eurocracy (and by extension towards Germany) in Czech public opinion and in Czech elites. The European Commissar for enlargement, G. Verheugen, was particularly conscious of this situation. In the decisive accession phase he made efforts to reduce the tension that culminated in a rift between the France-Germany tandem and the candidate states during debate (February-March 2003) on material support for the USA in its attack on Iraq.[61]

The East European states including the Czech Republic justifiably saw the United States as the guarantor of the democratic development of Central Europe and a source of support in debate on the future order of the region. Ultimately it had been the United States that had made the decisive contribution first to the creation and then to the restoration of an independent Czechoslovakia in the course of the 20th century. Currently this pro-American attitude has been confirmed in connection with the armed intervention against Iraq, which provoked a split between the USA and France supported by Germany. The East European countries backed the USA even at the cost of potentially complicating their accession to the EU. One reason was evidently their still living memory of the key role of the United States in the disintegration of the Soviet Empire.

This situation reflected a larger sensitive issue, i.e. that the new regime of mutual relations between Western and Eastern Europe could be perceived as either "imposed" or "negotiated".[62] Germany's commitment to enlargement and its position make it the key power when it comes to ensuring that the new system of international relations should be "negotiated", and this requires Germany to show restraint in the exploitation of instruments of dominance and hegemony.[63] The relationship of Germany and its neighbours in East Central

---

[60]   *Patterns of Migration in Central Europe.* 2001. Wallace, C. – Stola, D. (eds.). Houndsmills: Palgrave. 86.

[61]   G. Verheugen defended the candidate states that expressed a pro-American position in the Iraq crisis. (After some Euro-MPs had sharply criticised the support of the East European states for the American intention to attack Iraq). Verheugen added that "Eastern Europe had deep ties to the USA because they remembered the American role in the removal of communist regimes." Verheugen defends right of candidates to support American policy. *České noviny* (www.ceskenoviny.cz). ČTK 17. 3. 2003.

[62]   See Hyde-Price, A. "Negotiated or imposed order in Central Europe?", in *Germany and European Order.* 211–213.

[63]   For example by shifting the institutional frameworks of the functioning of the political system, state and local government, models of management though the activities of foundations etc. Hyde-Price. A. *Hegemony*

Europe is in fact best understood precisely in terms of hegemony, but what is crucial is that Germany is not exercising its hegemonic power unilaterally, but that its foreign and security policy is being solidly built into a series of close strategic partnerships via multilateralism. According to Hyde-Price, this means that Germany has become a team player out of conviction, not just because its inhabitants have accepted multilateralism as a moral principle, but because multilateralism provides the most effective foreign and security policy in a world of interdependent dependences.[64]

Despite this, or perhaps just because of it, Czechs have problems with Germany. The policy of the new Czech political elites towards Germany developed out of pre-1989 dissident circles and was formed by debates (consciously seeking a new concept of Czech relationship to Germany, see the debate on Danubius's Theses or the Prague Appeal) that took place away from the mainstream of Czech society. The Czech public could not in fact understand why two days after his election Václav Havel headed for the FRG on his first foreign trip. This distance between the elite and the rest of society soon widened and the trend has been continuing.[65]

Reasessment of the expulsion of Germans from Czechoslovakia was part of thinking on the transition of Central Europe from totalitarian rule to democracy, as has been discussed above (the debate on Danubius's Theses). The confrontation between these rather abstract conceptions and the prospects for pursuing their implications in the real political world revealed the gap between the political elites emerging from dissent and the rest of the Czechoslovak/Czech population (J. Rupnik). This gap has been a source of increasing difficulties in the process of search for settlement between Czechs and Germans as the superficial political consensus post-1989 disappeared in the years that followed.[66]

---

in Central Europe. 213–216, defines the difference between dominance and hegemony. He cites Otto von Bismarck, who defined hegemony as an unequal relationship between a great power and one or more smaller states which is nonetheless based on the legal and formal equality of all the states concerned. Bismarck's definition emphasises the important difference in the way the great power exercises influence on smaller states. This is based on a relation of leadership and following, not the principle of ruler and ruled. Unlike a relation of pure dominance, hegemony depends very much on "shaping the milieu" in a way conducive to hegemony.

[64] Rummel, R. "The German Debate on International Security Institutions", in *European Security and International Institutions after the Cold War*. 1995. Carnovale, M. (ed.). New York: St. Martin's Press. 193.

[65] For more detail see Rupnik, J. – Bazin, A. "La difficile réconciliation tchéco-allemande". *Politique étrangère* 2/2001 (Avril-Juin). 353–370.

[66] In reality the period of euphoria was very brief and ended as early as 1991 in the preparatory phase of the Treaty on Good Neighbourly Relations and Friendly Co-operation. For more detail on this theme see the chapter on the Treaty with Germany in his memoirs by Dienstbier, J. 1999. *Od snění k realitě* [From Dream to Reality]. Prague: Lidové noviny. 282–300. Dienstbier writes that from immediately after the unification of Germany, the role of the Bavarian CSU, which had decided to adopt a higher profile of support for the expellees, was ever more strikingly in evidence. He writes that, "the outlines of an alliance of hardliners in the FRG and this country are beginning to emerge, and this would not benefit the climate in Europe." What is disturbing when we assess the earlier and current situation is the repeated hesitation and vagueness in

Nervousness caused by constant postponements on the German side to the signing of a Czech-German Treaty in 1991–92, as well as the repeated demands of the expellees' organisations for compensation for loss of property and right to homeland, prompted a group of 30 deputies of the Czechoslovak Parliament to send a letter to the four great powers requesting confirmation of the *Potsdam Agreement*, specifically Heading 13 on the transfers of ethnic Germans. The powers concerned confirmed the Potsdam decisions, although in the case of the USA and Great Britain with the reservation that they could in no way comment on the terms of the text of the treaty between the CSFR and Germany, which was a bilateral matter.[67] The request for the opinion of the former members of the Allied coalition made sense because the FRG does not recognise the Potsdam Agreement as binding in international law (on the grounds that the documents accepted at the Potsdam Conference were allegedly merely signed by heads of states and governments, were not presented to parliaments for ratification, were not published in official treaty collections and "according to universal rules... a state that has not been party to an agreement cannot be bound by such an agreement").[68]

Despite Article IV of the *Czech-German Declaration* of 1997, following up the Treaty of 1992, which states that, "Both sides therefore declare that they will not burden their relations with political and legal issues which stem from the past,"[69] pressure for the repeal of President Beneš's Decrees continued. In a resolution of the 15th of April 1999, the European Parliament challenged the Czech

---

the attitudes of the federal government; it confirms the contents agreed by the two governments as it were reluctantly and always after a long process of prevarication, perhaps under pressure of circumstances. In the informed observer it produces the impression that there are some other, hidden goals in German foreign policy for which some manoeuvring space needs to be created. On this theme Dienstbier writes that Kohl's constant postponements had the effect of encouraging German nationalists. A similar impression is given by statements like those made on the TV programme *Bonn-direkt* on the 25th of August 1991 by the chairman of the CSU and then federal minister of finance, Theo Waigel: "Claims for the payment of war damages (made on the CSFR side) are unjustified and not internationally admissible... On the other hand the Czech side is refusing to talk about the Sudeten Germans' claims to compensation... the Czech side must think long and hard about how matters will look if Czechoslovakia wants to join the European communities." Here we can already hear the openly threatening tone that was to be used again and again in the future. This is hardly the way to promote the birth of a new Europe for which German politicians so often appeal. In this situation it is not surprising that Czech foreign policy should seek support from the USA.

67   "Stanoviska USA, Velké Británie, Ruské federace a Francie k Postupimské dohodě" [The Positions of the USA, Great Britain, the Russian Federation and France on the Potsdam Agreement], in *Právní aspekty odsunu sudetských Němců*. Supplement III. 103. See also *Komu sluší omluva* [Who Should Apologise]. 1992. (Collective of authors). Prague: Erika. 208–210.

68   As is well-known, by unconditional capitulation the defeated Nazi Germany forfeited its legal subjecthood in international law – but the FRG has always rejected this. See Fastenrath, U. "Who is bound by the Potsdam Agreement? The Allies adopted a series of heterogeneous provisions." *Frankfurter Allgemeine Zeitung*. 20th March 1996. See also *Česko-německé vztahy po pádu železné opony*. 1997. Rada pro mezinárodní vztahy. 71–72.

69   Text of the Czech-German Declaration on Mutual Relations and their Future Development of the 21st of January 1997, see ibidem. 22–23.

government, "to repeal the laws and decrees of 1945 and 1946 relating to the forced transfer of ethnic groups from the former Czechoslovakia."[70] The inclusion of this sentence was pushed through by CSU deputies in the European Parliament (including B. Posselt, current president of the Sudetendeutsche Landsmannschaft and president of the *Pan-European Union*). A month later, on the 19th of May 1999, the Austrian parliament, (*Nationalrat*) passed a similar resolution declaring the incompatibility of the laws and decrees on the postwar expulsion from the former Czechoslovakia and the former Yugoslavia (Slovenia) with European law.

Austrian politicians seized on the theme, raised from the start especially by the Governor of Carinthia Jörg Haider in relation to the CR and Slovenia, whose president Milan Kučan expressed disquiet at the exploitation of the issue both by Austria and the Italian *Northern League*.

Bavaria, particularly its conservative nationalist political leadership in which the Sudetendeutsche Landsmannnschaft has an influential place, has a key role in backing revisionist opinion in the Danubian region. The SL president Bernd Posselt has been promoting the view that the Sudeten German question is not soluble on the basis of bilateral Czech-German relations, but only multilaterally in a European context. He has threatened that the Sudetendeutsche Landsmannschaft will step up activities in this regard (the challenge to the presidential decrees has already been made in the European Parliament) in the process of EU enlargement so as to ensure that "no postwar settlement will remain necessary and a just international legal order will prevail in Europe." According to Posselt, the solution to the Sudeten German question is "a question of the European Union's essential conception of itself", because the expulsion of the Sudeten Germans affects not just the CR and Germany, but Austria, Hungary and Croatia as well.[71]

Posselt deems the resolution of the Sudeten German question to be a "positive signal for Mitteleuropa", and in this context it is clearly very important to identify what the concept of *Mitteleuropa* currently concretely means. On the Czech side the supporters of this concept are concentrated around the review *Střední Evropa/Central Europe*, which has been coming out since 1985, initially as a samizdat magazine but since November 1989 as an official journal with the subtitle *Review for Central European Culture and Politics*.

The first issue declared that the journal "has no synthesising ideal of Central Europe", but as the years went by the contours of such an ideal began to emerge in its contents. The following extract offers an idea of the publisher's

---

[70] Resolution of the COM (98)0708 – C4–0111/99 adopted on the 15th of April 1999 by the European Parliament. Point 7.

[71] "Posselt in Wien: Sudetendeutsche Frage multilateral lösen!" *Sudetendeutsche Zeitung*. 12. 4. 2002.

vision of Central Europe and the role of Czechs: "...Why should we, who for centuries had the closest possible relations and contacts with Vienna, starting with our aristocrats and ending with our artisans and students, be supposed to watch apathetically as Vienna and Budapest, between which there was never such a tradition, draw together? It must surely be quite clear to all of us that if Central Europe is some day to become a political reality again, its centre will be in Vienna."[72]

German influence has been returning to Central Europe and with it the need for a sober assessment of the situation. "Central Europe" has suddenly ceased to be a matter of mild nostalgia for the golden age of the Habsburg multinational state and the all-embracing cosmopolitanism of the literary cafés of Vienna, Prague and Budapest, and has reappeared surprisingly fast in the world of modern geo-politics, where there are emerging signs of a "new" system of Central European conditions and relations. The change has been manifest in quite explicit form in the claims of some Bavarian conservative Christian politicians that the *post-war European order in fact no longer exists*.[73] Of course, the presence of the conservative nationalist wing in German politics is hardly new, or something that has unexpectedly emerged after the collapse of bipolarism, but its influence is increasing in the new system for reasons that include major changes in German society (public opinion) in the era of the "Berlin" republic. Everything suggests that *the German public and its politicians consider the era of penance to be over*.[74] The controversy over the setting up of a Berlin *Centre against Expulsions* is just one more step in the process of the re-nationalisation of German identity. From the point of view of Germany's eastern neighbours (including the CR) the key question is to what extent and in what form the "European factor" will remain a component of this identity. Or whether Germany may not succumb to the temptation to extricate itself from European integration structures (which some member states continue to see as the best insurance against

---

[72] Kučera, R. 1989. *Kapitoly z dějin střední Evropy* [Chapters from the History of Central Europe]. München: Nationalausschuss in Deutschland e.V. 127.

[73] Examples of ideas of the revision of the results of the Second World War have been multiplying. One instance to stand for many is material in the SL's newspaper *Sudetendeutsche Zeitung*, where we find the assertion, "The results of the Second World War are dead, vanquished by reality through the complete failure of the communist system. Everything that was agreed at Yalta lies in the dustbin of history. If Yalta is dead, then "Potsdam" is deader than dead (if we have to use this illogical comparative)." Wildt, G. "Ergebnisse des Zweiten Weltkriegs". *Sudetendeutsche Zeitung*. 26. 4. 2002. 2.

[74] Informed observers have been expecting such a development since the 1990s. See e.g. the view, that "German foreign policy is not informed only by neighbourly altruism... Supporting the incorporation of Central Europe into the Western world is probably its last act of atonement for the crimes committed against the peoples of this region." Cook, J. "Obchodování a lítost" [Trading and Regret]. *Týden* 3/1997. 53–55 (taken from *Business Central Europe*).

German expansionist recidivism) or at least to adapt them to the needs of its own goals and interests.

Another possible way forward for Germany, according to current indications, is the attempt to shift the conflict-ridden themes of flight and expulsion/ *Flucht und Vertreibung* into the field of culture, as suggested by the most recent trend in German-Czech and German-Polish dialogue. A. Krzemiński points out that as early as the end of the 1990s there were tectonic shifts in Polish public opinion, leading to demands for "an end to the frivolity of the policy of reconciliation." In Poland, the building of the Berlin Holocaust monument was regarded as a way of reducing the victims of German mass slaughter in German minds simply to one single group – Jews, and the Centre against Expulsions as an institution for the falsification of the causes and consequences of the war unleashed by Hitler and waged by the German people.

The very idea of the Berlin Centre was viewed by the majority in Poland as an expression of historical revisionism and the deliberate blurring of the relationship between the authors and the victims of the war.[75] The re-discovered historical memory, or identity of the "Berlin" republic, is evidently coming up against the roused identities of its eastern neighbours. Continual emphasis on the "German way" is summoning up memories of the sadly famous "Sonderweg" notion of Germany destiny and is accompanied by a certain historical revisionism, and visible shift of attention from the victims of German Nazism to the German victims of the war: the Allied bombing of German cities, the rape of German women in 1945, the cruel conditions in which the Russians kept German prisoners of war, and of course the flights, expulsions and transfers.[76]

I doubt that those who took part in the debate launched by Kundera and developed in the interaction between domestic dissident circles and the exile ever envisaged this kind of outcome. The intellectual concept of a shared Central European intersection of cultures, which was in its time fashionable and after the fall of the Soviet imperium became a magic formula that seemed capable of real application, has been collapsing under the impact of newly found identities (this does not apply only to Germany) that seem to represent a spontaneous reaction to integrational and globalising trends, and the knowledge that *there is no escape from the past*. Yet in the post-revolutionary euphoria, it had genuinely seemed only a matter of time before everyone would look back on the crimes and human tragedies of the Second World War in a framework tran-

---

[75] Krzemiński, A. "Zápas o paměť" [The Struggle over Memory]. *Kafka (journal for Central Europe)* 3/2004. The theme of expulsion. 59–60.

[76] Ibidem. 59.

scending national memory, and the recollection of the sufferings of one's own people and other peoples would be viewed through "European eyes".[77]

Here it may be appropriate to quote words published in 1988 by the exiled historian and philosopher Bedřich Loewenstein: "The intact national self-satisfaction and sense of righteousness of the French, Poles, Russians, and most recently the newly expressed longing of the West Germans for a history like all the other nations − a history that need not be avoided like the executioner's house, the continual flaring up of nationalist orgies, nation egoism, chauvinist hatred for foreigners... all this, it seems, hardly signals the end of nationalism. On the contrary, is it not the case that precisely in a time *of supranational integration* processes, global strategies, cosmopolitan technological and consumer advances, and prefabricated habits, *national* characters are necessary? Is it not possible that the speed of innovation, the hectic succession of fashions and movements actually demands an anchorage in the national past, in the feeling of homeland, in folklore and regionalism?"[78] Fifteen years in advance, Loewenstein seems to have identified and captured the coming period of search for all kinds of identity that we are witnessing today.

Undoubtedly there is a great deal of truth in these insights, but not the whole truth. Loewenstein goes on more dubiously to argue that a past conceived in one or another way is ceasing to be functional and poses a question that in the context of continuing pressure on the Czech Republic sounds somewhat out of place: Does the Czech nation today need a nationalist ideology, does it need a national history in order to make its way in the world? I must say that I am quite amazed to see an equation being made between national history and nationalist ideology by an author who once wrote the essay on, "The German War Experience and the Irrational Critique of Civilisation."[79] The history of a nation, after all, is not only the source of nationalist myths in the sense of the "invention" and justification of national existence, but also a supremely necessary source of reflection on the nature of national community and an integrating factor in the positive sense of the word. This is particularly valid for Czech society, the permanent threat to which has been entirely real (especially in the course of the 20th century).

---

[77] Ibidem. 58. In this context Krzemiński points out that "Peter Glotz is the second most important person (after Erika Steinbach) behind this project (i.e. the Centre against Expulsions), and this fact in itself shows how far the German search for identity has shifted in the ten years of new German sovereignty". Krzemiński, A. "Mezi renacionalizací a evropeizací – polský pohled na Německo" [Between Renationalisation and Europeanisation – a Polish perspective on Germany]. *Internationale Politik und Gesellschaft* 1/2004. 15.

[78] Loewenstein, B. "České dějiny a národní identita (sedm tezí)" [Czech History and National Identity (seven theses)]. *Svědectví* 83–84/1988 (XXI). 573.

[79] Loewenstein, B. "Německý válečný zážitek a iracionální kritika civilizace". *Československý časopis historický*. 1969. 521–547. See also Holub, R. C. "The Memories of Silence and the Silence of Memories: Post-war Germans and the Holocaust". *German Politics and Society*. 1/spring 2000 (XVIII). 105–123.

Daniel Cohn-Bendit (a student rebel leader in the storms of 1968 and now a member of the European parliament) has spoken of the dangerous tendency to keep on waging yesterday's battles.[80] In his view, "certain movements have been activated in Germany, and have provoked ideological reactions in the CR, and this shows that there is a prevalent tendency to repeat the last battle." J. Rupnik and other political scientists and politicians have also noted a striking change of atmosphere in relations between the CR and Germany.

The weekly paper *Sudetendeutsche Zeitung* regularly presents the positions and opinions of the leaders of the expellees' organisations and also politicians who express views of the Sudeten German question in a way that conforms to the opinions of the SL.[81] Study of these statements shows that the concept of *Mitteleuropa* (or geopolitical visions of Danubian territory inspired by it), is the ideological axis of revision of the post-war order as envisaged in conservative nationalist circles with which the Sudetendeutsche Landsmannschaft has ideological links and affinities. For the moment, the dispute over the plan for a *Centre against Expulsions*, which is promoted by the *Federation of Expellees* led by E. Steinbach, supported by P. Glotz but particularly by the Christian Democratic parties CDU/CSU, has become the symbol and focus of these revisionist endeavours.

---

[80] "Diskusi o dekretech by měla ukončit konference" [The Conference should end discussions on the decrees], interview with D. Cohn-Bendit. *Právo*. 13. 5. 2002.

[81] It is curious that among SL functionaries one can hear the view that the *Sudetendeutsche Zeitung* does not represent the real spectrum of opinion among the expellees and their organisations. Yet the formula at the top of the paper reads "Die Zeitung der Sudetendeutschen Landsmannschaft" and the official press organ of the organisation is surely the platform for the life and spectrum of opinion of the expellees. If it contradicted the demands of the publishing organisation, its publication would be halted. Such is the logic of the publisher's policy.

President Václav Havel giving a speech on the 11th of November 1993.

10 The Return of Freedom (and History) – 1989

From the start the new Czechoslovak Republic was aware of the fundamental importance of relations with a Germany in the throes of reunification. The foreign minister, Jiří Dienstbier, proceeded on the principle set out in the dissident group *Charter 77's* position of 1985[1] which included the assertion that the solutions to the German and European problem were essentially two sides of the same coin. The very positive attitude of the representatives of the new Czechoslovak foreign policy to German partners was formed by this opinion, which had been shared for years in dissident milieux.

In a TV broadcast on the 23rd of December 1989, Václav Havel, still in the capacity of citizen and not yet president, followed up this policy by saying that "We have a duty to apologise to the Germans who were transferred after the Second World War. Because it was an act that very harshly deprived several million people of their homes and it was in fact an evil that was a reprisal for a preceding evil."[2]

---

[1]   *Pražská výzva* [The Prague Appeal]. 11. 3. 1985. The text includes the passage "Let us then openly accord to the Germans the right to freely decide whether and in what form they want to unite their two states within their current borders. After Bonn's eastern agreements and after Helsinki, the conclusion of a peace treaty with Germany could potentially become an important instrument of positive transformation in Europe. Since the end of the Second World War the German question has been one of the keys to peace in Europe and the revival of European identity... the collective memory of the present generations is affected by the long-term development of the German question, and however much memory sleeps in stagnant conditions, it will wake up the moment that the question is brought to mind, and will begin to manifest itself dynamically." Dienstbier, J. *Snění o Evropě* [Dreaming of Europe]. 1990. Prague: Lidové noviny. 63. For full text of the Prague Appeal by Charter 77 see *Česko-německé vztahy po pádu železné opony.* 53–55.

[2]   Video recording from ČsT news: *Rudé právo.* 3. 1. 1990. (See also *Česko-německé vztahy po pádu železné opony.* 1/1997. 25.)

The visit of German president Richard von Weizsäcker to Prague on the 15th of March 1990 was intended to symbolise a new start in relations between Czechs and Germans. In an address on the anniversary of the German invasion of the CSR, Weizsäcker sought to overcome the historical tension between the two nations: "We Germans are very well aware how important it is that our unification should not give rise to old or new concerns among our neighbours. We will and shall take their feelings, the feeling with which they accompany our development, very seriously... Through our words and deeds we wish to convince people that Germany unity is not only democratically legitimate, but will promote the spirit of peace in Europe."[3]

In the same period, however, almost immediately following the Velvet Revolution, the debate was opened directly from the German side with a call for an apology (M. Streibl, 14th of December 1989) for the transfer of the Sudeten Germans. In otherwise favourably developing relations between the CSFR and FRG, the issue again became a problem as a result of the demands of the Sudetendeutsche Landsmannschaft, stepped up especially after the prime minister Marián Čalfa had talks with the SL spokesman Franz Neubauer in December 1989.[4]

At a press conference in January 1990, the Bavarian prime minister declared (once again) that Bavaria had already demonstrated its friendship with Czechoslovakia by taking in a great many transferred Germans after the war. From the very outset, the new Czechoslovak foreign policy-makers encountered the specific factor of Bavarian patronage of the expellees, which the CSU actively promoted in the long-term both in internal land policy and especially in the external policy of Bavaria and the federal republic.

The Sudetendeutsche Landsmannschaft interpreted Havel's words not as as an expression of regret in the course of an appeal for reconciliation, but as an admission of guilt in the legal sense of the word. What followed from the SL side was not a reciprocal expression of goodwill but ultimative demands for compensation and the annulment of the Beneš's Decrees (denazification laws). Nor did the German federal government react to the goodwill gesture, and so traditional Czech fears that the Germans were playing dishonestly for the time needed to ratchet up demands seemed fatally confirmed.[5] The warm words of the German president at Prague Castle were soon corrected by the reality of Czech-German relations.

---

3   Dienstbier, J. *Od snění k realitě*. 56–58.

4   Kural, V. "Peripetie v česko-německých vztazích" [Peripetias in Czech-German Relations]. *Mezinárodní politika* 4/1996. 12–14.

5   Wagnerová, A. "Nevypočitatelnosti symbolické politiky" [The Unpredictability of Symbolic Politics]. *Listy* 3/1995. 11. The property claims of the Sudeten German organisations were published in comprehensive form after 1989 under the title. "Gesichtspunkte zur Entschädigung der Sudetendeutschen durch die ČSFR". *Sudetendeutsche Zeitung*. 10. 1. 1992.

A stormy public debate followed in which besides academically argued positions many deeply emotional opinions were voiced by members of the Czech public, who more or less overwhelmingly rejected Havel's apology and took the view that the transfer was not revenge but a just action approved by the victorious powers of the Allied coalition.[6] The Treaty between the Czech and Slovak Federal Republic and the Federal Republic of Germany on good Neighbourhood and Friendly Cooperation, signed on the 27th of February 1992 at Prague Castle by Václav Havel and Helmut Kohl, was intended to embody a fundamental turning-point in Czech-German relations. An integral part of the treaty was an accompanying letter identically worded in the Czech and German versions which included the declaration, "The two sides agree in proclaiming that this treaty does not relate to property questions."[7]

The Opening of Dialogue and the Division of the State

In an effort to unblock the difficult matter of property demands, Havel had proposed a "package" of related steps intended to resolve the situation in Czech-German relations.

In return for the satisfaction of Czechoslovak persecution claims, the writing off of Czech trade debts to the former GDR and the loan of two miliard crowns, Czechoslovakia was willing to consider the possibility of the return of those

[6]   See M. Klen's hunger strike in January 1990 as a protest against the views of Havel. Klen later rather changed his views and was appointed a member of the Co-ordination Council of the Czech-German Discussion Forum. In an article written shortly before his death, 20th of March 1998, he wrote, "At the time when the Declaration was being drawn up I tried to influence its content, but this was a lost cause from the start. After its signing and approval I saw its completely fundamental flaws, mainly to the disadvantage of Czechs. With a huge effort of self-denial, however, I took it on board as a fact and decided to try to exploit as far as possible those few points in it that could potentially be of benefit to both sides." It should be noted that the necessarily compromise text of the Declaration was to cause disappointment on the German side too.

[7]   In the debate in the Czech-Slovak federal parliament that preceded the signing of the Czech-German Treaty, Ulrich Irmer (a member of the *Bundestag* foreign committee) asserted, "We were unable to agree on the question of mutual property claims and on the invalidity of the Munich Agreement. I fully agree with colleagues who said that the treaty should not mention questions of property rights." In the same debate Christian Schmidt (the foreign-policy spokesman of the CSU parliamentary group in the *Bundestag*) said: "If we want to avoid the mistakes of many peace agreements signed in this century then we must be willing to include affected groups and minorities. And to support the Sudeten Germans' demands (regarded in this way) to be able to collaborate – for example young people too. I think that we ought to take a look at some models of minorities in border areas of Europe... Their (the German minority in Denmark's) cultural autonomy – this is an ideal model for Europe." *Československo-německý dialog ve Federálním shromáždění ČSFR* [Czechoslovak-German Dialogue in the Federal Parliament of the CSFR]. 1991. Prague: Ústav mezinárodních vztahů. 10–11. In its comment on the Treaty of 1992 the Sudeten German Council considered it progress that, "Joint responsibility for the preservation of German culture in the Sudeten German areas and the German minority in the CSFR (lies in) the avowal of the common past and common future of Germans and Czechs." *Český-Böhmen Expres*. 1992.

Sudeten Germans who expressed the wish to settle in the CSR. They would be able to apply for Czechoslovak citizenship and permitted to take part in coupon privatisation on equal terms. According to this proposal, Germany would in exchange definitively renounce property claims and recognise Munich as null and void.[8]

Chancellor Kohl had not, however, responded to Havel's suggestions. Indeed, the chancellor's prevarications in terms of stated opinions and constant postponements had provided time and political room for intervention by the Bavarian CSU, whose chairman T. Waigel proclaimed on the 25th of August 1991 that, "the Czech side must of course think long and hard about how these matters will look (i.e. property compensation of Sudeten Germans – author's note) if Czechoslovakia wants to join the European community, because this is naturally pertinent to the self-evident legal principles that exist in Europe and in the EC."

Arguments threatening the blocking of the expected Czechoslovak (later Czech) application to join West European communities were to be heard many times again from the Bavarian political stage, right up to the moment of the CR's accession to the EU. The culmination of systematic obstructionism came when the CDU/CSU deputies in the European parliament voted against the admission of the CR to the EU in June 2003.

In 1991 the Bavarian government commissioned Prof. F. Ermacora to draw up an expert opinion on the Sudeten German Question. This opinion included the assertion that Czechoslovakia had an obligation to compensate the Sudeten Germans[9], whose claims were addressed neither by the Treaty of 1973 nor the Treaty on the Unification of Germany. Ermacora argued that the Sudeten German right to self-determination, which was the basis of their right to homeland and free disposition of property, remained in force. In this context, F. Neubauer declared that right to homeland was more fundamental than property questions, but that of course the right to property "settlement" would automatically arise from the right to homeland. At this point it was already clear that the "conciliatory" rhetoric of the Sudetendeutsche Landsmannschaft was verbal camouflage and that behind it the emergent contours of property claims and power-political aspirations in regard to the CSFR could easily be detected.

One sentence in the 1992 Treaty between the CSFR and the FRG opened up the possibility that Czech-German dialogue on the ethical and moral aspects of the transfer of the Bohemian Germans might also include talks on settle-

---

8   Dienstbier, J. *Od snění k realitě*. 283.
9   On F. Ermacora's detailed legal analysis see: Pavlíček, V. – Suchánek, R. "O některých otázkách majetkových nároků v česko-německých vztazích". 75–128.

ment of property rights.[10] Demands for the annulment of the Beneš Decrees[11] were at first voiced only at meetings on the civic level. The theme was regularly raised by the spokesman and federal president of the Sudetendeutsche Landsmannschaft F. Neubauer and his successors B. Posselt, J. Böhm and other leaders of the expellees' organisations.

These opinions essentially continued to be based on the *Position on the Sudeten German Question* (20 points), described in detail earlier in this study, and the Statutes of the Sudetendeutsche Landsmannschaft. Later, however, demands for the annulment of the presidential decrees were regularly raised in connection with accession negotiations at government level by the FRG, Austria and subsequently also Hungary, thus giving the impression of the kind of gradualist intensification of pressure with which Czech foreign policy had unhappy historical experience. The Sudeten German organisations in Germany and Austria were as keen to exploit the preparatory phase of the accession of the CR to the EU to pursue their goals as they had been to use the pre-accession talks for the same purpose. These SL activities to a large extent devalued the partial positive results of the post-November-1989 Czech-German dialogue at civic level. For more detail on the development of attitudes in Czech society, see the last chapter.

Post-1989 calls for a reconciliation based on Christian ideals, understanding and forgiveness were repeatedly heard from the Sudeten German side, but this (it seemed) was only ever to be attained under certain conditions to be fulfilled by the Czech side.

Ideas of conciliation were expressed in comprehensive form for example in the joint declaration of Czech and Sudeten German Christians, "Czech-German Neighbourhood Must be a Success", published at the turn of 1991/92.[12] Consensual in tone, the proclamation has strong affinities with the positions of the *Ackermann-Gemeinde*. It includes formulation of attitudes to the two ba-

---

[10] "Let us, however, turn our attention to the demythologisation of the nationalism that is represented by the figure of E. Beneš... who contributed so strikingly to the ethnic and cultural devastation of Central Europe and to delivering Czechoslovakia up to the mercies of the Stalin system. All the proposals that Beneš made to the Sudeten German side up to 1938 were designed above all to demonstrate to the Western powers that it was essentially impossible to negotiate with Germans." Similar invectives very much in the spirit of the arguments of Henlein's SdP have been typical in expressions of the perspective of the SL for the whole conciliation period after 1989. Prinz, F. "Benešův mýtus se rozpadá" [The Beneš Myth is Disintegrating] (Text of a lecture given in the Sudeten German House in Munich on the 27th of November 1991 to the Sudeten German Council). *Střední Evropa* 24/1992 (VIII). 42–43.

[11] An overview of selected decrees relating directly to the subject of the Bohemian Germans is included in the supplement. Also see e.g. *Dekrety prezidenta republiky 1+2*.

[12] *Erklärung sudetendeutscher und tschechischer Christen zur Gestaltung der deutsch-tschechischen Nachbarschaft.* 1991/92. Paragraph II. Munich/Prague: Ackermann-Gemeinde.

sic theses of the Sudeten German question (right to homeland, property restitution).

"Return to the CSFR would mean moving the centre of gravity of life to an environment that could hardly be experienced by anyone as homeland. The retrospective return of illegally confiscated property would be possible only in forms and on a scale that would tend to disappoint the hopes now awakened... The expulsion of people who today enjoy the assets concerned is absolutely out of the question. Under these circumstances voluntary personal sacrifice is ready to hand as a contribution to a conciliatory new start."

Another passage[13] states, however, that "criminal lawlessness cries out for redress according to legal principles." How then can we understand the logic of an otherwise conciliatory text? From the excerpts quoted it is obvious that "real" conciliation can occur only on the condition that the Czech side radically reassesses its position and proclaims the transfer of the German-speaking inhabitants of the CSR to have been "criminal lawlessness". If it did so, the Czech side would be denying the whole causal logic of the development of the historical events, causes, course and consequences of the Second World War.

If the issue is not one of physical return to an environment that "could hardly be experiened as homeland", nor of material compensation, then what is the meaning of the term "redress according to legal principles"? It is hard not to get the impression that the verbal juggling is simply intended to veil a complex of demands in innocent-sounding phraseology, behind which the old familiar gradualist "step-by-step" tactic is once again in evidence. It is not surprising that all the other conciliatory experiments have failed to win much trust on the Czech side.

Further on in the proclamation we find the claim that, "the German share in the creation of culture and the economy in our country (meaning the CR) must be re-incorporated into the image of our history (meaning the history of the Czech Lands – author's note)."

In fact, the reincorporation of the German contribution into the history of the Bohemian Lands has already been happening on a large scale and the process will undoubtedly continue. The number of academic and popularising articles and books on the subject published in the CR since 1989 is convincing proof of this. It should also be noted that the theme of Czech-German relations and the Sudeten German question was already a subject of interest in Czech milieux in the 1960s, and so there has been an existing base for the renewed concern both in terms of theme and researchers and publicists.

---

[13]   Ibidem. Paragraph I.

The Czechs-Germans symposia that have been held regularly since 1991 in Jihlava by the Ackermann-Gemeinde and the Bernard Bolzano Foundation may be considered quite a representative example of Czech-Sudeten-German dialogue in the Czech Republic. In the 1990s the symposium was a kind of precursor of the later "post-Declaration" discussion forums, but with the difference that the openness of the debate in Jihlava was not constrained by diplomatic considerations related to the actual state of Czech-German relations.[14]

The activities of the church and associated organisations, in some cases (A-G) building on pre-1989 contacts in the Czech Lands, have been playing an important role on the Sudeten German side. One of the first initiatives was the meeting between the A-G and leading representatives of Czech Catholicism on the 16th–18th of March 1990 in Marktredwitz. In the years 1991–94 the Ackermann-Gemeinde in cooperation with the Czech Christian Academy organised regular talks in Mariánské lázně/*Marienbäder Gespräche*, on particular pre-defined themes.[15]

Permanent dialogue between the A-G and the Czech Christian Academy has been continuing since 1995 in the Premonstratensian Monastery in Teplá.[16] It has found only limited response in Czech society, however, and has had no very significant effect on public opinion in the CR.

Co-operation on a church basis has been intensive in Czech-German relations, as shown for example by the attendance of the Archbishop of Olomouc Jan Graubner at the 53rd Sudeten German Days in Nuremberg, where he also celebrated a mass. In the CR reactions to this initiative were mixed and mainly negative. In this context, we should mention a common statement of principles drawn up by representatives of the Protestant Church of the Bohemian Brethren and the German Protestant Church.[17]

In addition to this, there have been a number of other elements of dialogue at the civic level, with a significant role played by the Social Democratic Seliger-

[14] The content of the discussions at the Jihlava *Češi-Němci* symposia is available in the series of collections published by the B. Bolzano Foundation and include even papers that could not be delivered at the symposia for reasons of time.

[15] For example: Textbooks and Czech-German Neighbourhood, Jews in the Sudetenland, Homeland as a Condition for Life, etc. See the conference collections published by the Czech Christian Academy.

[16] Rzepka, W. "Úvod" [Introduction], in *Mariánskolázeňské rozhovory/Marienbader Gespräche* [Mariánské Lázně Conversations]. 1998–2001. Series of editions of lectures. Prague: Česká křesťanská akademie/Ackermann-Gemeinde. 7.

[17] "Although we may be sorry about it, return to earlier conditions is not possible: what we have all lost has to be set down to war losses." Smíření mezi Čechy a Němci/*Versöhnung zwischen Tschechen und Deutschen*. 1996. Hannover: EKD (Evangelische Kirche in Deutschland) Texte, 36. For other documents see EKD. *Der Trennende Zaun ist gebrochen/Rozdělující zeď je zbořena* [The Dividing Wall has been Demolished]. 1998. Leipzig: Verlag GAW.

Gemeinde, the Adalbert Stifter Verein focused on cultural exchange[18] and other associations. All the same, the the circle of people involved in regular meetings is small, as in the cases mentioned earlier.

Volkmar Gabert (an important Sudeten German Social Democratic politician, who died in February 2003), the president of the Seliger-Gemeinde of Social Democrats, signed the appeal *Conciliation 95*, because he was convinced of the need for talks between representatives of the Sudeten Germans and the government of the Czech Republic with the aim of achieving at least a "symbolic gesture" from the Czech side indicating some desire to redress the past violation of rights. At the same time, he rejected any kind of violation of the borders and sovereignty of the CR in the implementation of right to homeland; he insisted that the right could only be fulfilled in the framework of the CR and with there being no question of creating a free Sudeten state or the cession of territory to the FRG.[19]

The Declaration and Conditional Reconciliation

If we are seeking the contours and content of the Sudeten German question as these are understood by the leaders of the individual organisations of the Sudetendeutsche Landsmannschaft, we need to quote the following text: "The chief political principle of the Sudeten Germans, and of all expelled Germans, was and is the rejection of revenge and reprisals; instead they are asking for compensation for the damages arising from the expulsion, the right to homeland and self-determination."[20]

Any survey of views on the current form of the Sudeten German question must include the major German political party the SPD, which tends to be regarded as an ally among Czechs. In fact it cannot be pretended that the SPD's line on the matter is close to the Czech position. This has been demonstrated for example during the talks at the conference of ministers of culture of Central European countries in Warsaw on the 22nd–23rd of April 2004. Evidently following on from the Gdansk Declaration issued by the German president Johannes Rau and the Polish president Aleksander Kwaśniewski on the 29th of October 2003, the German minister of culture Ch. Weiss (SPD) appealed for the setting up of a European network of centres against expulsions with a headquarters at

---

[18] Research shows that it is precisely cultural values that are most easily shared and broaden contacts at civic level.

[19] See interview with Volkmar Gabert. *Rudé právo*. 24. 6. 1995.

[20] *Sudetoněmecká otázka: krátký obrys a dokumentace* [The Sudeten German Question: A brief outline and documentation]. 1987. München: Sudetendeutscher Rat. 16.

the Viadrina University in Frankfurt (Oder) – a suggestion that the representatives of the other countries rejected.

The demand that the theme of expulsion be Europeanised entails an inadmissible narrowing of the historical study of modern conflict, in which forced migration and population transfers were only a part of the suffering of the civilian population of European countries as a result of 20th-century wars. To expulsions we must add the extermination of the Jewish population, the "final solution of the Czech question", the terror associated with occupation in various European states, and massacres of civilians in the Ukraine, Poland, Yugoslavia and elsewhere. Only in the full context of the tragedy of the two "European" wars can Germany and her Eastern neighbours come to share their historical memories in a way that has a genuine therapeutic effect.

R. Scharping (former chairman of the SPD) likewise expressed a tendentious view of the past in a speech that he made on the 5th of April 1994 in Prague: "I venture to declare that the problem of the Sudeten Germans as we know it from the past, above all in the orders of magnitude of 1918, 1938 and 1945, no longer exists. But there still exists trauma on both sides and averting our eyes from it will not make it pass; indeed to do so is to risk that it will poison general relations. I say therefore with all openness, that the matter is no longer one of reviving some past; it is not now about retrospective burdening of relations with compensation demands. But it is a matter of including the Sudeten Germans in talks to bring lasting reconciliation; it is about offering them involvement where bridges should be built, for example in cross-border regional collaboration... in joint foundations... and also in the joint development of a view on history that is not concerned just with division into black and white, good and evil."[21] Once again we see the return of a situation of misunderstanding that is actually itself the result of a situation in which, despite all attempts at synthesis, parallel stories and interpretation of the same events of a common history remain present.

Examination of a cross-section of the views of the leaders of Sudeten German organisations at various different positions on the political spectrum shows that there is substantial agreement between them on the key fact of the expulsion of the German-speaking population of the former Czechoslovakia, and that all the political parties of the FRG (with the exception of the PDS) continue to support them (if to a modified extent). Despite the fact that this retrospective overview deliberately passes over the extreme views and attitudes of the members of the small but active Witikobund, it is clear that on the Ger-

---

[21]   Full text of the speech in *Mezinárodní politika* no. 5/94 – documentary supplement.

man side shift in opinion has been only minimal in the course of the intensive "conciliation" activities of the 1990s.

Despite the end of the Cold War, the SL continues to pursue demands defined by Franz Neubauer at the 45th Sudeten German Day in Nuremberg, when he explained the core demand for right to homeland: "By right to homeland we understand the right to live in our homeland and to be able to develop our lives freely and in every way on the basis of the secured rights of national groups in our mother tongue while cultivating our own culture; the right to homeland naturally means much more than freedom of movement and freedom to settle in the states of the European Union, to which the Czech Republic will certainly one day belong. The right to homeland cannot simply be removed by reference to the European freedom to settle anywhere."[22]

Further clarification of the demands can be found in the recommendations of K. Heissig: "The Sudeten Germans should be granted generous personal autonomy on the territory of the Czech Republic, and in return should renounce territorial autonomy. The Sudeten Germans should be allowed to return to the Czech Lands and the Czech state should support this act on territories earlier settled by Germans – the Sudeten Germans should recognise the homeland right of all groups of the population that have settled there in the meantime. The European Community's settlement right does not accommodate the right to homeland (sic)."[23] Neubauer further demanded that "the Sudeten Germans be allowed access to the Czechoslovak media, politics, the economy and the spiritual life of the CSFR."[24]

The Sudeten German organisations are not monolithic in views. The leaders of the Ackermann-Gemeinde, Adalbert Stifter Verein and other associations have indicated differences of opinion, but no significant organisation in Sudeten German circles has yet decided to distance itself fundamentally from the Sudetendeutsche Landsmannschaft. The only partial exception is the A-G, in the sense that it has repeatedly expressed regret (A. Otte, H. Werner) for the Sudeten German movement's role in the destruction of the CSR and subsequent occupation of the Czech Lands by Nazi Germany. Although in the period after the official Joint Czech-German Declaration there have been signs of differentiation of opinion on the Sudeten German side (the Brannenburg Theses of the Seliger-Gemeinde or the Ellwangen Declaration of the Ackermann-Gemeinde),

---

22 From F. Neubauer's speech at the 45th Sudeten German Day in Nuremberg on the 22nd of May 1994. *Střední Evropa* 41. 46.

23 Heissig, K. "Sudetoněmecká budoucnost v Čechách a na Moravě" [The Sudeten German Future in Bohemia and Moravia]. *Střední Evropa* 33. 23.

24 Translation of Neubauer's address from the Frankfurter Allgemeine Zeitung. *Přítomnost* 4/1991. 13.

none of the organisations in the Sudetendeutsche Landsmannschaft have yet revised their support for the 20-point political programme.

The demands of the Sudeten Germans have not been officially submitted to the government of the Czech Republic (or its federal predecessor) in comprehensive form, but from the foregoing account we can get an idea of their probable content and direction. In this way we can therefore attempt a "reconstruction" of the Sudeten German question as it is understood by the subjects associated in the Sudetendeutsche Landsmannschaft and represented on the Sudeten German Council.

In view of the fact that the SL leaders have been repeatedly demanding direct negotiation with the government of the CR without preliminary conditions but also without specifying their own initial positions for any such talks, one cannot help asking what the talks would be about, and what the point of them would be, if the political programme and demands of the Sudeten German organisations are essentially based on the claim to right to homeland/*Heimatrecht* arising from the right to self-determination/*Selbstbestimmungsrecht*.[25]

The reasons for change in the initially fairly tolerant attitude of the Czech public to the Sudeten German positions included the delays in the drawing up of the *Declaration* and the debate itself, together with the greater media coverage of the SL demands. The commentaries published in Lidové noviny (a leading Czech daily) might be taken as a model example of the gradual hardening of the views of the Czech public and elites in the "Declaration" discussion.[26]

A speech on Czech-German relations made by V. Havel on the 17th of February 1995 in the Carolinum (Charles University), was a striking accelerating

---

[25] See the expert opinion of Ermacora, F. *Rechtsgutachten über die Sudetendeutschen Fragen.*

[26] As examples among many we should here mention at at least Třeštík, D. "Bloudění v Teutoburském lese" [Going Astray in the Teutoburg Forest]. *Lidové noviny*. 14. 6. 1995, Putna, M. C. "Smiřovací jehňátka" [Lambs of Conciliation]. *Lidové noviny*. 20. 2. 1996. 2. The philosopher V. Bělohradský's opinions on the German problem developed in a highly distinctive way (see also preceding chapter). He identified the dilemma of reunified Germany's search for identity and its connection with a Czech national identity in process of redefinition (as the direct result of the division of the CSFR and establishment of a separate Czech state), in the following terms: "Will a united Germany want to belong to an ex-centric Europe, to that Western, relativist and liberal "démos", or will it succumb to its old demands, which whisper in its ear that it ought to be the "middle kingdom" in which European identity is above all something "ethnic"? In my view Germany's neighbours must support those Germans who regard the Western orientation of their state to be definitive and liberating. We Czechs, however, are prevented from doing this by the iron curtain between us and those Germans that has been created by the Sudeten-German attempt to monopolise dialogues." Bělohradský, V. "Německo a excentrická Evropa" [Germany and Ex-centric Europe]. *Lidové noviny*. 13. 7. 1993. "The purpose of the political concept of the problematic nature of German and the need for common supervision of Germany is to create a new dividing line in Europe on a criterion that is different from before. To divide it into states allegedly identifying with the ethnic principle (Germany) and the others. This is a demand for the disintegration of what has been achieved by joint labours in Europe over the last almost fifty years." Doležal, B. "Pohled na Němce: přísně střežit a pozorovat" [The View on Germans: strictly guard and observe]. *Mladá fronta Dnes*. 12. 9. 1995.

factor in the "Declaration" stage of Czech-German but above all internal Czech discussion. Reacting to the hardened attitudes of the SL, Havel declared: "The post-war transfer is a subject on which we can have different opinions – and my critical opinion is generally known, but we must never take the transfer out of its historical context and see it in isolation from all the horrors that preceded it and led to it... the evil of the transfer was just the sad outcome of the evil that preceded it. There can be no dispute over who it was who first let the djinn of real nationalist hatred out of the bottle."[27]

This was followed by an appeal, *Conciliation 95*, signed by 105 Czech and German, mostly Christian-orientated intellectuals calling for direct negotiations between the Czech government and the organisations of the Sudeten Germans: "We therefore propose the immediate opening of talks between the Czech government and the political leadership of the Sudeten Germans... that those expellees who still wish to do so should be allowed to return... the creation of a Czech-German foundation with state participation for the purpose of funding concrete projects in the Czech borderlands."[28] The content of this appeal was defended by Petr Pithart on the pages of Lidové noviny: "Talks at government level with the political representatives of the Sudeten Germans would indeed be a non-standard step, but what happened between us was not standard either."[29]

The basic demand in the appeal, i.e. direct negotiation between the Czech government and the SL, was rejected by all the major political parties of the CR, as were other similar appeals.

The extensive and at times emotionally heated and passionate debate accompanying the drafting (especially in the final phase of formulation of the text) and signing of the Czech-German *Declaration* showed the sensitivity of the issue of Germany as direct partner and neighbour in Czech society. The negotiation of the Treaty on Good Neighbourly Relations and Friendly Co-operation of 1992, the Declaration on Mutual Relations and their Future Development of 1997 and all further bilateral negotiations always involved complications and difficulties (the need for verbal and definitional tight-rope walking that essentially reflected the real situation), which inevitably led most politicians to an evasive approach, usually with an appeal to the claim that mutual relations were orientated to the future.

---

[27]   Havel, V. 1997. "Češi a Němci na cestě k dobrému sousedství" [Czechs and Germans on the Path to Good Neighbourly Relations], in *Rozhovory o sousedství* [Conversations on Neighbourliness]. Prague: Karlova univerzita. 36.

[28]   For the full wording of Smíření 95 mezi Čechy a sudetskými Němci/Conciliation 95 between Czechs and Sudeten Germans see *Česko-německé vztahy po pádu železné opony*. 58.

[29]   Pithart, P. "Smysl výzvy Smíření 95" [The Rationale of the Conciliation 95 Appeal]. *Lidové noviny*. 18. 4. 1995.

The last sentence of Article 4 is considered the key formulation of the Declaration, i.e. "Both sides therefore declare that they will not burden their relations with political and legal questions from the past."[30] The problem resides in the different interpretations of this sentence, which the Czech side understands as finally drawing a line under the conflict-ridden past, whereas the German side considers it the first step to the "reassessment" of the past with the aim of revising the "problematic decisions" of the past, this time without fear of property demands. The snag is that the property matters are not addressed either by the Declaration (which is only a demonstration of good will on both sides) nor by the Treaty of 1992, which was accompanied by letters from both foreign ministers, J. Dienstbier and H.-D. Genscher, stating under point 2) that both sides declare that the treaty is not concerned with property questions.[31]

The attempt to remove the memory factor from Czech-German relations, which was the rationale of the German-Czech Declaration on Mutual Relations and their Future Development of 21 January 1997, therefore remained once again stuck at the halfway mark. The whole exercise had been inspired by Richard Holbrooke, who on a short working visit to Prague in June 1994 had suggested to the Czech leaders (V. Klaus, J. Zieleniec, A. Vondra) the need to calm Czech-German relations especially as concerned the "Bavarian factor" so as to ensure that Germany would not cause difficulties in the process of the planned admission of the CR to NATO.[32]

Despite the quantity of activities directed to rapprochement (the great majority inspired by the Sudeten German or German side) brought by the post-1989 developments, for the entire period it was clear that the official positions at government level had moved only a little closer, with great difficulty, or not at all.[33] In relations between the CR and the FRG, the Sudeten German question cannot be underestimated. In the end it was precisely this point of contention that remained open in both bilateral treaties (1973, 1992) and complicated the drawing up of the Czech-German Declaration. Basic dissensions springing

---

[30] For the full text of the Czech-German Declaration on Mutual Relations and their Future Development see *Česko-německé vztahy po pádu železné opony*. 23.

[31] For the full wording of the letters of the foreign ministers accompanying the 1992 Treaty see Ibidem. 21.

[32] Here my sources are the verbal contributions of the main negotiators of the *Declaration*, A. Vondra and P. Hartmann, at the specialist conference "Vývoj česko-německých vzathů od Česko-německé deklarace z roku 1997" [The Development of Czech-German Relations since the Czech-German Declaration of 1997], organised to mark the fifth anniversary of the signing if the *Declaration* by the *Co-ordinating Council of the Czech-German Discussion Forum* in Berlin, 7th–8th March 2002.

[33] Everything suggests that the search for acceptable verbal formulas that allow each side to defend its own position still predominates over any serious (and perhaps doomed) attempt to integrate the two different interpretations of the modern history of Czech-German relations. Václav Klaus drew attention to a certain disproportion both in terms of themes and the composition-profile of participants in Czech-German dialogue in his speech to the conference Tolerance místo intolerance [Tolerance in place of Intolerance] in Ústí n. L. For the full text of his speech see *České noviny*. http://www.ceskenoviny.cz. 28. 3. 2004.

from different interpretations of key events (see the analysis above) cannot be overcome even by a variety of conciliatory initiatives (A. Vollmer, Conciliation 95 etc.), and this continues to complicate CR-FRG bilateral relations that are co-operative at the civic and regional level.

It is not only in the upper storeys of politics that the factor of the past plays a role. On the contrary, no agreement, international declaration nor political declaration can change the state of the historical consciousness of the two societies, or immediately transform the "culture of memory and remembering".[34] Nor can the problem be solved by historians, who can only modestly help in "historicising" the traumas of the past, for example by joint efforts to ensure the quality of the history books and remove simplistic pictures of the enemy.[35] Historians can hardly be expected to provide the answer to problems with which the politicians are unable to cope and on which the politicians often even refuse to comment consistently.

The different legal interpretations of key determining moments such as the Munich Agreement, the Potsdam Agreement and the ensuing transfer of the Sudeten Germans represent divergent standpoints in Czech-German relations (arising from the opposed legal positions of the two sides) that are so difficult to bridge that it is understandable that Czech politics should try to leave this "conflict-ridden field" to the experts. On the German side, however, we witness the opposite approach, with the politicians (especially those of the CDU/CSU) exploiting the potential of the theme of the expellees to win themselves "political points".

On the basis of personal experience of various conciliation initiatives, I consider the only viable starting point for any progress in Czech-German relations to be a clear, initial statement of the fundamental divergence, which cannot be wished away by any magic verbal formula. In a situation where neither party is able or willing to abandon its own viewpoint, the only way out is to respect this situation as the initial definitional framework of further cooperation. Ex-

---

[34] Kunštát, M. "Faktor minulosti v současných česko-německých vztazích" [The Factor of the Past in Current Czech-German Relations]. *Mezinárodní politika* 11/2001. 7.

[35] These possibilities too are complication-ridden and limited. For example, immediately after the Velvet Revolution, people came up with the idea of producing a reinterpreted "conciliatory" concept of history, to be developed and formulated at quite short notice by a mixed Czech-German Joint Committee of Historians. The plan was for this to be the basis of a new textbook of "common" history. The result was an outline sketch for an account of Czech-German history since the 19th century entitled *Konfliktní společenství, katastrofa, uvolnění*, which was published in 1995. Some compromise formulations of key historical events were adopted in the text of the Czech-German Declaration. The re-working of textbooks continued on both sides in very limited ways. For more detail on the theme see the articles by Beneš, Z. "České dějiny 20. století v německých učebnicích dějepisu" [20th-Century Czech History in German Textbook Historiography] and Weger, T. "Analýza českých učebnic dějepisu" [An Analysis of Czech Textbook History], in *Mariánskolázeňské rozhovory: Učebnice a česko-německé sousedství* [Textbook and Czech-German Neighbourhood]. 1998.

perience of Czech-German cooperation at local and regional level suggests that this pragmatic approach is workable and that it is up to the Sudetendeutsche Landsmannschaft to accept and come to terms with it. In the current circumstances of growing sympathy for the expellees in part of German society, however, I believe any expectation that the SL will do so easily to be unrealistic.

Modified Regionalism and Ethnic Minorities

Since the collapse of the bipolar order in international affairs there has been a certain revival of the principle of self-determination. After the disintegration of the Soviet Union, its multinational territory has become an area of actual and potential conflict on an ethnic basis. Yugoslavia fell apart in a chain reaction of ethnic wars and purges. The situation in Kosovo or Bosnia Herzegovina, where armed international peace-keeping forces are engaged, continues to be fraught with difficulty.

The international community, which has made use of the doctrine of self-determination in the cause of decolonisation, is now having problems finding persuasive reasons why it should refuse to grant the same right to own ethnic state to the peoples of the former Eastern bloc.[36] The Sudetendeutsche Landsmannschaft exploited the international situation of the 1990s, when ethnic cleansing took place n the Balkans, in its attack on the Beneš Decrees, by making a simplistic and context-blind parallel between the transfer (in German terminology the flight and expulsion) and the ethnic purges in the former Yugoslavia, which could allegedly have been prevented (as in the case of the former Czechoslovakia) by the prompt grant of the right to self-determination. These Sudeten German arguments, however, entirely ignore the requirement of international law that a nation aspiring to self-determination must pursue its will, "only by non-violent means and in line with constitutional law, while respecting the territorial integrity of the state in which self-determination is sought."[37]

Self-determination continues to be an "elastic" political concept rather than an automatically applied principle of international law.[38] It gives rise to a whole series of problems, above all over which ethnic groups are to be considered eligible to exercise the right of self-determination and on what criteria. The

---

[36] Lord, Ch. "Národnostní menšiny v Evropě a ve světě – politické otázky" [National Minorities in Europe and in Global Political Questions]. *Via Europa* 1/1996. Brussel/Prague. 15. Gottlieb, G. "Nations Without States". *Foreign Affairs* 3/May-June 1994 (LXXIII). 100–112.

[37] Malenovský, J. *Mezinárodní právo veřejné.* 88.

[38] "Its international legal foundation is dilapidated and the limited time in which it has been applied in practice makes it impossible to prove that any customary norms have emerged yet." Ibidem. 87.

demands of peoples and ethnic groups for their own states continue to be problematic and from the point of view of international relations tend to be destabilising in nature. The practice of the European Union gives precedence to the protection of civic rights (including the rights of national/ethnic minorities) over changes of borders, which it considers inviolable despite the fact that they are undergoing *denationalisation* as a consequence of integration processes.[39]

In the period 1981–1987 the European Parliament passed a series of resolutions concerned variously with protecting and supporting regional languages and cultures in Northern Catalonia, recognising independent local radio stations, building up regional television in Friesia, protection of the Catalan language at university, on television and so on, all mainly in the field of language rights.[40]

In 1990 a Belgian deputy for the Flemish area, Jaak H.-A. Vandemeulebroucke unsuccessfully put forward a resolution (83–0690/90) to change European law on national minorities so as to secure the right of nations to self-determination and impose on the European community an obligation to actively afford the right of self-determination to every European people. The text proposed the adoption of a *Charter on National Minorities* that would implicitly include:

- the right of ethno-national groups to the protection of their cultural, social and political rights,
- the right to free use of regional languages in private, social and economic agreements and also in public life, in relations with administrative authorities and courts.

Although Vandemeulebroucke's proposal was not accepted, it became part of what is known as the Stauffenberg Report, which is important because it defines national minorities, specifies the rights of individuals and communities, sets out the obligations of member states and confirms their legal protection. In relation to potential demands that might be raised by the Sudeten German national group in regard to the Czech Republic following the accession of the CR to the EU, four factors defining an ethnic group are worth noticing:

- presence in the member state for several generations must be proven,
- it must differ from the rest of the population linguistically, by history and/or religion,

---

[39] Essentially we can distinguish between two basic trends in thought on the role of the borders of national states. One sees borders as lines of difference, and the other regards them as areas of transition. For more detail see Van Dijk, H. "State Borders in Geography and History", in *Nationalising and Denationalising European Border Regions, 1800–2000*. 1999. Knippenberg, H. – Markusse, J. (eds.). Dordrecht/Boston/London: Kluwer Academic Publishers. 36.

[40] Gilbert, G. "The Council of Europe and Minority Rights". *Human Rights Quarterly* 18/1996. 160–189.

- it must have a distinctive cultural identity,
- it must form a demographic minority in the member state.[41]

Judging by European Community documents on the subject of national minorities,[42] it is obvious that the interpretation of rights is not unambiguous, and the main reason for the ambiguity is the desire to avoid providing a reason for the repetition of the conflict situations of the inter-war years 1919–1939, when special agreemens were made on the protection of minority rights that were abused by Nazi Germany to pursue expansionist aims under the excuse of defending the rights of ethnic Germans living on the territory of the states of Central and Eastern Europe.

The philosophy of current international protection of human rights gives precedence to the rationally conceived interest of the individual over the abstract social interest. It is therefore not surprising that the European Convention on Human Rights and Fundamental Liberties of 1950 contains no provision that would directly guarantee the rights of minorities. According to current international law, the rights of minorities take the form of individual rights. "By the rights of minorities is actually meant the rights of their individual members, although the exercise of such rights usually has a group dimension that cannot be overlooked." This individualist conception of the rights of minorities is the basis for both the Pact on Civil and Political Rights and the Framework Convention of the Council of Europe on the Protection of National Minorities of 1995.[43]

The programme document of 1994 *Charta Gentium et Regionum*[44] (European Charter of Nations and Regions – the so-called Brno Programme), drawn up by the Munich *Internationales Institut für Nationalitätenrecht und Regionalismus* which is close to Sudeten German circles, elaborates a principle of self-determination

---

[41]   Yacoub, J. "Mezinárodní právo a menšiny" [International Law and Minorities]. *Via Europa* 1/1996. 10.

[42]   The Framework Convention on the Protection of National Minorities of 1995, The European Charter for Regional or Minority Languages of 1992, both documents produced and approved in the framework of the Council of Europe. Among political documents – Recommendation no. 1201 of the Parliamentary Assembly of the Council of Europe 1993 and others. For more detail see Malenovský. J. *Mezinárodní právo veřejné* (general section). 87–90.

[43]   Ibidem. 107–108.

[44]   *Charta Gentium et Regionum – Brünner Programm.* (Überarbeitete Auflage). München: INTEREG. For the latest version of the text see: http://www.intereg.org/cms/index.php?page=draft-english. The programme was approved at an international symposium in Brno in 1994, and has been translated into 28 languages and presented (edited by R. Hilf) at another congress in Mariánské Lázně in 1997. The preamble explaining the goal and rationale of the document was signed by F. Esterbauer and J. Stingl. It asserts that the minimum demand for minorities is self-determination for peoples and regions including language rights and cultural autonomy, but also personal autonomy through territorial autonomy up to federalisation. The framework of self-determination is interpreted here in the European spirit of the principle of subsidiarity as a means to "prevent excessive concentration of power at the central level". Ibidem. 7–8.

adjusted to the integration principles of the European Union with a "subtle" shift of view. This shift in the current conception of national minority rights is not at first sight wholly evident. Nonetheless, a close look at the *European Charter of Nations and Regions* shows a return to the group/collective concept of the rights of national group, which is presented in the introduction as the first step to the resolution of internal and inter-state conflicts. Its proponents express the conviction that by applying the principle of subsidiarity, cross-border cooperation between Euro-regions and the sidelining of the antiquated model of the centralist national state and its sovereignty, they can achieve a model of unity combined with the maintenance of the distinctive character of smaller units by the implementation of their group rights, autonomy and self-determination.

The preamble to the text states that "a minimum of group rights is necessary by reason of the fact that individual equality for members of ethnic minorities is otherwise merely formal and not real, and so it is necessary to protect the group identity that in practice serves individual equality."

In the section entitled "Minimum Provisions" we find the following passage: "Borders limiting the freedom of the individual should be broken down as far as possible: for example by means of borders extending beyond regions, the possibility of *dual or regional land citizenship* if this is requested and useful for reducing conflicts and identity problems, and above all by means of the further development of European citizenship – especially for ethnic communities."

In the section devoted to autonomy, we read in Article 7 that, "The constitutional autonomy of ethnic groups and regions (federalism), mediating original statehood, may in addition assist in the attainment of a high degree of identity, self-determination and joint decision-making."

Finally Article 8 focuses entirely on the principle of self-determination and states that, "Apart from the issue of the existing extent of peoples' rights to self-determination under international law, self-determination must become the prevailing principle of organization in order to avoid foreign domination of large and small peoples, ethnic groups, and regions."[45]

According to these ideas (shared by leaders of the expellees' organisations, and specifically the Sudetendeutsche Landsmannschaft on whose claims they in fact build), the principle of self-determination is an inseparable part of the basic principles of European regionalism. Every region (meaning above all border regions), and not only regions equipped with the right to self-determination, should have the power to decide via free voting on the political system to which it wishes to belong and on its political status in the framework of that system, including the definition of the borders of a given region (which need

---

[45]   Ibidem. 7, 44–45.

not necessarily respect the borders of existing states), and in this context what is to be taken into account first and foremost is the ethnic point of view, followed by historical factors, geographical influences and finally economic criteria – in that order. In terms of powers of jurisdiction and influence, the regional institutions should be granted decision-making competences on the same scale as central bodies (with the use of the principle of subsidiarity).

A regionalism conceived on these lines (highly European lines on the face of it) makes possible the survival of nationalist ideas of the kind pursued and implemented by the Sudeten German movement in the 1930s – including the principle of national self-determination. The same notions are returning to the political scene, but this time the idea is for them to be achieved through the use of the instruments of European integration. Once again the suggested means is a plebiscite (referendum) on the territories affected, i.e. the tactic exploited by inter-war Germany for the destabilisation of international relations and border changes (Henlein's SdP repeatedly demanding a plebiscite in the Sudetenland on the model of the Saarland). Although the definitional framework of international relations has changed radically (Germany today is a democratic state and part of the Euro-Atlantic community), the experience of the past in mutual relations cannot be entirely ignored.

In retrospect, and with account taken of the role played by the principle of national self-determination in the conflict between the Czechs and the Sudeten Germans, the difficult position of international law with respect to national minority rights is all too plain. Nonetheless, what we need to hold on to as key is the fact that in the view of international law today the rights of minorities are individual in nature. Even if minorities can be defined by objective social features independent of the will of their members, this does not make a minority a subject in international law. The rights of minorities in reality mean the rights of the individual members of a minority.

The right to self-determination remains part of discourse in the field of international relations, however, because not even in the conditions of the contemporary world have clear answers been found to the questions aptly formulated by the acknowledged international security theorist P. Hassner: What is a nation/people? Which groups have a right to form nation states? On what basis should the international community decide between conflicting demands and criteria of historical legitimacy, self-determination, economic viability and/or regional security? Using which specific principles should border changes and population transfers be decided?[46]

---

[46] Hassner, P. "Beyond Nationalism and Internationalism", in *Ethnic Conflict and International Security*. 1993. Brown, M. E. (ed.). Princeton: University Press. 139. The concept of the right to self-determination has been elaborated in a range of publications that refer to principles of international law and the claim that the right

Until such time as these questions find satisfactory answers, the right to self-determination will contine to keep emerging in international relations as a complicated factor generating risk situations – and by no means only in the relations between Czechs and Sudeten Germans.

The Dual Interpretation of History

With the end of the Cold War, in which Germany had been on the side of the victorious democracies, the political leaders of the Sudeten Germans felt that the moment had come to reopen their cause at the level of Czech-German relations. The patronage extended to the Sudeten Germans by the federal land Bavaria made it natural for the task of pursuing their demands to be taken up by the Bavarian ruling party, the CSU; through the mediation of the CSU, the Sudetendeutsche Landsmannschaft has made considerable headway both on the German national political scene and in the European Parliament via the *European Peoples Party*.[47]

The fundamentally different views of the two sides on the key problems of Czech-(Sudeten)German relations, and the opposition between the two standpoints, Czech (A) and Sudeten German (B) on the key situations of their common history can be set out as follows:

A: **The establishment of Czechoslovakia** in 1918 was the culmination of the revival of Czech national consciousness and the efforts of the Czechs to obtain its own state.

B: The year 1918 was the beginning of national/ethnic oppression and lack of freedom for Germans, Slovaks and other ethnic minorities on the territory of the new CSR.

---

was denied to the Sudeten Germans in 1918. The most detailed is the study commissioned by the Sudeten German Council: Ermacora, F. *Rechtsgutachten über die Sudetendeutschen Fragen*. The same author has written other works on the right to self-determination – Ermacora, F. 1978. *Nationalitätenkonflikt und Volksgruppenrecht*. München: INTEREG. 38–49. On this theme see also Kimminich, O. 1996. *Das Recht auf die Heimat*. Bonn: Bund der Vertriebenen.

[47] The *European People's Party* was founded in 1976. Its leading founder members are the CDU and Bavarian CSU. In the very first elections to the European Parliament the EEP won 107 mandates out of an overall number of 410. Currently the EPP fraction is the strongest in the European Parliament. The rapporteur for the EP foreign committee for the CR is Jürgen Schröder (CDU). In the published programme principles of the EPP the issue of self-determination is treated as follows: "For this reason the right of nations to self-determination and to the free exercise of collective rights cannot be claimed in a way that would mean denying someone the right to the performance and enjoyment of his individual rights. Because the right to self-determination is a noble expression of justice." Kubes, M. – Kučera, R. *Evropská lidová strana. European People's Party*. 73.

A: **The First Czechoslovak Republic** was a democratic state that guaranteed equality and equal political representation to all its citizens.

B: The First Czechoslovak Republic was not a democratic state; it was a multi-national/ethnic society constituted as the nation state of a fictively constructed majority nation, the Czechoslovak nation.

A: **The Munich Agreement** was the betrayal of Czechoslovakia by the Sudeten Germans, France and Great Britain.

B: The Munich Agreement was the correction of the mistaken decision of the Versailles Peace Conference after the First World War, and the misguided policy of Czechoslovak governments during the First Republic.

A: **The sufferings and losses** of the Czech population resulting from the aggressive policy of Hitler's Germany, were evils for which former Czechoslovak citizens of German nationality bear responsibility (guilt).

B: The Sudeten Germans were victims of Hitler's Germany, because as in the case of Czechs, the decisions of Munich were taken without their participation. As a group, the Sudeten Germans bear no responsibility for the Occupation and the institution of the Protectorate of Bohemia and Moravia and the Slovak state, or for the administration of these entities, since like the Czechs the Sudeten Germans were granted no autonomy in the totalitarian Nazi system.

A: **The Transfer of the Germans** from Czechoslovakia was a historical necessity after the experiences of the years 1938–1945 and was carried out on the basis of the decision of the Potsdam Conference.

B: The Transfer, a euphemism for the expulsion of three million people from their homes and homeland, was the expression of traditional Czech hatred for Germans.[48]

This summary presents in deliberately very stark and probably rather oversimplified form the diametrically opposite views of the two sides on the key events that preceded the dramatic divorce of 1945–6 and continue to be the basis of conflict.

The gulf between the two views can be illustrated more discursively by the following text, which expresses the standard historical interpretation of the Sudeten German Question according to the Sudeten German Council (in the late 1980s):[49]

"The Sudeten German question concerns the Sudeten Germans and the territory of 27,000 km² formerly inhabited by them, which is today incorporated into

---

48 Overview taken from Hahn, E. *Sudetoněmecký problém – obtížné loučení s minulostí.* 184.

49 *Sudetoněmecká otázka – krátký obrys a dokumentace.*

the Czechoslovak Socialist Republic (published in 1987 – author's note). In 1919 the Sudeten Germans, appealing to the right to self-determination, wished to be incorporated into the German Reich together with the Austrian Germans. The victorious powers forebade the unification of purely German territories in one state under threat of deployment of armed forces. They granted the Sudeten territory to a new state that presented itself to "its Germans" under the official title "Czechoslovak Republic" (CSR). The Sudeten Germans were thus denied the right to self-determination and the Sudeten German question came into existence... Another of the causes leading to the Munich Agreement was the fact that since the founding of Czechoslovakia the Sudeten Germans had been forced to tolerate illegality and lawlessness... The expulsion, with its accompanying circumstances and consequences, meets the evidential basis of deportation of civilian population from occupied territory, which according to the institutions of the International Military Tribunal in Nuremberg (of 8th August 1945) to which the CSR also subscribed, is punishable as a crime against humanity, or as a war crime." This interpretation of the modern common history of Czechs and Germans shows plainly that the SL had retreated not an inch from the attitudes that had brought Sudeten German politicians into permanent conflict with the Czech political leadership.

The associations of expelled Germans from Eastern and Central Europe have had a substantial influence on the domestic and foreign policy of the FRG, especially in the 1950s as around 12 million ethnic German refugees and expellees were gradually being integrated in all the occupation zones of Germany.[50]

The Sudeten Germans, numbering around 2.9 million, formed the second largest group of expellees after the Silesians (3.2 million). The scale of the problem presented by the integration and social acclimatisation of the new arrivals is witnessed by the fact that in 1950 every third unemployed person in Germany came from the ranks of the expellees. Nonetheless, the "economic miracle" brought the highly motivated expellees substantial social advance and they came to be regarded in the FRG as a "structural growth factor". With economic success came political influence, and this has had consequences for the domestic and by extension the foreign policy of the FRG with which foreign-policy makers in the Czech Republic are now having to come to terms. The economic prosperity of the FRG and successful integration has naturally led more and more expellees to lose interest in their original political goal. According to a sociological survey[51] conducted in early 1996, around a quarter

---

50   Geissler, R. 1992. "Flüchtlinge und Vertriebene aus den Ostgebieten", in *Die Sozialstruktur Deutschlands*. Bonn: Bundeszentrale für politische Bildung. 296.

51   EMNID im Auftrag des Spiegel: *Was wollen die Sudetendeutschen?* Results of a sociological survey conducted in January-February 1996 by the EMNID Agency in Mainz on a selected sample of 2,400 people.

of expellees and their children and grandchildren show interest in the activities of the Sudetendeutsche Landsmannschaft, and of these only ten percent regularly attend the annual SL rallies (*Sudetendeutscher Tag*). The substantial percentage of young people in this latter group is surprising. According to the survey, young people of up to 24 form a quarter of these "die-hard" supporters. The percentage of young people who would like to return permanently to the land of their parents, even at the price of giving up German state citizenship, is roughly the same. More than fifty percent of Sudeten Germans (54%) do not feel themselves to be represented by the Sudetendeutsche Landsmannschaft and its political programme. This large group might be regarded as having the potential to exercise a positive influence on Czech-German relations, but it has no consistent and coherent political organisation capable of acting as a subject in political dialogue like the SL.

The regular raising of Sudeten German problems by individual politicians and groups on the Czech political scene and by the leaders of the Sudetendeutsche Landsmannschaft indicates that the issue is an important factor at national and regional level, and it also has a broader international dimension. The cross-border functions of European border-region communities that are gradually being introduced and developed through intensive cooperation between the CR and the FRG at all levels are playing a positive role in the ongoing integration of the CR into European structures. One of the basic conditions for the accession of the CR is the resolution of conflicts in border areas, including ethnic problems. The Sudeten German question is charged with potential for conflict both from the social point of view (ethnic peace in the borderlands) and the geographical point of view (the integrity of the CR and the stability of property-law relations in the borderlands), and so it is very undesirable for themes likely to mobilise ethnic passions to be brought up in the sensitive phase of the accession of the CR to the European Union. For this reason, at the annual conference of the *Co-ordination Council of the Czech-German Discussion Forum* in Munich in February 2003, Günter Verheugen, the commissioner for EU enlargement to the East, asked the SL and its leader J. Böhm to show restraint.

Memory as part of the present. The return of a transport of (Czech) citizens of the Protectorate
of Bohemia and Moravia after conscription for forced labour in the industry of the Third Reich.

11 Memory as Part of the Present

The preceding brief outline in no way exhausts all the current contexts and connotations of the transfer of the Sudeten Germans from the CSR as a "historical memory" factor in Czech-German relations. One aspect that we have not yet considered is its role in forming attitudes to Germany among present-day inhabitants of the Czech borderlands. Persistent pressure from the Sudeten German organisations has had the effect of making the transfer an issue in the thinking (views and attitudes) of the local population. It has caused a radicalisation of attitudes (the establishment of the *Kluby českého pohraničí*/Czech Borderland Clubs (KČP)) but also introduced elements of provincialisation into Czech-German relations where problems otherwise tend to be posed as national or international European matters.

Creation of the civic association of Czech Borderland Clubs has been a specific defensive response to the opening up of the Sudeten German question on the Czech political scene. Since 1992 clubs have been formed throughout the Czech borderlands to organise activities for "the defence of the Czech borderlands from the pressure of Germanisation". Their umbrella association puts out a regular (bi-monthly) bulletin entitled *Hraničář* [Borderer] which can be regarded as its main media platform and has a viewpoint that can be illustrated by its positions on the Czech-German Declaration. Briefly summarised – The Declaration should be focused exclusively on the future – the Potsdam Agreement drew a historical line that is non-negotiable – the Beneš Decrees are a pillar of the legal order – the property claims of the Sudeten Germans must be rejected on principle together with their other demands.[1] According to the KČP secretariat, the association has tens of thousands of members and sympathisers.

In the public opinion surveys *Pohraničí* [Borderlands] 1996 and 1997, 5–6% of respondents expressed agreement with the KČP, and around a third of respondents were aware of their existence. Quite possibly rather more citizens share the views of the Clubs, which have a nationalist programme and are strongly left-wing in orientation, than the surveys suggest (the same applies to the voter base of the Communist Party of Bohemia and Moravia as it emerges from polls), because people may not want to be considered political extremists or nationalists by the researcher. In this respect sociological surveys like electoral polls have certain inevitable limits as evidence.

Jacques Rupnik has argued that "we must distinguish between the essential discussion of history, including the transfer, and political or legal attempts to settle scores or challenge the results of the Second World War".[2] He then refers approvingly to the approach of the Poles, arguing that they have greater respect for this distinction than Czechs and so have been able to find an acceptable *modus vivendi* in relations with Germany (including recognition of the Oder Nisa border at the 4 + 2 negotiations). In the same context, he praises the long-term efforts of the joint French-German Commission of Historians set up on the basis of the need to understand the views of the other side and only then to formulate conclusions that might have an influence on public opinion.

The case of the Czech Republic is different from both these examples, however, and for at least two reasons. First, France and Poland are priority partners for Germany in an integrated Europe in a way that the Czech Republic is not. Second, in neither instance are the former enemies separated by anything like the "field of tension" created by the Sudeten German organisations, which have a clear-cut programme of revision of the post-war settlement. Neither the ethnic Germans expelled from the territory of Poland and former East Prussia, nor the Allemagnes from Alsace-Lorraine, have a position of influence or a consistent political programme comparable with that of the Sudetendeutsche Landsmannschaft.

The election campaigns in 2002 in both the CR and Germany undermined the "tranquilising" formula of reference to "re-evaluation" of the past that had since 1989 been deployed at inter-governmental level. It is clear that pressure from the expellees had caused an eruption of the theme into high politics. The Sudetendeutsche Landsmannschaft had evidently decided that their "moment

---

[1]   "K otázkám česko-německých vztahů – Stanovisko severočeské rady KČP z 20. 1. 1995" [On Questions of Czech-German Relations-the Standpoint of the North-Bohemian Council of the CCB of the 20th of January 1995]. *Českomoravský hraničář* 65.

[2]   J. Rupnik in an interview for *Lidové noviny*. 5. 5. 1995. 8.

of stardom" had arrived, both because of a change of mood in German society in attitudes to the expellees and their fate, and more broadly to the Second World War altogether, and because the situation offered the last chance to obstruct the accession of the Czech Republic to the European Union.

Eva Hahn(ová) has drawn attention to the major role of the German media in the course of Czech-German dialogue. More specifically, she shows how two newspapers – the *Sudetendeutsche Zeitung* ("an aggressive organ of simple-minded agitation") and the *Frankfurter Allgemeine* (high-brow, one of the leading European dailies), took similar attitudes in their accounts of 20th-century Czech history despite their differences in intellectual level. In her opinion, both papers make use of similar stereotypes and pictures of history. Furthermore, in view of its influential readership (Germany's political and cultural elites), she considers the *Frankfurter Allgemeine Zeitung* to be the most important mediating link between the Sudeten German organisations and the general German, possibly even the European public.[3]

Hahn describes how over one year, between the 52nd and the 53rd Sudeten German Day in 2001 and 2001, developments occurred that may be summed up in four points, which I present here in shortened form.

- The demand for the revocation of the Beneš Decrees was made a prominent theme by the rightwing press, especially on the pages of the *Frankfurter Allgemeine Zeitung*, and occasionally in *Die Welt* or the *Rheinische Merkur*. The impression of a major real problem was constructed, when in fact what was happening was just medialisation of the demands of the Sudetendeutsche Landsmannschaft supported by rightwing political parties in Bavaria, Austria and Hungary. Large sections of the German public and especially the liberal-left press did not embrace or support these demands.
- The demand for the "revocation of the Beneš Decrees" was usually accompanied by negative stereotyping of the image of Czech society, which is pre-

---

3   Hahn, E. 2003. "Španělské vesnice a české větrné mlýny: požadavek zrušení Benešových dekretů v německých médiích" [Strange Backward Dumps and Czech Windmills: the demand for the abolition of the Beneš Decrees in the German media], in Mink, G. – Blaive, M. 2003. *Benešovy dekrety* (Budoucnost Evropy a vyrovnávání se s minulostí) [The Beneš Decrees (The Future of Europe and settlement with the past)]. Prague: CEFRES. 76–77. On the basis of a content analysis of texts in the *FAZ* the author presents several examples from the electoral period in 2002 when almost every issue contained pieces on the theme of the "Beneš Decrees" that encouraged emotive support for this demand (Czech Policy Gone Astray, Prague Cynicism, Czech Parliament Legitimates Genocide etc.). Different views almost never appear and the protagonists are presented as defenders of "human rights" (Riess-Passer: Beneš Decrees are not Compatible with Human Rights). The problem is not presented as a complicated matter, but one-sidedly as the consequence of alleged Czech simple-mindedness. (B. Kohler in the article National Front: And here we have speechifying about alleged threats that can easily spark off the primordial Czech fear of opening up the "German question", simple-minded nonsense.) Ibidem. 80.

sented either as incomprehensibly backward, or infected with the communist bacillus and fighting fantasy battles against the windmills of an imagined German threat.

- The image of Czech society presented included the idea that it was divided into a majority succumbing to error and unable to grasp the obvious justice of the demand for the annulment of the decrees, and an isolated handful of enlightened Czech intellectuals (whose brave positions were considered high treason).
- The role of the Sudeten German organisations as the main actor in the current difficulties in Czech-German relations was progressively suppressed. The German media avoided description of the specific history and cultural historical traditions of the Sudeten Germans, but also of the political goals of the Sudetendeutsche Landsmannschaft. Almost nothing was written about the conservative nationalist (or extreme right-wing) views of people in the Witikobund.[4]

We cannot but agree that there are resonances with the situation in Czech-German relations in the 1930s, when there was also a deep gulf between left and right in attitudes to the CSR. In the 1930s negative stereotypes of Czechs were reinforced by slogans about the injustice of the Versailles Diktat and the denial of the right of self-determination to the "suffering" Sudeten Germans, while today the excuse is the "genocidal Beneš Decrees" supported by the "legally unsustainable" Potsdam Agreement, and the "expelled" Sudeten Germans right to homeland and collective return on the basis of the right of self-determination.

Of course, every comparison applies only in part (at the very least, Germany then and Germany today are quite different entities) but "a look into the world of the German media suggests that while much has changed in cultural-historical models in relation to Czech neighbours, unfortunately much has not changed".

Cautious Friendship

Germany both integrates and divides the Czech political scene. This was abundantly true in the crisis years of the mid-20[th]century, and following the unification of Germany it is once again very obvious. Although conditions today

---

4   Ibidem. 82–85.

are so different, traditional fears of the powerful neighbour remain present in the consciousness of Czech society, and these fears are specifically focused on the Germans expelled from the Czech lands after the Second World War. Yet in general, the prevailing attitude to reunified Germany in Czech society may with a certain simplification be characterised as "cautious friendship". This is the result of a number of factors, acting in parallel and sometimes against each other, to which I shall return later.

Since 1989 the attitudes of the population of the Czech Lands to Germany have been moulded by geopolitical changes following the fall of the "iron curtain". The two most important such changes are Soviet/Russian withdrawal from Central Europe (symbolically confirmed by the dissolution of the Warsaw Pact) and the unification of the two parts of Germany on the 3rd of October 1990. Germany embarked on the road to return to the status of major European power, its progress in this respect accelerated by its economic power and important role as leading protagonist in European integration processes. The population of the Czech Republic responded to the new features of the Central European geopolitical situation in the context of its historical experience.

At the start, sympathy in Czechoslovakia for the prelude to German unification (which actually started in Czechoslovakia in the summer of 1989 when the streets of Prague were full of the dozens of Trabant cars abandoned by East Germans seeking asylum in the grounds of the West German embassy) was demonstrable. In 1990, this sympathy was manifest as the new Czech government offered unconditional support for German reunification.[5]

As the international weight of their German neighbour continued to increase, however, Czech voices were to be heard asking the question: "May not Germany, in the context of integration processes, and even if this time by peaceful means, try once again to gain control of the whole Central European zone and enforce what are purely its own interests there?"[6]

The Czech Republic joined the process of European integration late, and with the handicap of decades of isolation from the modernisation processes that the Western European states had undergone in the post-war period. In that era it had in fact been Germany that had experienced the most drastic changes, starting with the constitution – with the direct involvement of the Allied pow-

---

[5]   Very soon, however, serious problems came up in negotiations for the treaty between the FRG and the CSFR. Dienstbier comments, "More than ninety percent of the text of the treaty was in fact negotiated almost instantly. There remained a thick line set against the claims of the Sudeten Germans, Munich, the confirmation of the continuity of Czechoslovakia, and provisions on the status of minorities. But on these issues, no movement was possible." Dienstbier, J. *Od snění k realitě*. 284.

[6]   Handl, V. – Kural, V. – Reiman, M. 1997. "Česká republika a Německo" [The Czech Republic and Germany]. *Česká zahraniční politika*. Prague: Ústav mezinárodních vztahů. 153.

ers – of two new political state subjects: the Federal Republic of Germany and the German Democratic Republic.

The two Germanies and the Czech Lands (as part of former Czechoslovakia) developed along different lines and to different extents in the post-war period, and the result was the different levels of social consciousness that have been contributing significantly to the difficulties in the process of Czech-German rapprochment since 1989.

Leaving aside the diametrically different initial starting line of a market system in West Germany and a centrally directed economic system in CSR, one crucial difference arose from West Germans' decades of social experience of neighbouring states of the Western Allied coalition – i.e. the gradual fading of resentment and lightening of the burden of the past in mutual relations. Increasing rapprochement between yesterday's enemies in the Western alliance was greatly encouraged by the situation of the Cold War and the integrating effect of the threat posed by an expansionist Soviet Empire. Czech-German relations had missed this historic chance of greater understanding (if we put on one side "proletarian internationalism" between the CSSR and GDR) and the examples of the ambitiously conceived projects of German-French rapprochement (and of German rapprochement with other Western European states, if on a lesser scale) have been of limited use as a model for them. Furthermore, these examples were built to a considerable extent on the strong political personalities of Chanceller Konrad Adenauer and Charles de Gaulle.

If in Germany the Czech state tends to be described as a difficult and antagonistic partner (especially although not only by authors from the Sudeten German group), the same applies vice versa. At the citizen level we can identify a certain irritability in the reactions of Czechs to the activities of richer visitors and commercial partners from neighbouring Germany. Especially in the border areas of the CR it is not uncommon to hear emotive complaints that Germans are buying up properties and lands on the cheap using Czech "front men" to evade regulations, or the expression of fears of becoming "strangers in our own country" etc.

At the level of bilateral relations, the state of social consciousness is also partially reflected by the media, which has attracted frequent criticism for the way in which it reports on Czech-German relations (in 1996 for example, a survey of people in the borderlands found that 87% of respondents thought that the Czech mass media's reporting on Germany was partially or wholly flawed). A more objective perception of mutual relations has not been encouraged by the German media either, which takes an interest in the Czech Republic mostly with regard to the post-war transfer of Sudeten Germans or else occasionally with the Czech-German borderlands as a source of small and organised crime, and prostitution. This kind of narrow and negative perspective is unlikely to change the stereotypes through which Germans view Czechs.[7]

Investigation of the attitudes of the Czech population to Germany has also revealed a tendency to emotional formulation in the case of Czech-German disputes, for example over the definition of the borders between the CR and FRG (existing border – state border), and the interpretation of historical events in the not-so-distant past (transfer – expulsion, the role of the Sudeten Germans in inter-war Czechoslovakia and their share in the destruction of the independent republic etc.). Antagonism is often implicit in double terminology (e.g. expulsion – transfer) where diametrically different interpretation of the problem is obvious even in the words regularly employed (see preceding chapter).

If theories of the close connection between the foreign and domestic policies of states are correct, then the Czech-German relationship presents an entirely model situation, and what is more a situation characterised on both sides by a tendency for attitudes to be highly emotionally coloured. In this context we can see the force of K. Boulding's view[8] that a nation's idea of itself and of other nations is formed not just by specific historical events, but also by how these have been processed in the form of historical memory.

What is often termed the Munich syndrome[9] is latently present in Czech society. Those who actually remember Munich and the impact it had on their

---

[7] The role of the media is definitely a whole separate theme in Czech-German relations and generalised judgments are risky before deeper studies have been carried out. All the same, existing content analyses suggests that the media has tended to have a negative effect. For example the study of the content of articles on Czech-German relations on the pages of the *Frankfurter Allgemeine Zeitung* from Feb. 1995 to May 1996 clearly identifies the tendency to look at the problems from the perspectives of the "conservative revolution", which has been bringing national ideology back onto the German political scene, including the demand for the preservation of the German language as "the most important bearer of the culture of the nation", but also care for German minorities in other countries. The authors of the study state that two thirds of all articles on the theme focus on the expulsion of the Sudeten Germans from CSR and the others also relate to the theme in one way or another. The picture of the Czech past conveyed by the *FAZ* is selective and one-sided in choice of theme and interpretation. The articles by G. Facius in the newspaper *Die Welt* or K. P. Schwarz's TV documentary "Transfer – the Expulsion of the Germans from Czechoslovakia", broadcast on the 23rd of March 1996 by the TV station ARD are similarly tendentious. Kaiser, D. – Šitler, J. "Novodobé české dějiny v zrcadle Frankfurter Allgemeine Zeitung" [Modern Czech History in the Mirror of the Frankfurter Allgemeine Zeitung]. *Dějiny a současnost* 5/1996. 15–19.

[8] Boulding, K. "National Actors and International Interactions (Nonrational Factors in Foreign Policy)", in Rochester, J. M. – Pearson, F. S. 1998. *International Relations*. New York: Random House. 200.

[9] One possible if extreme interpretation of the symptoms of the *Munich Syndrome* is presented as a motto passage quoted at the start of his book by Boris Čelovský: "the slow but irresistible feeling of symbiotic inclination on the part of the victim of an act of violence to its perpetrators. This delusive mental state is more often than not provoked by kind gestures from the perpetrators; the victim obstinately believes in their benevolence. The symptoms usually remain latent for whole decades." Freiberger, S. "Ein Beitrag zur Diagnostik einiger psychopatologischen Phänomena in der Beziehung zwischen ungleichen Partnern", in Čelovský, B. 1997. *Mnichovský syndrom* [The Munich Syndrome]. Ostrava: Syndikát novinářů. Motto in the introduction. Rather similar arguments based on psychoanalytical concepts of the relationship between perpetrators and victims regularly appear in the theoretical review, *German Politics and Society* published by the well-known

lives are most directly affected, but in fact the historical experience of voluntary renunciation of state sovereignty and national identity has influenced the social consciousness of generations to come.[10]

The opening of the borders and the mass opportunity for Czech citizens to gain first-hand experience of the political and economic conditions in the Federal Republic of Germany have helped to overcome many prejudices and wrong interpretations. Concurrently, however, the development of Czech-Sudeten dialogue after 1989 has caused striking dissensions in Czech society and confirmed a significant section of the public and newly constituted political elites in the view that the demands of the Sudetendeutsche Landsmannschaft (right to homeland and self-determination, the revocation of the Beneš Decrees, Czech acknowledgement that the transfer was an act of lawlessness etc.), could in their consequences potentially threaten the stability and integrity of the CR. The revival of historical resentments has a negative influence on the attitudes of Czech society to Germany.

Negative experiences from the past are not, however, the whole story in the current development of Czech views of role of Germany. Since 1989 there has been much to suggest that Czech society is quite capable of gradually moving forward from the historically formed and collectively shared stereotypes of the powerful neighbour. Surveys of public opinion show that Czechs see Germany as the closest (and a desirable) economic partner and political partner with whom we ought to maintain the closest possible cooperation.

Immediately after 1989 the attitudes of people in the CR to Germany were affected by the general euphoria at the sudden fall of the barriers between the two parts of Europe. Germany in particular, with its visibly successful economy, opened up for the Czech population a western world of prosperity and luxury, and this encouraged the rather naive idea that simply by dismantling its the totalitarian regime the CR would be able to share all these wonders almost overnight.

This uncritical admiration and naive faith in historical miracle (to which the political elite succumbed as well – let us just recall the claims that Czechoslovakia would be an integral part of Western structures and share their standard of living within ten years, or indeed Václav Klaus's assertion in the mid-nineties that the transformation was already complete) paved the way for later deep disappointment and disillusion. This "coming down" process affected not only attitudes to Germany but to other countries; Czech society came to take a somewhat sceptical view of Euro-Atlantic political, economic and military structures

British-American press *Berghahn Books*, New York/Oxford and edited by the prestigious *The Center for German and European Studies* at the University of Berkeley in California.

[10] See *Studie o sudetoněmecké otázce.*

and the benefits of joining NATO, and above all support for entry into the European Union declined, falling by May 2002 to a mere 40%.[11]

This drop in support for EU membership arguably also had something to do with the pressure of a number of German politicians and media for the annulment of the Beneš Decrees. After all, since Germany has been the leading protagonist for the enlargement of the EU eastwards (it bound itself to support the CR's accession and is fullfilling its obligation), it is not unnatural or unlikely that Czech citizens should see a link between German support for Czech accession and the pressure to make accession conditional on solution of the Sudeten German question, and so perceive EU entry as a threat to the sovereignty of their own state.

The situation is further complicated by the fact that Czech national consciousness is itself rather shaky and its confidence has been undermined. Czechs view themselves with a degree of scepticism, as well as other nations and international institutions. In this lack of confidence we see the effects of decades of isolation from the workd of advanced Western civilisation, as well as of the traumas of 1938 (the Munich syndrome), 1948 (the failure of democratic parties and politicians) and 1968, when the Soviet invasion put an end to a process that might otherwise have started modernising trends leading to greater contact and convergence with Western Europe.

Instead of the uninterrupted development of the national economy, and gradual incorporation into European integrational structures acccompanied by development of a pluralist democratic system, what befell Czechoslovakia following 1948 was the destruction of the structures of civil society and the decimation of the social groups and classes (the independent farmers, the middle class) that had been bearers of political culture and factors cultivating the social-political environment of a country advanced by the standards of the day, even if marked by war and occupation.

Particularly in the context of Czech-German relations, however, equally important was the fact that a key component of the population and political elite of the Czech lands had already been destroyed in the period of the Protectorate of Bohemia and Moravia by the Nazi occupation forces. A substantial proportion of the Jewish community of the Czech Lands had identified with German language and culture, or been bilingual, and in terms of opinions formed a bridge between Czech and German milieux. Indeed, in this respect the Jews of Czechoslovakia could be regarded as a kind of cultural cornerstone. They might have positively influenced postwar developments in the Czech Lands

---

[11]   See the results of the survey conducted in April 2002 by the CVVM agency. Three fifths of respondents believe (March 2002) that the debate on the Beneš Decrees has a negative effect on Czech-German relations. *Czech Press Agency.* 10. 5. 2002.

(moderating aggressive anti-German sentiments), and might have been able to play a positive role in finding a *modus vivendi* between Czechs and Germans post-1989[12], had they not of course been wiped out by Nazi Holocaust. Generally, this *drastic interference in the continuity of the social structure* removed an important social group that had made a fundamental contribution to the distinctive cultural environment of the Czech Lands, enlarging its horizons and multiplying its points of contact above all vis-a-vis the German-speaking countries and their advanced culture.

This too is one of the roots of the persisting disputes between Czechs and Germans. If today people speak of the practical impossibility of reviving the old multicultural character of the Czech Lands, this is not just because of the transfer of the Germans. Before the war there were three, not just two important cultural elements in the Czech Lands, and all but a remnant of the Jewish community was entirely entirely destroyed by the Nazis under the Occupation.

The Historical Roots of Attitudes to Germany

In the modern era, geographical and social conditions in a large area of Europe were so complicated that a population did not have to move anywhere for its status as part of national/ethnic majority or minority to vary with the size or type of whole within which majority or minority status was defined. I.e. whether this "whole" was a complex multinational state, an integral state/province, a group of countries or a region, district or town. Neither Czechs nor the Germans in the Czech Lands were willing to be satisfied with the position of national/ethnic political minority and they struggled to prevent that eventuality with all the means at their disposal.

As an ethnic community with attributes of own national identity, Czechs had by the turn of the 19th/20th century developed an almost complete social struc-

---

[12] Suda, Z. 1995. *The Origins and Development of the Czech National Consciousness and Germany*. Prague: Central European University. 49. A research project in the second half of the 1990s in the CR focused on the witnesses who had survived the Nazi extermination of the Jews. The result included the finding that both Czech and German were spoken in the majority of Jewish families in the inter-war period, even though most of the parents had attended German schools in the time of the Austro-Hungarian monarchy. In the young Czechoslovak Republic Jews hoped to find and in most cases found the possibility of real equality. A striking majority of families (68 percent) had considered themselves Czech Jews and did not feel that a high degree of assimilation and predominantly Czech orientation was in conflict with their Jewish sense of identity. Hyndráková, A. – Lorencová, A. "Postoje českého obyvatelstva k Židům ve 30. a začátkem 40. let ve vzpomínkách pamětníků" [The Attitudes of the Czech Population to Jews in the 1930s and 40s in the Recollections of Contemporaries], in *Fenomén holocaust* [The Holocaust Phenomenon]. (Collection). 1999. Prague/Terezín. 113–114.

ture including all the basic groups and classes of modern society.[13] By this time the national community also had an internally structured and differentiated political elite and range of parties and associations. The increased self-confidence of the Czech elites was making it possible for them to move from "defensive" nationalism to the active development of a distinctive modern Czech approach and culture, including contributions to science, scholarship and the arts that bore international comparison. "All the basic political lines of reform (in the Habsburg Monarchy) were also running up against the intensifying Czech-German national rivalry in the Czech Lands."[14]

In this context we can agree with Z. Suda's contention[15] that Czech social-national consciousness is "over-historicised", by which he means that the idea of a continuous shared historical experience has played a key role in maintaining the cohesion and solidarity of modern Czech society (one example is the national myth of the three centuries of the Habsburg Yoke). We will find few nations (perhaps with the exception of Poland) in which consciousness of historical tradition has been such an important constitutive and sustaining factor of national identity. Asking Czechs to as it were close the book of their past (both glorious and tragic) in the interests of a new partnership orientated purely to the future inevitably sounds to many like a demand that they lose their collective memory. However, the problem is not only in the Czechs and their historically anchored identity (in which there is undoubtedly an element of myth), but also and above all in the historicising arguments of the expellee organisations.[16]

---

[13] Kořalka, J. 1996. "Proměnlivý vztah většin a menšin. Národnostní otázka" [The Changeable Relationship between Majorities and Minorities. The Nationality Question], in *Češi v Habsburské říši a v Evropě 1815–1914*. 143.

[14] Ibidem. 124.

[15] Suda, Z. *The Origins and Development*. 42.

[16] From the great quantity of materials published by the expellee organisations we can mention as typical at least two: *Die Tschechoslowakei. Das Ende einer Fehlkonstruktion*. 1993. Eibicht, R.-J. (ed.). Berg: VGB-Verlagsgesellschaft Berg. In the introduction to this collection, to which prominent representatives of the SL (and Witikobund) contributed, we find the claim that the division of Czechoslovakia is once more returning the Sudeten German question to the centre of discussion. "Two new states have been established in Central Europe. A new situation has arisen and so many Sudeten Germans are supporting not just conciliation but historical settlement." Opinions challenging the very existence of the Czech state are present in the subtext and even openly. A second example is the published catalogue of the exhibition *Sudetští Němci. Etnická skupina v srdci Evropy* [Sudeten Germans. An Ethnic Group in the Heart of Europe]. 1994. Kraus, H. (ed.). München: Sudetendeutscher Rat. This includes a quotation of the words of R. Lodgman von Auen in his speech to the National Assembly on the 1st of June 1920, expressing the view with which the SL identified: "This state came into being at the expense of historical truth. The great powers who made the decisions were deceived about the true state of affairs. The Czechoslovak Republic is the result of unilateral Czech arbitrary will. The German territories (meaning the border areas of the Czech Lands) were occupied illegally and disarmed by force." (26) This text also refers to the standpoints of the German political parties, all in support of the expellees. "The CDU is of the opinion that the Sudeten German question has not been settled by the illegal expulsion of the Sudeten Germans from their original homeland. The principle of the national and

After 1945, Germany (or more precisely the FRG) underwent deep systemic changes, initially under the aegis of the Western Allied occupation administrations[17] and later as a result of dynamic processes in the conditions of a market economy and pluralist democratic parliamentary system. For example, there is general admiration for the principle of "co-operative federalism", which in the FRG's political system means practical application of the constitutional principle that requires central political direction with decentralised government.

German federalism is not just an instrument to protect regional autonomy, but also creates an additional checking mechanism on power through the vertical division of its exercise. This principle retains and maintains a functional centre of power (the federal government) while distributing a significant degree of authority to lower links in the political system.

The application of this principle results in effective mechanisms to safeguard the democratic character of decision-making processes in the FRG. It is questionable whether Czech society really sees and appreciates the depth and pervasiveness of the changes that German politics has undergone. Surveys of Czech opinion and attitudes to Germany indicate that at best Czechs appreciate it only partially. The main reason is that they are simply not informed about the mechanisms of decision-making in German politics, but the expellees and their organisations play a part here, because in the eyes of the Czech public they tend to represent (but also overshadow and obscure) Germany, even though they plainly form the most conservative part of the most conservative wing of the German political spectrum.

It is unfortunately thanks to the Sudetendeutsche Landsmannschaft that the ethno-cultural concept of the nation in the sense of *Volksgemeinschaft*, antagonistic to "the patriotism of the constitution" (J. Habermas), has repeatedly been instrumentalised in Czech-German relations. It is only a slight exaggeration to say that the expellee organisations separate Czechs from Germans by creating a "force field" of potential conflict between them. While on the German side the expellees are considered links between Czech and German environments, Czech society (with some exceptions), sees their role as the complete opposite.

It is of course true that the democratic Germany of today is a completely different partner compared to the Germany of national socialism or the Weimar

---

state continuity of Germany in its 1937 borders does not exclude a national and constitutional solution on the basis of right to homeland and self-determination for Sudeten Germans." Ibidem. 80.

[17] As an example of the abundant literature see e.g. Zink, H. 1974. *The United States in Germany 1944–1945*. Westport: Greenwood Press. Schubert, K. – Wagner, J. "Federalismus a nové teritoriální členění" [Federalism and the New Territorial Subdivision]. *Politologický časopis* 1/1997. 74. "The German federalist structure was entirely newly created after the end of the Second World War: on the basis of the Potsdam Agreement the Allied powers reconstructed the independence of the territorial wholes in the hope that this would have democratising effects."

Republic. The Czech problem in relation to Germany, however, is above all the group of expelled Sudeten Germans who while only a small minority in German society have a serious influence on Czech-German relations by virtue of their specific position in German society and politics. As a consequence of the foregrounding of expellee themes the Czech-German relationship constantly returns to the past and is much too focused on the Sudeten question. Concentration on the Sudeten problem puts the emphasis on conflict, and misunderstanding.[18]

Although sympathy for Germany has persisted in the attitudes of the Czech population since 1989 (in surveys it is repeatedly expressed to a greater or lesser extent by two thirds of respondents), there are a number of reasons for frequently expressed fears and uncertainty, even though these are also encouraged by prejudices.[19]

These reasons include, first and foremost, the historical experience of Germany as a neighbour, but also the activities of the expellee organisations as reported in the media. This is borne out by a content analysis of articles on themes of Czech-German relations published in *Lidové noviny* in the years 1991–1993 (carried out at the Charles University Faculty of Social Sciences.)

Articles in this *LN* – a leading serious Czech newspaper reported/commented on mutual relations most frequently through the prism of the Sudeten German Question, with the *Sudetendeutsche Landsmannschaft* and its leaders appearing as the dominant representative as well as subject of the problem.[20] Mutual compensation was the most frequent theme of these articles (it was the subject of around a third of them). They were mostly informed by a retrospective view of Czech-German relations, and indeed this became a certain media stereotype.[21] We can indeed agree that the media interpretation of Czech-Ger-

---

[18] Rupnik, J. "Důležitou zkouškou jsou vždy druhé volby" [Second Choices are always an Important Test]. *Lidové noviny*. 5. 5. 1995. 8.

[19] Wagnerová, A. "Nevypočitatelnosti symbolické politiky". 10.

[20] Šmídová, O. "Česko-německé vztahy v zrcadle tisku" [Czech-German Relations as Reflected in the Press]. *S-Obzor* 4/1995. 40. In the period monitored there was an clearly increasing trend in the use of historically-based arguments which later culminated in the polemics accompanying the preparation of the Czech-German Declaration and most recently in the spring of 2002. "In the first two years following November 1989 the Sudeten problem was an important point in Czech-German relations, but now it is becoming the dominant issue overshadowing everything else in the process of coming to terms with the common past and negotiating prospects for the future. On the other hand not even at the rhetorical level is it easy to wrest the Sudeten German problem away from the collectivist nationalist concept in which it has developed for so long and which literally gave birth to it. The fact that the press is often ready to engage in polemic with the opinions of ideologues of the Franz Neubauer type, whose arguments are presented in such a classically nationalist spirit, means that the counter-arguments "naturally" continue on the same wave in similar ideological mode." It would be hard to find a better characterisation of the reasons why Czech-Sudeten-German dialogue goes round and round in a closed circle. The author's appeal for a de-ideologised, non-nationalising reinterpretation of the issue will evidently remain unheard for some time to come (if not forever).

[21] Ibidem. 41.

man relations is over-historicised. This has its reasons, as discussed earlier.[22] As mentioned above, content analysis of articles on the theme of Czech history, the Sudeten Germans and current Czech policy in the famous conservative-ori-entated German newspaper the *Frankfurter Allgemeine Zeitung* likewise shows the importance and dynamic role of historical stereotypes on the German side.[23]

The birth of the Czech Republic on the 1st of January 1993 was an event greeted with some confusion and unease in Czech society. Many Czechs were hesitant and lukewarm in their agreement to the division of a state whose foundation in 1918 and restoration in 1945 had meant the fulfilment of a centuries-old dream of statehood for the majority of the population of the Czech Lands. This study is not the place for a detailed account of the circumstances of the split, but like many others I consider that the break-up the CSFR to have been the result of the failure of the new political elites,[24] (foreign observers including some FDP and SPD politicians share this opinion). It led to a crisis of Czech national identity, especially because it happened in parallel with the shock of the systemic change to which Czech society was exposed by the sudden collapse of the authoritarian regime and opening up to the advanced Western world.

Although the "new" Czech Republic has in many respects continued the constitutional political tradition of Czechoslovakia, the sudden and for many the unwanted revival of purely Bohemian statehood has involved a certain crisis of identity. Czech social consciousness, already stressed by the deep economic and political changes involved in the transformation, has been compelled to absorb the new statehood as a fait accompli, and so to go back to roots that Czech society has no difficulty in perceiving, given its strong historical anchorage, but has found it difficult to endow with new contemporary forms and meaning. To make matters even harder, this has happened at a time when Czech social elites

---

[22]   The correlation between more tolerant attitudes to Germany and higher levels of education is confirmed for example by a qualitative survey conducted among students of the Philosophical and Education faculties of Charles University in Prague (100 respondents). Two thirds of the respondents considered Czech-German relations to be good or very good, and 59% said that they could understand the point of view of the Sudeten Germans. A rather surprising 46% of respondents said that their view of Germany was wholly or partly influenced by its national socialist past. *Prager Zeitung*. 19. 6. 1997. 9.

[23]   "The picture of the Czech past conveyed by the FAZ is strikingly selective and one-sided both in choice of themes and in their treatment. Modern Czech history is viewed exclusively through German nationalist eyes, i.e. in the polarised scheme of Czechs versus Germans. This kind of picture of modern Czech attitudes, in which the Germans are presented exclusively as victims and the Czechs as perpetrators, is not limited just to the *FAZ* (they dominate the commentaries of Karl-Peter Schwarz). The articles of Gernot Facius in *Die Welt* do not differ much from the *FAZ* in their tendencies." Kaiser, D. – Šitler, J. "Novodobé české dějiny v zrcadle Frankfurter Allgemeine Zeitung". 18–19.

[24]   Jičínský, Z. – Škaloud, J. 1996. "Transformace politického systému k demokracii" [The Transformation of the Political system to Democracy], in Šafaříková, V. (et al.). *Transformace české společnosti 1989–1995*. Brno: Doplněk. 111.

are deeply divided in their views of the national community, state and history in the post-modern era.[25]

In the context of Czech-German relations, I consider two reasons for the strains on Czech national identity arising from the break up of the CSFR to be relevant. First, a substantial proportion of Czechs linked their sense of their own identity with the Czechoslovak state. This was evidently one of the reasons why the Czech political elites found it so hard to comprehend Slovak arguments on the Slovak need to abandon a state union with which they were allegedly unable to identify. If the new political elites found it difficult to come to terms with this situation, then it was a great deal harder for many ordinary Czechs. Not all Czechs have come to terms with the new reality to this day.[26] While generally Czech society has in practice accepted the division of the state unexpectedly easily, it is symptomatic that voices were raised warning against the step in its possible foreign political implications (see e.g. Jiří Dienstbier and others).

Second, Czech society has always tended to define its identity in the referential framework of attitudes to Germany and loss of union with the Slovaks may make this more of an issue for a Czech state. There are many stereotypes about Germans and Germany that are stored in the deeper levels of Czech consciousness and attitudes and form an *ethnically mobilising potential* which is activated in moments of real or even just imagined threat from Germany.

Immediately after the Velvet Revolution, the euphoria and the strong influence of Czech publicists calling for empathy for the Sudeten Germans and their post-war fate as interpreted by Bohemus, Podiven, Danubius and others, meant that for a time the mobilising potential of an identity formulated by tradition (in the sense of historical memory) spontaneously receded into the background. This phase lasted roughly up to the mid-1990s. As a result of long-term isolation from the world, Czechs were tending to succumb to the spirit of exaggerated self-criticism that in any case was constantly demanded of them through the media by prominent ex-dissident intellectuals, and President Václav Havel himself.[27]

---

[25] With a certain level of simplification (and using Anthony Giddens' terminology and typologisation) we might speak of Czech social elites as having a low degree of integration, i.e. relatively little in the way of shared ideals and a consciousness of solidarity that would allow them to exercise a major influence on the dynamics of the processes taking place in public space. For more detail see Pecka, E. "Doslov" [Epilogue], in Jodl, M. 1994. *Teorie elity a problém elity* [Theories of the Elite and the Problem of the Elite]. Prague: Victoria Publishing. 122.

[26] See e.g. The repeatedly expressed views of Petr Uhl, who insisted on his right to retain both Czech and Slovak citizenship and argued for this on both objective and subjective grounds. Similar views characterise the group of intellectuals around the Czech-Slovak journal *Mosty*.

[27] "Good relations between nations, and so our reconciliation too, can be based only on the cooperation of free citizens, resisting the temptation to form a crowd under collectivist banners and conjure up the spirit

In short, historical resentment based on the conflicts of the past was overlaid by a spirit of *nostra culpa* combined with an admiring vision of Germany and a rather naive faith that the Czech state would very rapidly enjoy the Western prosperity and functioning democracy exemplified by Germany. Czechs were hardly the only people to be intoxicated by the vision of a conflict-free world rid of the Soviet imperium (let us remember Francis Fukuyama and his essay *The End of History*), but in the Czech case it had the specific effect of leading them to temporarily forget the image of Germany as the enemy and instead to see Germans as self-confident, clever, educated, rich, reliable, honourable and so forth. This often uncritical admiration primarily affected people in the age category under thirty. Conversely, Czechs tended to accuse themselves of a whole range of corresponding faults and even, in self-flagellating mode, of being the epitome of negative attributes (envious, malicious, lazy, unreliable, poor, unable to stand up for themselves).[28]

The atmosphere of Czech "soul-searching" was encouraged by a number of prominent pundits who held up a one-sidedly unflattering mirror to Czech society. A characteristic example was Petr Příhoda's *Our Germans* on the ethnic aspects of the expulsion of the Sudeten Germans. I certainly do not regard it as illegitimate to pose questions about the ethnic core of the transfer (or forced evacuation, in the words of the Declaration). What is problematic is to judge the transfer from the perspective of the contemporary concept of human rights while entirely refusing to set it in historical context, the consequent branding of the transfer as an act of genocide and finally the making of misleading claims about the collective guilt of Czechs (despite the fact that Příhoda's central thesis is the rejection of the collective guilt of Germans) and their moral failure as a whole.

What is more, Příhoda's account and those like it confuse *three levels of the fact of the expulsion*: the historical, the moral, and the contemporary political.[29] The author as it were discreetly omits to mention that the trauma of the transfer was preceded by the no less tragic trauma of the situation of brutal threat to the very existence of the Czech nation, as the direct consequence of the destruction of an independent Czechoslovakia.[30] The wide-ranging and detailed discussion

---

of tribal confrontation in their shadow. …On the Czech side this is a strange and generally provincial combination of fear of Germans and servility to them, and of course the inability of many to free themselves from the straitjacket of prejudices that have been cultivated in society for so long." Havel, V. "Češi a Němci na cestě k dobrému sousedství". 39–40.

[28]   Zich, F. 1996. *Národnostní a etnické vztahy v českém pohraničí – obraz Čecha, Němce, Rakušana a Roma ve vědomí obyvatel* [National and Ethnic Relations in the Czech Borderlands – The image of the Czech, German, Austrian and Roma in the consciousness of the population]. Prague: Sociologický ústav AV ČR. WP 96:4. 19.

[29]   Kučera, J. "Česká historiografie a odsun Němců" [Czech Historiography and the Transfer of the Germans]. *Soudobé dějiny* 2–3/1994. 369.

[30]   "Specifically, the Czech trauma of the [possible] extinction of the Czech nation, which haunted the pre-1848 revivalist generation, was after 1939 shared in Czech circles, which could see in advance that if Germany was

on the transfer as the key issue of the post-war attitude of Czechs to Germans which took place in dissident circles at the end of the 1970s and 1980s was not repeated after 1989 in its full breadth and depth of differentiation of opinion. The opinions that received the most publicity were those that one-sidedly demanded penitence and revision of the act of transfer. I quote again from Příhoda: "It can be asked how it was possible that a nation of Central Europe with a thousand-year Christian tradition in a few weeks descended to the level of pagan barbarism and at the same time to the state of depersonalisation that is the distinguishing mark of modern totalitarianism. This is a question that we Czechs should be asking today. And we should not be satisfied with mere scientific explanation."[31]

Příhoda is untiring in his efforts to persuade Czech society and the politicians that there has been some huge conspiracy of silence about our sins against the Sudeten Germans and so there is a need for a "creative approach" to history that pays no attention at all to the historically conditioned nature of political decisions. "The most important consequence of the expulsion is the burden of collectively denied bad conscience. We speak not of expulsion but of transfer in order to displace its moral dimension. The majority in Czech society profess moral relativism, (which) renders them incapable of recognising, judging and naming even a completely contemporary evil, and so stands in the way of moral regeneration. This is why the Czech political leadership lacks imagination and ethos, and has gambled on populism."[32]

All that such calls for immediate and one-sided revision of the Czech position on the Sudeten German have really managed to do, to paraphrase A. Krzemiński and apply his insights to the CR, "is to revive in Czech society the German spectre, which from 1989 had appeared to belong to the past". Krzemiński has written on the similar effect in Polish society produced by the demand for the establishment of a Centre against Expulsions in Berlin. In Poland this project was considered a provocation. In Polish-German relations the dispute over the centre was primarily about the German vision of the history of the war, the erosion of the sense of proportion and link between consciousness of German guilt and German suffering arising from a war unleashed and lost.[33] In the Czech Republic the dispute over the transfer of the Sudeten Germans is primarily about the proportionality of guilt and punishment for the destruction of democratic

---

victorious, the very existence of Czechs as a nation was lost." From a letter from R. Luža to L. Hejdánek, in *Češi, Němci, odsun.* 162.

[31] Příhoda, P. "Naši Němci. (O jejich vyhnání a zrodu totalitní moci v Čechách)" [Our Germans (On their expulsion and the rise of totalitarian power in the Czech Lands)]. *Přítomnost* 4/1990. 22.

[32] Příhoda, P. "Nezvládnuté minulosti" [Unmastered Pasts]. *Kafka (journal for Central Europe)* 13/2004. Single-theme issue devoted to "expulsion". 22–23.

[33] Krzemiński, A. "Zápas o paměť". 58–61.

Czechoslovakia. I emphasise that I am well aware of the differences between the Czech and Polish contexts and make the comparison above all to highlight the current consequences of historical memory for perceptions of Germany and the Sudeten German Question.

Views involving wholly unacceptable generalisation (ahistorical disregard for causality in history, the instrumentalisation of ethical principles and demand for "creative" political decision-making) became widely medialised after 1989 at a time when one value system in Czech society had collapsed and another had not yet fully emerged. The result was a deepening of confusion and doubts about the legitimacy of a sovereign state (and what is more a a sovereign state that had now split) that had allegedly sinned so fatally against a large group of its own inhabitants.

"Self-criticism" conceived in such an extravagant way could not have had cathartic effects even had Czech society possessed resources comparable to those of Germany (social prosperity, a functioning pluralist system with established political parties, a mature civil society, decades of continuity in the develoment of the social pillar of the middle class and power elites etc.).

Eva Hahn, for example, has argued that, "Traditional stereotypical fears prevent Czech from regarding Germans as political partners in a self-confident manner. If the Czechs stopped seeing themselves as a nation oppressed for centuries by Germans, defeated at the White Mountain and sold by their former Germany-speaking fellow citizens to Hitlerian Germany, they might be able to notice the culturally and politically diverse society of contemporary Germany and stop regarding the Bonn government as a power centre on whose arbitrary caprice the solution of the Sudeten German problem depends."[34]

We can agree with this, but for this enlightenment to have happened would have required Czech commentators and the media in the course of the 1990s to have conveyed an objective picture of Germany society and the full spectrum of German political views. This did not happen and the question arises of whether ignorance was the only reason why not.

Hahn suggests what she believes to be one source of the difficulty Czechs have in setting the expellee problem in German context. She notes that the German past and the German present are composed of a far larger number of worlds that are far less dependent on each other and more closed to each other than Czechs are used to in their own conditions. Czechs therefore tend to see the history of Germans in the Czech Lands as far more "representative" of Germany and Germans than it actually was or is. In fact the history of the

---

[34] Hahn, E. "Češi, Němci, ostatní" [Czechs, German, the Others], in *Sudetoněmecký problém: obtížné loučení s minulostí*. 216.

Bohemian Germans represents just one specific area of the history of the German-speaking world, but is at the same time a part of the history of the Czech Lands. It is in this duality that Hahn identifies the specific feature of the Czech-German past that encourages the use of blanket stereotypes about Germans and Germany on the basis of conflation of German, Czech-German and Sudeten German history.[35]

However tempting this theory, it cannot be entirely accepted, because it fails to take account of the many examples of linkage and intersection between these three "types of history" (some of which I have pointed out in preceding chapters). Furthermore, historical actors and their actions participate in events that become one history (or past); this can certainly be interpreted in the frame of reference of Czechs, Sudeten Germans or "greater" Germany, but I consider it artificial (even though I am aware of basic differences as well as overlaps) to construct these as territorially separate histories.

Opinion surveys show that Czech society is gradually coming to differentiate between Germany and the expelled Germans. While there is a slow growth in friendliness and tolerance towards Germany, attitudes towards the demands of the SL remain cool to openly negative. This view has its rational core (even if there is some admixture of emotive stereotypes), which as a historian Hahn undoubtedly realises. The development of the post-1989 dialogue between Czechs and "their", former Germans has not exactly been conducive to differentiated perceptions of a Sudeten German community that still presents itself through the SL as monolithic in opinion. The only exception here is the position (set out in March 1988) of the German Circle of Friends of German-Czech Understanding/*Freundeskreis deutsch-tschechischer Verständingung*, which notes that only about 8% off the expellees are members of organisations forming the SL and rejects the SL as the exclusive representative of the expelled group. Yet the fact remains that the influence of the *Circle of Friends* is limited to a few tens or hundreds of people. Its significance lies in the mere fact of its existence rather than in the number of its supporters.[36]

---

[35] Hahn, E. – Hahn, H.-H. 2002. *Sudetoněmecká vzpomínání a zapomínání* [Sudeten German Remembering and Forgetting]. Prague: Votobia. In regard to Eva Hahn I regard it as necessary to note the significant change in the overall tone of her assessment of Czech-Sudeten-German relations in studies published at an interval of six years. If Eva Hahn had published her more recent study in 1990, it might have had a very healthy effect on the course of Czech-Sudeten German relations. As it is, this is more a book of "belated reportage", but is nonetheless a valuable contribution to the understanding of Sudeten German circles and their intellectual background.

[36] The Circle of Friends of German-Czech Understanding regularly publishes a bulletin carrying information about its activities (e.g. The regular Meetings on the Gold Road), and sometimes opinion pieces on significant events in Czech-German relations. See *Informator* – occasional circular of the Club/Rundbrief des Freundeskreises deutsch-tschechischer Verständigung. The club published a critical view of the form in which the SL information office in Prague had been set up, in March 2003.

Everything suggests that the constitutive element of Sudeten-German collective identity in relation to the Czech Lands continues to be the dogma of ethnic struggle/*Volkstumkampf*. According to Hahn, this is still the lens through which Sudeten Germans perceive and describe Czech-German relations.[37] Czechs are not on the whole well informed about this Sudeten German perspective (the views that appear regularly in the *Sudetendeutsche Zeitung* are very rarely presented in the CR), but even so they tend not to identify the expellee ideology with democratic Germany. I therefore consider it misleading to regard the majority Czech rejection of Sudeten demands as an expression of mass anti-German sentiment in Czech society and ethnic intolerance (which in the 1990s was the almost fashionable claim of some Czech publicists calling for the revision of "old" points of view – but also of the hard core of the SL).[38] On the contrary, there is plenty of evidence in Czech society of an ability to differentiate between different aspects of Czech-German relations when forming judgments.

Fears of Germany – A Reduced State Syndrome?

Research on inter-ethnic relations is confirming the general principle[39] that an ethnic group's increasing consciousness of its own unequal position leads to the hardening of negative stereotypes of the "other" and a heightened sense of threat. L. Hagendoorn argues that the conflict potential of inter-ethnic relations is affected by factors of ethnic "competition", among which he identifies the combination of power of numbers, social position (economic, political and cultural power), historical role and international ties. The Czech attitude to Germans is undoubtedly affected by the fact that the Germans are seen as the former "rulers", politicians, economists or cultural rivals, and sometimes the representatives of a "fifth column" (in the case of the Sudeten Germans).[40]

Research into the way that opinion stereotypes are used in inter-ethnic relations indicates that these stereotypes are multi-dimensional and involve response to specific characteristics of the target group. The sheer process of comparison between Czechs and Germans in conditions of relative deprivation

37 Hahn, E. – Hahn, H.-H. *Sudetoněmecká vzpomínání a zapomínání*. 11.
38 That the continual repetition of these claims is not without effect in German society is suggested by the views of a young left-wing journalist as presented by A. Wagnerová: "You Czechs have got rid of all your minorities over the centuries. You expelled the Sudeten Germans, you got rid of the Slovaks and now you want to do the same with the Roma." Wagnerová, A. "Nevypočitatelnosti symbolické politiky". 10.
39 Hagendoorn, L. 1997. "The Perception of National and Ethnic Outgroups as a Threat in Central and Eastern Europe". Paper for the ESF Conference. February 1997. Prague.
40 For more detail see L. de Jong's classification of groups of ethnic Germans in Central and Eastern Europe set out above.

(arising among Czechs above all from consciousness of the economic "inadequacy" symbolised in simplified form by the the marks/euros and crowns exchange rate), strengthens tendencies to adopt nationalist attitudes and negative stereotypes. In this respect they are to a greater or lesser degree a response to social reality.[41]

The interpretation of the attitudes of Czech society to the Germans is not such a simple matter, however, because the opinions expressed need not necessarily represent only a tendency to defensive nationalism but may to a certain extent be an expression of patriotism, which we may regard as a positive emotional tie representing consciousness of group solidarity and identification with language, national and cultural environment – i.e. expressions of national identity.[42]

The problem of Czech national identity in relation to Germany resides in the fact that all the basic factors have changed: above all, Germany itself has changed (it is now a developed democracy with many mechanisms built into the political system to prevent possible nationalist recidivism), the geopolitical situation has changed (the reunified Germany has become an ally not an enemy, but at the same time its influence has grown), and finally Czech society itself has changed, even if deeper structural changes have not yet occurred in social consciousness and it shows some elements of continuity and even inertia.

A research project on Czech national identity[43] in the mid-1990s identified some basic features of Czech society in its attitudes to foreigners which undoubtedly also affect views of Germans. First and foremost, it is important to bear in mind that Czech society has been unusually and unprecedentedly ethnically homogeneous (94.8% of the population identify as ethnic Czechs) since the expulsion of the German-speaking population of the Czech Lands and the destruction (or permanent flight) of most of the Jewish population in the Holocaust. The "typical member" of Czech society is a Czech-speaking person with Czech citizenship, of Czech origin, who has lived most of his life in his place of birth, has close ties to it, no aspirations to move anywhere else, and little or no personal experience of life abroad. He therefore naturally tends to have feelings of "fear, caution and distrust" towards foreigners (Kostelecký, Nedomová, 1996).

Also identified, however, were certain expressions of a "defensive structure" of national identity which goes beyond such feeling and actively seeks to reject

---

[41]   Ibidem.

[42]   Scruton, R. 1989. *Slovník politického myšlení* (heslo Nacionalismus) [Dictionary of Political Thought (entry for Nationalism)]. Brno: Atlantis. 75.

[43]   Kostelecký, T. – Nedomová, A. 1995. *Czech National Identity – Basic Results of National Survey*. Prague: Sociologický ústav AV ČR. ISSP, Research Project, 1,111 respondents, data collected in November 1995 (chance selection method).

foreign influence.[44] These may be more the consequence of relatively recent experience of the double loss of sovereignty (1938 and 1968) than of a desire to enforce a "splendid isolation". In the 1990s these 'defensive" elements of social consciousness were most in evidence in relation to Russia, as the successor state to the Soviet Union and according to the majority of Czechs a continuing potential threat to state sovereignty (the persisting effects of the invasion of Czechoslovakia by Warsaw Pact armies in 1968).

Germany remained in second place in the order of potential threats. The progressive deterioration of Czech-German relations from the high point of 1989/90, which reached its lowest point so far in the spring of 2002 as a result of pressures for the revocation of the Beneš Decrees, encouraged the trend of growing distrust for the large neighbour, and we might expect changes in attitude at the civic level to reflect this "new" state of Czech-German relations.

Graph 1: Reasons for the failure to achieve a settlement in Czech-German Relations

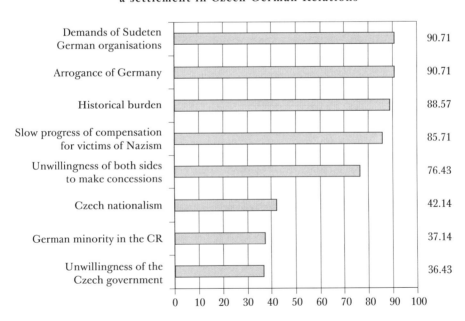

Category	Value
Demands of Sudeten German organisations	90.71
Arrogance of Germany	90.71
Historical burden	88.57
Slow progress of compensation for victims of Nazism	85.71
Unwillingness of both sides to make concessions	76.43
Czech nationalism	42.14
German minority in the CR	37.14
Unwillingness of the Czech government	36.43

Source: *Analysis and the expected development of border areas CR/FRG. Research Project of the Ministry of Foreign Affairs of the CR. Gaius/TNS Factum 2003.*
Source: *Sociological survey of the Czech Borderlands CR/SR – 2003*

---

[44] J. Křen noted the defensive reaction in Czech society to the perception of its own history back in 1988 and suggested that it was *inter alia* a consequence of the crisis of history (the discipline) in both West and East. "The attitude of the public to history seems today to have split in two. Both sides, the lack of interest and the interest, in many respects have a common cause. This is above all a defensive reaction to the crisis of history and the writing of history." Křen, J. 1992. *Historické proměny češství*. Prague: Karolinum. 9.

Nonetheless, in a survey of opinion conducted in the Czech borderlands in October 2003, 23% of respondents expressed the view that a settlement had already essentially been reached in Czech-German relations, with half saying that they considered a partial settlement had been reached.[45]

Another finding of the mid-1990s survey on national identity was that in practical life people in the CR make no distinction between citizenship and nationality/ethnicity. By a "real Czech" is meant someone who automatically possesses Czech citizenship and nationality. In fact this finding, if confirmed in the future, could be seen as involving an element of tolerance rather than the reverse.

Attitudes display two traditionally frequently noted features of Czech national character (if we concede the value of this construct just in the sense of a typology expressing tendencies to take certain attitudes): pragmatism and scepticism. The survey on national identity, like other surveys (e.g. conducted in the Czech borderlands[46]), confirms that Czechs are highly self-critical. One of the main reasons for low valuation of own nation was a lack of individual unmediated experiences with members of other nations.[47] A basis for distinction between the characters of different nations (however much the construct may be regarded as hypothetical) clearly has a place in the Czech social consciousness. Images of other nations or ethnic groups differ significantly. Hence the national aspect (in the neutral sense), expressed by the term "national character" may be considered a relevant part of the thinking and attitudes of ordinary people.

Both the *National Identity* project and surveys of attitudes to the Germans in the Czech borderlands suggest that the Czech population suffers from a syndrome that may with a certain hyperbole be called, "undermined or inadequate national self-confidence". People are markedly critical in their views of the supposed features of Czech "national" character and are similarly critical of their own contemporary state. Their sources of national pride/self confidence in order of importance are first the history of the Czech state, then art and literature, and third sports successes.[48] By contrast economic performance, the functioning of the political system and other indicators are rated poorly.

---

[45] 18% thought that there and been no settlement and 12 % had no opinion. See the results of a sociological survey conducted in all 13 districts of the Czech borderlands adjoining the FRG. The size of the sample of 789 respondents meets the criteria of a representative survey. The research was carried out as part of the project, "The Civic Dimensions of Czech-German Relations in the Phase of Czech Accession to the European Union – with an emphasis on the border areas." *CR Academy of Sciences Programme of Support for Targetted Research* (identification code IBS7028301).

[46] Zich, F. *Národnostní a etnické vztahy v českém pohraničí.*

[47] Ibidem. 20.

[48] Results of the surveys *The Czech Borderlands 91–96* and *Česká národní identita 95* [Czech National Identity 95]. Czech self-image was explored by research projects using the method of semantic differential, in which the

A closer examination of the structure of Czech national consciousness suggests that essentially there exist two sources of "self-confidence". The first is the *cultural type* (history, art, literature, sport, science, technology), i. e. everything that is the result of the long-term development of society and exists relatively independently of the government and political system. The second type of pride (or its absence) is based on *evaluation of the current state* of the Czech Republic. The degree of pride expressed correlates with the personal profile of respondents.[49] This is a finding relevant to the formation of the attitudes of Czechs to Germans. The personal characteristics of respondents (age, level of education, social situation, political orientation) have an important bearing on their levels of tolerance in regard to Germans (and foreigners in general).

Germany Unified and Emancipated

The subject of German identity is very large and complicated and the aspects that we touch on here are only those with a direct bearing on the Czech-German relationship.

As the key determining moment in the modern history of Germany, the ever-returning theme of the Nazi era and its crimes has fundamentally affected German national identity and is an integral element in the search for German national identity. Throughout the post-war era, most Germans connected their identity with the newly integrated form of Europe, since this identification allowed them to distance themselves from the tragic past and share democratic values with their allies in NATO and European organisations.

Surveys have nonetheless shown that citizens of the FRG have not ceased to be proud of being Germans[50] and this pride has grown stronger since the reunification of the country in 1990. In this context some authors speak of a "substitute" identity characterising the post-war development of German society in the Cold War period when Germans were seeking a way to distance themselves from the Nazi era.

The current phase of the process of "coming to terms with the past" is the result of the trend in an increasingly confident, reunited Germany to seek emanci-

tendency of Czechs to exaggerated self-criticism emerged through the respondents' attribution to Czechs of negative characteristics (insincerity, unhelpfulness, unreliability, dishonesty etc.). For details see Ibidem. 17–20.

49   Kostelecký, T. – Nedomová, A. *Czech National Identity*. 10.

50   Noelle-Neumann, E. – Köcher, R. 1987. *Die verletzte Nation* (Über den Versuch der Deutschen, ihren Charakter zu ändern). Stuttgart: Deutsche Verlags-Anstalt. 29 ff. An international comparative survey showed that in the mid-1980s the number of Germans (83%) expressing pride in their own state, its history and achievements (83%) was similar to the proportion in other major Western nations (Great Britain, France, Italy etc.).

pation from the past. Even members of the former rebel generation of 1968 are refusing to continue to see Germans simply as perpetrators, and through the reinterpretation of the historical factor of the flight and expulsion/*Flucht und Vertreibung* of ethnic Germans from Central and Eastern Europe are discovering a large group of Germans who were themselves victims of the conflagration of the war. It is as if by finding sympathy with this group and a new perception of their tragic destiny, Germany is finding redemption from the feelings of guilt that for decades traumatised a society which now wants to be finally rid of the stigma of Nazism.[51]

Not only the rightwing conservative part of the political spectrum but the left too has started to feel this sympathy for the expellees. The symbolic turning point in German culture in this respect was the literary "event of the season", Günter Grass's novel *Im Krebsgang* about the fate of a young German woman escaping from East Prussia in the last months of the war on board the ship *Wilhelm Gustloff*, which was torpedoed by a Russian submarine. Most of the refugees perish and the others in one way or another suffer the hard lot of refugees. A whole range of similar stories are appearing and the theme of flight and expulsion has been dominating the German media market.[52] Another theme that German society is currently re-evaluating is the Allied bombing campaign against Nazi Germany. In the light of the large numbers of civilian casualties German authors and journalists are now writing about "air terror"[53] and the massacre of innocents.

The Germans' new view of their own history evidently springs from their sense of need to grasp the modern history of their country with moral confidence, and this requires that the vision of a nation of "perpetrators" be transformed into the vision of a nation of "victims". This change has been aptly characterised in an article entitled *Die Deutschen als Opfer* (The Germans as Victims) in the weekly, *Der Spiegel*.

---

[51] "I soon discovered that the barrier (in Czech relations) has been created by a piece of history that we – the generation of 1980, hadn't taken enough interest in. Back then we felt a keen sense of solidarity with human rights, with the victims of expulsion everywhere in the world, but we weren't aware of the fate of of of expellees in our own country." "The master work of reconciliation" (interview with s A. Vollmer). *Nová Přítomnost* 9/1996. 10.

[52] G. Knopp's television documentary series *Flucht und Vertreibung* achieved viewing figures that exceeded all expectations. Other important literary works on the theme included among many others W. Kempowski: *Echolot* or T. Dückers: *Himmelskörper*. The new interest in and intepretation of the theme of flight and expulsion is examined in the article "Die Deutschen als Opfer". *Spiegel* 13. 25. 3. 2002. 36–64, and the single-theme issue of the theoretical review *Die Neue Gesellschaft-Frankfurter Hefte 12*. Dezember 2002. "Das Thema: Friedensordnung Europa-Flucht und Vertreibung".

[53] See e.g. the series of articles "Der Bombenkrieg gegen die Deutschen" in the weekly *Der Spiegel* 2–5/2003, or Friedrich, J. 2003. *Der Brand. Deutschland im Bombenkrieg 1940–1945*. Propyläen Verlag. Hage, V. 2003. *Zeugen der Zerstörung* (Die Literatur und der Lufkrieg). S. Fischer Verlag. Nossack, H. E. 2002. *Der Untergang*. Suhrkamp Verlag. Neillands, R. 2002. *Der Krieg der Bomber*. Berlin: Quintessenz Verlag, aj.

Thus, more than a half century after the end of the Second World War, a theme that seemed to have been long forgotten has caused a great stir in the normal calm of the Berlin Republic. The psychologically less burdened post-war German generation (including the left, which had hitherto held back), started to take a deeper interest in flight and expulsion.[54] This internal change could not but have consequences for the further course of Czech-(Sudeten) German dialogue, since it led to reinterpretation on the German side of the external social and political framework of mutual relations between the Czech Republic and Germany.

Intellectually, the road to the new situation had been opened much earlier by the (already mentioned) "dispute of the historians", which took place in the 1980s particularly on the pages of the papers *Die Welt* and the *Frankfurter Allgemeine Zeitung* and raised the problem of interpretation of the Nazi period and attitude to the Holocaust. At this point conservative historians (but also a number of politicians) were seeking to "reinterpret" or "normalise" German history and so permit the development of a more confident and politically ambitious sense of national identity. With German reunification this is indeed happening. This time the debate has involved not just a group of conservatively orientated historians, but influential groups of liberal German intellectuals, and – to judge by the mass response to the theme of flight and expulsion in German society, a considerable part of the general public in the FRG. There are signs, however, that the historical consciousness of Germans will continue to be ambivalent and very variable between groups (for example apart from differences related to political orientation and age, there are also significant divergences in view between inhabitants of the old and the new federal lands).

There are some fears that several key figures such as Joschka Fischer who are critics of the radical nationalists will be leaving government after the next elections and so will no longer be in a position to actively influence German politics and put brakes on the revisionist campaigns of the "Young-German right" that might ultimately detrimentally affect the democratic civil and peaceful foundations of Germany in the cause of "nation, ethnic self-definition, the power state and hegemony".[55]

It would be a mistake to see the undeniable sense of national identity as merely an internal feeling of ethnicity (this applies both to Germans and Czechs). The perception of what is specific to the nation is something that

---

[54]   "The expulsion was on of the biggest taboos of post-war history, and strictly avoided by the left including Günter Grass. The mass response to the novel is attested by the fact that in the first five days after it was launched on the market on the 5th of February 2002 it sold 110,000 copies." See Hojdová, K. "Günter Grass šlape na paty Potterovi" [Günter Grass Close on the Heels of H. Potter]. *Lidové noviny*. 23. 2. 2002.

[55]   Fischer, J. 1995. *Risiko Deutschland*. München: Knaur. See the "Czech Republic and Germany".

changes in terms of content and with regard to historical-social circumstances. This applies to Germany to the highest degree. Different variants and traditions of German nationalism have existed beside each other for a long time and have come to the fore in particular different situations. However much they overlap, they are rarely identical. Culturally, economically and politically they represent different kinds of nationalism that have found reponse and application in Germany over the last two centuries. Margaret Thatcher, for example, shares the view that since Bismarck's unification of Germany, Germany has lurched unpredictably between aggression and self-doubt.[56]

Instrumentally politicised nationalism came into play in many forms, from the ultra-liberal to the extremely reactionary. The nationalist or Pan-Germanist variant reached its peak in the Nazi era but represented only one of the possibilities. In addition, the very definition of Germany itself underwent transformations and was regularly the subject of discussion by the nationalists themselves.[57]

In view of the fact that the earlier "dispute of the historians" over modern German history has contributed to the formation of a renewed German identity, it is illuminating to quote the opinions of one of the main protagonists in the dispute, E. Nolte. Central to his position is the shift of emphasis from Nazism to communism, as a basis for a relativising approach to the question of guilt. "What characterised the theory of German guilt was its one-sidedness. It is unconditionally necessary to get over this one-sidedness, because it is unjust to put all the blame on the Germans. The decisive year of the 20th century is after all not 1933, but 1917. The positive consequence of getting free of the feeling of guilt will be that we shall not have to reconcile ourselves to the Americanisation of the world, the Americanisation of civilisation, but will fight for our identity and difference. National socialism represented a revolt against the American standardising hegemony... it is possible that at the end of this century Germany will become the leading nation in Europe. National socialism is an inheritance that Germany must not entirely throw away."[58]

---

[56] Thatcher, M. "Německý problém a rovnováha síly" [The German Problem and the Balance of Power], in *Roky na Downing Street*. 541.

[57] Evans, R. J. *Rereading German History*. 214.

[58] Nolte, E. – Interview in the newspaper *La Stampa*, 19. 5. 1993. See Bělohradský, V. "Proti státu Evropa" [Against the Europe State], in *Společné pohledy na Evropu* 14. 1998. Mayer, F. (ed.). Prague: CEFRES. 79–80. Four years later Bělohradský took an even more trenchant line: "The European Union is being abused (he refers to E. Stoiber) as the loud trumpet of German viewpoints, and the deputy Posselt presents himself as the holder of the keys to Europe – something that is in scandalous violation of the ideal of European unification." "Noví výrobci křivých rovnítek" [The New Manufacturers of Crooked Measuring Rods]. *Právo*. 25. 5. 2002. By contrast G. Craig argues that the need to seek a new German identity, emancipated from the shadow of the Nazi era that had constantly fallen on all post-war generations of Germans, had emerged and been expressed much earlier than at the moment of unification. He cites M. Stürmer. "Germany needed a new way of teaching history that would be consensual and would promise "direction signs to identity" and give the Germans "the chance to recognize themselves again". Craig, G. A. 1991. *The Germans*. London/New York: Penguin Books. 340.

There is much in V. Bělohradský's view that the rational core of German historical revisionism is the need for Germans to be able to identify with their history and for Germany to become a normal nation state. The current interest of German society in ethnic Germans and their flight and expulsion in the years 1944–1946 supports the relevance of this idea. It is with this pragmatic that Nolte reinterprets the evil of Nazism as just a response to the violence, humiliation and irrationality brought into European history by the First World War and communism.[59]

However, it is impossible not to question whether the theory of German search for a normal history is compatible with the pro-European rhetoric and arguments of Germans as the "engine of European integration". Bělohradský replies by citing Helmut Kohl: "I feel myself to be a German European and a European German. These two things are inseparable." Bělohradský sees this two-track German patriotism as a rhetoric that hides the real problem, i.e. "the united Germany is progressively becoming a normal nation state which is tough in the defence of its specific national interests".[60] He finds some evidence for this view in German policy in the conflict situations of the former Yugoslavia and the South Tyrol.

We find T. G. Ash expressing a similar view: "Since Germany has recovered the full sovereignty of a nation state there are arresting contradictions between – let us say – the architecture of Berlin and the rhetoric of Bonn. Indeed, Germany is finding itself in political-psychological conditions that can be characterised only in Faustian terms – two souls in a single body.[61]

The Return of Mitteleuropa?

Just before the introduction of the single European currency, the political leaders of Germany made it clear in private that currency union was the price for the unification of Germany. The unspoken answer to the question of why Ger-

---

[59] The way in which Sudeten German intellectuals pose the historical and legal question of the transfer is also part of the revisionist context. The revisionist concept of the transfer can be characterised as follows: Nazism and the expulsion of the Sudeten Germans are aspects of the same history. The typical revisionist position is that Czechs need to admit that they sinned in the same way as the Nazis, that the Czechoslovakia of Masaryk and Beneš, just like Hitler's Germany, committed crimes against humanity, which we can now resolve in a new "democratic European spirit". Bělohradský, V. "Revizionismus a německá identita" [Revisionism and German Identity]. *Lidové noviny*. 12. 6. 1995.

[60] Bělohradský, V. *Společné pohledy na Evropu*. 78. The author at the same time points out the potentially negative consequences for German foreign policy: "The revisionists are dragging pro-European and liberal Germans back to "conventional identity", back to the tribal concept of the state that is the tragedy of German political culture." Bělohradský, V. "Revizionismus a německá identita".

[61] Ash, T. G. "Europe's Endangered Liberal Order". *Foreign Affairs* 2/March-April 1998 (LXXVII). 37–58.

many had to give up her Deutschmark was – because Germans cannot trust themselves.[62] But the younger generation are asking "Why not?" Many of them see no reason why the Germans should be tied like Odysseus to the mast to prevent themselves being seduced by the sirens' song. Many are convinced that Germany is a proper liberal state of civilised Europe, an equal among equals, and has a claim to be regarded as such.

Public opinion surveys indicated that Germans were against giving up the DM because they saw in it a symbol of postwar advance, the economic power of the new Germans, the economic expression of renewed national identity.[63]Several months after the introduction of the Euro in 2002 German retailers started showing prices in marks alongside euros, in order to capitalise on the mood of a German public nostalgic for the period of price stability of the German currency.

The spectrum of views on the possible future development of the role of Germany (and the attitude of the German public to European integration) is wide and diverse. At one end of the spectrum are those who emphasise with suspicion that Germany is the only big nation in Europe to define itself ethnically (V. Bělohradský). At the other, economic arguments are presented to show that Germany's deliberate self-restraint and caution is reassuring its immediate neighbour states (including the CR), and confirming its support for the concept of interdependence, and that it would now be far too costly for Germany to abandon this policy in some third attempt to create a German economic empire on the European continent.[64]

Having learned from the past, Germany is exercising its influence on the post-communist countries of Eastern and Central Europe in a far more cultivated and refined way, exploiting not only the financial power of the German economy but also the advanced state of its political institutions and its civil society. It is clear that the power elites of Germany respect the lessons of modern history. German foreign policy functions in two ways applied in parallel, i.e. traditional governmental foreign policy goes hand in hand with German social foreign policy/*gesellschaftliche Aussenpolitik*. Most big German institutions run their own foreign relations.[65] Characteristically, they make binding agreements

---

62   Ibidem. 58.

63   Ibidem.

64   Berghahn, V. 1996. *Quest for Economic Empire*. Providence/Oxford: Berghahn Books. 33. On this theme Bělohradský adds, however, that "Many Europeans believe that on the contrary Europe is increasingly disappearing under Germany, and that this is the main problem of the post-bipolar order in Europe. On German lips the word Europe is always a threat – that is the constant of European history from Bismarck to Kohl. Let us notice it". Bělohradský, V. "Evropa jako výhružka" [Europe as a Threat]. *Lidové noviny*. 14. 6. 1995.

65   Of fundamental importance in this context is the role of German political and cultural foundations operating in the countries of Central and Easter Europe, which represent instruments of external influence on the course of transformation processes. Foundations embody the continuity of the long-term practice employed

with partner institutions in other countries, and this strengthens or creates models (agendas) of trans-national relations.[66] This technique provides German political actors with abundant opportunities to intervene indirectly in the environment of the domestic politics of Central European states without risking offence or a charge of arrogance. This is the distinctive style of contemporary German foreign policy, which is "becoming institutionalised and internalised" (Jeremiah Riemer).[67] One example has been the creation of the electoral systems in the Central European countries, in which the German CDU and SPD parties took an intensive part, as did the British conservatives or the American democrats and republicans.[68]

The role of German lawyers in the drawing up of constitutions for the states of Central and Eastern Europe has been similarly substantial yet discrete. Foundations of the different political parties of the FRG operate in the Czech Republic and other countries of the region and German institutional models are likewise evident in the economy and financial sphere. The independent *Deutsche Bundesbank* has had a very strong formative role on the creation and development of national banks.

There is a good deal of evidence that expressions of "revived" German national identity are influencing the formation of the fundamental principles of the post-communist states of Central and Eastern Europe, not excluding the Czech Republic. The question remains the extent to which the individual aspects of this new interdependence are planned or simply expressions of the *spontaneous predominance* of the German template as the functionally most advanced political and economic model for the area concerned. Probably there is a degree of combination of the planned and spontaneous in each case.

In terms of Germany's economic role in the region, however, the evidence for German resurgence is more limited. Despite an imposing growth in trading ac-

---

by Germany since the times of Bismarck, i.e. the funding of so-called middle-mediating organisations that function at home and abroad in matters that would otherwise be affairs for government, although if government intervened in them directly this would provoke complications in bilateral relations. "Germany developed ideal instruments to project its interests and authority abroad. They are the party-affiliated foundations (hereafter referred to as political foundations. (See chapter 5: Agents of Projection: German Political Foundations.) Another important instrument of informal German influence in Central Europe is the "broad cultural compatibility" of the area in which the German language used to be the *lingua franca.*" Phillips, A. L. "Agents of Projection: German Political Foundations", in *Power and Influence after the Cold War*. Lanham/ Boulder/New York/Oxford: Rowman & Littlefield Publishers. 119–128.

66 Katzenstein, P. *Mitteleuropa – between Europe and Germany*. 24–25.

67 Also notable are this author's views on the transformations of the political system of post-war Germany in the context of the extensive debate on the Holocaust/Shoah in the later 1990s, in which he draws attention to the problematic nature of attributiing guilt to the post-war generation of Germans, who as Kohl remarked, were "granted the pardon of being born late". Riemer, J. M. "Grace? Under Pressure?" (The Goldhagen Controversy after Two Years), in *Germany's Difficult Passage to Modernity*. 1999. Lankowski, C. (ed.). New York/Oxford: Berghahn Books. 212–226.

68 Katzenstein, P. *Mitteleuropa – between Europe and Germany*. 25.

tivities since 1990, Germany has achieved only a one third share of the foreign exchange of goods and volume of investments in Central European countries.[69] It should be remembered here that exports represent the vital element of the German economy. The lasting *export character of the German economy* was the answer to the post-war division of the country and loss of part of German territory to Poland. In the 1980s West Germany became the biggest world exporter, which also meant considerable dependence on the world market, over which Germany had little control.

In the light of this fact, there is no need to view German activities in Central Europe as simply a recidivist return to a former expansionism. Pressures to maintain economic growth in the conditions of a globalised economy are urgent in Germany as in other countries. This may be the main reason why the German economy took such rapid action in the first months of the 1990 with the result that *joint-ventures* involving German firms formed 30–40% of such ventures in Poland and the former Czechoslovakia. At the same time Russia's share of foreign trade with the countries of Central Europe fell drastically, reflecting the political changes and the disruption of the economy of the former Soviet Union.

The relatively low figures for German trade with Central and Eastern European countries might also be interpreted as the result of cautious attitudes to Germany on the side of the partner states (including the CR), whether based on prejudice or long-term experience with their big neighbour. Fears of Germany are finding expression in a number of European states. For example in Poland.[70] Similar suspicions about the goals of the German economy have been voiced in British politics. Let us remember, for example, Margaret Thatcher's regular confidential consultations with leading British and American historians on whether the new Germany was genuinely different from the old.[71] Cautious,

---

[69] Ibidem. 26.

[70] The growing demands of the German minority in Opole Silesia, which already has a substantial share in local government and where in line with the Polish-German Treaty many of its demands have been met, have been very badly received by Polish society, which is aware of the surprising relative foot-dragging in German fulfilment of treaty obligations to the Polish minority in Germany. Lesiuk, W. "Dánsko-německé zkušenosti z využití demokratických metod při řešení národnostních problémů etnického pomezí a interetnické poměry Opolského Slezska" [Danish-German Experiences of the use of democratic methods to solve nationality problems of the ethnic border and interethnic relations in Opole Silesia]. *Slezský sborník* 2/1994. 132.

[71] The fundamental turning point of the reunification of Germany was preceded at the beginning of the year 1990 by dramatic discussions that took place in the group of historians invited to her official summer residence Chequers by the British prime minister Margaret Thatcher. There was much talk of the cruelty, aggression and unreliability of Germans in history. The popular cabinet minister N. Ridley let himself get carried away in the debate and compared H. Kohl to Hitler, and had to resign as a consequence. All this reflected the widespread fears in the Conservative Party at the prospect of a new role for Germany. Evans, R. J. *Rereading German History*. François Mitterrand's statement that "Czechs, Poles and Hungarians will not want to be under exclusive German influence, but will need German help and investment" were prophetic. In the same context Thatcher recalls the speed with which H. Kohl seized the chance to act independently, so that as

distrustful attitudes to Germany are regularly voiced by some politicians, intellectuals and businessmen in France, Britain and the Netherlands.[72]

Fears are sometimes expressed that the businessmen and bankers of the new Germany are pursuing some version of the earlier *Grossraum Politik*. These are rather contradicted and sidelined, however, by the obvious fact that the foreign policy and the economy of the FRG represent many different interests that often cancel each other out and in which no one has managed to demonstrate any unifying direction aimed at German dominance in Europe. The fears of Germany's neighbours are less reactions to anything in current German policy and more extrapolations of historical experience with the expansionist concept of Germany's role in Europe, occasionally encouraged by the statements of a few German politicians (for example Klaus Kinkel's comment on the Potsdam "protocol" or the support voiced by leaders of German political parties for the expellee organisations).[73]

In France, debate on the "German question" became more intense at the end of the 1980s (although it has been continuing uninterrupted since 1945). Controversial issues in this context included the attitude of German diplomacy on the eve of the collapse of Yugoslavia, and also the suggestion made by F. W. Christians (*Deutsche Bank*) to Eduard Shevardnadze that Kaliningrad (earlier *Königsberg* – East Prussia) should be "Europeanised" as a "centre for the exchange of people, ideas, capital and goods". The ever-suspicious French press saw this as a sign of far-reaching ambition, especially in combination with the idea that the city could be attractive for settlers from the ranks of the Volga Germans (deported by Stalin to Central Asia and Siberia).

Although a whole range of German scientists, intellectuals and politicians, and above all the real functioning of a pluralist democratic political system, testifies to the deep and pervasive rebirth of Germany, the doubts remain. In

---

early as February 1990, without consulting the allies he gained Gorbachev's agreement to the principle that "the Germans themselves must decide on the unity of the German people". Thatcher, M. *The Downing Street Years*. London: Harper/Collins. 545. In talks with M. Thatcher on the 20th of January 1990 French President F. Mitterrand said that the Germans had a right to self-determination but did not have a right to upset the political reality in Europe. He complained that the Germans were rejecting every mention of caution as an affront to them and added that he was disturbed by the so-called German "mission" in Central Europe. Ibidem.

[72] Berghahn, V. R. "German Big Business and the Quest for a European Economic Empire in the Twentieth Century", in *Quest for Economic Empire*. 2.

[73] We have already mentioned the formalised acts of support for the expellees by all the parties in the German political spectrum. Here we may cite the view of Eva Hahn, supported by a series of sociological surveys conducted in the American occupation zone, that "almost all Germans regard the transfer of Germans from Eastern Europe to be unjust and illegal". The general disagreement of German society with the transfer was confirmed by the foreign policy of the FRG, which did not reconise the post-Munich German citizenship of the former Czechoslovak citizens. Nor did it recognise the legitimacy of the transfer with all the consequences arising from it. Hahn, E. – Hahn, H.-H. *Sudetoněmecká vzpomínání a zapomínání*. 18–19, 206.

this respect the reserved attitudes of sections of Czech society to Germany do not seem to me to constitute any special deviation from European attitudes and context in general.[74]

One theme often mentioned in connection with Germany (especially by politicians of the new member states of NATO and the European Union such as Poland or the Czech Republic) is the transatlantic dimension, understood as an insurance against any potential deviation of German policy from the "straight and narrow".

This situation has been explored in some detail by R. Kagan, who argues that the possibility of a sliding back into the past is precisely what disturbs Europeans even though Europe is meanwhile moving ahead. He claims that Europeans, above all the French and Germans, are not entirely sure whether the problem earlier known as the "German problem" has yet been truly solved. Neither Mitterrand's France nor Thatcher's Britain was enthusiastic at the prospect of the reunification of Germany after the Cold War. Each of these countries had to be persuaded and reassured by the Americans, just as four decades earlier British and French leaders had to be persuaded to agree to the re-admission of Germany to the international community. As the various and often very different proposals for a future European constitution show, the French are still unsure whether they can trust the Germans, and the Germans are still unsure if they can trust themselves.[75]

Fears of Germany do not persist only in Czech society (as a result of Czechs' alleged inability to come to terms with their own past), as some journalists seek to imply. Ultimately these fears are one of the motors for attempts to deepen European integration (including Germany's own fears about itself). In a speech at the Humboldt University in Berlin on the 12th of May 2000, Joschka Fischer warned that the European project had to succeed, because how else could the "risk and temptation objectively given by the size of Germany and its central position" be overcome. Kagan argues that the historical "temptation" of Germany continues to linger at the back of the minds of many Europeans.[76]

These fears are creating almost incredible situations. For example, when Chancellor Gerhard Schröder rejected George Bush's appeal for European sup-

---

[74] They are for example comparable with the long-term reserved and pragmatically motivated attitude of the Dutch towards Germany, as shown by surveys of public opinion. See Verheyen, D. "The Dutch and the Germans: Beyond Traumas and Trade", in Verheyen, D. – Søe, Ch. 1993. *The Germans and Their Neighbours*. Oxford: Westview Press. 59–80.

[75] Kagan, R. 2003. *Labyrint síly a ráj slabosti* [The Labyrinth of Power and the Paradise of Weakness]. Prague: Lidové noviny. 84.

[76] Ibidem. 85. Kagan is a respected scholar at the *Carnegie Endowment for International Peace* and his views should be taken seriously not only because of the depth of his analysis but also because they express to a significant extent the views of the American neo-conservative elite on how to solve the problems of the contemporary world and the role of the United States.

port for the USA's intervention in Iraq, saying that such matters should be solved "by the German method", this disquieted Germany's smaller neighbours even more than it did the United States. Kagan sees some irony in the fact that the chancellor's mere mention of the "German method" can alarm Europeans even when it is meant to express German pacificism and neutrality. As is obvious, attitudes to and assessments of German foreign policy coloured by "reminiscence" are far from the exclusive speciality of Czechs allegedly suffering from an inferiority complex.

All the same, Germany cannot really be expected to carry on demonstrating its "purity of intention" to its partners forever (especially in a situation when a large body of German society and political elites shares the view that Germany's penitence has been quite long enough and convincing enough already). Inevitably then, we shall have to reckon with the continuing subliminal presence of historical experience on the side of those partners, including the CR.

Election campaign in the village of Hinterhermsdorf close to the border with the Czech Republic.
The inhabitants distance themselves from right-wing extremists.

12 Germany and the Sudeten German Question in the Eyes of Public Opinion

In the later 1990s (1996–1999), a systematic continual survey was conducted in the Czech border areas (and partly on a national basis) on the attitudes of the Czech population to Germany. The survey focused on a few of the most important aspects of Czech-German relations, i.e. frequency of contact between citizens of the two states; perception of the influence of Germany on the accession of the Czech Republic to the EU; how citizens rate the role of the Czech-German Declaration; attitudes to the Sudeten German question; and how citizens rated the role of Germany as an important political, economic and culture partner/neighbour of the Czech Republic. A research survey in 2003 on the attitudes of members of local elites on both sides of the CR border with the federal lands of Saxony and Bavaria showed the German local leaders to be far more reserved about the progress of cooperation than their counterparts on the Czech side. Overall, cooperation at the level of towns and communities (sport, tourism, culture, education) was rated best, while cooperation on economic and security matters was rated poorly.[1]

The survey project was designed to provide Czech foreign-policy makers with a complex picture of the way in which Czech society sees relations with our most important neighbouring country, and so it takes particular account of

---

[1] For more detail see Research Project of the Ministry of Foreign Affairs of the CR (RB 6/5/3). *Analýza a předpokládaný vývoj hraničních oblastí ČR-SRN* [The Analysis and Anticipated Development of the Border Areas of the CR-FRG]. 2003. (Collective of authors). Unpublished study. Houžvička, V. 2004. Pohraniční oblasti v kontextu bilaterálních vztahů České republiky a SRN [The Border Areas in the Context of the Bilateral Relations of the CR and FRG], *Mezinárodní politika* 2/2004. 21–24.

the specific feature of bilateral relations known as the Sudeten German Question. The burden of history in mutual relations (although this is showing a tendency to fade in the younger age groups) continues to have emotional potential for the social mobilisation of Czech society if basic foreign-policy decisions are not in line with collectively shared opinions and attitudes (regardless of whether these opinions are considered to be rationally based or myths reproduced by the propagandist interpretation of the modern history of Czech-German relations).[2]

The results of the research indicated several basic features and trends that may be regarded as key determinants from the point of view of the long-term attitudes of Czech society to its German neighbour. Most of the public see current official relations between the Czech Republic and the Federal Republic as good.

The long-term trend of positive rating of mutual relations both at governmental and citizen level may be said to be continuing. Particularly in the border areas, activities in the framework of the CBC-PHARE and INTERREG programmes, and partnerships between schools and institutions, youth exchanges, town and community twinning and other forms of cooperation are having beneficial effects, as is the involvement of German businesses in the borderlands. All the same, from follow-up surveys of Czech-German relations at local and regional level (e.g. a survey of the intensity of inter-community cooperation on the Czech-Saxon border conducted by IÖR, Dresden in 1999[3]) it is clear that optimistic expectations of cooperation are strikingly higher on the Czech side. The pragmatic perceptions and evaluations of the situation that we encounter on the German side of the border in both Bavaria and Saxony are something of a corrective to the official optimism promoted by the Czech media.[4]

---

[2] For more detail on the results of research on Czech public opinion on Czech-German relations see the bulletin *Česko-německé souvislosti* [Czech-German Contexts] 1,2/2004. This was published in Czech, English and German versions by the Institute of Sociology, Academy of Sciences of the CR as part of the project "Občanská dimenze česko-německých vztahů ve fázi vstupu ČR do Evropské unie s důrazem na pohraniční oblasti" [Civic Dimensions of Czech-German Relations in the accession phase of the entry of the CR into the European Union with an Emphasis on Border Areas]. Academy of Sciences of the CR programme of support for targetted research and development. See also the project's web pages at http://www.borderland.cz.

[3] *Interkommunale Zusammenarbeit im böhmisch-sächsischen Grenzraum.* 1999. Müller, B. (ed.). Institut für Ökologische Raumentwicklung e.V. Texte Nr. 131. Dresden/Ústí n. L./Prague. Similar conclusions emerge from questionnaire surveys of representatives of local and regional elites conducted in the summer of 200 on the Czech-German borders in the Euro-region *Krušnohoří/Erzgebirge* and on the German-Polish borders in the Euro-region *Pro Europa Viadrina* as part of the project "The Role of Germany within the East Central Europe". Institute for German Studies. University of Birmingham.

[4] The findings of a survey conducted in 2003 on both the Czech and German side of the border show clearly that the German respondents (members of local elites) are much more sparing than their Czech counterparts in their praise when rating mutual relations. Co-operation on the level of towns and communities, and sometimes in sport, culture and education, is generally rated most highly. On the German side there is

Table 3: Assessment of the Development
of Czech-German Relations 1994–1998 (data in %)

In the period just gone by relations between the CR and FRG	1994 Sept.	1995 Feb.	1996 Feb.	1998 Feb.
Have definitely improved	9	9	2	6
Have tended to improve rather than worsen	40	37	12	53
Have remained the same	30	37	45	–
Have tended to worsen	9	8	26	14
Have definitely worsened	2	1	5	2
Don't know	10	8	10	25

Source: *Continual Survey IVVM 1994–1996. SOFRES/Factum 1998.*

Both ordinary citizens and representatives of state and local self-government bodies on the German side of the border consider the main obstacles to be Czech partners' lack of financial resources and legal-administrative incompatibilities between the Czech and German border areas. At the general level, members of the elites pick out three factors/sources of obstacles to German cooperation with neighbours to the East: these are language problems, different mentalities and economic disparity.

The long-term trend in the opinions of Czech society on the development of Czech-German relations is clear from the following graph. Over the long-

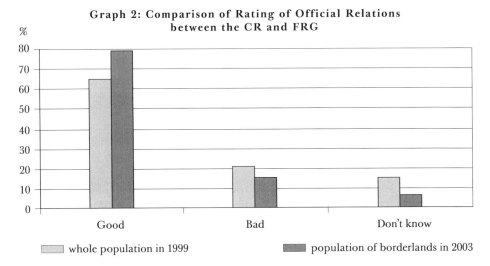

Graph 2: Comparison of Rating of Official Relations between the CR and FRG

whole population in 1999   population of borderlands in 2003

Source: *Analysis and the expected development of border areas CR/FRG. Research Project of the Ministry of Foreign Affairs of the CR. Gaius/TNS Factum 2003.*

notably more scepticism as regards cooperation in economic and security fields *Analýza a předpokládaný vývoj hraničních oblastí ČR – SRN.*

term, the majority of respondents consider Czech-German relations to be satisfactory; graduates, people with a right-wing political orientation and business
people are more likely than others to rate relations as good. The proportions of
opinions at the extreme ends of the spectrum, i.e. the view that Czech-German
relations are outstanding or entirely bad, have remained very small over the
years of survey.

In 2001, 76% of respondents considered relations with Germany to be good
or fairly good, and so it is clear that the relatively optimistic view of Czechs
on relations with their big neighbour is continuing into the new century. The
majority of Czechs consider relations with Germany to be economically advantageous and beneficial, and hope that it is possible to live in peace and quiet
with Germans. A certain caution persists, however, as we can see from the more
than 50% agreement with statements like: we must never allow ourselves to forget the Occupation; *Germany is a tough partner that does not give you anything for
nothing; Germany is first and foremost expanding its political and economic influence
eastwards; we must always be wary of Germans.*

Over the 1990s, the long-term trend of perceiving Germany as a politically
and economically strong partner with whom cooperation is advantageous continued. This trend indicated Czech respect for its Western neighbour, the efficiency of its economy, and its position on the international scene. A note of caution expressing historical experience with Nazi expansionism remained present
in attitudes, and also a certain doubt as to the goals of the German state with
regard to Central and Eastern Europe (in connection with Germany's active
support for the entry of the CR into the EU, which it had undertaken to give by
the 1992 Treaty with the CSFR).

Two thirds of respondents thought that Germany was striving to extend its
political and economic influence into Central and Eastern Europe, and almost
60% took the view that we should always be wary of Germans. *Two thirds, however, rejected the idea that Germany was a source of threat.* The number of people
who do believe that Germany is a potential threat to the Czech Republic, and
that we are always helpless against it, doubled to 20% of respondents in 1999
(in 1997 it was around 10%). Germany is considered a tough partner in negotiations (84%), and this, in combination with the view that we ought to show more
pride in relation to Germany, suggests a Czech lack of necessary self-confidence
in dealings with our larger neighbour. This lack of self-confidence is likewise
a long-term feature of Czech attitudes.

*Contacts with Germany are most often based on family or friends. Work and busi-
ness contacts with German firms are also important.* At citizen level, much the most
frequent reason for contacts with Germany was family or friends (24%). Work
as a reason for contacts was stated by 7% of respondents. In the border areas

the proportions are markedly higher. For example, in 1996 (the research pro-ject CR-FRG Borderlands) 48% of respondents said they had relatives or friends in Germany with whom they were in touch, and around 10% had work contacts.

Research in 1998 (on the specific group of people engaged in developing cross-border cooperation, i.e the *opinion leaders* type) showed an even higher proportion: 63% of respondents said that they had relatives and friends in Ger-many and as many as 68% that they had contacts arising from work.[5]

The predominant public view is that the quality of Czech-German cooperation is af-fected by the conflict-ridden past, differences in the efficiency of the economy, and dif-ferences in standard of living (compare this with the findings of a British project at the University of Birmingham which concluded that the barriers to cross-border coopera-tions were: language competence, mentality and economic inequality). In general, these factors may be regarded as obstacles to mutual cooperation in Czech-German relations generally, and not just in the border region issue.

The longitudinal programme of survey in the Czech borderlands includes a question on the perceived obstacles to Czech-German cooperation, and this allows us to see how opinions have developed since 1993. When comparing data, it needs to be borne in mind that the 1999 data are from a nation-wide sur-vey, while all the other data comes from the Czech border areas with Germany.

The table shows the public has been gradually attributing less and less im-portance to all types of obstacle in Czech-German relations with the exception of historical events, which have clearly been coming to the fore in attitudes. This is evidently a consequence of "return" to the past not just in Czech-Ger-man discourse but in European context, with the unintended consequence of an increasing tendency to "fight the battles of the past over again" (Daniel Cohn-Bendit).

In the nation-wide survey, the *historical memory* factor emerged as almost equal in weight to the economic obstacles to cooperation represented by the purchasing power of the currency and prices. Economic barriers can be ex-pected to diminish in importance as the Czech economy performs better, or possibly also as a consequence of continuing difficulties in the German econ-omy. Concurrently, however, the trend in attitudes indicates the long-term development of (or rather the return of) the factor of *the historical memory of Czech society*. In part this may be a spontaneous expression of the search for

---

[5] In this context it must, however, be emphasised that the two samples of respondents (in 1998 and 1999) were selected on a different basis and that a comparison between them has only qualified value. It mainly shows the difference between citizens personally involved in developing a new type of cross-border com-munity between the Czech Republic and Germany and an ordinary sample of citizens. Greater frequency of contacts in Germany is only to be expected among the former.

own identity in conditions of a value vacuum, and in part a reaction to the activities of the Sudetendeutsche Landsmannschaft in its attempts to exploit the phase of preparatory negotiations for Czech accession to the EU to get its claims adopted as positions of the EU organs (specifically the claim that the Beneš Decrees are incompatible with the legal norms of the *aquis communitaire*).

Table 4: Overview of Development of Views on the Factors Influencing Czech-German Co-operation

	1993	1994	1996	1997	1999	2003
Different language	44	39	47	43	36	42
Different national character	52	46	50	55	42	47
Efficiency of economy	83	73	79	78	70	70
Conflict-ridden past	40	44	57	62	69	70
Political system/interests of state	30	34	30	45	42	38
Inadequate transport communications	41	33	26	25	26	23
Lack of information	55	30	25	27	27	25

Note: the data present percentual share of answers expressing agreement in % according to surveys in the districts of the Czech-German border region.
The data for 1999 are taken from a longitudinal survey. Source: Instutute of Sociology, Academy of Sciences of the Czech Republic, longitudinal survey ČR (Department of Czech Borderland).

In Czech society, social consciousness and national identity (or mentality) have a strongly historicising character (see above for this issue as approached by Z. Suda and others), which is conditioned by the circumstances of its historical development and the competitive nature of Czech co-existence both with Germans in the Czech Lands and the powerful Germany as neighbour. Historical memory forms the emotional element in attitudes to Germany, and this is deep rooted. Another reason for the increasing historicisation of attitudes to Germany is the way that the Sudeten German organisations (especially the Sudetendeutsche Landsmannschaft) frame their own arguments: this is itself extemely historical and able to activate the conflictual potential of Czech-German relations, which had earlier been pushed into the lower layers of social consciousness. In any case, history has been returning in wider contexts (see particularly the theme of the holocaust), and not just in Czech-German relations.

The return of a historicising mode of thought (associated with demands for change in existing interpretations of key events in history) is encouraged by the *media* (repeated demands for the revocation of the Beneš Decrees, the re-opening of the Sudeten German question in Czech politics etc.) but also by the experience of sobering-up from the euphoric vision of conflict-free relations after 1989.

The long-term trend of historicising attitudes to Germany among the public should be taken into account by foreign-policy makers in the context of demands for the re-evaluation of important decisions taken by the former Czechoslovakia with regard to the Bohemian Germans. Czechs have a tendency to see Germany as a country that has the same or a greater influence than the other member states of the EU on the question of the acceptance of the CR into the European Union.

This further long-term feature of attitudes to the role of Germany in the process of the acceptance of our republic into the European Union has evidently rested on the perception of the FRG as a strong and at the same time a desirable partner. The graph below shows Czech views of the intensity of the influence of Germany on admission of the Czech Republic to the EU.

Graph 3: Comparison of the level of influence of Germany with that of other EU member states on the course of the CR's accession to the European Union

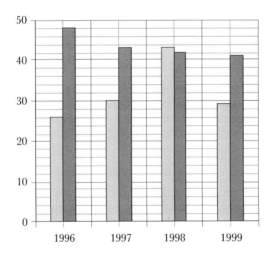

Note: The lefthand columns show the percentage of respondents who thought the FRG has greater capacity to influence our admission to the EU, while the righthand column gives the percentage of those who thought that the FRG has the same influence on the admission of the CR as other EU member states.
Source: *Institute of Sociology, the Academy of Sciences of the CR, (Department of Czech Borderland). Longitudinal Research Project of the Ministry of Foreign Affairs of the CR: Attitudes to Germany and the Sudeten German Question, 1997–1999.*

The results over time show a relatively stable, consistent and realistic evaluation of the role of Germany in the course of the Czech Republic's preparations for accession to the European Union. Between 40–50% of respondents have continued to believe that the FRG has the same influence as other member states on the Czech Republic's accession to the CR.

Graph 4: Share of views of the CR's entry to the EU among inhabitants of the Czech Borderlands adjacent to Bavaria and Saxony

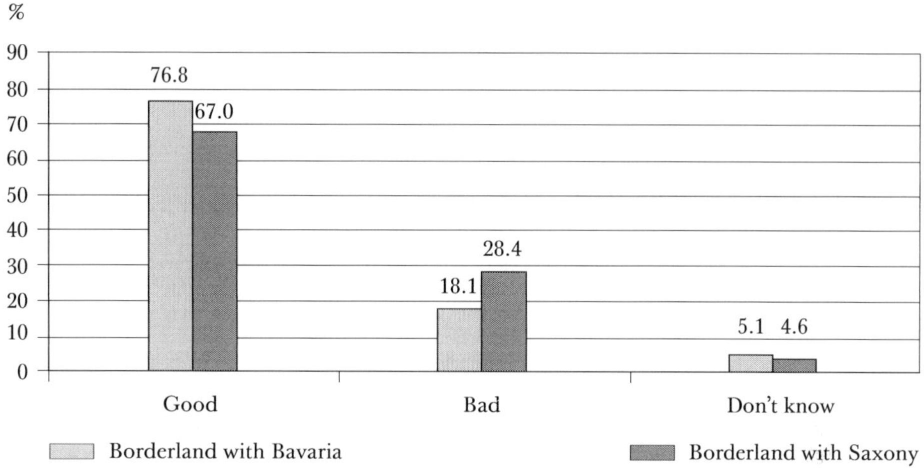

%

	Good	Bad	Don't know
Borderland with Bavaria	76.8	18.1	5.1
Borderland with Saxony	67.0	28.4	4.6

Borderland with Bavaria   Borderland with Saxony

Source: Institute of Sociology, the Academy of Sciences of the CR (Department of Czech Borderland) with Factum/Invenio, research survey Czech-German relations on the edge of EU accession, 2003–2005.

The public was relatively sceptical on the question of whether the Czech-German Declaration had managed to resolve the disputed points from the past. Given that in 1999 almost half those questioned believed that the Czech-German Declaration had not managed to resolve the contentious issues of the past (although we should note that 28% had no opinion or did not feel qualified to judge), then the Czech-German Declaration, designed above all as a gesture of goodwill towards both the German and Czech public, cannot be said to have achieved its goals.

Earlier, expectations on the Czech side had in fact been quite optimistic. This is attested by answers to a question about the rationale and necessity of the Declaration that was included in the Borderland survey in 1996 when the Declaration was being drawn up. More than 84% of respondents said that they believed the Declaration was necessary to improve the current state of Czech-German relations. Thus although the media often challenged the need for the Declaration at the time, the reactions of the public were notably positive. In response to a question about the aims of the Declaration, two types of answer predominated: improvement of Czech-German relations and the resolution of disputes arising from the past. The basic message of the Declaration – the need to turn away from the contentious past and look to the future – seems to have resonated with the opinions of the Czech public, although judging by the results of later survey, the Declaration did not succeed in its purpose.

The following graph presents the pattern of answers to the question: Do you think that the declaration on relations between the FRG and the Czech Republic has resolved the disputed questions of the past?

Graph 5. Has the Czech-German Declaration closed the problems of the past?

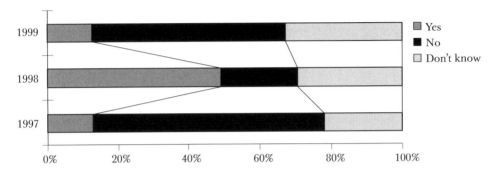

Source: Institute of Sociology, the Academy of Sciences of the CR, (Department of Czech Borderland). Longitudinal Research, Project of the Ministry of Foreign Affairs of the CR: Attitudes to Germany and the Sudeten German Question, 1997–1999.

A notably optimistic rating of the role of the Czech-German Declaration emerged in the survey of the group of local elites conducted in the Czech-German borderland in 1998. By contrast, the results of a nation-wide survey conducted in 1999 showed almost the same level of pessimism about the effects of the declaration as the survey of inhabitants of the borderland in 1997. In this respect, and in fact not only in relation to this particular question, there are signs that attitudes to Germany among Czechs in the borderlands differ much less from the national average than has been supposed. Rather than residence in the the borderland or the interior, the differentiating factors in attitudes to Germany seem to be position of respondents in the hierarchy of the social structure, level of information and political orientation.

Following the Declaration, the question of whether Czech-German reconciliation (constantly demanded by the SL but also a number of journalists, political scientists and historians) had actually occurred became a relevant one. In March 2001, the Centre for Research of Public Opinion at the Institute of Sociology of the Czech Academy of Sciences asked the public, "Do you think that Czech-German reconciliation has occurred?" A total of 57% of respondents answered "definitely yes" or "probably yes". In 2003, among the inhabitants of the border areas with Germany, 18% of respondents agreed with the statement that a settlement had not yet been achieved in Czech-German relations, and 47% believed that it had been achieved only partially.

Those who believed that reconciliation had yet to be achieved were then asked "What stands in the way of Czech-German reconciliation?". The order of the reasons that they gave is the precise opposite of those presented by the Sudetendeutsche Landsmannschaft and most of the opinions repeatedly presented in the media (constant demands for the revocation of the Beneš Decrees). In first place among obstacles to "conciliation" as seen by Czechs we find the historical burden of mutual relations (35%) this is followed by the Sudeten Germans (20%), the arrogance of Germany (also 20%), a lack of will on both sides (13%) and finally the settlement of war damages (12%).

The answers confirm the trend that had already been evident in the continual surveys conducted by the Ústí nad Labem region Czech Borderland team of the Institute of Sociology of the Czech Academy of Sciences, as described above. These sociological surveys make it clear that demands for the revocation of the Beneš Decrees and the re-evaluation of the fact of the transfer do not respect the collectively-shared opinions of Czech society.

Most of the Czech public saw the Sudeten Germans as a serious problem.

A question on the seriousness of the Sudeten German problem was included for the first time in the Borderlands survey in 1996, when more than 90% of respondents replied that they considered the theme to be a serious or partly serious problem of Czech-German relations. Three years later, more than 60% of respondents held the same view when questioned in a nation-wide survey. Despite this marked fall in the percentage giving this answer, it is clear that Czech society sees the Sudeten German question as a serious factor in Czech-German relations. It should be pointed out here, however, that there is a relative absence of social and ethnic hostility to Sudeten Germans. The research suggests that the prevailing attitude is one of indifference in this respect (e.g. three-quarters of respondents would not mind having a Sudeten German family living next door).

Most people agree that the post-war decrees of President Beneš that formed the legal basis for the transfer of the Sudeten Germans and the confiscation of their property should remain on the statute book.

A total of 66% of respondents agreed that the presidential decrees should be left in force. This figure invites comparison with the results of the 1998 survey of local elites in the borderland, since while this was a group strongly motivated to positive attitudes to Germans, 80% of them still agreed that the decrees should be left on the statute book. CVVM (the Czech Centre for Research of Public Opinion) put the question of whether the Beneš Decrees should be left in force in a survey at the time of heightened debate during the election campaign in the spring of 2002. In March 2002 as many as 67% believed they should be left in force, and in May 2002 as many as 71% of respondents. These results show, *inter alia*, that the question of the Sudeten Germans and their forced departure from the Czech Lands has a significant ethnically mobilising potential, as we have seen in preceding chapters.

The transfer of the German-speaking population from the border areas of the former Czechoslovakia is regarded by the majority of Czechs as right. A large group of respondents have reservations about the way it was conducted.

From the very start of the continual (tracking) surveys of the attitudes of inhabitants of the Czech borderlands (and later on a nationwide basis by the SOFRES/Factum, IVVM and CVVM agencies) a question has been included to identify views on the transfer of the Bohemian Germans.[6] This gives us a rare chance to assess the stability of opinion over quite a long time period, because data from a continual survey has much more substantial value as evidence than isolated data from one-off surveys on very specific themes.

The graph shows the trend in the the the attitudes of Czech society to the key question in Czech-Sudeten German relations represented by the question of the transfer of the Bohemian Germans after the Second World War. Three consistently well-represented views characterise majority opinion.

Table 5: Development of Attitudes to the Post-War Transfer of the German Population out of the Czech Lands

	1991	1996	1999	2003
Right, they helped to destroy the CSR	27	30	29	43
Right, but I have reservations about the way it was done	39.5	43	35	29
Wrong, but the great powers made the decision	6	11	12	15
Wrong	6	2	4.5	2.5
Wrong and cruel	3	3	2	1.5
Don't know/no opinion	14	8	17	8

Note: the data present percentual share of answers expressing agreement according to surveys in the districts of the Czech-German border region. The data for 1999 are taken from a national survey.
Source: Institute of Sociology, Academy of Sciences of the CR, longitudinal survey CR/FRG Borderlands, 1991–2005.

---

[6]   The research project of the Foreign Ministry of the CR *Reflexe sudetoněmecké otázky a postoje obyvatelstva českého pohraničí k Německu* [Reflection of the Sudeten German Question and the Attitudes of the Population of the Czech Border Areas to Germany], 1996–1999, produced a range of findings both on the current form of historical memory, including the factor of the historical burden in Czech-German relations, and on the process of emergence of new attitudes to Germany as an ally in the North Atlantic Alliance and geographically the closest EU partner, whose position significantly influenced the decision to accept the Czech Republic into this most important of communities of European states. For purposes of comparison, the findings of a number of other surveys conducted by sociological departments and institutions using at least partially relevant methodology and fulfilling the basic criteria for representativeness of samples have been used. Despite this, the author is aware of the pitfalls of comparing and conflating the results of differently angled projects, and has done so simply with a view to achieving a synthesising view of the way that Czech society (especially but not exclusively in the border areas) has been reacting to the Sudeten German question. In detail see: Houžvička, (ed.) 1997. *Reflexe sudetoněmecké otázky a postoje obyvatelstva českého pohraničí k Německu.* Praha: Sociologický ústav AV ČR.

The first group, which for the whole period monitored *has varied around 30%*, agrees with the view that the transfer/expulsion of the Bohemian Germans was a just action because of the destructive role of the Henlein movement in the period before the outbreak of the Second World War.

The second group, which remains the largest throughout the period of surveys, agrees with the view that the transfer was just, but has reservations about the way it was carried out. In the Czech borderlands, this view is held consistently by a majority of *around 40%* of respondents, while in the nationwide survey of 1999 the figure was a little lower, at 36%. The first and second groups together constitute a consistent two-thirds majority of Czechs agreeing with the transfer.

The third group also has clear views, i.e. that the transfer was unjust but that it was decided by the victorious powers; 10–12% of respondents consistently hold this view. 6–7% of respondents consider that the transfer was unjust and cruel. Not even in the 1998 survey, when the sample group was that of local elites expressing marked tolerance towards Germans and Germany, did the proportion of respondents who believed the transfer to be wrong exceed 6%.

In each of the three opinion groups there was a similar representation of age and educational categories, although slightly more people of retirement age and people with a leftwing political orientation agreed with the the transfer. Consistently over time there were more graduates in the group approving the transfer but with reservations about how it was carried out.

The table and commentary makes it clear that the society-wide consensus approving the transfer is lasting in character and that any radical re-assessment of the issue would provoke considerable internal political tension inside Czech society. In February 2001 the CVVM agency put the question in this way: "There is debate over whether the transfer of the Sudeten Germans after the war was just. Do you think it was: 47% stated that it was "just", 23% stated the variant "It was unjust but a line must be drawn under the past", and 8% stated that it was unjust and there was a need to apologise or even return property. [7]

In 1999 the nation-wide survey first included a question on the possibility of collaboration with Sudeten German organisations in the interests of the development of the borderlands: 54% of respondents favoured the possibility and 32% in the 2005.

The most frequently favoured possibilities for solving the problem of the Sudeten Germans have included over the long term (in repeated surveys) apology, Václav Havel's expression of apology, and most recently cooperation with the Sudeten German operations in the interests of development of the borderlands.

7   Kunštát, D. Prezidentské dekrety a odsun očima české společnosti. Česko-německé souvislosti [Czech-German connections] 1/2005. 4–6. http://www.borderland.cz

Graph 6: View on Questions Concerned
with Settlement of Disputes from the Past

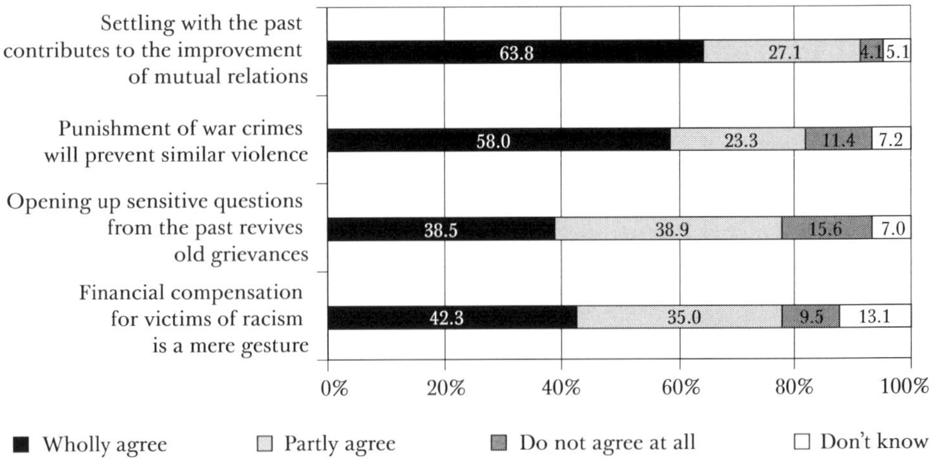

Settling with the past contributes to the improvement of mutual relations	63.8	27.1	4.1 5.1
Punishment of war crimes will prevent similar violence	58.0	23.3	11.4 7.2
Opening up sensitive questions from the past revives old grievances	38.5	38.9	15.6 7.0
Financial compensation for victims of racism is a mere gesture	42.3	35.0	9.5 13.1

■ Wholly agree   ▢ Partly agree   ▨ Do not agree at all   ☐ Don't know

Source: *Institute of Sociology, the Academy of Sciences of the CR (Department of Czech Borderland) with Factum/Invenio, research survey Czech-German relations on the edge of EU accession, 2003–2005.*

Table 6: Development of Views on the Possible Solutions
to the Sudeten German Question

	1991	1996	1999	2003
An apology is enough	24	55	46	57
There should be no negotiation with representatives of the Sudeten Germans	18	18	29	32
Support investment	14	20	28	28
The Declaration is the basis for a solution	x	33	32	48
Our dispute will be solved by the entry of the CR into the EU	x	13	31	30
Let it be and it will sort itself out	18	10	26	23
Return property to the expellees	2	2	6	8
Provide the expellees with compensation	3	7	13	15

Note: *figures indicate proportion of answers agreeing with statement in %, 1999 data are from nation-wide survey; – question not posed.*
Source: *Institute of Sociology, Academy of Sciences of the CR, longitudinal survey Borderlands CR/FRG–9, 1991–2005*

The most striking turning-point in the long-term trend of Czech public attitudes to possible ways to solve the Sudeten German question is the virtual doubling (1991–1996) of support for Havel's apology for the transfer of the Sudeten Germans. This change is quite significant, particular taking into account the markedly negative reaction of the public at the turn of 1989/1990. Support for Havel's expression of apology peaked in 1996 at 55% and has since gradually fallen to 46% in 1999. Nation-wide, roughly a third of respondents shared the view that the Sudeten German problem would be solved by the entry of the Czech Republic into the European Union, or by the Czech-German Declaration. In the borderlands the proportion of respondents holding these views has been lower over the long term, varying around one fifth of respondents. The rather fatalistic attitude (although not without a pragmatic element) that the problem will solve itself if left alone, continues to be taken by roughly a quarter of respondents. The proportion selecting this view has consistently risen…

Almost a half of respondents do not agree with the view that the government should negotiate directly with representatives of the Sudetendeutsche Landsmannschaft. This question was first posed in the survey in 1999 and the proportion of respondents who reject the idea of negotiation is less arresting than the proportion who replied "don't know" – 77%. This signals an instability of opinion which to a certain extent follows on from the findings of the preceding surveys in 1996 and 1998, when over 70% and 60% (respectively) took the view that it was not at all clear what the policy of the government towards the Sudeten Germans actually was. There are several possible hypotheses to explain this situation, and I consider two of these to be the most important:

- Since 1989, for various reasons the Czech government has not presented its standpoint on the demands of the Sudeten German organisations in a way that citizens of the CR find sufficiently comprehensible and persuasive,
- the mass media in the Czech Republic have not been able or willing to interpret the view of the official state bodies in a way that would enable citizens to gain a clear view of their content and argumentation.[8]

---

[8]   It was not until May 2002 that thanks to the initiative of the Minister of Culture P. Dostál an official publication on the matter was published. This was the book by a team of Czech historians *Rozumět dějinám*, which was distributed free of charge (in a 25,000 copy print-run) to schools, libraries and educational facilities. Although this has been a welcome step, it was a notably belated and partial response from Czech official bodies to the massive propagandist and media campaign aimed at winning Czech public opinion for the revisionist side. We should not, though, forget the fundamental works published by several Czech and German historians (some of them cited in this study) that in the course of the 1990s contributed to objective understanding of the problem of Czech-Sudeten-German relations. Concerned groups of the Czech public also developed their activities, for example the Svaz bojovníků za svobodu [Union of Fighters for Freedom] and their periodical *Národní osvobození* and the Club of Czech Historians which issues a bulletin publishing statements of principle, e.g. Pánek, J. – Pešek, J. "Historikové proti znásilňování dějin" [Historians against the Violation of History]. Special supplement to the *Zpravodaj Historického klubu* 2/2001 (XII).

The conflictual past of Czech-German co-existence remains present long-term in the attitudes of the population of the Czech Republic and forms the current background to mutual relations. The political orientation of respondents is an important differentiating factor (again in long-term perspective) of Czech attitudes to Germany and the Sudeten German question. In the 1990s, people with rightwing political orientations were strikingly friendlier in their attitude to Germany, as were people with higher education and qualifications and people up to thirty years old. By contrast a reserved attitude to the benefits of cooperation with Germany and caution in assessment of its role in Central Europe often correlated with leftwing political orientation. Since 2000 this pattern has been changing and rightwingers too have been expressing a greater level of distrust for Germany that is evidently linked to the escalating debate on modern history.

These trends should not be regarded as a rigorous rule, however, because citizens orientated to the political centre, which has been and still is very ill-defined and unstructured in the CR, often choose attitudes *ad hoc*, without deeper consideration of all the implication and connections, which in any case an averagely informed person is not able to judge (intuitive assessments with an admixture of attitude stereotypes plays a certain part here). With the growing pressure of the SL for the revocation of the Beneš Decrees, and with the accession of the CR to the EU, rightwing voters and the ODS (Civic Democratic Party) have also been taking a more aggressive position on the issue, and this trend culminated in the 2002 Spring election campaign with a stress on the defence of national interests (see for example some of Jan Zahradil's speeches).

The federal chancellor Helmut Kohl and prime minister Václav Klaus signing the Czech-German Declaration in Prague on the 21st of January 1997. In the background the German foreign minister Klaus Kinkel and the later Czech ambassador to Germany R. Jindrák.

13 The Czech-German Relationship between Past and Future

A book that has tried to identify the basic contours and milestones in Czech-German relations can hardly end with some simple and unambiguous conclusion. What can be said, however, is that while Germans and Czechs now find themselves on the common trajectory of an integrated Europe and Euro-Atlantic community, history remains a presence and the shadows of the past still have the power to return.

The regular appearance and discussion of Sudeten German issues on the German and Czech political scenes, and of the leaders of the Sudetendeutsche Landsmannschaft, suggests that this an important factor in bilateral relations. Meanwhile, the cross-border dimension of the local communities of the border areas, which is being progressively created through intensive cooperation between the CR and Germany on both state and regional/local level, is playing a significant part in the ongoing integration of the CR into European structures.

In this situation the Czech-Sudeten-German issue has been playing an important role in bilateral CR-FRG relations, especially in connection with the EU demand for resolution of ethnic and border conflicts in a spirit of moderation. We can assume that the text and formulation of the Declaration as the basic document containing the positions of the two sides in a balanced (and therefore compromise) form, will be the basis for all future mutual steps to reduce the burden on Czech-German relations. President Václav Klaus's speech on the 64th anniversary of the start of the German occupation of Czechoslovakia was likewise formulated in the spirit of the Declaration: "In both the CR and in Germany we ought to know how to say 'this happened, today we cannot change the past, from the standpoint of today these were unacceptable actions'. Let us turn to the future and support steps that ensure mutual cooperation, friendship and understanding."[1]

The Sudetendeutsche Landsmannschaft has yet again failed to respond in kind to the president's conciliatory gesture, which for example, shows willingness to respond to the recommendation of the European Parliament as a result of a detailed debate on the Beneš Decrees). The way in which the SL opened a Prague Office (25th of March 2003) immediately after Klaus's speech is yet another illustration of the lack of credibility and the rigidity of the ideas of this organisation. Although B. Posselt had voted against the admission of the CR to the EU in the foreign committee of the European Parliament only a short time before, in Prague he did not hesitate to declare ceremoniously that, "the office is a part of dialogue and the process of establishing contacts with Czech society."[2]

A peculiarity usually overlooked is the fact that neither at the time of its culmination at the end of the 1930s, nor in the post-war period, has the Sudeten German question been understood on the German side as a classic border conflict. On the contrary, the German side always emphasised that it considered the historical borders of the Czech Lands to be determined and beyond dispute.

The Sudeten German questions remains a potential source of conflict both from the social point of view (ethnic peace in the borderlands) and the geopolitical point of view (the integrity of the CR and stability of property-law relations in the borderlands). Growing external pressure on the Czech Republic from Bavaria, Austria and Hungary to revoke the Beneš Decrees, which are in fact the denazification laws of Czechoslovakia, escalated by means of a media campaign and forced the Czech Parliament to issue a declaration of principle on the 23rd of April 2003. Hitherto latent historical resentments evidently had the power to ethnically mobilise not only Czech society as a whole but part of its political elites very fast.[3]

It is precisely the Sudeten German demands as expressed in the form of the argument and vocabulary of the leaders of the Sudetendeutsche Landsmannschaft that have been awakening in Czech social consciousness memories of the 1930s and the political crisis that ended the existence of an independent CSR. Whether or not Sudeten German demands represent political extremism,

---

[1] *Češi a Němci, smiřme se (Obracejme se do budoucnosti)* [Czechs and Germans, Let us be conciliatory (Let us turn to the future)]. Text of V. Klaus's speech at Prague Castle. *Lidové noviny.* 15. 3. 2003. 3.

[2] The decrees belong in the dustbin of history, claims B. Posselt. in *Lidové noviny.* 26. 3. 2003.

[3] See e.g. the petition *Stop nacionalismu* [Stop Nationalism]. March 2002, and the "counter petition" *Stop demagogii* [Stop Demogogy]. April 2002.

it is clear that they fuel growing doubts about the trustworthiness of the policy of Germany towards the countries of Central and Eastern Europe, especially the Czech Republic. In my view this is the core of the latent situation of conflict in Czech-German relations.

The majority in Czech society regard the wartime past, Nazism and the Sudeten German movement as a closed chapter. In this respect the prevailing concensus runs through all generations. However, the continuing revival of historical resentments on the side of the Sudetendeutsche Landsmannschaft has already been provoking a defensive reaction on the Czech side. This is evident, for example, in the founding of the Czech Borderland Clubs and the Circle of Czech Citizens expelled from the Czech borderlands in 1938, and the Club of Czech Historians, as well as the activation of the Union of Fighters for Freedom.

These organisations bring together thousands of people who lived through Nazi persecution and the flight of Czechs from the territory of the former Sudetenland after its "incorporation" into the Third Reich. In the course of the 1990s, arguments mounted up from both sides for new clashes of opinion that found expression even in the public forums of Czech-Sudeten-German dialogue. (See for example the present author's clash with H. Sehling at the symposium in Liberec in November 1992, the argument between L. Dobrovský, then the Chancellor of V. Havel President's Office, and R. Hilf, former Secretary of Lodgman von Auen at the Jihlava Czechs-Germans conference in April 1995, the heated discussions associated with the drawing up of the Czech-German Treaty in 1991–1992 or the Declaration in 1995–1996, disputes on the form of a project comparing the denazification legislation of the former Czechoslovakia with that of other occupied European countries in the Co-ordination Council of the Czech-German Discussion Forum and other examples). The course of these and other disagreements confirm the power of the Sudeten German question to mobilise nationalist elements in relations between the CR and FRG.

The Czech public sees the Sudeten German demands as an important part of Czech-German relations. For example, the survey showed that as early as the mid-1990s two thirds of respondents considered the Sudeten German question to be a serious problem in Czech-German relations. [4] While the Borderland survey found that economic disparity (purchasing power, currency, prices) came first in the order of perceived barriers to mutual relations, the historical burden of the Czech-Sudeten-German conflict remained a neuralgic point in relations between the FRG and the CR and by the end of the 1990s had as much weight as economic disparity in attitudes to Germany.

---

[4] *Vztahy české společnosti k Německu* [Attitudes of Czech Society to Germany]. cited survey Naumann/Gabal.

Czechs and Germans were never entirely unconflictual neighbours in the past and it cannot be expected that the relationship will be entirely conflict-free in the future. Searching for a *modus vivendi* is a very long-term matter and may turn out to a permanent state of affairs. This was well expressed back in 1895 by the Czech national economist and politician J. Kaizl, who commented that "It is not necessary for us to like each other; what we need is to tolerate each other."[5]

Reactions to current Czech-German relations and the part played by the Sudeten German question are two parts of the same whole. While the two components are not entirely identical, they are inseparable. The results of surveys showing substantial change in the way people see Czech-German relations at the same time demonstrate that the past is still more or less latently present in their minds.

This historical dimension is anchored in the second half of the 19th century and the disputes of the time over the emancipation of the Czechs within the Habsburg Empire, followed by the establishment of an independent Czechoslovakia, the attempt by the Bohemian Germans to secede with their territory from the state at its birth, and their second, successful attempt after the tragedy of Munich in 1938, leading to the setting up of the occupation regime of the Protectorate of Bohemia and Moravia and ultimately to the transfer of the German-speaking population of the Czech Lands. All this represents the burden on Czech-German relations that today finds its concentrated expression in what is known as the Sudeten German question.

There is no doubt that it is precisely this aspect of mutual relations that for the majority of Czech society has the potential to accelerate the emergence of ethnic nationalism as a defensive instrument and expression of historical experience with the demands of the Sudeten national/ethnic group/*Sudetendeutsche Volksgruppe*. Negative tendencies in attitudes to the Sudeten German demands have the power to impact significantly both on relations to Germany and Germans in general, and on the attitude of the Czech population to the German national minority living in the CR.

A development of this kind might seriously threaten the trust that still predominates in the CR in relation to the Federal Republic of Germany. Two thirds of respondents in surveys continue to express trust for Germany as a state that poses no threat to the CR. On the other hand, it is also clear from surveys that the same proportion of Czech citizens (65%) at the same time express fears about the possible instability of the democracy and political system of the FRG. This is an opinion expressed by respondents in all age groups, who

---

[5]   Křen, J. *Konfliktní společenství.* 18.

evidently do not rule out the resurgence of political extremism in Germany, or some deviation from track towards a special vision of German destiny of the former "Sonderweg" kind.

It remains the case that successive federal governments have supported the larger (CDU/CSU) or lesser (SPD/Greens coalition) property and political demands of the SL. Of course, we can hardly overlook the basic difference between G. Schröder's luke-warm or even dismissive attitude to the demands of the expellee organisations, which he had already expressed when premier of Lower Saxony, and the open support of the Bavarian premier E. Stoiber, who is a serious candidate for the position of federal chancellor in the next elections. It is hard to determine how far the individual political parties express supportive attitudes out of a real sense of the obligation to defend the interests of German citizens (including the expellees) imposed on them by the *Grundgesetz*, and how far this attitude is just a reflection of the need to win votes in an atmosphere of postmodern re-evaluation of modern German history. We can also speculate as to how far another motive might be the "re-discovered" vital interests of the Federal Republic of Germany as regards Eastern neighbours, since this possibility cannot be ruled out. It would seem, however, that we cannot entirely separate one aspect from another, since in practical politics they form a fairly seamless web.

The continuing absence of clear definition in the German government position (caused to a certain extent by the legal relationship of the state to private property claims) on this matter may reinforce the trend in Czech society to distrust German intentions towards the east. Any continuing connections (in the sense of threatened conditions) made between the accession of the CR to the EU and property-law matters and demands for historical and moral re-evaluation of the transfer may well result in increasing Czech suspicion of the aims of German activities (including the economic) in the CR, and may entirely devalue the positive consequences of post-1989 dialogue.

I consider it quite fundamental that the SL rejected the wording of the Czech-German Declaration (as it had also rejected the wording of the 1992 Treaty), which clearly formulated a distancing from the past with the stress on the need to build relations of trust for the future. Views aired on the fifth anniversary of the Declaration confirmed the existing indications that the two sides had different interpretations of the document, and at a meeting of the Co-ordinating Council of the Czech-German Discussion Forum (in March 2002 in Berlin), calls were for the first time publicly made for the "negotiation" of an improved document, on the grounds that the Declaration was already out of date.

Many statements made by Sudeten German leaders like J. Böhm (stolen property must be returned), F. Neubauer (illegality must be condemned)[6], or R. Hilf (there will be no legally binding closure of the question of the Sudeten Germans), express or hint unmistakeably at goals that the SL is pursuing by exploiting the strength of the ties between the expellees and the Christian democratic parties, the CDU/CSU. The political weight of the latter is based not just on their position on the Bavarian, and in some contexts in the German and Austrian wider political scene, but in wider context on their position as part of the grouping of European Christian Democratic parties that is one of the strongest in the European Parliament. It is precisely here that we can identify the source of the influence of the expellees' organisations and the difficulties to which Czech foreign policy has been exposed in the preparatory phase of negotiations on the accession of the CR to the European Union. The fact that the CDU/CSU Euro-MPs voted against the admission of the Czech Republic to the European Union must be considered an ungracious (or rather unfriendly) gesture that was the culmination of the dispute over the Beneš Decrees (however much the bluntness of the step was subsequently smoothed over by "full explanation" of its "true" meaning).[7]

In the context of ongoing discussions about the historical and ethnic aspects of the transfer, it is nonetheless essential to bear in mind that the act of transfer is approved (as the logical outcome of the identification of the great majority of Sudeten Germans with Henlein's Sudeten German Party and the Nazi goal of destroying democratic Czechoslovakia) by a massive majority of Czechs, i.e. consistently over time by two thirds of the population of the CR, even if a proportion have certain reservations about how the transfer was conducted. It can therefore be said that any political party that decided on a radical re-evaluation of the transfer would essentially be committing political suicide. A demonstra-

---

[6]   A concise summary of the SL position was formulated in an interview with V. Žák by the Landsmannschaft spokesman F. Neubauer. Neubauer states that, "A solution demands a series of political decisions that can only be taken by the government and parliament. The Forum can suggest these, but cannot carry them out. What is crucial for us is that through its constitutional organs the Czech state should unambiguously condemn the expulsion of 1945 and 1946. Our goal is to achieve a unanimous evaluation of these events with the Czech side and an agreement on what follows from this shared evaluation." Neubauer, F. "Bezpráví musí být odsouzeno" [Illegality must be condemned]. *Listy* 2/2000. 23–26.

[7]   B. Posselt was uncompromising in his rejection of the presidential decrees, and criticised not only Czech politicians but also Chancellor Schröder for unwillingness to deal with the Sudeten German question. At the 52nd Sudeten German Rally in Augsburg Posselt declared that the Landsmannschaft leadership would seek to defend and pursue the interests of the Sudeten Germans not just with the federal government but also in the European Union. He warned the Czech government "not to delude itself that the Czech Republic would be able to become a member of the EU without revoking the Beneš Decrees, which were the basis for the expulsion and disenfranchisement of 3.5 million Sudeten Germans." Interview with B. Posselt "Jsem motorem rozšíření EU na východ" [I am the motor for EU expansion to the East]. *Lidové noviny*. 2. 8. 2001. 9.

bly lasting factor of public opinion may not be admirable in every way, but pragmatically it is an effective part of the creation of political will. This plays an important role in both Czech and German policy. On the Sudeten German side too there are examples of the excommunication of those who challenged the monolithic consensus of opinion of the community.[8]

Judging by the available public statements of the Sudeten German leadership, it is evident that there has been almost no essential modification of the views that brought the Sudeten German Party and politicians into fatal conflict with the majority of the representatives of the political spectrum of pre-war Czechoslovakia. For example, the introduction to the exhibition *Sudeten Germans – An ethnic group in the heart of Europe*, speaks of Czechoslovakia as a mistaken construction of the Versailles treaty and presents the transfer as genocide, which is a completely unacceptable interpretation.[9]

In a similar uncompromising spirit, the map in an official publication of the Sudeten German Council challenges the border on the Oder-Nisa line and speaks of territory "under Polish administration", while also employing German geographical names on principle etc. All this, together with the results of surveys of the attitudes of the population of the CR to Czech-German relations, makes it clear that their future development cannot be based exclusively on Czech- Sudeten-German dialogue. The latter can have benefits only in the context of objective and serious Czech-German debate on the disputed point of Czech-German history as the condition for further progressive incorporation of the Czech Republic into Euro-Atlantic structures.

From the practical point of view, convergence of perspective requires more intensive cross-border contacts at the local and regional level, language teaching, the exchange of young people, the founding of businesses with mixed capital backing and efforts to achieve a much greater level of mutual knowledge and information, the lack of which has been very evident in surveys. And all this must be pursued in conditions of partnership relations and dialogue conducted with mutual respect, without categorical demands for Czech penitence.

---

[8] See e.g. The fate of the Sudeten German Social Democrat J. W. Brügel, author of the thorough study *Deutsche und Tschechen*, or R. Zischka who in 1965 criticised the SL spokesman W. Jaksch, saying, "He is mistaken in supposing that all Sudeten Germans, and above all the social democrats, are willing to take part in that holy war that he wants to wage on the ridges of the Šumava between the free West and the barbarism of the East. With the 50 billion that Jaksch wants to devote to ensuring that the East is returned to the West, and indeed just with money generally, it is not possible to solve the problems that have arisen as a consequence of Hitler's war and its end. It is not that simple." The letter of a forgotten Bohemian German democrat, in Hahn, E. – Hahn, H.-H. *Sudetoněmecká vzpomínání a zapomínání*. 73.

[9] Among other publications see also: Coll. 1993. *Die Tschechoslowakei – Das Ende einer Fehlkonstruktion. Die Sudetendeutsche Frage bleibt offen*. Berg: VGB-Verlagsgesellschaft.

Instead of a conclusion

but also for the sake of clarity, I summarise the content of this study in a number of basic theses characterising the different phases of the Czech-Sudeten-German conflict.

- In the changing political and national environment of the Habsburg Monarchy at the end of the 19th and beginning of the 20th century, liberalism was increasingly coming into conflict with nationalism, with liberalism ever more often sacrificed in the defence of the nationalist demands of Austrian Germans. Their nationalist agenda spread from the regions known as the Südmark via academic circles in Graz and Vienna into North Bohemia, where it found particularly strong support. The spirit of national radicalism was exemplified by the Pan-German programme championed by Georg von Schönerer, who even at the height of his political influence had the support of only an unconvincing minority of Austrian Germans overall, but who won a disproportionately large following in the peripheral parts of the monarchy, in linguistically mixed areas (border territories of ethnic overlap and conflict). The fanatical antisemite von Schönerer was elected to the Imperial Council by voters from the Cheb and Opava regions of Bohemia. In content, the programme of his Pan-German antisemitically orientated party strikingly resembled the later programme of the NSDAP. The political milieu of Bohemian Germans was over the long term "emotionally predisposed" to respond to racially and nationally intolerant arguments.
- The project of *Mitteleuropa* conceived as a vision of German dominance in Central Europe represented the "rediscovery" of the Holy Roman Empire of the German Nation and its modernisation in the conditions of the Central Europe of the 20th century. F. Naumann was striving to harmonise the interests of Austro-Hungary and the German Reich and hoped that if this could be done then the others, including Czechs and Hungarians, would join this Central European core. He saw all the demands of the emancipated Czech political nation through the lens of the power ambitions of the Austrian-German interest; in his view an independent state for Czechs was out of the question. He did not accord the right to survival to small nations without a state of their own in the territory between Germany and Russia.
- The concept of national self-determination, proclaimed by Woodrow Wilson at the beginning of 1918 as the organising principle for the post-war order of Central Europe, seemed in the eyes of Austrian (and Sudeten) Germans to be in effect "self-determination so long as this does not mean pan-German unification". However imperfect and problematic from the point

of view of practical implementation, the principle of self-determination made possible the creation of a chain of independent (republican) successor states as the only alternative to a Pan-German order with a hegemonic Germany that inclined to authoritarian forms of political decision making. Unfortunately the spread of democracy did not automatically mean the end of expansionist ambitions on the part of states, as Wilson had believed, and the right to self-determination soon created new seedbeds of conflict in the complicated conditions of the ethnically divided and quarrelsome Central Europe.

- The Sudeten Germans were a politically highly organised group that had enjoyed a dominating influence in the Czech Lands up to the establishment of the CSR. They rejected the principle of civic individual rights and civil liberties as inadequate and insisted on a tribal concept of the collective rights of ethnic Germans. As a result their conflict with Czechs accelerated as soon as the Czechoslovak state was founded.

- During the 1930s, the various factors making for national radicalism among minority Germans throughout Central and Eastern Europe were all present in the case of the Sudeten Germans to the maximum extent. These were the geographical factor (proximity of territory to Germany), the ethnic factor (intensity of ethnic rivalry and tension arising from it), and the economic factor (level of economic difficulty and decline in a territory). In the Sudetenland all these factors mutually reinforced each other in their effects.

- The idea of the transfer of the German-speaking inhabitants of the CSR to the territory of Germany developed in the course of the Second World War. The views of British experts and of the home resistance in the Czech Lands were key factors in determining the adoption of the idea. The resettlement plans were agreed on by Beneš's government in exile in London together with other exile governments of occupied European states, the United States, the European Advisory Committee and other organisations. As reports of Nazi terror on occupied territories mounted up, far more drastic ideas than transfer appeared in British reports in the years 1942–1945, for example that Germans expelled from East Prussia and Upper Silesia should "be allowed to disappear in Siberia". Beneš's ideas on the post-war expulsion of the Germans did not deviate from or go beyond the frame of reference of the policy of the Western Allies and their political culture at the time, in which re-settlement and exchanges of population were considered legitimate means of solving ethnic conflicts and preventing their recurrence in the future.

- The defeat of Nazi Germany brought a fundamental qualitative rebirth of German political culture and the structure of political power, but certain conservative nationalist tendencies remain present in the part of the German political spectrum with which the activities and political demands of the expellee organisations have connections. Although German foreign policy makes no territorial or property-right claims against the Czech Republic, the "expellee factor" forms part of the German negotiating position.

- In the Sudetendeutsche Landsmannschaft the Witikobund retained a dominant ideological influence (and to a certain extent a direct influence through the presence of W-B members in important SL positions). The W-B is an organisation that carries on the political tradition of the Spann wing of the Sudeten German Party, and the so-called Kameradschaftsbund (which intellectually draws directly on the ideology of *Volkstumpkamf*). In line with the legacy of O. Spann, efforts are made to advance members of a spiritual elite into key positions where they can propagate political radicalism in Czech-German relations (the CSR as a mistake of the Versailles system, the validity of the Munich Agreement, the transfer as genocide, Potsdam as a mere protocol without legal binding force and not an agreement, the illegality of the Presidential Decrees and so on).

- As a consequence of the extensive programme of integration of groups of expellees into German society, most expellees have ceased to nurse ambitions to return to their former territories (something that would undoubtedly destabilise the political balance of the Central European region). All the same, this whole study is premised on the thesis that the factor of the expellees and their influence on German domestic and foreign policy has a certain specific role that Czech foreign policy is compelled to take into account. The course of the preparatory negotiation of treaty documents on Czech-German relations since 1989 (The Treaty on Good Neighbourly Relations and Friendly Co-operation, the Declaration) was proof of this. It is also a thesis repeatedly confirmed by the complications that the activities of the European People's Party have caused in the final phase of the accession of the CR to the EU. Despite the reservations of the CDU/CSU parties, however, the Federal Republic of Germany fulfiled its treaty obligation to support Czech membership of the European Union.

- Research surveys on public opinion in the Czech Republic show that the population clearly distinguishes between attitudes to Germany (its culture, economy, political system) and the problem of the expulsion of the Sudeten Germans from the former Czechoslovakia. Two trends in opinion are arising from this differentiation: the positive perception of Germany as a desirable partner especially in the field of economic and cultural cooperation, but in parallel a rejection of the demands of the Sudetendeutsche Landsmannschaft for so-called conciliation or settlement.

- The conflict-ridden past of Czech-German relations remains present in the consciousness of the Czech population in the form of an ethnic mobilising potential that reacts sensitively to disputes in bilateral relations, as was demonstrated in the course of the controversy over the presidential decrees which culminated in 2002 with the negotiation of the conditions for the admission of the CR to the EU.

Bibliography

Akten zur deutschen auswärtigen Politik 1918–1945. Series D. Vol. IV. 1964. Bonn: G. Hermes. 266.

Analýza a předpokládaný vývoj hraničních oblastí ČR–SRN [The Analysis and Anticipated Development of the Border Areas of the CR–FRG]. 2003. (Collective of authors). Unpublished study. Published part Houžvička, V. "Pohraniční oblasti v kontextu bilaterálních vztahů ČR a SRN" [The Border Areas in the Context of the Bilateral Relations of the CR and FRG]. *Mezinárodní politika* 2/2004. 21–24.

ANDĚL, Josef – BAUTZ, Rudolf – FILIP, Ota – KNOBLOCH, Edward. 1947. *Hromadné hroby v Čechách* [Mass Graves in Bohemia]. Prague: Ministerstvo informací.

BALLING, Mads Ole. 1991. *Von Reval bis Bukarest.* (Statistisch-Biographisches Handbuch). Kopenhagen: Citation Verlag.

Československo-německý dialog ve Federálním shromáždění ČSFR [Czechoslovak-German Dialogue in the Federal Parliament of the CsFR]. 1991. Prague: Ústav mezinárodních vztahů.

Československo-sovětské vztahy v diplomatických jednáních 1939–1945 [Czechoslovak-Soviet Relations in Diplomatic Negotiations 1939–1945]. (Documents). Němeček, Jan – Nováčková, Helena – Šťovíček, Ivan – Tejchman, Miroslav (eds.). Vol. II (July 1946–March 1945). 1998. Prague: Státní ústřední archiv.

Češi a sudetoněmecká otázka 1939–1945 [Czechs and the Sudeten German Question 1939–1945]. 1994. (Documents). Vondrová, Jitka (ed.). Prague: Ústav mezinárodních vztahů.

Charta Gentium et Regionum – Brünner Programm. (Überarbeitete Auflage). 1994. Munich: INTEREG.

DEJMEK, Jindřich. 2000. *Československá zahraniční politika v roce 1938* [Czechoslovak Foreign Policy in 1938]. Vol. 1–2. Prague: Ústav mezinárodních vztahů/Karolinum/Historický ústav Akademie věd ČR.

DEJMEK, Jindřich – NĚMEČEK, Jan. 2003. *Československá zahraniční politika v roce 1936* [Czechoslovak Foreign Policy in 1936]. Vol. 2. Prague: Ústav mezinárodních vztahů/ Karolinum/Historický ústav AV ČR.

"Dekrety prezidenta z hlediska současnosti a práva" [The Presidential Decrees from the Perspective of the Present and Law] (text of expert opinion of the CR government). *Právo*. 15. 5. 2002. 10.

Deutsches Vermögen im Ausland (Dokumentation). 1951–1955. Bände I–III. Bonn: Bundesministerium für Justitz.

Dokumentation der Vertreibung der Deutschen aus Ost-Mitteleuropa. Vol. IV/1: Die Vertreibung der deutschen Bevölkerung aus der Tschechoslowakei. 1957. Bundesministerium für Vertriebene, Flüchtlinge und Kriegsbeschädigte (ed.). 204.

Documents on the Expulsion of the Sudeten Germans. 1953. Turnwald, Wilhelm K. (ed.). Munich: University Press, Dr.C.Wolf&Sohn.

Documents on German Foreign Policy, 1918–1945, from the Archives of the German Foreign Minister. 1949–54. Published jointly by the British Foreign Office and the U.S. Department of State. Series D (1937–1945). 8 vols. Washington: U.S.G.P.O., and London: H.M.S.O.

Encyklopedie osobností Evropy [Personalities of Europe]. 1993. (Collective of authors). Prague: Nakladatelský dům OP. 616–617.

Erklärung sudetendeutscher und tschechischer Christen zur Gestaltung der deutsch-tschechischen Nachbarschaft. 1991/92. Paragraph II. Munich/Prague: Ackermann-Gemeinde.

FREMUND, Karel. 1961. *Chtěli nás vyhubit* [They Wanted to Exterminate Us]. Prague: Naše vojsko.

FRIŠTENSKÁ, Hana – SULITKA, Andrej. 1994. *Průvodce právy příslušníků národnostních menšin v České republice* [Guide to the Rights of Members of National Minorities in the Czech Republic]. Prague: Demokratická aliance Slováků v ČR.

FROWEIN, J. A. – BERNITZ, U. – KINGSLAND, Q. C. 2002. *Legal Opinion on the Beneš Decrees and the Accession of the Czech Republic to the EU.* Working document of the General Directorate for Research. European Parliament: Luxemburg.

GELLERMANN, Günther W. 1995. *... a naslouchali pro Hitlera. Tajná říšská záležitost: odposlouchávací centrály Třetí říše* [...and they listened in for Hitler. A secret Reich affair: The tapping centres of the Third Reich]. Brno: Bonus A.

GOEBBELS, Joseph. 1992. *Deníky 1938* [Diaries 1938]. Liberec: Dialog.

HABEL, Fritz P. 1984. *Dokumente zur Sudetenfrage.* Munich: Langen Müller.

HAJDŮ, Vavro – LÍSKA, Ladislav – ŠNEJDÁREK, Antonín. 1964. *Německá otázka 1945–1963.* [The German Question 1945–1963]. (Documents and materials). Prague: Nakladatelství politické literatury.

HARNA, Josef – ŠEBEK, Jaroslav. 2002. *Státní politika vůči německé menšině v období konsolidace politické moci v Československu v letech 1918–1920* [State policy towards the German minority in the period of the consolidation of political power 1918–1920]. Prague: Historický ústav AV ČR.

HITLER, Adolf. 1995. *Monology ve Vůdcově hlavním stanu* 1941–1944 [Monologues in the Fuehrer's Main Tent]. Prague: Aurora.

HOFFMANN, Roland J. – HARASKO, Alois. 2000. *Odsun – Die Vertreibung der Sudetendeutschen.* Munich: Veröffentlichung des Sudetendeutschen Archivs.

HRBEK, Jaroslav. "Americký dokument o odsunu Němců z Československa. Final Report. Transfer of German Population From Czechoslovakia to U.S. Zone, Germany." *Historie a vojenství* 5/1995 (XLIV). 139–171.

Interkommunale Zusammenarbeit im böhmisch-sächsischen Grenzraum.1999. Müller, B. (ed.). Institut für Ökologische Raumentwicklung e.V. Texte Nr. 131. Dresden/Ústí n. L./ Prague.

JECH, Karel – KAPLAN, Karel. 1995. *Dekrety prezidenta republiky 1940–1945* [Decrees of the President of the Republic 1940–1945], sv. I+II. Brno: Doplněk.

JIŘÍK, Václav. 2000. *Nedaleko od Norimberku* (z dějin retribučních soudů v západních Čechách) [Not far from Nuremberg (from the history of retributive courts in Western Bohemia)]. Cheb: Svět křídel.

"K otázkám česko-německých vztahů – Stanovisko severočeské rady KČP z 20. 1. 1995" [On Questions of Czech-German Relations-the Standpoint of the North-Bohemian Council of the CCB of the 20th of January 1995]. *Českomoravský hraničář* 65.

KAISER, Vladimír. 1998. *Intolerance-Intoleranz* (Češi, Němci a Židé na Ústecku 1938–1948) [(Czechs, Germans and Jews in the Ústí Region 1938–1948)]. Ústí nad Labem: Albis International.

KOHNOVÁ, Jana. 1969. *Člověk a lidská práva* [Man and Human Rights]. (UN Documents on Human Rights). Prague: Horizont.

Komu sluší omluva (dokumenty, fakta, svědectví) [Who is owed an apology (documents, facts, testimonies)]. 1992. (Collective of authors). Prague: Nakladatelství Erika.

KRÁL, Václav. 1964. *Die Deutschen in der Tschechoslowakei 1933–1947*. Prague: Nakladatelství Československé akademie věd (Acta occupationis Bohemiae and Moraviae).

KURTH, K. O. 1952. *Documents of humanity (during the mass expulsion)*. Goettingen/The Goettingen Research Committee.

Letáky z roku 1848. 1948. Novotný, Miloslav (ed.). Prague: Sfinx.

MEJDROVÁ, Hana. 1997. *Trpký úděl – Výbor dokumentů k dějinám německé sociální demokracie v ČSR v letech 1937–1948* [A Bitter Fate – Collection of documents on the history of the German Social Democratic Party in the CSR 1937–1948]. Prague: Ústav mezinárodních vztahů.

Mezinárodní konference 1943–1945 [International Conferences 1943–1945]. (Documents). Prague: Svoboda.

Minulost našeho státu v dokumentech [The History of Our State in Documents]. Státní ústřední archiv. 1971. Prague: Svoboda.

Mnichov v dokumentech I, II [Munich in Documents 1,2]. 1958. Prague: Státní nakladatelství politické literatury.

"Návrh řešení menšinové otázky v ČSR. Prozatímní memorandum o řešení sudetoněmecké otázky" [Proposal for a Solution to the Minority Question in the CSR. A provisional memorandum on the solution of the Sudeten German Question'], drawn up by J. Císař. Study department of the Czech Foreign Ministry. London. *Češi a sudetoněmecká otázka*. 264–265, 272–278.

NOVOTNÝ, Karel 1996. *Edvard Beneš – Odsun Němců z Československa* [Edvard Beneš-The Transfer of the Germans from Czechoslovakia]. Prague: Dita.

OLBERT, Franz. 1992. *Cesta ke smíření* [The Road to Conciliation]. (Documents 1948–1991). Prague: Institut pro středoevropskou kulturu a politiku.

PECHÁČEK, Jaroslav. 1984/1996. *Masaryk – Beneš – Hrad* [Masaryk-Beneš-the Castle]. Prague/München: České slovo/Faun.

POTOČNÝ, Miroslav. "Mezinárodní právo a transfer Němců z Československa" [International Law and the Transfer of the Germans out of Czechoslovakia], in *Právní aspekty odsunu sudetských Němců*. 14.

POTOČNÝ, Miroslav – ONDŘEJ, Jan. 1995. *Dokumenty mezinárodního práva* [Documents of International Law]. Prague: Univerzita Karlova.

Pražská výzva [The Prague Appeal]. 11. 3. 1985.

R. W. Seton-Watson and His Relations with the Czechs and Slovaks – R. W. Seton-Watson a jeho vztah k Čechům a Slovákům. Documents 1906–1951. Vols. I, II. 1995. Rychlík, Jan – Marzik, T. D. – Bielik, M. (eds.). Prague/Martin: Ústav T. G. Masaryka/Matica slovenská.

RYCHLÍK, Jan. "Memorandum Britského královského institutu mezinárodních vzathů o transferu národnostních menšin z roku 1945" [Memorandum of the British Royal Institute of International Relations on the Transfer of National Minorities 1945]. *Český časopis historický* 4/1993. 612–631.

Schicksalfrage Osteuropa. Referate auf der Landeskonferenz der S-G zu Weissenburg/Bayern am 30. 6.–1. 7. 1956. Undated and with no place of publication given. 22.

ŠNEJDÁREK, Antonín. "Dokumenty o vzniku tzv. Generálního plánu Východ" [Documents on the Origin of the so-called General Plan East]. *Československý časopis historický* 3/1961.

ŠNEJDÁREK, Antonín. 1968. *Druhá světová válka v dokumentech a fotografiích, I+II* [The Second World War in Documents and Photographs, I +II]. Prague: Svoboda.

STACKELBERG, Roderick – WINKLE, Sally A. 2002. *The Nazi Germany Sourcebook* (an anthology of texts). London/New York: Routledge.

SUM, Antonín. 1996. *Osudové kroky Jana Masaryka* [The Fateful Steps of Jan Masaryk]. Prague: Státní ústřední archiv.

"Transfer obyvatelstva v ČSR (Desetibodový plán E. Beneše k transferu sudetských Němců z Československa)" [The Transfer of Population in the CSR (E. Beneš's Ten-Point Plan for the Transfer of the Sudeten Germans from Czechoslovakia]. November 1943. London.

"Transfer of Population from Czechoslovakia" (Beneš's memorandum with Nichols' note to Roberts of the 28th of January 1944), in Brandes, D. *Cesta k vyhnání 1938–1945.* 223, 240.

Die Tschechoslowakei. Das Ende einer Fehlkonstruktion. 1993. Eibicht, R.-J. (ed.). Berg: VGB-Verlagsgesellschaft Berg.

URBAN, Rudolf. 1943. *Tajné fondy III. sekce. Z archivu ministerstva věcí zahraničních Republiky česko-slovenské* [Sectret Collections of the 3rd Section. From the archives of the Foreign Ministry of the Czecho-Slovak Republic]. Prague: Orbis.

Válečné deníky Jana Opočenského [The War Diaries of Jan Opočenský]. 2001. Čechurová, J. – Kuklík, J. – Čechura, J. – Němeček, J. (eds.). Prague: Karolinum.

WAGNEROVÁ, Alena. 1993. *Odsunuté vzpomínky* [Transferred Memories]. Prague: Prostor.

Wenzel Jaksch, Patriot und Europäer. (Documents). 1967. Kern, Karl (ed.). Munich: Die Brücke Verlag.

White Paper – on the Human Rights. 1977. CDU/CSU Group in the German Bundestag. *Situation in Germany and of the Germans in Eastern Europe.* Bonn.

List of literature and sources used

Allen, Martin. 2003. *Podraz na Hitlera a Hesse* [The Hitler-Hess Deception]. Brno: JOTA Military.

Als Feuer vom Himmel fiel. (Der Bombenkrieg gegen die Deutschen). *Spiegel special* (das Magazin zum Thema) 1/2003.

Alter, Peter. 2000. *The German Question and Europe – A History*. London: Arnold, New York: Oxford University Press.

Alter, Peter. 1994. *Nationalism*. London/New York/Sydney: Arnold.

Amort, Čestmír. 1965. *Heydrichiáda* [The Heydrichiad]. Prague: Naše vojsko/Svaz protifašistických bojovníků.

Anderson, Malcolm. "History And Territory", in *Frontiers*. 1996. Cambridge: Polity Press. 23.

Anderson, Malcolm. 2000. *States and Nationalism in Europe since 1945*. London/New York: Routledge.

Ash, Timothy Garton. "Does Central Europe Exist?" *New York Review of Books*. 9. 10. 1986.

Ash, Timothy Garton. "Europe's Endangered Liberal Order". *Foreign Affairs* 2/March-April 1998 (LXXVII). 37–58.

Ash, Timothy Garton. 2000. *History of the Present*. New York: Random House.

Ash, Timothy Garton. 1992. *Středoevropan volbou*. [A Central European by Choice] Prague: Institut pro středoevropskou kulturu a politiku.

Ash, Timothy Garton. *Rok zázraků* [Year of Miracles]. 123.

Augstein, R. (ed.) 1991. *Historikerstreit. Die Dokumentation der Kontroverse um die Einzigartigkeit der national sozialistischen Judervernichtung*. Munich/Zürich: Piper.

Azcárate, P. de. 1945. *League of Nations and National Minorities*. Washington: Carnegie Endowment for International Peace.

Barša, Pavel – Strmiska, Maxmilián. 1999. *Národní stát a etnický konflikt* [The Nation State and Ethnic Conflict]. Brno: Centrum pro studium demokracie a kultury.

Bartoš, Josef. 1986. *Okupované pohraničí a české obyvatelstvo 1938–1945* [The Occupied Borderlands and the Czech Population 1938–1945]. Prague: Svaz protifašistických bojovníků.

Bartošek, Karel. 2003. *Češi nemocní dějinami* [Czechs the Sick Men of History]. Prague/Litomyšl: Paseka.

Bauer, František. 1994. *Hitlerův Můj boj očima historiků I* [Hitler's My Struggle in the Eyes of Historians I]. Prague: UNIVERS.

Becher, Peter. "Staré a nové představy – na obou stranách" [Old and New Ideas-on both sides]. *Listy* 2/1997 (XXVII). 53–55.

Becker, Josef – Knipping, Franz. 1986. *Power in Europe?* Berlin/New York: Walter de Gruyter.

Bělohradský, V. "Evropa jako výhružka" [Europe as a Threat]. *Lidové noviny*. 14. 6. 1995.

Bělohradský, V. "Německo a excentrická Evropa" [Germany and Ex-centric Europe]. *Lidové noviny*. 13. 7. 1993.

Bělohradský, Václav. "Noví výrobci křivých rovnítek" [The New Manufacturers of Crooked Measuring Rods]. *Právo*. 25. 5. 2002.

Bělohradský, Václav. "Poučení z Mnichova" [The Lessons of Munich]. *Právo* – Literary supplement. 1. 10. 1998.

BĚLOHRADSKÝ, Václav. "Proti státu Evropa" [Against the State of Europe], in *Společné pohledy na Evropu* 14. 1998. Mayer, F. (ed.). Prague: CEFRES.

BĚLOHRADSKÝ, V. "Revizionismus a německá identita" [Revisionism and German Identity]. *Lidové noviny*. 12. 6. 1995.

BĚLOHRADSKÝ, Václav. "Sjednocené Německo a Západ: tři lekce" [United Germany and the World: Three lessons] (series of articles). *Lidové noviny*. 12.–14. 6. 1995.

BENEŠ, Edvard. 1948. *Demokracie dnes a zítra* [Democracy Today and Tomorrow]. Prague: Čin.

BENEŠ, Edvard. 1968. *Mnichovské dny* [The Days of Munich]. Prague: Svoboda.

BENEŠ, Edvard. 1995. *Odsun Němců* [The Transfer of the Germans]. Prague: Společnost E. Beneše/Svaz bojovníků za svobodu.

BENEŠ, Edvard. 1947. *Paměti – Od Mnichova k nové válce a k novému vítězství* [Memoirs – From Munich to a New War and a New Victory]. Prague: Orbis.

BENEŠ, Edvard. 1946. *Šest let exilu a světové války* (Projevy). [Six Years of Exile and World War]. Prague: Družstevní práce.

BENEŠ, Edvard. 1927. *Světová válka a naše revoluce* [The World War and Our Revolution]. I–III. Werstadt, J. – Opočenský, J. – Papoušek, J. (eds.). Prague: Orbis/Čin.

BENEŠ, Edvard. 1947. *Úvahy o slovanství* [Reflections on Slavdom]. Prague: Čin.

BENEŠ, Zdeněk. "České dějiny 20. století v německých učebnicích dějepisu" [20th-Century Czech history in German Textbook Historiography]; WEGER, T. "Analýza českých učebnic dějepisu" [An Analysis of Czech Textbook History], in *Mariánskolázeňské rozhovory: Učebnice a česko-německé sousedství* [Mariánské Lázně Conversations: Textbook and Czech-German Neighbourhood]. 1998. *Die Beneš-Dekrete*. 2002. Coudenhove-Kalergi, Barbara – Rathkolb, Oliver (eds.). Wien: Czernin Verlag.

Benešovy dekrety – záměrně živený spor [The Beneš Decrees – a deliberately nourished dispute]. *Přísně tajné* 3/2002.

BERGHAHN, Volker R. 1996. *Quest for Economic Empire*. Providence/Oxford: Berghahn Books.

BERNADOTTE, Folke. 1946. *Konec Německa* [The End of Germany]. Prague: Melantrich.

BEROUNSKÁ, Olga. 1969. "Postavení a činnost přesídleneckých organizací a zejména sudetoněmeckého landsmanschaftu v SRN po 2. světové válce" [The Status and Activity of the Expellee Organisations and Especially the Sudetendeutsch Landsmannschaft in the FRG after the Second World War], in *Severní Čechy a Mnichov*. Ústí n. L.: Pedagogická fakulta. 241.

Bez démonů minulosti [Without the Demons of the Past]. 2003. Richter, Karel (ed.). Prague: Rodiče, s. r. o.

BIMAN, Stanislav. 2003. *Kdo byl kdo v Říšské župě Sudety 1938–1945* [Who was Who in the Sudetenland Reichgau]. Vol. 1 (A–B). Ústí nad Labem: Albis International.

BIMAN, Stanislav – CÍLEK, Roman. 1976. *Partie hnědých pěšáků* [A Band of Brown Infantry Men]. Ústí nad Labem: Severočeské nakladatelství.

BIMAN, Stanislav – CÍLEK, Roman. 1989. *Poslední mrtví, první živí* [The Last Dead, the First Living]. Ústí nad Labem: Severočeské nakladatelství.

BIMAN, Stanislav – MALÍŘ, Jaroslav. 1983. *Kariéra učitele tělocviku* [The Career of a PE Teacher]. Ústí nad Labem: Severočeské nakladatelství.

Biographies in the Borderland. 2002. Zich, František (ed.). Prague: Sociologický ústav AV ČR.

BIRKETT, Justice. "International Legal Theories evolved at Nuremburg". *International Affairs* 23 (1947). 317–325.

BLAIVE, Muriel – MINK, Georges. 2003. *Benešovy dekrety* [The Beneš Decrees]. Praga: CEFRES.

BLEY, F. 1897. *Die Weltstellung des Deutschtums*. München: Lehmann. 20.

BLUMENWITZ, Dieter. "Benešovy dekrety z roku 1945 z hlediska mezinárodního práva" [The Beneš Decrees of 1945 from the Perspective of International Law], in *Edvard Beneš a střední Evropa*. 1994. Drda, A. (ed.). Prague: Institut pro středoevropskou kulturu a politiku.

BLUMENWITZ, Dieter. 1985. *Der Prager Vertrag*. Bonn: Kulturstiftung der deutschen Vertriebenen.

BLUMENWITZ, Dieter. 2001. *Vorschlag einer Minderheiten-schutzbestimmung in der Charta der Grundrechte der Europäischen Union*. Munich: Internationales Institut für Nationalitätenrecht und Regionalismus.

BOEHLING, Rebecca. 1996. *A Question of Priorities*. Providence/Oxford: Berghahn Books.

BOHÁČ, Zdeněk. 1993. *České země a Lužice* [The Czech Lands and Lusatia]. Tišnov/Budyšín: Nakladatelství Sursum/Společnost Cyrila a Metoděje.

BOHMANN, Alfred. 1975. *Menschen und Grenze* (Band 4). Köln am Rhein: Verlag Wissenschaft und Politik.

BOHMANN, Alfred. 1959. *Das Sudetendeutschtum in Zahlen*. Munich: Sudetendeutscher Rat.

BOLDT, Frank. "Základy a důsledky německé Ostpolitik" [The Principles and Consequences of German Ostpolitik]. *Dějiny a současnost* 2/1991. 41–46.

BOLDT, Frank – HILF, Rudolf. 1992. *Bayerisch-böhmische Nachbarschaft*. Munich: Bayerische Landeszentrale für politische Bildungsarbeit.

BORÁK, Mečislav. 1998. *Spravedlnost podle dekretu, Retribuční soudnictví v ČSR a Mimořádný lidový soud v Ostravě (1945–1948)* [Justice according to Decree, Retribution Justice in the CSR and the Special People's Court in Ostrava (1945–1948)]. Ostrava: Tilia.

BORODZIEJ, Włodzimierz. "Polská historiografie o vyhnání Němců" [|Polish Historiography andt he Expulsion of the Germans]. *Soudobé dějiny* 2/1997. 306–326.

BOULDING, Kenneth. "National Actors and International Interactions (Nonrational Factors in Foreign Policy)", in Rochester, J. M. – Pearson, F. S. 1988. *International Relations*. New York: Random House. 200.

BŘACH, Radko. 1996. *Československo a Evropa v polovině dvacátých let* [Czechoslovakia and Europe in the mid 1920s]. Prague/Litomyšl: Paseka.

BŘACH, Radko. 1994. *Smlouva o vzájemných vztazích mezi ČSSR a SRN z roku 1973* [The Agreement on Mutual Relations between the CSSR and the FRG of 1973]. Prague: Ústav pro soudobé dějiny AV ČR. 73.

BRAND, W. 1969. *Zwanzig Jahre Witikobund*. Beiträge, kleine Reihe des Institutum Bohemicum. Munich: Ackermann-Gemeinde. 30.

BRANDES, Detlef. 1999. *Češi pod německým protektorátem* [Czechs under the German Protectorate]. Prague: Prostor.

BRANDES, Detlef. 2002. *Cesta k vyhnání 1938–1945* [The Road to Expulsion 1938–1945]. Prague: Prostor.

BRANDES, Detlef. 2003. *Exil v Londýně 1939–1943* [Exile in London 1939–1943]. Prague: Karolinum.

BRAUMANDL, Wolfgang. 1985. *Die Wirtschafts und Sozialpolitik des Deutschen Reiches im Sudetenland 1938–1945*. Nürnberg: Helmut Preussler Verlag.

BRENNER, Michael. 1997. *After the Holocaust-Rebuilding Jewish Lives in Postwar Germany*. Princeton: Princeton University Press.

BROD, Toman. 1992. *Československo a Sovětský svaz 1939–1945* [Czechoslovakia and the Soviet Union 1939–1945]. Prague: Listopad/Práce/SPB.

BROD, Toman. 1990/91. *Operace velký podvod I+II* [Operation Major Deception I+II]. Prague: Magnet.

BROKLOVÁ, Eva. 1992. *Československá demokracie 1918–1938* [Czechoslovak Democracy 1918–1938]. Prague: SLON.

BROKLOVÁ, Eva. "Dvě Hitlerovy lži o Československu" [Two of Hitler's Lies about Czechoslovakia], in *Spory o dějiny* I. 1999. Bednář, M. (ed.). Prague: Masarykův ústav AV ČR. 49.

BROKLOVÁ, Eva. "Německá a československá meziválečné demokracie" [German and Czechoslovak Inter-War Democracy]. *Politologická revue* 2/1995. 17–28.

BROKLOVÁ, Eva. "Nevyužitá příležitost v minulosti" [An Unexploited Opportunity in the Past]. *Lidové noviny*. 26. 3. 1994. IV.

BROKLOVÁ, Eva. 1999. *Politická kultura německých aktivistických stran v Československu 1918–1938* [The Political Culture of the German Activist Parties in Czechoslovakia 1918–1938] Prague: Karolinum.

BROWN, MacAlister. 1959. "Fifth Column in Eastern Europe". *Journal of Central European Affairs*. July 1959 (XIX).

BROWN, Martin D. 2003. *Dealing with Democrats. Decision-making and policy formation within the British Foreign Office's Central Department with regard to the Czechoslovak political exiles in Britain and the Czechoslovak question, 1939 to 1945*. Downloadable from web.

BROWN, Martin D. "Forcible Population Transfers – A flawed legacy or an unavoidable necessity in protracted ethnic conflicts? The Case of Sudeten Germans". *RUSI (The Royal United Services Institute for Defence Studies) Journal* 4/August 2003 (CIIL). 81–87.

BROWN, Martin D. 2004. *"Never complain, never explain". The Foreign Office's influence on the formation of British Policy in regard to Anglo-Polish-Czechoslovak relations in exile, 1939–1945*. Unpublished paper. 1–13.

BROWN, Michael E. 1993. *Ethnic Conflict and International Security*. Princeton/New Jersey: Princeton University Press.

BRUBAKER, Rogers. "National Minorities, Nationalizing States and External National Homelands in the New Europe". *Daedalus* 2/1995 (CXXIV). 107–132.

BRÜGEL, Johann W. 1962. "Die Aussiedlung der Deutschen aus der Tschechoslowakei". *Vierteljahreshefte für Zeitgeschichte* 8. 134–164.

BRÜGEL, Johann W. "German Diplomacy and the Sudeten Question before 1938". *International Affairs* 3 (July)/1961 (XXXVII). 328–331.

BRÜGEL, Johann W. "Die Sudetendeutsche Frage auf der Potsdamer Konferenz". *Vierteljahreshefte für Zeitgeschichte*. 1962. 56–61.

BRÜGEL. Johann W. 1967/1974. *Tschechen und Deutsche I+II*. Munich: Nymphenburger Verlagshandlung.

BRUNNER, Georg. 1996. *Nationality Problems and Minority Conflicts in Eastern Europe*. Gütersloh: Bertelsmann Foundation Publishers.

BUCHHEIT, Lee C. 1978. *Secession-The Legitimacy of Self-Determination*. New Haven and London: Yale University Press.

BULMER, Simon – JEFFERY, Charlie – PATERSON, William E. 2000. *Germany's European Diplomacy*. Manchester/New York: Manchester University Press.

BURGHARDT, Andrew F. "The Bases of Territorial Claims". *Geographical Review* 63/1973. 225–245.

BUSEK, Erhard. "Česko-rakouské paralely" [Czech-Austrian Parallels]. *Nová přítomnost* 6/1996. 2–4.

BUSEK, Erhard. "Střední Evropa v budoucí evropské konfederaci" [Central Europe ina Future European Confederation]. *Střední Evropa* 37/1994.

CALLEO, David. 1978. *The German Problem Reconsidered*. Cambridge/London/New York/Melbourne: Cambridge University Press.

CAPLAN, Richard – FEFFER, John. 1996. *Europe's New Nationalism*. New York/Oxford: Oxford University Press.

ČEJKA, Eduard. 1997. *Československý odboj na Západě 1939–1945* [The Czechoslovak Resistance Struggle in the West 1939–1945]. Prague: Mladá fronta.

ČELOVSKÝ, Bořivoj. 2001. *Konec českého tisku?* [The End of the Czech Press?]. Ostrava: Tilia.

ČELOVSKÝ, Bořivoj. 1999. *Mnichovská dohoda 1938* [The Munich Agreement 1938]. Ostrava: Tilia.

ČELOVSKÝ, Bořivoj. 2000. *Politici bez moci* [Politicians without Power]. Ostrava: Tilia.

ČELOVSKÝ, Bořivoj. 2002. *Strážce nové Evropy* [Guardians of the New Europe]. Ostrava: Tilia.

ČELOVSKÝ, Bořivoj. "The Transferred Sudeten-Germans and their political activity". *Journal of Central European Affairs*. April 1957 (VI). 127–149.

ČERNÝ, Bohumil. "Edvard Beneš a odsun Němců z ČSR" [Edvard Beneš and the Transfer of the Germans from the CSR]. *Dějiny a současnost* 3/1969 (XI). 10–12.

ČERNÝ, Bohumil. "Schwarze Front v Československu (1933–1938)" [The Schwarze Front in Czechoslovakia (1933–1938)]. *Československý časopis historický* 3/1966. 328–357.

ČERNÝ, Václav. 1992. *Paměti 1938–1945. Křik koruny české* [Memoirs 1938–1945. The Cry of the Crown of Bohemia]. Brno: Atlantis.

CESAR, Jaroslav – ČERNÝ, Bohumil. "Iredentistické hnutí německých buržoazních nacionalistů z ČSR v letech 1918–1929" [The Irredentist Movement of the German Bourgeois Nationalists from the CSR in the years 1918–1929]. *Československý časopis historický* 6/1961. 789–831.

CESAR, Jaroslav – ČERNÝ, Bohumil. 1960. *Od sudetoněmeckého separatismu k plánům odvety* [From Sudeten-German Separatism to Plans for Revenge]. Liberec: Severočeské krajské nakladatelství.

CESAR, Jaroslav – ČERNÝ, Bohumil. 1962. *Politika německých buržoazních stran v Československu v letech 1918–1938, I+II* [The Politics of the German Bourgeois Parties in Czechoslovakia in the Years 1918–1938, I+II]. Prague: Nakladatelství ČSAV.

Češi a Němci, smiřme se (Obracejme se do budoucnosti) [Czechs and Germans, Let us be conciliatory (Let us turn to the future)]. Text of V. Klaus's speech at Prague Castle. *Lidové noviny*. 15. 3. 2003. 3.

Češi – Němci [Czechs – Germans]. 1991–2000. (Series of collections of the papers presented at the I-VIII symposia in Jihlava). Prague: Prago-Media-News.

Češi – Němci – odsun [Czechs-Germans-Transfer]. (Discussion by independent historians). 1990. Černý, B. et al. (eds.). Prague: Academia.

Česká zahraniční politika (úvahy o prioritách) [Czech Foreign Policy (Considerations on Priorities)]. 1997. Kotyk, Václav (ed.). Prague: Ústav mezinárodních vztahů.

České národní aktivity v pohraničních oblastech první Československé republiky [Czech national activities in the border areas of the first Czechoslovak Republic]. 2003. Šrajerová, O. (ed.). Ostrava: Filozofická fakulta Univerzity F. Palackého/Slezský ústav Slezského muzea/Nakladatelství Tilia.

Československá vlastivěda [Czechoslovak National History]. Vol. 5. The State. 1931. Prague: Sfinx.

Československé dějiny v datech [Czechoslovak History in Dates]. 1986. (Collective of authors). Prague: Svoboda.

Československý výběr (Baťova cena čsl. Novinářství 1937) [*Czechoslovak Selection* (Baťa Prize for Czechoslovak Journalism 1937)]. Zlín: Nákladem společnosti "Tisk".

Česko-německé vztahy 1945–2000 [Czech-German Relations 1945–2000]. (Collection of conference papers). 1999. Prague: Kruh občanů České republiky vyhnaných v roce 1938 z pohraničí.

Česko-německé vztahy po pádu železné opony [Czech-German Relations after the Fall of the Iron Curtain]. Prague: Sešity Rady pro mezinárodní vztahy 1/1997.

CHÁSZÁR, Edward. "The Problem of National Minorities before and after the Paris Treaties of 1947". *Nationality Papers* 2/1981 (IX).

CHÉRADAME, André: *L'Europe et la question d'Autriche au seuil du XXe siècle*. 1901. See new reproduction of the book by Nabu Press, 2010.

CHMEL, Rudolf. "Maďarský komplex a trinanonský syndróm" [The Hungarian Complex and the Trianon Syndrome]. *Listy* 5/2001 (XXXI). 33–37.

CHURAŇ, Milan. 2001. *Postupim a Československo – mýtus a skutečnost* [Potsdam and Czechoslovakia – Myth and Reality]. Prague: Libri.

CHURCHILL, Winston. 1992–1995. *Druhá světová válka* [The Second World War], I–VI. Prague: Lidové noviny.

COBBAN, Alfred. 1969. *The Nation State and National Self-Determination*. London/Glasgow: Collins.

COHEN, G. B. 2000. *Němci v Praze 1861–1914* [The Germans in Prague 1861–1914]. Prague: Karolinum.

COHN-BENDIT, D. "Diskusi o dekretech by měla ukončit konference" [The Conference should end discussions on the decrees] (Interview). *Právo*. 13. 5. 2002.

Coming to Terms with the Past, Opening up to the Future. (Discussion Papers in German Studies). 1998. Handl, V. (ed.). University of Birmingham: Institute for German Studies. *Die Constitution* 33. 29. 4. 1848. 503–504.

COOK, J. "Obchodování a lítost" [Trading and Regret]. *Týden* 3/1997. 53–55 (taken from *Business Central Europe*).

COUDENHOVE-KALERGI, Richard N. "Češi a Němci (Německá otázka v Československu)" [Czechs and Germans (The German Question in Czechoslovakia)]. *Střední Evropa* 7/1991 (XXI). 52–56.

COUDENHOVE-KALERGI, Richard N. 1993. *Pan-Evropa*. Prague: Panevropa.

COWELL, Alan. "Memories of Wartime Brutalities Revive Czech-German Animosity". *The New York Times*. 6. 3. 1996.

CRAIG, Gordon A. 1962. *Europe since 1815*. New York: Knopf. 10–11.

CRAIG, Gordon A. 1991. *The Germans*. New York/London: Penguin.

CRAIG, Gordon A. 1982. *The Germans*. New York: Putnam's Sons.

CRAIG, Gordon A. – LOEWENHEIM, Francis L. 1994. *The Diplomats 1939–1979*. Princeton, New Jersey: Princeton University Press.

DANILEVSKY, Nikolai Y. 1869. *Russia and Europe*.

DAVIDSON, Eugene. 1959. *The Death and Life of Germany*. New York: Alfred A. Knopf.

Dějiny a současnost 4/1999 – Téma: Od Mnichova k válce [History journal, theme: From Munich to the War].

Dějiny Československa v datech [History of Czechoslovakia in Dates]. 1968. (Collective of authors). Prague: Svoboda.

DEJMEK, J. 2001. "Britská diplomacie, Československo a Sudetoněmecká strana" [British Diplomacy, Czechoslovakia and the Sudeten German Party], in *Moderní dějiny* 9. Prague: Historický ústav AV ČR. 166.

DEJMEK, Jindřich. 2002. *Československo – jeho sousedé a velmoci ve XX. století* [Czechoslovakia – its neighbours and the great powers in the 20th century]. (Selected chapters from the history of Czechoslovak foreign policy). Prague: CEP.

DEJMEK, Jindřich. "Edvard Beneš – obtížná cesta k politické biografii (historiografický přehled)" [Edvard Beneš – The difficult path to political biography (historiographical overview)]. *Český časopis historický* 3/2003. 624–662.

DEJMEK, Jindřich. 1998. *Historik v čele diplomacie Kamil Krofta* [A Historian at the Head of Diplomacy]. Prague: Karolinum.

DEJMEK, Jindřich. 2003. *Nenaplněné naděje (politické a diplomatické vztahy Československa a Velké Británie 1918–1938* [Unfulfilled Hopes (the political and diplomatic relations between Czechoslovakia and Great Britain 1918–1938)]. Prague: Karolinum.

DEJMEK, Jindřich – KUKLÍK, Jan – NĚMEČEK, Jan. 1999. *Kauza tzv. Benešovy dekrety. Historické kořeny a souvislosti* [Controversy: The So-called Beneš Decrees. Historical Roots and Contexts]. Prague: Historický ústav AV ČR.

DELFS, Silke. "Heimatvertriebene, Aussiedler, Spätaussiedler". *Aus Politik und Zeitgeschichte*. November 1993. B 48/93. 26.

DEMANDT, Alexander. 1990. *Deutschland Grenzen in der Geschichte*. Munich: Verlag C. H. Beck.

DENIS, Ernest. 1931. *Válka (Příčiny bezprostřední a vzdálené – Otrávení národa – Smlouva)* [The War (Immediate and Remote Causes – The Poisoning of the Nation – Agreement)]. Prague: Nakladatelství Šolc a Šimáček.

DEUTSCH, Karl W. 1981. "On Nationalism, World Regions and the Nature of the West", in *Mobilization, Center-Periphery Structures and Nation-Building*. 1981. Rokkan, Stein – Torsvik, Per (eds.). Bergen/Oslo/Tromsö: Universitetsforlaget. 51–93.

DEUTSCH, Karl W. "Social Mobilisation and Political Development". *American Political Science Review* 55/September 1961. 493–514.

Deutsche und Tschechen. 1993. Informationen zur politischen Bildung 132. Bonn: Bundeszentrale für politische Bildung.

Deutschland bei Beginn des 20. Jahrhunderts. 1900. Von einem Deutschen. Berlin: Militär-Verlag R. Felix. 41.

DIENSTBIER, Jiří. 2000. *Od snění k realitě*. Paměti 1989–1999 [From Dream to Reality. Memoirs 1989–1999]. Prague: Lidové noviny.

DIENSTBIER, Jiří. 1990. *Snění o Evropě* [Dreaming of Europe]. Prague: Lidové noviny.

DILKE, Sir Charles. 1887. *l'Europeen*. Paris: Quantin. 183.

DOBEŠ, J. "Nolte a studium dějin fašismu" [Nolte and the Study of Fascism], in Nolte, E. 1999. *Fašismus ve své epoše*. Prague: Argo. 671–672.

DOBRÝ, Anatol. 1959. *Hospodářská krize československého průmyslu ve vztahu k Mnichovu* [The Economic Crisis of Czechoslovak Industry in relation to Munich]. Prague: Nakladatelství Československé akademie věd.

DOLEŽAL, Bohuslav. "Pohled na Němce: přísně střežit a pozorovat" [The View on Germans: strictly guard and observe]. *Mladá fronta Dnes*. 12. 9. 1995.

DOLEŽAL, Jiří. 1966. *Jediná cesta* [The Only Way]. Prague: Naše vojsko/SPB.

DRÁBEK, J. "Glosy k procesu s henleinovskými poslanci a senátory" [Glosses on the trial of the Henleinian deputies and senators]. *Dnešek* 46 (I.). 6. 2. 1947. 727–729.

DÜHRING, E. 1881. *Die Judenfrage als Racen, Sitten und Kulturfrage*. Karlsruhe/Lepizig.

EČER, Bohuslav. 1946. *Jak jsem je stíhal* [How I Prosecuted Them]. Prague: Naše vojsko.

EČER, Bohuslav. 1946. *Norimberský soud* [The Nuremberg Court]. Prague: Orbis.

Economic Consequences of the Size of Nations. 1960. Robinson, E. A. G. (ed.). London: Macmillan & Co. Ltd., New York: St. Martin's Press.

Edvard Beneš – Vzkazy do vlasti [Edvard Beneš – Messages to the Homeland]. 1996. Šolc, J. (ed.). Prague: Historický ústav Akademie věd ČR.

Edvard Beneš a střední Evropa [Edvard Beneš and Central Europe]. Drda, A. (ed.). 1994. Prague: Institut pro středoevropskou kulturu a politiku.

EICHLER, Richard W. "Vom kulturellen Profil der sudetendeutschen Volksgruppe", in *Rechtsstaat-Kulturerbe-Volksgruppe*. (Schriften der Sudetendeutschen Akademie der Wissenschaften und Künste, Band 1). Munich: Verlagshaus Sudetenland. 45–64.

EKD – Evangelische Kirche in Deutschland. 1998. *Der trennende Zaun ist abgebrochen* (Zur Verständigung zwischen Tschechen und Deutschen). Leipzig: Verlag des Gustav-Adolfs-Werks.

ELSÄSSER, Jürgen. 2003. *Der deutsche Sonderweg*. Munich: Diederichs.

EMERSON, Rupert. "Self Determination". *American Journal of International Law* 65/1971. 459–475.

ENSOR, R. C. K. "Mein Kampf and Europe". *International Affairs* 18/1939. 486.

ERMACORA, Felix. 1978. *Nationalitätenkonflikt und Volksgruppenrecht*. München: INTEREG. 38–49.

ERMACORA, Felix. 1991. *Rechtsgutachten über die Sudetendeutschen Fragen*. Innsbruck/Wien.

ERMACORA, Felix. 1995. *Die Sudetendeutschen Fragen (Rechtsgutachten)*. München: Verlagshaus Sudetenland.

ERMACORA, Felix. 1984. "Völker, Volksgruppen, Minderheiten im Ringen um Identität", in *Forschung und Praxis in den Sudetenländern*. Band 5. Munich: Verlagshaus Sudetenland. 19–24.

EVANS, Richard J. 1997. *Rereading German History 1800–1996* (From Unification to Reunification). London/New York: Routledge.

Europa von A bis Z. 2002. Weidenfeld, Werner – Wessels, Wolfgang (eds.). Bonn: Bundeszentrale für politische Bildung.

Evropa očima Čechů [Europe through the Eyes of Czechs]. 1997. Hahn, E. (ed.). Prague: Nakladatelství Franze Kafky.

Exil a domov [Exile and Homeland]. *Historické listy* 4/1995. Prague: Společnost Historických listů.

FARLEY, Lawrence T. 1986. *Plebiscites and Sovereignty*. Westview/Boulder/London: Mansell Publishing Ltd.

FASTENRATH, U. "Who is bound by the Potsdam Agreement? The Allies adopted a series of heterogeneous provisions". *Frankfurter Allgemeine Zeitung.* 20· 3. 1996.

FEDER, G. 1932. *The Program of the Party of Hitler*. Munich. 18.

FEIERABEND, Ladislav K. 1996. *Politické vzpomínky, III* [Political Memories, 3]. Brno: Atlantis.

FEIS, Herbert. 1960. *Between War and Peace (The Potsdam Conference)*. New Jersey: Princeton University Press.

FEJTÖ, François. 1998. *Rekviem za mrtvou říši* [Requiem for a Dead Empire]. Prague: Academia.

Fenomén holocaust [The Phenomenon of the Holocaust]. (Conference collection). 2001. Prague/Terezín: Task Force for International Cooperation on Holocaust Education, Rememberance and Research.

FIALA, Petr. 1995. *Katolicismus a politika* [Catholicism and Politics]. Brno: Centrum pro studium demokracie a kultury.

FIALA, Petr. "Sudetští Němci a politika" [Sudeten Germans and Politics]. PROGLAS 4/1995 (VI). 6–10.

FIALOVÁ, Ludmila – HORSKÁ, Pavla (et al.). 1998. *Dějiny obyvatelstva českých zemí* [History of the Population of the Bohemian Lands]. Prague: Mladá fronta.

FISCHER, J. 1995. *Risiko Deutschland*. Munich: Knaur.

FISCHER, J. –PATZAK, V. – PERTH, V. 1937. *Ihr Kampf: Die wahren Ziele der Sudetendeutschen Partei*. Karlsbad: Verlagsanstalt Graphia. 73.

FISCHER, Otokar. 1927. *Belgie a Německo* [Belgium and Germany]. Prague: Filosofická fakulta University Karlovy.

Die Flucht – Über die Vertreibung der Deutschen aus dem Osten. 2002. Aust, Stefan – Burgdorff, Stephan (eds.). Stuttgart/Munich: Deutsche Verlags-Anstalt.

FOERSTER, Friedrich Wilhelm. 1948. *Evropa a německá otázka* [Europe and the German Question]. Prague: Nakladatelství Universum.

FOOT, Michael R. D. 1997. *S.O.E. Stručná historie Útvaru zvláštních operací* [SOE, A Short History of the Special Operations Executive]. Brno: Bonus A.

FORD, G. S. *American Historical Review*. LVII (1951–52).

Four Fighting Years. 1943. Czechoslovak Ministry of Foreign Affairs (ed.). London/New York/Melbourne: Hutchinson & Co. (Publishers).

FRANZEL, Emil. 1997. *Sudetendeutsche Geschichte*. Augsburg: Bechtermünz.

FRANZEN, K. Erik. 2002. *Die Vertriebenen-Hitlers letzte Opfer*. Berlin: Ullstein Taschenbuch Verlag.

FREIBERGER, S. "Ein Beitrag zur Diagnostik einiger psychopatologischen Phänomena in der Beziehung zwischen ungleichen Partnern", in Čelovský, B. *Mnichovský syndrom* [The Munich Syndrome]. Ostrava: Syndikát novinářů. Motto in the introduction.

FREISTAAT SACHSEN. 1999. *Zu Hause in Sachsen Die Sorben*. Neschwitz: Sächsisches Statsministerium für Wissenschaft und Kunst.

FRIEDRICH, J. 2003. *Der Brand. Deutschland im Bombenkrieg 1940–1945*. Propyläen Verlag.

GAJANOVÁ, A. 1967. *ČSR a středoevropská politika velmocí 1918–1938* [The CSR and the Central European Policy of the Great Powers 1918–1938]. Prague: Academia.

GALANDAUER, Jan. 1990. "Předmluva" [Preface], in Masaryk, Tomáš G. *Česká otázka* [The Czech Question]. Prague: Svoboda.

GALANDAUER, Jan. 1988. *Vznik Československé republiky* 1918 [The Birth of the Czech Republic 1918]. Prague: Svoboda.

GEBEL, Ralf. 2000. *"Heim ins Reich!" Konrad Henlein und der Reichsgau Sudetenland (1938–1945)*. Munich: Oldenbourg Verlag.

GEBHART, Jan. "Migrace českého obyvatelstva v letech 1938–1939" [Migration of the Czech Population in 1938–1939]. *Český časopis historický* 3/1998 (IVC). 561–573.

GEBHART, Jan – KUKLÍK, Jan. 1996. *Dramatické i všední dny Protektorátu* [Dramatic and Ordinary Days of the Protectorate]. Prague: Themis.

GEBHART, Jan – KUKLÍK, Jan. 2004. *Druhá republika 1938–1939* [The Second Republic 1938–1939]. Prague/Litomyšl: Paseka.

GEBHART, Jan – ŠEDIVÝ, Ivan. 2003. *Česká společnost za velkých válek 20. století* [Czech Society in the Great Wars of the 20th Century]. Prague: Karolinum.

GEISSLER, Rainer. 1992. *Die Sozialstruktur Deutschlands*. Opladen: Westdeutscher Verlag GmbH.

GELLNER, Ernest André. 1993. *Národy a nacionalismus* [Nations and Nationalism]. Prague: Nakladatelství Jaroslav Hříbal.

GELLNER, Ernest André. "Nacionalismus a politika ve východní Evropě". *Mezinárodní politika* 4/1993. 20–24.

Germany's Difficult Passage to Modernity. 1999. Lankowski, Carl (ed.). New York/Oxford: Berghahn Books.

GILBERT, G. M. "The Council of Europe and Minority Rights". *Human Rights Quarterly* 18/1996. 160–189.

GILBERT, G. M. 1971. *Norimberský deník* [Nuremberg Diary]. Prague: Mladá fronta.

GILDEA, Robert. 2003. *Barricades and Borders. Europe 1800–1914*. Oxford/New York: Oxford University Press.

GISEVIUS, Hans Bernd. 1948. *Cesta do pekel* (Až k hořkému konci) [The Road To Hell (Right to the bitter end)]. Prague: Atheneum.

GLAESSNER, Gert-Joachim. 1999. *Demokratie und Politik in Deutschland*. Opladen: Leske+Budrich.

GLETTLER, M. – LIPTÁK, Ľ. – MÍŠKOVÁ, A. 2002. *Nacionálno-socialistický systém vlády* (Ríšská župa Sudety, Protektorát Čechy a Morava, Slovensko) [The National Socialist System of Government (The Reichsgau of the Sudetenland, the Protectorate of Bohemia and Moravia, Slovakia)]. Bratislava: Academic Electronic Press.

GLOTZ, Peter. 2003. *Die Vertreibung (Böhmen als Lehrstück)*. Munich: Ullstein.

The Goldhagen Effect – History, Memory, Nazism – Facing the German Past. 2000. Elley, Geoff (ed.). Ann Arbor: The University of Michigan Press.

GOLDSTEIN, Erik. 2002. *The First World War Peace Settlements 1919–1925*. London/New York/Toronto/Sydney: Pearson Education.

GOODRICK-CLARKE, Nicholas. 1998. *Okultní kořeny nacismu* [The Occult Roots of Nazism]. Prague: Votobia.

GORDON, Helmut. 1990. *Die Beneš-Denkschriften*. Berg: Druffel-Verlag.

GOTTLIEB, G. "Nations Without States". *Foreign Affairs* 3/May-June 1994 (LXXIII). 100–112.

GRANT DUFF, Shiela. 1939. *Europe And the Czechs*. London. 129.

GRANT DUFF, Shiela. 1942. *A German Protectorate. The Czechs under Nazi Rule*. London. 196.

GREGOROVIČ, Miroslav. 1995. *Kapitoly o českém fašismu* (fašismus jako měřítko politické dezorientace) [Chapters on Czech Fascism (Fascism as a measure of political disorientation)]. Prague: Lidové noviny.

GROBELNÝ, Andělín. 1989. *Národnostní politika nacistů a český průmysl* [The Nationality Policy of the Nazis and Czech Industry]. Ostrava: Profil.

GROSCURTH, H. 1970. *Tagebücher eines Abwehroffiziers 1938–1940*. Stuttgart: H. Krausnick/H. C. Deutsch.

Gross-Deutschland und Mitteleuropa um das Jahr 1950. Von einem Alldeutschen. 1895. Berlin: Thormann.

GROSSER, T. 1998. "Integrácia odsunutých v Spolkovej republike Nemecko" [The Integration of Expelled Germans in the Federal Republic of Germany], in *V rozdelenej Európe*. 40.

GRUBEN, Hervé de. "Belgian Views on the German Treaty". *International Affairs* 23/1947. 326–335.

GRULICH, Rudolf. 1999. *"Ethnische Säuberung" und Vertreibung als Mittel der Politik im 20. Jahrhundert*. Munich: Internationales Institut für Nationaltätenrecht und Regionalismus.

GRÜNWALD, Leopold. 1986. *Sudetendeutscher Widerstand gegen den Nationalsozialismus*. Benediktbeuren: Riess-Druck Verlag.

GRÜNWALD, L. "Die Ursache der Katastrofe von 1938–1939 in der "grosstschechischen" bzw. Tschechoslowakischen Einstellung der Gründer der Republik", in *Wir haben uns selbst aus Europa vertrieben. Tschechische Selbstkritik an der Vertreibung der Sudetendeutschen*. 1985. Munich: Sudetendeutsche Stiftung. 13.

HAAS, H. "Konflikt při uplatňování nároků na právo na sebeurčení" [The Conflict in Claims to the Right of Self-Determination], in Mommsen, H. – Kováč, D. – Malíř, J. – Marková, M. *První světová válka a vztahy mezi Čechy, Slováky a Němci*. 176–177.

HABEL, Fritz P. 1996. *Eine Politische Legende*. Munich: Langen Müller.

HABEL, Fritz P. 2002. *Die Sudetendeutschen*. Munich: Langen Müller.

HACKE, Christian. "The National Interests of the Federal Republic of Germany on the Threshold of the 21st Century". *Aussenpolitik/German Foreign Affairs Review* 2/1998 (IL). 5–25.

HAFFNER, Sebastian. 1998. *Německá revoluce 1918–1919*. Brno: Bonus Memorabilia.

HAFFNER, Sebastian. 1995. *Od Bismarcka k Hitlerovi* [From Bismarck to Hitler]. Prague: Votobia.

HAGE, V. 2003. *Zeugen der Zerstörung* (Die Literatur und der Luftkrieg). S. Fischer Verlag.

HAHN, Eva. "Španělské vesnice a české větrné mlýny: požadavek zrušení Benešových dekretů v německých médiích" [The Strange Backward Dump and Czech Windmills: the demand for the abolition of the Beneš Decrees in the German media], in Mink, G. – Blaive, M. *Benešovy dekrety* (Budoucnost Evropy a vyrovnávání se s minulostí). 76–77.

HAHN, Eva. 1999. *Sudetoněmecký problém: obtížné loučení s minulostí* [The Sudeten-German Problem: A Difficult Leave-Taking with the Past]. Ústí nad Labem: Albis International.

HAHN, Eva. "Sudetskí Nemci v nemeckej spoločnosti: polstoročie politických dejín mezi 'vlasťou' a 'domovom'" [The Sudeten Germans in German Society (a half-century of political history between "homeland" and "home")], in *V rozdelenej Európe*. 78.

HAHN, Eva – HAHN, Hans-Henning. 2002. *Sudetoněmecká vzpomínání a zapomínání* [Sudeten German Remembering and Forgetting]. Prague: Votobia.

HÁJEK, Jiří. 1993. *Hitlerův Mein Kampf* [Hitler's Mein Kampf]. Liberec: Dialog.

HÁJEK, Jiří. 1983. *Setkání a střety* [Encounters and Clashes]. Köln am Rhein: INDEX.

HAJŠMAN, Jan. 1928. *O špionáži* [Espionage]. Prague: Česká grafická unie.

HAJŠMAN, Jan. 1947. *V drápech bestie* [In the Claws of the Beast]. Prague: V. Neubert a synové.

HAJŠMAN, Jan – FILLA, Emil. 1934. *Hlídka české maffie v Holandsku* [The Czech Maffie Patrol in Holland]. Prague: Nakladatelství Orbis.

HALE, J. 1975. *Radio Power: Propaganda And International Broadcasting*. Philadelphia: Temple University.

HALL, John. "Nationalism: Classified and Explained". *Daedalus* 3/1993 (CXXII). 1–28.

HALL, Rodney Bruce. 1999. *National Collective Identity*. New York: Columbia University Press.

HAMAN, Aleš. "Masochistický pohled na české dějiny" [The Masochistic View of Czech History]. *Dějiny a současnost* 3/1992. 59.

HAMANN, Brigitte. 1999. *Hitlerova Vídeň* [Hitler's Vienna]. Prague: Prostor.

HANCOCK, M. Donald. 1989. *West Germany – The Politics of Democratic Corporatism*. New Jersey: Chatham House Publishers, Inc.

HANDL, Vladimír. "Německý multilateralismus a vztahy k státům visegrádské skupiny" [German Multilateralism and Relations with the States of the Visegrad Group]. *Mezinárodní vztahy* 1/2003. 5–27.

HANDL, V. – KURAL, V. – REIMAN, M. 1997. "Česká republika a Německo" [The Czech Republic and Germany]. *Česká zahraniční politika*. Prague: Ústav mezinárodních vztahů. 153.

HARVIE, Christopher. "Comparative Studies on Governments and Non-Dominant Ethnic Groups". *European History Quarterly* 2/April 1995 (XXV). 269–283.

HASSNER, Pierre. "Beyond Nationalism and Internationalism", in *Ethnic Conflict and International Security*. 1993. Brown, M. E. (ed.). Princeton: University Press. 139.

HASTINGS, Max – STEVENS, George. 1985. *Victory in Europe*. London: Weidenfeld and Nicholson.

HAUNER, Milan. "Czechoslovakia as a Military Factor in British Considerations of 1938". *Journal of Strategic Studies*. 1978.

HAUNER, Milan. 1993. "The Czechs and Germans: A One-Thousand Year Relationship", in Søe, Ch. *The Germans and Their Neighbours*.

HAUNER, Milan. "Dopis redakci" [Letter to the Editor of The New York Review of Books]. *Svědectví* 89/90. 381.

HAUNER, Milan. "Edvard Beneš a USA 1939–1942" [Edvard Beneš and the USA 1939–1942]. *Soudobé dějiny* 1/1996.

HAUNER, Milan. "Německo a střední Evropa" [Germany and Central Europe]. *Mezinárodní vztahy* 4/1994. 34–40.

HAUNER, Milan. "Sověti a obrana ČSR?" [The Soviets and the Defence of the CSR?]. *Soudobé dějiny* 1/1997. 134–141.

HAUNER, Milan. "Září 1938: Kapitulovat, či bojovat?" [September 1938: To capitulate or to fight?]. *Svědectví* 49/1975.

HAUSHOFER, Karl. 1939. *Grenzen in ihrer Geographischen und Politischen Bedeutung.* Heidelberg/Berlin/Magdeburg: Kurt Vowinckel Verlag.

HAVEL, Václav. 1997. "Češi a Němci na cestě k dobrému sousedství" [Czechs and Germans on the Path to Good Neighbourly Relations], in *Rozhovory o sousedství.* 36.

HAVEL, Václav. "Český úděl?" [The Czech Destiny?]. *Svědectví* 74/1985 (XIX). 338–343.

HAVRÁNEK, Jan. 1979. "Češi v severočeských a západočeských městech v letech 1880–1930" [Czechs in North Bohemian and West Bohemian Towns 1880–1930], in *Ústecký sborník historický.* Ústí nad Labem: Severočeské nakladatelství.

HEISSIG, Kurt. "Sudetoněmecká budoucnost v Čechách a na Moravě" [The Sudeten German Future in Bohemia and Moravia]. *Střední Evropa* 33. 23.

HEJL, Vilém. 1990. *Rozvrat – Mnichov a náš osud* [Breakdown – Munich and Our Fate]. Prague: Univerzum.

HEMMERLE, Rudolf. 1996. *Sudetenland Lexikon.* Augsburg: Bechtermünz Verlag.

HENRIKSON, Alan K. "The Map as an Idea: The Role of Cartographic Imagery during the Second World War". *The American Cartographer* 1/1975 (II). 19–53.

HERDE, Georg – STOLZE, Alexa. 1987. *Die Sudetendeutsche Landsmannschaft.* Köln: Pahl-Rugenstein.

HERLEMANN, H.-H. "Vertriebene Bauern im Strukturwandel der Landwirtschaft", in *Die Vertriebenen in Westdeutschland.* 128.

HERMAND, Jost. 1995. *Der alte Traum vom neuen Reich* (Völkische Utopien und Nationl-sozialismus). Frankfurt a. M.: Betz/Athenäum.

HEYDEN, Günther. 1960. *Teorie životního prostoru* [The Theory of Living Space/Lebensraum]. Prague: Orbis.

HEYDERHOFF, J. – WENTZCKE, P. 1970. *Deutscher Liberalismus im Zeitalter Bismarcks. Eine politische Briefsammlung.* Vol. 1 (1925). Reprint. 494.

HEYWOOD, Andrew. 1994. *Politické ideologie* [Political Ideologies]. Prague: Victoria Publishing.

HILF, Rudolf. "Das deutsch-tschechische Gesprächsforum". *Bayern-intern* 5 (25. August 1998).

HILF, Rudolf. 1996. *Němci a Češi.* Prague: Prago-Media.

HILF, Rudolf. "Plán pro střední Evropu: Jak předejít nacionální sebedestrukci" [A Plan for Central Europe. How to Prevent National Self-destruction]. *Střední Evropa* 35/1993.

HILF, Rudolf. 1951. *Die Presse der Sudetendeutschen nach 1945 und ihre Stellungnahme zum Schicksal der vetriebenen Volksgruppe.* (Dissertation). Munich.

HILF, Rudolf – RABL, Kurt. 1984. *Volksgruppenrecht und Minderheitenschutz.* Munich: INTEREG.

HILL, Norman. 1945. *Claims to Territory in International Law and Relations.* London/New York/Toronto: Oxford University Press.

"Historikové proti znásilňování dějin (Stanovisko Sdružení historiků České republiky)" [Historians against the Violation of History (Position of the Association of Historians of the Czech Republic)]. 2002. Kocian, Jiří (ed.). *Zpravodaj historického klubu,* special supplement 2/2001 (XII).

HITCHCOCK, Edward B. 1948. *Zasvětil jsem život míru* [I Dedicated My Life to Peace]. (Biography of Edvard Beneš). Prague: Jaroslav Podroužek.

HLAVAČKA, Milan. 1987. *Podivná aliance* [A Strange Alliance]. Prague: Mladá fronta.

HNÍK, F. M. "Záznam o rozhovorech v Chatham House" [Record of Discussions at Chatham House], in *Češi a sudetoněmecká otázka*. 239.

HOBSBAWM, Eric J. 1990. *Nations and Nationalism since 1780*. Cambridge University Press.

HOBSBAWM, Eric J. "Rakousko a střední Evropa" [Austria and Central Europe]. *Lettre Internationale* 5/1992. 52–53.

HOCH, Karel. 1946. *Pangermanismus*. Prague: Orbis.

HOENSCH, Jörg K. "Othmar Spann, Kameradschaftsbund a Sudetoněmecká vlastenecká fronta" [Othmar Spann, the Kameradschaftsbund and the Sudeten German Patriotic Front]. *Dějiny a současnost* 5/1999. 31–35.

HOENSCH, J. K. "Issues, going beyond an overall assessment", in *Coming to Terms With the Past, Opening up To The Future*. 35.

HOFFMAN, Jaroslav. 1996. *"Mnichov" a sudetoněmecký textilní průmysl* ["Munich" and the Sudeten German Textile Industry]. Ústí nad Labem: Univerzita J. E. Purkyně. 31.

HOFFMANN, Roland J. 1996. *Die Anfänge der Emigration aus der Tschechoslowakei 1948*. Prague: Sešity Ústavu pro soudobé dějiny.

HOJDOVÁ, K. "Günter Grass šlape na paty Potterovi" [Günter Grass Close on the Heels of H. Potter]. *Lidové noviny*. 23. 2. 2002.

HOLUB, R. C. "The Memories of Silence and the Silence of Memories: Post-war Germans and the Holocaust". *German Politics and Society*. 1/spring 2000 (XVIII). 105–123.

HON, J. – ŠITLER, J. 1996. "Trestněprávní důsledky událostí v období německé nacistické okupace Československa a v době těsně po jejím skončení a jejich řešení" [Criminal-law consequences of events in the period of German Nazi occupation of Czechoslovakia and and immediately thereafter and the way these were handled], in *Studie o sudetoněmecké otázce*. 165–179.

HORAK, Stephan M. 1985. *Eastern European National Minorities 1919–1980*. A Handbook. Littleton-Colorado: Libraries Unlimited, INC.

HOUSE, E. M. – SEYMOUR, Ch. 1921. *What really happened at Paris*. New York.

HOUŽVIČKA, Václav. "Česko-německé pohraničí v nových souvislostech" [The Czech-German Borderlands in New Contexts]. *Politologická revue* 2/1996. 87–102

HOUŽVIČKA, Václav. "Deset let diskusí mezi Čechy a sudetskými Němci" [Ten Years of Discussions between Czechs and Sudeten Germans]. *Mezinárodní politika* 6/2001. 21–22.

HOUŽVIČKA, Václav. "Euroregions as Factors of Social Change within the Czech-German Borderland", in *Räumliche Auswirkungen des Transformationsprozesses in Deutschland und bei den östlichen Nachbarn*. 1997. Musil, Jiří – Strubelt, Wendelin (eds.). Opladen: Leske+Budrich.

HOUŽVIČKA, Václav. "Germany as a Factor of Differentiation in Czech Society". *Czech Sociological Review* 2/1998 (VI). 219–239.

HOUŽVIČKA, Václav. "Historická dimenze vztahu Čechů a Němců" [The Historical Dimension of the Relationship between Czechs and Germans], in *Vytváření přeshraničního společenství na česko-německé hranici*. 2000. Zich, F. (ed.). Prague: Sociologický ústav AV ČR. 137–153.

HOUŽVIČKA, Václav. "Mitteleuropa – between Europe and Germany". *Czech Sociological Review* 2/1998 (VI). 261–264.

HOUŽVIČKA, Václav. 1998. "Německo a vstup do NATO jako diferenciační faktor české společnosti" [Germany and Accesion to NATO as a Differentiating Factor in Czech Society], in *Vztahy Spolkové republiky Německo ke státům střední Evropy.* 241–265.

HOUŽVIČKA, Václav. "Německo na sklonku bonnské éry – hledání nové identity" [Germany towards the end of the Bonn era – the search for a new identity]. *Mezinárodní vztahy* 1/1999. 21–28.

HOUŽVIČKA, Václav. "Pohraniční oblasti v kontextu bilaterálních vztahů ČR a SRN" [The Border Areas in the Context of the Bilateral Relations of the CR and FRG]. *Mezinárodní politika* 2/2004. 21–24.

HOUŽVIČKA, Václav. "Postoje obyvatel Chebska k Němcům" [The Attitudes of the Population of the Cheb Region to Germany]. *Mezinárodní politika* 4/1993. 72–75.

HOUŽVIČKA, Václav. "Poválečné Německo – tehdy v nulté hodině" [Postwar Germany – Zero Hour]. *Mezinárodní vztahy* 2/2000. 92–95.

HOUŽVIČKA, Václav. "Die Sozialen Folgen des Austausches der Bevölkerung in den tschechischen Grenzgebieten", in PLASCHKA, Richard G. – DRABEK, Anna (Zentraleuropa-Studien). 1997. *Nationale Frage und Vertreibung in der Tschechoslowakei und Ungarn 1938–1948.* Wien: Verlag der Österreichischen Akademie der Wissechschaften.

HOUŽVIČKA, Václav. 2002. "Suverenita, hranice, integrace – konflikt zájmů?" [Sovereignty. Borders, Integration-Conflict of Interests?], in *Současná česká společnost.* Prague: Sociologický ústav Akademie věd ČR. 307–321.

HOUŽVIČKA, Václav. "Sudetoněmecká otázka a vztahy Čechů k Německu (hlavní poznatky sociologických výzkumů v letech 1996–1999)" [The Sudeten German Question and the Attitude of Czechs to Germany (Main findings of sociological surveys in the years 1996–1999)]. *Mezinárodní vztahy* 4/2000. 94–102.

HOUŽVIČKA, Václav 1996. *Sudetoněmecká otázka v názorech a postojích obyvatel českého pohraničí* [The Sudeten German Question in the Views and Attitudes of the Population of the Czech Borderlands]. Working Papers, WP 96:2. Prague: Sociologický ústav AV ČR.

HOUŽVIČKA, Václav. "Wie Tschechen die Deutschen wahrnehmen", in *Nachbarschaft* (Interkulturelle Beziehungen zwischen Deutschen, Polen und Tschechen). 2001. Roth, Klaus (ed.). Münster/New York/München/Berlin: Waxmann. 79–97.

HOUŽVIČKA, Václav. "Změnilo opětovné sjednocení Německa vnímání jeho dějin?" [Has the reunification of Germany changed the perception of its history?]. *Mezinárodní vztahy* 2/2002. 93–99.

HOUŽVIČKA, Václav (ed.) 2012. *Odsun Němců z Československa 65 let poté.* [The Transfer of the Germans from Czechoslovakia 65 Years after]. Brno: Centrum pro studium demokracie a kultury.

HRBEK, Jaroslav. "Mnichov jako dilema evropské strategie" [Munich as a Dilemma of European Strategy]. *Dějiny a současnost* 6/1998. 24–27.

HRBEK, Jaroslav. "Nacistické Německo očima českého čtenáře" [Nazi Germany through the Eyes of a Czech Reader]. *Dějiny a současnost* 4/1996. 2–4.

HROCH, Miroslav. 1999. *Na prahu národní existence* [On the Threshold of National Existence]. Prague: Mladá fronta.

HROCH, Miroslav. 1999. *V národním zájmu* [In the National Interest]. Prague: Knižnice Dějiny a současnost.

HRUŠKA, Emil. 2002. *Pohoří divočáků aneb sudetoněmecké kapitoly* [The Mountains of the Wild Boar or Sudeten German Chapters]. Prague: Futura.

HÜBL, Milan. 1990. *Češi, Slováci a jejich sousedé* [Czechs, Slovaks and their Neighbours]. Prague: Naše vojsko.

HUDSON, Ray – WILLIAMS, Allan, M. 1999. *Divided Europe* (Society and Territory). London/Thousands Oaks/New Delhi: SAGE Publications.

HUNTER, James. 1983. *Perspective Ratzel's Political Geography*. Lanham/New York/London: University Press of America.

HYDE-PRICE, Adrian. 2000. *Germany and European Order (enlarging NATO and the EU)*. Manchester/New York: Manchester University Press.

HYNDRÁKOVÁ, A. – LORENCOVÁ, A. "Postoje českého obyvatelstva k Židům ve 30. a začátkem 40. let ve vzpomínkách pamětníků" [The Attitudes of the Czech Population to Jews in the 1930s and 40s in the Recollections of Contemporaries], in *Fenomén holocaust*. 113–114.

HYRŠLOVÁ, Květa – KURAL, Václav. 1999. *Češi a Němci společně proti Hitlerovi* [Czechs and Germans Together against Hitler]. Prague: Exhibition catalogue. *Die Identität der Deutschen*. 1983. Weidenfeld, Werner (ed.). Bonn: Bundeszentrale für politische Bildung.

Identität, Integrität, Integration (Tschechien und Mitteleuropa). 1997. Kipke, Rüdiger (ed.). Münster: LIT Verlag.

IGNOTUS, Paul. "Czechs, Magyars, Slovaks". *Political Quarterly* 40/1969. 188.

Irredentism and International Politics. 1991. Chazan, Naomi (ed.). London/Boulder: Lynne Rienner Publishers/Adamantine Press.

IRVING, David. 1997. *Norimberk – poslední bitva* [Nuremberg – The last battle]. Prague: Grafoprint-Neubert.

JACOB, James E. "Ethnic mobilization on the Germanic periphery: The case of the South Tyrol". *Ethnic Groups* 3/1981. 253–280.

JAKSCH, Wenzel. 2000. *Cesta Evropy do Postupimi* [Europe's Road to Potsdam]. Prague: Institut pro středoevropskou kulturu a politiku.

JAKSCH, Wenzel. Spoluobčané, jde o všechno [Fellow citizens, everything is at stake]. *Národní politika*. 14. 9. 1938.

JANČÍK, Drahomír. 1990. *Německo a Malá dohoda* [Germany and the Little Entente]. Prague: Univerzita Karlova.

JANOWSKY, Oscar I. 1945. *Nationalities and National Minorities (with Special Reference to East-Central Europe)*. New York: The Macmillan.

JASPERS, Karl. 1991. *Otázka viny (Příspěvek k německé otázce)* [The Question of Guilt (A Contribution to the German Question]. Prague: Mladá fronta.

JAWORSKI, Rudolf. "Aktuální diskuse o střední Evropě v historické perspektivě" [Current Discussion on Central Europe in Historical Perspective]. *Listy* 4/1990 (XX). 28–33.

JAWORSKI, Rudolf. 1996. *Friedrich Naumann a Češi* [F. Naumann and the Czechs]. Prague: Centrum liberálních studií.

JAWORSKI, Rudolf. "Mezi politikou a trivialitou – Sudetoněmecké grenzlandromány, 1918–1938" [Between politics and Triviality – the Sudeten-German Frontiersmen]. *Dějiny a současnost* 1/2004. 28.

JAWORSKI, Rudolf. "Obzvláštní truchlohra mezi Čechy a Němci" [The Particular Trag- edy between Czechs and Germans]. *Dějiny a současnost* 5/1996. 42–45.

Je již český právní řád v souladu s právem Evropské unie? [Is the Czech Legal Order now in Compliance with the Law of the European Union?]. 2002. Prague: Friederich Ebert- Stiftung e.V.

JEDERMANN, František. 1990. *Ztracené dějiny* [Lost History]. Prague: Institut pro středoevropskou kulturu a politiku.

JIČÍNSKÝ, Zdeněk – ŠKALOUD, Jan. "Transformace politického systému k demokracii" [The Transformation of the Political System towards Democracy], in Šafaříková, Vlasta (et al.). 1996. *Transformace české společnosti 1989–1995*. Brno: Doplněk.

JONG, Louis de. 1956. *The German Fifth Column in the Second World War*. London: Rout- ledge & Kegan Paul.

JOPPKE, Christian. 1999. *Immigration and the Nation-State*. Oxford: Oxford University Press.

Journal of Contemporary History – Special issue on Nationalism 1/1971 (VI). "Unsatisfied Nationalism". Seton-Watson, Hugh (ed.).

JOZA, Jaroslav. "Mnichov a severní Čechy" [Munich and North Bohemia]. *Terezínské listy* 18/1990. 74–92.

Judgment of the International Military Tribunal for the Trial of German Major War Criminals- Nuremberg. 1946. London: His Majesty's Stationery Office.

JUNG, Carl G. 1994. *Duše moderního člověka* [Modern Man in Search of a Soul]. Brno: Atlantis.

JUNGHAHN, Otto. 1931. *National Minorities in Europe*. New York: Covivi/Friede Publishers.

KADLEC, Čeněk M. 2001. *Hry o hranice* [Games over the Border]. Chrást u Poříčan: self- published.

KAGAN, R. 2003. *Labyrint síly a ráj slabosti* [The Labyrinth of Power and the Paradise of Weakness]. Prague: Lidové noviny. 84.

KAISER, Daniel – ŠITLER, Jiří. "Novodobé české dějiny v zrcadle Frankfurter Allgemeine Zeitung" [Modern Czech History in the Mirror of the Frankfurther Allgemeine Zei- tung]. *Dějiny a současnost* 5/1996. 15–19.

KÁŇA, O. "Instituce a organizace protičeskoslovenské iredenty" [Institutions and Organisations of the Anti-Czechoslovak Irredenta], in *Severní Čechy a Mnichov*.

KANSTEINER, Wulf. "Mandarins in the Public Sphere" (Vergangenheitsbewältigung and the Paradigm of Social History in the Federal Republic of Germany). *German Politics and Society* 3/1999 (XVII).

KAPLAN, Karel. 1990. *Pravda o Československu 1945–1948* [The Truth about Czechoslova- kia 1945–1948]. Prague: Mladá fronta.

KARLGREN, Anton. 1945. *Henlein, Hitler a československá tragedie* [Henlein, Hitler and the Czechoslovak Tragedy]. Prague: Nákladem Samcova knihkupectví.

KÁRNÍK, Zdeněk. 1968. *Habsburk, Masaryk či Šmeral?* [Habsburg, Masaryk or Šmeral?] Prague: Svoboda.

KÁRNÝ, Miroslav. 1991. *"Konečné řešení"- genocida českých židů v německé protektorátní poli- tice* [The "Final Solution" – The Genocide of the Czech Jews in German Protectorate Policy]. Prague: Academia.

KATZENSTEIN, P. J. 1997. *Mitteleuropa – between Europe and Germany*. Oxford, Provi- dence: Berghahn Books. 4.

KAZBUNDA, Karel. 1995. *Otázka česko-německá v předvečer velké války* [The Czech-German Question on the Eve of the Great War]. Prague: Karolinum.

KERSHAW, Ian. 1992. *Hitlerův mýtus* (image a skutečnost v Třetí říši) [The Hitler Myth (Image and Reality in the Third Reich)]. Prague: Iris.

KERSHAW, Ian. 2004. *Making Friends with Hitler.* London: Allen Lane/Penguin Books.

KERTESZ, Stephen D. 1956. *The Fate of East Central Europe.* Notre Dame-Indiana: University of Notre Dame Press.

KIMMINICH, O. "Benešovy dekrety (posouzení z mezinárodněprávního hlediska)" [The Beneš Decrees (considered from the perspective of international law]. *Střední Evropa.* 44/45 (1994). 55.

KIMMINICH, O. 1996. *Das Recht auf die Heimat.* Bonn: Bund der Vertriebenen.

KISSINGER, Henry. 1994. *Diplomacy.* New York: Simon and Schuster.

KLÁŠTERKOVÁ, Lenka. "Role německy vysílajících stanic ve vývoji Sudet v letech 1923–1938" [The Role of Stations Broadcasting in German in the Development of the Sudetenland 1923–1938]. *Dějiny a současnost* 2/1999. 42–44.

KLÍMA, Arnošt. 1994. *Češi a Němci v revoluci 1848–1849* [Czechs and Germans in the Revolution of 1848–1849]. Prague: Nebesa.

KLIMEK, Antonín. 1996/1998. *Boj o Hrad, I+II* [The Struggle for the Castle I+II]. Prague: Panevropa.

KLIMEK, Antonín. 1989. *Jak se dělal mír roku 1919* (Československo na konferenci ve Versailles) [How Peace was made in 1919 (Czechoslovakia at the Versailles Conference)]. Prague: Melantrich.

KLIMEK, Antonín – KUBŮ, Eduard. 1995. *Československá zahraniční politika 1918–1938* [Czechoslovak Foreign Policy 1918–1938]. (Chapters from the history of international relations). Prague: Institut pro středoevropskou kulturu a politiku.

KLIMKO, J. 1986. *Politické a právne dejiny hraníc predmníchovskej republiky (1918–1938)* [The Political and Legal History of the Pre-Munich Republic (1918–1938). Bratislava: Veda. 146.

KLINGEMANN, Hans-Dieter – HOFFERBERT, Richard I. "Germany: A New Wall in the Mind?". *Journal of Democracy* 1/January 1994 (V). 30–44.

KLIOT, Nurit – NEWMAN, David (eds.). 2002. *Geopolitics at the End of the Twentieth Century.* London/Portland: Frank Cass.

KNICKERBOCKER, H. R. 1935. *Bude válka v Evropě?* [Will there be War in Europe?]. Moravská Ostrava: Nakladatelství Julia Kittla.

KNIGHT, David B. – DAVIES, Maureen. 1987. *Self-Determination (An Interdisciplinary Annotated Bibliography).* New York/London: Garland Publishing, Inc.

KOCÍCH, Milan. "K mezinárodněprávním aspektům ochrany národnostních menšin v předmnichovské ČSR" [International legal aspects of the protection of national minorities in the pre-Munich CSR]. *Právněhistorické studie* 21/1978. Prague: Academia.

KÖHLER, Manfred. "Germans Happy to Say They Like Being Proud". *Frankfurter Allgemeine Zeitung.* March 25, 2001.

KOHN, H. 1953. *Pan-Slavism. Its History and Ideology.* Notre Dame: University of Notre Dame.

KOKOŠKA, Jaroslav – KOKOŠKA, Stanislav. 1994. *Spor o agenta A-54* [The Dispute over Agent A-54]. Prague: Naše vojsko.

KOMLOSYOVÁ, Andrea – BŮŽEK, Václav – SVÁTEK, František. 1995. *Kultury na hranici/ Kulturen an der Grenze.* Wien/Waidhofen an der Thaya: Promedia Druck und Verlagsgesellschaft/Waldviertel Akademie.

Konfliktní společenství, katastrofa, uvolnění (náčrt výkladu česko-německých dějin od 19. století) [Community of Conflict, Catastrophe, Disengagement (sketch of an interpretation of Czech-German history since the 19th century)]. Prague: Ústav mezinárodních vztahů.

KONING, Hans. "Germania iredenta". *The Atlantic Monthly.* July 1996. http://www.theatlantic .com/iisues/96jul/germania/germania.htm

KONRÁD, Ota. "Zásadní proměna Německo teprve čeká" [The Basic Transformation of Germany is yet to Come]. *Lidové noviny.* Supplement Orientace. 23. 10. 1999. 19.

KOŘALKA, Jiří. 1996. *Češi v habsburské říši a v Evropě 1815–1914* [Czechs in the Habsburg Empire and in Europe 1815–1914]. Prague: Argo.

KOŘALKA, Jiří. 1969. *Co je národ?* [What is a Nation?] Prague: Svoboda.

KOŘALKA, J. "Mitteleuropa Friedricha Naumanna jako plán německé hegemonie v Evropě za první světové války" [The Mitteleuropa of Friedrich Naumann as a Plan for German Hegemony in Europe during the First World War]. *Dějiny a současnost* 1/2003. 14.

KOŘALKA, Jiří. 1961. *Protičeskoslovenský revanšismus v historigrafii (bibliografie)* [Anti-Czechoslovak Revanchism in Historiography]. Prague: Historický ústav ČSAV.

KOŘALKA, Jiří. 1985. "Vztah rakouského státního patriotismu a velkoněmecké ideologie k Čechům v první polovině 19. století" [The Attitude of Austrian State Patriotism and Greater German Ideology to Czechs in the First Half of the 19th Century], in *Ústecký sborník historický.* Ústí nad Labem: Severočeské nakladatelství. 241–262.

KOŘALKA, Jiří – POKORNÝ, Jiří. "Česká společnost 19. a 20. století a čeští historikové" [19th- and 20th-Century Czech Society and Czech Historians]. *Český časopis historický* 4/1990 (IIXC). 572–576.

KORBEL, J. 1977. *Twentieth Century Czechoslovakia: The Meaning of Its History.* New York: Columbia University Press.

KORČÁK, Jaromír. 1938. *Geopolitické základy Československa* [The Geopolitical Foundations of Czechoslovakia]. Prague: Orbis.

KOSCHMAL, Walter – NEKULA, Marek – ROGALL, Joachim (eds.). *Češi a Němci. Dějiny – kultura – politika* [Czechs and Germans. History-Culture-Politics]. 2001. Prague/ Litomyšl: Paseka.

KOSÍK, KAREL. "Třetí Mnichov?" [A Third Munich?]. *Listy* 6/1992 (XXII). 35.

KOSTECKI, Wojciech. 1999. *Ethnicity and Autonomy in East-Central Europe: In Search of Advanced Conflict Prevention.* University of Cambridge: Faculty of Social and Political Sciences.

KOSTELECKÝ, T. – NEDOMOVÁ, A. 1995. *Czech National Identity – Basic Results of National Survey.* Prague: Sociologický ústav AV ČR. ISSP.

KOSTELECKÝ, Tomáš – NEDOMOVÁ, Alena. 1996. *Národní identita* [National Identity]. Working Papers, WP 96:9. Prague: Sociologický ústav AV ČR.

KOZÁK, Jan B. 1968. *T. G. Masaryk a vznik Washingtonské deklarace v říjnu 1918* [T. G. Masaryk and the Origin of the Washington Declaration in October 1918]. Prague: Melantrich.

KRAFT, Daniel – KÖSER, Helmut (et al.). 1999. *Kde domov můj/Wo ist meine Heimat*. Dresden: Brücke Stiftung.

KRÁL, Václav. 1975. *Dny, které otřásly Československem* [Days that Shook Czechoslovakia]. Prague: Naše vojsko/SPB.

KRÁL, Václav. 1964. *Zločiny proti Evropě* [Crimes against Europe]. Prague: Naše vojsko/SPB.

KRALLERT-SATTLER, Gertrud. 1989. *Recht und Verwaltung, Lastenausgleich*. Kommentierte Bibliographie zum Flüchtlings- und Vertriebenenproblem in der Bundesrepublik Deutschland, in Österreich und in der Schweiz. Wien: Braumüller.

KRAUS, Ota – KULKA, Erich. 1966. *Noc a mlha/Nacht und Nebel*. Prague: Naše vojsko/SPB.

KRČMÁŘ, J. 1923. "Právní základ československé republiky" [The Legal Basis of the Czechoslovak Republic], in Tobolka, Z. V. *Politika I*. 208.

KREJČÍ, Oskar. 2000. *Geopolitika středoevropského prostoru* [The Geopolitics of Central Europe]. Prague: Ekopress.

KREJČÍ, Oskar. 1997. *Mezinárodní politika* [International Politics]. Prague: Victoria Publishing.

Křen, J. "Češi a Němci: kritické poznámky" [Czechs and Germans: Critical notes], in *Češi, Němci, odsun*.

KŘEN, Jan. 1963. *Do emigrace* [Into Emigration]. Prague: Naše vojsko.

KŘEN, Jan. 1992. *Historické proměny češství* [Historical Transformations of Czech Identity]. Prague: Karolinum.

KŘEN, Jan. 1990. Konfliktní společenství Češi a Němci 1780–1918 [The Conflict-Ridden Community of Czechs and Germans 1780–1918]. Prague: Academia.

KŘEN, Jan. "Odsun Němců ve světle nových pramenů" [The Transfer of the Germans in the Light of New Sources]. *Dialog* 4–6/1967.

KŘEN, Jan. "Revanšisté s demokratickou minulostí" [Revanchists with a Democratic Past]. *Československý časopis historický* 9/1961. 42.

KŘEN, Jan. "Střední Evropa nahlížená z Čech" [Central Europe Viewed from Bohemia]. *Reportér* 9/1990. (Documentary supplement XII–XVI).

KŘEN, Jan. 1969. *V emigraci* [In Emigration]. Prague: Naše vojsko.

KŘEN, Jan. "Vrchol a konec Benešovy politické dráhy" [The Climax and End of Beneš's Political Career]. *Dějiny a současnost* 5/1968 (X). 34–38.

KŘEN, Jan – BROKLOVÁ, Eva. 1998. *Obraz Němců, Rakouska a Německa v české společnosti 19. a 20. století* [The Image of Germans, Austria and Germany in Czech Society of the 19th and 20th Centuries]. Prague: Karolinum.

KROFTA, Kamil. 1934. *Das Deutschtum in der Tschechoslowakischen Geschichte*. Prague: Orbis.

KROFTA, Kamil. 1939. *Z dob naší první republiky* [From the Times of our First Republic]. Prague: Jan Laichter.

KRZEMIŃSKI, Adam. "Zápas o paměť" ["The Struggle over Memory"]. *Kafka (journal for Central Europe)* 13/2004. 58–63.

KRZEMIŃSKI, Adam. "Zwischen Renationalisierung und Europäisierung – Ein polnisches Blick auf Deutschland". *Internationale Politik und Gesellschaft* 1/2004. 11–26.

KUBES, Milan – KUČERA, Rudolf. 2002. *Evropská lidová strana* [The European People's Party]. Prague: Institut pro středoevropskou politiku a kulturu.

KuBŮ, Eduard. "Zátěž dějinného dědictví, chybné kalkulace, osudová neschopnost, či neúprosná logika vývoje?" [The Burden of Historical Inheritance, Mistaken Calculations, Fateful Incapacity or the Inexorable Logic of Development?]. *Soudobé dějiny* 2–3/1995. 254–268.

KUČERA, Jaroslav. "Česká historiografie a odsun Němců" [Czech Historiography and the Transfer of the Germans]. *Soudobé dějiny* 2–3/1994. 369.

KUČERA, Jaroslav. "Mezi Wilhelmstrasse a Thunovskou" [Between the Wilhelmstrasse and Thunovská St.]. *Český časopis historický* 2/1997. 387–409.

KUČERA, Jaroslav. "Statistik auf dem Holzweg: Einige Bemerkungen zu Berechnungen der sudetendeutschen Vertreibungverluste", *in Nationale Frage und Vertreibung in der Tschechoslowakei und Ungarn 1938–1948*. 1997. Plaschka, Richard G. (ed.). Wien: Verlag der Österreichischen Akademie der Wissenschaften.

KUČERA, Rudolf. "Frakce evropské lidové strany (křesťanských demokratů) a evropských demokratů v Evropském parlamentu" [The European People's Party (Christian Democrats) Fraction and European Democrats in the European Parliament]. *Střední Evropa*. Special issue Evropská lidová strana a evropští demokraté. March 2002.

KUČERA, Rudolf. 1989. *Kapitoly z dějin střední Evropy* [Chapters from the History of Central Europe]. Munich: Tschechischer Nationalausschuss in Deutschland e.V.

KUKLÍK, Jan. 1998. *Londýnský exil a obnova československého státu 1938–1945* [The London Exile and the Restoration of the Czechoslovak State 1938–1945]. Prague: Karolinum.

KUKLÍK, Jan. 2002. *Mýty a realita takzvaných Benešových dekretů* [Myths and Reality of the so-called Beneš Decrees]. Prague: Linde.

KUKLÍK, Jan – NĚMEČEK, Jan. 2004. *Proti Benešovi!* [Against Beneš!]. Prague: Karolinum.

KULISCHER, Eugene M. 1948. *Europe on the Move (War and Population Changes, 1917–47)*. New York: Columbia University Press.

KULKA, E. 1964. *Frankfurtský proces* [The Frankfurt Trial]. Prague: Naše vojsko.

KUNDERA, M. "IV. sjezd SČSS" ["The 4th Congress of the Czechoslovak Writers' Union"]. *Svědectví* 29–32/1966–67 (VIII) (reprint). 493.

KUNDERA, Milan. "Český úděl" [The Czech Fate]. *Svědectví* 74/1985 (XIX). 343–350.

KUNDERA, Milan. "The Tragedy of Central Europe". *The New York Review of Books*. 26. 4. 1984.

KUNDERA, Milan. "Z kulturního testamentu střední Evropy" [From the Cultural Testament of Central Europe]. *Listy* 3/2000 (XXX). 89–90. (Reprint of article first published in *Listy* 6/1978.)

KUNŠTÁT, M. "Faktor minulosti v současných česko-německých vztazích" [The Factor of the Past in Current Czech-German Relations]. *Mezinárodní politika* 11/2001. 7.

KÜNZL-JIZERSKÝ, Rudolf. 1947. *V diplomatických službách* [In Diplomatic Service]. Prague: J. R. Vilímek.

KURAL, Václav. "Ještě několik glos" [Some Further Glosses], in *Češi, Němci, odsun*. 316.

KURAL, Václav. "K problému tzv. Grundplanung O.A." [On the Problem of the so-called Grundplanung O.A.], in *Historie okupovaného pohraničí 1938–1945* [A History of the Occupied Borderlands 1938–1945]. 2000. Radvanovský, Z. (ed.). Ústí nad Labem: Univerzita J. E. Purkyně. 217.

KURAL, Václav. 1993. *Konflikt místo společenství (Češi a Němci v československém státě 1918–1938)* [Conflict instead of Community (Czechs and Germans in the Czechoslovak State 1918–1938)]. Prague: Ústav mezinárodních vztahů.

KURAL, Václav. 1994. *Místo společenství konflikt (Češi a Němci ve Velkoněmecké říši a cesta k odsunu 1938–1945)* [Conflict instead of Community (Czechs and Germans in the Greater German Reich and the Road to the Transfer 1938–1945)]. Prague: Ústav mezinárodních vztahů.

KURAL, Václav. "Mohli jsme se bránit?" ["Could We have Defended Ourselves?"]. (Extract of study *Rok 1938. Mohli jsme se bránit?*). *Přísně tajné* 5/2003. 99–110.

KURAL, Václav. "Peripetie v česko-německých vztazích" [Peripetia in Czech-German Relations]. *Mezinárodní politika* 4/1996. 12–14.

KURAL, Václav. "Případ čs. květnové mobilizace v roce 1938" [The case of the May mobilisation in 1938]. *Přísně tajné* 4/2002. 25–26.

KURAL, Václav. 1992. *Rok 1938. Mohli jsme se bránit?* [1938. Could We have Defended Ourselves?]. A (non-sale) publication for the needs of the Czechoslovak Army.

KURAL, Václav. 1997. *Vlastenci proti okupaci – Ústřední vedení odboje domácího 1940–1943* [Patriots against the Occupation – the Central Leadership of the Home Resistence 1940–1943]. Prague: Karolinum/Ústav mezinárodních vztahů.

KURAL, Václav – RADVANOVSKÝ, Zdeněk (et al.). 2002. *"Sudety" pod hákovým křížem* [The Sudetenland under the Swastika]. Ústí nad Labem: Albis International.

KUTNAR, František. 2003. *Obrozenské vlastenectví a nacionalismus* [Revivalist Patriotism and Nationalism]. Prague: Karolinum.

KVAČEK, Robert. 1988. *Diplomaté a ti druzí* [Diplomats and the Others]. Prague: Panorama.

KVAČEK, Robert. 1976. *Historie jednoho roku* [The History of One Year]. Prague: Mladá fronta.

KVAČEK, Robert. 1966. *Nad Evropou zataženo. Československo a Evropa 1933–1937* [*Clouds over Europe.* Czechoslovakia and Europe 1933–1937]. Prague: Svoboda.

KVAČEK, Robert. 1958. *Osudná mise* [Fateful Mission]. Prague: Naše vojsko/SPB.

KVAČEK, Robert. "Předmluva k novému vydání" [Preface to a new edition], in Morrell, Sidney. 1995. *Viděl jsem ukřižování* [I Saw the Crucifixion]. (The Sudetenland 1938–39). Brno: JOTA.

KVAČEK, Robert. "Tesařovo kritické tázání" [Tesař's Critical Campaign]. *Literární noviny* 53/2000. 18.

KVAČEK, Robert – VINŠ, Václav. "K německo-československým sondážím ve třicátých letech" [On the German-Czechoslovak Probes in the 1930s]. *Československý časopis historický* 6/1966. 880–896.

LADAS, Stephen P. 1932. *The Exchange of Minorities: Bulgaria, Greece and Turkey.* New York: The Macmillan Company.

LAGARDE, P. de. *An die Deutschen.* Berlin: Deutsche Buch-Gemeinschaft.

LAGARDE, P. de. 1892. *Deutsche Schriften.* Göttingen: Dietrich Verlag. 110.

LAMBERT, Peter. "German Historians and Nazi Ideology. The Parametres of the *Volksgemeinschaft* and the Problem of Historical Legitimation, 1930–1945". *European History Quarterly* 4/1995 (XXV). 555–582.

LAŠTOVIČKA, Bohuslav. 1961. *V Londýně za války. Zápasy o novou ČSR 1939–1945* [In London during the War. The Struggles over the New ČSR 1939–1945]. Prague: SNPL.

LE GLOANNEC, Anne-Marie. "The Unilateralist Temptation. Germany's Foreign Policy after the Cold War". *Internationale Politik und Gesellschaft* 1/2004. 27–40.

LEHMANN, Hans Georg. 1995. *Deutschland-Chronik 1945 bis 1995*. Bonn: Bundeszentrale für politische Bildung.

LEMBERG, Eugen. "Aufbau und Führung einer Volksgruppe im Exil. Das sudetendeutsche Problem heute". *Der Neue Ackermann* 1/1953 (IV).

LEMBERG, Hans. "Etnické čistky – řešení národnostních problémů?" [Ethnic Purges – a solution to nationality/ethnic problems?]. *Listy* 2/1993. 98.

LEMBERG, Hans. 1999. *Porozumění Češi – Němci – východní Evropa 1848–1948* [Understanding Czechs-Germans-Eastern Europe 1848–1948]. Prague: Lidové noviny.

LESIUK, W. "Dánsko-německé zkušenosti z využití demokratických metod při řešení národnostních problémů etnického pomezí a interetnické poměry Opolského Slezska" [Danish-German Experiences of the use of democratic methods to solve nationality problems of the ethnic border and interethnic relations in Opole Silesia]. *Slezský sborník* 2/1994. 132.

Lettre Internationale 5/1992. Theme: Austria and Hungary. Prague: Lidové noviny.

LIND, Michael. "In Defense of Liberal Nationalism". *Foreign Affairs* 3/1994 (LXXIV). 87–99.

LIPSTADT, Deborah E. 2001. *Popírání holocaustu* [Holocaust Denial]. Prague/Litomyšl: Paseka.

Listy 5/1998 (XXVIII). Theme: Anniversary of the Munich Agreement.

LOCKHART, Robert Hamilton Bruce. 2003. *Jan Masaryk – osobní vzpomínky* [Jan Masaryk. A Personal Memoir]. Krnov: Vladimír Kořínek.

LOCKHART, Robert Hamilton Bruce. 1948. *Přichází zúčtování* [Comes the Reckoning]. Prague: Fr. Borový.

LOCKHART, Robert Hamilton Bruce. 1936. *Ústup ze slávy* [Retreat from Glory]. Prague: Fr. Borový.

LOEWENSTEIN, Bedřich. *České dějiny a národní identita* [Czech History and National Identity]. *Svědectví* 83–84/1988 (XXI). 567–611.

LOEWENSTEIN, Bedřich. "Německý válečný zážitek a iracionální kritika civilizace" [The German War Experience and the Irrational Critique of Civilisation]. *Český časopis historický* 1966. 521–547.

LOEWENSTEIN, Bedřich. 1991. *O nacionalismu a revolucích* [On Nationalism and Revolutions]. Prague: Lidové noviny.

LOEWENSTEIN, Bedřich. 1998. "Vlastenectví jako otevřený projekt" [Patriotism as an Open Project], in *Češi a Němci 150 let po Bolzanovi*. Prague: Prago-Media-News.

LÖFFLER, Horst. 1997. *...und zogen in die Ferne*. Wien: Österreichische Landsmannschaft.

LORD, Ch. "Národnostní menšiny v Evropě a ve světě – politické otázky" [National Minorities in Europe and in Global Political Questions]. *Via Europa* 1/1996. Brussel/Prague. 15.

LORENZ, Chris. "Beyond Good and Evil? The German Empire of 1871 and Modern German Historiography". *Journal of Contemporary History* 4/October 1995 (XXX). 729–765.

LOUDA, Vlastimil. 1948. *Politika soustavné zrady* [The Policy of Systematic Betrayal]. Prague: Svaz osvobozených politických vězňů.

Low, Alfred D. 1984. *The Anschluss Movement, 1918–1938. Background and Aftermath (Bibliography)*. New York/London: Garland Publishing, Inc.

LUDWIG, Emil. 1931. *Bismarck*. Prague: Melantrich.

LUKEŠ, Igor. "Bože, vrať nám císařství" [God, give us back the empire]. *Respekt*. 25.–31. 1. 1993. 6.

LUKEŠ, Igor. "Mimořádná vojenská opatření v květnu 1938: nová interpretace" [Special Military Measures in May 1938: A new interpretation]. *Historie a vojenství* 5/1995 (XLIV). 79–97.

Luža, Radomír. 2001. *Československá sociální demokracie* (kapitoly z let exilu 1948–1989) [Czechoslovak Social Democracy (chapters from the years of exile 1948–1989)]. Prague/Brno: Československé dokumentační středisko/Doplněk.

Luža, Radomír. 1964. *The Transfer of the Sudeten Germans*. New York University Press.

Lvová, Míla. "Dvacet let o Mnichovu v naší ideologii a vědě" [Twenty Years of Munich in our Ideology and Science]. *Revue dějin socialismu* 3/1969.

Lvová, Míla. "K otázce tzv. objednaného ultimata" [On the Question of the so-called ultimatum produced to order]. *Československý časopis historický* 3/1965. 333–334.

Lvová, Míla. 1968. *Mnichov a Edvard Beneš* [Munich and Edvard Beneš]. Prague: Svoboda.

MACARTNEY, C. A. 1968. *National States and National Minorities*. New York: Russell & Russell.

MACKENZIE, Compton. 1947. *Dr. Beneš*. Prague: Družstevní práce.

MAIER, Charles S. 1997. *The Unmasterable Past. History, Holocaust, and German National Identity*. Cambridge/Massachusetts/London: Harvard University Press.

MALÁ, Irena – KUBÁTOVÁ, Ludmila. 1965. *Pochody smrti* [The Death Marches]. Prague: Nakladatelství politické literatury.

MALENOVSKÝ, Jiří. 1993. *Mezinárodní právo veřejné* [International Public Law]. Brno: Doplněk.

Máme národní zájmy? [Do we have national interests?]. 1994. Valenta, Jiří (ed.). Prague: Ústav mezinárodních vztahů.

MANDLER, Emanuel. 2001. *Češi i Němci – legendy, spory, realita* [Czechs and Germans – Legends, Disputes, Reality]. Prague: Libri.

MANDLER, Emanuel. "Střední Evropa jako oběť?" [Central Europe as a Victim?]. *Nová přítomnost* 6/1996. 14–15.

MANN, Golo. 1993. *Dějiny Německa* 1919–1945 [A History of Germany 1919–1945]. Prague: Český spisovatel.

Mariánskolázeňské rozhovory/Marienbader Gespräche [Mariánské Lázně Conversations]. 1998–2001. (Series of editions of lectures). Prague: Česká křesťanská akademie/Ackermann-Gemeinde.

MARKOVITS, Andrei S. – REICH, Simon. 1998. *Das deutsche Dilemma*. Berlin: Alexander Fest Verlag.

MARKOVITS, Andrei S. – REICH, Simon. 1997. *The German Predicament: Memory and Power in the New Europe*. Ithaca: Cornell University Press.

MARSHALL, Barbara. 2000. *The New Germany and Migration in Europe*. Manchester/New York: Manchester University Press.

MASAŘÍK, Hubert. 2002. *V proměnách Evropy* [In the Transformations of Europe]. Prague: Paseka.

MASARYK, Tomáš G. 1990. *Česká otázka* [The Czech Question]. Prague: Svoboda.

MASARYK, Tomáš, G. 1920. *Nová Evropa – stanovisko slovanské* [The New Europe – the Slav Viewpoint]. Prague: Nákladem Gustava Dubského.

MASARYK, Tomáš G. 1925. *Světová revoluce* [The World Revolution]. Prague: Orbis.

MATĚJČEK, Jiří – MACHAČOVÁ, Jana. 1999. *Sociální pozice národnostních menšin v českých zemích 1918–1938* [The Social Position of National Minorities in the Czech Lands 1918–1938]. Opava: Slezský ústav Slezského zemského muzea.

MAZUR, Arnošt. 1963. *Kořeny fašismu sudetských Němců v Československu* (bibliografický výběr sudetik z let 1918–1939) [The Roots of the Fascism of the Sudeten Germans in Czechoslovakia (bibiographical selection of Sudetica from the years 1918–1939)]. Opava: Slezský ústav ČSAV.

McGOWAN, Lee. 2004. *Radikální pravice v Německu (od roku 1870 po současnost)* [The Radical Right in Germany (from 1870 to the present)]. Prague: Prostor.

MEAD, Walter R. "Coming to Terms with the New Germany". *World Policy Journal*. 1990. Fall. 593–638.

MEINECKE, F. 1908. *Weltbürgertum und Nationalstaat*. Leipzig.

MELLOR, Roy E. H. 1991. *Nation, State and Territory*. London/New York: Routledge.

MERRITT, Anna J. – MERRITT, Richard L. 1980. *Public Opinion in Semisovereign Germany*. Urbana/Chicago/London: University of Illinois Press.

Sudetendeutscher Atlas. 1954. Meynen, E. (ed.). München: Verlag der Arbeitsgemeinschaft zur Wahrung sudetendeutscher Interessen.

MEYER, Henry Cord. 1955. *Mitteleuropa in German Thought and Action 1815–1945*. The Hague: Martinus Nijhoff.

MEZIHORÁK, František. 1997. *Hry o Moravu* (separatisté, iredentisté a kolaboranti 1938–1945) [Playing for Moravia (separatists, irredentists and collaborators 1938–1945)]. Prague: Mladá fronta.

Mezinárodní politika 11/2001. Theme Czech-German Relations. Prague: Ústav mezinárodních vztahů.

MIKULE, Vladimír. "Dekrety prezidenta republiky a nynější právo" [The Decrees of the President of the Republic and Current Law], in *Právní aspekty odsunu sudetských Němců.*

MIKULE, Vladimír. 1996. "Dekrety prezidenta republiky po padesáti letech" [The Decrees of the President of the Republic after Fifty Years], in *Studie o sudetoněmecké otázce*. Prague: Ústav mezinárodních vztahů.

MILLER, David Hunter. *My Diary at the Conference of Paris*. Vol. XIII. 96. Vol. XVI. 15.

MÍŠKOVÁ, Alena. "Hitler, holokaust, a 'obyčejní Němci'" [Hitler, the Holocaust and "Ordinary Germans"]. *Dějiny a současnost* 5/1997. 27–30.

MÍŠKOVÁ, A. "Nadšení i rozčarování ve jménu vůdce-osvoboditele" [Enthusiasm and Disillusion in the Name of the Fuhrer/Liberator], in Zimmermann, V. *Sudetští Němci v nacistickém státě*. 572–573.

MÍŠKOVÁ, Alena. 2002. *Německá (Karlova) univerzita od Mnichova k 9. květnu 1945* [The German (Charles) University from Munich to the 9th of May 1945]. Prague: Karolinum.

Mitteleuropa between Europe and Germany. 1997. Katzenstein, Peter (ed.). Providence/Oxford: Berghahn Books.

MLYNÁRIK, Ján. 2000. *Causa Danubius*. Prague: Vydavateľstvo Danubius.

Mnichov 1938 [Munich 1938], I-III. Blodig, V. – Vostřelová, E. (eds.). 1988. Prague: Svaz protifašistických bojovníků.

Mnichovské trauma 1938 [The Munich Trauma 1938]. Lidové noviny – special supplement. 30. 9. 1998.

MOMMSEN, Hans. 1963. *Die Sozialdemokratie und die Nationalitäten Frage im habsburgischen Vielvölkerstaat.* Wien.

MOMMSEN, Hans – KOVÁČ, Dušan – MALÍŘ, Jiří – MARKOVÁ, Michaela. 2000. *První světová válka a vztahy mezi Čechy, Slováky a Němci* [The First World War and Relations between Czechs, Slovaks and Germans]. Brno: Matice moravská.

MOMMSEN, Wilhelm. 1996. *Bismarck.* Prague: Votobia.

MORAVCOVÁ, Dagmar. 2001. *Československo, Německo a evropská hnutí 1929–1932* [Czechoslovakia, Germany and the European Movement 1929–1932). Prague: Institut pro středoevropskou politiku a kulturu.

MORAVEC, Emanuel. 1942. *Das Ende der Benesch-Republik.* Prague: Orbis Verlag.

MORAVEC, Emanuel. 1936. *Obrana státu* [The Defence of the State]. Prague: Svaz čs. důstojnictva.

MORAVEC, Emanuel. 1941. *V úloze mouřenína* [In the Role of the Moor]. Prague: Orbis.

MORAVEC, František. 1990. *Špión, jemuž nevěřili* [The Spy They Didn't Believe]. Prague: ROZMLUVY Alexandera Tomského.

MORRELL, Sydney. 1939. *I saw the Crucifixion.* London: Peter Davies.

MORGAN, Roger. 1974. *The United States and West Germany.* London: The Royal Institute of International Affairs/Oxford University Press.

MORGENBRODOVÁ, B. "Česká otázka v říškoněmecké publicistice 1914–1918" [The Czech Question in Reich German Political Writings], in Mommsen, H. (et al.). *První světová válka a vztahy mezi Čechy, Slováky a Němci.* 179–194.

MOULIS, Miloslav "Výbor pro dějiny národně osvobozeneckého boje" [Committee for the History of the Fight for National Liberation], in *Occursus, Setkání, Begegnung.* 1996. Pousta, Z. – Seifter, P. – Pešek, J. (eds.) Prague: Karolinum. 20–25.

MÜLLER, Helmut (et al.). 1995. *Dějiny Německa* [A History of Germany]. Prague: Lidové noviny.

MÜLLER, Helmut (et al.). 1995. "Konference ve Wannsee a 'konečné řešení židovské otázky'" [The Conference at Wannsee and the "Final Solution of the Jewish Problem"], in *Dějiny Německa* [History of Germany]. Prague: Lidové noviny. 299–230.

MÜLLER, Jan. "Český tiskový trh ovládají zahraniční vydavatelé" [The Czech Press Market is Controlled by Foreign Publishers]. *Lidové noviny.* Supplement Média a komunikace. 9. 2. 1998.

MÜLLER, Karel. 2002. Češi a občanská společnost [Czechs and Civic Society]. Prague: Triton.

MÜNZ, Reiner – OHLIGER, R. 1998. *Path to Inclusion: The Integration of Migrants in the United States and Germany.* Oxford: Oxford University Press.

Národnostní otázka v Československu po roce 1918 [The Nationality Question in Czechoslovakia after 1918]. (Collection – internal print). Opava: Slezský ústav ČSAV.

MUSGRAVE, Thomas D. 1997. *Self-Determination and National Minorities.* Oxford: Clarendon Press.

Nationalising and Denationalising European Border Regions, 1800–2000. 2000. Knippenberg, Hans – Markusse, Jan (eds.). Dordrecht/Boston/London: Kluwer Academic Publishers.

NAUMANN, Friedrich. 1915. *Mitteleuropa*. Berlin: Druck und Verlag von Georg Reimer.

NEBESKÝ, Jiří J. K. 2003. *Příběh lágru* [The Story of the Camp]. Hranice: Tichý typ.

NEILLANDS, Robin. 2002. *Der Krieg der Bomber*. Berlin: Quintessenz Verlag.

NĚMEC, Petr. "Český národ a nacistická teorie germanizace prostoru" [The Czech Nation and the Nazi Theory of the Germanisation of Territory]. *Český časopis historický* 4/1990 (IIXC). 535–558.

NĚMEČEK, Jan. "Benešovy vzkazy do vlasti" [Beneš's Messages to the Homeland (review of publication in brackets)]. *Soudobé dějiny* 4/1996. 555–560.

NĚMEČEK, Jan. 2003. *Od spojenectví k roztržce* [From Alliance to Split]. Prague: Academia.

NEUBAUER, F. "Bezpráví musí být odsouzeno" [Illegaility must be condemned]. *Listy* 2/2000. 23–26. *Die Neue Gesellschaft-Frankfurter Hefte12*. Dezember 2002. "Das Thema: Friedensordnung Europa-Flucht und Vertreibung".

NEUMANNOVÁ, Jana. "Média bojují o regiony" [The Media Fight for the Regions]. *Týden* 15/2001. 92–93.

NOELLE-NEUMANN, Elisabeth. "The German Revolution-The Historic Experiment of the Division and Unification of a Nation as Reflected in Survey Research Findings". *International Journal of Public Opinion Reserach* 3/1991 (III). 237–259.

NOELLE-NEUMANN, Elisabeth – KÖCHER, Renate. 1987. *Die Verletzte Nation*. Stuttgart: Deutsche Verlags-Anstalt.

NOLTE, Ernst. 1999. *Fašismus ve své epoše* [Fascism in its Epoch]. Prague: Argo.

NOSSACK, H. E. 2002. *Der Untergang*. Suhrkamp Verlag.

NOVÁK, Miloslav. 1995. *Kancléř Adenauer* [Chancellor Adenauer]. Prague: Irma.

NOVÁK, Otto. 1987. *Henleinovci proti Československu* [The Henleinians against Czechoslovakia]. Prague: Naše vojsko/SPB.

NOVOTŇÁK, Miliduch M. 1945. *Lužičtí Srbové* [The Lusatian Serbs]. Prague: F. Kosek.

Occursus – Setkání – Begegnung [Occursus – Meeting – Begegnung (Collection in honour of the 65th birthday of Jan Křen)]. 1996. Pousta, Zdeněk – Seifter, Pavel – Pešek, Jiří (eds.). Prague: Karolinum.

OČENÁŠEK, Ludvík. 1919. *Na pomoc dohodě* [To the Aid of the Entente]. Prague: self-published.

OHLBAUM, Rudolf. 1981. *Bayerns vierter Stamm* – die Sudetendeutschen. München: Aufstieg-Verlag.

OLBERT, Franz. 1988. *Ackermann-Gemeinde-Weg und Ziel*. Schriftenreihe der AG, Heft 24. Munich: Ackermann-Gemeinde, Hauptstelle.

OLIVOVÁ, Věra. 1968. *Československo v rozrušené Evropě* [Czechoslovakia in a Disrupted Europe]. Prague: Svoboda.

OLIVOVÁ, Věra. "K historii československo-rakouské smlouvy z roku 1921" [On the History of the Czechoslovak-Austrian Agreement of 1921]. *Československý časopis historický* 2/1961. 198–219.

OLIVOVÁ, Věra 1998. *Manipulace s dějinami první republiky* [The Manipulation of the History of the First Republic]. Prague: Společnost Edvarda Beneše.

OPOČENSKÝ, Jan. 1931. *Umsturz in Mitteleuropa*. Hellerau bei Dresden: Avalun-Verlag.

ORT, Alexandr. 1994. Edvard Beneš. *Diplomat a politik* [Diplomat and Politician]. Prague: Společnost Edvarda Beneše.

Österreichs Zusammenbruch und Wiederaufbau. 1899. Munich: Lehmann. 20.

O'SULLIVAN, Noël. 1995. *Fašismus* [Fascism]. Brno. Doplněk.

OTÁHAL, M. "Ferdinand Peroutka – muž přítomnosti" [Ferdinand Peroutka – Man of the Present]. *Slovo k historii* 33/1992. 20.

OTAVA, Jan – TIGRID, Pavel. "Zpráva o stavu střední Evropy" [Report on the State of Central Europe]. *Svědectví* 89–90/1990 (XXIII). 227–260.

PALKOVSKÝ, Karel. 1946. *Londýnské epištoly* [London Epistles]. Prague: Václav Petr.

PALLIS, A. A. "Racial Migrations in the Balkans during the Years 1912–1924". *Geographical Journal* 66/1925.

PÁNEK, Jaroslav. "Historiografie, historické vědomí a odpovědnost" [Historiography, Historical Consciousness and Responsibility]. *Zpravodaj historického klubu* 2/1999 (X). 5–14.

PÁNEK, Jaroslav – PEŠEK, Jiří. "Historikové proti znásilňování dějin" [Historians against the Violation of History]. Special supplement to the *Zpravodaj Historického klubu* 2/2001 (XII).

PARKER, R. A. C. 2000. *Churchill and Appeasement.* London/Oxford: Papermac (Macmillan Publishers Ltd.).

Patterns of Migration in Central Europe. 2001. Wallace, C. – Stola, D. (eds.). Houndsmills: Palgrave. 86.

PAULOVÁ, Milada. 1938. *Tomáš G. Masaryk a Jihoslované* [Tomáš G. Masaryk and the South Slavs]. Prague: Československo-Jihoslovanská liga.

PAULOVÁ Milada. 1968. *Tajný výbor (MAFFIE)* [Secret Committee (MAFFIE)]. Praha: Academia.

PAVLÍČEK, Václav. "O amnestiích, zákonu č. 115/1946 Sb. a aktech odporu proti Německu" [On Amnesties, Law no. 115/1946 and Acts of Resistance to Germany]; PAVLÍČEK Václav. "Evropské hodnoty a dekretální normotvorba" [European Values and Creation of Norms by Decree], in *Je již český právní řád v soualdu s právem EU?.* 39–46.

PAVLÍČEK, Václav. 2002. *O české státnosti* [On Czech Statehood]. Prague: Karolinum.

PAVLÍČEK, Václav. "Odmítnout dekrety je jako uznat protektorátní řád" [To reject the decrees is like recognising the Protectorate's legal order]. *Právo.* 1. 10. 1998. 9.

PAVLÍČEK, V. – SUCHÁNEK, R. "O některých otázkách majetkových nároků v česko-německých vztazích" [Some Questions of Property Claims in Czech-German Relations], in *Krajanské organizace sudetských Němců v SRN* [Compatriot Organisations of the Sudeten Germans in the FRG]. Prague: Ústav mezinárodních vztahů. 82–83.

PÁTA, Josef. 1919. *Lužice* [Lusatia]. Prague: Nakladatelství J. R. Vilímek.

PEARSON, Frederic S. – ROCHESTER, J. Martin. 1988. *International Relations.* New York: Random House.

PEDERSEN, Thomas. 1998. *Germany, France and the Integration of Europe.* London/New York: Pinter.

PEKAŘ, Josef. 1923. *Omyly a nebezpečí pozemkové reformy.* Praha: Vesmír.

PFAFF, Ivan. 1993. *Sovětská zrada 1938* [The Soviet Betrayal 1938]. Prague: Naše vojsko.

PFAFF, Ivan. "Tragédie plná omylů (kritický portrét Edvarda Beneše)" [A Tragedy Full of Errors (A critical Portrait of Edvard Beneš)]. *Reportér* 9/1990. (Supplement I–XII).

PFOHL, Ernst. 1987. *Ortslexikon Sudetenland.* Nürnberg: Helmut Preussler Verlag.

PECKA, Emanuel. "Doslov" [Epilogue], in Jodl, M. 1994. *Teorie elity a problém elity* [Theories of the Elite and the Problem of the Elite]. Prague: Victoria Publishing. 122.

PECKA, Emanuel. 1994. "Sociologické teorie elity" [Sociological Theories of the Elite], in *Politické elity v Československu 1918–1948*. Ediční řada sešity USD. Vol. 20. Prague: Ústav pro soudobé dějiny AV ČR.

PECKA, Jindřich. 1995. *Váleční zajatci na území Protektorátu Čechy a Morava* [Prisoners of War on the Territory of the Protectorate of Bohemia and Moravia]. Prague: Ústav pro soudobé dějiny AV ČR.

PEDERSEN, Thomas. 1998. *Germany, France and the Integration of Europe* (a realist interpretation). London/New York: Pinter.

PERMAN, Dagmar. 1962. *The Shaping of the Czechoslovak State. Diplomatic History of the boundaries of Czechoslovakia, 1914–1920*. Leiden: E. J. Brill.

PEROUTKA, Ferdinand. 1991. *Budování státu I–IV* [The Building of the State 1–4]. Prague: Lidové noviny.

PEROUTKA, Ferdinand. 1993. *Byl Edvard Beneš vinen?* [Was Edvard Beneš Guilty?] Prague: H&H/Společnost E. Beneše.

PEROUTKA, Ferdinand. 1927. Kdo nás osvobodil? [Who Liberated us?] Prague: Svaz národního osvobození.

PERSSON, Hans Ake. 2001. *Rhetorik und Realpolitik*. Berlin: BERLIN VERLAG Arno Spitz.

PEŠEK, Jiří. "20. století – doba nucených migrací, vyhnání a transferů" [The 20th Century – a Time of Forced Migrations, Expulsions and Transfers]. *Dějiny a současnost* 1/2002.

PEŠEK, Jiří. "Nacifikace německých univerzit" [The Nazification of German Universities]. *Dějiny a současnost* 3/1995. 33–37.

PEŠEK, Jiří. "Poválečné osudy Němců v Polsku pod drobnohledem" [The Postwar Fates of Germans in Poland under the Microscope]. *Soudobé dějiny* 3/2003. 351–356.

PEŠKA, Zdeněk. "Historický vývoj mezinárodní menšinové ochrany před světovou válkou" [The Historical Development of Protection for Minorities before the World War]. *Zahraniční politika*. 1929. 1168–1182.

PEŠKA, Zdeněk. 1932. *Národní menšiny a Československo* [National Minorities and Czechoslovakia]. Bratislava. 38.

PEŠKA, Zdeněk. "Otázka národnostních menšin na pařížské konferenci" [The Question of National Minorities at the Paris Conference]. *Zahraniční politika* 1929. 1168–1182.

PEŠKOVÁ, Jaroslava. 1997. *Role vědomí v dějinách* [The Role of Consciousness in History]. Prague: Lidové noviny.

PETRÁŠ, René. "Mezinárodněprávní ochrana menšin po první světové válce" [The International Legal Protection of Minorities after the First World War]. *Historický obzor* I.–II./2000. 31–40.

PHILLIPS, Ann L. 2000. *Power and Influence after the Cold War*. Lanham/Boulder/New York/Oxford: Rowman & Littlefield Publishers, Inc.

PICHLÍK, Karel. "Poválečná Evropa v představách T. G. Masaryka v exilu" [Postwar Europe in the Ideas of T. G. Masaryk in Exile], in Mommsen, H. – Kováč, D. – Malíř, J. – Marková, M. *První světová válka a vztahy mezi Čechy, Slováky a Němci*. 53–62.

PICHLÍK, Karel. 1968. *Zahraniční odboj 1914/1918 bez legend* [The Czech Resistance Abroad 1914/1918 without Legends]. Prague: Svoboda.

PITHART, Petr. "Šetřme své dějiny" [Let us Spare our History]. *Svědectví* 89–90/1990 (XXIII). 300–314.

PITHART, Petr. "Smysl výzvy Smíření 95" [The Rationale of the Conciliation 95 Appeal]. *Lidové noviny.* 18. 4. 1995.

PITHART, Petr – PŘÍHODA, Petr. 1998. *Čítanka odsunutých dějin* [Tranfer History Reader]. Prague: Nadace Bernarda Bolzana.

PLICHTA, Dalibor. 1999. *Národ a národnost v čase globalizace* [The Nation and Nationality in the Time of Globlisation]. Prague: JOB Publishing.

PLICHTA, Dalibor. 1996. *Nesmířenost a nesmiřitelnost německé politiky* [The Unreconciled and Unreconcileable Character of German Policy]. Prague: Fénix.

PODIVEN (the pseudonym of a collective of authors: P. Příhoda, P. Pithart, M. Otáhal, M. Pojar, T. Brod). 1991. *Češi v dějinách nové doby* [Czechs in the History of the Modern Age]. Prague: Rozmluvy. 400.

POHLE, Heinz. "Der Rundfunk als Instrument der Politik", in *Zur Geschichte des deutschen Rundfunks von 1923–38.* 1955. Hamburg: Hans Bredow Institut. *Stín šoa nad Evropou* [The Shadow of the Shoah over Europe]. 2001. Pojar, Miloš (ed.). Prague: Židovské muzeum.

Politika. Co má vědět o Československé republice každý občan [Politics. What Every Citizen Ought to Know about the Czech Republic]. 1925. Tobolka, Zdeněk Václav (ed.). Prague: Nákladem "Československého kompasu", tiskařské a vydavatelské akc. společnosti.

POSSELT, B. (Interview). "Jsem motorem rozšíření EU na východ" [I am the motor for EU expansion to the East]. *Lidové noviny.* 2. 8. 2001. 9.

Potsdam After Twenty-Five Years. *International Affairs* (Special issue) 3/July 1970 (IVL).

POVOLNÝ, M. "Mnichov po patnácti letech" [Munich after Fifteen Years]. *Tribuna* (The bulletin of the Czechoslovak Foreign Institute in Exile). Sept.–November 1953. 10–12.

POVOLNÝ, M. "Šedesát pět let od Mnichova" [Sixty Years after Munich]. *Slezský sborník* 3/2002. 264–270.

Právní aspekty odsunu [Legal Aspects of the Transfer]. 1995, 1996 (enlarged edition). Matějka, D. (ed.). Prague: Ústav mezinárodních vztahů.

PŘÍBRAM, J. "Příběh s nedobrým koncem" [A Story with a Bad Ending], in *Češi, Němci, odsun.* 46.

PŘÍHODA, Petr. "Naši Němci. (O jejich vyhnání a zrodu totalitní moci v Čechách)" [Our Germans (On their expulsion and the rise of totalitarian power in the Czech Lands)]. *Přítomnost* 4/1990. 22.

PŘÍHODA, Petr. "Nezvládnuté minulosti" [Unmastered Pasts]. *Kafka (journal for Central Europe)* 13/2004. Single-theme issue devoted to "expulsion". 22–23.

PRINZ, F. "Benešův mýtus se rozpadá" [The Beneš Myth is Disintegrating]. (Text of a lecture given in the Sudeten German House in Munich on the 27th of November 1991 to the Sudetendeutscher Rat). *Střední Evropa* 24/1992 (VIII). 42–43.

PRÖLL, K. 1890. *Die Kämpfe der Deutschen in Oesterreich.* Berlin: Lüstenöder. 7.

Prostor 23/1993 (VI). Theme – Revived Czech statehood, not to speak (preferably) of the nation.

PUTNA, Martin C. "Smiřovací jehňátka" [Lambs of Conciliation]. *Lidové noviny.* 20. 2. 1996. 2.

QUAM, Louis O. "The Use of Maps in Propaganda". *The Journal of Geography* 1943 (XLII). 21–32.

RÁDL, Emanuel. 2003. *O německé revoluci – K politické ideologii sudetských Němců* [On the German Revolution – The political ideology of the Sudeten Germans]. Prague: Masarykův ústav Akademie věd ČR.

RÁDL, Emanuel. 1993. *Válka Čechů s Němci* [The War of the Czechs with the Germans]. Prague: Melantrich.

RADVANOVSKÝ, Zdeněk. 1998–2003. *Historie okupovaného pohraničí 1938–1945* [A History of the Occupied Borderlands 1938–1945]. Vols. I-VII. Ústí nad Labem: Univerzita J. E. Purkyně.

RAKOVÁ, Svatava. 1983. *Politika Spojených států ve střední Evropě po první světové válce* [The Policy of the United States in Central Europe after the First World War]. Prague: Academia.

RASCHHOFER, Hermann "Das Münchener Abkommen". *Volk und Reich* 19/1946. 313–320.

RASCHHOFER, Hermann *Die tschechoslowakischen Denkschfriten für die Friedenskonferenz von Paris 1919/1920.* 1937. Berlin.

RASCHHOFER, Hermann. 1953. *Die Sudetenfrage.* Munich: Isar Verlag.

RAŠÍN, A. Řeč dr. A. Rašína v Nymburce. *Národní listy.* 7. 1. 1920.

RAŠKA, Francis Dostál. 2002. *The Czechoslovak exile government in London and the Sudeten German issue.* Prague: Karolinum.

RATAJ, Jan. 1997. *O autoritativní národní stát* [On the Authoritarian Nation State]. Prague: Karolinum.

RATZEL, Friedrich. 1897. *Politische Geographie.* Munich/Berlin: R. Oldenbourg Verlag.

RAUSCHNING, H. *Mluvil jsem s Hitlerem* [I talked with Hitler]. 1946. Prague: Nová osvěta.

REDLICH, J. 1920. *Das österreichische Staats- und Reichs- problem I.* Leipzig. 30. *Cesta do katastrofy (Československo-německé vztahy 1938–1947)* [The Road to Catastrophe (Czechoslovak-German Relations 1938–1947)]. 1993. Řezanková, Ivona – Kural, Václav (eds.). Prague: Ústav mezinárodních vztahů.

Redrawing Nations (Ethnic Cleansing in East-Central Europe 1944–1948). 2001. Ther, Philipp – Siljak, Ana (eds.). Lanham/Boulder/New York/Oxford: Rowman & Littlefield Publishers, INC.

Reflexe sudetoněmecké otázky a postoje obyvatelstva českého pohraničí k Německu [Reactions to the Sudeten German Question and Attitudes of the Population of the Czech Borderland to Germany]. 1997. Houžvička, Václav (ed.). Prague: Sociologický ústav AV ČR.

RICHTER, Karel. 1994. *Sudety.* Prague: Fajma.

RIEMER, J. M. "Grace? Under Pressure?" (The Goldhagen Controversy after Two Years), in *Germany's Difficult Passage to Modernity.* 1999. Lankowski, C. (ed.). New York/Oxford: Berghahn Books. 212–226.

RIPKA, Hubert. 1939. *Munich: Before and After.* A fully documented Czechoslovak Account of the Crises of September 1938 and March 1939. London. Victor Gollanz Left Book Club. Not for sale to the public.

RIPKA, Hubert. "Záznam rozhovoru s A. Edenem" [Record of a Conversation with A. Eden], in *Češi a sudetoněmecká otázka.* 172.

RITTER, G. 1965. *The German Problem: Basic Questions of German Political Life, Past And Present.* Columbus: Ohio State University.

ROCK, David – WOLFF, Stefan. 2002. *Coming home to Germany*. New York/Oxford: Berghahn Books.

ROKKAN, Stein. "Models and Methods in the Comparative Study of Nation-Building". *Acta Sociologica* 2/1969 (XII). 53–73.

RÖPKE, W. 1946. *The German Question*. London: Knopf.

ROSENSTEIN-RODAN, P. N. "How much can Germany Pay?" *International Affairs* 21/1944. 469–476.

ROUSSO, H. L. "L'Épuration. Die politische Säuberung in Frankreich", in *Politische Säuberung in Europe. Die Abrechnung mit Faschismus und Kollaboration nach dem Zweiten Weltkrieg*. 1991. Henke, K.-D. – Woller, H. (eds.). Munich. 216–219.

Rozhovory o sousedství [Conversations about Neighbourhood]. (A series of speeches given in the Karolinum in 1995). 1996. Klener, Pavel (ed.). Prague: Univerzita Karlova.

Rozumět dějinám [Understanding History]. 2002. Beneš, Zdeněk – Kural, Václav (eds.). Prague: Gallery.

RUMMEL, R. "The German Debate on International Security Institutions", in *European Security and International Institutions after the Cold War*. 1995. Carnovale, M. (ed.). New York: St. Martin's Press. 193.

RUPNIK, Jacques. "Důležitou zkouškou jsou vždy druhé volby" [Second Choices are always an Important Test]. *Lidové noviny*. 5. 5. 1995. 8.

RUPNIK, Jacques. – BAZIN, Anne. "La difficile réconciliation tchéco-allemande". *Politique étrangere* 2/2001 (Avril-Juin). 353–370.

RUPPEL, Willy. 1943. *Soumrak ženevských bohů* [The Twilight of the Genevan Gods]. Prague: Orbis.

RŮŽIČKOVÁ, Monika. "České noviny v cizích rukou (diskusní panel)" [The Czech Newspapers in Foreign Hands (discussion panel)]. PRINT&PUBLISHING 46/1999. 42–45.

ŠABATA, J. "Masarykova Nová Evropa" [Masaryk's New Europe] (preface), in Masaryk, T. G. *Nová Evropa*. 19.

SALOMON, Dieter "Od rozpadu podunajské monarchie do konce druhé světové války (1918–1945)" [From the Collapse of the Danubian Monarch to the End of the Second World War (1918–1945)], in *Tisíc let česko-německých vztahů*. 191.

SALZBORN, Samuel "Zwischen Volksgruppentheorie, Völkerrechtslehre und Volkstumskampf. Hermann Raschhofer als Vordenker eines völkischen Minderheitenrechts". *Sozial Geschichte*. 21 3. 2006. 29–52.

ŠAMALÍK, František. 1996. *Úvahy o dějinách české politiky* [Reflections on the History of Czech Politics]. Prague: Victoria Publishing.

ŠATAVA, Leoš. 1994. *Národnostní menšiny v Evropě* [National Minorities in Europe]. Prague: Ivo Železný.

SCHECHTMAN, Joseph B. 1971. *European Population Transfers* 1939–1945. New York: Russell.

SCHECHTMAN, Joseph B. 1962. *Postwar Population Transfers in Europe* 1945–1955. Philadelphia: University of Pennsylvania Press.

SCHECHTMAN, Joseph B. "Postwar Population Transfers in Europe: A Survey". *The Review of Politics*. April 1953 (XV). University of Notre Dame. 151–178.

SCHIEDER, Theodore "Die deutsche Frage", in *Meyers Enzyklopädisches Lexikon*. 1972. (Collective of authors). Mannheim: Meyers.

SCHIEDER, Theodore 1957. *Die Vertreibung der deutschen Bevölkerung aus Ost-Mitteleuropa IV/1.* Bonn. 17.

SCHMID, Thomas. "Cutting Through the Mental Fire Wall". *Frankfurter Allgemeine Zeitung* 3/April 2001 (website English edition).

SCHMIDT, Dieter A. 1998. *Franz Josef Strauss Symposium.* 19. Internationale Fachtagung für Politik und Strategie. Munich: Hans-Seidel-Stiftung.

SCHMIDT, Helmut. 1997. *Na společné cestě* [On a Common Road]. Prague: PRAGMA.

SCHMIDT, Paul. 1997. *Paměti Hitlerova tlumočníka* [The Memoirs of Hitler's Interpreter]. Brno: Barrister&Principal.

SCHÖPFLIN, George. "Nationalism and National Minorities in East and Central Europe". *Journal of International Affairs* 1/1991 (VL). 51–65.

SCHRÖDER, Gerhard. "Německá spolková vláda a země střední a východní Evropy" [The German Federal Republic and the Countries of Central and Eastern Europe]. *Svědectví* 29–32/1966–67 (VIII), (reprint Dialog, Frankfurt am Mein). 15–23.

SCHUBERT, Klaus – WAGNER, Jürgen. "Federalismus a nové teritoriální členění" [Federalism and the New Territorial Subdivision]. *Politologický časopis* 1/1997 (IV). 69–82.

SCHULZE Wessel, M. 1997. "Střed je na Západě – střední Evropa v české diskusi osmdesátých let" [The Centre is in the West – Eastern Europe in Czech Discussion of the 1980], in *Evropa očima Čechů.* 73–77.

SCHUMACHER, Rupert – HUMMEL, Hans. 1938. *Vom Kriege zwischen den Kriegen.* Stuttgart: Union Deutsche Verlagsgesellschaft.

SCHUSCHNIGG, Kurt von. 1947. *Requiem v červeno-bílo-červené* [Requiem in Blue-White-Red]. Prague: Aventinum.

SCHWEIGLER, Gebhard L. 1975. *National Consciousness in Divided Germany* (With an Introduction by Karl W. Deutsch). London: SAGE Publications.

SCHWELB, Egon. *Obnovení právního pořádku* [The Restoration of a Legal Order]. 1945. London. Spolek československých advokátů v zahraničí.

SCRUTON, Roger 1989. *Slovník politického myšlení* (heslo Nacionalismus) [Dictionary of Political Thought (entry for Nationalism)]. Brno: Atlantis. 75.

ŠEDIVÝ, Jaroslav. 1997. *Černínský palác v roce nula* (Ze zákulisí polistopadové zahraniční politiky) [The Černín Palace in Year Zero (Behind the scenes of post-November 89 foreign policy)]. Prague: Ivo Železný.

ŠEDIVÝ, Jaroslav. "Multilaterální aspekt problému německé menšiny na našem území v r. 1945" [The multilateral aspect of the problem of the German minority on our territory in 1945], in *Právní aspekty odsunu sudetských Němců.* 7.

SEIBT, Ferdinand. 1993. *Německo a Češi* [Germany and the Czechs]. Prague: Academia.

SEMENESCU, Carmen. 1998. *Minority Communities and the Concept of Autonomy in Eastern Europe.* Working Draft of the project GSFI (Ethnicity and Autonomy). Unpublished paper. University of Cambridge.

SERENY, Gitta. 2001. *The German Trauma.* London/New York: Penguin Books.

SETON-WATSON, Hugh. 1982. *Eastern Europe between the Wars 1918–1941.* London: Westview Press/Boulder.

SETON-WATSON, Hugh. 1977. *Nations and States.* Boulder: Westview.

SETON-WATSON, Robert. W. "The German Minority in Czechoslovakia". *Foreign Affairs* XVI (July). 1938. 651–666.

Severní Čechy a Mnichov [North Bohemia and Munich]. 1969. Hájek, J. (ed.). Liberec/Ústí nad Labem: VŠST/Pedagogická fakulta.

ŠÍMA, Jaroslav. 1945. *Českovenští přestěhovalci v letech 1938–1945* [Czechoslovak Migrants 1938–1945]. Prague: Vydavatelství Societas.

ŠIMEČKA, Milan. "Jiná civilizace?" [A Different Civilisation?]. *Svědectví* 89–90/1984–1985 (XIX). 350–356.

ŠKÁBA, J. "Národní organisace v Československé republice" [National Organisations in the Czechoslovak Republic]. *Československá vlastivěda* V. *Stát*. Prague: Sfinx/B. Janda. 244.

SKILLING, H. Gordon. 1995. *T. G. Masaryk proti proudu 1882–1914* [T. G. Masaryk against the Current 1882–1914]. Prague: Práh.

SLAPNICKA, Helmut. 1999. *Die rechtlichen Grundlagen für die Behandlung der Deutschen und der Magyaren in der Tschechoslowakei 1945–1948*. Munich: Internationales Institut für Nationalitätenrecht und Regionalismus.

SMELSER, Ronald M. "At the limits of A Mass Movement: the Case of the Sudeten German Party, 1933–1938", in *Bohemia* (Jahrbuch des Collegium Carolinum). Band 17. 1995. München/Wien: Oldenbourg. 254–255.

SMELSER, Ronald M. 1975. *The Sudeten Problem 1933–1938*. Volkstumpolitik and the Formulation of Nazi Foreign Policy. Middletown: Wesleyan University Press.

ŠMÍDOVÁ, Olga. "Česko-německé vztahy v zrcadle tisku" [Czech-German Relations in the Mirror of the Press]. *S-Obzor* 4/1995. (IV). 37–46.

Smíření mezi Čechy a Němci [Reconciliation between Czechs and Germans]. 1996. Hannover: Kirchenamt der Evangelischen Kirche in Deutschland (EKD).

SMITH, Anthony D. "Nationalism and the Historians". *International Journal of Comparative Sociology* 1–2/1992 (XXXIII). 58–80.

SMITH, Anthony D. 1991. *National Identity*. London: Penguin Books.

SMITH, Anthony D. 1995. *Nations and Nationalism in a Global Era*. Cambridge: Polity Press/Blackwell Publishers.

SMITH, Anthony D. – WILLIAMS, Colin. "The national construction of social space". *Progress in Human Geography* 7:4. 1983. 503–518.

SMITH, Gordon – PATERSON, William E. – MERKEL, Peter H. 1989. *Developments in West German Politics*. London: Macmillan Education Ltd.

SMUTNÝ, František. "Byl jsem velitelem transportu odsunutých" [I was commander of a transfer transport]. *Národní osvobození* 25–26/2004. 13.

SMUTNÝ, Jaromír. 1996. *Svědectví prezidentova kanceléře* [The Testimony of the President's Chancellor]. Prague: Mladá fronta.

ŠNEJDÁREK, Antonín. The Beginnings of Sudeten German Organisations in Western Germany after 1945. *Historica* 8 (1964) 235–52.

ŠNEJDÁREK, Antonín. 1964. *Revanšisté proti Československu* [Revanchists against Czechoslovakia]. Prague: Naše vojsko.

ŠNEJDÁREK, Antonín. "Tajné rozhovory Beneše s Německem v letech 1936/37" [Beneš's Secret Talks with Germany in 1936/7]. *Československý časopis historický* 1/1961.

So oder so. Řešení české otázky podle německých dokumentů 1933–1945 [The Solution of the Czech Question according to German documents 1933–1945]. 1996. Čelovský, Bořivoj (ed.). Ostrava: Tilia.

SOBOTA, Emil. 1931. *Das tschechoslowakische Nationalitätenrecht*. Prague. 43.

Sociologický časopis 1/1992 (IIXXX). Theme – Nationalism.

Šolc, Jiří. 1994. *Ve službách prezidenta* [In the Service of the President]. Prague: Vyšehrad.

Šolle, Zdeněk. 1998. *Století české politiky – od Palackého k Masarykovi* [A Century of Czech Politics – from Palacký to Masaryk]. Prague: Mladá fronta.

Šolle, Zdeněk – Gajanová, Alena. 1969. *Po stopě dějin (Češi a Slováci v letech 1848–1938)* [On the Trail of History (Czechs and Slovaks 1848–1938]. Prague: Orbis.

Sommer, K. "Průběh a výsledky pozemkové reformy v pohraničí českých zemí" [The Course and Results of Land Reform in the Border Areas of the Czech Lands], in *České národní aktivity v pohraničních oblastech první Československé republiky.*

Šolle, Zdeněk. 1998. *Století české politiky – od Palackého k Masarykovi* [A Century of Czech Politics – from Palacký to Masaryk]. Prague: Mladá fronta.

Soudobé dějiny 2–3/1996. Theme – The Transfer in Czech Historiography.

Soukup, Josef. 2002. *Germania od porážky ke sjednocení* [Germania from Defeat to Unification]. Prague: Riopress.

Soukupová, Blanka. 2002. "Češi-Židé: židovství, češství a československství po vzniku Československé republiky. K identitě a mentalitě asimilující se menšiny" [Czechs-Jews: Jewish, Czech and Czechoslovak Identity after the Founding of the Czechoslovak Republic. On the identity and mentality of a minority in process of assimilation], in *Studie k sociálním dějinám* 9. 2002. Machačová, J. – Matějček, J. (eds.). Opava: Slezské zemské muzeum.

Spiegel Special (das Magazin zum Thema) 1/2003. "Der Bombenkrieg gegen die Deutschen". Hamburg: Spiegel Verlag-Rudolf Augstein.

Spory o dějiny III [Controversies out History III]. 2000. Bednář, M. (ed.). Prague: Masarykův ústav.

Šrámek, P. "Odhodlání versus loajalita" [Resolution versus Loyalty]. *Soudobé dějiny* 1–2/2004. 56–87.

Srb, Vladimír. "Obyvatelstvo Československé republiky v letech 1918–1938" [The Population of the Czechoslovak Republic 1918–1938]. *Demografie* 1/1998. 3–22.

Staněk, Tomáš. 1993. *Německá menšina v českých zemích 1948–1989* [The German Minority in the Czech Lands 194801989]. Prague: Institut pro středoevropskou kulturu a politiku.

Staněk, Tomáš. 1991. *Odsun Němců z Československa 1945–1947* [The Transfer of the Germans from Czechoslovakia 1945–1947]. Prague: Naše vojsko/Academia.

Staněk, Tomáš. 1996. *Perzekuce 1945* [Persecution 1945]. Prague: Institut pro středoevropskou kulturu a politiku.

Staněk, Tomáš. 1996. *Tábory v českých zemích 1945–1948* [Camps in the Czech Lands 1945–1948]. Ostrava: Tilia.

Stargardt, Nicholas. 1994. *The German Idea of Militarism (Radical And Socialist Critics 1866–1914)*. Cambridge: Cambridge University Press. 150.

Steed, Henry Wickham. 1927. *Třicet let novinářem* [Thirty Years a Journalist] I+II. Prague: Orbis.

Stern, Josef P. 1992. *Hitler – vůdce a lid* [Hitler – Fuehrer and Volk]. Prague: Knihovna Lidových novin.

"Střední Evropa a Slovensko" [Central Europe and Slovakia] (thematic edition). *Nová přítomnost* 6/1996.

STRMISKA, Zdeněk. "Výsledky nezávislého průzkumu současného smýšlení v Československu" [The Results of Independent Survey of Current Sentiments in Czechoslovakia]. *Svědectví* 78/1986 (XX). 265–334.

Studie o sudetoněmecké otázce I, II [Studies on the Sudeten German Question 1,2]. 1996, 1998. Kural, V. (ed.). Prague: Ústav mezinárodních vztahů.

STÜRMER, Michael. 2002. *The German Empire*. New York: The Modern Library (Random House).

ŠUBRT, J. 1908. *Vývoj a život českých menšin* [The Development and Life of Czech Minorities]. Vols. 1, 2. Most: Severočeské menšinové knihkupectví a nakladatelství.

SUDA, Zdeněk. 1995. *The Origins and the Development of the Czech National Consciousness and Germany.* (Working Paper). Prague: Central European University.

SUDETENDEUTSCHER RAT E.V. 1971. *The Sudeten German Problem in International Politics.* München:Universitätsbuchdruckerei und Verlag Dr.C.Wolf & Sohn.

Sudetoněmecká otázka – krátký obrys a dokumentace [The Sudeten German Question – A short outline and documentation]. 1987. München: The Sudetendeutscher Rat.

Sudetští Němci – etnická skupina v srdci Evropy [Sudeten Germans – An ethnic group in the heart of Europe]. 1994. Kraus, Heinz (ed.). München: Sudetendeutscher Rat.

ŠULC, Zdislav. 1990. *Jak se zrodil západoněmecký "hospodářský zázrak"* [How the West German "Economic Miracle" was Born]. Prague: Práce.

Survey of International Affairs 1939–1946. Hitler's Europe. 1954. Toynbee, A. – Toynbee, V. M. (eds.). London. 18, 589.

Svědectví. Double issue 70–71/1983 (XVIII). Theme – The First Republic of Czechoslovakia.

Svědectví 93/1992 (XXV). Theme – Nationalism as a modern drug.

SYNDIKÁT NOVINÁŘŮ. "Pluralita regionálního tisku je v ČR ohrožena!" [The Plurality of the Regional Press in the CR is in Danger!]. *Britské listy.* 13. 3. 2002.

SZABO, Stephen F. – NITZE, Paul H. 1999. *Germany: Strategy and Defense at a Turning Point.* Washington: The American Institute for Conteporary German Studies. (http://www .aicgs.org/IssueBriefs/szabo.html).

SZEFER, Andrzej. "Tzv. sudetská otázka roku 1938 ve světle nejnovější západoněmecké literatury (1970–1982)" [The Sudeten Question in 1938 in the Light of the Most Recent West German Literature (1970–1982)]. *Slezský sborník* 3/1985 (LXXXIII). 193–201.

SZPORLUK, Roman. 1981. *The Political Thought of Thomas G. Masaryk.* Boulder/New York: East European Monographs/Columbia University Press.

TÁBORSKÝ, Eduard. "Beneš a náš osud" [Beneš and our Fate]. *Svědectví* 89–90 (XXIII). 85–118.

TÁBORSKÝ, Eduard. Naše cesta [Our Road. On Sudeten Germans issue.]. Č. 4. April 1954.

TÁBORSKÝ, Eduard. *Naše věc* [Our Cause]. 1946. Prague: Melantrich.

TÁBORSKÝ, Eduard. 1947. *Pravda zvítězila* [Truth Prevailed]. Prague: Družstevní práce.

TÁBORSKÝ, Eduard. 1981. *President Beneš Between West and East, 1938–1948.* Stanford: Hoover Institution Press.

TABOUIS, Geneviève. 1967. *Předehra k tragédii* [Prelude to Tragedy]. Prague: Svoboda.

TAYLOR, Alan John Percival. 2001. *The Course of German History.* London/New York: Routledge Classics.

TAYLOR, Alan John Percival. 1966. *The First World War*. London/New York: Penguin Books.

TETENS, T. H. 1961. *The New Germany and the Old Nazis*. New York: Random House.

TESAŘ, Jan. "Emanuel Moravec aneb logika realismu" [Emanuel Moravec or the Logic of Realism]. *Dějiny a současnost* 1/1969 (XI).

TESAŘ, Jan. 2000. *Mnichovský komplex – jeho příčiny a důsledky* [The Munich Complex – Its Causes and Consequences]. Prague: Prostor. 20–27.

THATCHER, Margaret. 1993. *The Downing Street Years*. Prague: Naše vojsko.

Tisíc let česko-německých vztahů [A Thousand Years of Czech-German Relations]. 1995. Bauer, F. (ed.). Prague: Panevropa.

TOBOLKA, Zdeněk Václav. 1936. *Politické dějiny československého národa od r. 1848 až do dnešní doby* [A Political History of the Czechoslovak Nation from 1848 to the Present]. VIII (1879–1914). Prague: Nákladem "Československého kompasu", tiskařské a vydavatelské akc. společnosti.

TOMÁŠEK, Dušan – KVAČEK, Robert. 1995. *Causa Emil Hácha*. Prague: Themis.

TOMEŠ, J. Solitér čs. diplomacie [The Solitaire of Czechoslovak Diplomacy], (Postscript in Masařík, H. *V proměnách doby*). 361–362.

TOMUSCHAT, Christian. "Die Benesch-Dekrete – ein Hinderniss für die Aufnahme der Tschechischen Republik in die Europäische Union?", in *Je již český právní řád v souladu s právem EU?* [Is the Czech legal order now in harmony with EU Law?]. 2002. (Collective of authors). Prague: Friedrich-Ebert Stiftung e.V. 70–98.

TOYNBEE, Arnold J. "Czechoslovakia's German Problem". *The Economist*. 10. 7. 1937. 72–74.

The Treaty of Versailles. 1998. Boemcke, Manfred F. – Feldman, Gerald D. – Glaser, Elisabeth (eds.). Cambridge/Washington: Cambridge University Press.

TŘEŠTÍK, Dušan. "Bloudění v Teutoburském lese" [Going Astray in the Teutoburg Forest]. *Lidové noviny*. 14. 6. 1995.

TŘEŠTÍK, Dušan. 1999. *Češi, jejich národ, stát, dějiny a pravdy v transformaci* [Czechs, Their Nation, State, History and Truth in Transformation]. Brno: Doplněk.

TŘEŠTÍK, Dušan. 1999. *Mysliti dějiny* [Thinking History]. Prague/Litomyšl: Paseka.

Die Tschechoslowakei – Das Ende einer Fehlkonstruktion (Die sudetendeustche Frage bleibt offen). 1993. Eibicht, Rolf-Josef (ed.). Turmer-Verlag.

TUDJMAN, Franjo. 1997. *Dějinný úděl národů* [The Historical Destiny of Nations]. Prague: HF Studio.

TURNWALD, W. K. 1954. *Renascence or Decline of Central Europe*. Munich: University Press Wolf & Sohn.

URBAN, Otto. 1982. *Česká společnost 1848–1918* [Czech Society 1848–1918]. Prague: Svoboda.

URBAN, Otto. "Masarykovo pojetí české otázky" [Masaryk's Conception of the Czech Question]. *Československý časopis historický* XVII. 545.

URBAN, Otto. 1943. *Z tajných fondů III. sekce* (Z archivů Ministerstva zahraničí Republiky Česko-Slovenské) [From the Secret Funds of the 3rd Section (From the archives of the Foreign Ministry of the Czecho-Slovak Republic)]. Prague: Orbis. 12.

UHLE-WETTLER, Franz. 1999. *Das Versailler Diktat*. Kiel: Arndt. *V rozdelenej Európe. Česi, Slováci, Nemci a ich štáty v rokoch 1948–1989* [In a Divided Europe. Czechs, Slovaks, Germans and their States in the Years 1948–1989]. 1998. Kováč, Dušan – Křen Jan – Lemberg, Hans (eds.). Bratislava: AEP.

VAN DIJK, H. "State Borders in Geography and History", in *Nationalising and Denationalising European Border Regions, 1800–2000*. 36.

VEITER, Theodor. 1984. *Nationalitätenkonflikt und Volksgruppenrecht im ausgehenden 20. Jahrhundert*. Band I-III. Munich: Internationales Institut für Nationalitätenrecht und Regionalismus.

Velké dějiny – malý národ [Great History – Small Nation]. 1995. Boldt, Frank (ed.). Prague: Český spisovatel.

VERHEYEN, D. "The Dutch and the Germans: Beyond Traumas and Trade", in Verheyen, D. – Søe, Ch. 1993. *The Germans and Their Neighbours*. Oxford: Westview Press. 59–80.

VERHEYEN, D. 1999. *The German Question*. Boulder/Oxford: Westview Press. 8.

VERHEUGEN, Günter [press agency news]. "Verheugen hájil právo kandidátů na podporu americké politice" [Verheugen defends right of candidates to support American policy]. *České noviny* (http://www.ceskenoviny.cz). ČTK 17. 3. 2003.

Verlust der Heimat Aufgabe für Europa. 1945–1985. Heft 33 (1986). Munich: Schriftenreihe der Ackermann-Gemeinde.

Die Vertreibung der deutschen Bevölkerung aus der Tschechoslowakei. 1994. Augsburg: Weltbild Verlag.

Die Vertriebenen in Westdeutschland (in 3 Bänden). 1959. Lemberg, Eugen – Edding, Friedrich (eds.). Kiel: Ferdinand Hirth.

VESELÝ, Jiří (et al.). 1983. *Azyl v Československu 1933–1938* [Asylum in Czechoslovakia 1933–1938]. Prague: Naše vojsko/SPB.

VESELÝ-ŠTAINER, Karel. 1947. *Cestou národního odboje* [The Road to National Resistance]. Prague: Sfinx Bohumil Janda.

VINŠKOVSKÁ, Monika. 1998. *Odsunutí Němci z Podbořanska* [Transferred Germans from Podbořany]. Unpublished degree thesis. Ústí n. L.: Pedagogická fakulta Univerzity J. E. Purkyně. 47.

VLIELAND, Maxine. *Deutsch-Englisches Gespräch Forum*. (Proceedings). Königswinter Conference in Berlin. 13.–15. 3. 1997.

VONDROVÁ, Jitka. "Několik poznámek k tématu 'Cesta k odsunu sudetských Němců z Československa'" [A Few Notes on the theme of "The Road to the Transfer of the Sudeten Germans from Czechoslovakia"]. *Soudobé dějiny* 4/1995. 629–635.

"Vorurteile-Stereotype-Feindbilder (Gegen rechtsextreme Vorurteile)". *Informationen zur politischen Bildung* 271. 2-Quartal 2001.

Vyhnání Čechů z pohraničí 1938 [The Expulsion of the Czechs from the Borderlands 1938]. 1996. Zelený, Karel (ed.). Prague: Ústav mezinárodních vztahů.

Vynútený rozchod. Vyhnanie a vysídlenie z Československa 1938–1947 v porovnaní s Polskom, Maďarskom a Juhosláviou [Forced Parting of the Ways. Expulsion and Resettlement from Czechoslovakia 1938–1947 in comparison with Poland, Hungary and Yugoslavia]. 1999. Brandes, Detlef – Ivaničková, E. – Pešek, J. (eds.). Bratislava: Veda, vydavatelstvo SAV.

Vztahy Spolkové republiky Německo ke státům střední Evropy [Relations of the FRG to the States of Central Europe]. 1998. Handl, Vladimír – Hon, Jan – Pick, Otto et al. (eds.). Prague: Ústav mezinárodních vztahů.

WAGNEROVÁ, Alena. "Nevypočitatelnosti symbolické politiky" [The Unpredictability of Symbolic Politics]. *Listy* 3/1995 (XXV). 8–12.

WASBURN, Philo C. 1992. *Broadcasting Propaganda* (International Radio Broadcasting and the Construction of Political Reality). Westport: Praeger Publishers.

WEIRICH, M. 1938. *Staré a nové Československo* [Old and New Czechoslovakia]. Prague. 163.

WEIZSÄCKER, Richard von. 2000. *Čtvero zastavení*. Prague: Prostor.

WERTHEIMER, M. 1924. *The Pan-German League, 1890–1914*. New York.

WIESENTHAL, Simon. 1994. *Spravedlnost nikoli pomstu* (Paměti) [Justice not Revenge (Memoirs)]. Ostrava: Sfinga.

WILDT, G. "Ergebnisse des Zweiten Weltkriegs". *Sudetendeutsche Zeitung*. 26. 4. 2002. 2.

WINKLER, Pavel. 1996. "Dekrety prezidenta republiky z období 1940–1945. Majetkoprávní otázky ve vztahu ke Spolkové republice Německo" [The Decrees of the President of the Republic 1940–1945. Questions of property rights in relation to the Federal Republic of Germany], in *Právní aspekty odsunu sudetských Němců*. 21–40.

WINKLER, Pavel. "K dopisu Sudetoněmeckého krajanského sdružení poslancům Evropského parlamentu" [On the Letter from the Sudetendeutsche Landsmannschaft to Members of the European Parliament]. *Mezinárodní politika* 3/1995. 29–30.

WISKEMANN, Elizabeth. 1967. *Czechs and Germans*. London/Melbourne/Toronto: Macmillan – New York: St Martin's Press.

WISKEMANN, Elizabeth. 1968. *The Europe I Saw*. London/Glasgow: Collins.

WISKEMANN, Elizabeth. 1956. *Germany's Eastern Neighbours*. London/New York/Toronto: Oxford University Press.

WITTMANN, Fritz. "BdV-Bundesversammlung 1997". *Deutscher Ostdienst* 20, 39. Jahrgang 16. 5. 1997. 4–6.

WOHLSTETTER, Albert. "Illusions of Distance". *Foreign Affairs* 2/1968 (IVL). 243–255.

WOLFF, Stefan. 2000. *German Minorities in Europe*. New York/Oxford: Berghahn Books.

WRIGHT, Q. "The Munich Settlement and International Law". *American Journal of International Law* 1/1939 (XXXIII). 12–32.

YACOUB, J. "Mezinárodní právo a menšiny" [International Law and Minorities]. *Via Europa* 1/1996. 10.

YAPOU, Eliezer. 1981. "The Autonomy That Never Was: The Autonomy Plans for the Sudeten in 1938", in Dienstein, Yoram. *Models of Autonomy*. New Brunswick/London: Transactions Books.

YESTER, Stanislav. 1937. *Třetí říše nastupuje* [The Third Reich Rises]. Prague: Svaz čs. důstojnictva.

Za nové Československo [For a New Czechoslovakia]. (A collection of articles, speeches and documents). 1944. Bernard, V. (ed.). Moscow: Vydavatelství cizojazyčné literatury.

ZAJÍČEK, Karel. 1946. *Československo a Norimberský proces* [Czechoslovakia and the Nuremberg Trials]. Prague: Ministerstvo informací.

ZAJÍČEK, Karel. 1947. *Český národ soudí K. H. Franka* [The Czech Nation Judges K. H. Frank]. Prague: Ministerstvo informací.

ZAYAS, Alfred-Maurice de. 1977. *Nemesis at Potsdam*. London/Henley and Boston: Routledge & Kegan Paul.

ZEMAN, Zbyněk A. B. 1964. *Nazi Propaganda*. London: Oxford University Press.

ZEMAN, Zbyněk. 1998. *Vzestup a pád komunistické Evropy* [The Rise and Fall of Communism in Europe]. Prague: Mladá fronta.

ZEMAN, Zbyněk. 2000. *Edvard Beneš – politický životopis* [Political Biography]. Prague: Mladá fronta.

ZICH, František. 1996. *Národnostní a etnické vztahy v českém pohraničí – obraz Čecha, Němce, Rakušana a Róma ve vědomí obyvatel* [National and Ethnic Relations in the Czech Borderlands – the Image of the Czech, German, Austrian and Roma in the Consciousness of the Population]. Working Papers, WP 96:4. Prague: Sociologický ústav AV ČR.

ZICH, František. 1996. *Národnostní a etnické vztahy v českém pohraničí – obraz Čecha, Němce, Rakušana a Roma ve vědomí obyvatel* [National and Ethnic Relations in the Czech Borderlands – The image of the Czech, German, Austrian and Roma in the consciousness of the population]. Prague: Sociologický ústav AV ČR. Working Papers, WP 96:4. 19.

Židé v Sudetech [Jews in the Sudeten Land]. (Conference collection). 2000. Otte, A. et al. (eds.). Prague: Portál (Česká křesťanská akademie).

ZIMMERMANN, Volker. 2001. *Sudetští Němci v nacistickém státě* [Sudeten Germans in a Nazi State]. Prague: Prostor.

ZINK, Harold. 1974. *The United States in Germany*. Westport: Greenwood Press.

ZITELMANN, Rainer. 1993. *Adolf Hitler a jeho cesta k moci* [Adolf Hitler and his Rise to Power]. Prague: Agentura V.P.K.

"Zrušte dekrety, znělo z Norimberku." ČTK. *MF Dnes*. 20. 5. 2002. A/3. ["Declare the Decrees void, the message from Nuremberg"].

SELECTION OF INTERNET ADRESSES RELEVANT TO THE SUDETEN GERMAN QUESTION (RETRIEVED AUGUST 2013)

archive.today – http://web.archive.org/web/20020617142817

http://www.borderland.cz

http://www.czechembassy.org/servis
  Web pages of the Ministery of Foreign Affairs of the Czech Republic.
  Decrees of the President of the Republic – documentation for the European Parliament.
  German-Czech Declaration on Mutual Relations and their Future Development.

http://www.britannica.com/bcom/eb/article/printable/html
  Czechoslovak region, history of Czechoslovakia.

http://www.sudetendeutsches-archiv.de
  Comprehensive information on past and present publications directly or indirectly related to the theme of the Sudeten German Question.

http://www.Zeitgeschichte-online.de
  Rohlíková, S. "Die Zwangsaussiedlung der Deutschen und ihre Widerspieglung in den gegenwartigen tschechisch-deutschen Beziehungen".
  Datenbank der Literaturdokumentation

http://www.Herder-Institute.de
  Comprehensive data base including links and references to literature on the theme.

http://www.sudeten.de/sites/a
  Web pages of the Sudetendeutsche Landsmannschaft.

http://GermanPolitics&.Society-journals.berghahnbooks.com/access

http://www.bund-der-vertriebene.de/willkommen.htm
  The web pages of the Union of the Expelled (Bund der Vertreibene), the umbrella organisation for all the compatriot organisations of ethnic Germans expelled at the end of the Second World War from the countries of Central and South-East Europe.

http://www.deutsche-aussenpolitik.de
  Deutsche Aussenpolitik is an Internet portal of the University of Trier which provides comprehensive information on the foreign policy of the Federal Republic of Germany. *Auswärtiges Amt,* the official web pages of the Federal Ministry of Foreign Affairs provides the full text of documents, agreements, official speeches and so on.

http://www.german-foreign-policy.com
  Regular analysis and information on the activities of German foreign policy. This is produced by a group of independent journalists and experts monitoring Germany's efforts to achieve the position of great power in economic, political and security fields.

http://www.cap.uni-muenchen.de
  The *Centrum für Angewandte Politikforschung* (CAP) provides detailed information about the projects and other activities of the Centre for Applied Political Research at the Ludwig Maximilian University, which is orientated particularly to the theme of European integration (Young People and Europe. The Bertelsman Politics research group and others.).

http://www.iep-berlin.de
  The web pages of the Berlin *Institute for European Politics* (Institut für europäische Politik), which is one of Germany's leading research centres on European politics.

http://www.aicgs.org
  The web pages of the American Institute for Contemporary German Studies which is based in Washington D.C. It supports the study and discussion of relations between Germany and the United States. Its cross-section interdisciplinary approach exploiting comparative methods is cultivating the dialogue between the two states.

http://www.ifd-allensbach.de
  The prestigious *Institut für Demoskopie* in Allensbach was founded in 1947 and conducts research into public opinion using a statistical-psychological approach to study the attitudes and opinions of German society to political, economic, cultural and social themes and problems. It undertakes monthly surveys for the newspaper Frankfurter Allgemeine Zeitung.

PERIODICALS, NEWSPAPERS, EDITIONS

Český časopis historický, 1984–2000

Soudobé dějiny, 1993–2001

Střední Evropa, 1991–2002

150 000 slov (texts from elswehere, Cologne INDEX, Prague: Lidové noviny)

Dějiny a současnost, 1967–1969, 1991–2002

Svědectví, 1966–1992

Listy, 1990–2002

Historické listy, 1992–1995

Proglas, 1991–1998

Přítomnost + Nová Přítomnost, 1990–2002

Slezský sborník, 1984–2001

Historie a vojenství, 1993–1998

Právo (daily newspaper)

Lidové noviny (daily newspaper), 1990–2002

Literární noviny – Literární listy – Listy, 1968–1969

Sudetendeutsche Zeitung, 1995–2002

Bohemia, Zeitschrift für Geschichte und Kultur der böhmischen Länder 17, 41/2, 42

Mezinárodní politika, 1990–2002

Mezinárodní vztahy, 1991–2002

The Czechoslovak daily press from the autumn of 1938 – Sept. Oct. (Munich Crisis):
    Národní politika, Pražský list, Polední Halo, A-Zet Pondělník, Telegraf, Večerník Práva lidu, Lidové noviny, Večerní České slovo, Polední list

Prostor 31/1996. Monothematic edition: Německo, náš osud? [Germany, our Fate?]

Prostor 35/1997. Monothematic edition: Češi a Rakušané [Czechs and Austrians]

BEITRÄGE-KLEINE REIHE, edition series, published by the Institutum Bohemicum

KULTURELLE ARBEITSHEFTE, edition series, published by the Bund der Vertriebenen-Vereinigte Landsmannschaften und Landesverbände

Paneuropa Deutschland, 1992–1998

Paneuropa Intern, 1996–2000

Wittikobrief, 1995–2000

Bibliographical Note

A complete bibliography on the theme of Czech-German relations and the role played in them by what is known as the Sudeten German Question would fill a whole separate and lengthy publication. Although I have tried to identify and include all important works, limits of time and the space of just one book, as well as limitations of access to foreign book funds, has meant that it has not been possible to create a truly comprehensive list of relevant literature.

Many studies could only be obtained using the inter-library loan service of the Czech State Scientific Library in Prague and Ústí nad Labem, and of the joint library of the Sociology and Philosophy Institute of the Czech Academy of Sciences.

Grant projects of the Czech Ministry of Foreign Affairs and some foreign institutions enabled me to visit the libraries of the University of Cambridge, the Royal Institute of Foreign Affairs (Chatham House) in London, the University of Birmingham and the University of Essex, which have funds providing an overall view of the theme of the states of Central Europe and ethnic conflicts in the context of international relations.

In this connection I think it useful to draw attention primarily to valuable works on the subject of so-called *Volkstumkampf*, German ethnic minorities abroad. Among these works I would highlight L. de Jong (The German Fifth Column in the Second World War). Ronald H. Smelser (The Sudeten Problem 1933–1938). H. C. Meyer (Mitteleuropa in German Thought and Action 1815–1945) and R. Luža (The Transfer of the Sudeten Germans). Very valuable documents, insights and personal testimony from a Sudeten German democrat who worked during the Second World War in the ministry of foreign affairs of the Czechoslovak government in exile are contained in J. W. Brügel's two-volume work, Tschechen und Deutsche.

One particularly valuable source of comparison of the relations between Germany and her neighbour states is the collection of studies, The Germans and their Neighbours, edited by D. Verheyen and Ch. Søe; this shows convincingly that it is not just the

Czech Republic, or Czechs as a nation, that have problems with the historical burden of relations with Germany (as some publicists have claimed since 1989), but other nations too, typically for example the Dutch.

On the theme of transfers and exchanges of population in the 20th century, S. Ladas (The Exchange of Minorities: Bulgaria, Greece and Turkey), J. Schechtman (Postwar Population Transfers in Europe) and E. Kulischer (Europe on the Move) are particularly outstanding sources of information on which to base a rounded and balanced view.

The *Canadian Review of Studies in Nationalism* series, published by Garland Publishing Inc., is a quite unique source of bibliographical data on the various different sets of themes involved in research on nationalism. Specifically in relation to Germans in the Czech Lands, it effectively augments and complements the materials of the working group for the German question at the Historical Institute of the Czechoslovak Academy of Sciences that were published in the 1960s, and the bibliographical selection of Sudetica from the years 1918–1939 published by the Silesian Institute of the Czechoslovak Academy of Sciences, likewise in the 1960s.

D. Perman's The Shaping of the Czechoslovak State is a pivotal work on the birth of the independent Czechoslovakia. The diaries of D. H. Miller, legal advisor to the UD delegation at the Paris conference, and especially Vol. XIII, New States (Minorities), which were originally published in a very small number of copies for study purposes, are essential sources on the course of negotiations at the Versailles Conference include. For decades these were almost inaccessible through ordinary channels, but currently they are available on the Web.

After the Nazis came to power in Germany Czechoslovakia found itself under permanent pressure both in the field of foreign politics and as a result of the mounting demands of the Sudteten German party. Czechoslovakia looked to Great Britain and France for international support, but growing support in British governing circles for a policy of appeasement proved fatal for the existence of the CSR. There is a great quantity of literature on the subject but I would highlight three studies in particular: Ian Kershaw, Making Friends with Hitler; R. A. C. Parker, Churchill and Appeasement, and P. Neville, Hitler and Appeasement.

After the outbreak of war representatives of the governments of occupied countries met in exile in London. Although these provisional governments (existing, but without effective powers in their own territories) theoretically had freedom of decision-making, in the circumstances of the war conflict they essentially took their lead from British war plans and goals. This applied to the Czechoslovak government in exile led by Edvard Beneš as much as to the others. A ground-breaking study of the relationship between the Foreign Office and the Czechoslovak government in exile in London in the years 1939–1945 has been published by M.D. Brown under the title, Dealing with Democrats.

Finally I would like to draw attention to the very compendious, dual-language edition of documents, Odsun (Transfer)/Vertreibung published by the Sudeten German Archive. The edition is a unique achievement that presents key documents (or extracts from them) from the whole period from 1848 up to 1945, when the final Czech and Germans finally parted ways with the transfer of most of the Sudeten Germans in what was the dramatic end to the era of "coexistence and quarrel" between the two nations in the Czech Lands.

Despite some persisting gaps in research and publication, Czech historians at home and in exile have produced work that, overall, covers the entire period from the mid-19th century to the present (J. Kořalka, J. Křen, V. Kural, R. Kvaček, T. Pasák, J. Rataj, T. Staněk, B. Čelovský, E. Broklová, J. Gebhart, B. Černý, J. Tesař, J. Kučera, J. Němeček, J. Dejmek, J. Kuklík, V. Smetana, Z. Zeman, F.D. Raška and others). This has provided the basis of knowledge for Czech interpretation of the modern history of Czechs and Germans and their conflicts, on which this work relies. Unfortunately, with only a few exceptions these studies are not available in English translations. One of the aims of the English translation of this book has been to bring at least part of this body of knowledge and argument to the attention of interested readers abroad.

Naturally we canot overlook the fundamental contribution of German historians, including outstanding works by D. Brandes, F. Seibt, J. Hoensch, V. Zimmermann, R. Gebel and others. Since 1990, cooperation between Czech, German and Slovak historians has been developing to the full in the framework of the Mixed Czech-German and Slovak-German Commission of Historians, and individual results are published in a special series by the Albis International publishing house.

List of Appendix Documents

A Note on the Appendix Documents

This monograph is devoted to Czech-German discourse over the whole period 1848–2004, and to some extent involves consideration of entire Central European context. The period saw the gradual formation of the Czech political nation and the emergence of a complete Czech social structure including the development of social elites, creating the conditions for the political emancipation of the national community in the framework of the Austro-Hungarian monarchy. There then followed the establishment of an independent Czechoslovak Republic in 1918, the German annexation of the borderlands of the CSR as a result of the Munich Agreement of 1938, the occupation of the Czech Lands by Nazi Germany, the communist takeover in 1948 and the restoration of democracy after 1989.

From just this very brief list of historical events it is obvious that the choice of documents cannot be comprehensive and must inevitably draw on very different kinds of source, and not exclusively archives. The selection was made with a view to providing readers abroad an insight, at least in the form of illustration, into the idiom and argumentation of opinions of the time, and the attitudes of key actors in Czech-German relations.

In addition to editions of archival sources, I have considered it necessary to include a limited number of texts from the media, especially where it is desirable to give readers a taste of the content of period polemics, including their style and vocabulary. This applies to the texts of various civic, political and academic initiatives in the period of the Cold War, when a range of opinions and standpoints, representing the positions of both individual and groups and organisations on the Czech and German side, were published in the media.

I shall make special mention of the document known as the Grundplanung O.A here, because its authenticity has been the subject of repeated disputes between some Czech and German historians. The basic reason for doubts is the fact that this planning document attributed to the Sudeten side carries no date or signature by concrete author/s. Nonetheless, the diction of the text and the argumentation of the basic proposed methods for solving the Czech-Sudeten German dispute show a striking degree of consonance with other documents that demonstrably come from Sudeten German Part circles. One example might be K. Von Neurath and S.S. Obergruppenführer K. H. Frank's memorandum to Hitler dated the 28th of August 1940, which set out proposals for the individual phases of the process of progressive liquidation of the Czech nation. The memorandum *On the Solution of the Czech Problem*, dated the 18th of September 1938, which in content continues the line of planning in the Grundplanung

O.A., was demonstrably produced in the headquarters of the Sudeten German Party, as was the situation report of 18th of May 1938.

Both J. Drábek, the public prosecutor in the case of K. H. Frank, and the important Sudeten German politicians and opponent of the Nazis J. W. Brügel, inclined to belief in the authenticity of the Grundplanung O.A. I consider it significant in this context that in the summer of 1938 the Fuhrer's deputy Rudolf Hess, entrusted with the direction of German groups abroad, was in active contact with the leader of the Sudeten German Party in Czechoslovakia Konrad Henlein, and coordinated his actions with the Nazi leadership of the Third Reich. This fact was explicitly mentioned in the verdict of the International Military Tribunal in Nuremberg. The middle-man between Hitler and Henlein was Hess, and Hess was present at a three-hour discussion between K. H. Frank and Henlein and Hitler on the 28th of March 1938. For these and other reasons I share the view that the Grundplanung O.A. is an authentic planning document, and so it has been included in the appendix.

Wherever possible, I have given priority to texts taken from reliable, reviewed academic sources, and in some cases texts authenticated by institutions that deal with international relations in a serious and responsible way (Ministries of Foreign Affairs of the Czech Republic and Germany, and some foundations active in the field of foreign policy).

I. The New Europe

No criticism of the Allies?

I anticipate the objection that I am criticising Germans and Austrians but am silent about the Allies.

What entitles me to do so is the context of my arguments: it is the Germans not the Allies who are offering themselves as teachers, leaders, saviours of the nations and humankind, and so we have a duty to observe them attentively, especially when they are forcing their culture down our throats with their heavy artillery. The German is a strange mixture of pedagogue and soldier – first he gives you a lecture on salvation and spirit and then he lands a punch in your face (or perhaps the other way round).

I would have things to say about the French, English, Americans, Russians and so forth, including plenty of criticisms – I have already demonstrated that in my study of Russians and in my critical work at home in our ethnic conditions. I have never been a national chauvinist, and I am not even a nationalist – I have more often said that from my youth my perception of nationality has been social and moral – for me the repression of nationality is a sin against humankind and humanity.

My conclusions are not and cannot be that we must adopt either French or English or some other Western culture; the only issue here can be one of a synthesis from all the cultural elements and components developed by all nations. This synthesising is something on which the philosophers and experts of all nations are already engaged, and many people are doing it in practical life (migrants, traders and anyone who has the chance to get to know other nations, minorities). Internationalism is not just easy contact with the world outside, but precisely that cultural synthesis.

The German element will be incorporated into this synthesis, and it will be no small part of it. Inasmuch as the issue now is the political foundation of this cultural synthesis, however, we cannot accept German Prussianism, and we must turn to the models of French, American, English democracy: the West in this respect sets the overall trend but not the individual details of future development.

We are told that one nation, one state must be the leader, the first. Supposing that this is true, that one state will still be primus inter pares,[1] not set over the others – the organisation of Europe will be democratic not aristocratic. The

---

[1] First among equals.

medieval idea of aristocratic, theocratic imperialism has been overcome by the philosophical, church, political and social revolution of the modern age.

The new modern age? In fact we are in a transitional period and are suffering all the concomitant difficulties: the fact that the transition is only half complete and the new era has not yet quite arrived, and let us hope that this war, forcing all mankind to revise its history and endeavours, will prompt all the nations to conscious work for themselves and the whole of humanity. Inasmuch as we know it and can learn from it, history has only been going on for a a few thousand years, and what is that in comparison with the infinite series of millennia that astronomers promise for our planet! Mankind is truly at the beginning of his development; since the 18th century, philosophers of history in all nations have been declaring the period following the Great French Revolution to be the beginning of a new era, the modern epoch generally. This war and its horrors have been a great shock to our conscience, and let us decide for humanity.

Despite all the laws of historical development, we still have freedom to make this decision; awareness of laws of history is not passive fatalism. Volentem ducunt fata, nolentem trahunt...[2]

However scientifically conscientious, my philosophical attempt to understand the war will not be free of the personal element, personal sympathies and antipathies.

From my youth I have tried to get to know the cultural achievements of all nations. Apart from the foundation given by my own nationality I have become familiar not just with the classical world, but with all the principal national cultures of the present. Educated in German schools, I learned diligently and much from geniuses such as Lessing and Goethe. At the same time I found a way into the French and English world – French and English philosophy (apart from the the classical, mainly Platonic) were my school; German philosophy, especially Kant, I only came to understand later.

From the Slav world, I owe much to many Russians and Poles, and also South Slavs. Italians and Scandinavians have fertilised my understanding and also expanded my horizons.

Throughout my life I have been a diligent, passionate reader and conscientious observer of contemporary world affairs. If I had to say which culture I consider the highest, I would say the Anglo-American: at least, my time in England during the war and my very critical observations of English life have convinced me that overall the English come closest to the ideals of humanity. I had the same impression of American life. By this I do not mean that English and American civilisation is the dearest to me – that is a different question.

---

[2]   Fate leads the willing, and drags the unwilling.

I see and feel the shortcomings of us Slavs, but I love Slav mistakes and virtues. In the same way France has always attracted me, even though I found much to criticise and condemn, just as I have condemned our own national flaws and shortcomings.

I have always respected German culture, but have rarely felt at home in it. I have been unable to get enthusiastic about it. Prussia in particular I cannot bring myself to love, but I try to be just to it. If there is something I truly hate, it is that Austrianness, or more precisely that Habsburg Vienneserie, that decadent Aristocratism chasing after a tip, that false, low Habsburgism, that non-ethnic and yet chauvinistic hotchpotch of people of official Vienna. I do not like Prussianism but I find it preferable even with its rough barracks spirit and its hungry ruthlessness of the parvenu; after all, even Kaiser Wilhelm with his dilettante speeches and his playing at foresight unintentionally did more for democracy than that silent "bloody sovereign", proud of being the most perfect aristocrat in the world – a man quintessentially base.

I am hopeful that at least some of my numerous German friends will agree with me.

Source: Masaryk, Tomáš, G. 1994. *Nová Evropa* [The New Europe]. Brno: Doplněk. 140–142.

II. The CSR in Mortal Danger

Sir Nevile Henderson's Memorandum on British Policy towards Germany

This 13-page memorandum, dated May 10, 1937, had been written before Henderson took up his appointment in Berlin at the end of April in that year, but it was not until August that he sent it privately to Sir Orme Sargent, Assistant Under-Secretary at the Foreign Office. The Foreign Office, in forwarding a copy to Halifax before his visit to Germany in November, noted that "we gather that it still substantially represents his views." The important paragraphs are these:

"The obstacles to an Anglo-German understanding are, it is true, extraordinarily formidable. Quite apart from Germany herself, the Nazi régime, her traditional mentality and character and her inevitable urge towards unity and expansion, it is not to the interest-for obvious reasons-either of Italy or of Russia to witness its consummation. And, though it is difficult not to feel convinced that it would be to her ultimate interest, it will be exceedingly hard to obtain the cooperation of France, who has her own ideas as to what is her own best national policy. Yet can we go forward without France? It would seem therefore that the first objective must be to convince France that she must and can rely on us to guarantee her security as part of an understanding with Germany ... The alternative, however disagreeable and only as a last resort, would then be a direct Anglo-German understanding based on French security and integrity but including some guarantee of neutrality in the event of a Russo-German conflict ...

"Expansion in the East is an elastic term. If the national integrity and independence of her (Germany's) neighbours were safeguarded, His Majesty's Government would not be justified in actively objecting to a political and economic predominance which the German armies and German industry and population will in any case ensure of their own volition.

"As regards Austria, it is conceivable that sooner or later she will wish of her own free will to be reunited (sic) to Germany. Even today she would never take sides against Germany in a world struggle. She may be anti-Nazi, but she is assuredly German ... If the movement for union were to come from within Austria herself and not from pressure from without-as it well might eventually if, for instance, Schuschnigg were to disappear and Nazism become more tolerant. His Majesty's Government would find it morally impossible to contest the right of Austria as a nation to dispose of her own fate. In the end we may well be faced there with a 'fait accompli' which we could not prevent and which we would be regarded as having opposed in vain. Danzig is likely to revert to Germany in much the same way, and ultimately Memel.

"As regards the Sudetendeutsche and the other numerous German minorities in Europe, the best prospect for a peaceful solution lies firstly in a greater political wisdom than the Czechs themselves have hitherto displayed and in more energetic action than the League of Nations has yet shown in respect of the effective protection of minorities. Only so can we hope to ensure the maintenance of the promise which … might today, but possibly not tomorrow, be extracted by us from Hitler.

"In any case, whatever may have been possible yesterday, it is most improbable that any attempt to achieve an understanding with Germany has today even a faint chance of success except on the following minimum basis:

a) an undertaking that if and when – but only when – Austria herself honestly and spontaneously desires it, we shall not oppose the Anschluss;
b) the recognition in principle of Germany's right to own colonies and an eventual arrangement whereby some part of say West Africa is allotted to her;
c) an assurance that His Majesty's Government has in principle no jealous objection to German economic and even political predominance in Eastern Europe provided Hitler undertakes to abide by his public assurances of May 21, 1935 (that he would seek peaceful revision of the Treaty of Versailles). In return for these concessions and economic assistance, we could ask Hitler to implement the proposals which he made at the time of the remilitarisation of the Rhineland as contained in the German memorandum of March 7th, 1936, including Germany's return to a reformed League of Nations. Perhaps we should try to make this last desideratum our real starting point.

"Whether an advance on these lines commends itself or not to His Majesty's Government or is compatible with British international moral and legal conceptions, it would still be highly unwise to allow the present system of drift to continue … The conviction that Britain is barring the way to Germany in every direction, however legitimate, is deepening. More and more Germans are beginning to feel that, since conciliation has failed, war with Great Britain will again have to be faced if Germany is to realise her destiny …

"If Germany is blocked from any Western adventure – and Mr. Eden's definite public declaration that Great Britain would regard as a casus belli in future any aggression not only against Belgium but against France and Holland has made the position crystal clear in this respect – have we the right to oppose German *peaceful expansion* and evolution in the East? ...

"Surely our right course is to be prepared to submit, provided we secure peace in the West, without too great discomfort to the surge and swell of restless Pan-Germanism in Central and Eastern Europe. It is true that the idea of leaving a comparatively free hand to Germany eastwards will alarm and dissatisfy a section of public opinion both informed and uniformed (sic) in England. Yet what other practical course is open to us if we are to avoid the insane fatalistic folly of setting our course for another war? Even if we beat Germany again the result, after another period of chaos, would be the same as today. Unlike Great Britain and France, or even Italy since 1914, Germany as a political entity is still incomplete. Nothing we can do or say can make black white. The restlessness of Germany in the 20th century is inevitable and will make itself intensely disagreeable, particularly to Russia and Italy, as well as to the smaller States, but not necessarily to Great Britain, in spite of the out-of-date premiss as regards British opposition to any predominant Power in Europe ...

"Is not the present limit-of-what-is-possible an agreement with Germany which, while going far in the direction of her aspirations (and some must legitimately be conceded to her), still binds her to respect vital principles? ... We have at long last realised ourselves that the League of Nations, collective security and Treaty engagements constitute no reliable substitute for a Navy and Air Force capable both of defending Great Britain from invasion or attack and of making her due influence felt in the world. Would it not be equally wise to admit at once, without further delay, that Germany is now too powerful to be persuaded or compelled to enter into an Eastern Pact, that a certain German predominance eastward is inevitable, and that peace in the West must not be sacrificed to a theoretically laudable but practically mistaken idealism in the East ... To put it quite bluntly, Eastern Europe emphatically is neither definitely settled for all time nor is it a vital British interest and the German is certainly more civilised than the Slav, and in the end, if properly handled, also less potentially dangerous to British interests – one might even go so far as to assert that it is not even just to endeavour to prevent Germany from completing her unity or from being prepared for war against the Slav provided her preparations are such as to reassure the British Empire that they are not simultaneously designed against it ..."

The Foreign Office, in a note dated October 13, 1937, sharply re-pudiated Henderson's views.

Whether or not we believe that territorial expansion by Germany is in any event inevitable, we should, by making any such intimation to the German

Government, run the gravest risks of disturbing the stability of Europe, and bringing about hurriedly and out of season developments which should preferably take place, if they must, in their own good time, when the hour is ripe. Europe is in a tense and potentially unstable condition. What keeps it from immediate collapse more than anything else is the closeness of the Anglo-French connection, the published programme of British rearmament, and a lingering doubt in the minds of some Governments whether, in fact, Great Britain would refrain from armed intervention if trouble arose. Austria and Czechoslovakia occupy a special position in Europe and they are regarded by the world at large as tests or symbols of the direction in which the world is likely to move. Any intimation on the part of His Majesty's Government to Germany of her possible acquiescence in territorial changes to Germany's benefit would almost certainly at once become public property and would set up reactions in the minds of European Governments which might bring the European card-castle tumbling down ... "The position so far as we are concerned is as follows: 1) any territorial change in Central and Eastern Europe, even if it comes slowly and in good order, is certain to have political effects in Europe which it is not possible to assess, but which might well be to our disadvantage; 2) we are not (though we do not publicly say so) prepared to intervene by force of arms to prevent it; 3) the object of our policy is to keep the situation as steady as we can, without bringing ourselves face to face with war. The situation is therefore one of great delicacy, in which the resources of diplomacy are, thanks to our backwardness in rearmament, our chief instrument – unless it be our fortunately still powerful prestige. The problem is one for the most delicate handling, and it is unlikely that anything but confusion could result from any sudden plunge into a new policy of open undertakings to make concessions to Germany ..."

Throughout the Munich Crisis and beyond, the British Government balanced uneasily between the advice given by Henderson and that of the Foreign Office. Henderson, Sir Robert Vansittart's choice as Ambassador to Germany, never ceased privately to voice the views expressed in his memorandum, and though he was occasionally rebuked, he was neither recalled nor repudiated. One wonders how much of the British Ambassador's memorandum "leaked" to Russian eyes, and whether it affected Soviet policy in the years ahead.

Report by Dr. Hubert Masařík of the Czechoslovak Ministry of Foreign Affairs on the Czech Delegation's Stay in Munich[3]

At around ten o'clock Mr. Gwatkin summoned the ambassador Dr. Mastný and myself into Sir Horace Wilson's room. There, in the presence of Mr Gwatkin and at the wish of Mr. Chamberlain, Wilson explained the basic features of the new plan and gave us a map with the districts that were to be immediately occupied outlined on it. In response to my comments, instead of explaining he merely pointed out twice that he was unable to add anything to the explanatory notes on the plan. He paid no attention to our remarks about towns and districts that were important to us. When he left the meeting we remained alone with Mr. Gwatkin; we both explained to him again and in detail why corrections were necessary. His most important comment was his reply to Ambassador Mastný to the effect that the English delegation was favourable to the new German plan. As he again began to speak about the difficulties that had revealed themselves in negotiating with Hitler I said that all depended on the readiness of the Western powers. Mr. Gwatkin answered in a solemn tone, "If you do not accept you will have to settle your affairs with Germany quite alone. Perhaps the French will tell you this in pleasanter form, but believe me they share our wish – they disinterest themselves."

At half past one we were summoned to the conference room where those present were Neville Chamberlain, Daladier, Sir Horace Wilson, Léger, Gwatkin, Mastný and I. The atmosphere was oppressive. The verdict was to be pronounced. The Frenchmen, visibly agitated, seemed to be thinking about the effect on French prestige. Mr. Chamberlain, in a long introduction, mentioned the agreement that was to be reached, and handed Dr. Mastný the text so that he might read it aloud. During the reading of the text we asked at some points for explanation. Thus I asked Léger and Wilson to explain "preponderantly German Character" in Article 41, – but Léger said nothing about a percentage, and said only that it would mean a majority according to propositions accepted by us. Mr. Chamberlain also confirmed that this was just a matter of the application of the plan accepted by us. At Article 6, I asked M. Léger if we were to see in this a clause for the protection of our vital interests, as had been promised in their propositions. M. Léger replied in the affirmative, but that this would only be small in extent and would be within the competence of an international commission. The ambassador Mastný asked Mr. Chamberlain whether the Czechoslovak member of the commission would have the same voting right as the others, to which Chamberlain assented. To the question

---

3   DPDSV. I, no. 37; report of H. Masařík.

whether an international or English force would be deployed in the plebiscite belt we got the answer that this matter was not yet fully decided. The participation of a Belgian and Italian force was also under consideration. While Ambassador Mastný discussed secondary matters with Mr. Chamberlain (who yawned uninterruptedly and without embarrassment), I asked MM Daladier and Léger if they expected an utterence about or an answer to the agreement from our Government or whether they expected some statement or answer on the part of our government on the agreement presented to us. Daladier, visibly agitated, did not answer. Léger, on the other hand, answered that the four statesmen had not much time. He added hurriedly that no answer on our part was expected. And that our Government on the same day and at the latest by 5 p.m. must sent its representative to Berlin to the sitting of the International Commission. On Saturday our officer must go to Berlin to immediately negotiate the evacuation of the first belt. The situation was becoming really oppressive for everyone present, it has been sufficiently brutally explained to us, and by a Frenchman, that the verdict was without the right of appeal or possibility of alteration. Mr. Chamberlain no longer concealed his fatigue. After the perusal of the text we were given a second map, with small corrections; we took our leave and departed. The Czechoslovak Republic, as defined by the Treaties of 1918, had ceased to exist… In the lobby we talked with M. Rochat, who asked me about the possible consequences at home; I said briefly that I did not exclude the worst, and that the possibility had to be reckoned with.

Munich, 30th of September at 4.00 in the morning.

Source: *Mnichov v dokumentech* [Munich in Documents]. 1958. Prague: SNPL. 268–269.

Conference on the Sudeten German Question in Berlin

Translation of document 2788-PS.
Office of the US Chief Prosecutor.

Strictly secret.	Strictly secret.
(Guidelines on treatment omitted)	POL I 789 g/N
Strictly secret.	

Notes on Conference,
held on the 29th of March 1938 at 12.00 in the Foreign Ministry on the question of the Sudeten Germans

The conference was attended by the gentlemen named on the attached list.

The Reich minister opened proceedings by emphasising the necessity to keep the conference a complete secret. He also explained that in the context of the guidelines issued by the Fuehrer himself to Henlein personally yesterday, two questions were especially important in for the direction of the activities of the Sudeten German Party:

- The Sudeten Germans must be aware that behind them stands a nation of 75 million, which will not tolerate the continuing oppression of the Sudeten Germans by the Czechoslovak government.
- It is the task of the Sudeten German Party to formulate and present to the Czechoslovak government the demands that it recognises as necessary for the achievement of the privileges that the Party asks for.

In this context, the Foreign Minister declared that it could not be the task of the Reich government to supply Konrad Henlein, whose position as the leader of the Sudeten Germans has been expressly recognised and repeatedly confirmed by the Fuehrer, with detailed proposals on what to ask from the Czechoslovak government. What is necessary is to present a maximal programme, implementation of which would provide the Sudeten Germans with full freedom. Premature acceptance of the agreement of the Czechoslovak government seems to be dangerous; this would on the one hand give the impression abroad that a solution had been found, while on the other hand would only partially satisfy the Sudeten. There is a need for wariness, because on the basis of experience from the past the assurances of Beneš and Hodža cannot be trusted. A final goal of the negotiations of the Sudeten German Party with the Czechoslovak government should be to avoid joining the [Czechoslovak] government by raising and progressive specification of demands. In the negotiations it is necessary to proclaim clearly that it is the Sudeten German Party itself and not the Reich government that is negotiating with the Czechoslovak government. The Reich government must not give the Prague government, or London or Paris, the impression that it is the defender or mediator of Sudeten German demands. It is a condition to be taken for granted that during future negotiations with the Czechoslovak government the Sudeten Germans will remain under the strict control of Konrad Henlein, will maintain calm and discipline and will avoid ill-considered actions. The assurance that Konrad Henlein has given in this respect is satisfactory.

After this general account by the Reich minister, the Sudeten German Party's demands vis a vis the Czechoslovak government, as set out in the supplement, were debated and basically approved. For the purpose of further collaboration, Konrad Henlein was requested to maintain the closest possible contact with the Reich minister and the Head of the Central Office for Ethnic Germans (Leiter der Volksdeutschen Mittelstelle), and likewise with the German ambassador in Prague as the local representative of the foreign minister. The task of the German ambassador in Prague will be to indicate that the demands of the Sudeten German Party are reasonable, not officially but more in private conversations with Czechoslovak politicians. Without expressing a direct interest in the extent of the party's demands.

Towards the end of the meeting there was discussion of whether it would not be useful for the Sudeten German Party to co-operate with other minorities in Czechoslovakia, especially with the Slovaks. The foreign minister decided that it should be left to the will of the party to maintain free contact with other minotity groups, if it proves useful for the latter to initiate the same approach.

Berlin, 29th of March 1938.
R (parafa).

Source: *Československo a norimberský proces* [Czechoslovakia and the Nuremberg Trials]. 1946. Prague: Ministerstvo informací. 306–307.

This is about the whole question of the CSR

A programme document of the Sudetendeutsche Partei (Sudeten German Party) of 1938 indicates that the final goal of German policy is the complete destruction of the Czech nation.

Basic Planning O. A.[4]

I. General Comments

1. Editorial:
a) This basic planning is principally concerned with standpoints on national-ity/ethnic policy. Foreign policy, military and other considerations are men-tioned only where they touch on nationality policy concerns.
b) This basic planning is in no way intended to be exhaustive in the form pre-sented. The plans outlined need to be developed in much greater depth and breadth through special studies devoted to different geographical areas and areas of expertise.
c) New events may give rise to new standpoints and new possibilities. These will require an active and flexible approach. These basic standpoints must, however, be taken into account in all circumstances.

2. Fundamental:
a) In this fundamental case of conflict, the issue is not just the Sudeten Ger-man problem, but the whole question of Czechoslovakia in its present form. The whole complex may be divided into: the question of the historic "lands of the Bohemian Crown" (Bohemia, Moravia, the rest of Silesia i.e. Krnov, Opava, Těšín) on the one hand – hereinafter we shall call them the "Bohe-mian Lands", and on the other hand the question of Slovakia and Carpathian Ukraine.
b) As far as the Bohemian Lands are concerned, the German Reich must once again implement Reich Law on the basis of a thousand years of historical facts, wholly incorporating these lands up to the old Reich border valid until 1866 (The Small Carpathians). Historical justification for this claim must form the basic line of all internal political and foreign political propaganda throughout the whole action (Bohemia – "Citadel of Germany" in the Mid-dle ages; in order the first lands in the German Reich; the "heart of Germa-

---

4   Undated, document found in the archive of Henlein's Political Office at the Castle of Sukorady. The contents
     of the document suggest that it was probably drafted between May and August 1938.

nia"; Moravia, representative of the Margravate in the quartered coat of arms of the First Reich, and so on). In justifying the necessary action it is essential to reiterate with special emphasis the fact that by its alliance with Moscow Czechoslovakia[5] is increasingly creating in Central Europe a Bolshevik epicentre spreading fire and infection of the first degree, which is primarily directed against the German Reich, and so its removal will serve to consolidate European peace. Reference to the Bolshevik threat, like the historical justification, requires so much emphasis because it demonstrates the uniqueness of the case of the Czechs, and so other neighbouring nations can be reassured on the basis of the historically exceptional situation of the Bohemian Lands. In addition, national/ethnic considerations must be put forward (e.g. Germans in the Bohemian Lands constitute more than a quarter of the overall population; by contrast, after the incorporation of the Bohemian Lands into the German Reich Czechs will constitute only approximately 8% of the total population of the Reich.) Geopolitical, transport and economic viewpoints must also be presented.

c) The question of Slovakia and Carpathian Ukraine demands a completely different treatment to that which is planned for the Bohemian Lands. The idea of returning Slovakia to Hungary must be rejected. The borders can be modified to the advantage of Hungary with an eye to ethnic considerations, but the status of Slovakia must not be essentially affected. Bratislava also belongs to Slovakia. The Bratislava bridgehead will fall to the *German Reich*. Slovakia should remain independent. Its very close connection to the German Reich and friendly relationship with Hungary would be taken for granted. Thus Slovakia and the Carpathian Ukraine will remain as bars separating Poland from Hungary, and for the German Reich this represents the bridge to the East. Carpathian Ukraine could later through German initiative be developed into a "Piedmont of the Ukrainians". The vital national rights of the Carpathian Germans need to be secured by the German Reich. To treat the Czechs and Slovaks in completely different ways would be an important chess move against Pan-Slav ideas. The German Reich should present itself as the guarantor of the Slovak strivings for independence, which is anchored in the Pittsburgh Agreement.[6] (Germania divide et impera.)

d) Our attitude to the problem of the Czech nation demands that the necessary German demands on the one hand should be carefully balanced with the

---

5   The derogatory expression "Tschechei" is used in the original (translator's note).

6   The Pittsburgh Agreement was the declaration of representatives of American Slavs, addressing Czech organisations in the USA in 1918, in which they express the wish for Slovakia to be given an autonomous status in the framework of establishing Czechoslovakia. In later years Slovak separatists from the ranks of Hlinka's People's Party, co-operating with the SdP, were to appeal to this declaration.

tactical needs of the international situation on the other. On the basis of our historical experiences and with regard to the mixing of blood, known since early German times, *we cannot regard Czechdom as a distinctive nation.* In the nineteenth century anti-German propaganda succeeded in alienating Czechs from their German living space. The reversal of this development is justified and is a vital necessity for the German Reich. Never again in history must a Czech national revival be allowed to occur. Any further possibility of such a revival must be destroyed at the roots. This is why it is necessary to suppress the Czech language. It is in the German interest that this language should completely disappear. In the course of armed struggle, however, it is crucial to choose the right tactical steps. Specifically in relation to extermination of the language – as a programme – there should be no talk of it at all. The less opportunity the enemy is given to pursue a mere language struggle, the easier it will be for us to crush Czech national consciousness. We must not underestimate the factor of language for national solidarity [community]; the identification of the language community with the term "nation" needs to be avoided, and in the course of events it may even sometimes be necessary to fight against this in the Bohemian Lands. Let us not neglect to find new, bold formulations of what national community means, and so to create – in place of the rooted factors of Czech national consciousness – a new solidarity that would firmly incorporate the younger elements and the elements capable of development from Czech national territory. The goal or the future must be as follows: to destroy Czech national consciousness, to penetrate into existing Czech language areas through German settlement, and to absorb (and also partly resettle) Czechs into inseparable spiritual and physical continuity with Germany. National [Volks] political measures against Czechdom demand from us the greatest art and energy in the application of the principles of volks struggle and organisational principles. It will be necessary to put our knowledge gained from our own German nationality struggle to the test. On the one hand putting the necessary measures into practice will start in the first hours and days of military actions, but on the other hand these must be systematically planned for whole generations in advance.

II. The Stage of Acute Escalation of the Conflict

The struggle of the Sudeten Germans is a just national struggle and is directed against the unnatural and uncultured tyranny of the Czechs and against the most malign and nonsensical creation of the dictators of the Agreement of 1919.

The Sudeten Germans' struggle for their existence naturally fundamentally affects the relations of the German Reich with Czechoslovakia. The German

Reich is the protective power of Sudeten Germandom. The question of the constitutional future of the Bohemian Lands will not be raised by the leader of the Sudeten Germans, but directly by the Reich.

The leader of the Sudeten Germans exhausted all possibilities for the peaceful solution of the Sudeten German question. Long before this, the question of Czechoslovakia was represented to the whole world as the most acute danger to real and lasting peace.

The leader of the Sudeten German Party is still asking for the holding of a plebiscite in Sudeten Germany, which is the last possibility of a peaceful solution to the question of state affiliation. The Czechs can be counted on to reject this demand.

It will then be necessary for the leader and Reich chancellor by agreement to judge that the time has come for the leader of the Sudeten German Party to take the crucial revolutionary step:

He will declare that the laws of the Czechoslovak state are not binding and appeal for the help of the European great powers (including Germany, if they signed the Treaty of St. Germain), or just of the German Reich.

It can be anticipated that in the most extreme case the Czechs will respond to this step with violent measures. In fact this will give the leader of the Sudeten German Party all the freedom of action [he needs]. Necessarily, the German Reich on the basis of ties of nationality then has the right and duty to intervene in Czechoslovakia.

The leader of Sudeten Germandom will forbid Sudeten Germans to undertake any service for the Czechoslovak state, especially armed service, and will declare all oaths of loyalty taken by Sudeten Germans to that state to be invalid. He may issue a call to arms against Czechdom.

III. The Period of Military Combat Actions

In all phases of development, the leadership of the German Reich will maintain the closest possible communication with the leader of Sudeten Germandom. The latter must secure the radio and other communications on safe territory. The leader of the Sudeten German Party will use the radio to issue the necessary orders, especialy instructions for Sudeten German men capable of fighting in the stage of the outbreak of war.

For the wehrmacht of the German Reich, the German national territory of Czechoslovakia is its *own country,* while the enemy country is Czech national territory (map).

Operational measures and combat actions will need to be conducted on that principle. In the spirit of the national/ethnic character of the conflict it will be necessary to undertake military actions on Czech national territory from the very first moment with the maximum intensity in the sense of total war. It will be necessary for the airforce to attack not only well-known key points of military transport, arms depots etc, but also densely populated seedbeds of Bolshevik and Hussite hatred.

The distribution of settlements and structure of population is such that the large centres of population on Czech national territory are for the most part also important industrial centres and transport nodes. This applies above all to Prague and its suburbs, and also to Plzeň, Kladno, Brno, Moravská Ostrava and finally also for smaller centres such as Pardubice, Hradec Králové, Mladá Boleslav, Tábor, Slaný, Česká Třebová, Olomouc, Přerov, Břeclav, Blansko and so on. The relatively sharp boundaries between town and village settlement on Czech territory will facilite effective, unremittingly conducted degradation of the Czech position by air and also by long-range artillery.

Should it prove necessary to use the air force and long-range artillery in areas of Sudeten German population, then steps should be taken on the basis of situation plans of settlements to ensure that the German population should as far as possible be spared (e.g. the destruction of railway buildings in Česká Lípa, Jihlava, or the bridge over the Labe at Litoměřice). On the basis of this principle, and ultimately also in the interests of military success, Sudeten Germans familiar with the country and the population will be allocated to the command staffs of the wehrmacht, down to battalion level, for advance into territory beyond the current Reich border.

Sudeten Germans fit to fight will assemble on the orders of the leader of the Sudeten Germans on Reich territory, units will be formed from them, and they will be deployed on the basis of agreement with the leader of the Sudeten Germans.

After the initiation of enemy actions it will be necessary to make repeated radio announcements in Czech to the effect that the lives and property of Sudeten fellow Germans are under the protection of the German Reich. The response to every enemy action must be on the principle, "an eye for an eye and a tooth for a tooth" in the ratio of one to ten. Enemy actions on the Czech side must be punished with bloody severity on the basis of standing (wartime) law.

As soon as combat actions are launched, vigorous subversive propaganda in the Czech ranks must begin. For this purpose, it is radio that first comes into consideration. It is necessary to train radio announcers, male and female, with excellent command of Czech. Another possible method is leaflets dropped from aircraft and proclamations hung up by the advancing armed forces may be considered. Prepare the texts!

This propaganda must be aimed primarily against the Czech intelligentsia (lawyers, professors, teachers, journalists etc.) which for 100 years has been preaching a false ideology to Czechs and has only brought Czechs unhappiness and disaster. The history of Bohemia – this is German Reich history. Treachery in Central Europe. Quote the statements of Czech rulers (the Přemyslid kings, the Elector George of Poděbrady and so on, up to the present day). The Bolshevik and Bolshevik-inclined Czech leaders must be attacked with all severity (especially in propaganda targeted at the rural population).

The abundant corruption scandals of the last twenty years must be properly exploited.

Slovaks must be promised their own independent state. Captured Slovak soldiers should be treated well. Poles and Hungarians (and of course also Carpathian Germans) must be regarded as liberated. Captured Czech soldiers should be formed into labour divisions as soon as possible and employed in the reconstruction of war territories.

On occupied Czech territory, the intelligentsia and Marxist leaders must be regarded as dangerous enemies. Memorials to Czech leaders, and especially Czech legionaries, must be destroyed.

As soon as Prague is in German hands, so long as the foreign political situation does not prevent it, the re-incorporation of the Bohemian Lands into the German Reich needs to be proclaimed officially. Any further Czech attempts at resistance can then be branded attempts at revolt, while the destruction of economic and other property can be branded sabotage.

External pacification will be achieved when the last military units on former Czechoslovak territory are liquidated. Nonetheless, further measures on Bohemian territory will demand the continuation of a military state of emergency.

IV. The Stage of Military Occupation

a) The timing of the destruction of the last enemy military units will also determine the moment when the reincorporation of the Bohemian Lands into the Greater German Reich is to be solemnly and with final validity established at Prague Castle in an act of state, calculated above all for the foreign audience. At the same time the completion of the Greater German Reich will be announced. In the order of cities Prague will receive the title, "City of the Completion of the Reich." Apart from necessary legal modifications relating to Slovakia and Carpathian Ukraine, the German Reich will became successor to the Czechoslovak state in international law. The leader of the Sudeten Germans, who has already since 1935 been internally recognised as gauleiter of the Sudeten Germans, will now also be appointed "Reich Governor for the Bohemian Lands". On Czech national territory the wehrmacht will continue to exercise governmental and administrative power in accordance with military standing law. As far as this territory is concerned, the status of the Reich governer will be that of advisor to the general in command. On Sudeten German territory (map), in his function of governor and gauleiter, his task will be to implement as speedily as possible a new internal political order in accordance with the principles of the NSDAP and the administrative order of the German Reich. Germans, including Sudeten Germans and primarily those with a command of the Czech language, will be appointed to all central positions of the former Czechoslovak state. The same applies to government at regional level and for autonomous organs. The wehrmacht will extend its competence to include Sudeten Germany such that this competence will be the same as on the territory of the old Reich, and will ensure that the Sudeten German military units cultivate the tradition of the former Austrian army.

b) On Czech language territory all the important measures to divide and fragment the Czech national/ethnic community will be introduced in the period of military government. A leader of the national struggle for the Bohemian Lands will be appointed for the purpose: he will have to be well acquainted with the strategy and tactics of national struggle and will have to be granted full decision-making power. As regards the details, the following measures must be introduced immediately: German to be the only publicly valid language All Czech schools and education to be closed indefinitely. The churches to be placed under strict supervision, and in the Czech areas their de-ethnicisation to be commenced without delay. The geographical names valid in the 19th century to be reintroduced and to be the only valid names. All Czech periodicals to be prohibited – if this has not already happened during the military combat actions. The military administration will publish a newspaper in Czech and in case of need will take care of the publication of propaganda materials in Czech. Special care must be taken in building up the police on Czech territory. Foreigners must be removed from the Bohemian Lands. They must be forbidden to settle there.

Czechs may be allowed to remain in the Sudeten German areas so long as they hold no public position or perform only subordinate functions. Special law continues to apply to them, however, and they are to be forbidden from any cultural or charitable activities. Czech emigration abroad should not be prevented in principle. As far as the assets of such emigrants are concerned, the principles applicable for the emigration of Jews may be used.

c) The necessary charitable measures on territory with a Czech population will be conducted exclusively by German organisations (The Red Cross and the NSV). In the large Reich concerns, above all the railways, post and other state concerns, basic replacement of personnel must be carried out on territory with Czech population as soon as possible. Czech staff will be dispersed throughout the territory of the Reich – the establishment of trustee directors for Czech banks, industrial concerns etc. In the same way all Czech associations and societies, especially those that have a national political character, will be placed under trustees whose task it will be to liquidate them. All cultural and scientific institutions will be placed under commissioners entrusted with transforming them into German institutions (universities, museums etc.) Czech bookshops will be closed, Czech libraries will be confiscated, and similarly the police on the basis of a strict cull will confiscate sources of Czech national history and literary/historical monuments in archives and collections. The whole military structure of the former Czechoslovak army will be liquidated. Officers, non-commissioned officers and the men of the Czech army will be stripped of their ranks and all pension rights. All other public officials/servants will likewise forfeit these rights. All economic and social measures will be carried out with account taken of the fact that large swathes of the Czech population (industrial workers) are to be resettled in non-Czech areas and that there is a need to support and encourage the immigration of large numbers of German population from the whole territory of the German Reich into Czech areas.

V. Further Measures after the Termination of Military Government
(Calculated as roughly a period of 5 years)

a) Political measures:
After the termination of military government, responsibility for government and administration will pass to the leader of the Sudeten German Party as the Reich Governor. His seat will be Prague.

The leader of the national struggle needs to be masked as the director of security; he will work under the direction of the Reich Governor but will have full authority in the remaining territory of the Reich and will be answerable to the Reich government. He will be chief of the general staff for all measures required for the liquidation of the Czech Question.

It would be advantageous to return (Silesian) Krnov and (Silesian) Opava, including Hlučín, to union with Silesia proper. Silesian Těšínsko will remain part of Moravia. Conversely it would be necessary to incorporate the country of Kladsko into Bohemia. Valtice and České Velenice will return to union with the Lower Danubian Gau.[7]

b) National measures and settlement policy:
Geographic planning should take the following principal ideas into consideration: the Oder-Labe canal and the Oder-Danube canal, and motorways, will form the directional lines for building German farming and industrial settlements. It will be necessary to establish a belt inhabited by Germans between the Czechs and Slovaks along the Oder-Danube canal. In the same way it will be necessary to connect Prague with German national territory lying in the north, Plzeň with territory in the west, Budějovice with national territory in the south, and also to secure the Dyje-Brno-Vyškov-Olomouc-Oder line by German settlement.

There will be a need to bring families with a large number of children from all parts of the Reich to settle territory inhabited by Czechs. This applies above all to large classes of employees of the post, railways and industry.

There is no need to prevent marriages between Germans and Czechs if the German upbringing of the children is secured. (With certain restrictions!)

c) Measures in agriculture and forestry:
The large farms expropriated from Germans by Czechs will be returned to their former owners, with a small percentage taken for agricultural settlement.[8] The land of large farms originally belonging to Czechs and foreigners will remain expropriate according to the conditions of the Czech land reform and will in large measure be placed at the disposal of projects for the settlement of farmers. The large forestry enterprises of similar kind will pass like all Czech state property into the ownership of the Reich. In the case of all other large Czech estates there will be wide-ranging land reform (appropriation of land). The purchase of German land by Czechs will be prohibited. Exceptions may be allowed only on the territory of the Old Reich with the exception of Silesia and Lower Danube. The Reich law on Inherited Farms is a German nationality measure and must not be allowed to lead to the consolidation of the Czech farm holdings. Appropriation measures will also be relevant in the case of the property of Czech farmers. A bank needs to be established to finance the buying up of Czech property by Germans. Agricultural industry (distilleries, sugar

---

[7] According to the provisions of the Versailles Peace Treaty of 1919, a few small revisions of the border were undertaken to the advantage of Czechoslovakia (Osoblaha, Hlučínsko, Vitorazsko). Up the 18th century the Kladsko territory was an integral part of Bohemia.

[8] Land reform, which involved appropriation of most of the land owned by the German nobility, was implemented after 1918.

refineries, mills) will be put under German trusteeship; the same applies to Czech co-operatives.

d) Measures in industry:

For national political reasons we have no interest in the economic development of Czech industrial settlements. For this reason we must devote more attention to new German settlements and try to ensure that the Czech industrial centres became stunted. The sources of raw materials and relevant industrial factories that are the property of Czech banks, concerns and joint-stock companies will be transferred into German ownership. Other private industrial firms will be put under German trustee administration in cases where this is in the interest of settlement and nationality policy. Such firms can be confiscated if the owners were evidently involved in the struggle against Germandom. As far as militarily important industrial firms are concerned, the military government will already have taken the necessary steps.

Czech banks will need to be liquidated and transformed into German banks. The same measures will be applied in the case of Czech wholesale companies and co-operatives (e.g. consumer co-operatives).

e) Cultural measures:

On principle only a German education system will exist, from nursery schools up to university. Reform of the curriculum of geography and history with special emphasis on the history of Bohemia as Reich history. There will be a need to fund holidays in the Reich for Czech children on the broadest possible social basis and for the longest possible time. The same applies to young people as regards stays in camps and specialist training.

German nursery schools must be set up everywhere as the necessary preliminary stage of national schools. Existing Czech public educational and information services and institutions will be liquidated definitively. German films need to be fully exploited. The radio must be brought into line with the other territories of the Reich.

Sports organisations will gradually be allowed to exist again, if German direction is ensured.

At certain German types of school and study courses in Vienna, Dresden and Wroclaw it will be necessary to provide teachers, lawyers, judges, doctors, priests etc. with an opportunity to gain a thorough knowledge of the Czech language, in order to facilitate German immigration to Czech territory. Examinations at all levels previously taken in Czech will no longer be valid qualifications. No one who does not have a thorough knowledge of the German language will be allowed to take any position in public service.

f) Military measures:

Numerous and strong garrisons and Reich labour camps will be established in Czech territory.

Czech conscripts will not undertake military service but must serve two and a half years in labour service, during which they will be divided into small groups among the German forces. The question of when it will become possible to conscript Czechs into military service is, among other things, a matter of generations. In any case, military service must represent a greatly desired honour for Czechs. Former Czech officers and men who loyally fulfilled their duty in the Austrian army must be supported. These may again be allowed to wear their old Austrian military decorations. The same approach should be taken to former civil servants in Austrian services, especially if they were persecuted by their own fellow countrymen for their attitude at the time.

On the other hand, its will be necessary to exclude Czech legionaries[9] from any kind of public functions and support. Cases of abuse of prisoners of war by legionaries should be investigated and punished.

g) Social measures:

The labour laws of the German Reich will be introduced as soon as possible into Czech national territory as well. The fight against unemployment will involve the arrangement of work in the Old Reich. Czech workers and employees in all occupations, but also farmers, who take jobs in the Old Reich and in the Alpine and Danubian countries will receive preferential treatment. (Help with resettlement, help for the household etc.). The same kind of preferential treatment can be extended to Germans who move to Czech territory.

It will be necessary to continue organising holiday events and help for children for the kind of Czech families whose behaviour is beyond reproach.

VI. Later Measures Envisaged

Once the Czech nation has been broken apart we have an interest in maintaining it in this state and in keeping the boundaries between Czech and German unstable, to the advantage of Germandom. This is how we shall ensure that large strata of the Czech population will officially identify with German nationality. For this reason we have to avoid any official recording of the state of Czech property in land registers, censuses etc. Uncompromising harshness will be in order against all attempts at resistance, whereas signs of readiness to co-

---

9   Legionaries were members of the Czechoslovak forces abroad formed in 1915–1918 in Russia, France and Italy, to fight against the Central Powers.

exist within Germany will be met with an open ear and open heart and effective action from our side. Anyone who who has once managed to find his way to us out of Czechdom during these pervasive upheavals, must be made to feel that we value him as a citizen of Germany and also as a compatriot.

On the basis of this principle, and using an individual approach, we should reckon eventually with the progressive introduction of the the DAF (Deutsche Arbeitsfront/German Labour Front), NSV (Nationalsozialistische Volks-wohlfahrt/National Socialist People's Welfare), HJ (Hitlerjugend/Hitler Youth) and other party bodies into Czech territory.

Source: *Chtěli nás vyhubit (dokumenty o nacistické vyhlazovací a germanizační politice v českých zemích v letech druhé světové války)*. They Wanted to Exterminate Us (documents on Nazi extermination and Germanisation policy in the Czech Lands in the Second World War). 1961. Prague: Naše vojsko/SPB. 29–40.

III. The Protectorate of Bohemia and Moravia

Memorandum on a Method for the Solution of the Czech Problem and the Future Ordering of Bohemian-Moravian Territory

(extracts from Appendix 2 of a document prepared by K. von Neurath and K. H. Frank, and presented to Hitler as a proposal for the progressive liquidation of the Czech nation).

Aim of the Memorandum

The Protectorate of Bohemia and Moravia was set up in a particular political situation and acquired its current legal and political form on the basis of that situation (14th April 1939). The question of whether the Protectorate headed by the Reich Protector is an appropriate solution to the Czech Problem, and whether it should therefore be retained or should be replaced by a different structure, has been raised in various quarters and is the reason why this memorandum has been drawn up. This memorandum is intended, in brief outline,

a) to identify the nature of the Czech Problem,

b) to analyse the current approach to it,

c) to examine the usefulness of proposed changes, and finally

d) to present an independent standpoint on the whole question.

The solution of the Czech Problem depends on making the correct decision. We therefore bear the responsibility for future centuries.

A. Character of the Czech problem

The character of the Czech problem is identifiable from

1. – a view of the geographical and ethnic map,

2. – a knowledge of racial conditions and

3. – the historical lot of the Czech nation.

The Czech people, who are part of the Western Slavs, is located not only in German political space but also in German national living space. Their location in this space rules out their political independence. The inability of Czechs to organise their own state permanently is a destiny given by their location. The Greater German Reich has to have the power of political decision-making over this space and its inhabitants. Arising from this is the question of the fate of the Czech people and the constitutional form of its incorporation into the Reich. (...) If their geographical position requires that Bohemia and Moravia be incorporated into the Reich, the racial profile of the Czechs makes it feasible to implement a *policy of assimilation, or as the case may be the policy of change of nationality [Umvolkung] for the greater part of the nation;* the past has ultimately shown that the Protectorate form of incorporation of Bohemia into the old Reich is a successful one (...)

B. **Our own viewpoint**
The goal of Reich policy in Bohemia and Moravia must be the complete Germanisation of the space and people. There are two possible ways of achieving this:

I. The total expulsion of Czechs from Bohemia and Moravia and their resettlement beyond the borders of the Reich, and the settlement of the vacated space by Germans.

Or

II. If the majority of Czechs are left in Bohemia and Moravia, it is necessary *to use various methods in parallel* serving Germanisation in accordance with a plan for X years. Such Germanisation presupposes:

1. change of nationality [Umvolkung] of racially suitable Czechs;
2. the expulsion of racially unsuitable Czechs and the groups of intelligentsia hostile to the Reich, or as necessary *special treatment* of these and all destructive elements;[10]
3. settlement of the vacated space by fresh German blood.

ad I.

I consider the expulsion of 7.2 million Czechs to be unfeasible,

a) because no territory in which they might be resettled is available;
b) because German people immediately able to fill the vacated space are not available;
c) because a highly civilised, economically and in terms of communication technology highly sensitive country in the heart of Europe cannot tolerate the disruption of its functions, and cannot tolerate a vacuum;
d) because people are Reich capital and in the new Reich we cannot do without the labour force of 7 million Czechs;
e) because the effects of the shock of such an expulsion on the other nations of the south-east is probably undesirable.

ad II.

Germanisation, however, can in my view be achieved by the three methods set out above. The successful assimilation processes of earlier centuries, by which the already mentioned equality of racial level of millions of Czechs with Ger-

---

[10] In answer to the question of what the term *Sonderbehandlung* (special treatment) meant, at his tribunal hearing K. H. Frank said "Sonderbehandlung means to have persons executed without a judicial verdict on the basis of state police findings of an evidential kind."

mans came about, and the force of attraction of the new Reich, make it possible and likely that several million Czechs can be brought to undergo a genuine change of nationality.

To separate those Czechs whose nationality can be changed from the racially inferior part of the Czech population is a task for investigative committees set up specially for this purpose. Possibly in the framework of the public health system. *Through systematically conducted political neutralisation and depoliticisation it is necessary first to achieve the political (mental) and then the national assimilation of the Czech nation, in order ultimately to achieve a real change of nationality.*

This process will have to take place both on the territory of the Protectorate itself and in the German interior. In all areas of the life of the nation it is necessary to apply resolute methods that are planned in a flexible, diverse and wide-ranging way. Here I indicate some of them in rough outline:

The Working Class:
Raising the standard of living – Participation in the social benefits of national socialism (DAF, KdF – Provision of basic advantages to those who identify with German nationality, the exclusion of any kind of defamation) – Generous *exchange of workplace with the Old Reich, including moving families* – To maintain a certain difference of conditions between the Old Reich and the Protectorate as a bait– *Sending maids to the Old Reich – also waiters, male servants, musicians etc.*

The Agricultural Population:
Participation of Czech farmers in German advantages favourable to the farming class, agrarian policy – A good market and price policy – *Right to own a heritable farm restricted to German farmers – (Settlements of German armed farmers[11] along the Eastern borders).*

Bourgeoisie:
Material support for business and trades – provide social benefits for the clerical (civil service) class – Individual possibilities – Promotion – *Award of decorations.*

Youth:
Fundamental change of school education – *Exorcise the Czech historical myth –* Upbringing in the idea of the Reich – No social advance without perfect knowledge of the German language – First the abolition of middle schools,

---

[11]   Armed farmer: (Wehrbauer) – these meant armed farmed settled on the boundaries of language areas or spheres of interest who were supposed to act as defences against neighbouring nations and strong points for further penetration (translator's note).

then national schools – Czech universities to be abolished forever, with only transitionally a "Collegium Bohemicum" attached to the German University in Prague – First compulsory two-year labour service, and then compulsory military service – Recognition of the great honour involved in permission to become German officers.

An ambitious land policy, the establishment of German points of support and bridges of German territory, above all the penetration of German national territory *from the north as far as the suburbs of Prague.*

The fight against the Czech language, which should become, as in the 17th and 18th centuries, just a colloquial language (dialect) and should entirely disappear as an official language.

Marriage policy following racial screening. The border gaus should be excluded from attempts to assimilate Czechs into the Old Reich. Apart from continuous recruitment for Germandom and the provision of benefits, it is necessary to use the toughest police methods including banishment from the country and special treatment for all saboteurs.

The principle of "carrot and stick"!
The employment of all these methods has a chance of success only when *one central Reich power with one man at its head* decides on its planning, direction and implementation. The direct subordination of the *"Lord in Bohemia"* to the Fuehrer clearly demonstrates the political nature of the office and task, and will prevent the political problem sliding into an administrative problem. Only in this way can the task be saved from the effects of sector ambitions and the pluralism of ministries and other Reich and party places. *The Czech is never impressed by anything but the direct deployment of Reich power.* With his political skill and with tactics that are the product of centuries of schooling, the Czech can easily exploit three or four different provincialisms, expecially since "Mother Prague" remains the political brain of the Czech people. For this reason, *every subdivision* of the territory of the Protectorate would violate this *fundamental law.*

Until such time as the changes of nationality achieve the desired effects, I therefore support:

1. The maintenance of the territorial integrity of the territory of the Protectorate as it is today. Minor modifications of the borders to the advantage of neighbouring gaus or for technical reasons are possible at any time (Plzeň, Moravská Ostrava, Jindřichův Hradec and so on).
2. The maintenance of one *single* ruling power of the Reich in Prague *with one single man* at the helm, who is directly subordinate to the Fuehrer and is equipped with all the necessary powers for Germanisation.

3. The gradual dismantling of the autonomy of the Czech state and an associated cautious, unobtrusive dismantling of the Czech state apparatus, starting with the highest offices, but with the retention of a Czech civil service and employees.

It is necessary to retain this body because,

a) in view of the shortage of officials we are unable to fill posts in 7,950 community administrations, 92 regional administrations and 2 provincial authorities with Germans, and because in the future Reich, given the huge tasks that will confront us, we shall be *forced to make wide-ranging use of Czechs.*

b) because the Czech administrative apparatus – even during the war – thanks to the German fist that runs it, is generally functional and will continue to function, and it will be the Czech responsibility to maintain it in the interests of calm and order for the Czechs themselves.

c) Because it is enough if we place a small but well-trained corps of German officials in all important key positions in higher administrative authorities and instead of dealing with minor details we issue orders and lead, which means *rule.*

My standpoint is based on the intention to Germanise the territory (Raum) and people in the Protectorate. For that reason it does not consider the question of the absolute "degradation" of the Czech people for racial reasons into a mere auxiliary nation (the askari position!) which would be under a social curse and with which marriages would have to be forbidden. I regard this *total degradation* to be unfeasible in practice and envisage only the use of *individual degradation* as a special method of *"special treatment"* in accordance with D II/2, On the basis of the conclusions of this memorandum, total degradation appears to be neither necessary nor desirable, because the solution of the Czech Question and with it the final pacification of the centuries-old *Bohemian-Moravian seedbed of conflict in Europe* can be achieved by the path proposed.

After a certain transitional period during which the process of change of nationality must be set in full motion on a unified basis, *there will no longer be anything standing in the way of the division of the territory of the current Protectorate among the existing gaus or the creation of new reichgaus.*

Prague, 28th of August 1940

Frank v. r. /=vlastní rukou/

Chtěli nás vyhubit (dokumenty o nacistické vyhlazovací a germanizační politice v českých zemích v letech druhé světové války). **They Wanted to Exterminate Us** (documents on Nazi extermination and Germanisation policy in the Czech Lands in the Second World War). 1961. Prague: Naše vojsko/SPB. 29–40, 68, 71–75.

Report of Capt. Alfgar Hesketh-Pritchard of the British Section of the Special Operations Executive (SOE), organizing training for actions in the rear of the enemy.

MOST SECRET.   22/1/42.

M

OPERATION   ANTHROPOID.

The operation ANTHROPOID, consisting of 2 agents was despatched by parachute on the night of 28/29th December, 1941.   They carried with them a package containing two metal boxes, the contents of which are shown in the attached schedule.

The object of the operation is the assassination of Herr HEYDRICH, the German Protector in Czechoslovakia and the small box contains equipment for an attack on him in car on his way from the Castle in Prague to his office.   The la rger box contains assorted equipment for alternative attacks by:-

(a) Getting into the castle,
(b) Getting into his office,
(c) Placing a bomb in his car or in his armoured
        railway train.
(d) Blowing up his railway train,
(e) Mining a road along which he is going to
        travel.
(f) Shooting him when he is appearing at some
        ceremony.

The time and place of this operation will be decided on the spot but the two agents concerned have been trained in all methods of assassination known to us.   They intend to carry out this operation whether or not there is any opportunity of subsequent escape.

This project is not known to the Czech organisation within the Protectorate.

Hesketh Pritchard
Capt
for Brigadier G. S.
22 . 1. 42

ENCL.

Source: Archiv Paměť a dějiny/TNA (photocopy).

IV. The Sudeten Question in the Cold War Period (1948–1991)

Pan-Europe (Martin Posselt)

Coudenhove's first article on the idea of Pan-Europe came out in September 1921. He gave it the revealing title, "Czechs and Germans". Here we read, "For the Czech Lands (Bohemia) the Czech-German oppositions has the same meaning as the Franco-German opposition for Europe. In both cases there are feelings of historical guilt, rivalry, vengefulness, hatred, blindness, pride, ambition and lies on both sides instead of the so-much-needed tolerance, love, forgiveness, understanding and cooperation."

The common interest of Germany, Czechoslovakia and the Deutschböhmen demands a shared struggle against Reich German, Czech and Deutschböhmen nationalism.

Fate has assigned to the Bohemian Germans the heavy lot of a national group separated from its own state community, which mean that they must be satisfied with the role of a minority. They are compensated for this hard political sacrifice by a European cultural mission: to become the intermediary between the two leading Central European peoples, a bridge between the Slav and German worlds. By their political situation the Bohemian Germans today are called on to become Europeans...

Source: Richard N. Coudenhove-Kalergi: *Pan-Evropa*. Doslov. 1993. Prague. 103.

The Eichstätt Declaration 1949

On the initiative of the Ackermann-Gemeinde, a number of prominent Sudeten Germans met in Eichstätt in Bavaria on the first Sunday in Advent of 1949 and signed the following declaration:

At a meeting of Sudeten German politicians and scientists, agreement was reached on a number of principles that they consider authoritative for the future orientation of the Sudeten German national group. These principles arise from their sense of responsibility as people active in politics and journalism. Their aim is to achieve closure of the tragic past and to establish a starting point for efforts to achieve the new order of the future.

The general spiritual crisis of our time was exacerbated by mistaken state-political constructions in Central Europe. The schematic application of the western concept of "nation state" to the supranational communities that had organically developed here gave additional rein to the forces of totalitarianism. With the resettlement and expulsion of whole ethnic groups this development reached its climax. Events since 1945 have disproved the theory that the ethnic unity of Central European states enforced by violence could guarantee a lasting world piece. On the contrary, it has led to the loss of independence of the states that commited the expulsions and has opened up the path to the west for eastern totalitarianism. It is not yet widely acknowledged that with the ideological penetration of Bolshevism there is also ongoing pan-Slavist-imperialist pressure on the West. The Asiatic supremacy from the East represents the most serious threat to European balance since the times of the migrations of peoples. Without active American intervention, catastrophe would already have overtaken Western Europe.

All attempts to save Europe and bring about a new European order must be based on recognition of these basic realities.

The current division of Germany and the whole of Europe is unsustainable. Either Eastern Europe will be won back for Western civilisation, or the whole of Western Europe will fall victim to Russian Bolshevism. This is no longer just a matter of the right of nations or national groups to self-determination, but of the right to self-determination for all Europe. We believe that it is still possible for this danger to be averted without the catastrophic effects of an atomic war, and that this can be achieved by the power of the moral resistance of all those menaced, and by the realisation of the ideal of a unified Europe. The fundamental precondition for this is German-French understanding. On the basis of this overall assessment, we consider the current struggle between West and East to be a fight for human rights on one side and against them on the other. The nations behind the Iron Curtain must realise that the reinstatement of their own rights and liberties is inextricably linked to the recognition and reinstatement of the right to homeland and home for all the expelled.

We do not want the progressive adoption of this view to be slowed down by accusations of collective guilt directed at the Czech or Polish peoples. We Sudeten Germans are asking not for revenge, but for justice. Although elementary knowledge of law demands the judicial punishment of all crimes, we do not wish to contribute to a situation in which these nations hesitate to free themselves from communist dictatorship out of fear of some collective vengeance.

Our demand, which cannot be subject to any statute of limitations, is for the return of our homeland in the language borders and settlement conditions of 1937. In this we respect the historical-geographical conditions of Bohemia,

Moravia and the Carpathian region. In the same way we acknowledge the ancient fateful alliance of the Danubian nations. No new European order can avoid a new constitutional arrangement of the Danubian territories nor of the other territories occupied and controlled by the Soviet Union since 1945. At the same time the question must also be one of establishing an acceptable relationship between Germany and its West Slavonic neighbours, one precondition for which is likewise the willingness of the Czechs and Poles to allow the expelled Germans to return to their homelands. All these tasks can be solved only within the framework of a federalist European order, which rules out any kind of hegemonic position for any great power. Our compatriots will certainly grasp that all their attitudes and actions must be subordinated to these foreign policy imperatives.

Guided by this ideal, we resolve to work within our national group and among all the expellees in such a way as to make our efforts to recover our homeland a part of the great struggle for the Christian-humanist rebirth of Europe.

Hans Schütz MdB[12], Dr. Hermann Götz MdB, Wenzel Jaksch, Reinhold Riedel, Dr. Wilhelm Karl Turnwald, Dr. Walter Becher, Dr. Gottfried Preissler, Dr. Eugen Lemberg, Richard Reitzner MdB, Dr. Walter Zawadil MdB, Dr. Walter Brand, Ing. Friedrich Brehm, P. Dr. Paulus Sladek, Dr. Rudolf Schreiber, Dr. Emil Franzel, Hermann Hönig, Dr. Walter Hergl.

Source: *Cesta ke smíření (Prameny k dějinám sudetoněmecké otázky)*. [The Road to Conciliation – sources on the history of the Sudeten German Question)]. 1992. Prague: Institut pro středoevropskou kulturu a politiku. 28–30.

The Bundestag Declaration on Protection of 14th of July 1950 (Reaction to the Prague Agreement of the 23rd of June 1950)

On the 23rd of June 1950 the ostensible government of the Soviet occupation zone of Germany, occupied by Russian forces, signed what is known as the Prague Agreement, in which the expulsion of the Sudeten and Carpathian Germans, which was inhuman and contrary to international law, is recognised as "unchangeable, justified and definitive". This moves the German Federal Assembly to declare once again that this ostensible government is neither politically nor morally entitled to speak in the name of the German people and make treaties in its name.

---

[12] MdB = Mitglied des Bundestages = deputy of the Federal Assembly.

The Prague Agreement is incompatible with the inalienable human right to homeland. The German Bundestag therefore resolutely protests against the abuse of the right to homeland of Germans from Czechoslovakia, who are under the protection of the German Federal Republic, and asserts that the Prague Agreement is invalid.

The German Bundestag welcomes the rejection of the Prague Agreement by the high commissioners. It appeals to the community of free nations to commit themselves in the spirit of the Atlantic Charter to achieving a peaceful order in which the natural rights of Germans too will be secured.

(Passed by all against the votes of the communist deputies – see stenogr. protocol 75th Meeting S.2689A)

Source: *Cesta ke smíření (Prameny k dějinám sudetoněmecké otázky)*. [The Road to Conciliation – sources on the history of the Sudeten German Question)]. 1992. Prague: Institut pro středoevropskou kulturu a politiku. 33.

The Dinkelsbühl Resolutions

7th Annual Meeting of the Ackermann-Gemeinde association in Dinkelsbühl in 1954

Eight delegates and members of the Ackermann-Gemeinde at its 7th annual meeting unanimously declared themselves in favour of the idea of setting up a Homeland Association (Landsmannschaft) and in favour of the organisational development of this idea. At the same time, those present emphasised that the Homeland Association could only be based on genuine cooperation between all existing parts of the national group, with the corresponding representation of all groups in the sense of organic activity both in the wider organisation and in the leadership of the Homeland Association. This is an essential condition, since otherwise there is a danger that the compatriot organisation might come into conflict with the basic law of the compatriot idea, which would necessarily lead to its fatal fragmentation.

All the delegates and members regard the "Working community for the protection of Sudeten German interests" as an extraordinarily effective instrument of political work for the whole national group, and one that even its opponents envy, and consider that its activity represents what is so far the maximum degree of cooperation achieved between the different political groups of Sudeten Germans. If this working community did not exist, political sense would dictate that it should be created.

"The working community for the defence of Sudeten German interests" and likewise the "working community of Sudeten German deputies" are essentially the most useful instruments for transmitting the foreign-policy demands and wishes of our national group to the executive organ for German foreign policy. Any impairment of the work of these associations serves the interests of the enemies of the Sudeten Germans.

It is in the interest of Sudeten Germans to expand both these associations and step up their activities in order to guarantee their political demands the greatest possible efficacy. The delegates expect that in the very near future all existing differences and problems will be overcome in the interest of the shared responsibility of all concerned for the common endeavours for a better future for the national group.

Source: *Cesta ke smíření (Prameny k dějinám sudetoněmecké otázky)*. [The Road to Conciliation sources on the history of the Sudeten German Question)]. 1992. Prague: Institut pro středoevropskou kulturu a politiku. 34.

"Standpoint on the Sudeten Question"

*adopted on the 15ᵗʰ of January 1961 by a plenary session of the Sudeten German Coun-
cil, and was confirmed on the 7ᵗʰ of May 1961 by the Federal Assembly of the Sudetendeutsche Landsmannschaft.*

Standpoint on the Sudeten German Question (The 20 Points)

I. Retrospects
1. The Sudeten Question – and so also the "Sudeten Crisis" of the autumn
   of 1938 – can be properly understood only against the background of the
   establishment of Czechoslovakia in 1918/1919.
2. For more than 700 years Germans have lived in Bohemia, Moravia and Silesia. Until 1806 these lands belonged to the Roman-German Empire, up to
   1866 to the German Confederation, and up to 1918 to Austro-Hungary.
3. With appeal to the right to national self-determination proclaimed by the
   American President Woodrow Wilson, the founders of Czechoslovakia
   succeeded at the peace negotiations in 1918/1919 in securing the severing
   of Bohemia, Moravia and Austrian Silesia from Austria and the severing
   of Slovakia and Sub-Carpathian Rus from the Hungarian Lands. Without
   respecting the right to self-determination, the founders of Czechoslovakia succeeded in bringing about a situation in which 3.5 million Sudeten

Germans and 1.3 million Hungarians, Ukrainians and Poles were declared, against their will, to be incorporated into a multi-ethnic state that was, however, consituted as a "Czechoslovak" nation state. In this way many decades of efforts to achieve a German-Czech settlement came to nought.

4. According to the Czechoslovak census of population of 1930, continuous Sudeten-German areas amounted to 50 political land districts, or 120 judicial districts with 3,338 communities with an average majority of German inhabitants of more than 80%. The overall extent of this territory was 25,775 km². In addition there were another 59 communities that were Sudeten German language islands. Another 313,666 Sudeten Germans lived in Czech language territory, where they formed local linguistic minorities.

5. In the framework of the Czechoslovak constitution that had been forced upon them, the Sudeten Germans tried in vain to achieve security for their economic, social and national existence, automony for their cultural life and a proportional share in state funds, state facilities and official positions in state administration. In the years 1926–1938 German parties participated in government of the Czech Republic and up to 1935 these participating parties represented 75% of Sudeten German voters. It was only the failure of these efforts, a state of social and economic crisis that became a long-term phenomenon, and the rejection of the proposals of the Sudeten German parties for autonomist solutions, that compelled the majority of Sudeten Germans, influenced by political and economic developments in the neighbouring German Reich, to strive for a different solution.

6. In 1938, just as at the end of the First World War, the Sudeten Germans were merely the object of the politics of the Great powers. Hitler played a dishonourable game with the destiny of the Sudeten Germans and exploited them for his own ends in the developments leading to the Munich Agreement. England and France would never have imposed on Czechoslovakia the obligation to cede Sudeten German territory, however, had the liberation of the Sudeten Germans from Czech domination not corresponded to the principle of the right to self-determination.

7. The destruction of Czech statehood and the freedom of the Czech nation by the national socialist regime in March 1939 was a contemptible, violent act against the right to self-determination, and we approve its remedy in the framework of international law and human rights without reservation. We also condemn without reservation all the measures and all the plans of the national socialist regime that were directed against human rights and against the national existence of the Czech people.

8. In 1945 expansionist Czech nationalism in alliance with Soviet imperialism exploited the collapse of the Third Reich to expel the Sudeten Germans

from their original settlement territory and to rob them of their national property. This step, accompanied by cruelties and murders, was a multiple violation of basic human rights and liberties.

9. Today 2 million Sudeten Germans are living in the Federal Republic of Germany, 1 million of them in Bavaria. Around 800,000 Sudeten Germans were transferred into the Soviet Occupation Zone of Germany, 140,000 are living in Austria, around 24,000 in other European countries and overseas, and around 200,000 in Czechoslovakia. Approximately 240,000 Sudeten Germans lost their lives during the expulsion.

10. The ongoing economic, social and political integration of the Sudeten Germans into the Federal Republic of Germany, and the gradual change of generations, will in no case lead to the de facto "settlement" of the Sudeten German question. Indeed, the consolidation of their material position is more often than not giving Sudeten Germans a chance to develop political activities and call for their rights. The dispersal of Sudeten Germans throughout Germany and their new social ties have meant that today the German nation is taking a more intensive interest in the Sudeten question than ever before.

II. Prospects

11. Not only the Sudeten Germans but the whole German nation will never be reconciled to the expulsion of the Sudeten Germans from the homes in which they lived for centuries. In the same way they will never acquiesce in the denial of freedom and independence to the Czech nation. Voices calling for justice and self-determination, and likewise for "revisionism in the name of freedom" will never fall silent.

12. In line with the Charter of the Expellees we reject any idea of revenge and retaliation. We do not recognise any collective guilt of the Czech people for our expulsion, and we judge all persons individually according to their present sentiments on the expulsion and according to the ends for which they are honestly striving today. For this reason we can reject the charge of "revanchism" with a clear conscience. By contrast we shall never give up our demands for the re-establishment of the right violated by the expulsion and for compensation for damages suffered.

13. We expect and trust that the Federal Government will never accept the expulsion and dispossession of more than three miliion German citizens from Bohemia, Moravia and Silesia, but will commit itself to act effectively on behalf of their rights in every direction. This also applies in the eventuality of the establishment of diplomatic relations with Czechoslovakia.

14. Our political efforts are grounded in the right to homeland and right to

national self-determination and in the framework of European integration, and independently of the disputed Munich Agreement of 1938.

15. We also recognise the natural indefeasible right of the individual to his legal place of residence, and likewise the indefeasible right of all nations, ethnic, racial and religious groups to live permanently in their original home territories (right to homeland). In our case we understand by this the right of the Sudeten German national group to return to its homeland and an undisturbed life in that homeland in free self-determination. Conditions in Europe – including mutual relations between the Federal Republic of Germany and Czechoslovakia – can be regarded as normalised only when this right is upheld.

16. We support the right to self-determination as the right of nations and national groups to freely determine their political, economic, social and cultural status. Decisions on the fate of the Sudeten Germans and their territories can be taken only with their explicit consent.

17. We honestly wish to contribute to peace between nations by the solution of the Sudeten German question. We consider the overcoming of the German-Czech dispute, which arises from the nationalism of the 19th century, to be a European task. For this reason we regard the best such solution to be one to which the two nations can freely agree.

18. In the special geographical conditions of Bohemian-Moravian-Silesian territory, the principle of the right to national self-determination allows of various different constitutional and international legal solutions. A solution corresponding to the right to self-determination is, however. incompatible with any sort of attempt to incorporate Germans and Slovaks into a centralistic Czech nation state, in which they would be accorded a subordinate position ("Czechoslovakism").

19. Constitutional community between the Czech and Slovak nation is not ruled out in advance provided that it rests on the basis of equal and free partnership, which means the free expression of the will of those involved, and provided that this is guaranteed by the community of the free nations of Europe.

20. The future relationship between Sudeten Germans, Czechs and Slovaks will be satisfactorily resolved only in the framework of European-wide integration. Its condition is conciliation between the German nation and its eastern neighbours conceived on a long-term basis.

Source: *Cesta ke smíření (Prameny k dějinám sudetoněmecké otázky).* [The Road to Conciliation – sources on the history of the Sudeten German Question)]. 1992. Prague: Institut pro středoevropskou kulturu a politiku. 35–39.

Text of the charter on the patronage of Bavaria over the Sudeten German national group *(from 6ᵗʰ June 1954) of 7ᵗʰ November 1962*

Cognisant of the centuries of historical and cultural ties between the Bavarian and Bohemian Lands and the relations of kinship between the Old Bavarians, Franks and Schwabians and the Germans in Bohemia, in Moravia and in Silesia, and as an expression of the recognition, on the part of the Free State of Bavaria and the Bavarian people, of the contributions of our fellow citizens from the Sudetenland, the Bavarian state government on the occasion of the 5ᵗʰ Sudeten German Day at Whitsun 1954 assumes patronage over the Sudeten German national group.

By assuming this patronage the Bavarian state government conveys to the Sudeten Germans expelled from their homeland above all its thanks for their valuable contribution to the building up of the Free State of Bavaria in the field of politics, culture and society, and likewise for the fact that they have proved themselves a reliable support for our free democratic order. The Bavarian state government regards the Sudeten German national group as one tribe among the Bavarian tribes and recognises the right of the Sudeten Germans to homeland and self-determination, which it will always support with the full weight of its influence. The Bavarian state government will always strive for the maintenance of the national identity of the Sudeten Germans and provide intellectual and financial support for their Landsmannschaft with its organisations as the representative of the Sudeten German national group in the fulfilment of their compatriotic political, cultural and social tasks.

Dr. Erhard
Prime Minister of Bavaria
Munich, 7ᵗʰ of November 1962

Source: *Cesta ke smíření (Prameny k dějinám sudetoněmecké otázky)*. [The Road to Conciliation – sources on the history of the Sudeten German Question)]. 1992. Prague: Institut pro středoevropskou kulturu a politiku. 40.

The Franken Declaration

On the initiative of the Opus Bonum association a symposium on developments in Czechoslovakia 1945–1948 was held on the 23ʳᵈ–26ᵗʰ of February 1978 in Franken in Bavaria.

Thirty years after the establishment of a totalitarian political dictatorship in Czechoslovakia, people who had to leave their country as political exiles have met here. This is a meeting of people driven from their country by the dictatorship of the CPCz in 1948 with people who were at that point in the political camp of the victors, and were driven from their land thirty years later, by the Soviet Occupation in August 1968 and the regime installed after it.

The meeting was motivated by the desire of all the participants to get over illusions and myths about the past and present of Czechoslovakia. Its participants took as starting point the awareness that the past cannot be erased from history or from the lives of individuals, and that mistakes and guilt cannot be changed retrospectively, but they also shared a conviction that the past need not be an insuperable burden for the future. In views of the past, nevertheless, truth must prevail – however painful it is to some. For the future, then, the will never to repeat the mistakes of the past must not be lacking.

February 1948 was a defeat for ideals of democracy and humanity, including democratic socialist ideals. It was the victory of the totalitarian principle, which denies the indivisibility of human rights and political liberties; this totalitarian principle progressively excludes more and more groups of citizens from democracy, puts them outside the protection of the law and ultimately deprives the whole controlled society of any rights.

After 1945 in Czechoslovakia millions of citizens of German nationality were the first to be placed outside the protection of the law, and the principle of retaliation prevailed over the principle of justice and right. After February 1948 citizens that the dictatorship saw as political opposition to communism were the next to be placed outside the law; in later years it came to be everyone who were critical of the ruling totalitarian power – until finally after August 1968, together with the other citizens it was a large proportion of the communists themselves.

The strategy of stripping groups of inconvenient citizens of their political liberties and rights continues to be a basic to totalitarian dictatorship in Czechoslovakia and the complete subjection of this country to Soviet supremacy. There can be no prospects for democracy or for national and state sovereignty unless it is overcome. Recognition of the indivisibility of human rights and political liberties for all citizens regardless of their faith, philosophical or political convictions can therefore be the starting-point for the future.

Charta 77 has shown that supporters of ideals of democracy and humanity have arrived at this realisation within Czechoslovakia. The supporters of these ideals who are living in political exile see the rationale of their future efforts as a matter of seeking to ensure that the indivisibility of human rights and political liberties should be a basic social recognised value regardless of differences of faith and philosophical and political conviction.

Signed:

Richard Belcredi, Alexander Heidler, Karel Kaplan, Antonín Kratochvil, Zdeněk Mlynář, Anastáz Opasek, Luděk Pachman, Jaroslav Pecháček, Vilém Prečan, Radoslav Selucký, Karel Skalický, Jiří Sláma, Rudolf Ströbinger, Pavel Tigrid.

Source: *Cesta ke smíření (Prameny k dějinám sudetoněmecké otázky)* [The Road to Conciliation – sources on the history of the Sudeten German Question)]. 1992. Prague: Institut pro středoevropskou kulturu a politiku. 44–45.

Manifesto of the Sudeten German Homeland Association and the Sudeten German Council *(of 3ʳᵈ of June 1979)*

Sixty years after the denial of their rights to self-determination by the Treaty of St. Germain, and more than thirty years after their expulsion, the Sudeten Germans are maintaining their solidarity as part of the German nation. They have made a major contribution to the reconstruction of the community from the ashes of the Second World War. In addition, they have developed pioneering ideas for a new free future order for nations and national groups.

Our thirtieth annual meeting compels us once again to draw attention to our position, our distinctive conception, our role and our goals.

1.
From the very start of the atomic age it has been the duty of all mankind to overcome the danger of atomic destruction by just, peaceful co-existence, which can be secured only when it is built on the partnership of free nations and national groups. This leading idea, also elaborated by the Sudeten Germans, must acquire the same importance as the principles of the right to self-determination and rights of national groups that they have represented for years.

2.

All nations and national groups have the right to self-determination. This right acquires a special significance when they have created and beautified their homeland by peaceful work for generations. This applies to the Sudeten Germans: It was not by the sword of the warrior but by the plough of the farmer, as peace-loving miners and citizens as artisans and merchants, that their forefathers moulded this land.

3.

These achievements, regardless of some agreements or treaties, justify the legitimate claim of the Sudeten Germans to their inherited homeland.

4.

The United Nations Organisation has recognised the validity of this claim in the case of other nations and national groups. For example it has acknowledged the claim of the Palestinians "to return to their homes and the return of stolen property", in Resolution no. 3236 of the 22nd of November 1974. On the principle of "the same right for all" we raised this demand for the 3 ½ million Sudeten Germans in a petition submitted on the 5th of December to the United Nations Organisation. The fact that we have never pursued our demand by violent means does not mean that it is less weighty. In a separate legal protest we are drawing attention to our claim to our confiscated private and public property.

5.

In an era when many nations and nation groups have got rid of colonial government and won freedom in the sense of the right to self-determination, the German nation or part of our nation must not be excluded from this development. It is therefore inadmissible that the rights and claims of the Sudeten Germans should be passed over or that decisions should be made that concern them without their consent. The situation in Europe – including the relationship between Germany and Czechoslovakia – will be normalised only when the rights and claims of the Sudeten Germans are taken into account.

6.

The right to the maintenance of identity corresponds to the right to homeland. All people who identify with a common homeland are entitled to defend and maintain this identity. For us Sudeten Germans, our identity is part of the identity of the whole German people and is legitimate reason for protection by the state. This fact is reflected in the Declaration on Protection passed in the German Bundestag on the 14th of June 1950 and in the patronage of Bavaria over the Sudeten Germans of the 6th of June 1954.

7.
We refer to the findings published by the Sudeten German Council and the Sudetendeutsche Landsmannschaft on the 15th January / 7th of May 1961 in "Twenty Points on the Sudeten Question" and we re-emphasise our wish to change the relationship between Czechs and Germans into real partnership on the basis of good neighbourship. This is possible only together with the Sudeten Germans.

8.
Partnership requires that the nations involved should condemn the crimes committed in their names. It is time that the Czech side too should condemn the crimes committed in their name, and specifically it is necessary that the Czech side clearly and unambiguously condemn the expulsion of the Sudeten Germans as an act in violation of international law. It is gratifying that well-known figures and groups of the Czech nation have already expressed views of this kind.

9.
In the 20th century violent expulsion became the scourge of nations. We are therefore in favour of an international ban on the policy.

10.
International laws for the protection of national groups are one of the means that can be used to prevent expulsions. The right of national groups also allows people in multi-national states to lead an autonomous, culturally and economically secured life.

11.
The right to self-determination of peoples, national groups and nations, makes possible the development of this self-determination in larger communities together with other nations. We Sudeten Germans have learned from historical experience, we have chosen this path and we shall follow it with foresight and energy. For the same reason we are supporting the vigorous building of a free Western Europe as the first step to a united Europe and to making partnership between continents a reality.

12.
A free Europe will also bring together the nations of our homeland areas and remedy the conditions that led Sudeten Germans to be expelled from their

homes and the Czechs and Slovaks to lose their freedom. The advantage of these nations lies not in separation but in new meeting.

13.

In this specific case, in the relations between the German nation and the Czech nation, we consider a solution freely decided on by both nations to be the best. A solution of this kind can be found even after the signing of the Prague Treaty of 1973.

14.

The New Europe that will arise on the basis of law and freedom will also include the territory of our homeland; young people above all will have a chance to transform the Sudeten areas once again into a healthy and flourishing part of our continent.

We, Sudeten Germans of 1979, once again avow our connection to our homeland, the land of our origin. The basis of our actions will continue to be truth, justice and freedom, in order that the peaceful coexistence of all nations can be made possible, and in order that the dream of a free homeland in a free Europe can become a reality.

Source: *Sudetoněmecká otázka [The Sudeten German Question]*. 1987. München: Sudetendeutscher Rat. 23. 31–33.

V. Documentation of Civic and Church Initiatives

The Prague Appeal of Charter 77 of the 11th of March 1985
(selected passages)

A democratic Europe, mature enough to manage its own affairs, cannot exist if any citizen, group or nation is denied the right to take part in decisions on events affecting not only their everyday life, but their very survival.

In cooperation and dialogue with everyone who genuinely wants to over-come the current dangerous situation, it will become possible for people and peoples to come forward with their own initiatives for disarmament, for crea-tion of nuclear-free belts and neutral zones, to stimulate the development of relations between individuals, groups, states, to support non-aggression pacts, renunciations of violence or nuclear arms, regional agreements of all kinds in-cluding e.g. some convergence between the EEC and Comecon, to act together to prevent an insensitive approach to the environment, to take governments at their word, to analyse their proposals and think through their consequences. In short: to encourage every individual, group and government initiative serving the ideal of the rapproachement and free union of European states and to reject steps that make this prospect more distant or compromise it.

Nor can we avoid some issues that have hitherto been taboo.

One of these is the division of Germany.

In the perspective of European unification, no one can be denied the right to self-realisation, and that applies to Germans as well. As with other rights, however, this right cannot be implemented at the expense of others, or without regard to their fears. Let us therefore declare plainly, that a way out cannot be found in any further revision of European borders. In the framework of European integration borders will be ever less important, but this too must not be interpreted as an opportunity for nationalist recidivism. Let us none-theless openly accord to the Germans the right to freely decide whether and in what forms they wish to unite their two states within their borders today. After Bonn's eastern treaties and after Helsinki the conclusion of a peace treaty with Germany could be one important instrument of positive transformation in Europe.

Source: Document of Charter 77, no. 5/1985. *Česko-německé vztahy po pádu železné opony.* Praha: Rada pro mezinárodní vztahy / Council for International Relations. 53–55. [Czech-German Relations after the Fall of the Iron Curtain].

VI. Czech-German Relations after the Fall of the Iron Curtain

Václav Havel's first public statement on the theme of the transfer of the Sudeten Germans
(Cited by the president of the FRG Richard von Weizsäcker in a Christmas broadcast on the 22nd of December 1989)

The Czech fighter for freedom Václav Havel, this year's bearer of our peace prize, was unable to come to its presentation in Frankfurt am M. At the beginning of November he therefore sent me a remarkable letter, from which I quote: "I personally – like many of my friends – condemn the expulsion of the Germans after the war. I have always considered it the most deeply immoral act which inflicted moral and also material damage not only on the Germans, but perhaps in even greater measure the Czechs themselves. When anger is answered by anger, it means that the anger is not suppressed but spread."

Source: Bundespräsidialamt Bonn; cited in: *Rudé právo,* 4th of January 1990

German-Czech Declaration on Mutual Relations and their Future Development (21st of January 1997)

The Governments of the Federal Republic of Germany and the Czech Republic,
    Recalling the Treaty of 27 February 1992 on Good Neighbourly Relations and Friendly Cooperation between the Federal Republic of Germany and the Czech and Slovak Federal Republic with which Germans and Czechs reached out to each other,
    Mindful of the long history of fruitful and peaceful, good-neighbourly relations between Germans and Czechs during which a rich and continuing cultural heritage was created,
    Convinced that injustice inflicted in the past cannot be undone but at best alleviated, and that in doing so no new injustice must arise,
    Aware that the Federal Republic of Germany strongly supports the Czech Republic's accession to the European Union and the North Atlantic Alliance because it is convinced that this is in their common interest,
    Affirming that trust and openness in their mutual relations is the prerequisite for lasting and future-oriented reconciliation, jointly declare the following:

I

Both sides are aware of their obligation and responsibility to further develop German-Czech relations in a spirit of good-neighborliness and partnership, thus helping to shape the integrating Europe.

The Federal Republic of Germany and Czech Republic today share common democratic values, respect human rights, fundamental freedoms and the norms of international law, and are committed to the principles of the rule of law and to a policy of peace. On this basis they are determined to cooperate closely and in a spirit of friendship in all fields of importance for their mutual relations.

At the same time both sides are aware that their common path to the future requires a clear statement regarding their past which must not fail to recognize cause and effect in the sequence of events.

II

The German side acknowledges Germany's responsibility for its role in a historical development which led to the 1938 Munich Agreement, the flight and forcible expulsion of people from the Czech border area and the forcible breakup and occupation of the Czechoslovak Republic.

It regrets the suffering and injustice inflicted upon the Czech people through National Socialist crimes committed by Germans. The German side pays tribute to the victims of National Socialist tyranny and to those who resisted it.

The German side is also conscious of the fact that the National Socialist policy of violence towards the Czech people helped to prepare the ground for post-war flight, forcible expulsion and forced resettlement.

III

The Czech side regrets that, by the forcible expulsion and forced resettlement of Sudeten Germans from the former Czechoslovakia after the war as well as by the expropriation and deprivation of citizenship, much suffering and injustice was inflicted upon innocent people, also in view of the fact that guilt was attributed collectively. It particularly regrets the excesses which were contrary to elementary humanitarian principles as well as legal norms existing at that time, and it furthermore regrets that Law No. 115 of 8 May 1946 made it possible to regard these excesses as not being illegal and that in consequence these acts were not punished.

IV

Both sides agree that injustice inflicted in the past belongs in the past, and will therefore orient their relations towards the future. Precisely because they remain conscious of the tragic chapters of their history, they are determined to continue to give priority to understanding and mutual agreement in the development of their relations, while each side remains committed to its legal system and respects the fact that the other side has a different legal position. Both sides therefore declare that they will not burden their relations with political and legal issues which stem from the past.

V

Both sides reaffirm their obligations arising from Articles 20 and 21 of the Treaty of 27 February 1992 on Good Neighbourly Relations and Friendly Co-operation, in which the rights of the members of the German minority in the Czech Republic and of persons of Czech descent in the Federal Republic of Germany are set out in detail.

Both sides are aware that this minority and these persons play an important role in mutual relations and state that their promotion continues to be in their common interest.

VI

Both sides are convinced that the Czech Republic's accession to the European Union and freedom of movement in this area will further facilitate the good-neighbourly relations of Germans and Czechs.

In this connection they express their satisfaction that, due to the Europe Agreement on Association between the Czech Republic and the European Communities and their Member States, substantial progress has been achieved in the field of economic cooperation, including the possibilities of self-employment and business undertakings in accordance with Article 45 of that Agreement.

Both sides are prepared, within the scope of their applicable laws and regulations, to pay special consideration to humanitarian and other concerns, especially family relationships and ties as well as other bonds, in examining applications for residence and access to the labour market.

VII

Both sides will set up a German-Czech Future Fund. The German side declares its willingness to make available the sum of DM 140 million for this Fund. The Czech side, for its part, declares its willingness to make available the sum of Kc 440 million for this Fund. Both sides will conclude a separate arrangement on the joint administration of this Fund.

This Joint Fund will be used to finance projects of mutual interest (such as youth encounter, care for the elderly, the building and operation of sanatoria, the preservation and restoration of monuments and cemeteries, the promotion of minorities, partnership projects, German-Czech discussion fora, joint scientific and environmental projects, language teaching, cross-border cooperation).

The German side acknowledges its obligation and responsibility towards all those who fell victim to National Socialist violence. Therefore the projects in question are to especially benefit victims of National Socialist violence.

VIII

Both sides agree that the historical development of relations between Germans and Czechs, particularly during the first half of the 20th century, requires joint research, and therefore endorse the continuation of the successful work of the German-Czech Commission of Historians.

At the same time both sides consider the preservation and fostering of the cultural heritage linking Germans and Czechs to be an important step towards building a bridge to the future.

Both sides agree to set up a Czech-German Discussion Forum, which is to be promoted in particular from the German-Czech Future Fund, and in which, under the auspices of both Governments and with the participation of all those interested in close and cordial German-Czech partnership, German-Czech dialogue is to be fostered.

Helmut Kohl, Klaus Kinkel, Václav Klaus, Josef Zieleniec
ČTK/Czech News Agency

Source: *Česko-německé vztahy po pádu železné opony (Dokumentace k česko-německým vztahům 1989–1997)* [Czech-German Relations after the Fall of the Iron Curtain (Documentation on Czech-German Relations 1989–1997)] 1997. Prague: Rada pro mezinárodní vztahy/Council for International Relations. 21–24.

Václav Havel: "Češi a Němci na cestě k dobrému sousedství"
[Czechs and Germans on the Road to Good Neighbourly Relations].
(From the speech of the President of the Republic, Charles University, Prague, 17th of February 1995)

1) If someone claims now and then that the Czechoslovak Republic as the fruit of the ripening self-consciousness and the self-liberation efforts of the Czechs and the Slovaks and a product of the Peace of Versailles was an error and, as such, a cause of the subsequent disasters, he or she only reveals his or her own ignorance. The birth of the republic cannot be ascribed only to the realism that paid regard to the desire of the Czechs and the Slovaks to develop their

identity, to free themselves from the rule of the Austro-Hungarian monarchy that failed to offer them an appropriate status, and to build their new, viable statehood on their association in one common state. What was no less, if not even more important was the fact that a modern, democratic, liberal state was purposefully created here on the basis of the values to which the entire democratic Europe of today is committed as well, and in which it sees its future. Its founding fathers expected that against the background of a growing stability of both the domestic and the international situation it would develop into a true civil state, growing out of a creative cooperation of all its citizens and of their respect for one another's national character. It is true that the Czechoslovak Republic had its weaknesses among other things, it never worked out a satisfactory solution to its nationalities problems but the roots of these weaknesses did not lie in the values that marked its birth, and showed it the way to go. They were the result of the inability of some of its political forces to act in a broad-minded manner and in the spirit of those values so as to solve the country's minor domestic problems before enemies of freedom turned them into major international problems. All that is well known and has been recorded, but it does not change in any way the fact that Czechoslovakia like France, today's Benelux countries, Switzerland and the Nordic nations was one of the few truly democratic and well-ordered states of continental Europe. Voices of personages such as Thomas Mann, whom along with thousands of other German democrats Czechoslovakia granted asylum after Hitler came to power, have testified to that. Thus, when the Czech Republic acknowledges its ties of continuity with Czechoslovakia this can only be to its credit.

2) It would be a dangerous oversimplification if the transfer of the Germans from our country after the war were to be perceived as the only item in the tragic coming to an end of the thousand years of Czech-German coexistence here. Physically, the transfer undoubtedly was the end of our life together in a common state, because it was with the transfer that that coexistence was actually terminated. But the lethal blow that caused its death was struck by something else: the fatal failing of a great part of our country's German-born citizens who gave preference to the dictatorship, confrontation and violence embodied in Hitler's national socialism over democracy, dialogue and tolerance, and while they were claiming their right to their homeland, they in fact renounced their home country. In so doing, they negated the outstanding accomplishments of the many German democrats who had helped build Czechoslovakia as their home. Whatever the deficiencies of the solution of the nationalities issue in prewar Czechoslovakia may have been, they can never justify that failing. Those who committed it turned not only against their fellow citizens, against Czechoslovakia as a state and their own status as citizens of that state; they turned

against the very foundations of humanity itself. They embraced a perverted racist ideology and began immediately to apply it in practice. It is marvellous that many descendants of our former German fellow citizens have understood that and are now working selflessly and patiently for a reconciliation between our peoples.

We can have different views on the post-war transfer of the German population, my own critical opinion is widely known, but we can never take that step out of its historical context, nor can we fail to see the connection between the transfer and all the preceding horrors that led to it. While until recently I believed this to be self-evident and therefore felt no need to stress it, I do have to say it clearly at present, now that people who ignore this fact or even call it in question are again being heard in Germany. I have already stated more than once in the past that evil is of an infectious nature and that the evil of the transfer was only a sad consequence of the evil which preceded it. There can be no dispute about who was the first to let the genie of national hatred out of the bottle. And if we, that is, the Czechs, are to recognize our share of responsibility for the end of the Czech-German coexistence in the Czech lands, we have to say, for the sake of truth, that we let ourselves become infected by the insidious virus of the ethnic concept of guilt and punishment but that it was not us who brought that virus, at least not its modern destructive form, into this country.

Source: *Česko-německé vztahy po pádu železné opony (Dokumentace k česko-německým vztahům 1989–1997)* [Czech-German Relations after the Fall of the Iron Curtain (Documentation on Czech-German Relations 1989–1997)] 1997. Prague: Rada pro mezinárodní vztahy/Council for International Relations. 29–30.

Statement of the Government of the United States on the question of the validity of the conclusions of the Potsdam Conference (*of 15th of February 1996*)

The decisions made at Potsdam by the governments of the United States, United Kingdom, and the then Soviet Union in July/August of 1945 were soundly based in international law. The conference conclusions have been endorsed many times since in various multilateral and bilateral contexts.

– The Conference recognized that the transfer of the ethnic German population of Czechoslovakia had to be undertaken. Article XIII of the Conference report called for this relocation to be "orderly and humane".

– The conclusions of the Potsdam Conference are historical fact and the United States is confident that no country wishes to call them into question.

– It would be inappropriate for the United States to comment on any current bilateral discussions under way between the Czech Republic and Germany.

United States Information Service

Source: *Česko-německé vztahy po pádu železné opony (Dokumentace k česko-německým vztahům 1989–1997)* [Czech-German Relations after the Fall of the Iron Curtain (Documentation on Czech-German Relations 1989–1997)] 1997. Prague: Rada pro mezinárodní vztahy/Council for International Relations. 43–44.

Czech-German Relations Must Flourish. Joint Declaration of Czech and Sudeten German Christians
(Prague/Munich, 18th of December 1991, excerpt)

The German signatories turn especially to Sudeten Germans with the wish that they should act as a connecting link between Czechs and Germans and not allow themselves to be pushed into the role of an obstacle to peace. The declarations of past decades that have striven to come to terms with the event of the expulsion in a spirit of conciliation must now bear fruit. This requires a level-headed attitude to the question of redress of wrongs.

– Return to the CSFR would mean moving the centre of gravity of life into an environment that could hardly be experienced as homeland. For that reason, demands of this kind, justified by right to homeland, should be supported only those who would really have the courage to take this step.

– The retrospective award of illegally confiscated property could only be practically realisable in forms and on a scale that would inevitably tend to disappoint the hopes now raised. After forty years of socialist planned economy the land is devastated. The expulsion of the people who today enjoy the assets involved is out of the question. Under these circumstances voluntary personal sacrifice as a contribution to a conciliatory new beginning is ready to hand.

– Such an attitude cannot be considered a betrayal of right, or a betrayal of obligations to ancestors who built the old homeland. Whether someone wants or may pursue a right is not a legal question, but a question of moral viewpoints. If a certain worldly good is to be justly assigned, a deed establishing peace has greater value than a fight over an object that is (no longer) a thing essential for life.

Source: *Česko-německé vztahy po pádu železné opony (Dokumentace k česko-německým vztahům 1989–1997)* [Czech-German Relations after the Fall of the Iron Curtain (Documentation on Czech-German Relations 1989–1997)] 1997. Prague: Rada pro mezinárodní vztahy/Council for International Relations. 56.

VII. From responses in the press

Klaus Kinkel rejects criticisms from Prague
(From an interview with the federal minister Klaus Kinkel)

C.G.: Kinkel wehrt sich gegen die Vorwürfe aus Prag
[...] Zu der zweiten Streitfrage, die Behandlung der Vertreibung, sagte Kinkel: "Ich habe die Verpflichtung, das Unrecht an den Sudetendeutschen mit in die gemeinsame Erklärung zu bringen". Die Prager Regierung *sei bisher nicht bereit,* in der Erklärung auszusprechen, daß durch die Vertreibung Unrecht *geschechen sei.*

Offenkundig hält Prag am Begriff der "zwangweisen Aussiedlung" mit Berufung auf das Potsdamer Abkommen fest. Nach deutscher Auffasung bedeutet das Potsdamer Abkommen nicht die rechtliche Anerkennung der Vertreibung, sondern war nur eine politische Erklärung. [...]

C. G. Kinkel rejects criticisms from Prague
[...] On the second disputed question – the way the expulsion is described, Kinkel said, "I have a duty to include the injustice to the Sudeten Germans in the declaration." The Prague government is said not yet to have been prepared to state in the declaration that an injustice was done through the expulsion.

Prague is evidently insisting with reference to the Potsdam Agreement on the use of the term, "compulsory de-settlement". According to the German view, the Potsdam Agreement does not mean the legal recognition of the expulsion, because it was only a political declaration. [...]

Note: In the original German the use of the passive voice – marked in Italic in the text – is diplomatically significant. I.e. The issue of an injustice being committed, rather than a formulation specifying who committed it.

Frankfurter Allgemeine Zeitung, 18th of January 1996

Source: *Česko-německé vztahy po pádu železné opony (Dokumentace k česko-německým vztahům 1989–1997)* [Czech-German Relations after the Fall of the Iron Curtain (Documentation on Czech-German Relations 1989–1997)] 1997. Prague: Rada pro mezinárodní vztahy/Council for International Relations. 68.

Who is bound by the Potsdam Agreement? The Allies accepted a series of heterogeneous provisions

Ulrich Fastenrath

[...]
In legal assessment and categorisation of international documents, what matters is not their titles but the will of the states involved, which has to be judged from a few small statements contained [in the Potsdam] documents and from the circumstances in which they were articulated. Here we shall not reach unambiguous conclusions. The Potsdam provisions are too heterogeneous. At the very least the agreement on setting up a Council of Foreign Ministers, on political and economic principles, on the system of control over Germany, on German reparations and on the Western border of Poland imply or might be held to imply a legal act. A legal significance might also be ascribed to the recognition of "the transfer to Germany of the German population or parts of it, which have remained in Poland, Czechoslovakia amd Hungary". In the case of all these provisions it is assumed that they will necessarily have to be fulfilled. Yet this in no way makes it impossible to argue that they are not binding legal provisions. In other places in the documents, facts or expressions are merely taken cognisance of, or other meetings, reviews or goals announced. Whether or not we consider the Potsdam Agreement to be an international legal agreement, clearly such sentences have no normative content and cannot be considered binding.

Arguments against the international legal binding status of the Potsdam Agreement include the later circumstances of its ratification procedures. These documents were signed only by heads of states and governments, and were not submitted to parliaments, which at least in the case of the American constitution is essential for treaties. Furthermore – unlike the other provisions of occupational legal norms – they were not included in official treaty collections. On the other hand, the three great powers always repeatedly stressed that their actions were based on the binding effects of the agreement. The Soviet Union even had it included in its treaty of friendship with the GDR of 1964. And it was especially the Soviet Union that saw in the Potsdam Agreement the basis of the post-war order, which was supposed to be binding on Germany too.

On the other hand, according to universal rules, a state that has not signed an agreement cannot be held to be bound by that agreement. Since Germany was not a party to the Potsdam Agreement, nor did it add its signature later, nor did the Federal Republic recognise any obligations arising from the agreement, it is not bound by it in international law.

In any case, the Federal government has always taken this position (unlike the government of the GDR, which was always referring to the Potsdam Agreement). And there is almost complete agreement that the Potsdam Agreement was never incorporated into German law even through the little known Article 139 of the Basic Law [the constitution of the FRG]. This Article relates only to the legal regulations of the occupation powers concerned with denazification and demilitarisation, and not to the agreement these powers made with each other. Of course, the German view was not shared by the victorious powers.

Frankfurter Allgemeine Zeitung, 20ᵗʰ of March 1996

Source: *Česko-německé vztahy po pádu železné opony (Dokumentace k česko-německým vztahům 1989–1997)* [Czech-German Relations after the Fall of the Iron Curtain (Documentation on Czech-German Relations 1989–1997)] 1997. Prague: Rada pro mezinárodní vztahy/Council for International Relations. 71–72.

VIII. Decrees of the President of the CSR dr. E. Beneš, relating to the Sudeten German issue

List of the Decrees of the President of the CSR dr. E. Beneš, relating to:

the punishment of some crimes and offences committed in the time of heightened threat to the republic (retribution),
the state citizenship of Germans and Hungarians,
confiscation and nationalisation of property without compensation.

ad 1) **Decree no. 16/1945, of 19th of June 1945** "concerning the punishment of Nazi criminals, traitors and their accomplices and concerning extraordinary people's courts" (known as the Great Retribution Decree). **Decree no. 138/1945, of 27th of October 1945** "concerning the punishment of some offenses against national honour" (known as the Small Retribution Decree).

ad 2) **Decree no. 33/1945, of 2nd of August 1945** concerning modification of state citizenship, in which Para 1, Point 1 contains the provision: "Czechoslovak state citizens of German or Hungarian ethnicity (nationality), who acquired German or Hungarian state citizenship in accordance with the regulations of the occupying power, on the day of acquisition of such state citizenship forfeited Czechoslovak state citizenship."

ad 3) **Decree no. 5/1945, of 19th of May 1945** "concerning the invalidity of some transactions involving property rights from the time of lack of freedom, and concerning the National Administration of property assets of Germans, Hungarians, traitors and collaborators and of certain organisations and associations." **Decree no. 12/1945, of 21st June 1945** "concerning the confiscation and expedited allotment of agricultural property of Germans, Magyars, as well as traitors and enemies of the Czech and Slovak nation."
Decree no. 22/1945, of 20th of July 1945, "on the settlement of the agricultural land of Germans, Hungarians and other enemies of the state by Czech, Slovak and other Slav farmers." **Decree no. 108/1945, of 25th of October 1945** "concerning confiscation of enemy property and concerning National Recovery Funds." **Decree no. 50/1945, of 11th of August 1945** "on measures in the field of film" and **Decrees nos. 100–103/1945, of 24th of October 1945** "on nationalisation of mines and some industrial enterprises", on "nationalisation of some enterprises of the food indus-

try", "on nationalisation of joint-stock banks" and "on nationalisation of private insurance companies."

Source: Winkler P. "Dekrety prezidenta republiky z období 1940–1945" ["Decrees of the President of the Republic 1940–1945"]. *Mezinárodní vztahy* 3/94. Prague: Ústav mezinárodních vztahů. 20–29.

The Decrees – An obstacle to the Admission of the Czech Republic into the European Union?

Christian Tomuschat
(extract from legal opinion on the decrees of President E. Beneš, commissioned by the European Commission in connection with the approval process for the entry of the CR into the EU)

To this day the so-called "Beneš Decrees" and other legal norms from the period immediately after Czechoslovakia regained its state independence, continue to burden the Czech Republic's relations to its neighbour states – Germany and Austria. As is well-known, after the end of the occupation by the forces of Nazi Germany, Czechoslovakia took political decisions and employed radical measures to punish the supposed disloyalty of the Sudeten German national group during the occupation. A series of legal norms were issued that led to the extensive removal of rights from unloved fellow citizens. The first step was a thorough confiscation policy which was formulated in three decrees of the president of the republic:

- Decree no. 5 of the 19th of May 1945 "concerning the invalidity of some transactions involving property rights from the time of lack of freedom and concerning the National Administration of the property assets of Germans, Hungarians, traitors and collaborators and of certain organisations and institutions."[13]
- Decree no. 12 of the 21st of June 1945 "concerning the confiscation and expedited allotment of agricultural property of Germans, Hungarians and also of traitors and enemies of the Czech and Slovak nation."[14]

---

[13]   In the German translation printed in: *Dokumentation der Vertreibung der Deutschen aus Ost-Mitteleuropa*. Vol. IV/1: Die Vertreibung der deutschen Bevölkerung aus der Tschechoslowakei. 1957. Bundesministerium für Vertriebene, Flüchtlinge und Kriegsbeschädigte (ed.). 204.

[14]   Ibidem. 225 (German translation).

- Decree no. 108/1945 of the 25th of October 1945 "concerning confiscation of enemy property and the National Revival Funds".[15] In addition, by the removal of Czechoslovak state citizenship the Sudeten Germans were excluded from the national community.
- Constitutional Decree no. 33 of the 2nd of August 1945 "concerning the regulation of the Czechoslovak state citizenship of persons of German and Hungarian nationality."[16] stripped all persons of German and Hungarian nationality of Czechoslovak state citizenship with retroactive force from the day when they acquired German or Hungarian state citizenship.

IV. Conclusions

The Main Conclusions of the considerations presented are as follows:
1) Neither the law grounded in the treaties of European communities nor the secondary law of the European communities provide any way that would make it possible to challenge the Beneš Decrees and the Law on Impunity of the 8th of May 1946.
2) Nor procedurally do the treaties of the community afford possibilities of legal protection that would make it possible for the Beneš Decrees and the Law on Impunity of the 8th of May 1946 to be reviewed by the standards of the acquis communitaire or general international law.
3) From the point of view of 2001, neither the confiscation decrees nor the decree on removal of state citizenship can be considered obstacles to the admission of the Czech Republic with a view to the demands placed on candidate counties in Article 49 of the EU Treaty.
4) The case of the Law on Impunity of the 8th of May 1946 is different in this respect. The indiscriminate refusal to prosecute by legal means criminal acts committed in a period between the 30th of Seoptember 1938 and the 28th of October 1945, fundamentally contravenes the demands of the international community for the protective function that is the obligation of every state.

Source: *Ist das tschechische Rechtssystem bereits EU-konform?* 2002. Prague: Friedrich Ebert Stiftung. 70, 95–96.

---

[15]   Ibidem. 263 (German translation).
[16]   Ibidem. 240 (German translation).

IX. Centre against expulsions

Chronological view of the development of discussion around
the Centre against Expulsions in German and European context
in the period 2000–2003

- 2000 – beginning of discussion on the so-called Centre against Expulsions (CAE). The CDU deputy and president of the Federation of Expellees Erika Steinbach and the former federal SPD acting secretary Peter Glotz, who was born in Cheb, start to campaign through a Foundation set up for the purpose for the founding of a CAE which, as they describe it, would be concerned with the phenomenon of expulsion in Europe in the 20th century. From closer study of the whole concept it is clear that the central point of the project is to be the expulsion of Germans from Central and Eastern Europe as a result of the Second World War. The "national" component of the centre is emphasised by its backers' demand that it be sited "in a central location in Berlin".
- The idea that discussion of the expulsions might be elevated to the level of setting up a kind of centre documenting (and as a memorial to) victims from the ranks of the expellees was to a considerable extent inspired by the ongoing discussion in the Bundestag of the plan for a national memorial to victims of the Holocaust.
- 2002 – on the initiative of the SDP deputy Markus Meckel and the CDU deputy Rita Süssmuth, at first as a certain "counterweight" to the "national" concept of the CAE, a proposal is put forward for the creation of a "European Centre against Expulsions, Forced Resettlement and Deportations", with the additional suggestion that the development of the concept of the centre would be the subject of dialogue with European partners (the CR and Poland are considered crucial).
- 16th May 2002 – The Bundestag supported, with the votes of deputies of the governing coalition (SPD and Greens), Meckel's proposal for setting up a "European" CAE. But the most important consequence of the debate in the Bundestag was the agreement of the German political parties that it was legitimate that some centre documenting the phenomenon of expulsion be established, and that it would be established in some form.
- 15th July 2003 – In the daily newspaper *Rzeczpospolita* a former Polish minister of foreign affairs, Prof. Władysław Bartoszewski, whose words have considerable weight in Polish public life, reacted to the CAE project. Prof. Bartoszewski emphasised that the past should be commemorated, but not in a one-sided way. At the same time he expressed a doubt (he had himself

been imprisoned in Auschwitz), as to whether the building of a CAE was not supposed to create the false impression that apart from the Jews the main victims of the Second World War had been Germans.

- 10th August 2003 – a "third" current of opinion enters the internal German debate in which the main dispute had been whether to set up a "national" or "European" CAE. This "third" current took the form of a petition initiated by the German historians and political scientists, some also from the circle of the Munich *Collegium Carolinum (*including the Hahns, husband and wife), casting doubt on the very idea of the CAE.

- August 2003 – for the first time the Chancellor Gerhard Schröder entered the debate in the media (statement for the media after a meeting of the federal cabinet), and the foreign minister of the FRG Joschka Fischer (interview for *Die Zeit*). Schröder's rejection of Berlin as a site for the CAE was generally interpreted as a rejection of the "national" concept of the CAE. Minister Fischer tried to direct the internal German discussion towards the question of German self-destruction and irreversible losses in the widest possible sense ("What have we done to ourselves, what have we lost by that?").

- 1st September 2003 – in a speech to Second World War veterans the Polish president Kwaśniewski expressed his openness to the European project of the building the CAE on the lines of Meckel's alternative. The Polish premier Miller also started to talk about the possibility of a "European variant" of a CAE. If previously the problem of a CAE had attracted comment mainly from historians, or sometimes former Polish politicians, this statement by Miller means an evident shift in the level of of Polish discussion.

- 8th September 2003 – at the Expellees' Homeland Day the federal president Johannes Rau expressed his views on the CAE question. He had decided to take on the role of moderator of the whole dispute, which he regarded as primarily internal political. He warned against its further escalation, expressed understanding for the fears of neighbours and stressed that the historical debate needed to be thoroughly contextualised.

- 15th September 2003 – in an important article entitled "Against a Europe of National Animosities", on the front page of the daily *Rzeczpospolita,* the Polish president made another contribution to the debate. Kwaśniewski expressed surprise that at a time when Poles and Germans were talking about current questions, like the common future, the relatively distant past seemed to be affecting relations more and more, and he noted that this problem had been opened by the German side, who were in this way trying to come to terms with their own past. Kwaśniewski stressed that it was impossible to listen to the way the Federation of Expellees interpret the past and say nothing. "A centre based in Berlin and devoted just to German expellees" was in his view a "bad idea, which is damaging for reconciliation". According to Kwaśniewski a CAE in Berlin, presenting above all the suffering of the Germans, would be a return to a "Europe of animosities between nations, in which history can all too easily be replaced by ideology."

- 16ᵗʰ September 2003 – An impatiently awaited conference on the question of the CAE was held at the offices of the daily newspaper *Rzeczpospolita*, and was attended by the President of the Federation of Expellees Steinbach and a whole range of politicians, diplomats, historians and publicists. All the important Polish media including several television stations covered the conference. The course of the conference confirmed the unshakeable opposition of Poland towards the national project of the Federation of Expellees, and in most cases to the project as such. While Steinbach insisted that Germans too had a right to memory and that the CAE would be open to all nations that had suffered, the Polish leaders were without exception convinced of the purely political background of the project and emphatically expressed their fears during discussion. Not once during the conference was there even the slightest mention of the Czech-German debate on post-war events.

- September 2003 – the theme of the CAE now entirely dominated the front pages of most Polish dailies. The theme was now discussed by journalists, publicists, and historians and politicans right across the political spectrum, including the president. Many commentaries were unable to avoid a highly emotional tone. On the other hand, the emotional character of the discussion was natural and given the historical contexts the issues are even more sensitive than in Czech-German discussion.

- 29ᵗʰ September 2003 – The Polish Sejm [parliament] approved an appeal to all European parliaments to resist the deformation of historical facts and attempts to give a distorted picture of responsibility for the unleashing of the Second World War. This was in fact a compromise document following from an earlier draft presented by the Law and Justice Party which had appealed to the government for an even more trenchant response to the effort to cast doubt on the course of certain historical events.

- 29ᵗʰ October 2003 – The joint "Declaration of Presidents Rau (FRG) and Kwaśniewski on a European Conception of the View of Expulsion of the 29ᵗʰ of October 2003" was issued in Gdansk. It declared that the horrors of the wars of the 20ᵗʰ century had led to the suffering of many millions of people – victims of resettlement, flight and expulsion, and so it was necessary to invest greater efforts in building a better future, while not avoiding reflection on the past. (quotation): *"The Europeans should together re-examine and document all cases of displacements, flights and expulsions that have taken place in the 20ᵗʰ century in order for their causes, historical contexts and consequences to become readable for public opinion. All this can be accomplished only in the spirit of reconciliation and friendship. This will unite us even more."* ("European dialogue").

- 27th November 2003 – publication of "Resolution of the Sejm of the Polish Republic of the 27th of November 2003 on the question of the establishment of a Centre for the Memory of European Nations under the Aegis of the European Council" – the document asserts that even though each nation has a right to its memory, this cannot be distanced from historical context. In its resolution the Sejm noted that the leaders of the USA, Great Britain and the USSR decided on the transfer at Potsdam and that the legal resettlement of the German population could not be compared with fascist crimes. It suggested that an institution should be set up that would be concerned with the criminal actions of the Hitlerian and communist totalitarian system – a *Centre for the Memory of the Nations of Europe* under the aegis of the Council of Europe. With this initiative the Sejm appealed to other states of the Council of Europe for support, but did not in fact follow up an alternative initiative of this kind.
- November 2003 – France had been carefully following the situation around the plan to build the CAE, but did not intend to become involved in it. According to French diplomacy, European-wide discussion on the theme of the CAE would provoke a whole series of reminiscences in probably every European country, and certainly no one would want that. The Germans allegedly never approached the French side on these matters. *(Generally the French prefer to avoid the theme, because they are afraid that it might spread to the Weimar Triangle (Russia-France-Poland))*
- December 2003 – the CDU deputy F. Pflüger put forward a "compromise" proposal for the CAE at the congress of expellees – CDU/CSU members in Berlin. He said that it was necessary to take into account Polish fears about lack of balance in the exhibition, and that the exhibition would draw attention to the fact that Poles were the first victims of the despotism of Nazi Germany. Nonetheless he added that the central subject should be the fates of the expelled Germans and that he considered the most appropriate location to be Berlin, but did not rule out Wroclaw or Sarajevo (towns that once had large German minorities) *(Note: in fact the first victim of Nazi despotism was the CSR.)*
- 11th December 2003 – the speech of the representative of the Chancellor's office K. Nevermann at the forum "Expulsion in the 20th century", held in the Berlin central office of the SPD. Nevermann asserted that Germany had excellent institutions studying German history in context (the *Haus der Geschichte* in Bonn, the *Deutsches Historisches Museum* in Berlin and numerous other institutions), which represented a guarantee of objectivity. In the

current situation he believed that a more helpful approach than building a new centre would be to exploit the existing infrastructure of academic and popular-academic institutions, and to do so with an eye to the fact that the FRG, CR, Poland other countries were becoming partners in the EU, and this would offer a real possibility for new ways of engaging with common themes relating to the past. ("We don't need a museum, we need European infrastructure.")

- 15th December 2003 – in an exchange with Wolfgang Schäuble during the debate on approval of the budget chapter of the German Foreign Ministry, the minister Joschka Fischer summed up the government's attitude to the German debate on coming to terms with the past, and the whole complex of relations to neighbouring states especially Poland. In response to Schäuble's mention of the problem of historical burdens (debate on the CAE), Fischer said that he regretted that a debate on the past conceived in this way had ever developed at all, and that originally he had underestimated the damage that this would cause e.g. to mutual relations with Poland. He also said that he was very much aware of the efforts that had been made by the SPD and the CDU/CSU in the post-war integration of refugees and expellees. He said that a similar unfortunate spirit of debate (i.e. similar to the spirit of Erika Steinbach's attitude at the debate on the CAE in Poland) had been evident in some quarters during the preparation of the German-Polish Border Treaty, but that had this Treaty not been approved, German unification would never have been achieved (he included a reference to the fact that Schäuble was well aware of this). Fischer finally said, "I appeal to the CDU/CSU, to understand that as a result of the way that the discussion is being conducted here, huge damage is being inflicted which is burdening the future. In the context of the generous European traditions, which despite all doubts this Union can boast, it surely must not be allowed to be this way."

Source: Report prepared by Department of the States of Central Europe of the Ministry of Foreign Affairs of the CR. April 2004.

The Gdansk Declaration
Declaration of Presidents J. Rau and A. Kwaśniewski of the 29th of October 2003 (working translation)

The Federal President Johannes Rau and the President of the Polish Republic Aleksander Kwaśniewski have today issued the following joint declaration in Gdansk:

In the 20th century, dozens of millions of Europeans suffered in effect of displacement, flight and expulsions. The Nations of Poland and Germany are particularly mindful of the atrocities experienced by the millions as the result of the war unleashed by the inhuman national-socialist regime. The death toll of those tragedies was counted in millions. Even greater numbers of European citizens suffered pain, humiliation and material losses. That brought about deep changes in many nation states and still has an impact on relations among our citizens. Displacements, flights and expulsions are part of Europe's history and hence part of its heritage. This bitter heritage should lead to the unification of our efforts for a better future. We must remember the victims and make sure that they were the last victims. It is every nation's natural right to cherish their memory, but it also is our duty to assure that remembrance and grief shall not be abused to again divide Europe. Thus, there is no room whatsoever for material claims, mutual accusations and the counterposition of the suffered losses and perpetrated crimes. The Europeans should together re-examine and document all cases of displacements, flights and expulsions that have taken place in the 20th century in order for their causes, historical contexts and consequences to become readable for the public opinion. All this can be accomplished only in the spirit of reconciliation and friendship. This will unite us even more. We call for an honest European dialogue on this important issue concerning our past and future. We expect that the persons who enjoy the highest moral authority, politicians and representatives of civil society shall be willing to participate in this dialogue. Their task will be to draw up recommendations as to the forms and structures of this European process of examination and documentation. We are confident that the outcomes of such a European dialogue will significantly contribute to mutual understanding and the deepening of our bond as citizens of Europe.

Source: *Bundespräsident Johannes Rau und der Präsident Aleksander Kwaśniewski haben heute in Danzig folgende gemeinsame Erklärung abgegeben (The federal president J. Rau and president A. Kwaśniewski today in Gdansk approved the following joint declaration):* Bundespräsidialamt-Pressemitteilung, Berlin, 29. 10. 2003

Adam Krzemiński: *The Struggle over Memory*

Why has the discussion around the Centre against Expulsions erupted with such fury in Poland precisely in the summer of the year 2003? After all, a year ago this debate was proceeding in a much calmer spirit. And ten or even seven years ago it would have been unthinkable. After the revolution in 1989, it seemed as though it would be only a matter of time before the crimes and human tragedies of the Second World War would be commemorated outside the narrow limits of national memory, and the sufferings of our own peoples and others would be recollected through "European" eyes.

The character of Polish-German rapprochement and cooperation after the fall of communism was not just a matter of the pragmatic convergence of the interests of the two states, but was also based on the Christian philosophy of reconciliation symbolised by the words of the Polish bishops addressed in 1965 to the German bishops: "We forgive you and we ask your forgiveness." It might therefore have been assumed that when Poland and Germany finally found themselves in the same Euro-Atlantic Europe, this common culture of historical memory would be something natural. Why then did the dispute over the Centre against Expulsions break out in 2003 with such intensity?

First of all: the Centre against Expulsions started to take on real form when the president of the foundation concerned and president of the Federation of Expellees Erika Steinbach announced that she had obtained a site in Berlin for this dubious project and that she rejected all the objections of opponents. This allowed her opponents to argue more persuasively that the memorial to the suffering of the expelled Germans, even if enlarged to include an exhibition recording the fates of other nations, would only open barely healed wounds and would stimulate a new wave of nationalisms. In other words, the unyielding position of Erika Steinbach and her allies mobilised the opponents of the Berlin variant, encouraged them and polarised their arguments.

Second: the year 2003 saw a general deterioration of Polish-German relations. The reason was the split in the North Atlantic Alliance and then division of the European Union into two camps on the issue of the American war in Iraq. The fact that Poland and Germany found themselves on opposite sides of this dispute weakened their will to look for compromises in other matters. After the unfortunate "Letter of the Eight" sent to Berlin and Paris, and the crude retort of President Chirac that the new states in the European Union had missed a good opportunity to "shut up", very arrogant commentaries appeared in the German press and these could no longer be held to be balanced by the mutual confidence – now deeply undermined – that had still been declared in the winter of 2002 by the two prime ministers. It is true that Gerhard Schröder and

Joschka Fischer emphatically distanced themselves from Erika Steinbach's project, but there was no longer an atmosphere congenial enough to enable both governments to support an alternative project, either in Wroclaw or in the form of a network of local museums and centres.

Finally third: the enlargement of the European Union to the East and the war in Iraq both fuelled a revival of nationalist moods in the two countries. In Poland in a referendum held on the 4th of June 2003 the majority voted for EU entry, but did so particularly thanks to the campaign stress on Polish national interests and the opportunity to throw up obstacles to the egotistic and inaccessible "hard core". In Germany, nationalist sentiment sharpened in the spirit of fears at the costs of extending EU membership to "poor relations". At the same time, however, the Germans were proud of having stood up to American hegemonism. The stress on the "German way" was accompanied by a certain historical revisionism, a clear shift of attention from the victims of German Nazism to the German victims of the war: to the Allied bombing of German cities, to the rape of German women in 1945, to the cruel conditions in which Russians held German prisoners of war, and of course to flight, expulsions and transfers.

The revival of nationalist moods also went hand in hand with criticism of the "kitsch of reconciliation", allegedly practiced in the 1990s (by Klaus Bachmann), and criticism of the superficial liturgy of friendship. Despite the almost ritual gestures of the politicians – symbolic meetings in historic locations and telegenic embraces – the societies had continued to view each other with distrust. The growth of sympathy for Germans in Poland towards the end of the 1990s visibly slowed down. And on thermometers of German sympathy Poles constantly found themselves near the bottom of the scale.

The lack of convincing symbols of the new good neighbourly relations, together with what were often humiliating procedures in the accession process to the EU, shifted Polish-German dialogue back to the genuinely or allegedly unsettled questions of the wartime past – from the compensation for Poles subject to forced labour to the question of the property rights of the transferred Germans and admission that they had suffered injustice.

At the end of the 1990s the "struggle over memory" in the Polish and German media started to overshadow discussions on the theme of the future of Polish-German neighbourly relations, still rated poorly as the titles of political pamphlets published in 2001 in Wroclaw attest: "Difficult Neighbourship", "Declare War on the Germans". The authors demanded the adoption of a tougher attitude towards the Germans and the end of the frivolous policy of reconciliation, and attacked its supporters – above all Andrzej Szczypiorski, popular in Germany – as German hirelings pandering to German opinion and blackening Poles.

This new tone was a result of tectonic shifts in Polish public opinion at the end of the 1990s. Regardless of the results of the elections (in 1998 parties that had emerged from the former Solidarity won the elections, and in 2001 a post-communist grouping), neo-conservatives were starting to gain the upper hand in Polish society. In foreign policy they are orientated above all to the Anglo-Saxon world, while at home they have been putting stronger emphasis on Catholic-nationalist, and certainly not liberal values. The new tone of Polish discussions likewise had a new emotional background.

Since the mid-1990s public discussion on the theme of Polish antisemitism has been appearing in regular waves. In 1994 a controversy broke out over anti-semitism in the time of the Warsaw Uprising in 1944. A year later there was the "battle of the cross" erected very close to the former Auschwitz concentration camp, and accompanying dispute over whether Auschwitz should be exclu-sively a symbol of the Holocaust. And finally in 2000 Jan Gross's book "Neigh-bours" provoked an extensive controversy over Polish antisemitism before and during the war, over the collaboration of Jews with the NKVD on territories occupied by the Soviet Union in September 1939, and over Polish involvement in anti-Jewish pogroms stirred up by the German occupiers on territories oc-cupied in July of 1941.

Jedwabne became a symbol of revision challenging the self-image of Poles as almost all noble victims of repression. Although in Polish post-war literature there had certainly been examples of the condemnation of Polish collaborators and antisemites who – as informers – blackmailed Jews in hiding or gave them up to the Gestapo, the anatomy of the pogrom in Jedwabne, analysed in detail in the media, was a great shock for Poles.

Such was the emotional background to the Polish controversy over the Cen-tre against Expulsions. In Poland the building of a holocaust memoral in Ber-lin was regarded as a way of reducing the victims of German mass murder in German consciousness to just one group – the Jews. As if the crimes committed against the Polish nation, from the systematic murder of the Polish elites of politicians, intellectuals, teachers, and priests, to the mass transfers in 1939, were now to be suppressed. It was argued that in German historical conscious-ness the building of a Centre against Expulsions in Berlin would then represent a moral counterweight to the holocaust (in line with the theories of Ernst No-lte in the "historians' dispute"), and all the more so if it was to stand (accord-ing to Erika Steinbach quoted in the *Leipziger Zeitung*) close to the Holocaust memorial and to be linked with it in terms of content. The Centre against Ex-pulsions was regarded as an institution for the falsification of the causes and results of the murderous war unleashed by Hitler and waged by the German people. In Poland there are fears that the granite slabs of the memorial and brick rotunda commemorating primarily the transferred Germans would raise German history, as victimhood, to the level of Polish history, and that Poles, whose history is on the margins of interest in Germany, would in German consciousness appear only in the role of originators of the expulsion – the greatest catastrophe in German history. Indeed, not only in the history of Germans, but of Ukrainians and Jews.

The idea of the Berlin Centre against Expulsions was mostly seen as an expression of historical revisionism and the deliberate whitewashing and so erasure of the relationship between the authors and the victims of the war. For part of the Polish public one ominous sign was the officious interest of the German media in the pogrom in Jedwabne in July 1941, in Polish antisemitism, in the persecution of the intelligentsia and the anti-zionist excesses in 1968, which forced nearly 30,000 of the last Polish Jews into emigration.

In 2003 these fears of a false picture of Polish history in German consciousness became linked to the evident collapse of domestic politics. The post-communist social democrats who had been ruling in Poland since 2001 found themselves in difficulties – not only because in 2002 they lost their coalition partner and Leszek Miller's minority government became dependent on the votes of the opposition, but also because a whole serious of corruption affairs and announcements of budget cuts drastically reduced its credit. In one year the SLD lost half of its supporters. In this situation there was basically no one to be found among the social democratic politicians who would be prepared to support a bold approach to the problem of how to commemorate the wrongs suffered by millions of people (not just Germans and Poles) who had been forced to leave their homelands in the 20th century.

While in conservative nationalist-catholic media the emotions were unleashed, the politicians of the SLD kept quiet for a long time. Naturally the latter were against the location of the Centre against Expulsions in Berlin, but which variant should they support? Far from Poland, ideally in Strassbourg under the wing of the Council of Europe, or preferably nowhere? It was not until September that the Polish prime minister Miller and not until October of 2003 that President Aleksander Kwaśniewski in a joint declaration with President Johannes Rau appealed for European discussion and cooperation on some way of commemorating the expelled that would not ignite former animosities and raise rival claims of every kind.

In Poland the idea of a Berlin Centre against Expulsions was seen as a provocation. At the same time, however, an internal Polish dispute over the philosophy of Poland's own history had been underway for some time. The "conservative republicans" stress the Polish tradition of tolerance and consider the noble republic of the period before the partition of Poland (from 1454 to the 18th century – translator's note) to be the prototype of the multinational and multiconfessional European Union. The Neo-Enlightenment camp, on the other hand, draw attention to the disastrous consequences of the counter-reformation in the 17th century, which not only cut Poland off from the Enlightenment and modernisation by provoking the neighbouring absolutist monarchies to aggression and the liquidation of Poland, but was also a source of xenophobia and intolerance – the proof of this being the expulsion of the Arians and the Bohemian Brethren, among them the teacher Jan Amos Komenský (Comenius).

In the dispute over the Centre against Expulsions in 2003, the issue was mainly one of the German perspective on war history, of an undermining of the perceived link between consciousness of German guilt and the German suffering that resulted from a war unleashed and lost. But it was at the same time a dispute about how to commemorate the fates of those people who had helped create the history of the country that now forms the Polish state and is not the historic homeland of the Poles alone. The regional societies, like the Olsztynian "Borussia", have been making an immense contribution by mapping in full and without falsification the local histories of the Poles, Germans, Jews, Roma, Ukrainians and other ethnic groups and individuals that in the course of centuries lived side by side in Pomerania, and in Mazuria, in Silesia, in Eastern Prussia and in Galicia. In 2004 "Borussia" won a Polish-German prize for this activity. Its work shows that it is possible to commemorate expulsion, deportation and resettlement in a very sensitive way – by joining forces and bringing together all kinds of different initiatives. It is not necessary to erect a grandiose monument than would only open wounds that have yet to heal entirely.

The whole dispute relates rather less to honouring the memory of the transferred Germans than to the political position of the Federation of Expellees, which despite the efforts of its individual members to co-operate, foster conciliation and restore monuments in some former German eastern territories, is generally perceived as a lobby seeking to exert moral, political and material pressure on Poland. Its current president Erika Steinbach, impervious to any criticism, and likewise organisations pressing for condemnation of the transfer, the nullification of the Beneš and Bierut Decrees and ultimately the return of property, have managed to revive in Poland a German spectre that after 1989 had seemed a thing of the past.

Source: *Kafka. Journal for Central Europe,* 13/2004 (Theme – expulsion). 58–63.

List of Maps and Graphs

Maps and Graphs

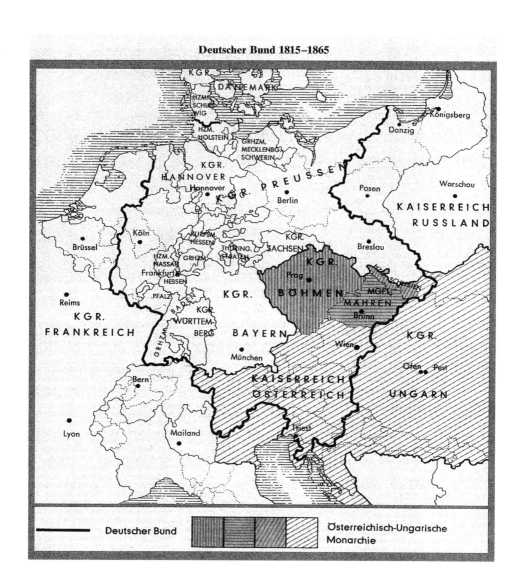

1. Map of the German Confederation 1815–1865

Source: Deutsche und Tschechen. Informationen zur politischen Bildung. No. 132.

Bonn: Bundeszentrale für politische Bildung 3.

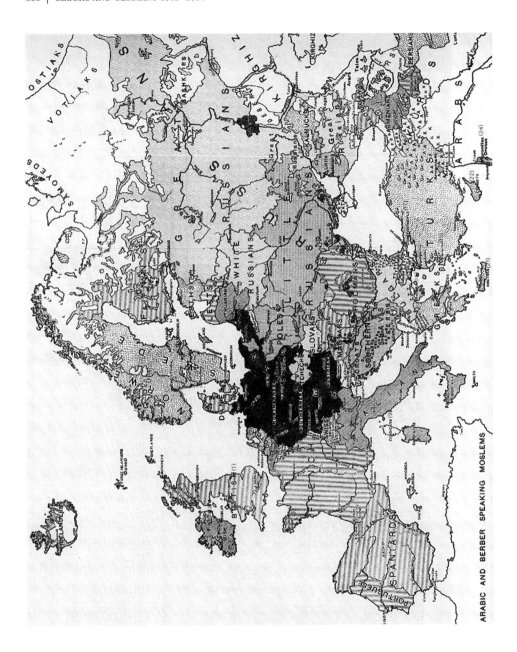

2. Map of the Nationalities of Europe
Source: Arnold J. Toynbee: *Nationality and the War*, London – Toronto 1915.

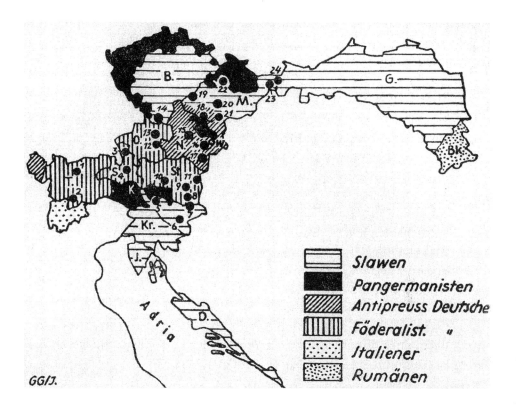

3. Map/schematic representation of national mentalities in the Habsburg monarchy
Source: A. Chéradame: *L'Europe et la question d'Autriche au seuil du XXe siècle*. 1901. See new
reproduction of the book by Nabu Press, 2010. Text inside the map: Slavs, Pan-Germans,
Anti-Prussian Germans, Federalists, Italians, Rumanians.

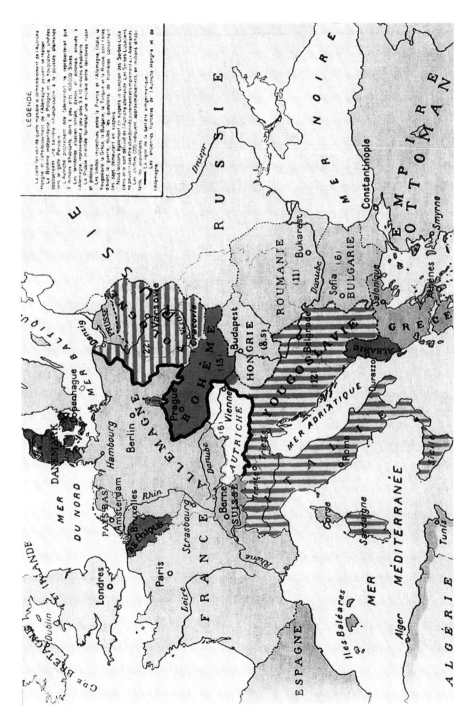

4. Maps of the National Council of the Czech Lands

Source: appendix to Masaryk's programme study *Nová Evropa – stanovisko slovanské*
[The New Europe – The Slav Standpoint], 1918.

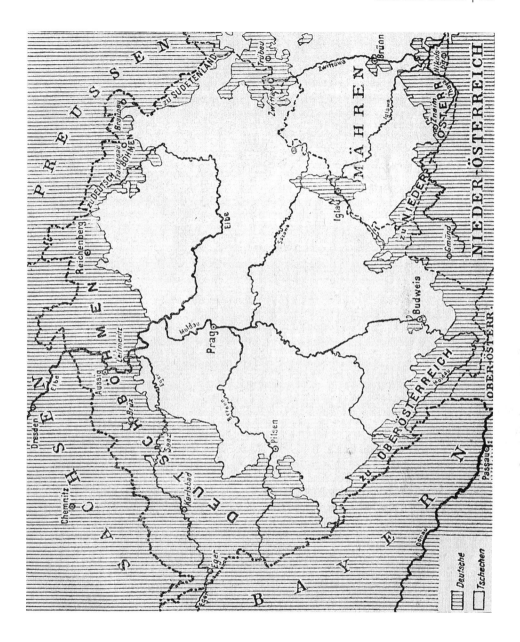

5. Map of German-Czech/Deutsch-Böhmen territories as conceived by Lodgman von Auen, published 1919. It essentially prefigured the extent of the Nazi annexations in October 1938. Source: Lodgman von Auen: Für die Selbstbestimmung Deutschböhmens. Wien: Alfred Halder. (Flugblätter für Deutschösterreichs Recht)

6. Map of Central and Eastern Europe after 1918. Territorial losses of the Central Powers
Source: Goldstein, E.: *The First World War Peace Settlements 1919–1925*. London – New York – Toronto – Sydney 2002. Map XV.

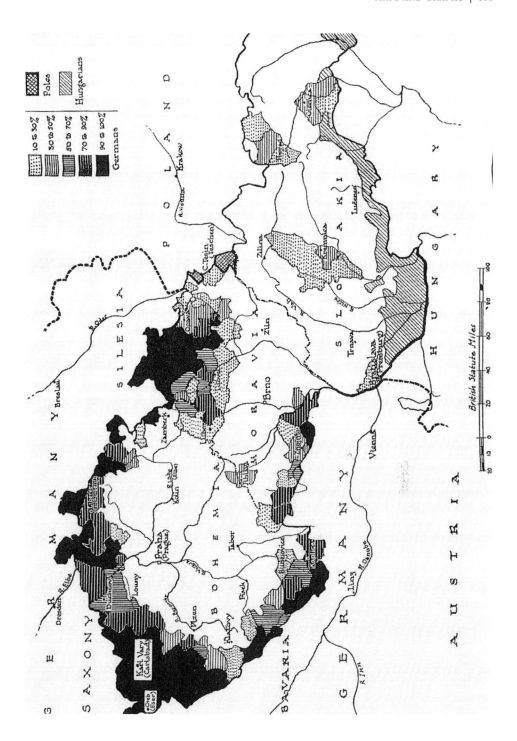

7. Map of the territorial distribution of ethnic minorities in inter-war Czechoslovakia.
Source: Chmelař: *The German Problem in Czechoslovakia*, Prague 1936.

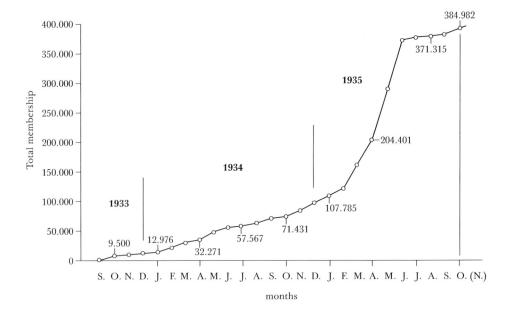

8. Growth in the number of members of the Sudeten German Party 1933–1935
Source: Sudeten German Party, Statistische Abteilung des Werbeamtes, Národní archiv,
Prague, 5-HS-OA/://:14.

9. Ethnographic map of Europe on the cover of a leaflet by Konrad Henlein. (French edition). Published by the K. H. Frank publishing house, Karlsbad – Leipzig 1938
Source: Verlag Karl H. Frank, 1938.

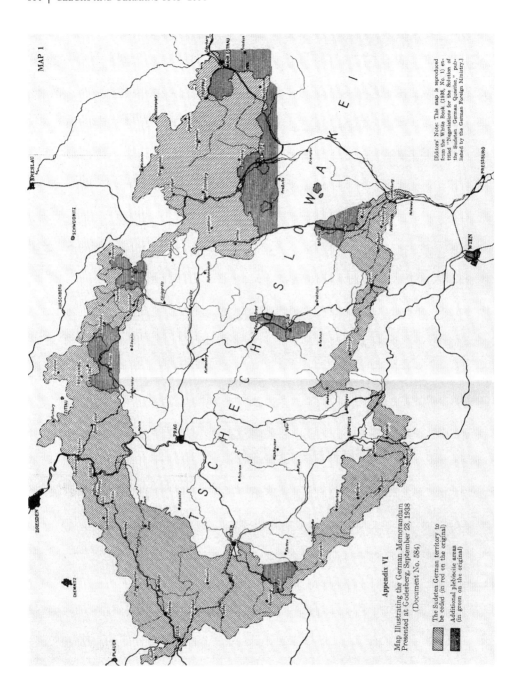

10. Map illustrating the German memorandum at Godesberg, September 23, 1938
Source: *Documents on German Foreign Policy, 1918–1945, from the Archives of the German Foreign Ministry.* 1949–54. Published jointly by the British Foreign Office and the U.S. Department of State. Series D (1937–1945). 8 vols. Washington: U.S.G.P.O., and London: H.M.S.O.

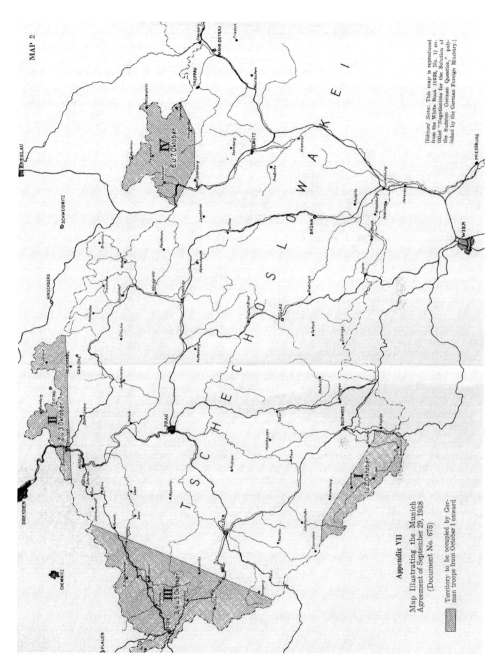

11. Map illustrating the Munich Agreement of September 29, 1938
Source: White Book (1938, No. 1) entitled "Negotiations for the Solution of the Sudeten German Question, published by the German Foreign Ministry. Via *Documents on German Foreign Policy, 1918–1945, from the Archives of the German Foreign Ministry.* 1949–54. Published jointly by the British Foreign Office and the U.S. Department of State. Series D (1937–1945). 8 vols. Washington: U.S.G.P.O. and London: H.M.S.O.

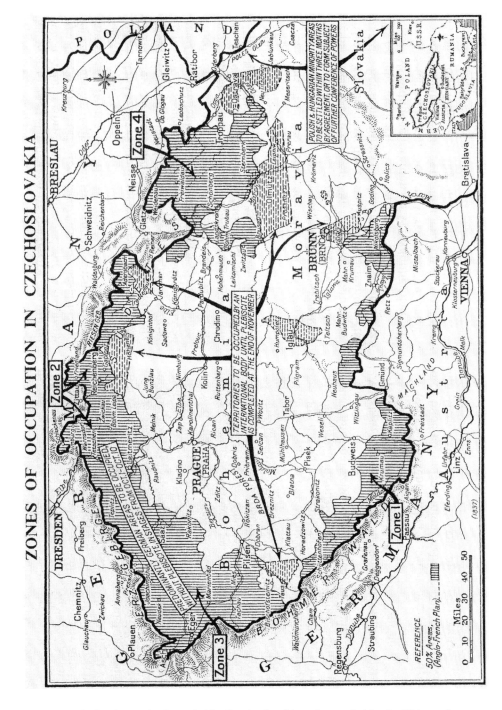

12. Map of the border territories ceded by Czechoslovakia and occupied by the Wehrmacht as a result of the Munich Agreement
Source: *The Times*, 1st Sept. 1938.

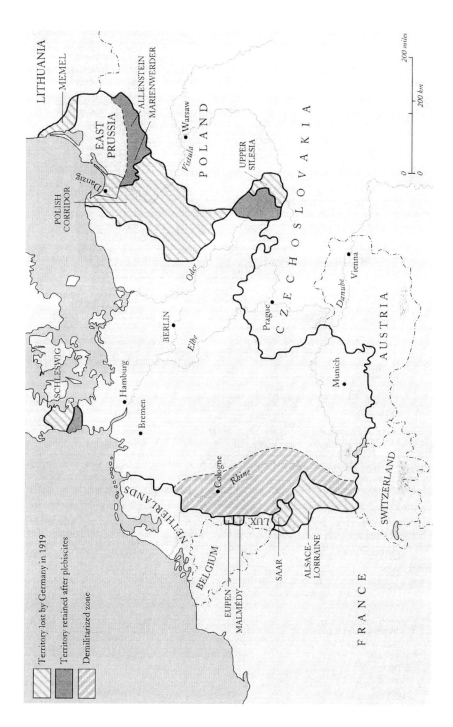

13. Map of Germany after the Treaty of Versailles
Source: Goldstein, E.: *The First World War Peace Settlements 1919–1925*. Longman: London – New York – Sydney – Toronto 2002.

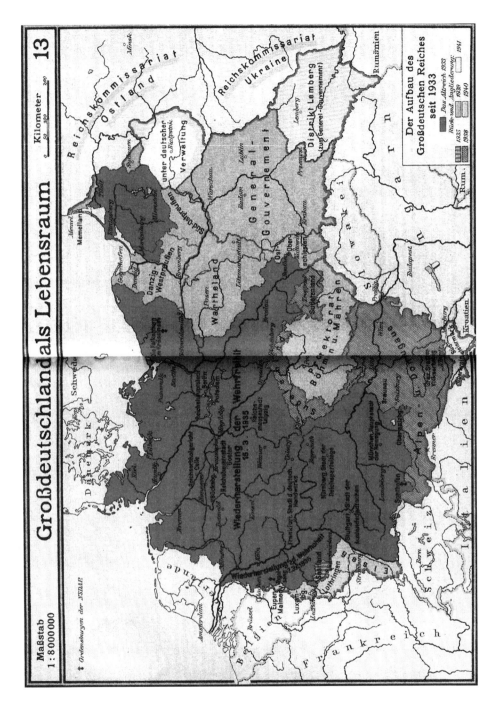

14. Map of the Building of the Third Reich 1941
Source: Collective, Kancelář pro oběti nazismu/Office for Victims of Nazism. 2004.
Nepřichází-li práce k tobě... – If work does not come to you..., Praha: Czech-German Fund
for the Future. 132–133.

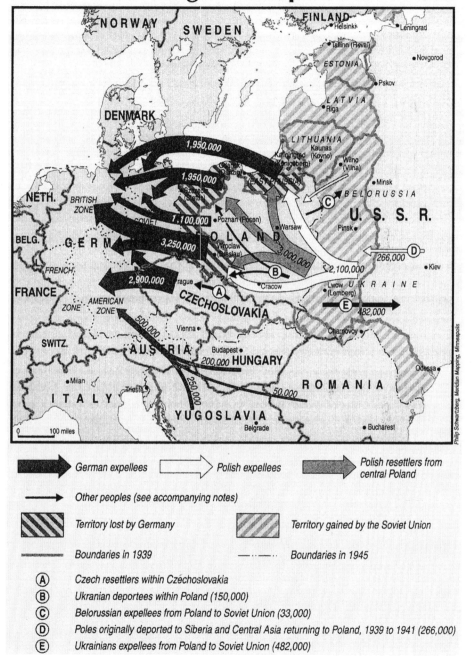

Ethnic Cleansing in Europe: 1944-1948

15. Map of flights and expulsions of the German-speaking population from Central
and Eastern Europe in the period 1944–1948
Source: Schwartzberg, P., Meridian Mapping, Minneapolis.

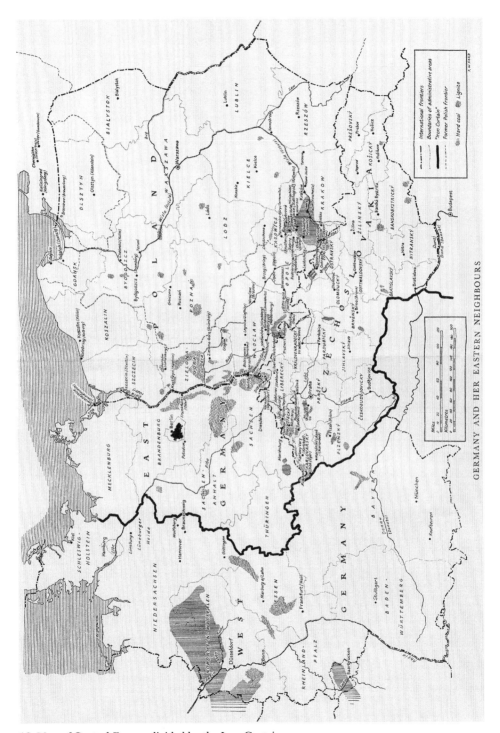

16. Map of Central Europe divided by the Iron Curtain
Source: Wiskemann, E., *East Germany and her Eastern Neighbours*. Oxford University Press. 1956.

17. Europe in 1914
Source: A.J.P. Taylor, *The First World War. An illustrated history*. London: Penguin Books, 1966, 18–19.

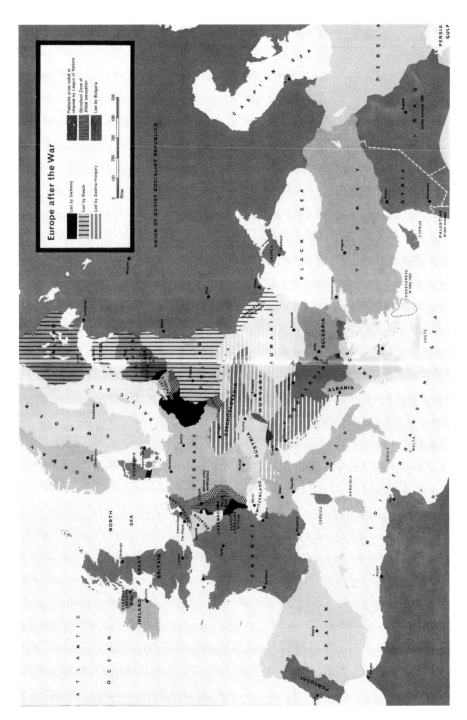

18. Europe after the War
Source: A.J.P. Taylor. *The First World War. An illustrated history*. London: Penguin Books, 1966, 20–21.

19. Map showing the territory of the European Union after the expansion to the east
on the 30th of May 2004. The beginning of a new stage in Czech-German co-operation
and good neighbourliness.
Source: Creative Commons.wikimedia. org. EU25-2005 European Union map.svg

List of Illustrations

Tables and Graphs

Index of Organisation Names

Society of Protestant Sudeten Germans (Gemeinschaft evangelischer
 Sudetendeutscher) 349
Sojusz Lewicy Demokratycznej *see* Democratic Left Alliance
State Institute for War Documentation (Rijksinstituut voor Oorlogsdocumentatie) 183
Strength Through Joy (Kraft durch Freude, KdF) 559
Sudeten German Academie of Sciences and Art (Sudetendeutsche Akademie der
 Wissenschaften und Künste) 349
Sudeten German Archive (Sudetendeutsches Archiv) 349, 528
Sudeten German Council (Sudetendeutscher Rat) 256, 349, 351–352, 354, 397, 405,
 415, 476, 531, 567, 573, 575
Sudeten German Homeland Association (Sudetendeutsche Landsmannschaft, SL) 275,
 309, 335, 340–341, 343, 345–346, 348–352, 354–359, 367, 389–390, 393, 396, 398–399,
 404–406, 409, 412, 414, 416–417, 420–422, 426, 429–431, 437–438, 459, 462–463,
 467–468, 470–471, 472, 474–476, 479, 531, 566–567, 573, 575
Sudeten German Homeland Front (Sudetendeutsche Heimatfront, SHF) 177–179, 200,
 224, 335
Sudeten German Party (Sudetendeutsche Partei, SdP) 148, 153, 168, 178–180,
 183–192, 194–196, 198–203, 206–207, 211–219, 221–226, 238, 240–241, 251, 253,
 269, 275–279, 284, 295, 307, 316, 335, 352–353, 399, 413, 475–476, 479, 533,
 543–546, 548, 552
Sudetendeutsche Akademie der Wissenschaften und Künste *see* Sudeten German
 Academie of Sciences and Art
Sudetendeutsche Heimatfront *see* Sudeten German Homeland Front
Sudetendeutsche Landsmannschaft *see* Sudeten German Homeland Association
Sudetendeutsche Partei *see* Sudeten German Party
Sudetendeutscher Heimatbund 172, 176
Sudetendeutscher Rat *see* Sudeten German Council
Sudetendeutsches Musikinstitut 349

Trades Bank (Živnobanka) 150
Treasury (United Kingdom) 300
Treugemeinschaft sudetendeutscher Sozialdemokraten 285, 287, 296

Union for the German East (Bund Deutscher Osten, BDO) 147, 281
Union Internationale des Associations pour la Société des Nations (Commission
 spéciale sur les minorités de race, de langue et de religion) 171
Union Interparlementaire (Commission des questions ethniques et coloniales) 171
Union of Fighters for Freedom (Český svaz bojovníků za svobodu) 467, 472
Union of Germans Abroad (Bund der Auslandsdeutschen, BdA) 173
United Nations 170, 262, 311, 325, 574
Ústav pro péči o přestěhovalce *see* Office for Care of Migrants
Ústřední matice školská *see* Central School Foundation
ÚVOD 272, 290

Verband der deutschen Volksgruppen in Europa *see* Association of German Ethnic
 Groups in Europe

Index of Personal Names

Václav Houžvička

Czechs and Germans 1848–2004

The Sudeten Question and the Transformation
of Central Europe

Originally published in Czech under the title *Návraty sudetské otázky*,
Prague: Karolinum 2005
Translation by Anna Clare Bryson-Gustová

Published by Charles University in Prague,
Karolinum Press, Ovocný trh 3, 116 36 Praha 1
Prague 2016
Cover and layout by Jan Šerých
Copyediting by Martin Janeček and Vendula Kadlečková
Indexes by Josef Schwarz
Typeset and printed by Karolinum Press
First reprint, First English edition

ISBN 978-80-246-2144-9 (Karolinum)
ISBN 978-80-7325-284-7 (CDK)

From reviews of the Czech edition

V. Houžvička's book on "The Returns of the Sudeten Question" is the most extensive study on this theme published in the Czech Republic since 1990. The problems that it addresses and its overall range go beyond the theme suggested by the title. The work is not simply a treatment of the Sudeten question since 1989, but an attempt to set it in the context of the whole perspective of Czech-German relations over the last century. The book is based on solid research, using both Czech and foreign sources and all the scholarly literature, which for understandable reasons is more extensive on the German than on the Czech side. In the last 15 years academic treatments of the subject have not kept pace with the development of polemic and media interest in the "Sudeten Question". Václav Houžvička's book therefore fills a definite gap and is of considerable value for the academic community both at home and abroad with an interest in "coming to terms with the past" and the use of history for contemporary political purposes.

The study has the major virtue of being on the intersection of several disciplines (history, sociology and international relations). This allows problems that are usually treated separately to be considered in their mutual implications: the work of historians on the Sudeten question and the transfer, the significance of this problem for Czech-German relations after 1990, and a sociological analysis based on surveys of public opinion (generally and specifically in the border regions). This last section of the study in particular offers new information about and interpretation of trends in the attitudes of Czech society, which the author relates to the role of the media (restricted, superficial and even completely tendentious reporting) and the domestic political scene. The study of Czech public opinion shows the limits of certain stereotypes, and at the same time illustrates expressions of defensive identity that are not by any means confined to the Germans, but reflect the attitudes of Czech society to foreigners and the outside world in general.

Prof. Jacques Rupnik, Director de recherches, CERI-Sciences Po, Paris;
Professor at College of Europe, Bruges (internal peer-review)

This is an exceptionally important book. It is the first summarising, academically grounded study of the history of German-Czech relations in the Czech Lands; it will probably become a standard work on the theme for future generations.

An investigation of German-Czech conflicts conducted and presented in the objective, evidence-based way that we see in Houžvička's work, reveals the long-standing problem as something that is neither obscure nor difficult to grasp. Houžvička thus offers not just an important contribution to the understanding of an often discussed but rarely analysed theme, but also a useful and inspiring contribution to future German-Czech discussions on the past.

Prof. Dr. Hans-Henning Hahn, Universität Oldenburg.
Bohemistik, Zentrum gegen die Vertreibung

It is at this point that Houžvička's text really comes into its own, for he provides a clear examination of the complex round of claims and counter claims that were exchanged between Czechoslovakia and West Germany during the Manichean climate of the Cold War – including the influence the „expulsions" exerted in the 1970s on Czechoslovak dissidents, many of whom sided with the Sudeten German interpretation of the past, not least because it was diametrically opposed to the version promoted by the Czechoslovak Communist Party. Moreover, Houžvička was personally involved in a range of Czech-German forums and negotiations during 1990s and these experiences lend the text a feel of authenticity. These are the views and opinions of a practitioner who has had his feet under the table and witnessed history unfolding at first hand.

Dr. Martin D. Brown, Richmond University.
British Czech and Slovak Review, 6, 2006